SOVIET-AMERICAN RELATIONS, 1917–1920

Volume II

The Decision to Intervene

Soviet-American Relations, 1917–1920

By *George F. Kennan*

Vol. I. Russia Leaves the War

Vol. II. The Decision to Intervene

SOVIET-AMERICAN
RELATIONS, 1917–1920

The
Decision
to Intervene

BY GEORGE F. KENNAN

PRINCETON, NEW JERSEY
PRINCETON UNIVERSITY PRESS

Published by Princeton University Press,
41 William Street, Princeton, New Jersey 08540

Copyright © 1958 by George F. Kennan

All Rights Reserved

Library of Congress Card No. 56-8382
ISBN 0-691-00842-6, pbk.
First Princeton Paperback printing, 1989

Princeton University Press books are printed on acid-free paper, and meet
the guidelines for permanence and durability of the Committee on Production Guidelines for Book Longevity of the Council on Library Resources

10 9 8 7 6 5 4 3 2 1, pbk.

Printed in the United States of America
by Princeton University Press,
Princeton, New Jersey

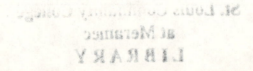

To

the memory of

two members

of

America's Foreign Service,

DEWITT CLINTON POOLE

and

MADDIN SUMMERS,

of whose faithful and distinguished efforts

in Russia on their country's behalf

this volume gives only an incomplete account

PREFACE

THIS volume is a direct continuation of the first volume of this series, which appeared under the title *Russia Leaves the War*. This being the case, there is no need to repeat or to expand the prefatory remarks which introduced the first volume.

I must, however, reiterate here the expression of my indebtedness to the librarians of the Institute for Advanced Study and of Firestone Library at Princeton University;

to the several sections of the National Archives of the United States which have aided my research on this volume;

to the Manuscripts Division of the Library of Congress;

to the Missouri Historical Society and the State Historical Society of Wisconsin;

to the Hoover Library of War and Peace at Stanford University, the Harper Library at the University of Chicago, and the Yale University Library.

In addition, I must add a word of gratitude to the Archive of Russian and Eastern European History and Culture and to the Oral History Research Office, both in the Butler Library at Columbia University in New York, where I received particularly valuable help in connection with this second volume.

I bear a special debt of appreciation to the families of David R. Francis, Allen Wardwell, Thomas D. Thacher, DeWitt C. Poole, and Arthur Bullard for making available memoir material used in this volume.

To Sir Llewellyn Woodward and to the Honorable Norman Armour I am indebted for their kindness in reading large portions of the manuscript and giving me their valuable comments, for the utilization of which I alone bear the responsibility.

CONTENTS

ILLUSTRATIONS

PLATES

[xi]

Illustrations

MAPS

The maps were drawn by R. S. Snedeker

SOVIET-AMERICAN RELATIONS, 1917–1920

Volume II

The Decision to Intervene

P R O L O G U E

*Велик был год и страшен год .... от начала же революции 2-й.
Был он обилен летом солнцемъ а зимою снегом, и особенно высоко
в небе стояли две звезды: звезда пастушеская — вечерняя Венера и
красный, дрожащий Марс.*

(Great was the year and terrible the year . . . that followed on the second
Revolution. It abounded with sunshine in the summer months, with snow
in the winter; and two stars stood out prominently in the heavens: the
shepherd's star—the evening Venus—and the red, vibrant Mars.)—*Opening words of the great and almost forgotten novel of the Russian civil war,
"Byelaya Gvardiya" (White Guard), by Mikhail Bulgakov*

THE month of March 1918 marked the beginning of the final crisis
of the First World War. In the preceding autumn the Allies had
been struck by two calamities: the crushing defeat of the Italians on
the Po and, even worse, the events in Russia—the collapse of the
Russian military resistance, the triumph of the Bolsheviki in Petrograd, the effective departure of Russia from the ranks of the warring
powers. Throughout the winter, while Germans and Bolsheviki
haggled at Brest-Litovsk over the terms of the peace, a relative quiet
prevailed on the western front. It was no secret that the Germans
were moving troops and transport from east to west on a massive
scale, in preparation for what they hoped would be a crushing and
decisive offensive against the Allied forces in France.

In London and Paris, beneath all the embittered tenacity which
three and a half years of war had bred, there was an undercurrent
of dull apprehension at the realization of the numerical superiority
the Germans would now be able to amass in the west. There was no
loss of determination—quite the contrary. It was realized that this
would be Germany's last great effort, and that if it were successfully
contained, the worst would be over. But it promised at least another
year of war, and further casualties on a fearful scale.

This appalling prospect, together with the forced lull in military

[3]

activity at the front, told heavily on the nerves of those concerned with the conduct of the war. The long exertion was now taking its psychic toll. Many people were wretchedly overworked and over-wrought. Tempers were frayed, sensibilities chafed and tender. There was, in some quarters at least, a loss of elasticity. Men did their work uncomplainingly, but in a fixed, dogged way, and found it difficult to take fresh account of their situation. February had witnessed a painful readjustment of senior command arrangements on the British side. Inter-Allied military relations were also strained and unsatisfactory, torn this way and that by a never-ending succession of resentments, suspicions, misunderstandings, and political maneuvers. Despite all formal titles and institutional devices, real unity of command was never fully achieved.

At 4:30 a.m. on March 21, after a night of particularly ominous stillness, six thousand German guns suddenly opened up, with a deafening thunder, on the British sector of the front. The dreaded spring offensive had begun. It represented the greatest single military operation ever mounted, to that date. It was designed to split the British sector from the French and to carry the German armies to the sea. The full weight of the attack fell on the British, already worn by years of unremitting losses, effort, and sacrifice. Within the ensuing forty days it was to cost the British army in France some 300,000 further casualties, more than a fourth of the entire force. Not until mid-June would the military situation be stabilized and the state of extreme danger overcome.

Small wonder, then, that as the German offensive got under way a note of sheer desperation entered into the calculations of the British military planners at the Supreme War Council with respect to Russia and the possibilities for reviving the eastern front. The war now hung by a thread. Who knew?—perhaps the thread lay in Russia; perhaps even a token revival of resistance in the east, even the slightest diversion of German attention and resources from the western front, would spell the difference between victory and defeat. If there were even a chance that this was the case, should not every possibility, however slender and implausible, be pursued?

❖

American forces had, as yet, been scarcely involved in the fighting in France. Nearly a year had now elapsed since the American declaration of war. Six American divisions were in France, but none of these had as yet been employed for active combat. Three (the 1st, the 26th, and the 42nd) had already entered the line on quiet sectors of the front, for training purposes; and a fourth (the 2nd) did so in March. American casualties totalled, to this date, 1,722, of which only 162 represented deaths incurred by enemy action in battle.

Against the background of this slenderness of combat commitment, the huge show of martial fervor that dominated the American domestic scene had something slightly forced and artificial about it. Not that the war had not exacted in America, too, a respectable toll of exertion, sacrifice, and sometimes even discomfort. There were such things as high prices, fuel shortages, transportation breakdowns, and manpower shortages. Europeans tended to underestimate both the difficulties of creating a great armed force from scratch in a country such as the United States and the seriousness with which Americans had thrown themselves into this effort. But there had of course been no visible bloodshed or destruction; the shadow of human losses on a mass scale did not yet lie across American society; the effort, thus far, had been primarily economic and organizational; there was no proper image in people's minds of the ghastly reality of modern war, destined in time to raise such heavy problems for all of western European civilization. For Americans, war still had the charm of newness and remoteness. And much of American life could continue, not substantially affected by the military effort.

The Giants—by late March—were in training in Texas, the Yankees in Georgia. Yale was on top in the intercollegiate swimming competition. Show business was still show business. Fifty legitimate stages still functioned robustly in New York City. The musical comedy of Chu Chin Chow could still be hopefully billed in the papers as the "Most Gorgeous, Gigantic, Colorful, Magnificent, Enthralling, Fascinating and Superb Spectacle Ever Known in History of Stage." Barnum and Bailey's circus—all eighty-five carloads of it —could still make its annual trek from Bridgeport to New York and parade as usual down Lexington Avenue on the way to the Garden. So long as such things could happen, one could tell one's self a hundred times a day that civilization was threatened, that humanity hovered on the brink of disaster; but it was hard to visualize it, and it tended at times to escape one's attention.

Perhaps it was partly in the subconscious effort to assure them-

selves of the reality of war that Americans gave themselves so prodi-
gally to the external manifestations of the martial spirit. Of course,
such things as commercial exploitation of the war theme and govern-
mentally inspired propaganda were abundantly involved. The market was flooded with war books. There was a thriving industry in the
production of patriotic baubles. The music stores resounded to the
strains of "Over There," "So Long, Mother," "Goodbye Broadway,
Hello France," and "I May Be Gone for a Long, Long Time." In
Madison Square Garden a "Grand Military and Naval Meet," offer-
ing "100 Thrilling and Instructive War Features" and ending with
massed bands playing "The Star-Spangled Banner" under the personal direction of John Philip Sousa, drew packed houses.

But most of what was said about the war came, quite spontaneously,
from the educated upper class of the day—from people who felt an
obligation to set the tone for public discussion and a need to show
themselves, as prominent figures, in the proper light in any given
situation. For such people, the war posed a difficult problem. American society had no tradition that could help it to accept a foreign
war with calmness and maturity. Its political philosophy—optimistic,
idealistic, impregnated with the belief that an invincible progress had
set in with the founding of the American state—had no comfortable
place for mass killing and destruction as an end of American policy.
There was no explanation for America's involvement in the war
which fitted with the basic assumptions of the American outlook
and at the same time permitted the adoption of a realistic image of
the enemy and recognition of the war as an integral part of the
process of history. It could not, in the American view, be anything
generic to human nature that had produced this confusion. Only a
purely external force—demonic, inexplicable, evil to the point of
inhumanity—could have put America in this position, could have
brought her to an undertaking so unnatural, so out of character, so
little the product of her own deliberate choice.

In the face of this preposterous situation, many people—particularly
those accustomed to talking and being listened to and setting the
tone—felt themselves thrust on the defensive. The sudden reality of
war did not square with what they had been telling people before;
they had a feeling, now, that they must vindicate themselves, must
show themselves adequate to the new situation. There was a sort of
mass running for cover; and "cover" was an impressive show of

noble indignation against the external enemy, coupled with the most unmeasured idealization of the American society whose philosophic foundation had been thus challenged. This was, somehow, the only wholly safe stance, the only one that gave protection against being drawn into dangerous depths of speculation and doubt where one would be quite alone, in moral isolation, and where there would be no stopping point, no terra firma.

The result was an hysteria, a bombast, an orgy of self-admiration and breast-beating indignation, that defies description. In one degree or another it took possession of press, pulpit, school, advertising, lecture platform, and political arena. The President's official statements were, whatever the merits of the political philosophy underlying them, restrained, moderate, and statesmanlike. But the same could not be said of private discussion. Never, surely, has America been exposed to so much oratory—or to oratory more strained, more empty, more defensive, more remote from reality. All was righteousness and hatred. The humorous magazines suddenly acquired that abysmal humorlessness that enters in when the effort is made to base humor on wrath. In the eminently respectable *Outlook,* editor-emeritus Lyman Abbott, himself a clergyman, denied the application of the principle of Christian charity to the Germans. In the halls of the Republican Club in New York City, distinguished citizens vied with one another every Saturday afternoon in forensic demonstrations of the wartime spirit: tales of German atrocities, largely without substance but eagerly credited, were worked to the limit; suggestions for a compromise peace were denounced from every conceivable angle; the guilt of every last German was demonstrated; "a hundred years of social and commercial ostracism" was demanded for the German people—retribution "down to the children's children." Insistence on unconditional surrender became an obligatory ritual. A major press scandal ensued when a speaker at the New York Peace Society was quoted as voicing, in response to a question, the opinion that the war would end in a compromise. Everywhere, people took it upon themselves to search among their neighbors for spies and saboteurs—with all the usual injuries and absurdities. The treatment of "hyphenated-Americans" and people with German names was cruel, undiscriminating, and often wholly disgraceful. America, it might be said, had little or nothing to be ashamed of in the substance of her war effort; but in the public discussion of it at home, in the interpretation it was given, and in the reflection it found in civic behavior, this was not America's finest hour.

The point was not that American society was devoid of virtues or that there had not been provocation for the situation in which she found herself. The point was that there was a total loss of balance and discrimination in the assessment of both homeland and enemy. A few faint voices (notably, William Forbes Cooley, in the *Bookman*) were raised on behalf of greater thoughtfulness and introspection about America's purposes and her future and a more mature scrutiny of the enemy's views and motives; but they were lost in the general din. The capacity for realistic self-appraisal was literally stifled in the debauch of patriotic demonstration. And by the same token, the image of the enemy became distorted to the point of absurdity. The real Wilhelminian Germany, with all its deficiencies, its accomplishments, its illusions, its bewilderment, and its tragedy, was lost from view; in its place there appeared the grotesque figure of the beastlike "Hun," personified by the unfortunate Kaiser, for whose real personality and significance in the pattern of the German war effort no trace of comprehension remained.

All this being the case, it will be understood why there was little real appreciation in the American public for the seriousness of the military situation in Europe and for the significance, in particular, of the German spring offensive. The United States being now formally engaged and her armies in training, Americans never doubted that the war would be won. There was still a naïve and old-fashioned belief in the efficacy of sheer physical courage and righteous anger as a source of victory. The humorous magazine *Life,* being anti-Wilson and regretting the failure of people to elect Theodore Roosevelt as a wartime President in his stead, ran—with the caption "It might have been"—the representation of an embattled Roosevelt, his face distorted with indignation, leaning over his desk and throttling a startled Kaiser. It was, you see, as simple as this. You needed only to be brave and angry and armed with a good conscience. Victory would be sure to ensue.

Because of this haziness about military realities, Russia's defection did not cause in America the same combination of bitterness and consternation that was experienced in England and France. The feeling among influential Americans was rather one of indignation

over Germany's exploitation of the situation at Brest-Litovsk, of pity
for the Russian people (regarded as somehow innocent of the whole
development and really still "on our side"), and of high resolve not
to "abandon Russia"—a resolve for which the only visible connection
with reality was the confidence in an ultimate victory over Germany
and the belief that this would somehow or other make all things
possible.

It was, of course, a corollary of this outlook that the phenomenon
of Soviet power had to be regarded as merely a product of German
intrigue. The Soviet government could not—in this view—reflect
popular feeling; for the Russian people were really with us and
would not have left the war of their own volition. Soviet power,
therefore, was to be regarded as evil. But there could not be two
independent and contesting centers of evil—the Kaiser and Lenin.
In the emotional world of an aroused democracy evil had always to
be singular, never plural. To admit the complex and contradictory
nature of error would be to admit the complex and contradictory
nature of truth, as error's complement; and this was intolerable, for
if there were two ways of looking at a thing, then the whole structure
of war spirit fell to the ground, then the struggle had to be regarded
as a tragedy, with muddled beginnings and probably a muddled
end, rather than as a simple heroic encounter between good and
evil; and it had to be fought, then, not in blind, righteous anger
but rather in a spirit of sadness and humility at the fact that western
man could involve himself in a predicament so unhappy, so tragic,
so infinitely self-destructive.

Even in official Washington, where emotion was tempered by
responsibility and by constant reminders of the fact of international
complexity, something of this same distortion tended to prevail. There
was no lack of willingness to seek the facts of the Russian situation
or to face them; but even here, understanding was constantly bedeviled by the inability to form a realistic image of the German
opponent. There was a tendency to exaggerate German ambitions
and the German role in Russia; to underestimate the disunity in the
German camp and the weaknesses and limitations that rested on the
German war effort; to underrate the phenomenon of Bolshevism
as an indigenous manifestation of Russian political realities; to regard
the confusions of the Russian scene as only another projection of

German evil; and to argue from this that the problems of Russia, like those of Europe proper, would find their solution automatically in an Allied victory over Germany.

✧

In Russia, the conclusion of the Brest-Litovsk Treaty had ushered in a new era. On the northern section of the old eastern front, there was now a precarious quietus, the Germans creating a species of western-European order along their side of the military demarcation line, turmoil and revolution prevailing on the other side. In the Ukraine, the Germans pressed forward vigorously the military advance they had begun prior to the Soviet capitulation. This they did on the strength of their earlier treaty with the Ukrainian Rada. But there was no formal agreement anywhere on what constituted the northern boundary of the area the Rada were supposed to control. The German forces stumbled at many points on communist detachments loyal to Moscow. Skirmishes ensued; protests flew back and forth. It was a dangerous, unstable situation. Few people, least of all the Soviet leaders, believed in its permanence. Good faith and confidence were utterly absent on both sides. General observance of the treaty rested, mutually, on a tortured, fragile expediency.

In Moscow, by late March, all was confusion, heterogeny, and motion. The move of the government from Petrograd to Moscow was now in progress. Almost hourly the overloaded trains lumbered into the Moscow yards—strings of battered, befouled passenger cars, bursting with human bodies, or open freight cars piled high with filing cases and office equipment—and disgorged their loads into the prevailing chaos. The newspapers, carrying daily lists of the new Moscow addresses of government bureaus, gave a certain impression of order and purpose; but the reality was different: cavernous, unheated halls, full of the wrong packing cases, the unremoved belongings of the evicted last tenants, broken telephone wires, shattered windowpanes, litter, filth, and distracted people in fur coats and muddy boots, fumbling around in the confusion. Only slowly, with a million creaks and interruptions, did the governmental machinery of the Russian state install itself and come into some sort of ordered motion in the new capital.

The cozy, comfortable, old-Russian city on the banks of the Moskva was not set up to absorb at once all the shocks of revolution and the invasion of new bodies and functions occasioned by the arrival of the government from Petrograd. Overcrowded and overwhelmed, it resembled a vast, disturbed ant hill. All day long the flood of brown-black garbed humanity—endless variations of khaki intermingled with the somber winter dress of the Russian civilian—flowed through the premises and thoroughfares of the city, inundating the public places, spilling out from the narrow sidewalks into the streets where the snow had now been pressed into thick coatings of blackish ice. People clung in dense swaying masses, like clusters of insects, to the platforms and footrails of the battered streetcar trains, groaning and jangling their way through the confusion.

Everywhere there was the excitement and bustle of revolution. Agitators and mobilizers stormed through the factories for the support on which the regime was so dependent. In innumerable barnlike rooms, reeking of *makhorka* and unaired clothing, Party committees argued their way, hoarsely and wearily but often with brutal effectiveness, through the fog of administrative confusion. All over the city, there was a savage struggle for housing space, with much unceremonious evicting of "bourgeois elements," but, as yet, little terror or brutality. In the old "Cavalier House" in the Kremlin, Lenin and Trotsky scurried up and down the corridors between their respective offices, and snatched hasty meals of salt pork, buckwheat grits, and red caviar between endless visits, meetings, and telephone calls. Overhead, at every quarter hour, the great Kremlin bells now played the opening notes of "The International," in place of "God Save the Tsar."

Yet the other side of life continued, too. Night clubs and restaurants did a frantic business. There was much despairing gaiety and much drowning of sorrows to the strains of gypsy music, on the part of people who sensed the end of their usefulness and their time. Fortune-tellers suddenly made fortunes such as they themselves never had foretold. The pulse of cultural life ran high, in defiance of all ulterior excitements. Chalyapin sang; Karsavina danced. In the Bolshoi Theater, the lights at the foot of the great curtain still dimmed (as for how many years to come?) to the opening strains of the indestructible "Swan Lake" and "Sleeping Beauty"; and proletarians and *bourgeoisie* sat side by side in the gilded boxes, spellbound and subdued, reconciled—for this brief hour—in a common fascination with the choreographic reenactment of the age-old encounter between chivalry and brutishness, the authenticity and relevance of which, for some reason, no one seemed inclined to question.

In this maelstrom of uprooted humanity, all the extremes were represented. Here the old fought with the new, the past with the future, the indigenous with the foreign. Here was a great city in the most acute conceivable spasm of change. And over it all—over the hatred, the hope, the despair, the conspiracy, the mysticism, the passion, and the cruelty—there presided the great flaring domes of the Kremlin churches, rooted in the dark, grim heritage of the Russian past, brooding silently and ironically, now, on the distracted city, confident, we may suppose, that change so rapid could never be wholly real, and that the ancient, barbaric Muscovy in which they had their origin could not fail to reassert itself, now that the Kremlin had again become the center of the Russian land.

❖

By contrast to Moscow, provincial Vologda was a quiet idyl. Here the life of the little colony of Allied diplomats, who had removed from Petrograd at the end of February, took a relatively tranquil course. The American Ambassador, Mr. David R. Francis, had now settled down in the big, wooden clubhouse which was to be his home and office for nearly five months. The place needed paint, and the arrangement of the rooms was not ideal; but life was quite tolerable. The wood fires crackled cozily in the big brick ovens. Outside, there was still the sound of distant church bells, and the creaking of sledge-runners on the snow-covered street. The staff, quartered variously around the town, came in daily, operated a miniature chancery in the building, and shared in the Ambassador's mess. What with the quest for food and drink, the lingering correspondence about the liquidation of the establishment in Petrograd, and the daily telegraphic exchanges with Raymond Robins, the American Red Cross chief in Moscow, there was enough to do. The evenings passed in cards and food and the swapping of anecdotes. Every Saturday afternoon the Ambassador held a reception for such high society as the town could produce. All in all, life quickly settled into a groove as restful as it was impermanent and misleading.

The Vologda diplomats had primarily a symbolic value. It was only their presence in Russia—no longer their activity—that was important. They were there as the living demonstration of the unwillingness of the Allies to admit complete defeat in the face of Russia's withdrawal from the war. They could do little more, for the moment, than to exist. It was elsewhere—in the Allied chanceries and in the contacts of Allied representatives in Moscow with the Soviet leaders—that the further clarification of the relationship between the Bolsheviki and the Allies would ensue.

✧

There are those today who see the winter of 1917–1918 as one of the great turning points of modern history, the point at which there separated and branched out, clearly and for all to see, the two great conflicting answers—totalitarian and liberal—to the emerging problems of the modern age: populousness, industrialism, urbanism. There is much to be said for this view. The one concept was indeed personified, and sharply defined, by Lenin; the other, dimly and less adequately, by Wilson. The one not only accepted but embraced the violent and total break with the past, the virtual destruction of man's social and political heritage, the unlimited belief in the power of contemporary man to understand his own problems and to chart his own course, the centralization of all social and political authority, the subordination of all local and individual impulses to a collective purpose, centrally defined, and the deliberate destruction of large elements of humanity in the interests of a predicted progress of the remainder. The other concept looked to ethical standards—largely religious in origin—as the foundation of all human progress; accepted as relevant to contemporary problems the wisdom and experience of former generations; believed that change, to be useful, must be gradual, organic, and non-destructive; rejected the need for violence against classes of people as such; viewed the individual as the end, not the means, of social organization; welcomed diversity of motive and interest—held, in fact, a superior wisdom to reside in the interaction of a great variety of human impulses—and preferred, generally, to bear with the imperfections of society, as handed down from the past, hoping that they could be gradually and gently bent to a better shape, rather than attempt to uproot and destroy them all at once, at the risk of uprooting and destroying God knows what else.

It was this tremendous dichotomy, universal in its implications and its appeal, that underlay the Russian Revolution and was now emerging, behind a thousand confusions, in the year 1918. It was to be the great issue of the coming half century. But it was not actually the issue of World War I—not the issue western European peoples and America were still fighting about. This last was a rivalry for position among European powers—a rivalry embracing such questions as the future of the Austro-Hungarian Empire and the place to be allotted to a recently unified and strengthened Germany, both within Europe and as a power on the oceans and trade routes of the world.

It was precisely for this reason—because two such different issues were involved—that so much confusion attended the initial encounter between the Allies and the Soviet government. This confusion is something Soviet ideologists have chosen to ignore and to conceal from their own charges. It makes a more dramatic case for world communism to paint a neat picture of the western powers of 1918 as terrified at the emergence of the communist ideology and absorbed in the effort to save themselves by stifling Soviet power in its infancy, than to admit to the reality of a world at war: tired statesmanship, aroused national feelings, military fixations, and confused issues.

But all these things did exist. Confusion was the predominant element in the external relations of Russia in 1918. It was from this confusion that the events to which this inquiry is addressed derived their immense, discouraging perplexity; but it was also from this that they derived the color, the drama, and the excitement that were peculiarly their own.

CHAPTER I

THE RUSSIAN NORTH

THE outbreak of the World War in 1914 effectively closed the Russian Baltic ports as channels of access for Russia to the Atlantic Ocean. Northern and western Russia were left with no direct maritime approach to the Atlantic other than by the bays and inlets of the Barents Sea, on the Arctic coast. As of 1914 there was only one port of any significance in this region. This was Archangel, situated at the head of the Duna Gulf on the White Sea.[1]

Founded in 1584 by Dutch merchants, Archangel soon developed into an important harbor for trade between Russia and the West. It served as an alternative to the port of Narva, on the Finnish Gulf, and its importance was of course greatest at those times when traffic through Narva was interrupted. In the eighteenth and nineteenth centuries a number of developments—Russia's acquisition of the Baltic provinces with the excellent and well-established port of Riga, the development of a new port at St. Petersburg, and the initial orientation of Russian railway construction toward the Baltic harbors—all served to diminish the activity and significance of Archangel. But at the beginning of the present century a railway was built linking Archangel to the general Russian railway system; and the activity of the port was spurred by the rapid growth of the British market for timber and forest products. By 1914 the place had become, despite its remote location, the administrative and commercial center for the entire Russian North. It had a population of nearly 50,000. It handled, to be sure, only a tiny proportion of Russia's foreign trade by value; but its shipments were large in bulk, and they involved a sizeable port activity.

[1] The exact transliteration is "Arkhangelsk." The customary English rendition —"Archangel"—will be used here, as the one most familiar to the English-speaking public.

[15]

Archangel is situated on the eastern bank of the Northern Duna (in Russian, Dvina) River, just at the point where that great stream broadens out into an island delta. Several channels wind their way another forty miles through the islands to the open water of the White Sea. The area is a fine natural port, with protected anchorage for hundreds of ocean-going vessels and with great expanses of potential dockside area. Town and harbor are laid out on the sweeping scale of all the newer Russian cities, and exhibit that careless generosity of the horizontal dimension which is the outstanding characteristic of the North Russian landscape generally.

In 1914 the docks and warehouses of the port already stretched for thirteen miles along both banks of the river. The town itself, though composed like all North Russian communities primarily of log structures, could boast of a main street, the Troitski Prospekt, conceived on the impressive pattern of the great Petrograd avenues. It extended for nearly three miles parallel to the river bank, and was lined with a number of relatively modern and permanent structures.

Aside from its remote location, Archangel's most serious handicap as a wartime port was its icebound condition throughout nearly half the year. Navigation closed, as a rule, in November, and could not be resumed until late May, sometimes even June. By use of modern icebreakers it was possible to whittle a few days off this icebound period at both ends. A certain further alleviation could sometimes be achieved by the use of discharging areas near the mouth of the delta. But the fact remained that the inner harbor, constituting the main dockside area, was normally closed to navigation for a period of nearly six months in each year.[2]

The activity of the port of Archangel increased greatly in the early war years, with the development of munition and supply shipments from the western Allies to European Russia. During the summer of 1916 more than six hundred vessels visited the port. In 1917, for the first time, American vessels—members of the rapidly growing war merchant marine—were included among the many ships arriving at Archangel with war supplies.

Prior to 1917 the United States had had no regular official representation at Archangel. There had been, in the earlier war years, only

---

[2] Ice conditions were troublesome not only in the delta of the Duna but also, on occasions, in the straits leading into the White Sea from the Barents Sea, where pack ice had a tendency to accumulate.

a local resident, a Danish businessman, who had performed American consular services as a side line, under the title of American Consular Agent. By the summer of 1917 the Dane had contrived, deservedly or otherwise, to get himself on the black books of the Allied intelligence services as a likely German agent. For this reason, and because American vessels were now beginning to visit the port, the United States government decided to replace the Consular Agent with a regular consular representative. Mr. Felix Cole, one of the young wartime vice consuls on the staff of the Petrograd Consulate, was accordingly detailed to Archangel in late summer. Cole, a Harvard graduate, had been five years in Russia on private pursuits prior to his entry into the service, and had a good working knowledge of the Russian language. With his arrival in Archangel the United States government acquired for the first time an independent source of information on developments in the northern area.

At the time of the Bolshevik seizure of power in Petrograd the Allies were interested in Archangel not only for its importance as a channel of entrance and egress for European Russia but also for the fact that here too, as at Vladivostok, war supplies shipped by the Allies to former Russian governments had accumulated in large quantity. At the great military discharging area of Bakaritsa, across the river from the city, and at the advance port of Ekonomia near the mouth of the delta, a total of 162,495 tons of such supplies had piled up and were awaiting removal at the end of 1917. These included valuable stocks of metals: 2,000 tons of aluminum, 2,100 tons of antimony, 14,000 tons of copper, 5,230 tons of lead, etc.[3] Not only had these supplies been provided by the Allies from their own scarce wartime stocks, but they had been in effect paid for as well by the Allies under the credits extended to Russian governments, and had been shipped in the extremely scarce Allied tonnage, desperately needed in other theaters of war. Quite naturally, the Allied governments felt a keen concern for the fate of these stores, and considered themselves entitled to have a voice in deciding what—in view of Russia's departure from the war—should be done with them.

The political situation at Archangel, in the weeks immediately following the November Revolution, was not dissimilar to that which

[3] National Archives, Foreign Affairs Branch, Petrograd Embassy 800 File, 1918; unsigned document dated March 20, 1918, entitled "Memorandum regarding Allied War Stores Lying at Archangel."

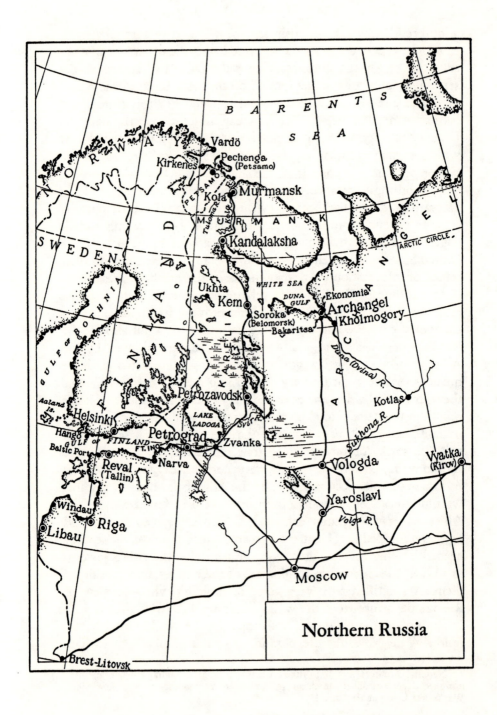

Northern Russia

prevailed in Vladivostok. Here, too, a remoteness from the Russian center, the prominent presence and interest of friendly Allied representatives, and the greater cosmopolitanism of a community oriented primarily to foreign trade and shipping, combined to retard the advance of the Bolshevik movement. To these factors there was added the extensive dependence of the city on food supply from overseas—a circumstance which became increasingly important with the dwindling of food shipments from the disorganized Russian interior.

In the face of these circumstances, the revolution at Petrograd found, initially, only a partial reflection in the situation at Archangel. Power was peacefully assumed, at the outset, by a so-called Revolutionary Committee, dominated by the moderate Social-Revolutionaries who—as the elections of delegates to the Constituent Assembly were soon to demonstrate—enjoyed a majority of popular support in the Archangel area. The members of this Committee and of the local municipal administration took a reasonable and friendly attitude toward the Allies and manifested from the start a readiness to solve mutual problems by discussion and agreement.

The Bolsheviki had no sooner consolidated their power in Petrograd than they set about to put an end to this unsatisfactory situation in Archangel. Immediately after the suppression of the Constituent Assembly in January 1918 there was despatched to Archangel a high-powered "Extraordinary Commission," headed by a Bolshevik commissar, M. S. Kedrov (Tsederbaum), who from this time on was to bear the major executive and military authority on behalf of the Soviet government for the Northern Region, and who was later to become the leading Soviet historian of the events surrounding the Allied intervention in that area.[4] The Extraordinary Commission was instructed, first, to assure complete Bolshevik control of the city and surrounding region and, second, to arrange for the immediate despatch to the interior of the war materials stored at Bakaritsa.

The reason for this last measure was presumably the desire of the Soviet leaders to get these materials to a place where they could

[4] In addition to a number of articles for Soviet periodicals, Kedrov wrote two books dealing with the events in the Russian North in the years immediately following the Revolution. The first, entitled *Za sovetski sever* (The Struggle for the Soviet North), Leningrad, 1927, dealt with the military operations against the Allied expeditionary force. The second, entitled *Bez bolshevistskogo rukovodstva* (Without Bolshevik Leadership), Leningrad Publishing Company "Krasnaya Gazeta," 1930, dealt with the development of the Murmansk situation.

themselves have easy access to them and where they would be safe from recapture by the Allies. The decision was taken without consultation with, or forewarning to, the Allied governments. It came almost simultaneously with the Soviet repudiation of the debts of the former Russian governments. This meant that in addition to appropriating the supplies for purposes which had nothing to do with Russia's war effort, now effectively at an end, the Soviet government was refusing to pay for them.

Kedrov and his associates lost no time in proceeding to the execution of their orders. On February 7 they succeeded, as Cole put it in one of his despatches, in "bulldozing" for themselves a majority in the Archangel Soviet. Using this leverage, they at once proceeded to abolish the Revolutionary Committee and to assume effective power, in the name of the Soviet, throughout the city and the surrounding region. The change was effected without bloodshed, and without immediate challenge to the position of the Allied representatives in the port.[5]

The political situation having been thus brought under control, the members of the Extraordinary Commission proceeded with similar despatch to the removal of the war stores. This was not easy, in view of the general economic disorganization and the low state of efficiency of the Vologda-Archangel railway. But here, as in so many other situations, Bolshevik ruthlessness and determination were effective; by late March shipments were going forward to the interior at the rate of about 3,000 tons per week. Most of them were routed to another storage site on the banks of the Sukhona River, near Vologda.

Early in January 1918, prior to the final Soviet seizure of power in Archangel, the moderate elements then in charge of the city had appealed to the British and American representatives for assistance in the supply of the region with food, pointing out that the Archangel district had received in 1917 only one-half of its usual supply from the Russian interior, and asking specifically for 35,000 tons of foodstuffs, mostly flour. In making this request, the members of the Revolutionary Committee were quite conscious of the Allied interest in the war materials stored at Bakaritsa and Ekonomia, and were clearly

[5] The authority of the Soviet continued to be halfheartedly challenged, for some time, by the non-Bolshevik city Duma; but this was a languishing center of resistance, and by summer it was pretty well eliminated from the picture.

Allen Wardwell

Wood-burning locomotive on Vologda-Archangel Railway

Archangel, from a tugboat on the River Duna

Shipping in Archangel harbor, 1918

prepared to agree that some of these stores should be released and returned to the Allies as a *quid pro quo* for the food. The British government responded, through its consul at Archangel, with a proposal to send two cargoes of food, in vessels so constructed as to be capable of penetrating the ice at least to the outer port, in return for which the Archangel authorities were to release sufficient quantities of war stores to make up return cargoes. By the time the British reply reached Archangel, however, the Extraordinary Commission had taken over and was busy carting the stores away. Not being particularly concerned for the comfort of a community predominantly anti-Bolshevik in its political sentiments, the leaders of the Commission proved deaf to all entreaties that the removals should cease. The British government, in a bit of wartime confusion, nevertheless despatched the two ships. They arrived in late April, only to find themselves compelled to lie idle in the roadstead for some two months, vainly awaiting settlement of the dispute over the war supplies.

In such circumstances it will readily be understood that the Bolshevik persistence in removing the supplies was intensely resented in Allied circles. What possible right, it was asked, could the Bolsheviki have to dispose over these valuable stores, sent to Russia at the expense and sacrifice of others for use in a purpose the Soviet government had now abandoned? To this grievance there was added, in many Allied minds, the suspicion that the removal of the stores was inspired by the Germans and that the materials would eventually end up in German hands.

So long as the port remained frozen, there was little that the Allies could do about it. The ice made any armed action unthinkable. It was this fact, together with the realization that with the thawing of the port in June the situation would change, that lent such urgency to the Bolshevik action in removing the stores. Meanwhile the matter naturally rankled in Allied minds and came to constitute one of the factors justifying, in the Allied view, military intervention for the protection of the Allied war interests in the North Russian area.

❖

In view of Archangel's brief navigation season, it had always represented only a partial alternative to the Russian Baltic ports, some of which were entirely ice-free in normal winters.[6] For this reason the decision was taken, early in the war, to supplement Archangel by the development of a new northern port which could be used the entire year.

The site chosen for the new port was a point on the Kola Inlet of the Murmansk coast, not far from the Finnish border. The Kola Inlet may be described geographically as the easternmost of the larger Norwegian fjords. Stretching some forty-six miles from the open sea to the confluence of the Tuloma and Kola Rivers, it resembles the fjords of the adjoining Norwegian coast in depth, narrowness, and relatively ice-free condition in winter—a product of the influence of the Gulf Stream. But it is extremely remote from all the Russian urban centers. In 1914 it was accessible to central Russia only via Archangel. Furthermore, as of 1914 there was nothing on the Kola Inlet in the way of a town or of a port adaptable to the handling of ocean-going traffic. The little village of Kola, the only inhabited place on the fjord large enough to claim the distinction of being a municipal entity, was wholly inadequate for this purpose. It was thus necessary not only to build an entirely new port city but to connect it with Russia proper by the construction of a new railway bridging the eight hundred miles of sparsely settled northern country, mostly swampland and tundra, that lay between Kola and Petrograd. Despite the obvious difficulty of implementing these projects in the face of the other wartime demands on Russian resources, they were—under the urging of the British—courageously put in hand. For the town, a site was selected on the eastern side of the fjord, some forty miles from its mouth, at a point where the steep, hilly banks receded from the water's edge to make way for a relatively flat, swampy basin.[7]

Construction was begun in September 1915 on both town and railway. In each case the operation was unavoidably hurried and makeshift. The railway construction, in particular, involved formidable difficulties. Twenty-five percent of the line had to be laid through

[6] Surely there are few subjects more widely misunderstood than that of Russia's reputed need for ice-free ports. The Russian Empire of the nineteenth century had, in addition to the Black Sea outlets, three Baltic ports (Libau, Windau, and the naval base of Baltic Port) that were normally ice-free. Russia's problem was not ice but rather lack of strategic control over the straits connecting her ports with the world ocean.

[7] This bit of flat land had previously been the site of a tiny fishing settlement called Romanov.

marshland. There were severe technical problems connected with permanently frozen subsoil. To avoid an even higher percentage of swampy foundation, forty percent of the line had to be laid out on curves. The waterways to be crossed seemed innumerable; when the line was completed there were sixteen yards of bridge to every one thousand yards of track. The long Arctic night had to be coped with, at a time when mobile electric illumination was not yet possible. Labor, food, and fodder for draft animals all had to be imported from a distance of hundreds of miles.[8] Despite these obstacles the line was completed, by the spring of 1917, to a point where it was possible to undertake a limited movement of traffic over its flimsy, winding, single track. And this achievement was matched by the completion of housing and port facilities at the new terminus on the bank of the fjord, crude and jerry-built in large part, but sufficient to make possible the loading and unloading of ocean-going shipping on a modest scale and the transshipment of the cargoes to and from the interior.

It cannot be said that the Murmansk of 1917–1918 was a prepossessing spot. Situated at the extreme northern latitude of sixty-nine degrees (approximately the same as the northern coast of Alaska, where it meets the Canadian border), it constituted, together with the nearby Norwegian town of Kirkenes, the northernmost of permanent urban settlements. It consisted solely of log cabins, wooden barracks, and storage sheds. Americans thought it resembled an early American logging camp. There was no sewage system, nor were there any paved streets. Open places tended to be littered with the debris of recent construction. Throughout the long winter the piles of frozen refuse grew higher and higher, only to melt and subside again with the advent of the late spring thaw and to join the sandy quagmires that served, perforce, as streets throughout the warmer season. As in all Arctic places, there was permanent daylight in the period of the summer solstice; but the air remained cool, and the sky was too often dimmed by clouds of mosquitoes emerging from the limitless swamps of the mainland.

One sensed on every hand the remoteness and desolation of the region. The rocky hills along the sides of the fjord, partly wooded

[8] For a description of the difficulties presented by the construction of the Murmansk line, see Alfred Knox, *With the Russian Army 1914–1917: Being Chiefly Extracts from the Diary of a Military Attaché,* Hutchinson & Co., London, 1921, Vol. II, pp. 501ff.

near Murmansk but becoming more and more barren as one pene-trated inland, were snow-covered and inhospitable to both beast and man throughout much of the year. The waters of the fjord were deep and cold—too cold for bathing even at the height of summer. At the head of the estuary, six miles from Murmansk, stood the ancient village of Kola, the former administrative center of the region. This little settlement, distinguishable from afar by its white stone church and citadel, huddled forlornly on the face of a great barren head-land separating the mouths of the two rivers that joined to form the fjord. Aside from this, there was no other human community worthy of the name within hundreds of miles of Murmansk. Even the sea to which the fjord descended was an empty one, frigid and mel-ancholy, leading only to the wastes and the silence of the Arctic.

Despite this extreme isolation, the new town of Murmansk had become, by the winter of 1917-1918, a fairly populous and busy place. Women, to be sure, were few. The amenities were wholly lacking. But there was already a population of nearly 5,000 people, including some 1,800 sailors (mostly naval) and an even larger num-ber of railway and port workers. Several Russian naval vessels, in-cluding the battleship *Chesma* and the cruiser *Askold,* were sta-tioned at the port. By the end of 1917 the demoralization of the Russian armed forces had proceeded to a point where the larger of these vessels were no longer operable. Their crews—idle, restless, excited by communist agitators—constituted a major source of un-rest and disorder in the community.

The use of Murmansk as a port had been inaugurated, during the course of the year 1917, by the visits of a number of ships bringing munitions and supplies from the western Allies. It would presum-ably have been used quite intensively during the winter and spring of 1918, while Archangel was icebound, had not the Bolshevik seizure of power in Petrograd put a stop to most of the shipments. Actually, it is questionable whether the railway could have coped successfully, in that winter, with any very large amount of traffic, even had the shipments come forward as originally planned. The line was still primitive and flimsy, operable only with great difficulty. Trains arrived at Murmansk, throughout the winter, on an average of less than once a week. For a passenger, the journey from Petrograd generally took five to nine days. Freight movement was still slower. Even this minimal achievement was made possible only by the fact that the soil was firmly frozen. Maintenance engineers looked forward with some apprehension to the thawing of the ground in the forthcoming summer.

In view of the inadequacy of the Russian naval units, the main burden of the naval defense of the Murmansk region had fallen to the British. British vessels had assumed, in 1916 and 1917, the major responsibility for anti-submarine patrol and mine-sweeping operations off the Murmansk coast. When the 1917 navigation season came to an end at Archangel, a small British naval force, commanded by Rear Admiral Thomas W. Kemp, was left to winter at Murmansk. The force consisted of the battleship *H.M.S. Glory,* which served as flagship, the cruiser *H.M.S. Vindictive,* and a group of six trawler-mine sweepers. The purposes which the force was intended at that time to serve, in the view of the Admiralty, were: the protection of the accumulation of stores at Archangel against possible German depredation, the similar protection of Russian vessels operating in the White Sea, and the protection of Allied nationals and refugees who used Murmansk as a port of exit from European Russia.[9]

Considering the part of the British in the development of Murmansk and the role they had assumed in the naval defense of the area, one cannot wonder that they felt a special sense of responsibility about what happened there, and considered themselves entitled, so long as the war might last, to a voice in the affairs of the port. This, too, must be borne in mind if the happenings of 1918 in this region are to be understood.

As at Archangel, the Bolshevik Revolution was slow to reach Murmansk. The city and surrounding region were largely a naval area. Extensive powers lay in the hands of the senior naval official, the so-called *Glavny Nachalnik,* Admiral K. F. Kyetlinski, a moderate and reasonable man, well inclined toward the Allies, and the United States in particular. Being popular with the rank and file of the naval garrison, he was permitted to carry on in the first weeks after the November Revolution and to exercise at least a portion of his normal authority. But beneath this surface arrangement there could be ob-

[9] Henry Newbolt, *History of the Great War, Naval Operations,* Longmans, Green & Co., London, 1931, Vol. v, Chapter ix, "Russia," pp. 301-333. Admiral Kemp had the advantage of considerable experience in Russia and a working knowledge of the language. He was not, however, viewed with great confidence by the American officials in Russia, who seem to have been unanimous in considering him excitable and impetuous.

served something of the same ferment that was taking place in the other Russian port cities just at this time. The local Soviet grew steadily in power; and the radical element in it, made up of the political leaders of the naval sailors and the local railwaymen, became daily more aggressive and intractable. In a community so closely connected as was Murmansk with the Allied war effort, such a development of the political situation could not fail to be the source of anxious concern to the Allied representatives on the spot.

✧

At the time of the November Revolution there were British and French representatives, of various capacities, in Murmansk, but no representatives whatsoever of the United States government. It is doubtful whether official Washington had ever known much, or cared much, about what went on at that remote point. But as the winter of 1917–1918 wore on, the force of circumstances began to compel a certain American participation in the affairs of the port; and a brief glance at the manner in which this participation came into being might be not without usefulness as an illustration of the prevailing atmosphere and of the casualness with which Americans contrive, on occasion, to back into confused and delicate political situations.

In mid-December 1917 there arrived in Murmansk two vessels carrying supplies for the American Red Cross missions in Russia and Rumania. The shipment destined for Russia consisted largely of canned milk, intended for the children of Petrograd.

In the absence of any American representative, the British made provisional arrangements for the removal of the cargo to the dock but wired at once to the Americans at Petrograd to send someone to look after the shipment. The head of the American Red Cross Commission in Petrograd, Colonel Raymond Robins, thereupon detailed one of his younger aides, Major Allen Wardwell, for this task.

Wardwell, a distinguished member of the New York bar, was one of the most useful of Robins' assistants in the Red Cross Commission. He was frequently used by Robins for trouble-shooting assignments away from the Russian capital. Vigorous, sensible, and of a patient and equable temper, he carried out these missions with tact and persistence, contriving both to remain aloof from the political and personal controversies that frequently wracked the American official colony and to keep on reasonably good terms with the various Soviet officials whose predisposition was essential to the accomplishment of his work. His diary—factual, cheerful, restricted almost entirely to things he saw or personally experienced—is a first-rate source of information on the doings and experiences of the Americans in Russia in 1918.[10]

After lengthy preparations, Wardwell managed to get off on January 2, 1918, traveling in a magnificent private railway car which Robins had wrangled from the Soviet authorities for the purpose. He took with him food for thirty days, an interpreter, and a Bolshevik sailor as bodyguard. The journey lasted five days and nights. It was so cold, Wardwell recorded in his diary, that the mercury in his Fahrenheit thermometer, suspended outside the train window, retired sullenly to the little ball at the bottom and occupied only a portion of that.

Wardwell arrived in Murmansk on the late evening of January 7. A dense fog was superimposed on the Arctic darkness. The temperature was thirty degrees below zero. After arranging for his car to be put on a siding, he set out to look for the British representatives. No one knew where they were to be found. A boy thought he knew where there were some French people. Together, the two set out into the impenetrable obscurity. After a mile of tramping through deep snow, the boy confessed himself hopelessly lost. But they ultimately stumbled, rather by accident, onto a log hut in which, to Wardwell's vast relief, they found three French officers and a lady playing cards. The French received Wardwell with that curious sense of brotherhood that seems to bind all westerners in the Russian presence, and took him to the British, who turned out to be living on a ship in the harbor.

The fog, so dense and so bitterly cold that Wardwell had the impression it was frozen to the ground, endured for two more days. Stumbling around in it on his various errands, he had at first only the most ghostly impressions of the vicinity. When it finally lifted, he was amazed, in the brief hours of daylight, at the winter beauty of the fjord and the surrounding hills, and overwhelmed—on the clear, cold nights—with the magnificence of the aurora borealis.

---

[10] I am indebted to the members of the Wardwell family for permission to draw on this valuable document, now on deposit with the Archive of Russian and Eastern European History and Culture, Butler Library, Columbia University, New York City.

With much difficulty, Wardwell rounded up his shipments, most of which had by this time been unloaded. It was none too soon. Pilferage was already extensive. By dint of long days of wrangling, threatening, arguing, cajoling, and checking up on the execution of promises—a process familiar to anyone who has ever tried to pilot shipments through the Russian transportation system in troubled times—he finally got the shipment unloaded, cleared, stowed into freight cars, placed under proper guard, and prepared for despatch southward.

Meanwhile, he was received in Murmansk, despite his Red Cross status, as the first American representative. He addressed, by invitation, a meeting of the Murmansk Soviet. He also paid a courtesy call on Admiral Kyetlinski. He found the Admiral to be a relatively young man, living with his wife and two small daughters in one of the few tolerable private residences the community had to offer. Kyetlinski had previously been stationed in the United States. The family had lived in Philadelphia, and had liked it there. They bore pleasant memories of the experience. They received the American visitor with kindness and hospitality.

After a night of wild last-minute confusions and false beginnings, Wardwell finally got his two trains started for Petrograd in the early morning hours of January 14. His own car was attached to the first of them, that of his interpreter to the second. On the 19th—very fast time in the circumstances—he proudly shepherded his caravan into the snow-covered railway yards at Petrograd.

Meanwhile, the American Embassy at Petrograd had taken steps to send to Murmansk, for the first time, a regular official of the United States government. It is illustrative of the lack in American circles of any political interest in the Murmansk region at that time that this was not a consular representative but a Passport Control Officer, whose function—matching that of the similar officials maintained there and in other Allied ports by the British and French—was merely to give aid and support to the masters of such American vessels as might arrive there, to keep an eye on Americans moving through the port, and to perform the various counterintelligence functions normally exercised by warring governments on friendly or Allied territory. Having no regular officers trained for this work, the Embassy had selected (and had unceremoniously commissioned, to this end, as a lieutenant in the army) another one of its special wartime employees: Mr. Hugh S. Martin of Meridian, Mississippi—a dashing young man of courtly but sanguine temperament, marked personal courage, and a very old-fashioned southern eloquence.[11]

Martin had already served as Passport Control Officer at Archangel during the summer navigation season of 1917. With the freezing up of that port, he had returned to Petrograd. In view of the prospective arrival of American vessels at Murmansk during the winter, it was now decided to detail him to that place. For some reason or other the Soviet authorities balked at this project and declined to give him the necessary permit for travel on the Murmansk Railway. (The reason for this—there already being British and French officials as well as British naval vessels at Murmansk—is difficult to imagine.) In any case, Martin was not to be thus easily put off. He returned by rail to Archangel, where he had only recently been, and where his presence was acceptable to the Soviet authorities. From there he proceeded to make his way, hiring peasant sleighs from village to village, across some two hundred and fifty miles of snowbound Arctic country to the little settlement of Soroka on the Murmansk Railway. There, far from the long arm of Petrograd and its permits, he found space in a northbound freight car. He arrived in Murmansk, after a total journey of some twelve hundred miles through the frozen Russian North, in early February, just in time to be present at, and to participate in, the first serious crisis in Murmansk's peculiar position between the western Allies and the Bolshevik authorities.

Like Wardwell, Martin was supplied with no instructions whatsoever of a political nature. He had had no personal preparation for the exercise of any political responsibility. He enjoyed no direct communication with Washington. His only source of instruction lay through a military attaché of the Embassy in Russia whose qualifications for the assumption of political responsibility were scarcely greater than his own. His presence at Murmansk rested on the happy confidence of official Washington that where it had not authorized political contact, no such contact could exist. Yet everyone in Murmansk looked to Martin as the spokesman for his government, and he was repeatedly placed in situations where even his silence would have been given a political interpretation. It is a tribute to the inher-

[11] Martin had, before coming to Russia, been for some years personal assistant to Senator John Sharp Williams, of Mississippi. Presumably, he owed his diplomatic clerkship to the influence of that redoubtable pillar of the Democratic Party.

ent virtues of the American character, rather than to methodology of American diplomacy, that people like Wardwell and Martin coped as well as they did with problems of the utmost complexity in which, as the future was to show, the American interest was not inconsiderable.

CHAPTER II

COMPLICATIONS IN MURMANSK

. . . You must accept any and all assistance from the Allied missions and use every means to obstruct the advance of the [Germans].—Trotsky, to the Murmansk Soviet, March 1, 1918

SHORTLY after Wardwell's departure from Murmansk, trouble had begun to develop with respect to the person of Admiral Kyetlinski.[1] He was, as it happened, a strongly liberal officer—a socialist, in fact, by persuasion. Even prior to the Revolution he had taken a lively interest in the well-being of the men under his command. He had continued, after the Revolution, to enjoy the sympathy and respect of the rank and file of the Murmansk naval garrison. This alone was probably sufficient to draw down upon him the jealousy and suspicion of the communist leaders in Petrograd. But beyond this, he had incurred special resentment in Bolshevik circles by the firmness with which, some months earlier, as head of a naval court-martial, he had condemned to death several revolutionary sailors who had made an effort to blow up the cruiser *Askold,* of which he was then the commander.[2]

Around the beginning of February orders were received from Petrograd by the local naval garrison that Kyetlinski was to be placed under arrest. Inquiry elicited the further information that the order was in connection with the *Askold* incident. The local sailors, now

---

[1] In attempting to reconstruct what took place at Murmansk in the ensuing weeks, the historian is greatly aided by the fact that these events form the subject of one of the few English-language secondary works dealing with the early period of Soviet-American relations. This is the valuable study by Professor Leonid I. Strakhovsky, *The Origins of American Intervention in North Russia (1918),* Princeton University Press, 1937. Although use has been made in the present study of the main sources to which Dr. Strakhovsky had reference, a special debt must be acknowledged to him for his initial development of these sources as well as for the general illumination brought to this subject by his careful and authoritative study.

[2] There has surely never been a navy in which such a crime, attempted in wartime, would not automatically have been punishable by death.

making their own decisions through their revolutionary committees, had no enthusiasm for the execution of this order. They contented themselves with putting a guard around the Admiral's house and assigning to him a personal bodyguard; and after a few days, even these measures were discontinued. Shortly thereafter Kyetlinski, walking alone in the port area, was suddenly set upon in a deserted area by two men in the uniform of naval ratings, who shot him down in cold blood and fled. Staggering to the nearest habitation, he died there twenty minutes later.

It was generally supposed, and with good reason, that the deed was the work of outsiders, and a consequence of the refusal of the sailors to take repressive measures against the Admiral. The local Soviet, obviously much embarrassed, termed it a "provocation" and suggested that it was the work of "counterrevolutionaries." This is most improbable. Allied officials, together with Kyetlinski's widow, suspected—characteristically and probably quite unjustly—the German hand, working through the agency of the Bolsheviki.

In general, the effect produced on the Allied representatives by incidents of this nature, so deeply shocking to all western liberal sensibilities, must not be underrated as a factor in the growth of their distaste and distrust for Bolshevik power.

Kyetlinski's murder had extensive consequences. It removed the only Russian official personally qualified to keep the local situation in order. It came as an unsettling shock to Admiral Kemp and the other British officials in the port, causing them to question the firmness of the power of the local Soviet in the face of German and other pressures hostile to the Allies. Above all, it raised in acute form the awkward question: who was now to exercise supreme authority in the area?

There were, by this time, in Murmansk three local bodies without whose collaboration and consent orderly government was scarcely possible. The first of these was the Murmansk Soviet, which in theory represented all the labor and socialist elements in the community. The Soviet was headed by an individual who was destined to play an important role in the unfolding of the entire Murmansk story— Aleksei Mikhailovich Yuryev. Yuryev, like most of the other actors in that drama, was then a newcomer to the Murmansk scene. He had been by profession, since the age of fourteen, an oiler and fireman, first on vessels of the Russian Volunteer Fleet and later, during the war, on American and British vessels. For a time during the war he had remained on shore in the United States. There he had apparently taken various jobs in different parts of the country. (He was able, in 1918, to understand much of what was said in English, though he spoke it only with difficulty.) He had arrived in Murmansk, as chief fireman on a Russian merchant vessel, in November 1917. An anarchist by persuasion, he had never, up to that time, been a member of the Russian Communist (then still called the Social-Democratic) Party. His political ideas were primitive and unschooled. Like most other Russian radicals, he thought of the Allies as "imperialists" and viewed them with neither confidence nor enthusiasm. (He had once been beaten up on a British ship, he claimed, for refusing to call the first mate "sir"; and the incident no doubt had something to do with his feelings about the British.) But he was practical enough to recognize the heavy dependence of Murmansk on the Allies for food and other supplies, as well as for defense against possible German encroachment. It was this practicality, together with his political inexperience and certain confusing events to be discussed shortly, that led him into a collaboration with the western Allies more intimate than his own political feelings would probably have warranted, and destined, as things worked out, to cause him bitter trouble in future years.[3]

The other two local bodies whose wishes had to be taken into account were the respective professional organizations of the railway workers and the naval sailors, known as the *Sovzheldor* (Union of Railway Workers) and *Tsentromur* (Central Soviet of the Murmansk Squadron). Both of these bodies feuded with the local Soviet over problems of administrative jurisdiction. Both were less friendly to the Allies than were the leaders of the Soviet itself.

The sailors—politically disoriented, undisciplined, and unable even to keep their own vessels operable—made a poor appearance generally. They were naturally aware of the disdain with which they

---

[3] On the collapse of the anti-Bolshevik movement in late February 1920, Yuryev remained in Murmansk and permitted himself to be taken prisoner by the triumphant Bolsheviki. Hailed before a military court on the charge of treason for his collaboration with the Allies, he defended himself with spirit and sincerity and succeeded, rather miraculously, in getting off with a prison sentence, subsequently commuted.

Professor Leonid I. Strakhovsky, the historian of the northern intervention, has described Yuryev to the writer as being, in 1918, "a colorful figure, tall, with dangling limbs, a long horse-like face and constantly smoking a large under-slung South African pipe."

were viewed by the relatively smart and well-disciplined crews of the foreign naval vessels in port. To this personal irritant there was added the intense political bias the Bolshevik agitators had already drummed into them. They viewed the Allied forces, throughout, with suspicion and hostility.

The Murmansk *Sovzheldor,* for its part, was only a branch of a parent union embracing the workers of the Murmansk line as a whole. Its members were constantly subject to the influence of the main headquarters, at Petrozavodsk, strongly Bolshevik in its outlook and highly suspicious of the Allied influence at Murmansk.

On the evening of February 12, two days after the murder of Kyetlinski, Admiral Kemp and the British Consul, Hall, met secretly with Kyetlinski's former aide, Georgi M. Vesselago,[4] and with the commander of the local land forces, Major General Nikolai I. Zvegintsev,[5] to discuss the measures that might be taken to assure the orderly administration and military security of the area in the light of Kyetlinski's death. Word had just reached Murmansk of the breakdown of the Brest-Litovsk negotiations. The possibility of some German action in the Petrograd area was in everyone's mind. Obviously, if the Germans were to take Petrograd, Murmansk would be cut off from mainland support and would become completely dependent on the Allies for supplies of every sort and for defense against possible German encroachments. It seemed plain to the four men that there was urgent need for the establishment in the Murmansk region of some orderly governmental authority which could collaborate with the British naval forces in assuring the security of the area. The decision was taken to ask the three local bodies—the

[4] Vesselago is now an American citizen. His memoirs were assembled, in 1918, in the form of a monograph entitled *Dokumentalnaya spravka iz moikh Murmanskikh bumag za 1917 i 1918 gg* (Documentary Digest from My Murmansk Papers 1917-1918). A copy of this monograph is in the National Archives, Foreign Affairs Branch, Washington. The Soviet government also obtained a copy of it as early as 1930, by processes probably known only to itself. (See Kedrov, *Bez bolshevistskogo rukovodstva, op.cit.*)

[5] Zvegintsev, former Commander of the Tsarskoye Selo Hussar Regiment of the Guards, was, like so many other people, a newcomer to the Murmansk scene. He had previously held no official position there. He had been sent there by the central Soviet authorities, with whom he remained on nominally acceptable terms up to the beginning of the intervention. He and Vesselago appear to have been the dominant personalities behind the Murmansk Soviet. Martin thought Zvegintsev "a man of remarkable intelligence, ability and energy." (National Archives, Foreign Affairs Branch, Petrograd Embassy file "Miscellaneous Confidential Information, 1918"; Martin's report of May 8, 1918.)

Soviet, the *Sovzheldor,* and the *Tsentromur*—to join in forming a so-called People's Collegium, which would take over Kyetlinski's powers in the area, and with which the Allies and the armed services could deal in matters of defense. This decision was communicated to Martin, who had just arrived in Murmansk, and to the chief of the local French Military Mission, Captain de Lagatinerie. Martin was thus plunged from the moment of his arrival into the political problems of the region.

The new Collegium was set up on February 16, with Vesselago as its executive secretary. Its authority was promptly confirmed by the Commander in Chief at Archangel, Somov, who still theoretically had over-all military authority over the entire northern area. Its relationship to the central Soviet authority was thus fuzzy from the outset.

At this point the situation was further complicated by the receipt, on or about February 18, of the news of the renewal of hostilities against Russia by the Germans. This confirmed the worst fears of both Allied representatives and Russian officials at Murmansk. It led them to expect the emergence of German forces at any time at the Petrograd end of the Murmansk Railway. By giving them a sense of common danger, it created among them—Russians and westerners alike—a sense of solidarity that contrasted sharply with the antagonism and suspicion by which relations between the Allied missions and the Bolshevik leaders in Petrograd were already marked.

❖

The news of the pending arrival at Murmansk of another vessel, the *Dora,* bearing foodstuffs consigned to the American Red Cross Commission, moved Robins to despatch Wardwell on a second expedition to Murmansk. Wardwell set off on February 15, again in his private railway car, and arrived in Murmansk on the 20th. He discovered that the British authorities, shaken by Kyetlinski's murder and by the German renewal of hostilities, had turned the *Dora* back as soon as she reached the Murmansk coast. Although they later thought better of this action and tried to recall the vessel, they were no longer able to get into touch with her, and she pursued her return journey to England.

This left Wardwell without any serious mission. He at once despatched a telegraphic report to Robins on the situation, and asked what he was now to do. But by this time all was turmoil and confusion in Petrograd. Robins had left the city before the message was received. There was no immediate reply. For the moment, therefore, Wardwell continued to reside in his car in the railway yard. Martin and a representative of the American Y.M.C.A., the Reverend Jesse Halsey, both lacking adequate accommodations, moved in with him.

On March 4, the little party was joined by another member of the Red Cross Commission, Major Thomas D. Thacher, accompanied by the commission's Cossack interpreter, Captain Ilovaiski.[6] Thacher was also, like Wardwell, a distinguished member of the New York bar (subsequently president of the bar association of New York City and judge of the New York State Court of Appeals) and one of several exceptionally able men on Robins' staff. Robins had sent him to Murmansk in order to place him in a position where he could leave Russia, if necessary, and deliver to William Boyce Thompson (former head of the Red Cross Commission to Russia) and other well-wishers abroad a personal account of Robins' latest experiences and views. On arrival in Murmansk, Thacher sent off a cable to Thompson, now in the United States, soliciting the latter's guidance with respect to his own further movements. While awaiting a reply, he, too, took lodgings with Wardwell in the railway car, which thus became a sort of American headquarters on wheels.

Life took a colorful course in the railway yards where the Americans were residing. From time to time trainloads of refugees, in boxcars, lumbered in from the distant south. Cosmopolitan Petrograd was now disgorging, in its extremity, all those international elements that had no place in the world of Bolshevism. No other quarters being available in Murmansk, the refugees remained in the boxcars, in the snow-covered yards. There were among them all shapes and sizes of humanity. The scenes recall, to the contemporary mind, the Lisbon of World War II. "We have nearly every nationality here now," Wardwell wrote on March 5,

it is a queer conglomerate crowd. There are French, Italians, English, a few Americans, Russians, Roumanians, Czechs and with the Chinese

[6] Thacher and Ilovaiski had left Petrograd together with Robins, on the occasion of the final departure of the Embassy from that city for Vologda. They had disembarked, however, from the official train at Zvanka, where the Murmansk line takes off from the Petrograd-Vologda line, and had made their way to Murmansk on one of the refugee trains, being kindly welcomed into a very crowded car full of Englishmen.

working on the railway and the Greeks and Finns . . . There are French officers and men, some Italian singers who bellow all day in their cars and once in a while sing in front of it in true operatic style with all the approved gestures. There is a famous singer of gypsy songs, a number of Russian aviators trying to sneak out of Russia to America, a Russian professor of mathematics . . . a cook from the American Embassy who comes from the West Indies and speaks English with a French accent . . .[7]

This condition, alleviated periodically by the departure of evacuation vessels, continued throughout March and part of April. Immediately after departure of one of the refugee ships the yards would be relatively peaceful and deserted, but soon the accumulation would begin again. On March 29 Wardwell wrote:

Life in the metropolis of the North to which all the social life of Russia, particularly of the foreign element, has flocked for this winter season, quieted down somewhat after the departure of the "Hunt's End," but has begun to boom again as the time for the departure of the next steamer approaches. The streets are filled with the elite of both sexes, and the temporary cooking outfits are coming into action again. Society tires of eating out of tins and cooking in the cars makes a mess, so stoves are placed in the open between the lines of cars and meals are cooked al fresco although the thermometer is well below freezing. The only danger is that cars may be switched about and dinner, when cooked, may be a long way from the dining room.[8]

Somehow or other, despite the chaotic circumstances, the lack of accommodations, the appalling sanitary conditions, and the severe climate, life moved on in the little far northern community. International concerts were even arranged, to tap the talents of Allied representatives and the transient population. Wardwell himself participated in one of these performances—one put on by the British contingent. He led off the program, in fact, by playing Nevin's "Ophelia" on the piano. Recalling the opera, ballet, and concerts he had been attending in Petrograd, he returned to his railway car that evening shaken by the artistic limitations of his own race. "Only the Anglo-Saxons could seriously do this thing," he recorded with a shudder, as he thought back on the performance; "it is the worst crime which has been committed in Russia!"

On one occasion (March 14), Thacher, accompanied by Ilovaiski,

---

[7] Wardwell MSS, *op.cit.,* Diary.
[8] *Ibid.*

attended a meeting of the Executive Committee of the Soviet. What was the occasion of this visit and what was actually said at it, we do not know. Thacher was asked for, and gave, his views on the current situation. Ilovaiski interpreted. Some months later Ilovaiski had an interview with the American Vice Consul at Stockholm, in which he boasted that he had only pretended to interpret Thacher's remarks, but had actually said what he knew Trotsky would have liked to have had Thacher say: that the United States would never permit Allied intervention in the Russian North and that the Allies ought to accord early recognition to the Soviet government and lend support to Soviet policies. Thacher had later learned of this distortion, Ilovaiski said, and had been greatly indignant; but it was then too late: he, Ilovaiski, had already wired his version of it to Moscow, where it had appeared in the Soviet press.[9]

This account, whatever the truth behind it, raises inevitably the uncomfortable question: on how many other occasions were these American representatives—ignorant as most of them were of the language in which the political life around them was transpiring—betrayed in this manner by their interpreters, and how much was added, in this way, to the confusion and misunderstandings of the time? The exact answer to this question we shall never know; but that a considerable measure of distortion was occasioned generally in the presentation of the American position by the dependence of the leading American representatives on Russian interpreters, each of whom had some ax of his own to grind, is scarcely open to doubt.

Thacher eventually received a telegram from Thompson telling him to proceed to London and to brief Mr. Dwight Morrow on the

---

[9] War Department Archives, Records Branch, The Pentagon, Washington, report to SECSTATE, September 13, 1918.

Ilovaiski's ruse was obviously a move aimed at the British; and it must have displeased them greatly. It was surely with the blessing of the Soviet authorities that Ilovaiski functioned as an interpreter for the Red Cross Commission; and it must be assumed that he was a Soviet agent. But the British may not have been wholly blameless with respect to Ilovaiski's evident desire to toss the bone of contention between them and the Americans. Two days before this meeting with the executive committee, Wardwell had paid a visit to the British Consulate with Ilovaiski. He subsequently wrote in his diary: "There were a number of English there. It is quite appalling the things they say right in front of Ilovaisky. They have no tact whatsoever." (Wardwell MSS, *op.cit.,* Diary.)

This was not the first complaint by Americans over the lack of effort on the part of the British to conceal their contempt for, and disparagement of, the Russian armed forces.

situation, after which he could return to the United States. He got off
with a vessel that left on March 22.

Wardwell had first thought to leave with Thacher; but on March
16 he received a message from Thompson advising him to remain
for the time being in Russia since there might be important work
for him to do.[10] This was soon supplemented by a telegram from
Robins (now in Moscow) telling him to return to Petrograd and
wind up the Red Cross work in that city. He remained in Murmansk
until March 30.

❖

To return to the development of the political situation in Murmansk: the apprehension experienced by the Allied officials there at
the reports of the final Brest-Litovsk crisis in late February was
heightened by the simultaneous arrival of the first vague and distorted reports of the civil war that had broken out in Finland. Hostilities between Whites and Reds in Finland had erupted with the
move of the Finnish Communists, in mid-January, to seize power
throughout the country, following the precedent set by the Bolsheviki in Petrograd. On January 28 the Reds had seized power in Helsinki and had forced the non-communist government to flee. Marshal Carl Gustaf Mannerheim, who had been entrusted by the uprooted government with the defense of the new republic against the
communist bid for power, finding himself confronting a hopeless
Red preponderance in the south, had gone to north-central Finland
and had set about to create in that area a nucleus of resistance to the
Finnish Reds and to the bolshevized Russian garrisons in Finland by
whom they were supported. By dint of prompt and daring action, he
had succeeded by the end of January in disarming the disaffected
Russian garrisons in the immediate vicinity of his hastily improvised
headquarters.[11] By mid-February all of north-central Finland, including the Finnish-Swedish border point of Torneo-Haparanda, at
the head of the Gulf of Bothnia, was in his hands.

In itself, there was no reason why Mannerheim's initial success

[10] *Ibid.*, Diary.
[11] It is interesting to note the similarity of this development to that which took
place simultaneously in Rumania, where the Rumanian army was obliged, for reasons
of its own security, to disarm and expel the disaffected Russian troops in Moldavia.
A similar development, it will be recalled, had taken place in Harbin.

should have alarmed either the Russians or the Allied representatives at Murmansk. A former Tsarist officer with a long and distinguished record of service in the Russian army, Mannerheim was neither pro-German nor pro-Entente. He was simply pro-Finnish. He had, initially, no intention of appealing to the Germans for aid, nor was he even aware, in February, that any such appeals had been made from other Finnish quarters.[12] The Reds, strongly supported by the new Soviet regime in the neighboring Petrograd area, had an important head start. The task that loomed before Mannerheim in February 1918—namely, liberating the entire southern part of Finland from communist control—was in itself a great and dangerous venture, certain to tax to the full all the resources he could conceivably muster. The gratuitous assumption of any further and unrelated military burdens in another direction, such as serious offensive operations against the Murmansk Railway or the Allied position at Murmansk, was the last thing that would have entered his mind in this initial stage of the Finnish Civil War, even had the political motivation been present.

It is true that Mannerheim was, at the time of the resumption of the German offensive against Russia, already making use in part, and would soon use in its entirety, the German-trained Finnish battalion known as the "Königliches Preussisches Jägerbatallion 27." This unit was made up of some 1,800 young Finns who, anxious to liberate their country from Russian rule, had gone into training with the German army in the earlier years of the war, and had been used briefly by the Germans for combat on the eastern front near Riga in 1916. Upon the Bolshevik seizure of power in Petrograd and the Finnish declaration of independence that followed at the end of the year, the Germans promptly agreed to repatriate this unit to Finland, with its arms. Some sixty of these Jägers had already returned secretly to Finland by the middle of February and had entered into underground service there for the White cause. Another small contingent reached Finland on February 17. The main body of the corps arrived at Vaasa on the 25th.[13] At Mannerheim's insistence, and much to their own discontent, these men, instead of being permitted to go into action as a single fighting unit, were distributed throughout the newly formed units and used primarily as training officers

[12] G. Mannerheim, *Erinnerungen*, Atlantis Verlag, Zurich, 1952, p. 192.
[13] J. O. Hannula, *Finland's War of Independence*, Faber & Faber, Ltd., London, c. 1939, pp. 104–109.

and commanders. They were thus spread very thinly throughout the Finnish White forces. They were attached heart and soul to the Finnish cause, and were in no sense agents of German military power.

In addition to the Finnish Jägers, a few German officers were brought in together with the Jäger unit to occupy higher command positions for which the Finns lacked suitable men.[14]

The Jägers probably wore uniforms similar at least in part to those of the German army. This, together with the admixture of German names, was perhaps sufficient to give Allied intelligence officers from the start a somewhat exaggerated impression of the degree of German involvement in the Finnish White cause.

As will be seen in another chapter, certain detachments of Red Finns, driven out of central Finland by Mannerheim's operations, retreated in early March into the zone of the Murmansk Railway. Reconnaissance patrols of White Finns, evidently commissioned to keep track of these Red detachments, appeared in this area in early March. It is conceivable, though subsequent statements of the Finnish government render it doubtful, that one or another of these reconnaissance detachments of White Finns was commanded by one of the Jägers; and this, in turn, may have led to the rumors, soon current in Murmansk, that the Murmansk Railway, and Murmansk itself, were being attacked or threatened by "German-Finnish" units under German command. It is difficult to see what other substantiation these rumors could have had.

Another factor that might have had something to do with the early emergence of Allied fears about a German move against Murmansk was the fact that on February 10 (the very day of Kyetlinski's murder), the German High Command resolved, in view of the breakdown of the Brest-Litovsk negotiations, to despatch a regular German military force to Finland, and at once began preparations to do so. This was a secret decision, but rumors of it may conceivably have reached Allied circles in the ensuing days. The purpose of this German move was a double one, flowing from the necessities of the conduct of war.[15] First there was the desire to establish a mili-

[14] Rüdiger von der Goltz, *Meine Sendung in Finnland und im Baltikum,* Verlag K. F. Koehler, Leipzig, 1920, p. 37.

[15] See statements by both Hindenburg and Ludendorff, cited by Strakhovsky, *op.cit.,* pp. 18–19. Whether, in addition to this, the Germans had designs on Finland's independence is a question that does not need to be examined at this point; if they did, these designs were decidedly secondary to the military considerations involved.

tary position from which Germany could counter and frustrate any Allied move to use Murmansk as a base for the development of renewed military resistance to Germany on the eastern front. Plainly, a German position in Finland, on the flank of the Murmansk Railway, would render extremely vulnerable any Allied movement from Murmansk southward. Secondly, the presence of German forces in Finland would constitute an additional German threat to Petrograd and would thus increase German means of pressure on the recalcitrant and elusive Bolsheviki, on whose good faith—treaty or no treaty —the German High Command was not inclined to place any great reliance. The initial plans for the employment of these German forces included no offensive intentions against Murmansk itself, or even against the Murmansk Railway—in the absence of any Allied move toward Petrograd.

German forces were landed at the Aaland Islands on March 7. No landing was made on the mainland of Finland until April 3, at which time units were landed at Hängo. This was followed somewhat later by another landing just east of Helsinki. The German operations were confined to assistance to the Finnish Whites in liberating the southwestern and south-central portions of the country from communist control. At no time did they get nearer to Petrograd than about eighty miles. They remained hundreds of miles distant from the main stretches of the Murmansk Railway east and north of Lake Ladoga.

There is no evidence that an attack on Murmansk by German forces ever entered into German plans prior to the landing of the first regular British military force there on June 23, 1918.[16] Later, at a time when the Allies had extensive naval forces at Murmansk, the Germans would show a serious interest in the chances for obtaining naval control of the neighboring Petsamo; and later still, in late June, they would press the Bolsheviki (unsuccessfully) to combine with the Finnish White government in doing just what the Allies were worried about in March and April—in setting up, that is, a joint armed expedition, under German command, to expel the Allies from the Murmansk region. But these German undertakings were, in both cases, later reactions to moves the Allies had already made.

[16] This is not to be confused with the landing of a few British and French marines in early March, as related below.

Neither was ever actually carried through; and it is doubtful whether the second, in particular (the effort to organize a joint Finnish-Russian action against the Allies at Murmansk), would ever have been entertained had not the Allies already given every evidence of preparation to undertake a serious intervention with land forces in the Russian North.

Here, again, we have a good example of the tendency of warring powers to exaggerate the enemy's intentions and capabilities, to ascribe to him intentions that go beyond what he actually wishes to do, to take counteraction, then, against these fancied intentions, and thus in the end to provoke precisely the behavior that was initially feared. In March and April there was no serious danger of attack on Murmansk by Finns under German command; but by the time the British and French had spent some weeks acting as though there *were* such a danger, they had succeeded in conjuring it into a real existence.

The first of the misleading rumors and reports about the German threat began to reach Murmansk in late February just at the time of the establishment of the People's Collegium and the institution of close collaboration between the local authorities and the Allied representatives in the port.[17]

❖

The last days of February, marked as they were by a steady flow of sensational and alarming reports, some false, some true—that the Germans were marching on Petrograd, that the capital was being evacuated, that the government was fleeing to Moscow, etc.—naturally constituted a time of great excitement and apprehension in Murmansk. It was generally assumed, for a period of some days, that Russia would not accept the German terms; that there would be no peace; that Murmansk, cut off from the rest of Russia, would shortly be "on its own" and confronted, in some way or other, with direct German attack. The central Soviet authorities in Petrograd were at that moment far too harried and pressed to keep the remote outposts of the Soviet world informed of what was occurring or to give them any detailed guidance. It was not surprising, in these circum-

---

[17] Wardwell mss, *op.cit.*, Diary for February 28 records the circulation in British circles of rumors of "Finns with German officers" trying to reach Kandalaksha.

stances, that both Allied and Russian authorities at Murmansk took independent measures designed to put themselves in a position to meet the threatened danger.

On the Allied side, Admiral Kemp, at some time during the last days of February, wired to London requesting the immediate despatch of six thousand troops to Murmansk for the protection of the area. He informed Martin, and no doubt also the French representative, of this request and asked them to bespeak the support of their own military authorities.[18] The British government, hard-pressed to find adequate forces for the western front in the light of the forthcoming German offensive, did not accede at that time to the request for troops, but did respond by despatching a second warship, the cruiser *H.M.S. Cochrane,* to Murmansk, and by requesting the French and American governments to follow suit and to despatch warships of their own to that point.

This request came to the United States government in the form of a memorandum from the British Embassy to the Department of State. It was argued, on the basis of Admiral Kemp's report, that

. . . a serious situation exists there [i.e., in Murmansk] owing to the anti-Ally attitude adopted by the Bolsheviki garrison, and to the reported intention of the Finns who, acting at the instigation of the Germans, propose to advance on the Petrograd-Murmansk Railway.[19]

The memorandum was delivered at an awkward moment: on March 5, when everyone was in the throes of the crisis produced by the Allied proposals for Japanese intervention in Siberia. The matter had not been adequately prepared or explained. Washington's reaction (cleared, no doubt, with the President) was negative; no American warship would be sent "for the present."[20]

The French, on the other hand, responded by despatching at once the heavy cruiser *Amiral Aube,* which arrived in Murmansk in mid-March.

[18] David R. Francis MSS, Missouri Historical Society, St. Louis; telegram, Francis to SECSTATE, March 4, 1918.

[19] *Papers Relating to the Foreign Relations of the United States, 1918, Russia,* U.S. Government Printing Office, Washington, 1932, Vol. II, p. 469; Memorandum No. 232, March 4, 1918.

This series of government publications, the individual volumes of which appeared at varying dates, will hereafter be referred to simply as *Foreign Relations.*

[20] National Archives, War Records Division, Navy Branch, Record Group 45, Naval Records Collection of the Office of Naval Records and Library; telegram no. 3532, OPNAV to Sims, March 5, 1918.

Complications in Murmansk

The Murmansk Soviet, meanwhile, had also reacted, in its way, to the excitement of the final days of February. It had despatched on March 1 to the central Soviet authorities at Petrograd a telegram which was destined to have extensive consequences. The text was as follows:

The renewed attack by the German imperialists and capitalists gives grounds for anxiety for the security of the Murmansk region and railway. The Murmansk Soviet, concerned to defend the railway and the region against every form of attack, is setting up a socialist armed force. There are widely circulating rumors of the possible appearance of the Finnish White Guard and German partisan bands in the neighborhood of the railway. The representatives of the friendly powers, the French, American and English missions currently at Murmansk, continue to show themselves inalterably well-inclined toward us and prepared to render us assistance, running all the way from food supply to armed aid, inclusive. The Murmansk Soviet, in guarding the conquests of the proletariat, hesitates nevertheless to attempt to solve independently the question of the defense of the region and the railway, and it requests instructions from the central Soviet authority, particularly with regard to the forms in which aid in men and materials may be accepted from the friendly powers. Czech and French detachments, numbering some two thousand men, in process of repatriation to France, are at this time in transit along the Murmansk Railway.[21]

[21] Kedrov, *Bez bolshevistskogo rukovodstva, op.cit.*, p. 27.
Unless otherwise stated, translations from foreign language sources cited in this work are my own.
The text of this and other documents appearing in Kedrov's book will be found in French translation in the article by Mme. Alexandra Dumesnil entitled "L'Intervention des Alliés à Mourmansk (Mars-avril 1918)," *Revue d'Histoire de la Guerre Mondiale*, No. 1, January 1936 (Ancienne Librairie Schlicher, Paris, Alfred Costes, Editor), p. 44. Dumesnil took the texts from Kedrov.
As for the reference to Czech and French detachments, the number is probably greatly exaggerated. There appears to have been a movement of French technical military advisers and possibly one or two artillery detachments through Russia en route to France, following the collapse of the Rumanian front and the German-Rumanian armistice. Some of these people were en route to Murmansk as of March 1. There is no confirmation of any Czechs being on the railroad at this time; and it is likely that what this had reference to was really a detachment of Serbs, likewise in process of repatriation. The British Consul, Hall, told the representatives of the Murmansk Soviet on March 2 that a detachment of fifty English soldiers was at Kem (about halfway up the line from Petrograd to Murmansk) and that a larger detachment was expected in two days. What this referred to is utterly unclear. There is no other evidence of anything of this sort. Kem is a port on the White Sea. Conceivably this might have referred to men on a British vessel; but Kem, like Archangel, was normally wholly icebound at this time of the year. The reference will have to stand as one more example of the confusion and chaos of the time.

[45]

It was characteristic of the confusion of the moment that this message from the Murmansk Soviet reached Trotsky, at Petrograd, almost simultaneously with the misleading telegram from Kara-khan, at Brest-Litovsk, which caused the Soviet leaders to believe, over a period of some hours, that the Soviet delegation at Brest had been unsuccessful in its effort to capitulate to the Germans and that the latter now proposed to continue their march on the Russian capital and probably on Moscow as well (see Volume 1, Chapter xxiv). Trotsky's reply to the Murmansk Soviet, despatched on the evening of the same day (March 1), was evidently drafted in the brief period during which this misunderstanding persisted. Trotsky was there-fore writing under the erroneous impression that the German offen-sive was about to be ruthlessly pursued and that the fall of Petrograd was practically inevitable (the first sentences clearly reflect this mis-understanding). The message, destined to become a key factor in the subsequent development of the Murmansk situation, read as follows:

To the Murmansk Soviet, March 1/14, 21:25 o'clock.
PRIORITY.
The peace negotiations have apparently been broken off. Petrograd is menaced. All measures have been taken for defending the city to the last drop of blood. It is your duty to do everything to protect the Murmansk Railway. Whoever abandons his post without a fight is a traitor. The Germans are advancing in small detachments. Resistance is possible and obligatory. Abandon nothing to the enemy. Evacuate everything that has any value; if this is impossible, destroy it. *You must accept any and all assistance from the Allied missions* and use every means to obstruct the advance of the plunderers. Your Soviet must set an example of courage, firmness and efficiency. We have done everything possible for peace. The bandits are now attacking us. We must save the country and the Revolu-tion . . .

People's Commissar,
Trotsky.[22]

Since this message became the formal basis for much of the subse-quent course of action of the Murmansk Soviet, leading to the estab-lishment of intimate collaboration with the Allied powers and even-tually to a complete break with the Bolsheviki, it is no wonder that it was bitterly assailed by the Stalinist historians and exploited as

---

[22] Kedrov, *Bez bolshevistskogo rukovodstva, op.cit.,* p. 28. The italics were added by Kedrov.

grounds for the denunciation of Trotsky. Kedrov's own works afford, in their references to it, an interesting example of the progression of violence and distortion in the treatment of Trotsky and his actions by Soviet historians, as Stalin's personal power became consolidated. The references to the message in Kedrov's book, published in 1930, are relatively moderate and understanding. The later references, contained in an article published in 1935 [23] commemorating the fifteenth anniversary of the termination of the civil war in the north, are violently abusive, and portray Trotsky's action in despatching this message as a wholly undisciplined, highly suspicious, and probably treasonable act.

In the book Kedrov stated:

The telegram, drafted in somewhat panicky tones, reflected the prevailing bewilderment in Soviet circles in connection with the renewed German offensive. . . . The telegram was, unquestionably, a serious political error, since it (1) obliged the recipients to accept every sort of collaboration from the imperialists of the Entente, not limiting this acceptance by any conditions; (2) it brought confusion into the relations between the soviets of the Murmansk region and the Olonets and Archangel *guberniyas,* in that it authorized the Murmansk Soviet alone to conduct negotiations with the "Allies," to assume leadership in the defense of the whole vast region, and to guard the entire Murmansk Railway, failing at the same time to apprise the other provincial centers of the measures taken; and (3) it legitimatized the work of those persons who . . . were endeavoring to establish a common front with the "Allies." . . .[24]

Having made these points, Kedrov went on to examine the general Party line prevailing at that time with respect to the acceptance of assistance from the Allies, including the statements of Lenin and Trotsky himself, and to demonstrate that this Party line never envisaged actually inviting foreign armed forces onto the territory of the Russian Soviet Republic. Thus Trotsky, Kedrov concluded, in drafting this telegram

. . . deviated a tiny bit to the right from the line laid down by the Central Committee, and that little deviation, miniscule [*malyusenki*] in itself, consisting of the single redundant expression "any and all" . . . without any modifications or exceptions, had extremely serious consequences, since it implanted in the minds of the worker and peasant masses the illusion

[23] Moscow *Pravda,* February 21, 1935.
[24] Kedrov, *Bez bolshevistskogo rukovodstva, op.cit.,* pp. 28–31.

of the possibility of conducting a revolutionary war against the German imperialists side by side with the brigands of Anglo-French imperialism.

It can scarcely be doubted that Kedrov's analysis is substantially correct, if taken in relation to the *general* policy of the Central Committee at that time. There is no reason to believe that at any moment of the Brest-Litovsk crisis other than precisely these hours on March 1 would Lenin himself have been inclined to give Soviet assent to any movement of regular Allied forces onto territory claimed by the Soviet government; for he viewed the Allies as no whit less evil and menacing than the Germans. His general purpose, throughout this period, was to purchase, by the concessions of the Brest-Litovsk Treaty, a breathing-space during which Soviet power could be strengthened; and there was, at that time, still hope that this could be accomplished. The Central Committee, in any case, had not taken note in its policy directives of any contingency other than that of German acceptance of a Soviet capitulation, and there could thus have been no general policy directive by which acceptance of the entrance of Allied forces onto Soviet territory could have been rationalized.[25]

At a somewhat later date both Trotsky and Lenin, as we shall see, would go fairly far in acquiescing passively to the presence of Allied forces on shore at Murmansk, though they maintained at all times a formal position of protest against it. But this would be at a time when the landing was already an accomplished fact, beyond their power to alter, and when they had other reasons for not seeking too sharp and final a conflict with the Allied governments.

Nevertheless, Trotsky's reply to the Murmansk Soviet, constituting as it did an apparent sanction by the Soviet government of precisely the sort of collaboration already growing up between that body and the Allied commanders at Murmansk, gave a powerful impulse to the further development of this cooperation and caused it at once to take on a formality and intimacy which surely no one at the center— not even Trotsky—could have fully envisaged. On the day following

[25] The formula embodied in Trotsky's questions to Robins four days later, after signature of the treaty—a formula to which Lenin gave his consent (see Volume I, Chapter xxiv)—confirms this assumption, in that it merely inquires to what extent, in the opinion of the United States government, aid would be assured "through Murmansk and Archangel" *if* the Russians should refuse to ratify the treaty or *if* hostilities were to be renewed for any other reason, thus leaving the implication that Allied aid was desirable and discussable only in these contingencies.

receipt of the message, Vesselago lost no time in calling a new meeting of the People's Collegium, together with representatives of the Allied missions, to work out a more concrete program for the joint defense of the area. The danger envisaged was, it should be noted, primarily the fancied threat from Finland, not the possibility of a German advance up the railway from the south. The meeting was attended on the Allied side by Admiral Kemp, the British Consul, and a French military representative, Captain Charpentier. It led to the approval by those present of a so-called "oral agreement" which, after some refinement in one or two further sessions, came to embrace the following points:

1. The Murmansk Soviet should be considered the supreme power in the Murmansk region.

2. Supreme military power was to be in the hands of a Military Council, composed of one representative from the Soviet, one British, and one French.

3. The French and British undertook not to interfere in the internal affairs of the region, but they were to be kept informed, in appropriate ways, of all decisions of the Soviet having general applicability.

4. The French and British would do all in their power to assure the supply of the region with food and other materials.[26]

This agreement was accepted by Admiral Kemp, subject to the approval of his government. Whether such approval was ever actually given is uncertain.[27] In any case, military collaboration de-

---

[26] Kedrov, *Bez bolshevistskogo rukovodstva, op.cit.* The agreement is also summarized in Kedrov's *Pravda* article, *op.cit.* Kedrov charges, in the later *Pravda* article, that the Military Council was set up and made the supreme military authority with Trotsky's knowledge. No proof is offered for this assertion, which was not made in Kedrov's book; and there is no other evidence that this was so. The statement may be taken as probably a bit of deliberate propagandistic distortion.

[27] At the session of March 2 Kemp, according to Kedrov, told the others, "I will transmit to my government the conditions of the agreement and will say that I agree with them, and will extend aid on my part until the receipt of an answer from London." At the session on the following day, he said: "I transmitted your conditions to the British Government but have as yet received no answer to my telegram. I may say that the British Government is prepared to extend aid for the defense of the region but as far as other measures are concerned, I have not yet received authority to take them." Kedrov, *Bez bolshevistskogo rukovodstva, op.cit.,* pp. 34, 35.

Newbolt, Vol. v, *op.cit.,* pp. 313–314, describes the instructions given to Kemp at that time as follows:

". . . the despatch of troops from England seemed at the moment to be impossible. The Allies could not undertake the military defence of Murmansk, nor could

veloped along the lines envisaged. The Murmansk Soviet, in particular, seems to have proceeded on the theory that the agreement was a wholly valid one. The United States government, it will be noted, was in no way involved.

In the ensuing days the Military Council was formally constituted, the initial members being Lieutenant V. N. Brikke (first officer on the *Askold*) for the Russians, Captain Fawcett for the British, and Captain de Lagatinerie for the French. Vesselago came forward at the last minute with the further demand that the sessions of the Military Council be attended by three commissars, representing respectively the Murmansk Soviet, the *Sovzheldor,* and the *Tsentromur,* who would participate in the capacity of observers. To this demand, which plainly reflected the basic disunity among the Russians as well as the sharp suspicion with which the Allies were still viewed by the sailors and the more radical railway union leaders, the Allied representatives reluctantly acceded.

The establishment of the Military Council was followed by renewed activity on the Allied side at Murmansk. On March 7 the *H.M.S. Cochrane* arrived, to be followed on the 19th by the French heavy cruiser *Amiral Aube.* This brought the Allied naval force at Murmansk up to sizeable dimensions, including as it did a battleship and three cruisers,[28] aside from the smaller vessels, and placed it in the clearest sort of military domination over the local situation.

More important still, on March 6, just before the *Cochrane's* arrival, Admiral Kemp put ashore a small contingent of marines from the *Glory.* These were apparently supplemented, a day or so later, by another contingent from the newly arrived *Cochrane.* The exact number cannot be established. The entire landing party, even after addition of those from the *Cochrane,* probably ran to no more than 200.[29] The men simply went into barracks ashore. They appear to

---

they support any operations beyond the reach of the ship's guns. What was possible they were prepared to do. If the Russians would defend themselves, British bluejackets could be landed to stiffen the resistance against the Germans, but Admiral Kemp was not to share the executive command of the Russian forces, and must not forget that his main interests were the safety of the Russian men-of-war, the repatriation of refugees and the preservation of the Allies' stores at Archangel. . . ."

[28] The battleship *H.M.S. Glory* and the cruiser *H.M.S. Vindictive* had already been stationed there for some months.

[29] Martin reported it to Francis as "several hundred" (*Foreign Relations, 1918, Russia,* Vol. II, *op.cit.,* p. 470, Francis' telegram to SECSTATE, March 11). But in a report of May 8 (National Archives, Petrograd Embassy file "Miscellaneous Confidential Information, 1918," *op.cit.*) he said the British had some 200 troops in

have taken no part in the administration of the port or in the preservation of order in the community (although there were occasions on which Kemp had to threaten that they would be used if the local authorities did not take suitable action). Their presence matched, in a sense, that of a detachment of Allied legionnaires of Slavic nationality—either Czechs or Serbs [30]—stationed at Kola, several miles away. These were under French command. They were apparently kept ashore in barracks at the time of the Brest-Litovsk crisis, rather than evacuated, in the belief that their presence on shore, as an Allied force, would have a stabilizing effect.

The landing of the British marines was carried out very quietly and without fanfare. No public announcement of it was ever made, and accordingly no official explanation of the motives behind it was ever forthcoming. The western press seems not to have reported it; and there is not even any evidence that the Soviet government became aware of it until some time later. Admiral Kemp had authority from his government "to employ Allied forces under his command to prevent disturbance or anarchy locally if Allied interests were involved or threatened." [31] He could presumably have taken this action on his own responsibility, in the light of his judgment of the local situation. It is reasonable to suspect, however, that the action may have been not unrelated to news reaching the British government just at that time of the movement of a German naval force northward to the Aaland Islands.

The German press (which the Allied governments followed carefully) had carried as early as March 1 stories of Finland's request for German help.[32] On March 4 the governmental Swedish Telegraph Bureau had made the official announcement:

The German Minister, acting on instructions of his government, has notified the Minister of Foreign Affairs that Germany intends to send troops to Finland, at the request of the Finnish Government, in order to

---

barracks, in addition to a few gunners and engineers along the railway. While the date of the landing is variously given, Wardwell's diary confirms that the men went ashore on the 6th (Wardwell, MSS, *op.cit.*).

[30] These men were usually referred to as Czechs. Wardwell, who visited them, refers to them in this way. There is, however, no confirmation from other sources that any Czechs were ever sent to Murmansk. Western representatives were at that time not always very firm in their distinction between the two Slavic nationalities of Central Europe. The probability is that these men were Serbs.

[31] Newbolt, Vol. v, *op.cit.*, p. 314.

[32] *Frankfurter Zeitung* (Abendblatt), March 1, 1918.

suppress the existing revolt there, and that these troops will, with the agreement of Finland, make use of the Aaland Islands in the course of their operations.[33]

It will be noted that this announcement made it plain that the principal and ultimate purpose of the German action was a landing *in Finland proper* and that the use of the Aaland Islands was only subsidiary thereto. *The Times* of London had this story on March 4 together with a report that fifteen German naval vessels had been seen off the coast of Gotland, headed north, on March 2 and that this was believed to be the expedition to Finland. Naval intelligence reports were no doubt even more timely and circumstantial. From this it may be inferred that the British Admiralty was aware on March 3 or at the latest on March 4 of the movement of a considerable German naval contingent northward in the Baltic, and was under the impression that this was the beginning of an effective German military occupation of Finland itself. In these circumstances, it is not surprising that the British should have decided to land marines from their naval vessels in Murmansk, both as a precaution and as an earnest of their determination not to be driven out of that strategic area at the northernmost tip of Europe.

The British action was taken not only with the full agreement of the Murmansk Soviet but actually on its invitation. It was thus not a hostile act so far as the local authorities were concerned. But those who are searching for some event that can be called in the formal sense the beginning of the Allied intervention in Russia may wish to note this occurrence as probably the first actual landing of Allied forces on Soviet territory.[34]

It was not long before the independent action taken by the Murmansk Soviet began to lead to troubles and misunderstandings as between Murmansk and the Soviet authorities in the interior. On March 17 the Murmansk Soviet despatched to all the local authorities of the Murmansk region as well as to the town soviets along the Murmansk Railway a circular telegram apprising them of the establishment of the Military Council, declaring a state of military emergency, and summoning them to collaborate in the requisitioning

---

[33] *Berliner Tageblatt*, March 5, 1918.

[34] There have been statements that some British personnel were landed in late February at Aleksandrovsk, the receiving station of the cable to England, farther down the fjord. I have been unable to confirm this.

American Embassy group in Vologda
Front row, l-r: Jankewicz, F. F. McClelland, E. T. Colton, Livingston Phelps, Norman Armour, Captain E. Francis Riggs, Lieutenant Alfred W. Klieforth; back row, l-r: Philip Jordan, Philip Groves, Ambassador Francis, Earl M. Johnston, Lieutenant Colonel James A. Ruggles, Brazilian Chargé Kelsch

The clubhouse in Vologda, used as American Embassy, 1918

Allied diplomats in Vologda railway yard, March 1918
Front row, l-r: unidentified Soviet commissar, Japanese, Siamese, and Chinese envoys; back row, l-r: Ambassador Francis, Brazilian Chargé Kelsch

of arms and military stores for the forthcoming military effort against the Finns and Germans. To some of the local soviets—notably the strongly Bolshevik Soviet at Petrozavodsk on the southern stretch of the Murmansk Railway—this appeared as a summons, in effect, that they switch their allegiance from the Soviet government in Moscow to a group of people in Murmansk who had entered into treasonable relations with the Allies. Kedrov, in his history of the Murmansk situation,[35] described at length the ensuing exchanges between these local officials and Moscow, and cites certain of the documentation. His account, showing Trotsky as defending—in cryptic utterances—the action of the Murmansk Soviet and Stalin as attempting to correct Trotsky's mistakes and set things back on the proper rails, falls in too neatly with the obvious tendencies of Stalinist historiography to be fully creditable. One derives, from Kedrov's lengthy discussion and from the other evidence available, the impression that the arrangements made between the Murmansk Soviet and the Allies in early March went a bit further than anything Moscow had bargained for; that Lenin and Trotsky were mildly disturbed about the situation, but not enough to cause them to take energetic measures to correct it, particularly because they were not sure at that time that they would not require Allied aid against the Germans in the near future; and that certain elements within the party leadership, to whom Stalin may well have belonged, viewed the situation with even greater distaste, favored sharp and brutal measures to reestablish Moscow's authority and used their influence, wherever they could, to this end.[36]

Actually there would have been little possibility, at any time, for a reversal by the Murmansk Soviet of the line of policy on which it had embarked. The Allies disposed of more armed men in Murmansk than did the Soviet, not to mention the power of the Allied warships anchored in the fjord. Nor could the food supply of the

---

[35] Kedrov, *Bez bolshevistskogo rukovodstva, op.cit.*

[36] Kedrov, in his *Pravda* article on February 21, 1935, *op.cit.*, gives the text of an alleged telephone or telegraph conversation between Stalin and Yuryev, in which the latter was asked for explanations about the treaty concluded with the British. The document, the date of which is not given, does not make a very reliable impression as a historical source. It portrays Stalin as saying, in reply to Yuryev's explanations: "Now listen to our answer. It seems to us that you have been taken in a little [in Russian: *vy nemnozhechko popalis*]; now you have to get yourselves out of it. The English can . . . exploit the . . . situation and the aid they have actually extended as grounds for occupation." Stalin then goes on to tell Yuryev to get a written guarantee from the British and French that they will not proceed to any actual occupation.

region have been assured, at that time, by any means other than continued collaboration with the Allies. Petrograd, at the other end of the railway, was already hungering. The Allies would not have stood any nonsense, at that time, from the local Soviet, especially if they had suspected—as they would have if the orders had come from Moscow—the German hand behind it. For better or for worse, Murmansk, by virtue of factors geographic, strategic, and political, was in no position to follow Moscow in the departure from the Allied camp.

The Americans, ignorant as they were of the attitude of their own government, watched with some uneasiness the unfolding of these developments. They were not sure how much of this British activity represented agreed Allied policy and how much reflected special aspirations and designs of the British government. Wardwell and Thacher, in particular, imbued to some extent with Robins' outlook, also wondered how all this fitted in with the situation in central Russia and especially with the need to preserve some sort of an effective relationship with the Soviet government.

On the day of the landing of the British marines (March 6) Wardwell and Thacher, having learned only the day before that the British intended to take this step, took occasion to go out to the *Glory* and to pay a formal call on Admiral Kemp. When they arrived, the marine detachment was already lining up at the gangway, preparatory to going ashore. The Americans gave Admiral Kemp a full report of the happenings in Petrograd, based on Thacher's recent experiences. They told him that Francis, Robins, and some of the British representatives in Petrograd (here they had in mind, no doubt, Mr. Bruce Lockhart, the official British agent in Moscow) felt "that the only reliance was in Soviet power" [37]—that the Allies' only hope, in other words, for the restoration of any opposition to the Germans lay in the possibility that the Soviet government might itself yet decide to resist. They questioned, by implication, whether any action should be taken that might prejudice relations with the central Soviet authorities.

Kemp was, as Wardwell put it, "very courteous" and asked many questions. But he showed no disposition to defer in any way to his visitors' views. The marines were landed, as scheduled, the same day.

---

[37] Wardwell MSS, *op.cit.*, Diary. This was, after all, in the extremely unsettled period between the signing of the Brest-Litovsk Treaty and its ratification; and it is to be doubted that any of the participants in the discussion had any clear picture of the terms and meaning of the Soviet capitulation on March 3.

Complications in Murmansk

The following day (March 7) Martin attended a meeting of the Executive Committee of the Murmansk Soviet. He was not reassured by what he heard there. He came away reinforced in his suspicion that the British and the local Russian leaders were regarding the landing as purely a local matter, whereas in his opinion it had important implications for Allied policy toward Russia generally. The arrival, that same day, of the *Cochrane* led to further questionings among the Americans as to the extent of British plans and their possible effect on American interests.

This uneasiness was heightened, as the month wore on, by statements made to the Americans by the local Russian officials. The latter, Vesselago in particular, were growing apprehensive lest the new intimacy with the British become too one-sided and oppressive. They, too, were not fully comfortable in their minds about British intentions with respect to the Murmansk region. They voiced these misgivings quite freely to the Americans, and pleaded with the latter, privately, for despatch of an American warship to balance the British presence and to give reassurance against any unilateral line of action on the part of the British.[38] It must be said to the credit of the British that they were generous enough to recognize these fears and to welcome, themselves, the despatch of an American vessel as a means of reassuring the local Russian leaders.

The result of these stimuli was to cause Martin, at some time during the month of March, to recommend to Francis and to the American Military Attaché, Colonel James A. Ruggles, that an American ship be sent. Francis reported this to the State Department, specifically endorsing the recommendation. Ruggles also passed it on to the War Department, relaying Martin's view that American representation was needed "to allay suspicions held by some" that England was "acting for her own selfish interests." [39]

These messages were brought to the attention of the Counselor of the Department of State, Frank L. Polk, by the Russian desk officer, Basil Miles, on April 2, under a covering chit telling about the presence of British and French ships at Murmansk, about the Murmansk

---

[38] When Wardwell paid his farewell call on Vesselago on March 28, the latter told him that the Murmansk Soviet would welcome the despatch of an American warship "as it would go far to remove the apprehension that England was furthering her imperialistic designs." *Ibid.*

[39] For Francis' message, see *Foreign Relations, 1918, Russia*, Vol. II, *op.cit.*, p. 471, telegram no. 45, March 28, 1918, 11 p.m. Ruggles' message will be found in the Frank L. Polk MSS, Yale University Library, New Haven, Conn.

[55]

Railway's being threatened by the Germans and Finns, and about the British landing of marines, which, it was added, had been effected "with the full consent and approval of Trotsky." [40] Polk shunted the entire file to the Secretary of State, adding that "Several high military officers are strongly in favor of this step." The Secretary sent it on, without comment, to the President, who replied on April 4:

> I am willing that a warship should be sent to Murmansk, if there is one available near those waters, and I am willing to have its commander operate there; but . . . it would be wise . . . to caution him not to be drawn in further than the present action there without first seeking and obtaining instructions from home.

On the strength of this statement, the Navy Department went back at the British, through Admiral W. S. Sims, Commander of the American naval forces in European waters, to find out whether they still desired the presence of an American vessel at Murmansk. The answer was: they certainly did—a stronger force might be required there at any time, and there was a need to impress the Russians with Allied unity; Russian feeling for the United States was, after all, "somewhat more friendly than for Great Britain." [41]

Some difficulty was encountered in finding a suitable vessel. The modern ones were all employed on more urgent wartime duty. But all that was really needed here, it was thought, was to show the flag; and this, it was finally decided, could be honorably and effectively performed by Admiral Dewey's old flagship, the *U.S.S. Olympia,* then in American waters.

The *Olympia* was despatched in late April, under the command of Captain Bion B. Bierer. For his political instructions, Bierer was handed a copy of a telegram which Admiral Sims had sent to the Navy Department on April 13. [42] It read as follows:

> Instructions have been issued to the British Rear Admiral at Murmansk to take any steps which he may consider necessary and desirable with the forces at his disposal to protect and further the Allied interests generally, and to assist in recovering the Allied stores at Archangel. Instructions have also been given him that he is not to commit himself to land military

---

[40] This memorandum, and the President's reply, *ibid.*

[41] National Archives, Navy Branch, R.G. 45, *op.cit.;* telegrams 4605, April 5, 1918, OPNAV to Sims, and 6214, April 8, Sims to OPNAV.

[42] *Foreign Relations, 1918, Russia,* Vol. II, *op.cit.,* p. 488. This telegram was transmitted to the Secretary of State by Secretary Daniels on June 22.

operations away from the port, but subject to the above-mentioned restriction he may utilize the crew of the ships for the purpose of stiffening the local resistance against Germans if it be found practicable. The same instructions have been issued to the French senior officer. It is considered essential by the Admiralty that the Allied ships at Murmansk should be placed under the orders of the senior Allied commander, and that the ships be instructed to cooperate with him in carrying out the above instructions. I concur in the above and recommend that it be carried out.

It is clear from this message that Bierer was to be, while at Murmansk, under the command of his British colleague, Admiral Kemp, and was expected to cooperate with Kemp in protecting and furthering Allied interests, in recovering the Archangel stores, and in "stiffening the local resistance to the Germans." The President's injunction—that he should be careful about going further, without instructions—seems to have become lost, somewhere, in the shuffle.

CHAPTER III

SIBERIA IN MARCH 1918

. . . No doubt some day all this will be carefully studied and research scholarship will find documents and papers, reports of conversations and invitations to new policies, based upon supposed new facts, but when all has been disclosed that can be, Siberia will remain Sergeant Grischa. The Siberian situation will always illustrate the eccentricities of a remote and irrational emanation from the central madness of a warring world.—*Newton D. Baker, Foreword to William S. Graves, "America's Siberian Adventure, 1918–1920"*

DURING the winter of 1917–1918, while the Soviet delegates struggled with the German negotiators at Brest-Litovsk, the adherents of the new Soviet regime in Siberia, capitalizing on the success achieved in Petrograd and Moscow and aided by the unpreparedness and bewilderment of their opponents, succeeded in assuming effective power throughout Siberia.

In general, the communist seizure of power encountered only sporadic local resistance. Severe fighting occurred in Irkutsk in December. It was terminated by a Bolshevik victory. Another trouble spot was the town of Blagoveshchensk on the Amur River, adjacent to the Manchurian border. Here Bolshevik control, though first established without appreciable violence, was later opposed by dissident Cossack elements and strongly anti-Bolshevik portions of the town population, including a number of Japanese. There were strong hopes in anti-Bolshevik circles that the Chinese might intervene; but they remained passive, and the street fighting ended, as in Irkutsk, with a Bolshevik victory.

Only in one instance was there an attempt at something more than local political opposition to the Bolsheviki. This came from the adherents of the movement for Siberian autonomy, which had long had its center with some of the professors and intellectuals grouped around the sole Siberian university, at Tomsk, and had received new impetus from the February Revolution. A Siberian Regional Duma had been elected during the Provisional Government period, but had not yet come together when the Bolsheviki seized power. An attempt to convene the Duma at Tomsk on February 8, 1918 was at once suppressed by the Bolsheviki. A number of the delegates were arrested. Some of those who escaped arrest, meeting clandestinely before they took ·flight, made the gesture of electing, partly from among their own number and partly from absent persons presumed amenable to this honor, an underground executive cabinet bearing the ambitious title of "Provisional Government of Autonomous Siberia." This cabinet was headed by a somewhat obscure Social-Revolutionary figure, himself not a Siberian at all but a native of Odessa, Peter Derber. Derber at once fled, with a handful of associates, to Harbin, where he arrived in mid-March. There General Dmitri L. Horvat, General Manager of the Chinese Eastern Railway, contemptuously gave him a railway car to live in.

Derber had neither troops nor money. He was personally little known among the Siberian population. The railway car constituted, for the moment, his entire domain. But he did enjoy the halfhearted moral support of a considerable portion of the powerful S-R faction in western Siberia, and was not a negligible factor in the developing political situation in Siberia.

In Vladivostok, the presence of Allied warships in the harbor (Japanese and British since early January, joined on March 1 by the *U.S.S. Brooklyn*) had sufficed to forestall a complete and overt communist coup in the first weeks of Soviet power. But even here, the Bolsheviki soon became the dominant element in the local political situation. By early March all that remained of non-Bolshevik authority at Vladivostok was the moderately oriented *Zemskaya Uprava* (elected administrative organ) of the Maritime Province, a relic of the short-lived administrative arrangements of the Provisional Government. The *Uprava* was permitted by the local Bolshevik leaders to continue formally in existence, on the theory—no doubt— that its presence on the scene would weaken whatever incentive the Allied powers might have for an actual landing. But the *Uprava* had no means of enforcing its will, and its function remained more symbolic than real. The Vladivostok Soviet was already the most powerful of the local Russian bodies. The armed formations without whose collaboration no maintenance of order was possible—the military and naval garrisons and the municipal police—were, while generally undisciplined and demoralized, more under Bolshevik influence than any other.

It was not long, after the November Revolution, before the commercial undertakings and individual citizens of the Allied powers in the Russian Far East began to feel in small but irritating ways the hostility borne them by the Communists. The harassments and inconveniences proceeded in many instances from ostensibly irresponsible parties; but the local police, either sympathetic to the Bolsheviki or terrorized by them, failed to afford any appreciable protection. And no one had illusions as to the quarter from which the inspiration for these encroachments was coming.

This posed a difficult problem for the Allied consular representatives. They were as yet unwilling to recognize the Vladivostok Soviet or to deal with it as the responsible authority. Yet the moderate *Zemskaya Uprava,* to which they continued to take their protests, was powerless to help.

As an example of these difficulties, one may note an incident which occurred on the night of February 3–4, when some thirty armed men wearing military uniforms (presumably they were members of the local military garrison) raided the principal hostelry of the city, the "Hotel de Versailles," spent several hours in the building leisurely going through the effects of the guests, and finally made off with loot valued at something like one million rubles, including the passport and pocket money of one American visitor. Efforts were repeatedly made, during the course of the night, to interest the police in what was going on, but not one policeman could be induced to approach the vicinity of the building while the raid was in progress, nor was any serious investigation conducted afterwards.[1] It was perfectly clear that such incidents were taking place with the encouragement and connivance of the local Communists.

The victims of these harassments were in a number of instances Japanese citizens—and this despite the fact that Japanese warships lay at anchor in the harbor. How long the Japanese would continue

---

[1] National Archives, Foreign Affairs Branch, Vladivostok 800 File, 1918; telegram of February 4, 8 p.m. and despatch no. 206 of March 9, Caldwell to SECSTATE.

to show patience in the face of such provocation was of course a question in everyone's mind.

In addition to this, foreign firms throughout the entire eastern Siberian region found themselves by this time increasingly subject to various forms of extortion at the hands of local communist authorities who in this way exploited the police power now in their hands. To these communist officials, the commercial relations of their communities with foreign countries were entirely expendable. In early March some of the business houses in Vladivostok suspended operations entirely, in protest against such interference. The local Bolsheviki, in retaliation, arrested four members of the Chamber of Commerce and allowed it to be known that it was intended to send them as prisoners to Irkutsk for further investigation and punishment. On March 6, the consular corps publicly protested this action.[2]

Throughout the winter the Allied representatives continued to keep an anxious and watchful eye, so far as they could, on the enormous stock of war supplies (roughly four times the amount at Archangel) that had accumulated at Vladivostok. There was an incessant flow of rumors of attempts by the Bolsheviki to remove these supplies and deliver them into German hands. The vast quantity of the stores and the manner in which they were spread out over the port area rendered difficult any accurate observation of what was happening to them. Admiral Austin M. Knight, Commander in Chief of the Asiatic Fleet, after a study of the situation conducted in early March, immediately after his arrival at Vladivostok in his flagship, the *U.S.S. Brooklyn,* reported to Washington that there was no ground for anxiety on this score; but this did not stop the rumors or allay the suspicions of the other Allied representatives, who had no intimacy with the local Bolsheviki and had seen no reason to trust them.

Thus the situation in Vladivostok as of early March was one of growing tension: the Communists becoming increasingly resentful of the inhibitions placed upon them by the spectacle of the foreign warships in the harbor, the Allied consular representatives increas-

[2] Some idea of the attendant tension may be gained from the report sent to Washington that same evening by the American Consul, Mr. John K. Caldwell, to the effect that he thought there might be an attempt at counterrevolution during the night on the part of some 500 "White Guards." (*Ibid.,* telegram of March 6, 10 p.m.) The uprising did not materialize. The arrested businessmen were released the following day, and the incident passed off with no immediate further violence.

ingly irritated by the harassment of their nationals and the suppression of normal business activity in the port. Suspicion and antagonism were mounting on both sides.

❖

The situation in Manchuria, meanwhile, had reached a state of confusion and complexity which defies any brief general description. But there are certain elements of it worthy of mention in connection with the problems of American diplomacy at that time.

The news of the conclusion of the Brest-Litovsk Treaty and the almost simultaneous appearance in Harbin of the members of the "Derber government" stirred up a flurry of exchanges in Russian and Allied circles of the Far East over the question of the possible establishment by Horvat of a new Russian government. This naturally involved the question of whether this should be a coalition government, embracing representatives of the Derber group, who were socialists, or whether Horvat should attempt to take power initially, at least, as a personal ruler, basing himself on the conservative and largely monarchist circles to whom his own sympathies inclined. Despite the fact that it was still hypothetical, the question could not fail—in turn—to release the entire complex of conflicting political passions and interests that had been the undoing of the Provisional Government at the other end of the Russian Empire, plus a few more of a specifically local nature. There at once began an intensive milling around among the various elements involved: Horvat and his associates, the Derber group, committees of Russian residents of Harbin and other cities, Chinese officials at various levels, and the Allied consular and diplomatic representatives—Japanese, British, French—in Harbin, Peking, and Tokyo. To these last were added—quite prominently, in fact—the Russian diplomatic representatives of the recent Tsarist and Provisional Governments; for in the Far East, as in Washington, the old Russian diplomatic missions had continued to carry on. The Russian Minister at Peking, Prince Kudashev, and his colleague at Tokyo, Krupenski, both active and influential men, were still recognized, as was Bakhmeteff in Washington, by the governments to which they were accredited; and it was to them, particularly to Kudashev, that Horvat looked for political guidance.

At the end of March, as though the cooks already involved in this brewing were not enough, there was injected one more: Admiral

Aleksandr Vasilevich Kolchak, who was later to play so prominent and tragic a part in the anti-communist movement in Siberia. He had been on a special naval mission to the United States in the fall of 1917. Overtaken on the return journey by the news of the Bolshevik seizure of power, he had remained for some time in Japan. His introduction into the Manchurian scene was the result of the initiative of Prince Kudashev, who persuaded the British that Kolchak could be best employed, from the standpoint of the Allies, in the Russian Far East.

The interests, pressures, and considerations bearing on the possible creation of a government by Horvat were so varied and conflicting, and the real prerequisites for any such undertaking present only in so small degree, that nothing at all emerged in the month of March from these efforts, and very little later on. The Japanese, who had initially promised Horvat support in most categoric terms, became increasingly cool toward his fortunes as the weeks wore on, and began at a very early date to support the Derber group as well, playing them off against Horvat with the evident intention of promoting disunity in the Russian camp—a process that required little outside stimulus in any case. But the considerable volume of smoke that emerged from all this friction was enough to affect appreciably the international atmosphere.

The political climate of the Far East, it should be noted, was generally different from that of European Russia. To people in Harbin or Peking, the European war—the factor that affected so strongly the attitudes of the western Allied chancelleries—was remote and unreal. The fear of "driving the Russians into the arms of the Germans" that more than any other consideration moved the western governments to observe forebearance in their attitude toward the Bolsheviki, was scarcely present in the cities of the Far East. The general tone of discussion in Allied circles there was uninhibitedly anti-Bolshevik, to a degree that would have shocked the Washington statesmen, at least, had they been aware of it. The free and easy way in which the possible establishment of anti-communist governments was discussed in Allied circles throughout the Far East, at a time when no final decisions had yet been taken by the Allied governments as to their attitude toward Soviet power, provides a striking contrast to the desperate efforts being put forth simultaneously by Lockhart, Robins, and a portion of Allied officialdom in Russia to achieve some sort of *modus vivendi* with the Bolsheviki. The repercussions of all this anti-communist activity and intrigue in the Far Eastern capitals did much to confirm the suspicions with which the Soviet leaders were congenitally inclined to view the Allied governments and their offers of military aid.

Be it said to the credit of the official American representatives in the Far East that, having no authorization to enter into any of this trafficking, they kept pretty well out of it. With regard to conferences that took place in early April between Horvat and the Entente ministers at Peking, where decisions were taken that were thought at the moment to be of far-reaching significance, Horvat says in his *Memoirs:*

After an exchange of opinions the Ministers decided to support me and to co-ordinate their help through me. At my farewell visit, in the presence of our Minister, Prince Kudashev, this decision was confirmed by all the Allied Ministers, except the American Minister whom I had not asked for help because neither Mr. Stevens, nor the American Consul in Harbin had assisted in the anti-Bolshevik movement.[3]

The Stevens mentioned here was Mr. John F. Stevens, who had been head of the Advisory Commission of Railway Experts, sent to aid the Russian Provisional Government in 1917. He was now in Manchuria seeking useful employment for the American engineers of the Russian Railway Service Corps, commanded by Colonel George H. Emerson, which had been sent to the Far East just at the time of the Bolshevik seizure of power, in the hope that it could be helpful in restoring the efficiency of the Trans-Siberian Railway. The accession of the Communists to power in Siberia had made it impossible to carry out the original plan, and the engineers had been waiting idly in Japan, over the winter. At the end of February an agreement had been reached in principle with the Chinese government for the employment of these men on the Chinese Eastern Railway; and Stevens, together with Emerson and a portion of the Corps, came on to Harbin in March with a view to starting the work. In Harbin, Stevens, unavoidably suspected of having some secret political status and purpose, naturally became the object of a great many approaches from competing factions seeking American support. To

[3] Dmitri Leonovich Horvat, *Memoirs,* Manuscript in Hoover Institute & Library, Stanford; page 28 of Chapter x of the draft translation.

these he seems to have turned a consistently discreet and unreceptive ear. "Credit must be given to Mr. Stevens," Horvat wrote,

for strictly limiting his activities to helping the railways and for not interfering in politics. No one succeeded in drawing him into an open political conversation. Even now we do not know what his political views were and whether or not he sympathized with our movement. . . .[4]

At a later date there would be-charges by the Soviet government that Consul Caldwell at Vladivostok had conspired with members of the Derber group; but evidence cited to support the charges was of the flimsiest, and they cannot be credited. Admiral Knight, too, was treated to the appeals of Derber and his associates, and came even closer than did Caldwell to encouraging them beyond the point of discretion. But the government at Washington was in no wise involved in any of this. Repeatedly, it warned its representatives in the Far East to remain aloof from every form of interference in Russian internal affairs; and this the latter seem generally to have done—with commendable stoutness, considering the volume of entreaties and pressures to which they were subjected.

❖

One of the most serious of Horvat's problems, in the first months of 1918, was the presence at the western end of the Chinese Eastern Railway of the person and supporters of the young Cossack leader, Grigori Semenov.[5] Brief mention was made in Volume I (Chapter xxiii) of this colorful but sinister character. It now becomes necessary to have a closer look at him.

Having served in the Tsarist army and seen considerable service on other fronts during the early years of the World War, Semenov in the summer of 1917 persuaded the Provisional Government to let him return to his native haunts of the trans-Baikal area and attempt to set up there a volunteer detachment from among the local Mongols.[6] The little army post at Dauria, a few miles from the Man-

---

[4] *Ibid.*, p. 29 of Chapter x.

[5] Pronounced: Sem-yon'-off.

[6] This and the following data concerning Semenov are taken primarily from his own memoirs, published in China in 1938, under the title *O sebe, vospominaniya, mysli i vyvody* (About Myself, Memories, Thoughts and Conclusions). Semenov, through some unaccountable lack of vigilance, was caught in Manchuria by the Soviet forces in 1945 and hanged—a fate which, in view of the appalling cruelties he had perpetrated during the Civil War, cannot be regarded as too unnatural.

churian border on the railway line connecting the Chinese Eastern with the main line of the Trans-Siberian, was assigned to him as his headquarters. He was just beginning to assemble his force when the Bolshevik seizure of power occurred in Petrograd. The wave of bolshevization, marked by extreme indiscipline and defiance of the regular officers, soon began to sweep through the Siberian garrisons. Semenov at once came into sharp conflict with the Communists in Chita and Irkutsk and flatly defied their authority. That he was able to do this is attributable to his own bold and insolent temperament, his favorable geographic situation in the immediate neighborhood of the Manchurian border, and his ability to recruit a few followers from elements—Mongols, Cossacks, and prisoners-of-war—not under Bolshevik influence. How much may be believed of his own account of his early military exploits is uncertain. He claims, for example, that he and seven of his supporters succeeded, by a combination of surprise, bluff, and daring, in disarming and expelling from the neighboring border point of Manchuria Station the entire disaffected garrison of 1,500 men. The tale may be exaggerated; but there is nothing inherently impossible about it, given the chaotic and confusing conditions of the time. In any case, there can be little doubt that Semenov did succeed during the winter of 1917–1918, by one means or another, in removing most of the regular Russian military personnel from the immediate vicinity of Dauria, leaving him—for the time being—master of the local situation. Astride the last few miles of railway on Siberian territory, his rear as well as his left flank being covered by the Manchurian border, he was in a relatively favorable situation to defend himself from the Bolshevik forces in Chita and Irkutsk.

The Bolsheviki were of course intensely irritated by Semenov's defiance of their newly established authority. His unceremonious expulsion of the bolshevized local garrisons deprived the Communists of the trump card which everywhere else had been the key to their success. His position on the railway line gave him control of the direct connection from Irkutsk to Vladivostok and eventually forced the Communists to route all their traffic over the longer and less convenient Amur line.[7] Finally, his defiance impeded any extension of Bolshevik influence into Manchuria.

[7] The break in railway traffic from Chita into Manchuria and vice versa became

The awkwardness of this situation from the Bolshevik standpoint was illustrated in a rather startling manner by an incident which occurred in the beginning of December 1917. The Russian Communists had at that time not yet been expelled from the Chinese Eastern Railway zone; and their leader in Harbin, Arkus, attempted to proceed from Harbin to Irkutsk for consultation with the Bolshevik leaders at that point. When the train stopped at Dauria, Arkus was taken out, on Semenov's orders, and searched. When he remonstrated over this treatment, Semenov coolly had him executed on the spot. Semenov then took personally to Harbin the documents found on Arkus' body, and used them to persuade Horvat of the necessity for immediate action against the Communists. It was shortly after this, and possibly partly in consequence of it, that the Chinese intervened, as described in Volume 1 (Chapter xiv, pp. 303–306), and expelled the Russian Communists from Harbin. If anything more had been needed to seal Semenov's breach with the Communists, this incident would have supplied it.

Semenov's relations with the Chinese were also strained from the start. His use of Mongol supporters, drawn for the most part from what was nominally Chinese territory, was naturally alarming and offensive to the Chinese, who were hard put to it anyway to preserve the fiction of their sovereignty in the Mongol-populated territories along the Russian border.

In mid-January, Semenov made a visit to Harbin with a view to drumming up arms and support. He first appealed to Horvat, who received him politely and offered to accept his detachment as one of the regular Chinese Eastern Railway guard units and to support him accordingly. Horvat declined, however, to meet Semenov's immediate request for arms. Semenov's response was characteristic. With the aid of his own Mongolian bodyguard, he succeeded in stealing two artillery pieces from the mouth of a tunnel on the Chinese Eastern Railway, loaded them onto flat cars under the noses of Horvat's personnel, and shipped them off to his own little enclave on the Siberian border.

Despite this and other discourtesies suffered at Semenov's hands, Horvat was in too weak a position to break with him entirely. While

complete in early March. The first Trans-Siberian Express routed over the Amur line reached Vladivostok on March 6.

nothing was achieved on this first occasion, Horvat later gave him help of one sort or another and endeavored, with minimal success, to exert a friendly influence upon him. In later years he came to regret this misspent effort.[8]

Independent, insolent, abominably brutal and cruel in his methods, Semenov remained a constant embarrassment not only to Horvat but to all the more respectable elements in the anti-communist Russian community of the Far East. It was virtually impossible for the other Russians to cooperate with him; and there seems to be no record of anyone's having done so successfully. Yet none could begrudge him a certain admiration for the ruthlessness and audacity of his actions against the Bolsheviki; and his position on the western border of Manchuria served in many respects as a useful buffer between the communist authority in central Siberia and the vulnerable leased zone of the Chinese Eastern Railway, where the theory of special Russian administrative rights now hung by the most slender of threads.

Semenov's appeals for support were also addressed, in January 1918, to the representatives in Harbin of Japan and of the western Allies. With the Japanese, this approach had an immediate and enduring success. Semenov's situation and exploits suited them very well. His unmanageableness from the standpoint of Horvat and every other Russian authority helped to prevent the emergence of any single strong anti-Bolshevik force in the Siberian region. This fitted well with Japanese policy of the moment, to which any strong anti-communist movement in Siberia, with its inevitable claim to be treated by Japan as a friend and ally, would have been embarrassing. By providing a military check to the Bolsheviki in the trans-Baikal area and by cutting their communications to Manchuria, Semenov weakened the Bolshevik military potential in the Far Eastern portion of Siberia. This, too, was eminently agreeable to the Japanese. Finally, Semenov, with his Mongolian supporters, provided a countercheck to the Chinese in Mongolia and Manchuria and served to perpetuate a form of weakness and disunity in that area from which many Japanese hoped in the very near future to profit.

The Japanese therefore supported Semenov steadily from the time of his visit to Harbin in January. They assigned to his headquarters

[8] "God forgive me, but I decided to support Semenov . . ." Horvat ruefully confessed in his *Memoirs, op.cit.,* p. 17 of Chapter 10.

a liaison officer, Captain Kuroki, to whom Semenov conceived such personal devotion as he was capable of entertaining for another person. Kuroki did much to keep him in line with Japanese purposes. The Japanese also gave support in money and arms—just enough to keep Semenov in the running and to preserve his independence of Horvat and the other Russian anti-communists, not enough to permit him to become a serious aspirant for power in the Russian Far East.

On the French and British representatives, too, Semenov made a favorable initial impression with his accounts of his exploits against the Bolsheviki. The result was a considerable enthusiasm for him, at the outset, in the French and British camps. The British sent a liaison officer, Major Denny, from their military staff at Peking, and provided a certain amount of financial assistance in the late winter of 1918. The French likewise sent an officer, Captain Pelliot.[9] Between them the French and British managed to make available to Semenov a couple of field howitzers from the arsenal of the Peking Legation Guards.

While they lasted, the hopes placed by the British on Semenov were quite sanguine. But they soon came into conflict with the hopes entertained in London that the Bolsheviki could be brought to request Allied intervention.[10] It was apparent that the French and British support to Semenov was one of the main sources of Soviet suspicion of Allied good faith generally. British enthusiasm was further dampened, at an early date, by reports of the psychological effects of the excesses committed by Semenov's men on Siberian territory.

At the outset of 1918, Semenov's little force numbered only 556 men, including 51 officers, 380 Mongols (of whom 300 came from

[9] Or Pellier; sources vary.
[10] The hopes and misgivings of the British with regard to Semenov are well illustrated in the following telegram from the British Foreign Office to the British Minister at Peking, dated April 7, 1918:

"It is clear that our policy must be seriously prejudiced with the Bolshevist authorities, even fatally so, in the event of Seminov [sic], encouraged by the Allies, making an advance at this moment. Nor do we think it likely from the present and prospective composition of the forces under Semenov that they will be able to achieve very much from a military point of view.

"On the other hand, Semenov and his force will constitute a very useful adjunct to any occupying forces, both from a political and military standpoint, if and when intervention in Siberia, either by the Allies or by the Japanese alone, materializes. It will be better in the meantime for Semenov to wait, and to devote himself to the organization of his force without embarking on military operations pending the further development of the situation as to the intervention by the Allies in Siberia." (National Archives, State Department File 861.00/1448; enclosure to Reading's note to Lansing of April 8.)

the Chinese side of the border), and 125 Cossacks and other volunteers. He was soon to be joined by 300 stranded Serb war prisoners. This was about all that he was able to support, logistically. His greatest need, in this initial period, was for arms, particularly artillery.

Whatever could be gained in those early weeks by audacity, speed of decision, and ruthless brutality of execution, Semenov gained. But he was never able to command any popular support in the Siberian area surrounding his seat of operations, a fact which limited severely his possibilities for recruitment. Thus his force remained a tiny one, compelled to restrict itself largely to minor operations.

During February, taking advantage of the unpreparedness of his opponents, Semenov conducted a series of successful skirmishes with Bolshevik detachments in the area between the Manchurian border and the Onon River, 130 miles to the west. But by the end of the month the Bolsheviki were beginning to develop a more serious force in that area, and Semenov was pushed back into Manchuria. Here, under the nose of the passive Chinese commander, he disarmed and deported another undesirable Russian garrison and made himself thoroughly at home, to the intense embarrassment of the Chinese.

The Bolsheviki naturally at once complained to the Chinese about Semenov's use of Chinese soil as a "privileged sanctuary." A local Chinese-Bolshevik conference was convened at Matsiyevskaya (the Russian border station) in mid-March, on Soviet initiative, to discuss this situation. Semenov, sulking in the background, was not represented. An agreement was reached that for three weeks, i.e. up to April 5, he should not be permitted by the Chinese to recross the border. The Russians, meanwhile, would "restore order" on their side of the line. Direct railway traffic was to be resumed at once. Arrangements were made for normal Chinese-Russian border control.[11]

These provisions involved a good deal of empty face-saving on both sides. The main motives on the Soviet side were obviously to embroil the Chinese, if possible, with Semenov, and to gain time. The Chinese were in no position to execute their part of the bargain. Guessing this, the communist military leaders in the trans-Baikal region continued, despite the agreement, to press preparations for new operations against Semenov on a much larger scale, in the event that, as was to be feared, the Chinese should fail to restrain him and he, with Japanese support, should renew his incursions into the trans-Baikal area.

[11] Moscow *Izvestiya*, No. 51, March 19, 1918, p. 2.

Semenov, for his part, devoted himself during the month of March to building up his little force with a view to renewing the attacks on the Bolsheviki in Siberia as soon as his relative strength permitted.

✧

The conclusion of the Brest-Litovsk Treaty brought with it heightened attention on the Allied side to the prisoners-of-war of the Central Powers who were being held in Siberia.[12] The exact number of these is difficult to determine. In all of Russia there were some 1,600,-000 prisoners.[13] Eight hundred thousand has been frequently cited as the number of such prisoners held in Siberia at the time of the Revolution. This figure seems, in the light of available evidence, quite plausible. In any case the number ran into the hundreds of thousands.[14]

The great bulk of these prisoners were subjects of the Austro-Hungarian Empire, not Germans, and members of the non-Austrian portions of the Empire at that. Hungarians and Slovaks seem to have been particularly prominent among them. Of the 1,600,000 prisoners in Russia as of the beginning of 1918, not more than one-tenth were Germans, and only a portion of these were in Siberia. Of the captive officers, a higher proportion were Austrians and Germans than of the men.

Even before the conclusion of the Brest-Litovsk Treaty, these war prisoners were a source of great concern to the Allied representatives in Russia and their governments. Many of the prisoners were not confined behind barbed wire but were merely restricted to specific localities, where they were allowed freedom of movement and permitted to take various forms of employment. After ratification of the Brest-Litovsk Treaty, their status as prisoners-of-war technically lapsed and they became only "displaced persons." To Allied representatives traveling the Trans-Siberian Railway, they often appeared to be completely at liberty. In some instances they were employed in the guarding of their own camps, which involved bearing small arms.

[12] See Volume I, Chapter XII, pp. 283ff.

[13] Margarete Klante, *Von der Wolga zum Amur: Die tschechische Legion und der russische Bürgerkrieg,* Ost-Europa Verlag, Berlin, 1931, Chapter IV.

[14] James Bunyan, *Intervention, Civil War, and Communism in Russia, April-December 1918, Documents and Materials,* Johns Hopkins Press, Baltimore, 1936, p. 92. Taking his figures from the Soviet publication "Rossiia v mirovoi voine 1914-1918 g. v tsifrakh," p. 41, Bunyan indicates that there were about 920,000 prisoners in the Volga district and Siberia together.

This, too, did not escape the attention of Allied travelers. These circumstances, apparently supported in some instances by deliberate exaggeration, led very soon after the Bolshevik Revolution to many rumors and fears that these prisoners could in some way be used to capture Siberia for the Germans.

While the Brest-Litovsk Treaty provided (Article VIII) that prisoners-of-war on both sides were to be released for return to their homelands, this did nothing to quiet the apprehension of the Allied representatives about the prisoners in Siberia. In the first place, there was, for several reasons, no possibility of repatriating any great number of them at any early date; so that in the weeks immediately following conclusion of the treaty most of them remained at their places of detention or residence in Siberia. And since they were now officially released from their technical status as enemy aliens and prisoners-of-war, it was easy for the Allies to picture them as mobilizing and undertaking renewed military action, locally, on behalf of their governments.

The Bolsheviki began at an early date to conduct revolutionary propaganda in the camps with a view to winning over the allegiance of as many as possible of these men. These were, after all, the halcyon days of Russian Communism's view of itself not as a national but as a purely international movement, cutting across all national frontiers and embracing people on the basis of class rather than of nationality. There was thus no theoretical reason why the war prisoners should not be appealed to, just as were the Russians, to embrace the communist ideology and to throw in their lot with the Bolsheviki. A committee was formed in Moscow soon after the November Revolution to direct the conduct of such agitation among the prisoners. Agitators were sent to all the major camps and centers of concentration. Prisoners were pressed to declare themselves "Internationalists" (i.e., partisans of international communism), to renounce the authority of their native countries, and to take up arms with local Red Guard detachments.

These efforts to recruit the war prisoners into armed detachments became particularly vigorous and insistent just after ratification of the Brest-Litovsk Treaty, when the first efforts were being made to create a new Red Army. Persuasion was by no means the only method of inducement employed. In many instances the Communists seized the administration of the camps, reestablished under their own control the guarding of the camps where this had been abandoned in deference to the peace treaty, seized the funds and food supplies (including stores of the Swedish Red Cross), and distributed benefits and privileges in such a way as to put a premium on signing up with the communist cause. Their efforts were aided by the fact that considerable numbers of the prisoners belonged to socialist organizations in their own countries, and were not sure that they did not owe a debt of loyalty to the Russian socialists, whose spokesmen the Bolsheviki professed to be.

In the face of these efforts, the number of prisoners induced to sign up with the Communists remained remarkably small. The entire effort of recruitment was, in fact, a short-lived one. It was extremely unwelcome to the German and Austrian governments. It was terminated at the insistence of those governments, and the communist formations were broken up, as soon as the German and Austrian repatriation and welfare commissions (made possible by the Brest-Litovsk Treaty) arrived on the spot. The German commissions began to arrive at the end of May; the Austrian, some weeks later. The high point of communist organization of the prisoners was thus from the middle of March to the end of May.

The percentage of those joining the Communists was highest in the Siberian camps: and even there, at the peak of this development, they never amounted to more than about twenty percent of the total.[15] Many of these signed up only reluctantly and *pro forma*. Only a fraction of those who joined up were actually armed. Thus the number of armed prisoners remained extremely small. The best estimates, based on the observations of the Swedish Red Cross workers, placed the number of those armed in all of Russia at no more than 15,000, of whom 5,000 were in Turkestan alone. Thus in all of Siberia and the Volga region, there could not have been more than 10,000 armed prisoners—a tiny number, considering the vast extent of this territory. Among these, the Hungarians made up the largest national group, followed by the Czechs and Serbs. The Germans showed greater resistance to communist pressures than any other na-

---

[15] Elsa Brändström, the Swedish woman who played so prominent a part in the work of the Swedish Red Cross among the prisoners in Siberia, puts the total of those who signed up with the Bolsheviki, at one time or another in all of Russia, at about 90,000. This would represent only 5.6 percent of the total number. (Elsa Brändström, *Among Prisoners of War in Russia and Siberia*, Hutchinson & Co., London, 1929.)

tionality; and the number of them who bore arms in communist detachments must have been quite negligible. The very few Germans who did participate, however, had a tendency to assume leadership, both militarily and politically—a fact which may have helped to mislead Allied observers about the extent of German participation.[16]

It is most important to recognize that not only did the governments of the Central Powers have nothing to do with this recruitment but it took place against their wishes and against the violent opposition of the officer-prisoners in the same areas, to whom any yielding to these Bolshevik pressures appeared as outright treason. By no stretch of the imagination could the recruitment of these men into the Red Guard be considered an expression of the wartime policies of the Central Powers or a move taken in their interest.

The overwhelming majority of the recruits to the Bolshevik forces from among the war prisoners were taken directly into Russian communist units, where they served side by side with Russian personnel. There seems to have been only one instance where men of this sort were organized into a national unit; and this, as will be seen below, was soon regretted by the communist authorities.

Many rumors of the arming of the prisoners-of-war in Siberia reached the Allied representatives in European Russia and those who were stationed in Peking, in Manchuria, and in the Russian Far East. The reports that filtered through to the Far East were particularly prolific and spectacular. It was perhaps due to this circumstance that the American Legation at Peking chose to despatch to Siberia in mid-March the Military Attaché of the Legation, Major Walter S. Drysdale, to investigate the situation with respect to the reported arming of the prisoners. Drysdale had already made one journey of observation to Siberia earlier in the winter. Now he was to go again, and this time specifically to investigate the tales of the arming of the war prisoners.

Just at this time the Allied officers attached to the military missions in Russia proper were greatly stimulated and exercised by the talk

[16] See Klante, *op.cit.,* Chapter iv. Communist sources have given considerably higher figures for the number of those prisoners recruited into communist armed service (see Bunyan, *op.cit.,* p. 96) but these figures may have included many who signed up and were not actually armed. Klante's estimates, based on the observations of the Swedish Red Cross, would seem to be the most objective and reliable ones available.

of possible military collaboration between the Allied powers and the Soviet government. Agitated debates took place among them, particularly in February and March, concerning the desirability of giving military aid to the Bolsheviki. In these discussions the charges that the Bolshevik authorities were arming German and Austrian prisoners in the interests of the Central Powers naturally played a prominent part. If these charges were true, it was obvious that the Allies ought to be extremely cautious about giving any help in the establishment of the new Red Army. Lockhart and Robins, who strongly favored military collaboration with the Bolsheviki, found themselves constantly confronted with charges that the Bolsheviki were betraying the Allies by putting arms in the hands of the prisoners-of-war in Siberia.

Upon Lockhart's arrival in Moscow, immediately after ratification of the Brest-Litovsk Treaty, he and Robins asked Trotsky about the truth of these reports. Trotsky replied that there was no truth in them, but that it was useless for him to issue a denial: the Allies would place no faith in his words. He recognized the seriousness of the charge, however, and suggested that Lockhart and Robins send their own representatives to Siberia to investigate. He undertook to see that every facility was provided for such an investigation. Robins and Lockhart agreed.

The two men selected were Captain W. L. Hicks, for the British, and, for Robins, Captain William B. Webster [17] of the Red Cross Commission. No time was lost in getting the men off. Trotsky was as much interested as were Robins and Lockhart in scotching the rumors that the prisoners were being armed. A special train was made available the same day (March 19) to take the two men to Vologda, where their private car was to be attached to the Trans-Siberian Express.[18] They were accompanied by a Soviet commissar,

[17] Webster had already taken part in prisoner-of-war work in central Siberia, as a delegate of the American Embassy at Petrograd, in 1916–1917, and therefore had some familiarity with this territory.

[18] C. K. Cumming & W. W. Pettit, Editors, *Russian-American Relations, March, 1917–March, 1920, Documents and Papers,* Harcourt, Brace & Howe, New York, 1920; Robins' message to Francis over the direct wire, March 20, p. 105.

Texts of the various telegraphic reports sent by Webster to Robins during the course of this trip, as well as the text of the final report (April 26, 1918) of the two officers, together with some supporting material will be found, *ibid.,* pp. 165–187. The information concerning Webster's and Hicks's journey is taken, unless otherwise stated, from this source.

who had instructions to look after their comfort and to see that all went smoothly. Trotsky publicly announced the despatch of the officers.

Irkutsk, as the military center of Siberia and the focal point of most of the rumors, was selected by Webster and Hicks as their main destination. On the outward journey to that point they found things normal and quiet. There was no sign of any disturbing activity of war prisoners. At Perm (now Molotov) and Ekaterinburg (now Sverdlovsk) a few prisoners had, they were told, joined the Red Army; but these had no influence over its operation.

Arriving at Irkutsk on March 29, Webster and Hicks found Drysdale, who had reached that point three days earlier. He had made his way from Manchuria over the Amur Railroad and had visited the larger war prisoner camps in eastern Siberia. He had encountered no armed prisoners throughout this area and had found the various concentrations to be well guarded.[19] Reassured by this impression of Drysdale's observations, Webster and Hicks concluded that it was unnecessary for them to pursue their investigations beyond Irkutsk.

The three officers were disturbed, however, to discover that on March 28, just one day before the arrival of Webster and Hicks, there had arrived at Irkutsk a trainload of 500 Hungarian prisoners from Omsk, armed with machine guns and rifles, who were being sent to take part in the operations against Semenov. The Allied officers were naturally greatly interested in this news, and immediately made inquiries of the local Soviet authorities. They were told that these were Hungarian deserters who had embraced the communist ideology and thrown in their lot with the Bolsheviki. This, it appeared, was only the first of three batches. Two other groups, embracing 497 men, were still in Omsk but due to follow at a later date. To Drysdale, who personally interviewed some of the Hungarians, it was even intimated (quite erroneously) that there might be many more than just these 497.

[19] Strangely enough, in a message sent from somewhere in eastern Siberia on March 24, Drysdale had reported that prisoners "at Chita and northward" were armed and committing misdeeds, and were being ordered by their officers to join the Red Guard (*Foreign Relations, 1918, Russia,* Vol. ii, *op.cit.,* p. 91). This is in direct contradiction not only to the impression Webster and Hicks gained from Drysdale in Irkutsk, but also to an undated note written by Drysdale to Caldwell, apparently from Chita, in which he wrote: "The prisoners are not armed but some few have been convicted of Bolshevick ideas, but we can rest assured that there is no armed organization of Prisoners of War." (National Archives, State Department File 861.00/1711.)

This discovery led to disagreement between Webster and Hicks, on the one hand, and Drysdale on the other. Webster and Hicks were inclined to accept the Soviet explanation that these men were Communists and deserters. (There is every indication that this was correct.) Drysdale was skeptical, and insisted that the Hungarian unit was a possible threat to Allied interests. He left the same evening on the return journey to Peking, resolved to report—as he told the others—that Allied interests were being endangered.

The report which Drysdale submitted to the American Minister at Peking, Mr. Paul S. Reinsch, after his return on April 10, makes an odd impression; for the factual material included in it seems scarcely to justify the general conclusion arrived at: that the prisoners-of-war were a serious potential danger to Allied interests.[20] East of Irkutsk, Drysdale had found no evidence of any arming of prisoners on a serious scale. In the entire Pri-Amur District, he reported, there were only 13,000 prisoners, and their removal to Europe had already begun. At Chita, very few prisoners were being armed. Even with respect to Irkutsk he mentioned no evidence of any sizeable arming of prisoners beyond the one Hungarian detachment. As for the Germans: "We were unable to find a single armed German prisoner of war, and I believe that practically no German prisoners of war are armed." Such danger as existed, he admitted, was potential rather than actual. His grounds for the belief that the danger was serious appear to have lain exclusively in the boasts of the Hungarian Communists about the number of like-minded men they had left behind in Omsk.

In view of this disparity between existing fact and analysis of future prospects, it is not surprising that Drysdale's reports were variously interpreted. Reinsch, on reading the report, wired the Department of State that

There is no evidence of a concerted plan on the part of the Germans to control Siberia through the prisoners nor could such an attempt succeed. Earlier reports about armed prisoners were exaggerated; most of these reports came from one source in Irkutsk. . . .[21]

The Department of State, on the other hand, was informing Francis on the same day (April 10) that it had reports from Drysdale "show-

[20] National Archives, Department of State File 861.00/1870.
[21] *Foreign Relations, 1918, Russia,* Vol. II, *op.cit.,* p. 117.

ing conclusively that prisoners of war in Siberia are arming and getting beyond control." [22]

Following Drysdale's departure, Webster and Hicks had conferences (March 30 and 31) with the three senior Soviet officials in Irkutsk: Yanson, chairman of the Irkutsk Soviet; Yakovlev, chairman of the All-Siberian Soviet; and Strenberg, military commander of the Irkutsk District. Webster and Hicks brought up the matter of the Hungarian unit and drew attention to the concern bound to be caused in Allied circles by such arming of prisoners. The Bolshevik officials expressed understanding for this view. They insisted that the Hungarians from Omsk were the only ones who had been so armed. They were all Internationalists who had broken with their own government. They had already caused considerable trouble to the Bolsheviki. It was not proposed to use them for military operations or to permit them to act as an independent force. Nor would any further units of this sort be established. The Soviet officials were prepared to guarantee that not more than 1,500 prisoners would be armed in all of Siberia. They would be glad to submit to arrangements for continued inspection by the Allied consuls at Irkutsk.

The sole reason for arming the Hungarians, the Soviet officials maintained, was the threat presented by Semenov. They pleaded with Webster and Hicks for the exertion of Allied influence on the Chinese with a view to persuading them to exert authority over Semenov or at least withdraw protection from him, so that traffic could be resumed from Siberia into Manchuria over the direct rail route. They complained that it was only Allied support that was making it possible for Semenov to hang on. If the Allies would only cooperate in removing this thorn from their side, there would, it was implied, be no incentive to any further arming of prisoners.

On the following day, April 1, Webster and Hicks visited the large war prisoner camp in the neighborhood of Irkutsk. Here they found everything normal and only a few prisoners armed for purposes of guarding supply and munitions depots.

The two officers had planned to start their return journey on April 2; but on the morning of that day they were visited by Yakovlev, who

[22] *Ibid.*, p. 116. The Department was here no doubt referring particularly to a message from Drysdale, sent through the American Consul at Chita and received in Washington on April 8, stressing the danger of the prisoners getting out of hand and urging either pressure through the Soviet government or direct American action to correct the situation (National Archives, State Department File 861.00/1444).

urged them to participate as observers at a further Chinese-Bolshevik conference, to be held at the Manchurian border, over the Semenov problem. The Chinese, Yakovlev explained, had not lived up to the initial understanding of March 18. Semenov's scouts continued to operate across the frontier; railway traffic, contrary to agreement, had not been resumed. For some reason, Yakovlev thought Allied representatives from China would be present at the forthcoming conference, on the Chinese side. The help of Webster and Hicks, as Allied representatives who fully appreciated the Russian situation, would, Yakovlev argued,

. . . be invaluable in explaining the Russian point of view to the Allied delegates from the East, and proving to them that it is to the benefit of Russia and the Allies that this guerilla fighting should cease.

Somewhat rashly, one feels, in view of the obvious ulterior motive behind this Russian proposal, Webster and Hicks accepted the invitation. They joined the Soviet delegates [23] in their special train, and arrived with them at Matsiyevskaya, on the Manchurian border, on April 6. Since no Allied representatives showed up with the Chinese delegation, there was no reason for the two Allied officers to participate in the discussion. They functioned only as observers at the long hours of wrangling between the Russian and Chinese delegates. The results, they subsequently reported to their principals in Moscow, were "unsatisfactory, hazy, . . . indefinite" and inconclusive. The Chinese were prepared neither to take effective measures against Semenov themselves nor to permit Bolshevik forces to enter Manchuria in pursuit of him. In Chinese eyes this was a Russian quarrel; they did not propose to get involved. Semenov had got there first; now he could stay. Pressed by the Soviet delegates to explain their seeming indifference to what was transpiring on their own territory, the Chinese negotiators blamed it on "the Allies." Without the consent of the Allies "they could not possibly act against Semenov." (The term "Allies" plainly, in this instance, was largely a euphemism for the Japanese. But the British and French had given just enough support to Semenov to make it impossible to exempt them entirely from the operation of the Chinese reproach.)

[23] These were Yanson, and the well-known political commissar, Sergei Georgievich Lazo, who was local commander of the forces operating against Semenov. Lazo, who later had the misfortune to be burned alive by the Japanese in the firebox of a locomotive, became posthumously a Soviet hero and the object of much folklore.

The conference broke up on the same day, with a complete lack of agreement. No sooner had the train bearing the Chinese delegation receded across the plain than Semenov's mounted scouts appeared on the horizon. The Soviet party, including Webster and Hicks, hastily withdrew (leaving an armed detachment to deal with Semenov's scouts) and returned to Irkutsk.

Ten days later (April 12), Consul General Maddin Summers in Moscow was disquieted to learn from the local press that "early this week" British and American delegates had attended a conference between Chinese and Bolsheviki concerning Semenov. Evidently nothing had been said to him by Robins about the Webster-Hicks mission. Summers relayed the report to the Department the same day and inquired, "Can Department inform me who these delegates were and by whom sent?" The reply, on April 19, stated simply, "The Department knows nothing of any such conference." [24]

After further conferences in Irkutsk, Webster and Hicks returned to Moscow, where they rendered their report to their superiors on April 26. The report could not have been more pleasing to Robins and Lockhart or, for that matter, to Trotsky. Other than the Hungarians from Omsk, the two officers had found no prisoners armed for military purposes. There were minor instances where prisoners were being used as guards and bore small arms accordingly. They recognized that their view was contrary to that held by the Allied consuls in Irkutsk; but they questioned whether the latter were well-informed or impartial. The consuls, they argued, were "unanimously anti-Bolshevik in sympathy, had had nothing to do with the Soviet authorities personally, and had not even met Mr. Yakovlev. . . ." The consuls, they felt, drew their information from the old property-owning classes and were too busy with their own office pressures to get out and elicit the facts.

Webster and Hicks professed, in their report, full faith in the Soviet assurances that no further prisoners would be armed, in the absence of Allied intervention in Siberia—for which contingency the Soviet authorities naturally reserved full freedom of action. They warmly recommended economic aid for the Siberian Bolsheviki. "Cooperation on a commercial basis," they wrote in the concluding passage of their report,

[24] National Archives, State Department File 861.00/1592.

would not only tend to prevent Germany securing the Siberian raw products but would be the best point of contact we could secure, and the best influence we could use from a political standpoint.

Webster and Hicks doubtless underestimated the number of war prisoners who went over to the Communists and joined the Soviet units as individuals. They misunderstood in particular the situation at Irkutsk itself, where a body of armed prisoners appears subsequently to have made up a good part of the internal security force of the local communist regime. But they were correct in their conclusion that the Hungarians from Omsk were the only ones armed as a unit for any external military purposes. More important still, they were correct in their general deduction that there was no appreciable danger to Allied war interests from the Siberian prisoners-of-war. The governments of the Central Powers, after all, had had nothing whatsoever to do with this development. Very shortly, on the establishment of a German Embassy in Moscow at the end of April, the German government itself would protest against communist efforts to subvert the prisoners from allegiance to their own governments; Trotsky would issue a public order [25] instructing the Soviet authorities not to admit into the Red Army any volunteers from among foreigners who had not assumed Soviet citizenship; and existing Internationalist detachments would be broken up. These developments would have put an end to any "prisoner-of-war danger" even had there been one.

Had the Webster-Hicks report reached the Allied chanceries in good time and been given proper weight, much unnecessary confusion could have been avoided. But the report did not reach Washington before the end of April at the earliest. By this time events had moved on; and the conflict between the Allied governments and the Soviet regime had come to embrace new sources of bitterness and commitment on both sides. The reception of the report, furthermore, was evidently affected by Drysdale's contrary reactions and by the growing distrust in Washington of Robins' impartiality and soundness. Here again, the lack of an effective orderly arrangement for representation and information-gathering abroad prevented the United States government from assembling and utilizing cor-

[25] On April 20. Jane Degras, Editor, *Soviet Documents on Foreign Policy*, Oxford University Press, 1951, Vol. I, *1917–1924*, pp. 70–71.

rectly the best information available to it on a situation which was shortly to enter most importantly into the formulation of American policy.

❖

It is impossible to discover in the Siberian situation of early 1918 any central logic that served as the determinant of Allied interests and attitudes. The outstanding characteristics of this situation were its extreme complexity and instability. The internal-political condition in Siberia, in the wake of the two revolutions in European Russia, was confused, precarious, and obscure. Nor was there, among the manifold interests that animated the Allied powers in their approach to Siberian problems, any overriding single interest that could have lent unity to Allied purposes. The various Entente governments viewed Siberia, as Wilson suspected, primarily as a means to the attainment of ulterior ends of one sort or another; and among these various ends there was little in common. The Japanese were interested in building up their political and economic position on the Asiatic mainland. The French were interested in overthrowing the Soviet government and in salvaging something of the investment of their citizens in the Siberian and Manchurian railways. The British were interested in finding a new channel of access to the Middle Eastern theater of war—a channel that could check the German-Turkish advance upon a now powerless Russia. None of these powers, as Wilson correctly surmised, had any very benevolent interest in the Siberians for their own sake. Siberia was, in fact, primarily the battleground for a host of external stimuli and pressures. It had no internal unity, and it engendered no internal impulses strong enough to compete with those that came to it from outside.

The United States government was urged by Americans who knew Siberia (of these Mr. George Kennan [26] was perhaps the most authoritative and influential) to draw a distinction between Siberia and European Russia, to take a special interest in the great Siberian territory, to adopt a special policy toward it, and to attempt to salvage there what could not be salvaged in Russia proper.

There was much justification for such a view. Siberia's development had paralleled in many ways that of America's own North-

[26] The reference here, as explained in Volume I, is to George Kennan (1848–1924) who was a first cousin twice removed of the author of this study.

west. The feudal institutions and complexes of European Russia had scarcely penetrated to this great region. Its human atmosphere, emerging from frontier experiences not too dissimilar in many instances from those of the United States, was marked by a personal independence and a breezy informality that made Americans feel more at home there than in Russia proper, where the long tradition of Tsarist despotism had left so strong an imprint. America could well expect her leadership to be more welcome and more effective among the Siberians than among the Russians farther west. And she could expect to find among them a greater natural resistance to the weaknesses that had rendered European Russia so vulnerable to the contagion of Bolshevism.

Had such arguments had any palpable effect on the statesmen in Washington, it would be easier than it is to understand America's subsequent involvement in Siberia. Unfortunately, this was not the case. The President's approach to the problems of Siberia remained, like that of his chief advisers, undeviatingly high-minded and abstract, unpolluted by any distinctions of a geographic or local-political nature. Siberia, in Wilson's view, was a part of Russia, just as Manchuria was a part of China. The Siberians were Russians and entitled, as such, to be the objects of precisely those same sentiments of friendship and benevolence which, as the President thought, ought to lie at the heart of America's attitude toward Russia generally. If considerations based on the specific characteristics of Siberia, as a part of Russia, ever entered into Washington's handling of the Siberian problem, the record does not show it.

The confusions that marked America's subsequent involvement in Siberian affairs were the faithful reflection of the peculiar confusions to which that area was itself now the victim. And these were of such a nature that before them the inquiring eye of the historical philosopher, seeking always to discern order and unity in the processes of history, must retire in frustration. Of the Siberia of 1918 the only reasonable generalization that can be stated is that it was an unbelievable chaos.

CHAPTER IV

THE FIRST JAPANESE LANDING

THE evolution of Japanese policy with respect to Siberia up to March 1918 was traced briefly in Volume I. It now becomes necessary to return to this subject and to examine in somewhat greater detail, to the extent limited sources permit, the state of Japanese official thought and preparations during the month of March.

It will be recalled that the Japanese Foreign Minister, Viscount Ichiro Motono, had contrived in late February to create in the diplomatic chanceries of the Entente powers an impression that Japan was about to intervene in Siberia regardless of whether Washington could be prevailed upon to join in requesting and sponsoring the undertaking. It will also be recalled that this impression was incorrect: the preponderance of influential Japanese opinion remained at all times adverse to any major action by Japan in Siberia not supported by request and approval from the American side. The main consideration behind this reserve appears to have been a fear that Japan might, by undertaking such an action without American blessing, find herself caught up in a wearisome and economically exhausting occupational involvement in Siberia, while the Americans stood aside, preserved their own strength and resources in the Pacific area, disclaimed responsibility for Japan's discomfort, and withheld economic and financial aid.

By the first days of March even Motono had fallen in line with this basic position and reflected it, if somewhat grudgingly, in his statements to the Allied ambassadors. To Sir William Greene, the British Ambassador, who came in to see him on March 7 (the day Wilson's note of the 5th, questioning the wisdom of a Japanese intervention, was delivered in Tokyo [1]), Motono observed that

[1] See Volume I, Chapter XXIII.

. . . if the attitude of the United States made it impossible for Japan to obtain assistance from her financially and in such materials as steel, it would be very difficult for Japan to act on the invitation of the Allies, . . .

Unless there was assurance of the President's support it would perhaps be better, Motono said, "that action should be deferred." The situation in Russia was not urgent; it would be a pity if there were disagreement among the Allies.[2]

Greene's own report to his government of Motono's statements gives a good picture of the state of Japanese official opinion at that time:

. . . the former eagerness shown by the Minister for Foreign Affairs for intervention had been reduced by the element in the Cabinet, which includes the Prime Minister and the Minister of the Interior, who have doubts as to the endurance of the Allies and who consider that intervention is impracticable without financial and material assistance from the United States. If it is considered wiser to defer action, I do not think that to do so will necessarily disappoint the Cabinet who are satisfied with our action hitherto and who are especially pleased with us for not insisting on our demand for the participation of allied troops in intervention.

The General Staff continues to prepare to take action at short notice, . . .

This last sentence reflected a very important proviso to the Japanese position as described above. The Cabinet, while adhering to its unwillingness to act on behalf of the Allies in the absence of American agreement, had made two significant concessions to the desire of Motono and the army leaders for immediate and vigorous action in Siberia. First, it was agreed that Japan, while abstaining for the time being from participation in any action concerted with the Allies, should publicly reserve to herself the right to take independent action, on her own initiative and responsibility, should this at any time seem warranted for the protection of Japanese interests. The unwillingness to take action on behalf of the Allies at that moment was not, in other words, to be permitted to prejudice Japan's freedom to act at any time on her own, if she felt it to be in her interest to do so. Secondly, it was agreed that abstention from any major action at that time should not preclude the vigorous putting in hand of preparations, military and political, designed to place the Japanese

<hr />

[2] Woodrow Wilson MSS, Series II, Library of Congress, Washington; paraphrase of Greene's cable to Foreign Office of March 7, 1918.

[85]

government in a position to act promptly and effectively when and if the proper moment arrived.

Precisely what these preparatory measures consisted of does not appear from the record available for this present study; but it is evident that they included, in addition to the designation and readying of the necessary armed units, two steps that were of particular importance from the standpoint of American policy. These were:

1. the cultivation of a special bilateral agreement with the Chinese which would commit the latter to participation and co-responsibility in whatever venture Japan might undertake and would make possible Japanese use of the Chinese Eastern Railway for such a purpose; and

2. completion of plans for a preliminary landing at Vladivostok. An agreement of such a nature with the Chinese would, it was clear, increase China's obligation to Japan and her dependence on Japanese assistance. It would guard against China's being used by any other power as a means of obstructing fulfillment of Japanese purposes in Manchuria and Siberia. It would give to Japan, as China's ally in a Siberian venture, an excellent position from which to edge Horvat out of the picture and to move into Russia's place as the dominant power in the leased zone of the Chinese Eastern Railway.

It is clear, in the light of these plans, that the agreement concluded, at the end of February, between Stevens and the Chinese for employment of the Russian Railway Service Corps on the Chinese Eastern could not fail to make the Japanese most uncomfortable. It did not fit at all with the plan for cultivation of a special Sino-Japanese understanding with regard to a possible action in Siberia. It was particularly dangerous insofar as it might well appear to the Chinese as an alternative to the acceptance of the Japanese proposals. Nor is it likely that the Japanese fully understood or trusted American motives. Political innocence was, surely, the quality least apt to be understood in the arena of Far Eastern diplomacy at that time. It must have been extremely difficult, if not impossible, for the Japanese to believe that Washington's eagerness to see American engineers employed on either the Siberian or Manchurian railways reflected no other motive than a disinterested desire to bring the blessings of economic development to the peoples of these regions.

As for the preliminary landing at Vladivostok, there was evidently some ambiguity as to whether it was the landing itself, or just the preparations for the landing, which was envisaged as the measure preparatory to a larger intervention. The question appears to have remained without clear determination in Tokyo; but authorization was evidently given to Admiral Kato, at Vladivostok, to put forces ashore on his own responsibility if at any time he felt that they were urgently required for the protection of Japanese interests. Thus the decision as to when the preliminary landing should occur was left to flow from the unfolding of events on the spot, as seen and interpreted by the naval commander there.

These dispositions were clearly reflected in the Japanese reaction to President Wilson's note of March 5. The arrival of the note naturally brought matters to a head and necessitated a thorough review of the Japanese position. While the President's communication did not, to be sure, give the green light for a major action by Japan in Siberia, it was cast in a friendly and sympathetic vein. It was now plain that if Japan were to act, there would be regret, skepticism, and a disavowal of responsibility in Washington—but no actual protest or objection. This must have been seized upon by the proponents of intervention in Tokyo as an argument in their favor.

The whole matter was therefore gone over once more at meetings of the authoritative Advisory Council of Foreign Affairs held on March 9 and 15. But the basic position appears to have survived these deliberations without suffering any material change. The weight of official opinion continued to lean to the view that time and circumstances were not ripe for the sort of action the French and British were urging. This thought could be repeatedly detected in the statements of senior Japanese figures. Baron Shimpei Goto, the Minister of Interior, observed to Morris (March 2):

The previous Ministry declared war on Germany too soon; in this crisis we must . . . not . . . act too soon again.[3]

A similar opinion was voiced (March 15) by one of the most influential of the elder statesmen, Aritomo Yagamata:

It is too early now to send forces to Siberia. If we dare to send the army to Russian territory without her [America's] request, it will cause suspicion and disfavor in the United States, and we will not be able to expect her

---

[3] *Foreign Relations, 1918, Russia*, Vol. II, *op.cit.*, p. 72; from telegram of March 7, I a.m., Morris to SECSTATE.

help. Our armed forces are strong enough to confront the enemy, but I regret to say that we should depend greatly upon assistance from the United States and Great Britain in the form of military materiel and financial backing.[4]

The day after the second of these meetings of the Advisory Council (March 16), the Japanese made their reply to Wilson's communication of March 5. It was in the form of a confidential memorandum handed to American Ambassador Roland S. Morris.[5] Expressing appreciation for the frank and friendly tenor of the American communication, the Japanese memorandum continued:

It will be clearly understood that the intervention now proposed by the Allied Governments . . . did not originate from any desire expressed or any suggestion made by the Japanese Government. At the same time the Japanese Government have viewed with grave concern the chaotic conditions prevailing in Siberia and they fully realize the serious danger of the German aggression to which these regions are exposed. . . . they are prepared to entertain . . . any plan of action with which they may be approached by the Allied Governments. . . .

They, however, feel that the success of such undertaking will depend largely upon the whole-hearted support of all the great powers associated in the war against Germany. Accordingly, it is their intention to refrain from taking any action on which due understanding has not been reached between the United States and the other great powers of the Entente.

Having thus reasserted their unwillingness to act as mandatory for the Allies without American request, the Japanese government went on to stake out their claim to freedom of action for whatever operations they might find it necessary to take in their own interests:

. . . should the hostile activities in Siberia develop to such a degree as to jeopardize the national security or vital interests of Japan she may be compelled to resort to prompt and efficient measures of self-protection. The Japanese Government are confident that in such event they can count on the friendly support of the American Government in the struggle which may be forced upon them.

The memorandum ended with an assurance that any action the Japanese might be called upon to take in the Russian territory would

[4] This passage is quoted in a memorandum entitled "Origin of the Siberian Intervention, November 1917–August 1918" written, and kindly made available to me, by the Japanese historian, Mr. Chihiro Hosoya. He attributes it to a Japanese source (Biography of Yamagata Aritomo) by I. Tokutomi (1933), Volume II, pp. 987–989.
[5] *Foreign Relations, 1918, Russia,* Vol. II, *op.cit.,* pp. 81–82.

be "wholly uninfluenced by any aggressive motives or tendencies." The Japanese government, it was said, remained

. . . unshaken in the profound sympathy towards the Russian people with whom they have every desire to maintain the relations of cordial friendship.

The meaning of this communication was entirely clear: no major intervention by Japan as mandatory for the Allies, unless America assumed her share of the responsibility and the expense; full freedom for Japan to take action whenever and wherever she wished, in her own interests and at her own expense.

❖

In Washington, meanwhile, the French and British—wholly undeterred by the President's decision of March 5—kept up their drumming on the United States government for a change of the American attitude. The language of these continued urgings took so little account of Wilson's communication that one wonders whether the Allies realized at all the solemnity of decision that lay behind it. Implying as it did that the President's decision of March 5 was not to be taken seriously, this continued agitation of the matter showed a poor understanding of Wilson's psychology. It will, however, be recalled that this was just the time of final preparation and launching of the great German spring offensive in France. The desperation of the British and French planners in the face of this development has already been mentioned.

On March 12, only a week after Wilson's message was sent, the French Ambassador, J. J. Jusserand, was back at the State Department with another note urging intervention. Ignoring completely the President's recent communication, the French once more predicted the inevitability of Japanese intervention with or without Allied consent—possibly even by agreement with Germany. The familiar arguments were reintroduced: only by Allied agreement to the action, it was held, could Japan be induced to give the necessary guarantees for the postwar period. The hope was expressed that the United States would reexamine the matter, concur in the French view, and join in requesting the Japanese to intervene.[6]

[6] *Ibid.,* pp. 75-77. In this note, the French made the mistake of describing in somewhat glowing terms the prosperity and material resources of the Japanese, as

Polk, who received the French Ambassador, at once assured him that there was no possibility of any such reconsideration. After conferring with the President (at the Cabinet meeting on March 15), Lansing confirmed Polk's statement (March 16) in a polite but blunt note to Jusserand,[7] saying that it was not without respect for the French views and not without a most thorough study of the problem that the United States government was "unable at the present time to alter its opinion and attitude towards this question. . . ."

On the same day that Lansing sent this reply, the whole question of Siberian intervention was being warmed over once more: this time at an Allied diplomatic conference in London. Once more the reader is struck with the scant heed paid on this occasion to Wilson's note of March 5. The British Foreign Secretary, Mr. Arthur Balfour, who had now had Greene's account of Motono's statements, led off by stating that he no longer thought the Japanese would consent to act alone in the absence of United States support. What, then, was to be done? The French pleaded for a new joint approach to the President. Mr. Arthur Hugh Frazier, the American Diplomatic Liaison Officer to the Supreme War Council in Paris, summed up as follows the pattern of the discussion:

It is quite obvious that the French and Italians on the one hand and the English on the other regarded the subject . . . from different points of view, the French and Italians were all for prompt action and inclined to make light of the danger [of] antagonizing Russia; both Mr. Balfour and Mr. Lloyd George had evident misgivings as to the wisdom of the policy and the former especially was in favor of delay in the hope that possibly the invitation for Japanese intervention might come from the Russians themselves.[8]

This last reference to the possibility of a Russian request reflected the optimistic belief in such a development entertained and relayed to the western governments at that time by the three Allied contact men in Moscow, Lockhart, Robins, and Captain Jacques Sadoul of

---

reinforcement for the argument that the Japanese would be prepared to act alone, without American support and approval. Two days later, having learned from Tokyo that this was precisely the opposite of the Japanese position, the French sent a further note correcting the error, but still insisting on the desirability of intervention. (Wilson MSS, Series II, *op.cit.*)

[7] *Foreign Relations, 1918, Russia,* Vol. II, *op.cit.,* p. 80.

[8] National Archives, State Department File 763.72 Su/144, telegram no. 19, March 16, 11 a.m., signed Page, from Frazier for the President.

the French Military Mission. The sources of this belief will be discussed in the next chapter.

Despite the lack of basic agreement, the conference nevertheless decided, on French insistence, that Wilson should be approached once more, this time in the name of the Allied governments as a group. Balfour, despite his own misgivings, was commissioned to convey to Wilson the sentiments of the conference. The British Ambassador in Washington, Lord Reading, accordingly appeared at the White House on March 18 with Balfour's message.

The danger, Balfour stated, was now "great and imminent." Russia had destroyed her armed forces. Germany would never permit her to reconstruct them.[9] Her territory swarmed with hostile agencies; such energies as she still possessed were expended in internal conflicts. Russia, in short, was delivered up to the German invader and was at his mercy for unlimited exploitation. What was the remedy? Only Allied intervention—from the northern ports and from Siberia. But the Japanese alone were in a position to supply manpower and tonnage on any major scale for such a venture. It was the Japanese, therefore, to whom the request had to be addressed.

The conference recognized, Balfour continued, that there were weighty objections to this course. There was, admittedly, in Russia a fear of Japan. But this fear was baseless. If Japan intervened, it would be as the friend of Russia and the mandatory of the Allies. Her object would be "not to copy the Germans but to resist them."

No steps could usefully be taken, however, to implement this policy unless they had United States support. Without this support, it would be useless to approach the Japanese government, and even if the Japanese should consent to act without it, the action would lose half its moral authority.[10]

Colonel Edward M. House, the President's confidant and intimate adviser, was at that time ill in New York. Forewarned of the Allied step by the informal liaison officer of the British government in New York, Sir William Wiseman, House immediately asked his

[9] Ironically enough, the building of a new armed force was being inaugurated, that very day, by Trotsky; and, despite many German misgivings, it would proceed rapidly, from that time forward, without serious interference from the Germans. This German tolerance was to be explained, of course, only by the fact that the Germans were well aware that the Bolsheviki had no intention of resuming the war in the Allied cause.

[10] *War Memoirs of David Lloyd George,* Ivor Nicolson & Watson, London, 1936, Vol. vi, pp. 3175–3177.

son-in-law, Gordon Auchincloss, who was assistant to Counselor Frank Polk in the State Department, to get word to the President that he, House, had seen Frazier's report and that it had not changed his opinion. Reading was already with the President when House's message was delivered at the White House. Mrs. Wilson took the responsibility of having it sent in at once, while the meeting was still in progress.[11] Whether or not his views were affected by it, Wilson's reply to Reading was precisely that of House: "I have not changed my mind." [12]

That same day Lansing, still apparently unaware of the Allied step, sent to the White House a memorandum of his own on the same subject.[13] The proposal for a Japanese expeditionary force was continuing to be urged, he wrote, with varying degrees of earnestness by the British, French, and Italian governments, all of which desired to make Japan a mandatory of the Powers. He went on to stress, once more, the unfavorable psychological effect intervention would inevitably have on the Russians. All Russia, he thought, would become hostile: "There would be the charge that Russia had been betrayed by her professed friends and delivered over to the yellow race." The Russians might even turn, in their embitterment, to Germany.[14] Nor was there any reason to believe that the military effect of a Japanese intervention, from the standpoint of the World War, would be great. The supplies at Vladivostok were not being moved to the interior; there was no prospect of their being moved, in view of the disorganization of the railway.[15] In these circum-

[11] Wilson MSS, Series II, *op.cit.;* Auchincloss' note, with Mrs. Wilson's chit: "Thought you might want this while you were talking with Reading."
It is doubtful that Reading was able to support this *démarche* with any personal enthusiasm. "I have talked Sir William quite out of the proposal," House recorded in his diary on March 18, "and he, in turn, has shaken Reading's views to such an extent that the Ambassador could not put up any argument for his Government." (Edward M. House MSS, Yale University Library, New Haven.)
[12] *Ibid.*
[13] Nothing in the text of the memorandum indicated any knowledge on Lansing's part that Lord Reading was discussing this same matter with the President that day. Reading told him on the following day of his visit to Wilson. (Robert Lansing MSS, Library of Congress, Washington, Desk Diary, March 19.)
[14] One has here an interesting example of the way in which the war in the west dominated all Allied calculations at this time. While the French were arguing that lack of American consent to intervention would drive Japan into Germany's arms, Lansing was arguing that intervention would have precisely this effect on the Russians.
[15] Lansing had by this time received a reassuring report from Admiral Knight about the Vladivostok supplies.

stances, Lansing registered once more the conclusion he and House and the President had been voicing to each other with such monotonous regularity over the past weeks: ". . . it would seem unwise and inexpedient to support the request for Japanese intervention in Siberia." [16]

When Lansing's memorandum was returned the next day, it bore the notation: "With the foregoing the President entirely agrees."

The receipt, on March 20, of the Japanese reply to the note of March 5 naturally strengthened the President in his reluctance to contemplate any such move as the Allies were urging. The argument which had been used so effectively in late February, and which had brought him at one time so close to changing his position was, after all, that the Japanese were preparing to act anyway,[17] regardless of America's attitude. The Japanese reply now effectively disposed of this suggestion. Lansing and the President were both greatly pleased. Ambassador Morris was instructed to tell the Japanese government that the reply was "most gratifying" and that it removed any possibility of misunderstanding "which might otherwise arise." [18]

During the final days of March, appeals for intervention continued to reach Lansing and the President from many quarters, other than the Allied governments. A long message from Admiral Knight, in Vladivostok, was received on March 18. It contained no specific recommendation for immediate intervention but set forth in detail a plan for the allotment of missions among the Allied governments if and when intervention should finally be decided upon.[19] J. Butler Wright, now in Vladivostok on his way home from his post as Counselor of Embassy in Petrograd, wired his impressions of the trip across Siberia, and expressed himself as in favor of joint intervention.[20] Consul Charles K. Moser, in Harbin, was reporting that conditions in Siberia would be "unbearable . . . unless Allies intervene." [21] General William V. Judson, former Military Attaché

[16] Lansing MSS, *op.cit.*, Box 2 (Confidential Memoranda & Notes, April 15, 1915 to December 20, 1918, incl.)

[17] See Volume I, p. 476.

[18] *Foreign Relations, 1918, Russia,* Vol. II, *op.cit.*, p. 88.

[19] A further message from Knight, of the 23rd, indicates that he showed his plan to the Japanese Admiral at Vladivostok, who took note of it without enthusiasm and without comment (National Archives, Navy Branch, R.G. 45, *op.cit.*). The plan does appear, however, to have had an important influence on the dispositions made when intervention actually took place some months later.

[20] *Foreign Relations, 1918, Russia,* Vol. II, *op.cit.*, pp. 89-91.

[21] *Ibid.*, p. 93; telegram of March 29, 6 p.m., from Peking.

and Chief of the American Military Mission at Petrograd, called at the Department of State on March 20 and then set forth his views on paper for the Secretary. He was sure that a Japanese invasion of Siberia would throw Russia into German hands. He believed that a small United States force, acting alone, would have the opposite effect and would compel Germany to keep large forces on the eastern front. There were, he added, many possible intermediate courses and obviously some sort of compromise would be necessary. But the benefit would be proportionate to the extent that "American initiative and cooperation . . . were emphasized." [22]

A further jolt was received on March 21, when Lord Reading brought in certain messages from Irkutsk about the prisoner-of-war situation in Siberia, emanating from the Acting British Vice Consul there and from a French intelligence officer, Colonel Pichon. (This, it will be recalled, was less than a fortnight before the visit of Webster and Hicks to that place.) The British Vice Consul reported a great concentration of German prisoners about to take place at Irkutsk, and mentioned the number of 80,000.

Lansing was quite alarmed, and at once sent the messages to the President. [23] If the reports were true, he observed, this would place the problem of intervention in a different light. [24]

The President did not agree. "I am much obliged to you for sending these papers to me so promptly," he replied the next day (March 22),

but I do not find in them sufficient cause for altering our position. They still do not answer the question I have put to Lord Reading and to all others who argue in favor of intervention by Japan, namely, What is it to effect and how will it be efficacious in effecting it? The condition of Siberia furnishes no answer. [25]

Now, at last, it was Lansing's turn to argue. He went back at the President with a letter (March 24) in which, for the first time, he really came close to arguing in favor of intervention—though only on the hypothesis that the alarming reports about the prisoners were

[22] National Archives, State Department File 861.00/1353½.
[23] *Papers Relating to the Foreign Relations of the United States: The Lansing Papers, 1914–1920*, U.S. Government Printing Office, Washington, 1940, Vol. II, p. 357.
[24] Lansing MSS, *op.cit.*, Diary Blue Boxes, Box 2: Lansing Memoranda of March 22 and April 6.
[25] *Foreign Relations, The Lansing Papers*, Vol. II, *op.cit.*, p. 357.

correct. He posed for the President the question as to whether, if the reports proved true, there was anything to be lost

. . . by making Japan the mandatory of the Powers, and giving approval to her sending an expeditionary force into Siberia to oust the Germans and to restore Russian authority in that region? [26]

But Wilson was not so lightly shaken. He replied (according to Lansing's own record) that "he quite agreed but did not think the situation yet warranted change of policy." [27] The reports, as it turned out, found no clear confirmation; and things went on as before.

On April 1, Mr. Herbert Bayard Swope, co-editor and Washington correspondent of the *New York World,* solicited the President's approval for an interpretative article he proposed to write "to clear up doubt arising from contradictory reports of our attitude on the Japanese-Siberian situation." Swope proposed to state that

. . . America's non-assent to the suggestion of Japanese intervention in Siberia checked the original plan and that nothing is to be done along that line until there is *actual military necessity* for the step, in which case America will give her consent.

To this inquiry Wilson drafted a reply suggesting that Swope omit the words: "in which case America will give her consent." The President explained:

. . . I should like to leave that idea out, in view of the many impressions which are beginning to cluster around this extremely difficult and delicate subject.[28]

❖

It was against this background of feeling in Tokyo and Washington that the situation in Vladivostok moved rapidly, in the last days of March, to a crisis.

There were at this time four Allied vessels at anchor in the harbor: the *U.S.S. Brooklyn,* the Japanese cruisers *Asahi* and *Iwami,* and a British cruiser, *H.M.S. Suffolk.* Admiral Knight and the Japanese Admiral, Kato, were on pleasant personal terms. Knight kept his Japanese colleague informed of his instructions, his analyses of the

[26] *Ibid.,* p. 358.
[27] *Ibid.,* p. 357, footnote 47.
[28] Wilson MSS, Series II, *op.cit.;* Wilson's draft reply was dated April 2.

situation, and his views as to what ought to be done. Kato was perhaps somewhat bewildered by this openness; there is, in any case, no evidence that he fully reciprocated the frankness. "He is most courteous," Knight reported on March 23,

but appears to believe that compromise can be effected between extreme factions in Russia. I have seen no one who agrees with him nor has he any plan for affecting [sic] such compromise. . . . He states that he has no instructions from his government and knows nothing of its attitude but believes Japanese people are against intervention and his [government] cannot finance a campaign. . . .[29]

Whether the British commander had a greater intimacy with the Japanese Admiral, the record does not indicate. One is moved to suspect that he had. The Anglo-Japanese Alliance was, after all, still operative at that time; and there was formal reason for greater frankness with the British on the Japanese side. It may be surmised, furthermore, that British policies toward Siberia and Manchuria, being more openly political and obviously based at that time on England's interests in the remote European war, were less disturbing and more intelligible to the Japanese than was the baffling highmindedness of the American government.

A special tenseness seems to have come over the situation at Vladivostok toward the end of March. On the 24th the local Bolsheviki seized the telegraph office. The postal and telegraph employees, being strongly anti-communist, went on strike in protest. The services were thus paralyzed, with the result that the Allied consular representatives found themselves without communication with the outside world. They met at once and decided to insist on reestablishment of the services, at least for foreign representatives and residents. They agreed that if the effort failed, each would ask his own government whether "forceful intervention by men of war" would be considered. The Japanese intimated that in this contingency he would expect to receive a favorable reply. But Knight, consulted by the American Consul, was opposed to any use of force.[30] And within three days the Bolsheviki reestablished a partial service —just enough to take the edge off the Allied indignation.

[29] National Archives, Navy Branch; Subject File, 1911–1927, folder labelled "Russia; WA-6 Siberia, Conditions in Vladivostok 1917–1919."

[30] *Ibid.*, Foreign Affairs Branch, Vladivostok 800 File, 1918, *op.cit.;* draft telegram, unsent, Caldwell to SECSTATE, March 25.

Despite this partial concession, the atmosphere remained sultry. A new flurry of rumors now began to circulate concerning alleged German activity in the Far East and German-Bolshevik designs on the war stores. It was only ten days earlier that Knight, after completing his initial survey of the situation, had reported that there was "absolutely no present danger" that the stores might fall into German hands. A portion might be destroyed, he had conceded, since they were poorly guarded; but even this portion would not be large.[31] Now, however, he was shaken by the spate of new rumors. On the 26th he reported that orders had been received by the Russian port authorities, from both Moscow and Khabarovsk, to start shipping the munitions inland. The following day he wired that there was

. . . Marked unrest in city . . . with danger of conflict between Soviet . . . and conservatives. . . . Many Red Guards arriving from Khabarovsk reported at several thousand. Three German officers arrived here today and others believed to be in Vladivostok. Continued indications that munitions will be seized or destroyed. Situation very tense.

Prepared [to] land [to] protect Consulate.[32]

An equally grim report was sent on March 28. The Soviets, Knight reported, were now boasting of their strength. Supplies were being shipped out at the rate of forty carloads a day. The danger was such that it "may compel us to land." He recommended an increase in American naval strength at Vladivostok.[33]

Was there any substance behind these reports of impending measures to remove the stores? Possibly there was. Trotsky had just recently arrived in Moscow and had taken over the War Commissariat. His vigorous telegrams were now flying in all directions. Energetic measures were already being implemented to remove the Archangel stores to the interior. There was no reason why similiar measures should not have been put in hand at Vladivostok, where the accumulation was even greater and more valuable.

But there is no reason to suppose that the Germans had anything to do with any of this. Diplomatic and technical contact between Russia and Germany had not yet been resumed, at this point, after the recent Brest-Litovsk crisis. What was involved here was—if any-

[31] *Ibid.,* Navy Branch, R.G. 45, *op.cit.,* Knight to OPNAV, March 16.
[32] *Ibid.,* Knight telegram of March 27.
[33] *Ibid.,* telegram of March 28.

thing—a Soviet effort to secure the stores, for Soviet use, against Allied capture and removal. At the rate of forty carloads per day this would have taken, in the case of the Vladivostok stores, somewhere between three and four years.

The British commander received authorization from his government to concert with his Japanese and American colleagues whatever measures might be necessary to prevent removal of the stores. Knight, while "assuming" initially that it was his duty to cooperate, wired Washington (March 26) for confirmation that it wished him to do so. But Washington's reply (March 29) was characteristically negative. If the Japanese and British wanted to take such action, that, the Secretary of the Navy, Mr. Josephus Daniels, stated, was that; it was not clear why the United States should join them.

. . . During disturbed conditions in Russia this government most anxious that nothing be done that could in any way affect the confidence of the Russian people in our sincere desire to help them establish and maintain government of their own choosing.[34]

A second message was sent the following day, admonishing Knight to

. . . be careful to proceed on the principle that we have no right to use armed force except for the protection of Americans or . . . American interests. Take no action unless instructed by Department.[35]

At some time prior to the late afternoon of April 2, Knight informed Kato of Washington's disapproval of his joining in any operation to secure the stores.

According to Knight's reports the local situation was by this time "extremely tense." The local Soviet, he wired, was now convinced that the time had come for a complete assumption of power by the Communists; the Red Guards now numbered 3,000; more were expected to arrive shortly; 800 of them were quartered close to the place where the munitions shipped by the Allies were stored. There was talk that the foreign warships might at any time be fired upon.[36]

On April 2 Lord Reading came in to see Lansing, bringing a memorandum setting forth the views of the British government

[34] *Ibid.*, SECNAV to Knight, March 28; 20028.
[35] *Ibid.*, SECNAV to Knight, March 29; 17029.
[36] *Ibid.*, Knight's telegram of April 2.

about the Vladivostok situation. There was now, it was said in this memorandum, danger of a full communist coup at any time.

. . . The Bolshevists believe that, in the present political situation, the men of war in the port will not take any action except, possibly, to act for the protection of the foreign Consulates, and they realize that these vessels cannot afford any protection to the city without definite orders to that effect. . . . while they anticipate Japanese intervention some time or another, they expect to be able to gain complete control by immediate violent action.[37]

The memorandum went on to relate that the commander of the *Suffolk* was being instructed to act in concert with the Japanese and American commanders in preventing removal of the stores, and asked whether the United States was contemplating a similar step. We have no record of Lansing's answer, but may be sure it was negative.

On April 4th, at 11:00 a.m., several armed men in the uniform of Russian soldiers entered a Japanese shop in Vladivostok and demanded money. This being refused, they then shot and killed three Japanese. Early the following morning, Kato put a party of marines ashore for the purpose (as he put it in a written notification to the Russian officials) of protecting the lives and property of Japanese citizens in the city. A second Japanese contingent was landed later in the day, making a total of 500 men ashore. The British followed suit by putting ashore 50 men as a guard for their consular establishment.

Kato explained to Knight the same day that he had been unable to find any authority on shore to whom he could appeal for the protection of his nationals.[38] He had received information, he said, that Russian communist sailors had planned to loot the city; he thought the attack on the Japanese might have been a premature move in this direction. He had therefore acted under necessity. He had not received any further instructions from his government; but he expected an increase of his force by one more cruiser and three destroyers, to arrive April 6.[39]

The Japanese landing was not opposed in any forceful way by the

[37] *Ibid.*, Foreign Affairs Branch, State Department File 861.00/1435½.
[38] *Ibid.*, Navy Branch, R.G. 45, *op.cit.*, telegram, Knight to Navy Department, April 5.
[39] *Ibid.*, later telegram of same date.

Communists. They appear to have been caught completely by surprise. Two days later the Vladivostok Soviet, after hearing the report of one of its members who had been sent to consult the Allied consuls and to inquire the purpose of the move, decided there was nothing to do but to accept the situation, under protest, and wait.[40]

Knight naturally watched the Japanese landing with the greatest interest. He did not question the good faith of the Japanese action. The landing appeared, he wired, to have been dictated by necessity. But he decided to take no parallel action at the moment. "Shall only land force if our interests are threatened," he wired to the Navy Department on the day of the landing,

. . . which is not the case at present. Have informed Japanese Admiral of my position and stated that any concerted action beyond protection of nationals must be arranged by our governments.[41]

Official Washington, too, was obliged to ask itself whether Admiral Knight should not be instructed to follow suit. The British Ambassador urged on Lansing (April 8) that instructions to this effect be sent to the Admiral at once.[42] There was strong support for this suggestion among Lansing's aides; but the Secretary was firmly opposed. The Japanese-British landing, he said in a memorandum to the President of April 10,

. . . in no way affects my opinion as to this Government's policy. . . .

I think it would be unwise, in view of the reports we have received, to permit American marines to land. The state of affairs in Russia proper is in my opinion against such a policy. In this I disagree with the judgment of Mr. Long, Mr. Miles and others who have this matter in charge in the Department.[43]

He added, somewhat irrelevantly, "I am entirely responsible for the present policy which is opposed to intervention by the Japanese in a mandatory capacity."

On April 15 Reading came in to assure the Secretary of the purely local character of the British and Japanese landings; and on April

[40] Vladivostok *Krasnoye Znamya*, No. 161 (65), April 9, 1918; Hoover Institute & Library, Stanford.

[41] National Archives, Navy Branch, R.G. 45, *op.cit.*, Knight's telegram of April 5.

[42] *Ibid.*, Foreign Affairs Branch; State Department File 861.00/1448.

[43] Lansing MSS, *op.cit.*, Diary Blue Boxes, Box 2. There is no record of Wilson's reply to this memorandum. The two men had discussed the matter the previous afternoon (Lansing's Desk Diary, entry of April 9). Lansing's position was obviously fully approved by the President.

17 the Japanese Chargé d'Affaires called and assured Lansing that his government was prepared to withdraw its marines again as soon as conditions might permit.

The Japanese marines were not, however, in fact withdrawn. They remained in Vladivostok throughout the ensuing weeks, patrolling the vicinity of the Japanese Consulate and to some extent the entire city. The Communists hotly resented their presence, and there was no lack of minor incidents; but the local Bolshevik leaders did not feel strong enough to challenge the Japanese and British at that time. They therefore swallowed their irritation and endeavored to place on their natural political impulses a restraint sufficient to avoid provocation for further Allied action.

Very soon thereafter the Vladivostok situation began to be complicated by another factor destined to have, in the end, a more decisive influence on the affairs of that city and region than did the presence of the Allied marines. This was the arrival there of the first of the Czech forces trying to make their way from European Russia over the Trans-Siberian Railway to the Pacific and thence, via the United States, to the western front.

❖

The news of the Japanese landing was naturally received with most intense alarm and suspicion by the Bolshevik leaders in Moscow. It was first taken as the beginning of intervention. Lenin at once despatched to the Vladivostok Soviet a message voicing this interpretation:

. . . We consider the situation to be very serious. . . . It is probable, in fact almost inevitable, that the Japanese will advance. Undoubtedly, the Allies will help them. We must prepare ourselves immediately, straining all our energies to this end.[44]

He then went ahead to outline a series of military preparations to be taken at once, and warned the Vladivostok Soviet that it could hope for help from Moscow only if it put these measures energetically in hand.

A statement was issued the same day (April 5) by the Soviet Commissar for Foreign Affairs, Georgi Chicherin, denying knowl-

[44] V. Melikov, "Lenin v grazhdanskoi voine, 1918–1920 gg" (Lenin in the Civil War, 1918–1920), *Voina i Revolyutsiya*, January–February, 1934, pp. 30, 32.

edge of the circumstances of the alleged murder of the Japanese citizens, stamping the incident as an obvious pretext, and charging the Japanese government with every sort of evil design with relation to Siberia.[45] The Japanese imperialists wished, Chicherin charged,

to strangle the Soviet revolution, to cut Russia off from the Pacific Ocean, to seize the rich territories of Siberia, and to enslave the Siberian workers and peasants. . . .

"What," he then asked,

are the plans of the other Governments of the Entente: America, England, France, and Italy? Up to the present their policy in regard to the predatory intentions of Japan has apparently been undecided. The American Government, it seems, was against the Japanese invasion. But now the situation can no longer remain indefinite. England intends to act hand in hand with Japan in working Russia's ruin.[46]

This query as to Allied intentions was not merely rhetorical. The Allied representatives in the city were called in by Chicherin the same evening to receive the Soviet complaint and a demand for explanations. He followed up this step the following day by a written note drawing attention to the unfavorable effect the landing was bound to have on relations between the Soviet Republic and the Allies. "The Commissariat considers it essential to remind you," it was said in this note,

of the extremely tense situation created by this action, which is obviously inimical to the Republic and its regime, and to point out . . . that the only way of putting an end to this state of affairs is the immediate withdrawal of the troops landed and that a precise explanation of your Government's attitude to the events which have taken place at Vladivostok is absolutely necessary as soon as possible.[47]

A special written communication was addressed to Robins personally. Mentioning

[45] Among other things, the Japanese were charged (not unjustly, as other evidence would suggest) with having instigated and spread rumors of the arming of the prisoners-of-war. In refutation of these rumors Chicherin cited the journey of Webster and Hicks, although these officers were still in the midst of their trip and their final report would not be rendered for weeks to come.

[46] Degras, Vol. I, *op.cit.*, pp. 67–68.

[47] *Ibid.*, pp. 68–69.

. . . the highly unfavorable influence which this forcible invasion of Russia by foreign military forces may have upon the relation between the Soviet republic and the country represented by you,

Chicherin proceeded to remind Robins of the "extremely tense situation" that had been created,

. . . and to point out once more that the only solution of the situation which has arisen is the immediate evacuation of the landed forces and the necessity of making a full and definite immediate statement of the attitude of your Government towards the occurrence which has taken place at Vladivostok.[48]

In a telegraphic exchange with Francis the following day (April 6), Robins described his reply to Chicherin and gave his reaction to the incident. He had spoken guardedly to Chicherin, he told Francis,

. . . of your efforts to prevent hostile intervention and your success with foreign representatives at Vologda, and what seemed to be the friendly purpose of allies. Urged that Vladivostok incident be treated as local and . . . be settled by friendly diplomacy. Later urged this same policy upon other leaders of government here. . . .[49]

It was evident, Robins continued in this message, that the Soviet government feared hostile intervention and would, if this were to take place, declare war on Japan. In that event the Russian resentment against Germany would be transformed into a far more bitter resentment against the Allies. "We are now," he continued,

at most dangerous crisis in Russian situation, and if colossal blunder of hostile Japanese intervention takes place all American advantages are confiscated. . . .

The Soviet leaders believed, Robins stated, that it was in America's power to prevent hostile intervention; if the Japanese were to advance, it would mean that America had consented. It was important that he, Robins, should be able to make some sort of reply to the Soviet government. Did the Ambassador have any instructions?[50]

[48] Foreign Relations, 1918, Russia, Vol. II, op.cit., p. 107.
[49] Cumming & Pettit, op.cit., p. 134.
[50] The following morning Trotsky received Riggs and repeated to him his expectation of "a confident statement from the Allies which will clarify aims of the Japanese in Vladivostok." He reiterated the suggestion he frequently made to the Americans: that the Japanese were in secret accord with the Germans (Foreign Relations, 1918, Russia, Vol. II, op.cit., p. 104).

Robins' message put Francis in a difficult position. He had, as usual, no word from his government as to its attitude. Yet he wished to quiet the Soviet government's fears. Not surprisingly—in the circumstances—he floundered. He sent Chicherin (through Robins, April 7) the following reply, which either he or someone else in Vologda at once divulged to the press:

Soviet government attaching undue weight to landing of Japanese, . . . There is thorough understanding among the allies concerning their intervention in Russia, including Japanese intervention, and that understanding is to the effect that there is no intention or desire on the part of any of Russia's allies to attach any of Russia's territory or to make an invasion of conquest. On the other hand the allies desire to see the integrity of Russia preserved and are willing and desirous to aid the Russian people to that end.[51]

In addition to this, Francis issued (April 9 or 10) a formal press statement of somewhat different tenor. The Soviet government and press, he declared, was

. . . giving too much importance to the landing of these marines which has no political significance but merely was a police precaution taken by the Japanese Admiral on his own responsibility for the protection of Japanese life and property in Vladivostok, . . . My impression is that the landing of the British marines was pursuant to the request of the British Consul for the protection of the British Consulate and British subjects in Vladivostok which he anticipated would possibly be jeopardized by the unrest that might result from the Japanese descent. The American Consul did not ask protection from the American cruiser in Vladivostok Harbor and consequently no American marines were landed; this together with the fact that the French Consul, at Vladivostok, made no request for protection from the . . . cruisers . . . unquestionably demonstrates that the landing . . . is not a concerted action between the Allies.[52]

Both of these statements got Francis into trouble—and for precisely contrary reasons. Official Washington was startled and horrified by the assertion, in the first of them, that there was full understanding among the Allies about intervention in Russia. The American press was prevailed upon, through the wartime censorship arrangements, to suppress the story; and Francis was delicately reprimanded. The Japanese, on the other hand, were stung by the

[51] Cumming & Pettit, *op.cit.*, pp. 135-136.
[52] *Foreign Relations, 1918, Russia*, Vol. II, *op.cit.*, pp. 116-117.

assertion, in the second statement, that the landing at Vladivostok was *not* a concerted action, and particularly by the inference that the British landing was something forced by the Japanese move rather than a parallel reaction to the local situation. On May 4 the new Japanese Ambassador in Washington, Viscount Ishii, delivered a note of protest about Francis' remarks, stressing the solidarity of the Allied representatives on the spot and quoting Admiral Knight as commending the Japanese action and as having said that if American citizens had been exposed to a similar danger, he would not have hesitated to resort to the same steps.[53] This communication, to which Lansing gave a polite and conciliatory reply, showed clearly what delicacy surrounded the entire episode, and how sensitive the Japanese were to the interpretation given to it in the outside world.

❖

The exact circumstances surrounding this first Japanese landing in Siberia remain in many respects obscure.

The Japanese government had warned, in its memorandum of March 16, that if "hostile activities" in Siberia developed to a point where Japanese interests were jeopardized, Japan would not hesitate "to resort to prompt and efficient measures of self-protection." The landing on April 5 would appear to be a very good case in point. Yet there is no confirmation that Tokyo had specifically ordered it or authorized it; everything points rather to the conclusion that it flowed from a decision taken locally, by Admiral Kato, on the basis of his standing instructions.

The incident of the murder of the three Japanese appears to have been genuine; but the evidence relayed by Knight for the existence of a general state of extreme tension just before the landing is singularly unconvincing, and bears strong earmarks of artificial inflation. It is plain, in particular, that the local Communists were taken quite by surprise by the Japanese action. Had the situation really been as reported to Knight by his informants, this would scarcely have been the case. Was the Admiral being deliberately misinformed from some quarter?

And what, if anything, was the relation to Kato's action of the information divulged to him by Knight less than two days before, that the United States government was not prepared to permit

[53] *Ibid.*, p. 151.

American marines to be landed? This gave him, of course, the assurance that a Japanese landing at that particular time would not be matched by any parallel American move. Would this not have been, in Kato's eyes, a consideration favorable to his own action? The British, after all, had requested the United States to take parallel action. The Japanese had not.

All these questions remain to be answered.

There is one question, however, to which a most definite answer may be given. Stalinist-Soviet historians have repeatedly portrayed the United States as one of the instigators of the landing. A. I. Melchin, for example, in the volume entitled *Amerikanskaya interventsiya v 1918–1920 gg*,[54] stated:

. . . Having made a deal in good time with their co-participants—the Japanese—for the future division of Russian territory, the American imperialists proposed a plan of action according to which Japan was to make a landing at Vladivostok. . . . The Japanese Government, under the protection of this same cruiser, the *Brooklyn* . . . carried out a landing at Vladivostok.

It may be stated without hesitation that in this allegation there is not a single iota of truth. The United States government had not the slightest forewarning of this particular Japanese action, nor did it ever voice, either before or after, any approval of it. The only surprising element in the American reaction was the minor degree of interest shown by the Washington statesmen in the background, motives, and implications of the Japanese move. One has the impression that a concern for the propriety of America's own position was far more prominent in the thinking of the President and his Secretary of State at that time than any concern for what actually took place in Siberia.

[54] (American Intervention, 1918–1920), Military-Naval Publishing Co., Moscow, 1951.

CHAPTER V

THE WRAITH OF ALLIED-SOVIET
COLLABORATION

But we ourselves henceforth shall be no shield of yours,
We ourselves henceforth will enter no battle.
We shall look on with our narrow eyes
When your deadly battles rage.
                    —*Alexander Blok, "The Scythians"*

THE situation that prevailed in the immediate wake of the ratification of the Brest-Litovsk Treaty heightened greatly the divisive effect which the nature and behavior of the new Soviet regime already exercised on the Allied representatives in Russia. Nowhere did this schism take sharper or more dramatic forms than among the small band of Allied representatives and officials stationed in Moscow in the period following the movement of the Soviet government to that city.

The reasons for this division are not hard to perceive. The Soviet leaders had suffered a severe shock from the resumption of the German offensive at the end of February and the first strong rumors of Japanese intervention following immediately on the heels of that event. They had, as yet, little faith in the efficacy of the Brest-Litovsk Treaty as a protection against further German encroachments. They feared that they would soon be confronted with some new crisis in which they would have no choice but to try to defend themselves, in a last-ditch struggle for the survival of communist power, against the implacable Germans, whose representatives they had treated with such studied and frivolous insolence at Brest-Litovsk. More important still, perhaps, they had put in hand a vigorous and serious effort, headed by Trotsky himself, now Commissar for War, to create a new communist armed force to replace the old army they themselves had demoralized and destroyed. The harsh school of necessity had already taught them that such a force, if it were to have any military meaning, could not be founded on disciplinary looseness—on soldiers' committees, votes, resolutions, and helpless commanders—such as they had forced upon the old army. They were quite serious, now, about creating a real armed force in the shortest possible time. They were prepared to make serious compromises and concessions to achieve this goal. But they had largely cut themselves off, or thought they had, from the sources of knowledge and skill within their own country necessary to create a new army. It was not at first supposed that many able ex-officers would wish to serve in a Bolshevik army, aside from the question of their reliability in point of class origin and ideology. The Soviet leaders, therefore, great as was their distaste for the acceptance of any aid from the Allied "imperialists," were not wholly disinclined to contemplate some use of Allied officers for purposes of training and guidance in the creation of the new force, provided this could be done without political concessions on their part and provided the officers in question could be kept in their place and prevented from exerting any ideological influence on the new formations.

In addition to this, the heads of the Soviet government were acutely fearful that a Japanese intervention might be added to their troubles in the west, and were anxious to forestall this eventuality at all costs. They were well aware that this was a matter in which the western governments, and particularly the United States, had some influence. They were also aware of the desperate eagerness with which certain elements in western officialdom, symbolized by Robins, Lockhart, and Sadoul, cherished the dream of military collaboration between the western Allies and the new Soviet power, as a possible means of restoring Russian resistance to Germany on the eastern front. They were quick to realize that by encouraging these hopes on the Allied side they might perhaps induce the Allies to put a restraining hand on the Japanese.

For all these reasons, the Bolshevik leaders were never more co-operative, correct, and obliging than in their dealings during the last days of March and the first days of April with that portion of the Allied official colony in Moscow which, they felt, was well-inclined toward them and favored the development of military collaboration. Toward this portion of American officialdom Trotsky and Chicherin in particular showed themselves, at this period, conciliatory, helpful, and frank. (Lenin was more reserved.) They were forthcoming with information of all kinds.

The effects of this forthrightness were dual. The Allied officials thus favored were naturally impressed and pleased by this manifestation of good disposition toward their persons. Some of them became in this way the first of a long series of western representatives in Russia who, finding themselves the object of unusual favor or courtesy at the hands of the Soviet authorities, were misled into believing that this was the result of some particular charm or impressiveness in their own personalities, and thus concluded that they had been endowed by nature with the key to the riddle of "How to get along with the Russians." But beyond this, these Allied officials found themselves, by virtue of their contacts with the Soviet Olympus, privy to information which enabled them better to assess the innumerable rumors of conditions in Russia generally and of the behavior of the Soviet authorities in particular with which the Allied missions were constantly being inundated from anti-Bolshevik sources. This served to instill in such men as Robins and Lockhart a certain contempt for the judgment of others who lacked this direct access to the Soviet authorities and who drew their information, or more often misinformation, very largely from the frustrated and embittered elements whose interests had been damaged by the Revolution.

These displaced groups and classes, the potential opposition to Soviet power, were now growing rapidly more vigorous and articulate. Numbed, initially, by the precipitateness of the Bolshevik seizure of power and by the sudden frustration suffered in the dissolution of the Constituent Assembly, the latent opposition to Bolshevism was only now beginning to crystallize and to discover its real power. Moscow was, in the spring of 1918, the initial center of this crystallization.

Unencumbered by the ponderous central bureaucracy and the aristocratic court society that had set the tone in Petrograd, the Moscow scene had been dominated in the final decades of Tsardom by the business circles and the liberal-academic world of the Moscow University. Even Moscow conservatism was more up-to-date, more progressive, closer to the modern industrial growth of the country, than that of Petrograd. For this reason Moscow was the spiritual center of the Constitutional-Democratic (Kadet) Party, the only strong non-socialist liberal party at the time of the Revolution. Although the operation of this party had been suppressed in Petrograd by the Bolsheviki even prior to the convening of the Constituent Assembly, and although two of its most distinguished leaders had been the victims of a peculiarly brutal assassination at the hands of the Kronstadt sailors in January, the strength of the party in Moscow was not yet fully destroyed by the spring of 1918. There remained, at the time the government moved to Moscow, a considerable undercurrent of Kadet influence and activity in the new capital.

In addition to this, many of the leaders of the Social-Revolutionary Party, most of them deputies in the suppressed Constituent Assembly (in which the S-R's had had a majority), had fled after the suppression of the Assembly to Moscow, where an underground existence was easier and more comfortable.

Finally, Moscow was the center of activity for many hundreds of officers of the old army who had suffered the supreme humiliation of being driven out of their own units and forced to flee in disguise (either in civilian clothing or by ripping off their own epaulets and masquerading as common soldiers) in order to escape being lynched by their own men. These officers, idle, frustrated, and seething with resentment, now milled around Moscow in a semi-underground status, mingling with the various political oppositionists and lending themselves to every possible scheme for bedeviling or overthrowing the Soviet authorities.

In March and April 1918, the Allied official community in Moscow having been fortified by the arrival of those who had accompanied the Soviet government from Petrograd, members of the opposition groups entered into many forms of contact with Allied representatives. There was as yet relatively little police repression in Moscow. Compared to the communist capital of a later date, the Moscow of early 1918 was a wide-open city, seething with counterrevolutionary sentiment and activity. Quite naturally, every bit of anti-Soviet information or gossip that could be picked up anywhere was rapidly relayed to the representatives of the Allies by the anti-communist factions; and it was usually embellished by the most uninhibited exaggeration. The impressions conveyed in this way centered, of course, around the thesis that the Bolshevik leaders were subservient to Germany and were deliberately abetting Germany's war effort. Acting on minds already made hyper-suspicious by the fixations and preoccupations of war, rumors along this line found ready credence in Allied circles and stimulated intense suspicion of the Soviet leaders in many quarters. The effect created was diametrically opposed to the impressions being gained by Robins, Sadoul, and the section of Allied officialdom that had close contact with the Bolshevik leaders.

This polarization of opinion among the Allied representatives in Moscow was supplemented by a further partial division between those stationed in the Soviet capital and those serving in other parts of the old Russian Empire. Whereas in Moscow there was at least one section of the Allied community that was well-inclined to the Bolsheviki and disposed to attempt to see things from their standpoint, the Allied representatives in the provincial cities, including Vologda, were almost universally hostile and suspicious toward the new Soviet power. They were often witnesses to the many real injustices and cruelties perpetrated by local Soviet authorities and their hangers-on in the early days of the revolution. In these provincial centers, the relatively intelligent and responsible Bolshevik leaders were not present to give explanations and promises of improvement, as they did to Robins, Lockhart, and Sadoul in Moscow. Finally, in many of these provincial towns the effect of the Revolution had been to injure the propertied classes but not to destroy them. Police control was sometimes even more lax than in the capital. In many instances, the former respected citizens of the towns were still physically present, to horrify the foreign representatives with the visual evidence of their sufferings and to pour into their ears, with that lack of critical reserve that characterizes the politically impassioned Russian, their tales of outrage and terror.

In the accounts of the undertakings and affairs of the Allied communities in Russia in the wake of the Brest-Litovsk Treaty, we will find at every hand evidences of this growing division and polarization of opinion among them, approaching at times the dimensions of a massive official schizophrenia and occasioning suspicions and antagonisms of the most tragic intensity. In the first six weeks following ratification of the treaty, it was still the pro-Bolshevik Allied officials in Moscow whose impressions and reports dominated the Allied camp. It is to these hopes and activities that this chapter is addressed.

The Wraith of Collaboration

The first matter to preoccupy the Allied officials after ratification
of the Brest-Litovsk Treaty was the possibility of Allied collaboration
in the creation of a regular Soviet armed force. This matter had been
vaguely touched on from time to time in the frantic discussions
which Robins and Sadoul had conducted with Trotsky and Lenin
in Petrograd, at the time of the resumption of the German offensive.
On March 8, just prior to the departure of the Soviet government to
Moscow, the American Military Attaché, Colonel James A. Ruggles,
and his assistant, Captain E. Francis Riggs, had visited Trotsky at
Sadoul's suggestion (see Volume i, page 506). In his telegraphic
report of this interview, Ruggles said:

... Trotsky ... and the majority of the Bolsheviks now seem convinced
that peace ... cannot be permanent. ...

Trotsky desires Allied assistance, especially American. ... Trotsky
now willing to reorganize army under rigid discipline, recalling Russian
Government officers and best class of Russian people but believes of first
importance that United States take the necessary steps to prevent action
by Japan or other Allies at this critical time. ...[1]

Ruggles strongly agreed that the Japanese should not be permitted
to intervene, but made no comment on the plea for military assistance.

When Robins proceeded to Moscow, at the time of the move of
the Soviet government, Riggs accompanied him, whereas Ruggles
returned to Vologda to remain with Ambassador Francis. Riggs
was already sympathetic to Robins' outlook, and shared in high
degree his optimism about the prospect for collaboration.

Robins' removal to Moscow was followed a few days later by that
of Sadoul. Lockhart, who had remained initially in Petrograd, also
came on to Moscow about March 16–17, accompanying Trotsky in
his private car when the latter, in his new capacity as Commissar
for War, left Petrograd to rejoin his associates in the Soviet government in Moscow.

Lockhart had in his entourage two young officers, Captain W. L.
Hicks (who later accompanied Webster to Siberia) and Captain
Dennis Garstan, a young cavalry officer who had been serving in

[1] Wilson MSS, Series II, *op.cit.*

Petrograd. Sadoul, on the other hand, was technically associated with the large French Military Mission headed by General Lavergne which, instead of accompanying the French Ambassador in his effort to leave Russia via Finland, likewise followed the Soviet government to Moscow. General Niessel, who had headed the French Military Mission in Russia up to that time, had now laid down his responsibilities with the ratification of the Brest-Litovsk Treaty. His successor, Lavergne, was less embittered by past happenings, and more receptive to suggestions for military collaboration with the Soviet government.

Altogether, therefore, there was assembled in Moscow immediately after ratification of the Brest-Litovsk Treaty quite a coterie of officials, both civilian and military, who were keenly interested in the possibility of Allied aid to the Soviet government and inclined to pursue hopefully every possibility that pointed in this direction. An informal committee, composed of Lavergne, the Italian Military Attaché General Romei, Lockhart, Riggs, and Robins, soon began to meet daily in Lockhart's quarters at the Hotel Elite and to serve as a sort of clearinghouse for these efforts.

The discussions concerning military aid were pressed vigorously from the moment of Trotsky's arrival on March 17. On the very next day Robins conferred with him and with Chicherin. Robins reported to Francis that the conference had been "most satisfactory." Trotsky had asked that five American officers be detailed at once "to act as inspectors of the organization, drill and equipment of the Soviet Army."[2]

The next day, Tuesday, March 19, Sadoul had a talk with Trotsky. He gained the impression that Trotsky intended to request of the United States, in addition to railway engineers and specialists, a dozen officers for purposes of inspection and instruction. Trotsky evidently said nothing about seeking military aid from France. "Trotsky is still sulking with us," Sadoul explained to his friend Thomas, and he thought he knew the reason for this; General Niessel, in his farewell call, had spoken harshly to Trotsky and had irritated and offended him.[3]

The large French military mission from Rumania, on its way

[2] Cumming & Pettit, *op.cit.*, p. 104.
[3] Jacques Sadoul, *Notes sur la Révolution Bolchevique,* Editions de la Sirène, Paris, 1920, p. 273.

home to France via Russia in consequence of Rumania's effective retirement from the war, was at this time in Moscow. It numbered several hundred officers. Sadoul had hopes that some of these men could be retained in Russia and detailed for work in the organization of the new army. He moved at once, therefore, to get American support in overcoming Trotsky's peculiar suspicions of the French. He went to Riggs (whom he described in one of his letters as "un excellent garçon, très francophile, que je manoeuvre facilement.") and persuaded him—or thought he did—that the use of the French officers was the only real solution.

The next morning, March 20, Riggs and Sadoul went to see Trotsky together. On this occasion, Riggs apparently supported Sadoul's suggestions, at least so far as the acceptance of French officers was concerned. In any case, Sadoul, whose enthusiasm—like that of Robins—often tended to override the precision of his understanding, came away from the interview with the impression that it was now established that these French officers would be accepted as Trotsky's closest collaborators, that they would have their offices next to his and would function simultaneously as a sort of "cabinet militaire" and department of plans and operations.

The following day, March 21, addressing the Moscow Soviet, Trotsky spoke publicly of the necessity for a modern army of 300,000 to 500,000 men, and of the unusual problems which this presented for the Soviet government. Later in the day Riggs had a further interview with him, and induced him to produce a written request to Ruggles (as Chief of the American Military Mission in Russia) for American assistance "in the work of the reorganization of the country which the Soviet Government is about to undertake." This letter asked for the assignment of railway experts to aid the Soviet government in the restoration of the efficiency of the railway network. It included a request for the assignment of one military liaison officer "for the study of military questions." But it said nothing about any military specialists for purposes of training and inspection.[4] Sadoul, evidently, had by now carried his point that this

---

[4] The substance of this letter was as follows:

"Comme suite aux entretiens que je viens d'avoir avec le Colonel Robbins et le Capitaine Riggs, j'ai l'honneur de demander, au nom du Conseil des Commissaires du Peuple, la collaboration technique américaine à l'oeuvre de la reorganization du pays que va entreprendre le Gouvernement des Soviets.

"Comme le Colonel Robbins et le Capitaine Riggs m'ont fait connaître la presence, ou en Siberie ou au Japon, d'un certain nombre de specialistes des chemins de fer

sort of aid should be drawn primarily from the resources of the large French military contingent then in the city.

Riggs was not entirely satisfied with this request. He approved the use of French military advisers but felt that there ought to be American ones as well. In forwarding Trotsky's letter to Ruggles, he urged that the American government also send "inspectors" (a term which appears to have meant, to those concerned, military advisers or instructors).

It was now Ruggles' turn to draw back. The French Military Mission, Francis reported on March 22 to the Department of State, had

. . . accepted government offer and is making assignment of officers for inspection of new army. Riggs . . . strongly recommends we do likewise, but Ruggles here undecided, as he is not thoroughly satisfied that new army is intended for German resistance.[5]

The Department of State, meanwhile, was entertaining misgivings even more serious than those of Colonel Ruggles. On March 23 the Department informed Francis that it had a report

. . . suggesting that Soviet leaders who have asked for military assistance must be suspected of acting on orders from German staff with a view to diverting Entente efforts from western front.

Francis' views were requested.[6]

Francis replied on March 26 with a frank confession of his own

---

et comme ils m'ont indiqué d'autre part que vous étiez d'accord avec Monsieur l'Ambassadeur des Etats Unis d'Amérique et le Gouvernement Américain pour apporter à la Russie l'appui dont elle a besoin, je vous prie de mettre en relations avec mon commissariat,

"1/ pour l'étude des questions militaires et pour la liaison avec vous, 1 Officier de l'armée Américaine.

"2/ pour l'étude du problème des chemins de fers de la Russie

A/ A Moscou—une unité de specialistes de chemin-de-fer en relations avec mon commissariat et le commissariat des Voies et Communications.

B/ En Russie /Européenne/ Une ou plusieurs unités de specialistes de chemin-de-fer.

C/ En Siberie—Une ou plusieurs unités de specialistes de chemin-de-fer. . . ." National Archives, Foreign Affairs Branch, Sisson Documents File, Box 1; Enclosure 22 to Despatch No. 1386 of July 15, 1918 to the Department of State.

[5] *Foreign Relations, 1918, Russia*, Vol. 1 (1931), p. 485.

[6] *Ibid.*, p. 486. This reaction on the part of the Department was probably the result of the information Lansing had been given on March 21 by the British, indicating great danger to Siberia from the German prisoners-of-war (see Chapter IV). The portions of the "Sisson Documents" material that had been wired from Petrograd in February may also have had something to do with it.

torn feelings. He had been shaken, he admitted, by the evidence of Soviet-German complicity suggested by the documents (see Volume I, Chapters xxi and xxii) unearthed in Petrograd shortly before by Edgar Sisson, first director of the American wartime propaganda program in Russia. He recognized that Sisson and his successor, Arthur Bullard, were both wholly convinced of the correctness of this thesis.[7] But Robins, he pointed out, had continued to maintain that the suggestion was absurd. "Probably Sisson and Robins both influenced," he concluded philosophically and quite accurately, "by pride of opinion and mutual animosity."[8]

During the ensuing days the reports from Riggs and Robins, as well as Sadoul's references to this subject in his private letters, were all happy and optimistic. On the 24th Sadoul stated that General Lavergne had been entirely won over to a conviction of the possibility and necessity of Allied aid in the reorganization of the Russian army.[9] Riggs reported on the 25th that thirty-eight officers (presumably French) were being assigned to help organize the Red Army, and that the Italians were going to bring ten from Italy.[10] On the 26th Sadoul wrote that "collaboration for the reorganization of an army" had already begun.[11] Robins confirmed this in a message to Francis on March 27.

Meanwhile, Francis and Ruggles in Vologda were trying to give some sort of response to Trotsky's request for the railway experts and for a military liaison officer. Francis wired Stevens (through the consuls at Harbin and Vladivostok) to send six units of railway engineers to Vologda immediately. The Department of State, to whose attention this message came, was at once alarmed by this interference in the affairs of the Railway Corps. It went back at Francis, on March 26, with a request to be told specifically what these railway men were to do and on what railways they were to work. Their services must not, after all, be permitted to facilitate

---

[7] This is not wholly accurate. Arthur Bullard's relation to the Sisson documents was always a very uncomfortable one. His views on this subject were set forth in a long, competent, and highly interesting memorandum for Colonel House entitled "German Gold," copies of which can be found in the National Archives as well as in the Arthur Bullard MSS, Firestone Library, Princeton.

[8] *Foreign Relations, 1918, Russia,* Vol. I, *op.cit.,* p. 487.

[9] *Quarante Lettres de Jacques Sadoul,* Librairie de L'Humanité, Paris, 1922, letter of March 24, 1918.

[10] *Foreign Relations, 1918, Russia,* Vol. I, *op.cit.,* p. 487.

[11] Sadoul, *Notes . . . , op.cit.,* p. 277.

communications between Germany and Russia. The original agreement with the Provisional Government, furthermore, had provided that the Railway Service Corps should be maintained by the Russian government. Was the Soviet government prepared to accept this obligation? [12]

Francis replied that he was sure the Soviet government would be ready to guarantee that the men would not be used in German interests, and expressed readiness to take responsibility for this himself. He thought it extremely desirable, he wired on March 29, that the capacity of the Trans-Siberian Railway in particular should be increased, for possible emergencies.[13]

The Department of State remained unconvinced by Francis' arguments, and held up authorization to Stevens to send the men. After the Japanese landing on April 5, Francis himself came to the conclusion that the situation had changed, and advised the Department on April 9 not to send them until relations with the Soviet government were "better defined." [14]

In addition to this effort to get railway engineers to European Russia in response to Trotsky's request, Francis, acting on his own responsibility, authorized Ruggles to instruct Riggs to join with the French and Italians in assisting in the organization of the new army. To the Department he gave a most curious explanation of his motives in taking this step. He did not believe, he wired (March 26), that the new army was really for defense against the Germans. Its real object was "resistance to all existing governments and promotion of socialism throughout the whole world." Nevertheless, it provided the "only hope for saving European Russia from Germany." His "real and confidential reason" for authorizing American collaboration was

. . . that army so organized can by proper methods be taken from Bolshevik control and used against Germans, and even [against] its creators if [they] prove . . . German allies. I anticipate not revealing last reason to Robins or Riggs. . . .[15]

[12] *Foreign Relations, 1918, Russia,* Vol. III (1932), p. 225.

[13] *Ibid.,* pp. 226–227.

[14] *Ibid.,* p. 229. A fortnight later Francis persuaded the Department to approve the despatch to Vologda, for purposes of consultation, of the Chief of the Railway Corps, Colonel George H. Emerson, with a few of his aides. Emerson left for Vologda in May, but, for reasons that will be described below, never got there.

[15] *Foreign Relations, 1918, Russia,* Vol. I, *op.cit.,* pp. 487–488.

Francis' reason, in other words, for authorizing military collaboration with the Soviet government was the private calculation, not divulged to Robins, that once a new army had come into existence with Allied assistance and with the use of a number of the older Russian officers, it might become a force in its own right and an agency for protection not only against the Germans but also against the Soviet government itself, in the event that the leaders of that government—as he still thought possible—proved to be German agents.

Actually, nothing came of Francis' rash and disingenuous authorization. Ruggles, instead of acting on it, chose to reinsure himself by asking the War Department for a policy directive. The War Department replied that a statement of governmental policy on this matter would be sent direct to Francis by the State Department.[16] With this, the matter had come full circle. There was nothing to do, now, but wait. Riggs was obliged to hold up on further discussions with Trotsky about the possibility of American military assistance.

On March 29, the little diplomatic colony at Vologda was joined by the French Ambassador, Joseph Noulens, and his official party. Noulens, it will be recalled, was as strongly anti-Soviet as Sadoul was attached to the principle of Allied-Soviet collaboration. Moreover, he was violently suspicious of Sadoul and resentful of his activities. Sadoul reciprocated these sentiments with vigor.[17] He had greeted with grateful relief his ambassador's absence from the scene, occasioned by the attempt to leave Russia at the end of February. "Blessed be the fair wind," Sadoul had written delightedly in mid-March, "that has carried M. Noulens off to Finland."[18] But now Noulens was back in Russia; and his influence, as was to be expected, immediately made itself felt in opposition to the military collaboration Sadoul was so busily promoting.[19]

[16] Cumming & Pettit, *op.cit.*, p. 119; message from Francis to Robins, March 28.

[17] See Volume I, Chapter XIX. Sadoul's opinion of Noulens, in retrospect, was expressed without inhibition in *Naissance de l'URSS*, Editions Charlot, Paris, 1946, pp. 278–279: "Noulens, French Ambassador, former Minister, boss of the radical party, typical elder politician of that time, a man of mediocre intelligence and of base soul, without conviction but not without wiles, was a notorious intriguer."

[18] *Quarante Lettres de Jacques Sadoul*, *op.cit.*, letter of March 24, 1918.

[19] According to R. H. Bruce Lockhart, *British Agent*, G. P. Putnam's Sons, New York, 1933, p. 248, Noulens at once disrupted the plan for using officers from the erstwhile French Military Mission to Rumania, and insisted that they all immediately resume their homeward journey.

Very soon after his arrival in Vologda, Noulens recorded contentedly in his memoirs, his diplomatic colleagues there "were made to see the dangers involved

The Wraith of Collaboration

Upon Noulens' arrival in Vologda, Francis at once arranged a luncheon for him, together with the Italian and Serbian Chiefs of Mission (the British Chargé d'Affaires, Lindley, had not yet arrived). On this occasion (March 31) the entire situation was gone over; the activities of the military and unofficial representatives in Moscow were taken under skeptical scrutiny; and it was recognized that some general rationale had to be evolved that could govern the position both of the representatives in Vologda and those in Moscow. There was general agreement, as Francis understood it, that an effort had to be made to smoke out the Soviet government on its attitude toward the Allies generally and particularly on its position with respect to intervention. The French and Italian Ambassadors thought that the first step ought to be a demand on the Soviet government that it cease the attacks on the Allied powers in the government-controlled press and rescind the decree of February 3, 1918 repudiating the debts of former Russian governments to the Allied powers. As for the discussions in Moscow looking toward military collaboration between the Allies and the Soviet government, there was a general feeling of discomfort, and a fear that the matter was getting out of hand. The envoys were worried, in particular, by information they had received to the effect that in the new Soviet army subordinate officers were still to be elected by committees of the rank and file—a system which the Allied representatives were unanimous in condemning as unworkable from the standpoint of adequate military discipline. It was decided, therefore, to instruct the military attachés at Moscow to come to Vologda for a conference with the chiefs of mission.

Francis reported the results of this meeting with his colleagues to the Department, including the French-Italian suggestion that a demand be made for the rescinding of the decree repudiating the debts of former Russian governments. He himself, he told the Department, was not convinced that the time had yet come for such a demand.[20]

The military attachés at once proceeded to Vologda. Conferences of these officers, together with their assembled diplomatic chiefs, took place on April 2 and 3.

---

in a cooperation with the Red Army." (Joseph Noulens, *Mon Ambassade en Russie Soviétique, 1917–1919*, Librairie Plon, Paris, 1933, Vol. II, pp. 55–56.)

[20] *Foreign Relations, 1918, Russia*, Vol. I, *op.cit.*, p. 491.

The upshot of these discussions was a "procès-verbal," reading as follows:

The Ambassadors of America, France and Italy came together today, April 3, with the Chiefs of Mission, the Military Attachés, and Captain Garstan of the English Army, to examine the situation. They are unanimously of the opinion that:

1. Japanese intervention is more than ever necessary in order to combat Germany;

2. Such intervention will not have its full effect unless it takes on the character of an inter-Allied intervention and unless the Bolshevik government can be led to accept it, for otherwise there will be certain risks involved;

3. Allied personalities who are in touch with Trotsky have the impression that it would probably be possible to lead him to accept Japanese intervention;

4. In taking account of these facts, the Ambassadors have found it opportune to adhere to the principle, laid down by the Chiefs of Mission and Military Attachés, of Allied collaboration in the organization of a Russian army against Germany, provided that definite adherence to this principle shall be withheld until after examination of the drafts of the decrees.

In the interval conversations will be put in hand with a view to obtaining guarantees concerning the true purposes of the Bolshevik government with regard to the Allies.

These guarantees shall be:

Acceptance of Japanese intervention;

Concession to Allied nationals of at least the same advantages, privileges, and compensations accorded by Russia to German subjects by the peace treaty of Brest-Litovsk.[21]

It will be noted that what Noulens had skillfully contrived to do in the course of these discussions was to make further progress in the matter of military collaboration dependent on the fulfillment of three prerequisites:

1. that the decrees setting up the new army should give assurance that adequate disciplinary standards would be enforced;

---

[21] Noulens, Vol. ii, *op.cit.*, pp. 56–57. Also *Foreign Relations, 1918, Russia,* Vol. ii, *op.cit.*, p. 111.

For some reason, Francis failed to transmit this document, and his report on the conference (*Foreign Relations, 1918, Russia,* Vol. i, *op.cit.*, p. 491) bears little resemblance to it. Ruggles, however, did transmit it to the War Department (National Archives, State Department File 861.00/1730½, Ruggles' report as received from the War Department on April 11).

2. that the Soviet government should extend to Allied nationals all the benefits promised to German nationals by the Brest-Litovsk Treaty; and

3. that the Soviet government should agree to intervention by the Japanese.

On April 5, immediately after the return of the military representatives to Moscow, the Department of State reacted to Francis' report of the initial luncheon meeting with Noulens and included in its reply the statement of policy on military assistance which Ruggles had been told would be sent to Francis:

. . . Department regards any protests relative to repudiation of loans as grave error. . . . Protest would not influence Soviet and would only aid German propaganda. In same connection do not give Soviet promise military support as requested in queries submitted through you and through military attaché. This Government is conducting war against Central powers to safeguard free countries, small and great, from domination of German militarism. Its purpose to assist Russia already made clear. Department concurs in your general estimates of Bolsheviki, and approves your decision to feel your way to certainty before making positive recommendations.[22]

The reasoning behind this communication is obscure but not wholly invisible. The reference to the fact that the United States government was conducting war against the Central Powers to safeguard free countries from German militarism, plus the reference to its purpose to assist Russia, was evidently meant to indicate that the best way the United States could help Russia to defend herself against German encroachments was to help win the war in the west, which it was making every effort to do. It was implied, though not stated, that the United States was not convinced, as yet, that aid given to the Bolsheviki in the establishment of a new armed force would necessarily be efficacious in keeping Russia out of German hands—certainly, in any case, it would not be as efficacious as the defeat of Germany in the west.

[22] For this exchange see *Foreign Relations, 1918, Russia*, Vol. I, *op.cit.*, pp. 491, 495. The Department later weakened this interdiction slightly by a further message (May 2) saying that while it could make no agreement with the Soviet government and could give no effective military support, Ruggles might himself lend such assistance as Francis deemed to be "in accord with the spirit of the Department's instructions . . ." (*ibid.*, pp. 517–518).

This instruction naturally put an end to any further participation by Riggs in the discussions in Moscow about military aid.[23]

The negotiations between the other Allied powers and the War Commissariat looking toward Allied military assistance likewise petered out completely at an early date. The conditions laid down at the Vologda conference of April 3, together with Noulens' continued personal influence, were enough to prevent any further progress along this line by Allied initiative.

Actually, there is no evidence that the Soviet authorities took very seriously these talks, which were primarily the result of the enthusiasms of Robins and Sadoul. The Allied representatives appear, as on other occasions, to have derived a highly exaggerated and over-optimistic impression of what was really in the Soviet mind. Trotsky recalled, in 1925, that Sadoul had introduced to him the officers of the Allied military missions in Russia for the purpose of "establishing contact." He explained,

. . . My purpose in these negotiations was to obtain war material (at that time we were ignorant of the state of our own supplies).

But the negotiations, he added, had led to nothing. Why? Because Lavergne had "apparently" received instructions from Paris that the coming struggle was to be *against,* not *with,* the Bolsheviki.[24]

In his autobiography, published in 1930, Trotsky went on to relate that Lavergne had placed at his disposal two staff officers. These, he says sourly, he regarded as "more competent in military espionage than in military administration." He never had time to look at their reports. And as for the occasion on which Sadoul introduced to him the Allied officers who were supposed to aid him in the organization of the new army, well, he was unable to think of it later without an "embarrassed laugh." "We literally did not know what to say to each other." [25]

[23] The Department had, the day this instruction was issued, received word of the Japanese landing at Vladivostok. If it was to be anticipated that there was a possibility of military resistance by the Bolsheviki to the Japanese landing (and in view of the reports of extreme tension prior to the landing such a possibility could not be ruled out at this early hour), then, plainly, direct American military assistance to the Bolsheviki could easily place the United States in a position of direct military opposition to the Japanese. But whether this was in the Secretary's mind when he wired Francis is not apparent.

[24] L. D. Trotsky, *Sochineniya* (Complete Works), Moscow, 1926, Vol. xvii, Part i, pp. 672–673 (Hoover Institute & Library).

[25] Leo Trotzki, *Mein Leben,* S. Fischer Verlag, Berlin, 1930, p. 343.

This was, of course, a far cry from the excited hopes and dreams which Robins and Sadoul managed to invest in this possibility of Allied aid.

THE POSSIBILITY OF INTERVENTION-BY-SOVIET-INVITATION

If the first of the two main hopes that characterized the attempts at Allied-Soviet *rapprochement* in March and April 1918 was that the Soviet leaders would accept Allied collaboration in the reconstruction of a Russian army, the second was that they would either invite or consent to actual intervention in Russia by the forces of the Allied powers. The two concepts were closely linked and often interflexed in the thoughts and discussions of the actors in this drama, and might conceivably have been treated as a single subject. But the issues at stake in the two questions differed in significant respects, and for this reason it seemed preferable to examine them separately.

It will be recalled that the possibility of intervention with Soviet consent had, like that of military "collaboration," become the subject of discussion in the midst of the extraordinary alarums and excursions that marked the final days of February and the first two or three days of March, in connection with the renewed German offensive against Russia and the final signature of the Brest-Litovsk Treaty. It was noted in Volume I (Chapter xxiv) that Lockhart, wiring from Petrograd in the first days of March, encouraged his government to hope that if the Allies would abstain from independent action it might be possible to obtain a direct invitation from the Soviet government to the English and American governments "to cooperate in the organization of Vladivostok, Archangel, etc." [26] We have also noted the curious circumstances under which Trotsky was led to despatch, on March 1, a telegram to the Murmansk Soviet instructing them to "accept any and all collaboration from the Allied missions," and we have seen that this was interpreted in Allied circles as an expression of Soviet consent to at least a preliminary landing in that city.

The suggestions that intervention might take place by agreement with, or on invitation of, the Soviet government, coming just at the time of the opening of the great German spring offensive, were seized on by the British with that special eagerness which character-

[26] Francis MSS, *op.cit.*, Lockhart's report of March 5, 1918, to his government.

[123]

ized—quite naturally—their reaction to any idea that held out hope of detaining a larger number of German troops on the eastern front.

There was, it should be noted, some justification for hopes of this sort *in the period prior to final ratification of the Brest-Litovsk Treaty*. No one knew at that time whether the treaty would really be ratified and mutually observed. The Soviet leaders had indeed indicated, in the days of their greatest extremity prior to the signature of the treaty, that if the Germans were to continue the offensive and attempt to overthrow them by force of arms, they would, as a last and desperate expedient, contemplate the acceptance of Allied military aid. It was understandable, therefore, that in the Anglo-French diplomatic discussions that took place in London in the middle of March, just before ratification of the treaty, Balfour should have expressed himself as in favor of delaying intervention "in the hope that possibly the invitation for Japanese intervention might come from the Russians themselves." [27] Actually, even this hope, however understandable in the light of Lockhart's messages, was largely illusory. We have already noted, in connection with the Murmansk incident, that the Central Committee of the Party never seriously faced the question of acquiescing in any actual movement of Allied forces on the Soviet territory. There was, accordingly, no established Party position on this point. Nor was there any reason to believe that Lenin himself would ever have approved anything of this sort except in the dire extremity of an all-out German attack.

One might have thought, in these circumstances, that once the acceptance of the "shameful peace" had been forced by Lenin on his reluctant comrades, and the treaty ratified, all talk of Allied intervention by Soviet consent would have subsided. This, however, was not the case. In the intensive exchanges he conducted with Robins, Lockhart, Sadoul, and the Allied military representatives after ratification of the treaty, Trotsky continued to discuss this subject in such a way as to convey the impression that there was a real possibility that the Soviet government might, on certain conditions, agree to Allied military intervention. The conditions in question were even mentioned on at least two occasions, once at the end of March and again on April 7. On the first of these occasions, in a discussion with Sadoul, Trotsky defined the conditions as follows (we have only Sadoul's account and must allow for his passionate desire to see some

[27] See above, page 90.

sort of agreement reached between the Soviet government and the Allies):

1. The intervention should be carried out not exclusively by the Japanese but by the Allied powers acting together.

2. It should be strictly military—that is, there should be no interference in Russian domestic-political affairs, no flirting with the opposition groups as had been done in the case of the Ukraine and the Don Cossack territory (see Volume i, Chapter ix).

3. The Japanese must specify precisely what tribute they proposed to exact from Russia in the form of territorial and other concessions.[28]

This last stipulation, implying as it did that Japan's purposes were purely rapacious, was meant, of course, to have insulting overtones. In this early period the Bolsheviki derived enjoyment from phrasing their communications to the "imperialist" governments in such a way as to imply the assumption that the latter were guided by the worst possible motives, making it impossible for these governments to reply in substance without seeming to accept the assumption.

In a "long and violent discussion" which Trotsky conducted with the military representatives immediately after the receipt of the news of the Japanese landing (April 7), he appears to have added two more conditions to the above three. One was that there should be "loyal collaboration" in military questions, even though there might be no political recognition. This apparently referred to the various forms of military aid, short of direct intervention, which had been under discussion. The second was a most curious suggestion to the effect that if intervention was to serve the interests of both Russia and the Allies, the latter should "examine the possibility of territorial and economic concessions in their Far Eastern possessions."[29] What this meant, and to whom these concessions were to be given, is wholly obscure.

To Lockhart, too, Trotsky repeatedly gave encouragement along these lines, and here he seems to have been even more sanguine in his suggestions. On March 28 Lockhart reported that in a discussion the previous day Trotsky had himself mentioned "the possibility of allied troops being sent via Siberia to Russia," and had said Russia

---

[28] Sadoul, *Notes . . . , op.cit.*, pp. 284–285.
[29] *Foreign Relations, 1918, Russia*, Vol. ii, *op.cit.*, p. 114, from Francis' telegram no. 81, April 8, 7 p.m.

would welcome help from the Allied countries, now that she was involved in a life-and-death struggle. "Provided that the allies would give guarantees on certain points and that other allied forces were present," Lockhart reported, Trotsky thought "there was no objection to the use of Japanese troops." Lockhart went ahead to observe that

The attitude of the Bolsheviks toward the Allies is completely changed and it is most important that this should be realized. The change is of course due to the necessity for fighting. . . .[30]

This last referred of course to Trotsky's belief that the breathing-space would not last long.

Lockhart received further encouragement along these lines in the first days of April from the representative in Moscow of the Finnish communist government, Tokomatt, who considered that the Soviet government would have to accept help from the Allies because "they could hope for nothing from the enemy."[31]

Lockhart talked with Trotsky again on April 13, and quoted Trotsky in his report as having recognized that sooner or later Russia would be obliged to fight Germany and that the help of the Allies would be valuable when this time came. Trotsky, he reported to London on that day:

. . . invited the Allied Powers to submit as soon as possible a complete and proper statement of the support which they are in a position to offer and of the guarantees which could be given by them. If satisfactory conditions are reached, he thinks it would be both necessary and desirable to come to an agreement.[32]

In a further conversation on May 8, concerning the Murmansk situation, Trotsky said—according to Lockhart's report to the Foreign Office—

. . . that his Government was quite prepared to reach an arrangement with the Allies on the general lines which had already been indicated by myself and . . . he regretted that the views of the Allies had apparently not yet been presented in a more concrete shape, . . .

[30] National Archives, State Department File 861.00/1438½.
[31] Wilson MSS, Series II, *op.cit.,* Balfour telegram transmitted with Lansing letter of May 21.
[32] *Loc.cit.*

It will be noted that throughout these discussions Trotsky appears to have been animated by the assumption that resumption of full-fledged hostilities with the Germans was inevitable and imminent. The prevalence of the discussion of this possibility of intervention-by-invitation or intervention-by-consent appears, in fact, to be roughly coincidental with the period that elapsed between ratification of the Brest-Litovsk Treaty and the resumption of official German-Soviet contacts in May, during which time the Bolsheviki strongly doubted the durability of the Brest arrangements. The idea of accepting Allied aid was eventually laid to rest mainly by the revelation in these German-Soviet contacts that, unsatisfactory as these relations would continue to be, there was at that time no intention on the German side of using the German forces in Russia to destroy the Soviet regime. In addition to this there was also the growing deterioration in the relations between the Allied governments and the Soviet government which set in after the end of April (largely as a result of Noulens' influence and activities) and which remains to be related in later chapters.

By early May, therefore, the idea of intervention by Soviet invitation, or at least consent, had largely lost such reality as it ever possessed. By mid-May, even Lockhart admitted that the moment had passed. From that time on, the idea ceased to be seriously discussed in Moscow; and if it died more slowly, as was the case, in the Allied circles in the West, this was merely because people there were slow to realize the change that had come over the situation in Moscow.

Nevertheless, while it lasted, the belief in the reality of this possibility had important effects, both locally and on the discussion of the intervention problem in the Allied capitals.

Francis, for one, was much affected by it. While he never shared the unreserved optimism of Robins and Sadoul, he was persuaded that the possibility of intervention-by-invitation was one worth working for, and his entire attitude and personal policy from the time of the ratification of the Brest-Litovsk Treaty to the beginning of May were predicated on this calculation.[33] In this respect it should

---

[33] "I appreciate fully [the] mistakes of Soviet government and outrages practiced as reported by Summers and consuls," Francis wired to the Department on April 5, "but think best plan is to ignore same for the present in order to induce Soviet government to ask Allied assistance, so that when Allies enter Russia, will not meet with Soviet government's refusal, but Soviet government's welcome. . . ." *Foreign Relations, 1918, Russia*, Vol. III, *op.cit.*, p. 228.

be noted that Francis was following the advice not only of Robins but also of his own military representatives, Ruggles and Riggs, both of whom appear to have believed that the Soviet request for intervention was a real possibility and could easily be realized if the Allies seriously wished this to happen.[34]

The Consulate General in Moscow, on the other hand, never supported the thesis that intervention-by-invitation was a real possibility. Summers favored intervention without Soviet consent and believed that a joint enterprise of this nature would be "welcomed by the great majority of Russians." But he gave no encouragement to the belief that the Soviet government could be induced to ask for it or that such a request would be worth having even if it were conceivable.

It was the British government which was most affected by the prospect of intervention with Bolshevik consent. Throughout April and May the evidences of British thinking on the intervention problem, and the official British correspondence with other Allied governments, were permeated with this suggestion. The belief that the possibility was genuine, taken against the background of the desperate situation on the western front, was the real explanation for much of the persistence and urgency with which the British continued to agitate the intervention problem up to the end of May.

The British government was practically alone, among the Allied governments, in its preoccupation with this possibility. The French and Italians never warmed to it. The French were not averse to having the suggestion dangled before official Washington, if there was any possibility that it might be a useful means of easing Wilson into the acceptance of intervention in principle. But their desire, throughout, was for intervention without Soviet consent, and preferably with a view to overthrowing the Soviet government.

As for Wilson, at no time did he exhibit the slightest interest in this possibility. This was the one point at which he disagreed with House, who was impressed with the suggestion that a Soviet invitation might be forthcoming and thought it worth pursuing. The main

---

[34] See, among other things, Ruggles' telegram of May 1, 1918 to the War Department: "I believe . . . that we should negotiate with Bolsheviks *modus vivendi* by consent to immediate Allied intervention through Siberia and northern ports; . . ." *Foreign Relations, 1918, Russia*, Vol. 1, *op.cit.*, p. 517. This telegram appears to have been based on a recommendation from Riggs of April 25, cited in full in Strakhovsky, *op.cit.*, pp. 39–40.

reason for Wilson's lack of enthusiasm was, no doubt, his aversion to intervention generally, based on the belief that it would serve no serious military purpose and would antagonize the Russian people. This last effect, he surely thought, would be produced even though the Soviet government were to request the action—perhaps even more so.

The Japanese government likewise showed no interest in the possibility of a Soviet invitation to intervene. Plainly, if influential Japanese even entertained misgivings about entering Siberia by agreement with the western Allies, they certainly had no greater desire to see their freedom of action limited by any such agreement with the Soviet government. Even had they been willing to contemplate this alternative, they would have had no disposition to fulfill the conditions Trotsky had named. In mid-April the Vice Minister of Foreign Affairs in Tokyo told the French Ambassador there (in a marvelous example of diplomatic double talk) that while Japan would of course be prepared to give assurances that she would not interfere in the domestic affairs of Russia, he personally thought that these assurances

. . . should not be formulated with excessive clearness and precision, as any cooperation with the Maximalists would in his opinion be directly antagonistic to the contemplated goal which is to repress anarchy and combat the Germans. . . .[35]

The suggestion that there was a real possibility of Allied intervention by Soviet invitation or with Soviet consent not only played an important part in the discussion of the intervention problem among the Allied governments in the spring of 1918 but subsequently became a central factor in the reproach—so often levied at the Allied governments from liberal or left-wing quarters in the West—that they had spurned, either from shortsightedness or from motives of imperialistic greed, a perfectly acceptable alternative to the intervention they later undertook against the wishes and resistance of the Soviet government.[36] A particularly strong impression was made by

[35] *Foreign Relations, 1918, Russia*, Vol. II, *op.cit.*, p. 128, from French Ambassador's note of April 21.

[36] It is interesting to note that the Soviet propagandists and official historians, while evidently not loath to permit the inference to rest in the West that the Allied governments unjustly repelled the outstretched hand of Soviet friendship in the

a letter written by Lockhart to Robins on May 5,[37] designed to strengthen Robins' hand in further discussions with Francis. In this letter, Lockhart listed the points on which Trotsky had met the Allied governments halfway, and drew the conclusion that "a policy of Allied intervention, with the cooperation and consent of the Bolshevik Government, is feasible and possible." Robins took this home to the United States, where it was shown to a number of people and served to fan the suspicions that were already arising in many minds concerning the soundness of Allied policy towards Russia. Senator Hiram Johnson, speaking on the floor of the Senate on December 12, 1918, asked the Administration, rhetorically, whether it was true

. . . that the British High Commissioner . . . stated over his signature that the Soviet government had cooperated in aiding the Allies, and that he believed that intervention in cooperation with the Soviet government was feasible as late as the fifth of May, 1918?

Six years later the anonymous author of *Archangel: The American War with Russia,* a bitter firsthand account of the Archangel expedition,[38] was still able to say

. . . No spokesman for the administration, or anyone else, ever answered or attempted to answer this question.

In these circumstances it would seem desirable to inquire, in the interests of clarity throughout the remainder of this narrative, what —precisely—was the authoritative Soviet view on this subject; and for this it is best to turn to the position and opinions of Lenin himself.

---

early months of Soviet power, scarcely mention these negotiations about Allied aid in material designed for internal Soviet consumption. Where it is mentioned at all, this is done either (1) to prove that the Allies wished to embroil the Soviet government with the Germans (V. M. Khvostov & I. I. Mints, under editorial supervision of V. P. Potemkin, *Istoriya diplomatii* [History of Diplomacy], State Publishing House for Political Literature, Moscow, 1945, Vol. II, *Diplomacy in New Times* [*1872–1919*], p. 348), (2) to praise Lenin's skill at playing his adversaries off against each other (*ibid.,* p. 349), or (3) to make out a case that Trotsky was guilty of treachery (A. Berezkin, *S-SH-A: aktivny organizator i uchastnik voennoi interventsii protiv Sovetskoi Rossii* [*1918–1920 gg.*] [U.S.A.: The Active Organizer of and Participant in Military Intervention against Soviet Russia (1918–1920)], State Publishing House for Political Literature, Moscow, 1952, Second edition, p. 37).

[37] See below, Chapter VIII.

[38] Published by A. C. McClurg & Co., Chicago, 1924, p. 24. Published under "A Chronicler," the author was probably Mr. John Cudahy, later American Ambassador to Poland.

Lenin's views on the complex of problems affecting the relations of the Soviet government with the Allies at this juncture might be summed up as follows. The position of the new Soviet republic was difficult and dangerous in the extreme. The "peace" that had been achieved was onerous and highly unstable. Nevertheless, it provided the Soviet republic with a respite—a breathing-space—which was of immense value to it insofar as it gave it an opportunity to consolidate the new structure of power at home and, possibly, to exploit the hostilities and rivalries of the various "imperialist" powers in such a way as to delay, if not to prevent permanently, reprisals and attacks by any of them against the weak and struggling Soviet power. The Soviet government itself, prizing this breathing-space as its only real hope of salvation, had not the faintest intention of renewing military operations against the Germans. The instability of the Brest-Litovsk peace therefore did not lie in any attitudes or intentions on the Soviet side. The great danger lay in two possibilities: the first was that the German "war party, seduced by the momentary weakness of Russia and urged on by the German capitalists with their hatred of socialism and their appetite for plunder," [39] would win out in Germany and would insist in tearing up the peace treaty and attempting the complete conquest and subjugation of Russia. The second was that in the Far East, where a savage attack on Soviet power by the "imperialists" had thus far been prevented only by the rivalries and suspicions between the Americans and Japanese *bourgeoisies,* these last two forces might arrive at some sort of a dicker for sharing the spoils, which would permit them both to pounce upon Soviet Siberia and satisfy their economic appetites at Russian expense.

Three basic and overriding conclusions flowed, as Lenin saw it, from these appreciations. First, the real hope of the Soviet republic for permanent respite and survival lay only in the ripening and eventual fruition of social revolution in the West. Secondly, the continuation of the breathing-space, on which the survival of the Soviet republic now hung as on a thread, depended on the continuation of the hostilities and rivalries among the great imperialist powers —and this meant, among other things, a continuation of the great war. ("Our only chance, until the European revolution breaks out

[39] V. I. Lenin, *Sochineniya* (Complete Works), Fourth Edition, State Publishing House for Political Literature, Moscow, 1950, Vol. 27, *February–July 1918,* p. 209.

. . . is the continuation of the struggle of the gigantic imperialist powers. . . ." [40]) Thirdly, the only possible and correct policy for the Soviet regime, in these circumstances, was "to maneuver, to retreat, to bide one's time."

These last three expressions Lenin repeated time after time, on one occasion after another. In Russian, they consisted only of these three infinitive verbs, but their meaning cannot adequately be translated into English with equal succinctness. By "maneuver" (*lavirovat'*) Lenin had in mind the rapid and adroit tactical shifting of ground as well as the exploitation of the contradictions and rivalries between the various "imperialist" enemies. The word "retreat" (*otstupat'*) was used not in the literal military sense but in the broad political-military sense; and what Lenin meant by it was that while one should do everything within one's power to prevent encroachments against the Soviet republic by the "imperialist" governments, one should not permit one's self to be lured into taking positions which would force one to stand up and accept actual battle to the death on uneven terms with a superior adversary. What he meant was thus: "retreat—if no other course is possible but suicidal resistance." In other words: no heroics, no romantic and suicidal actions, preservation at all cost of the sheer existence of Soviet power, even if only on a reduced territory. Finally, in the expression "bide one's time" (*vyzhidat'*) Lenin had in mind exercising patience and waiting out the adversary through this dangerous period until the spread of world revolution might take the pressure off the Soviet republic.

The following summary taken from his "Six Theses concerning the Current Tasks of Soviet Power" and written at some time between April 30 and May 3, 1918, will give a good idea of the context in which Lenin used these expressions and the language with which he stated the propositions summarized above:

The international position of the Soviet republic is difficult and critical in the extreme, because the most deeply rooted interests of international capital and imperialism impel it to be inclined not only toward military pressure on Russia but also toward mutual agreement concerning the division of Russia and the strangling of Soviet power.

Only the sharpening of the imperialist slaughter of the peoples in western Europe and the imperialist rivalry of Japan and America in the Far East

[40] *Ibid.*, p. 259.

paralyze or restrain these tendencies, and they have this effect only partially and only for a limited and probably brief period.

For this reason the Soviet republic must, on the one hand, bend every effort for the most rapid possible economic rebuilding of the country, the increase of its defense capability, the creation of a mighty socialist army; and on the other hand, in international politics we are obliged to follow a course of maneuver, of retreat, and biding one's time until the moment when the proletarian revolution, now ripening more rapidly than before in a number of advanced countries, comes to fruition.[41]

The reader will note that in this basic formula there is not the slightest hint of a belief that there was anything to choose, morally and politically, from the Soviet standpoint, between the two "imperialist" camps then engaged in the great World War, nor the slightest substance for any rationale that would permit the inviting in of the troops of one of the imperialist powers onto Russian territory, as a counterweight to the other. Had Lenin regarded this as among the likely alternatives open to Soviet policy, he would surely—being the ideologically consistent person that he was—have phrased the basic formula on which he took his stand in such a way as to allow for this possibility. But nothing he said, not only in the statement quoted but in other references to international affairs during the weeks in question, could be taken by any stretch of the imagination as preparing his followers for the possibility of any such expedient. That one should play off the adversaries against each other was indeed an integral part of his concept; to invite the armed forces of one of the imperialist powers onto Soviet territory, however, with a view to pitting it against the forces of another, would have been plainly self-defeating. It was something that could be contemplated, if at all, only in conditions of most dire emergency and catastrophe—in the event, that is, that the breathing-space had already been brought to an end by some sort of outside action.

But this had not yet happened; and if any one thing is clear about Lenin's thinking at this time, it is that he did not want it to happen. He was profoundly opposed to any Soviet policy that would jeopardize in any way the continuance of the breathing-space. Yet this is precisely the effect that would have been produced by any invitation to the Allies to intervene in Russia.

[41] *Ibid.*, p. 282.

Lenin stated this very clearly in his "Theses on the Present Political Situation" (May 12–13):

Not by any means repudiating in general the idea of a military agreement with one of the imperialist coalitions against the other in cases where such an agreement would, without encroaching on the foundations of Soviet power, strengthen its position and paralyze pressure against it by some imperialist power, we at the given moment cannot enter on a military agreement with the Anglo-French coalition. Because what is really important for the members of that coalition is the removal of German forces from the west, which means the advance of many Japanese units into the interior of European Russia, and this condition is not acceptable, as it would mean the complete destruction of Soviet power. If an ultimatum of this nature were to be given to us by the Anglo-French coalition, we would reply with a refusal, because the danger of a Japanese move could be countered with less difficulty (or could be delayed for a longer time), than the danger of the occupation by the Germans of Petrograd, Moscow, and the greater part of European Russia.[42]

Sadoul recognized this same basic reality and could not, therefore, conceal his amazement, mingled as it was with pleasure, that Trotsky should be prepared to discuss with Allied representatives the possibility of an entry of Allied forces into Russia. "It is certain," he wrote, that when such a step became known, the Germans

. . . would take umbrage, would address to the Bolsheviki ultimatum after ultimatum and would begin a military advance which . . . would carry them very rapidly to the occupation of Petrograd and Moscow, which would mean to deprive the existing [Soviet] government of the industrial-worker elements on which it is almost exclusively basing itself.[43]

It is difficult to understand from a distance of nearly forty years how it was possible, in the face of this recognition and in the light of Lenin's statements, to believe that there was a serious possibility that the Soviet government might invite the Allies in. Lockhart and Robins were, after all, intelligent and sincere men. But their hopes bore the fevered quality of so many wartime calculations. Being partly dependent on Russian interpreters and secretaries, they did not read the Soviet press themselves and perhaps did not follow as carefully as they should have Lenin's statements to his followers on the internal front. Finally, they were unquestionably diverted

[42] *Ibid.*, p. 325.
[43] Sadoul, *Notes* . . . , *op.cit.*, p. 285; letter of March 30.

and misled by Trotsky's statements, which reflected partly his greater pessimism (as compared with Lenin) over the chances for prolonging the breathing-space, and partly, no doubt, his anxious desire to exploit Allied interest as a means of discouraging Japanese intervention.

CHAPTER VI

THE CZECHOSLOVAK LEGION

. . . the cards were not all on the table and will not be until the passion of this whole situation dies out and the truth is allowed to come forth. —Raymond Robins on the Czech uprising, "Bolshevik Propaganda, Hearings. . . ." (1919)

THERE was, in the unfolding of events as between the Allies and Russia in the summer of 1918, no single factor that played a more significant role than the unique armed force known subsequently as the Czechoslovak Legion. This being so, it now becomes necessary to examine the curious origins of this body of men, and the situation in which it found itself in the spring of 1918.

Before the World War there were numbers of Czechs and Slovaks residing in some of the larger Russian cities, as well as a few Czech colonists in the countryside in Volhynia. The resentment in the historic provinces against Austrian rule, the romantic nationalism that marked the liberal movement of the nineteenth century, and the Pan-Slavic tendencies proceeding from Russia, had all served to create a bond between Russia and the protagonists of Czech autonomy or independence. Even stronger was the sentimental attachment to Russia on the part of the Slovak intellectuals who resented the Hungarian predominance in their own homeland.

When the World War broke out a special unit was set up within the Russian army called the *Druzhina,* the rank and file of which was made up predominantly of men from the Czech colonies within the Russian Empire. The higher officers were chiefly Russians; but a few men of Czech origin who had been serving as regular officers in the Tsarist army were also attached to this unit and given officers' rank. The *Druzhina* took part in the battles of the eastern front both north and south of the Carpathians, being used primarily for reconnaissance work.

The Czechoslovak Legion

During the course of the war large numbers of Czech and Slovak soldiers fighting in the Austro-Hungarian armies either deserted to the Russians or were taken prisoner by them, the two phenomena being frequently almost indistinguishable. The leaders of the Czech colony in Russia, as also the representatives of the Czechoslovak National Council established in 1916 in Paris, pressed to have these prisoners incorporated, together with the *Druzhina,* into a new Czechoslovak force which could take part in the World War on the side of the Allies.

During the Tsarist period, the Russian government remained generally unsympathetic to these urgings. There was a natural reluctance in Petrograd to encourage centrifugal tendencies anywhere, even in the camp of the enemy. The Russian Empire, like that of the Hapsburgs, was a multi-national entity. It was plain that if the principle of self-determination became triumphant in the lands of the Danube monarchy, it could easily spread to Russia and create similar disaffection there.

With the overthrow of the Tsar's government in March 1917, these inhibitions ceased to exist. The Provisional Government took a more sympathetic attitude toward the Czechs and Slovaks and permitted the expansion of the *Druzhina* into an entire army corps through the rapid recruitment into its ranks of war prisoners and of Czechs and Slovaks working in Russian industrial plants. This unit, generally known as the Czech Corps, took part—and even distinguished itself—in the ill-fated Brusilov offensive in the summer of 1917. By the fall of the year it had grown to a point where it consisted of two full-fledged divisions, with some supporting service units.

Professor Thomas Masaryk, the future president of the Czechoslovak Republic, had come to Russia in May 1917 to weld the various Czechs and Slovaks in Russia into a single faction and to make arrangements, if possible, for the removal of the Corps to the western front. He remained there throughout 1917 and served during that period as spokesman for the Corps vis-à-vis the Russian authorities. The unfavorable outcome of Brusilov's offensive and the rapid disintegration of the Russian army that set in immediately afterward made it clear that there was no longer any military future for the Czechs on the eastern front. Masaryk therefore redoubled the effort to find some way for them to leave Russia and to join the Allied forces in France. Negotiations to this end were in progress when the Bolshevik seizure of power occurred. The Bolshevik move to take Russia out of the war, together with the break between the Soviet government and the Ukrainian Rada placed the Corps, then stationed in the Ukraine, in a most awkward and ambiguous position. The Czechs immediately proclaimed their neutrality in the face of the Russian civil conflict; but as the only large body of men on the eastern front that had retained its discipline, its unity, and its loyalty to the Allied cause, the Corps found its position near the front an exposed and—in view of the overwhelming superiority of the forces of the Central Powers on the other side of the line—a dangerous one.

In December 1917 an "autonomous Czechoslovak army," made up of Czechs from the western countries, was recognized by the Allied governments as a regular Allied force and was subordinated to the French High Command. In the course of the winter it was arranged that the Czech Corps in Russia should become an integral part of this Czechoslovak army, and agreement was reached with the French government that the Corps should be evacuated to France as rapidly as possible. In Petrograd, Masaryk conducted negotiations to this end with the Soviet authorities. But the uncertainties prevailing during the negotiations with the Germans were such that no definite arrangements could be made before the final conclusion of the Brest-Litovsk Treaty. The Corps was stationed, throughout this period, in the area around and including Kiev. Having retained—in contrast to the Russian forces around it—a satisfactory military discipline, it was used primarily for guarding war stores and ammunition dumps which otherwise, in view of the demoralization of the Russian soldiers, would have been left to the mercies of fate. By virtue of this function, plus the fact that it had seized extensive stocks of weapons from the enemy during the Brusilov offensive, the Corps was by this time relatively well armed.

From December to early February the Ukrainian territory on which the Czech Corps was stationed was, it will be recalled, under the somewhat tenuous rule of the Ukrainian Rada. It will further be recalled that on February 8 delegates of the Rada concluded a separate peace treaty with the Central Powers at Brest-Litovsk just at the moment when their capital, Kiev, was falling to the invading Bolsheviki. These developments complicated still further the position of the Corps. It now found itself on the territory of a government which had made peace with its enemy. When, a few days later, the Germans resumed the offensive against Russia and German land forces began to penetrate into the Ukraine, it was clear there was no time to be lost. It was decided, without further ado, to begin evacuation of the base area in the Ukraine and to seek exit from Russia via the Trans-Siberian Railway and Vladivostok. Believing on the basis of his own discussions with the Bolshevik leaders that they now had no objections to evacuation of the Corps via Vladivostok and supposing the Allied chiefs of mission (who had left Petrograd on February 28) to be also about to leave Russia by the same route, Masaryk left Moscow for Vladivostok on March 6, en route to America and Europe, with a view to arranging for the shipping necessary to transport the Corps from Vladivostok to Europe.

Meanwhile, the Corps was having a difficult time extracting itself from the western Ukraine. The German advance was so rapid that German forces intercepted its retreat at the railway junction of Bakhmach. In the days immediately following Masaryk's departure, sharp engagements were fought there—engagements in which the Czechs found themselves, by force of circumstances, fighting side by side with the Ukrainian Bolsheviki. With difficulty, the Czechs broke through the encirclement and continued their eastward movement in the direction of Kursk.

The Soviet government had, by this time, just completed its move to Moscow. On the first day of the meeting of the Congress of Soviets called to act on the ratification of the Brest-Litovsk Treaty, the Soviet of People's Commissars (*Sovnarkom*) found time to take cognizance of the situation of the Czech Corps. In what must—in the circumstances—have been very hasty and hectic deliberations, the *Sovnarkom* arrived at a formal decision to permit the Corps to proceed across Siberia and to depart from Russia via Vladivostok. This decision was communicated the following day, March 15, to the Czechs. A local agreement was at once made between the commanding officers of the Corps and the Bolshevik commander in the Ukraine, Antonov-Ovseyenko (later to be Soviet Minister in Czechoslovakia), for the entry of the Czechs onto the territory of the Russian Soviet Republic, with a view to their further transit eastward. On March 16, Antonov-Ovseyenko made an announcement acknowledging the "fraternal help" the Czechoslovaks had given to the Ukrainian proletariat "in their struggle against the imperialist looters," and said that the Bolshevik forces would "accept as a token of friendship the arms which the Czechoslovaks are leaving." [1]

This last referred to an important provision of the arrangements the Czechs had made with Antonov-Ovseyenko: namely, that they would, before starting on their journey to Siberia, surrender to the Bolshevik forces a portion of the arms they held. This surrender appears to have been carried out at Kursk, on the very day of Antonov-Ovseyenko's announcement, by such of the Czech contingents as had already reached that point. The first trainloads of semi-disarmed Czechs were then permitted to start on the long trek eastward in the direction of Siberia and Vladivostok.

Immediately after this, difficulties began to develop. The precise source of these difficulties is unclear. Eduard Beneš states in his memoirs that the attitude of the Soviet military authorities had changed as early as March 18, and that they began at that time to place difficulties in the path of the further eastward movement of the Corps—"their explanation being that the Czechoslovak Army might join Semyonov or the Japanese." [2] It seems likely that the hitch in the arrangements was the result of Trotsky's arrival in Moscow and assumption of the duties of Commissar for War on March 17. It was only natural that he, not having participated in the hasty decision of March 14 and having now the over-all military responsibility, should wish to review the terms on which the Czech force was to pass through Soviet territory. However that may be, it now became necessary for further negotiations to be conducted in Moscow in the ensuing days. While these talks were in progress, the movement of the Corps was delayed. The new negotiations led to a revision of the Soviet terms, spelled out in a telegram despatched by Stalin, as Commissar of Nationalities, to the Czechoslovak National Council on March 26. As set forth in this message, the Soviet government agreed to the evacuation of the Czechoslovak Corps via Siberia, but only on three conditions:

1. that the evacuation should begin at once;

2. that the non-communist Russian officers who still occupied the highest command positions in the Corps (referred to in the

---

[1] Bunyan, *op.cit.*, p. 80.
[2] Eduard Beneš, *My War Memoirs* (tr. Paul Selver), George Allen & Unwin Ltd., London, 1928, p. 355.

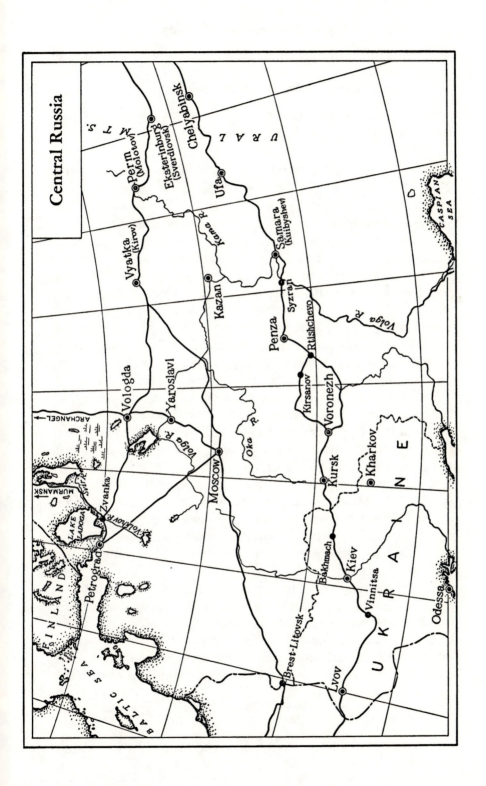

Central Russia

telegram as the "counter-revolutionary commanders") be immediately removed; and

3. that the members of the Corps should proceed

not as fighting units but as a group of free citizens, taking with them a certain quantity of arms for self-defense against the attack of counter-revolutionists.[3]

This decision was followed, the next day, by the conclusion at Penza (where the leading echelons of the Corps had now arrived) of a new and detailed agreement with the local Soviet military authorities, according to which each trainload of Czechs might have one armed company of 168 men, with rifles and a single trench mortar. Certain specified Russian commanders might, under this new agreement, be retained.[4] With the conclusion of this agreement, movement of the force began again. Once more the long trainloads of boxcars containing the Czech soldiers began to roll eastward from central European Russia toward the Urals and Siberia.

But the situation remained very delicate. The Czechs, being suspicious of Bolshevik good faith and well aware that once their weapons were abandoned they would be at the mercy of others, did not actually surrender all the arms they were supposed to surrender. Considerable quantities were retained and concealed in the trains.

The next serious impediment to the movement of the Corps arose from the shock produced in Moscow by the Japanese landing in Vladivostok on April 5. The leaders of the Soviet government feared that the Japanese move was the precursor of some full-fledged intervention. This being the case, they at once became suspicious of the eastward movement of the Czechs. On April 7 orders were issued to halt the movement of the Corps across Siberia. A few days later, when the excitement over the Japanese action had subsided, the order was rescinded.

But the movement of the Corps had by this time become the subject of much tension and confusion. Conflicting orders were issued by various Soviet authorities, central and local. The Czech command itself was now widely dispersed. There were confusing variations in the inclination and ability of individual Czech commanders and Soviet officials to adjust amicably the many problems

[3] Bunyan, *op.cit.*, pp. 81–82.
[4] These included, above all, General Dietrichs (Dukhonin's former Chief of Staff), General Kappel, and Colonel Ushakov.

and incidents to which the passage of the Corps gave rise. The fears and suspicions of the Czechs themselves, furthermore, were now growing apace.

For this hardening of the Czech position, there were several reasons that deserve to be noted.

There was, in the first place, the influence on the Czech officers of those few Russian commanders who had remained with the Corps. These were, to a man, anti-communist. To some extent, they were in touch with underground Russian oppositionist groups. Their influence was naturally committed to the encouragement of a stiffening of attitude on the part of the Czechs. On April 14, the commanders of the First Division of the Czech Corps, meeting at Kirsanov, not far from Penza, arrived at a secret determination that it was impossible to rely on any agreement with the Bolsheviki, and agreed that the Czechs must be prepared to force their own passage, if this should prove necessary. This decision, later to become the position of the Corps as a whole, was one on which the Russian officers may be presumed to have had an important influence.

Added to this were the intensive efforts being made just at that time by the Soviet authorities to propagandize and disaffect the war prisoners in Russia, with a view to inducing them to embrace the communist cause and to take up arms with local Red Guard units or the new Red Army. About mid-April—just at the time, in fact, when the Czech deliberations were in progress at Kirsanov—a congress of such disaffected prisoners was being held in Moscow. Some of the delegates were Czechs; and the purpose of the gathering —the conversion to the communist cause of as many as possible of the war prisoner community in Russia—was addressed no less to the Czechs than to the other prisoners. Not only at this conference but also on the spot, wherever the Czech units found themselves, intensive efforts were made by the Bolsheviki to penetrate the Corps, to alienate the men from their officers, and to induce them to remain in Russia and take up arms on the communist side.[5] These efforts naturally caused alarm and resentment among the officers of the Corps. They also tended to split the rank and file into bitterly hostile and antagonistic elements. Since the officers of the Corps were well

[5] The Moscow *Izvestiya*, No. 83, April 26, 1918, carried an account of these efforts to subvert the Czechoslovak Corps. The actual appeals to the men of the Corps were issued in the name of the Czechoslovak Section of the Russian Communist Party.

aware that the inspiration for these efforts came from the Soviet leaders themselves, it is no wonder that they were suspicious of the sincerity of the Soviet assurance of safe-conduct to Vladivostok, and reluctant—accordingly—to see the Corps surrender the last of its arms to the Soviet authorities.

A further source of Czech suspicion—and one that was to become increasingly important as the spring advanced—was the belief, or assumption, that the difficulties the Corps was encountering were the result of German pressure on the Soviet authorities. This suspicion was greatly heightened, at the end of April, by the news of the arrival in Moscow of the new German Ambassador, Count Mirbach. The thesis was, as will be seen in a later chapter, without foundation; but it permeated the Corps, caused the commanders to see in every Soviet official a concealed German agent and in every impediment arising in the path of the Corps a likely reflection of German designs.

❖

While the Corps was thus making its uneasy passage eastward, the growing realization of its relative strength and speculation about its possible uses were beginning to agitate the Allied governments at home and their representatives in Russia.

To the British military planners at the headquarters of the Supreme War Council the idea seems to have occurred, at about the time of the ratification of the Brest-Litovsk Treaty, that the services of the Czech units in Russia might be used to good effect either in connection with the Japanese intervention in Siberia on which these British officers had set their hearts or—possibly, and as a second alternative—in connection with the operations which they now thought would be necessary to protect the North Russian ports from German encroachment. On April 1, the British War Office approached the Czechoslovak National Council, through the French government, with a communication expressing doubt that the Czech Corps could actually get to Europe via Siberia and voicing the view that it ought, therefore, to be used in Russia or Siberia. The English military authorities, Beneš relates in his memoirs:

. . . held the opinion that it would be possible [for the Corps] to occupy Siberia in the region of Omsk, or else to proceed to Archangelsk where a military base could be established, from which communication with

Siberia could be maintained by way of Perm. Finally, it might be possible to pass beyond Baikal and join Semyonov, and this latter solution was the one which the English favoured.[6]

Beneš, after discussing the matter with the Chief of the French General Staff and with General Maurice Janin,[7] replied with a letter to Clemenceau opposing any alteration of the plans for removing the Corps to France.

This remained, throughout the spring, the position of the Czechoslovak National Council and (until June) of Clemenceau himself. It did not, however, cause the British military authorities, and some of the French staff officers, to be weaned from their attachment to the idea of using the Corps in Russia. A vigorous effort was made by the British side at the military level of the Supreme War Council to get the sanction of the Council for this scheme. The first result was the insertion of a reference to the Czechs in the draft of a Joint Note submitted by the British to the Permanent Military Representatives at some time around the beginning of April. In this document, apparently drawn up on the basis of a memorandum prepared by Brigadier General H. W. Studd, the British military planners set forth their concept of a Siberian expedition grouped around the Japanese—a concept which they were continuing to push tenaciously despite Wilson's opposition. The document envisaged the advance of an Allied expeditionary force from Vladivostok to the area of the Urals, and possibly the Volga. The Japanese were to form the "mobile base or nucleus" of this force; but they were to enjoy, it was envisaged, "the eventual assistance *of Czech and other elements which can be organized on the spot.*" [8]

This document was approved by the Permanent Military Representatives, as Joint Note No. 20, on April 8. General Tasker H. Bliss, the American representative, abstained from taking a position on it,

[6] Beneš, *op.cit.*, p. 357.

[7] General Janin, of the French army, had been stationed in Russia earlier in the war and had served as French military representative at the Russian field headquarters on the eastern front in 1916 and 1917. Here he had become acquainted with the affairs of the Czechoslovak units in Russia. At the end of 1917 the Czechoslovak National Council requested that he be designated by the French government as the over-all commander of the Czech forces everywhere, and this was done. He was subsequently, after the beginning of the intervention, sent to Siberia where he served as Chief of the French Military Mission and Commander in Chief of the French and British forces there. In the spring of 1918, however, he was still in Paris.

[8] National Archives, War Records Division, Record Group 120, Records of the American Expeditionary Forces (Supreme War Council papers). Italics added.

in view of the President's strong feelings that the Permanent Military Representatives ought not to concern themselves with political questions. And despite French acceptance of the Joint Note at the military level, the French government itself, and Clemenceau personally, remained undeviatingly averse to any diversion of the Czechs from the earliest possible passage to France.

Almost immediately after adoption of Joint Note No. 20 a new idea was broached which was evidently designed to achieve the retention of the Czech Corps in Russia without actually saying so. This was the idea of dividing the Corps, permitting all those who had already passed the Urals to continue toward Vladivostok, ostensibly for eventual removal to France, but routing the remainder to the ports of the Russian North—Murmansk and Archangel. Concerning the purpose of this proposed removal of a portion of the Corps to the Russian North there was, as we shall see shortly, some equivocation. The Czechs, and subsequently the Russians, were given the impression that the basic purpose was the evacuation of these units to France. There seems to have been no question, however, but that the thought uppermost in the minds of the authors of the project was that the removal to France might be long delayed and that meanwhile the units might come in handy for purposes of Allied occupation of the ports in question and the surrounding areas. It was then taken practically for granted in French and British military circles that military steps to keep these regions out of German hands [9] would soon be necessary.

By late April this scheme had found such favor in the thinking of French and British military authorities that it was brought up for formal consideration at both the military and political levels of the Supreme War Council. On April 27 the Permanent Military Representatives at the Council, convening at Versailles, discussed in detail for the first time—on French initiative—the question of the future of the Czech Corps. The upshot of their discussion was another Joint Note (No. 25) in which they took note of discussions that had

[9] The evidence of this will be found in the understanding of the scheme that was conveyed, at a very early date, to the operational echelons of the French and British forces. According to Newbolt (Vol. v, *op.cit.,* p. 318) the mission of the British instructor staff despatched to Murmansk in May was "to train and organize the Czech corps, expected to number about 20,000 men, which would then be employed for the defense of North Russia." Newbolt also says that a French officer who arrived in Murmansk in May proposed to station 5,000 of the Czechs at Archangel and another 4,000 along the Murmansk Railroad.

taken place between the French and British governments "on the subject of the transportation of [the] Czech contingents from Russia" and expressed the opinion

i. That there is everything to be gained by securing their transportation at the earliest possible date.

ii. That as the greatest possible rapidity can be assured by using Archangel and Murmansk, all Czech troops, which have not passed East of Omsk . . . should be despatched to those two ports.

A third point indicated that while these troops were waiting to be embarked

. . . they could be profitably employed in defending Archangel and Murmansk and in guarding and protecting the Murman railway.

Similarly, it was suggested, those troops which had passed Omsk might be used, as already recommended in Joint Note No. 20, to cooperate with the Allies in Siberia.[10]

The wording of this note, together with the fact that as much as six weeks later no serious move had yet been made by either government to provide shipping either at Vladivostok or at the northern ports, makes it very difficult to believe that the idea of dividing the Corps was anything other, in the minds of its authors, than a disingenuous one, designed to give perfunctory recognition to the principle of the eventual removal of the Czech units to France but actually to assure their availability for service in Russia in the event of Allied intervention.

Some days later (May 2), the subject came up for a rather confused discussion at the Fifth Session of the Supreme War Council itself, in Abbeville. The Allied statesmen had before them for consideration Joint Note No. 25 of the Permanent Military Representatives. Clemenceau, who clung consistently to the position that the Czechs should be removed to the western front as rapidly as possible, was evidently suspicious of the motives of the authors of the Joint Note. He had no objection to routing a portion of the Corps via the northern ports, but he did want them to be promptly removed to France. He therefore pressed energetically for a clear commitment on the part of the British to attempt to find the necessary shipping. The British representatives somewhat grudgingly agreed to do their best, but voiced pessimism about the chances of finding enough ships

[10] National Archives, War Records Division, R.G. 120, *op.cit.*

[147]

to remove the entire Corps. Lord Milner, British Secretary of State for War, urged that even in the case of Siberia the removal only of a portion of the Czech force should be envisaged and that

. . . the additional troops should be asked not to continue their journey to Vladivostok . . . but . . . should be detained near Omsk or Cheliabinsk.[11]

He took the position that it would suffice if the Supreme War Council were simply to accept Joint Note No. 25. Clemenceau, still unsatisfied, argued that it would be desirable to embody the results of the discussion in more precise terms than those of the Joint Note. At his insistence, a resolution was drafted purporting to clarify the views of the senior statesmen on the subject; and the Council ended up by approving both Joint Note No. 25 and the draft resolution. Actually, the resolution, like many another product of the harried deliberations of top level multilateral conferences, merely reflected the conflicting points of view without endeavoring to reconcile them, and brought no clarification into Allied policy. It read as follows:

(a) The British Government undertake to do their best to arrange the transportation of those Czech troops who are in Vladivostok or on their way to that port.
(b) The French Government undertake the responsibility for those troops until they are embarked.
(c) The British Government undertake to approach M. Trotsky with a view to the concentration at Murmansk and Archangel of those Czech troops not belonging to the Army Corps which has left Omsk for Vladivostok.[12]

The upshot of the Abbeville conference was thus an agreement that the Corps should be split, one part of it being directed to the Pacific and the other to North Russia. But no real agreement had been achieved between the governments as to the desirability of its prompt removal to the western front.

The matter was duly taken up with the Soviet authorities at Moscow, as the resolution had envisaged—not only by Lockhart but also, apparently, by Lavergne and Sadoul. As to the dates of these discussions, the identity of principal participants, the content of what was

[11] *Ibid.*
[12] *Ibid.*

Czechoslovak armored train on Trans-Siberian Railway

May Day, 1918

Foreground, l-r: unidentified figure, Charles Stephenson Smith (AP correspondent), Jacob Peters, Raymond Robins, D. Heywood Hardy. On the tank, second from left, Alexander Gumberg

Approaching one of the series of tunnels on the Trans-Siberian Railway along Lake Baikal

Characteristic scene along the Trans-Siberian Railway near Chita

conveyed to the Soviet authorities, and the precise reaction of the latter—evidence is conflicting and confusing.[13] The most that can be said with any certainty is that the matter *was* discussed; that the reaction of the Soviet authorities was not unfavorable; that Chicherin issued some sort of an order to the local soviets along the railway, designed to implement the scheme; and that nothing in the reports of the Allied representatives in Russia to their governments during the month of May suggested that any appreciable difficulties had arisen.[14] The Allied chanceries were thus left under the impression that the project was in process of implementation. Actually, it was almost immediately overtaken and vitiated, unbeknownst initially to the Allied governments, by a further series of events in Russia and Siberia, of which it now becomes necessary to take note.

❖

By the beginning of May the Czech Corps was spread out all the way from the Penza area, west of the Volga, to Vladivostok, where the first trainloads were just arriving. A new interruption of its progress had been ordered by Moscow on April 21—occasioned, apparently, by news that Semenov had started a new offensive in the trans-Baikal area. Once more, therefore, difficulties were placed in the way of its progress by local Soviet authorities; the trains idled in stations or on sidings; restlessness and tension grew on both sides.

The Czech commanders on the spot, meanwhile, remained in complete ignorance of the policy decision, arrived at by the French and British governments, to split the Corps. According to Bunyan's account, they were therefore amazed when they learned, at the beginning of May, that Chicherin had issued a new order authorizing release of the trains east of Omsk for further passage to Vladivostok

---

[13] Whoever feels the inclination to exercise himself in the untangling of contradiction in historical sources on a minor point will do well to examine the statements on these questions of Bunyan, *op.cit.*, p. 74; Noulens, Vol. II, *op.cit.*, p. 84; Sadoul, *Notes . . . , op.cit.*, p. 338; Lockhart, *op.cit.*, p. 269; and the American Military Attaché, Ruggles, in *Foreign Relations, 1918, Russia*, Vol. II, *op.cit.*, p. 158. There is some question whether the representatives in Moscow did not actually anticipate the deliberations of the Supreme War Council. Lockhart, as will be seen below, mentioned to Robins in a letter of May 5 that Trotsky had already agreed to send the Czechs to Murmansk and Archangel.

[14] Trotsky later indicated that he asked only for assurance that shipping would actually be provided to remove the Czechs from Murmansk and Archangel, but that since Lockhart was unable to give such assurance the talks remained "inconclusive." Trotsky, *Sochineniya*, Vol. XVII, *op.cit.*, pp. 478–480.

but providing that those west of Omsk should be routed to the northern ports.[15] The amazement and consternation of the Czech commanders was increased when, on May 8, they received word from the representative of the Czechoslovak National Council at Vologda, Mr. Straka, that Chicherin's order had been issued by agreement with the Allied representatives in Russia. Their state of mind being what it was, the idea of splitting the Corps and thereby weakening such strength as it possessed seemed to them preposterous. They at once sent two envoys, Maxa and Markovič, to Moscow to find out what it was all about. Arriving in Moscow on May 13, the two envoys were told by General Lavergne that the change in route did indeed reflect the wishes of the Allies. They also saw Trotsky, who promised them that the Soviet authorities would assist in the transport of the First Division to Archangel.

Maxa and Markovič were about to return to Omsk, with a view to putting the new arrangements into effect, when the entire situation was changed by the receipt in Moscow of the news of an incident which had taken place at Chelyabinsk on May 14.[16] As luck would have it, one of the Czech troop trains standing in the station at Chelyabinsk found itself side by side with a trainload of Hungarian prisoners being evacuated from Siberia for repatriation. A stone or a piece of iron was thrown from the Hungarian into the Czech train and one of the Czech soldiers was killed by it. The Czechs retaliated by lynching the man who had thrown the missile.[17] The Soviet authorities immediately set about to investigate the matter. Several Czech soldiers, whose collaboration was desired as witnesses, were arrested and incarcerated in the local jail. A Czech delegation was sent to demand their release. The members of this delegation were also arrested. Thereupon the Czechs, on May 17, took armed action, seized the local arsenal, and liberated their comrades.

Within a few days, as it happened, this particular incident was amicably settled with the local Soviet authorities. Had things been left to the two parties on the spot, the Czechs would presumably

[15] Bunyan, *op.cit.*, p. 85.

[16] See *ibid.*, pp. 85–86 for issuance of Chicherin's order and the further data mentioned above.

[17] The account of this incident, as reported by the local Soviet military commissar, Sadlutski, to the War Commissariat in Moscow, is given verbatim in Jaroslav Kratochvíl, *Cesta Revoluce*, Praha, Čin, 1928, pp. 550–551.

have continued peacefully on their journey. But meanwhile, the receipt of the news of the Czech action at Chelyabinsk produced a violent reaction in Moscow. Two representatives of the Czechoslovak National Council, Maxa and one other, were at once arrested and obliged to sign a telegraphic order to the commanders of the Corps, telling them that all arms were to be delivered up at once to the Soviet authorities. A further order was then issued by Trotsky as Commissar for War to the Siberian soviets, directing them to detrain the Czech troops and "organize them into labor artels or draft them into the Soviet Red Army." [18]

These orders left to the commanders of the Corps no choice but to see the Corps disarmed, disbanded, and placed at the mercy of the local communist authorities, or to proceed to a complete break with the Soviet government.

The incident at Chelyabinsk had happened to coincide with the convening in that city of a "Congress of the Czechoslovak Revolutionary Army." This gathering had originally been arranged for the purpose of establishing the future organization and command status of the Corps and considering the difficulties that had arisen in connection with its movement eastward. The Chelyabinsk incident, occurring in the same city, naturally preoccupied the attention of the delegates during the first days of the meeting. It brought home to them, in particular, the realization of the looseness of the discipline exercised by the central Soviet authorities over the local soviets in Siberia. In these circumstances, the proposal for a splitting of the Corps aroused the most intense indignation and suspicion among the delegates. Unanimously, in the face of the outraged protestations of the French military representatives present, they voted to reject the project and to defy, in this respect, even the wishes of the Czechoslovak National Council and the Allies. [19]

It was in the midst of these events that the Congress received, on May 23, the new directive from the representatives of the Czecho-

---

[18] Bunyan, *op. cit.*, p. 88. There seems to be some uncertainty as to whether it was really the news of the Chelyabinsk incident that led to the arrest of these Czech representatives. The influence of the Czech Communists was unquestionably a factor. One would think that the Chelyabinsk incident must at least have been an important background factor.

[19] Klante, *op.cit.*, pp. 143–145. Dr. Klante, in preparing her valuable study, had access not only to the personal papers of Elsa Brändström, the Swedish Red Cross representative in Siberia in the 1918 period, but also to the Archive of the Czechoslovak Legion, in Prague.

slovak National Council, then under duress in Moscow, to the effect that all arms were to be delivered up to the Soviet authorities. A resolution was at once passed defying this directive as well and proclaiming the intention of retaining the arms and continuing on to Vladivostok. By the time the Czech commanders left Chelyabinsk on May 24, to return to their units, it is clear that they had agreed among themselves on some sort of operational plans for "shooting their way through," to be implemented immediately and without further ado, to whatever extent might be necessary, upon their return to their posts.

The news of the Chelyabinsk resolution was received within a matter of hours in Moscow, where it had a violent effect on the Soviet leaders. They reacted at once. On May 25, Trotsky despatched to the local soviets along the Siberian railway a telegram which began as follows:

All Soviets are hereby ordered to disarm the Czechoslovaks immediately. Every armed Czechoslovak found on the railway is to be shot on the spot; every troop train in which even one armed man is found shall be unloaded, and its soldiers shall be interned in a war prisoners' camp. Local war commissars must proceed at once to carry out this order; every delay will be considered treason and will bring the offender severe punishment. . . .[20]

In relaying this order to the local soviets, the central Soviet military authorities in Siberia added:

. . . If your forces are not adequate to disarm them, do everything possible to stop the echelons: side-track them, take their locomotives, in urgent cases tear up the railway tracks. . . .

It will thus be seen that by May 25 matters had come to a complete break between the Soviet government and the Czech Corps. Hostilities were now inevitable, by decision of both parties.

There has been a good deal of argument, subsequently, as to whether Trotsky's order for the breakup of the Czech force preceded or followed the Czech decision to fight the way through. The argument is idle. The Czechs took their decision before they had knowledge of Trotsky's telegram. Trotsky, when he sent the telegram, *did* have knowledge of the resolution of the Chelyabinsk Congress. In this sense, it may be said that the Czechs began the

[20] Bunyan, *op.cit.*, p. 91.

uprising. But they did so against the background of a long series of complications, in which rumor, confusion, and mistakes on the part of all concerned—Czechs, Bolsheviki, and Allies alike—played a part.

On May 26, hostilities between the Czechs and the Bolsheviki broke out all along the railway line from Penza to Irkutsk.

✦

It has been, from the outset, the official communist thesis that the Allies instigated the Czech uprising. On May 29, only three days after the outbreak of the hostilities between the Czechs and the Bolsheviki, Sadoul reported in one of his letters that Trotsky was convinced the Czech action was the result of a conspiracy between the Allies and the Russian oppositionists, that it was directed by French officers, and that it represented a species of dress rehearsal for a future Japanese intervention in Siberia.[21] Soviet historians have continued to reiterate the same thesis, in one form or another, down to the present day. At first it was the French and British to whom these suspicions—or professed suspicions—related. Later, at the height of the anti-American campaign following World War II, the United States was insinuated into the ranks of the guilty.[22]

How much truth is there in these charges? In view of the importance of the uprising for subsequent Allied, and particularly

---

[21] Sadoul, *Notes* . . . , *op.cit.,* p. 369.

[22] As evidences of these allegations we may note the following.

The official Soviet "History of Diplomacy" says that the uprising occurred "on the orders of the Entente." (Khvostov & Mints, Vol. II, *op.cit.,* p. 383.)

A. V. Berezkin, in a work for which he received the Stalin Prize in 1950 (*op.cit.,* p. 44), speaks of the plans of the "imperialists" in 1918 for a struggle against the Soviet republic, allowing it to be inferred that the "imperialists" in question were primarily the leaders of the American government. He then goes on to say: ". . . In accordance with these plans the Czechoslovak uprising was to serve as a signal for the uprising of the *kulaks* on the Volga and in Siberia; it was to hasten the process of gathering and organizing counterrevolutionary forces in Russia with the purpose of overthrowing Soviet power and restoring the bourgeois-landowner system." At another point, Berezkin refers to the uprising as "organized by the Anglo-French-American imperialists."

A. Ye. Kunina, in a volume bearing the significant title *Proval Amerikanskikh planov zavoyevaniya mirovogo gospodstva v 1917–1920 gg.* (The Fiasco of the American Plans for Achieving World Domination), State Publishing House of Political Literature, Moscow, 1954, says (p. 48): ". . . As a result of the direct instigation of the representatives of the U.S.A., England, and France and with their financial support there was organized a counterrevolutionary uprising of the Czechoslovak Corps against Soviet power."

American, policy with regard to the intervention, one cannot refrain from examining this question.

We have already reviewed in some detail the discussions among the Allied chanceries of the future of the Czech Corps. We have seen that never, in the course of these discussions, was mention made of even the idea that the Czechs should rise up and challenge, alone, Soviet authority. Some of their Allied planners had envisaged their being retained, partly, in Russia; but no one had said anything about their starting a counterrevolution in May 1918. The Czech leaders abroad, notably Masaryk and Beneš, were still exerting themselves to achieve the earliest possible removal of the entire Corps to France.

But how about the Allied representatives in Russia?

The Corps, it will be recalled, had by this time become an integral part of the Czechoslovak army in France and was technically under French command. The senior French officials in Russia—military and political—bore the immediate responsibility of giving guidance, on behalf of the Allies, to the commanders of the Corps and to the representatives in Russia of the Czechoslovak National Council. In the circumstances, with the various units strung out in trainloads all the way from Penza to Vladivostok, these lines of authority had unavoidably become tenuous and confused. It was generally recognized that operative decisions had to be left largely to the commanders of the Corps, to be decided by them in the light of circumstances. The commanders, as we have seen, defied the French over the proposal to split the Corps. Nevertheless, the principle of the Corps' subordination through Masaryk and the Czechoslovak National Council to the Allied cause, and to immediate French command, was never seriously questioned.

It was easy, in the confusions of 1918, to assume, as many did, that anything was likely to be true except the obvious; and it is intriguing even today to search for possible secret lines of authority, ulterior to the regular channel, running from the Allies to the Czechs and transmitting the impulses that resulted in the outbreak of hostilities. But nothing in the actual record suggests that either Ambassador Noulens or General Lavergne was a figurehead, or that the overt and legitimate channel of authority was anything but the authentic one. French officers—one with the advance body which reached Vladivostok in late April and early May and two with the central body involved in the uprising—were stationed with the Corps for liaison purposes at the time the trouble broke out. Although their advice was sometimes overridden by the commanders of the Corps on grounds of urgent local necessity, their right to be there and to have a voice in the counsels of the Corps was never seriously disputed. The officers with the central body of the Corps, in the Volga-Urals area, were Major Alphonse Guinet and Captain Pascal. In the days immediately preceding the uprising, they were on the southern branch of the railway, running from Penza and Samara (now Kuibyshev) to Kurgan, over which echelons of the Corps were then being moved. They were attending, as observers, the Chelyabinsk Congress.

The French representatives in Moscow and Vologda were much disturbed by the news of the Chelyabinsk incident, by the subsequent arrest of the two representatives of the Czechoslovak National Council, and by the defiance of the order for evacuation of the First Division via Archangel and Murmansk. They correctly saw the entire project of the removal of the Czechs to the western front, the execution of which they were under instructions to assure, as jeopardized by this development. The senior officers of the French Military Mission in Moscow at once concluded that the Czechs must now be told firmly that they must accept the Soviet order to disarm and rely on the benevolence and good faith of the Soviet authorities to assure their further movement to Vladivostok.

On learning of the Chelyabinsk incident, the chiefs of the French Military Mission despatched—on their own responsibility—an officer-courier to Guinet and Pascal, with instructions to tell the Czechs to submit to Soviet requirements—in other words, to disarmament. Then, it seems, they proceeded to Vologda, to enlist Noulens' support for the position they had taken. Noulens gives the following account of his meeting with these officers at Vologda:

The representatives of the Military Mission came running from Moscow to ask us to accept Trotsky's conditions—the only way, they said, of obviating the effects of his anger. I joined with the other Allied Chiefs of Mission to hear their views. Their arguments did not affect my conviction. Taking the floor after their statement, I defended before my colleagues the contrary thesis: that the Czechs had the right to leave with their arms; this right ought to be respected.

[155]

The Military Attachés argued against my point of view with such a passion that one of them, the American, went so far as to say to me: "You would not speak this way if it was a question of French soldiers."

I protested vehemently that I had too much esteem and sympathy for the Czechs to wish to treat them otherwise than as our own soldiers. . . .[23]

As a result of Noulens' insistence it was decided, he says, to annul the orders to the Czech Corps to accept disarmament at the hands of the Bolshevik authorities. By this time, however, the officer-courier despatched by the French Military Mission had already left with the earlier orders. It became necessary, Noulens recounts, to send another officer to countermand this order and to tell the Czechs of the new decision.

So much for Ambassador Noulens' account. Let us note, once more, the timing of these events. All this took place shortly after the arrest of the two chief Czech representatives in Moscow on May 14–15. The first courier was apparently sent on the heels of that event. Raymond Robins, as will be seen in another chapter, also left Moscow on the evening of May 14 on his journey to the United States, via Vologda and Siberia. He must have passed through Vologda the following day, May 15. The conference in Vologda described by Noulens did not take place until some time between May 20 and May 25.

An American observer, Professor Edward Alsworth Ross, subsequently had the following to say in a book about the Russian Revolution:

It is certain that on the train which bore the American Red Cross Mission across Siberia in May [this obviously refers to the train on which Robins was traveling] there were Frenchmen who at every station where there were Czechoslovaks held long and confidential colloquies with the officers.[24]

Ross took this as evidence, in retrospect, that the French had been behind the uprising. Robins presumably gained a similar impression.

This incident may well stand as an example of the dangers of drawing general conclusions from isolated phenomena in complex situations. The conclusion seems inescapable that what Ross observed was actually the activity of the first French courier-officer, sent to

[23] Noulens, Vol. II, *op.cit.,* pp. 85–86.

[24] Edward Alsworth Ross, *The Russian Soviet Republic,* Century Co., New York, 1923, p. 135.

tell the Czechs to submit.[25] The second emissary, sent after the conference in Vologda, could scarcely have reached the Urals district before the Czech uprising. The best evidence is that he actually arrived there on or about the last day of the month, four or five days after hostilities had begun.

From all of this it may be inferred that while Noulens, at some time between the Chelyabinsk incident (May 14) and the Czechoslovak uprising (May 25), had succeeded in imposing on his own military advisers and on the Allied official community in Vologda his view that the Czechs should be told to resist disarmament and detrainment and to "shoot their way out" to Vladivostok, and while a French military representative was indeed despatched, on the heels of this conference in Vologda, to the Urals and Siberia to acquaint the Czechs with this decision, these events had nothing whatsoever to do with the origin of the uprising. As of May 25, the French representatives on the spot, Guinet and Pascal, were both still under the impression that it was the desire of the French government that the Czechs should avoid, even at the cost of being disarmed and detrained, every sort of military involvement with the Soviet authorities. Even had the second order reached these French liaison officers and the Czechs before the uprising, which it did not, its tenor was merely to the effect that the first order was cancelled and the Czechs were not to be *forbidden* to take armed action to assure their passage to Vladivostok. Nothing was said about their being encouraged to enter in any way into the Russian civil war or about their remaining in Russia to take part in Allied intervention. Such thoughts had no doubt been entertained by individual Allied representatives even before the uprising; they were indeed soon to gain general currency in Allied circles and to have a considerable effect on Allied policy *after the uprising had occurred;* but there is no evidence that they played any serious part in the guidance given to the Corps by the Allies in advance of the outbreak of hostilities.

It is worth noting that even Sadoul, despite his violent differences

---

[25] The original disposition of the French military representatives in Russia to see the Czechs continue to Vladivostok and not become involved in any action against the Soviet authorities finds confirmation in a message Ruggles, in Vologda, sent to the War Department on May 10. In this message Ruggles said that it was the intention of the French government to send these troops to France at the earliest possible moment and that none of them were to be used for policing the railroads or for collaboration with an Allied intervention "unless requested by Russia." *Foreign Relations, 1918, Russia,* Vol. II, *op.cit.,* p. 158.

with Noulens and his heavy misgivings over Allied policy generally, was convinced at the time that Trotsky was wrong in his belief that the Allies had instigated the insurrection. It seems never to have occurred to him (and this is in itself significant, for he was well acquainted with the affairs of the French Military Mission) that such instigation could conceivably have come from the responsible French officials in Moscow or Vologda. The only possibility that occurred to him was that Guinet and Pascal might have exceeded their competence and encouraged the Czechs to revolt; and this possibility he at once rejected on the basis of his personal knowledge of both of these officers. Guinet seemed to him to be by nature incapable of participation in such a conspiracy. Of the other, "my friend, Lt. Pascal," he wrote:

. . . Although I am legitimately suspected of sympathy for the Bolshevik government, I have nevertheless not lost all critical sense and my sympathy is not without reservations. The admiration entertained by Pascal, a Tolstoyan Catholic, for a movement of which he appreciates above all the evangelical value—an admiration which has remained strictly in the speculative sphere (Pascal has never known a Bolshevik)—does not predispose him to any military action against the Soviets. He is furthermore the most disciplined and loyal of soldiers. I am convinced that both in obedience to orders and by personal conviction he has respected the instructions of the Mission which . . . are certainly not to fan the flames, even if they are also not to extinguish them. I said all this to Trotsky. It is only too obvious that France would have everything to lose in so deplorable an adventure which could only end sooner or later in the crushing of the unfortunate insurgents. The only serious utilization of the Czechs is on the western front, where they are awaited with enthusiasm.[26]

Somewhat later, to be sure, Sadoul would write with considerable bitterness about the Allied involvement in the *further course* of the Czech uprising; but this bitterness related to things the Allies did— as will be seen in a later chapter—*after* the uprising had taken place.

Sadoul's belief in the innocence of Guinet and Pascal is fully borne out by what is known of their behavior at the time of the uprising. At the Chelyabinsk Congress Guinet strongly pressed the Czech delegates to submit to disarming and to accept the orders of the Czechoslovak National Council. Shortly after the outbreak of

---

[26] Sadoul, *Notes* . . . , *op.cit.*, p. 369. Pascal subsequently became a distinguished scholar in the Slavic field, and has recently occupied the position of Professor of Russian Languages, Literature and Civilization at the Sorbonne.

hostilities Guinet found himself in Omsk where, on May 31, he participated in a local conference with Czech and Soviet representatives. The purpose of this conference was to try to find some peaceful solution of the situation at Isil Kul, just west of Omsk. Here, a party of Czechs had entered into hostilities with a communist force, and a menacing military deadlock had ensued. The conference was attended by the American Vice Consul, Mr. L. S. Gray. The Soviet representative read out an intercepted telegram from the Czech commander at Chelyabinsk to other Czech commanders along the line, telling them

. . . the situation had developed to such an extent that the French control would have to be disregarded for the time.[27]

Guinet thereupon despatched a telegram to the Czechs at Isil Kul of the following tenor:

Your action forces the French Mission to wash its hands of this affair. It will be a disgrace for the Czechs to become involved in Russian difficulties. If the Czechs persist in their activities everything must end between them and the French Government. The Czechs must take no action whatever until the French Mission [which was leaving Omsk immediately] arrives in Isilkul.[28]

This message makes it abundantly clear that as of May 31, Guinet had received no instructions envisaging retention by the Czechs of their arms or action by them against the Bolsheviki in support of a possible Allied intervention.

In all this background of the uprising the Americans were in no way involved, other than by the fact that Francis, in conference with his Allied colleagues in Vologda, supported the French Ambassador in the view that the Czechs ought not to be required to submit to disarmament and detrainment. When the uprising occurred, the American official representatives in the Siberian cities, as we shall also see in a later chapter, did everything in their power, even to the point of embarrassing and irritating the Czech commanders, to compose differences between the Czech and the local Soviet authorities and to facilitate the peaceful passage of the Czech trains to

[27] Ernest Lloyd Harris Papers, files of the American Consul General in Vladivostok for the period 1918–1920, Hoover Institute & Library, Stanford; Gray's report of November 10, 1918 entitled "Political Situation in the Omsk District, covering period from May 1918 to date."
[28] *Ibid.*

Vladivostok. There is not the slightest indication that they had any foreknowledge of the uprising or encouraged it in any way.

So much for what must be taken as the primary evidence as to direct Allied involvement. In addition to this, we must take note of the further possibility, implicit in some of the statements from the communist side, that the uprising was the result of some sort of prearrangement between the Czechs and the Russian oppositionist parties, of which the Allies had knowledge and to which—despite their own contrary official position in the matter—they gave at least tacit encouragement.

It would carry us too far from the central theme of this study to attempt to describe at this point the various opposition groupings which were active in European Russia in the spring of 1918 and to reproduce and analyze in detail the individual bits of evidence concerning their relationship to the Allies and the Czechs. The nature and significance of this evidence might, however, be summarized as follows.

The Soviet historian P. S. Parfenov, in works published in the early 1920's, alleged that the central military staff of the Social-Revolutionary Party "learned" in April 1918 that Lavergne and Lockhart were engaged, together with members of a conservative underground officers' group, in working out plans for the overthrow of Soviet power and the restoration of Russian military resistance to Germany, and that these plans envisaged using the Czechs, in coordination with the Russian opposition groups, to seize the Siberian railways and destroy the Soviet forces in the Siberian area. Parfenov even speaks, in another place, of a meeting of April 14 at the French Military Mission in Moscow, where representatives of the British, French, Czechs, and Russian opposition groups were said to be present. Lockhart and a Captain Konshin, shown as being in contact with an underground officers' group in Novo-Nikolayevsk (now Novosibirsk), are specifically named as having been present.[29]

[29] P. S. Parfenov, *Grazhdanskaya voina v Sibiri* (The Civil War in Siberia), State Publishing House, Moscow, 1924. See also John Albert White, *The Siberian Intervention*, Princeton University Press, Princeton, 1950, pp. 249-250. White cites another volume by Parfenov: *Uroki proshlago, grazhdanskaia voina v Sibiri 1918, 1919, 1920 gg.* (Lessons of the Past, The Civil War in Siberia), Harbin, pp. 29-32. The name of Captain Konshin also appears in the "Sisson documents" (*The German-Bolshevik Conspiracy*, War Information Series, No. 20-October, 1918, Issued by the Committee on Public Information, George Creel, Chairman, Document No. 2)—a circumstance which does not contribute to the reliability of Parfenov's story.

A similar report is to be found in a despatch reviewing the history of the origins of the Kolchak regime in Siberia, written somewhat later (1919) by American Consul Alfred R. Thomson, who had been stationed at the key point of Omsk at the time of the Czech uprising. Thomson also mentions the presence of Lockhart and Lavergne at an alleged meeting of this nature, and goes on to say that the Czechs

... were to have been asked to begin their hostilities against the Bolsheviki later than they actually did; but the German Government ... urged Trotsky to disarm the Czecho-Slovaks, and thus precipitated the crisis earlier than had been designed.[30]

Parfenov's allegations, which do not appear to be substantiated by any proof or citation of source, make—on various counts—a highly unreliable impression. They could, in fact, have been written only by someone who was not familiar with the circumstances in which the Czech Corps found itself at that time and with its relations, generally, with the Allies. What is said about Lockhart and Lavergne accords with nothing else that is known (and a great deal *is* known) about the official endeavors and personal inclinations of those two men at the time. Thomson's statement, also proffered without any indication of source, was evidently based on secondhand accounts he had heard from Russian officials in Siberia in the Kolchak time; and cannot be taken as solid historical evidence. The reference to the German government, incidentally, is flatly incorrect, and represents simply the gossip then current in Siberia.

The closest friends of the Czechs, on the Russian political scene, were the Right S-R's. With them the Czechs had both an ideological bond (their sympathies lying—for the most part—somewhere between the "bourgeois" parties and the Bolsheviki) and an organizational bond—through the leaders in the Siberian section of the Russian cooperative movement. The cooperatives were largely a movement of the independent peasantry (particularly strong in western Siberia). They were naturally close to the S-R's, who were outstandingly the peasants' party. A number of leaders of the cooperative movement in Siberia were prominent in S-R circles. The Czechs concluded a contract with the Siberian cooperatives for the supply of food to the Corps on its movement across Siberia. This placed the commanders of the Corps in close touch with the cooperative

[30] Harris MSS, *op.cit.*, despatch of August 16, 1919 from Consul Alfred R. Thomson, on special detail at Omsk, to the Department of State.

leaders and the S-R's all along the line. Since the Czech uprising was immediately followed, and in some instances even accompanied, by uprisings of local Russian groups against the Bolsheviki—uprisings in which the S-R's played a leading part, especially at the outset—the question at once arises as to whether there was instigation of the Czech action by the S-R's.

There were two main centers where Russian groups took military and political action against the Bolsheviki in the immediate wake of the Czech action. In both instances, the S-R's were prominently involved. One was Samara, on the Volga; the other, central Siberia, in particular the region of Omsk and Novo-Nikolayevsk. In each case plans for an insurrection against the Bolsheviki by the S-R's and secret groups of ex-officers had been worked out long in advance of the Czech action. But in each case the target dates envisaged were ones considerably later than the end of May. There is no reason to doubt that the anti-communist leaders concerned— well aware of the situation of the Czech Corps, of its potential strength, and of the difficulties it was experiencing with the Soviet authorities—hoped that the Czechs would in some way contribute to their own contemplated actions.[31] But that was quite a different thing from instigating the Czechs to rise up on May 26.

In the case of the Samara group the best historical evidence indicates that the local underground S-R leaders had no idea that any Czech action was forthcoming at the end of May, and learned of it only subsequently by reports from Moscow. When they did learn of it, they at once got into touch with the Czechs, of course, in order to coordinate further actions.[32]

As for Omsk and Novo-Nikolayevsk, this was a very special situation. Novo-Nikolayevsk was not only the seat of the military staff of the S-R Party but the center, generally, of the underground officers' activity in Siberia. A leading figure in this activity was the young Russian officer Grishin-Almazov. Although the officer-con-

[31] In the foreword of a book by B. Solodovnikov on Gajda's part in the Siberian civil war (*Sibirskie avantyury i General Gaida* [The Siberian Adventures and General Gajda], Prague, n.d.) the following passage occurs: "As early as the beginning of May 1918 I met on one occasion in Moscow, in the apartment of the lawyer Vilenkin and in the presence of the Colonel of the General Staff N. Poradelov, with the well-known S-R, Colonel V. I. Lebedev, and gained the understanding that in preparing their uprising, the S-R's were placing hopes on the Czechoslovaks."

[32] M. V. Vishnyak, *Vserossiiskoye uchreditelnoye sobraniye* (The All-Russian Constituent Assembly), Publishing House "Sovremennyya Zapiski," Paris, 1932, pp. 148–149.

spirators were generally not of socialist persuasion and viewed the
S-R's with much suspicion, Grishin-Almazov believed, at that time,
in the necessity of a collaboration between the two groups in action
against the Bolsheviki. He therefore worked closely together with
the S-R military staff in the same city.

The commander of the central group of Czech trains, with headquarters at Novo-Nikolayevsk, was, as it happened, a young Czech
officer who was later to gain much notoriety as an adventurer and
fire-eater: Rudolph Gajda.[33] Strongly anti-Bolshevik and thirsting
for violent action, Gajda was the principal moving spirit behind the
decision taken at the Chelyabinsk Congress to defy the Bolsheviki
and fight the way out to Vladivostok. As a result of the obstacles
placed by the Soviet authorities in the path of the Czech movement,
his command had been detained at Novo-Nikolayevsk for some
time prior to the uprising. There he had become acquainted with
the underground Russian officers' group, whose views and impatience
for action he fully shared. Far from being pressed by them to take
action against the Bolsheviki, Gajda did his best to induce them to
rise up against the local Soviet authority, promising them Czech
support if they did. "You just start in," he is said to have assured
Grishin-Almazov, "and we'll take care of the Bolsheviki." [34] When
the Czechs themselves then decided to take action, Gajda at once
coordinated his activity locally with that of the Russian group, and
the two organizations moved together to overthrow Soviet authority
in the entire area from Omsk through Novo-Nikolayevsk to
Krasnoyarsk.

The Czechs, through their contacts with Gajda and others, were
well informed of the strength of the anti-Soviet sentiment in central
Siberia and of the existence of the underground officers' groups,
straining to seize power at the earliest possible moment. When, at
the Chelyabinsk Conference, they arrived at the decision to shoot
their way through if necessary, the Czechs had these circumstances
in mind. But their purpose at that moment was only to assure their
own security and safe passage. Aside from the purely local situation

---

[33] In addition to causing a good deal of trouble during the course of the Siberian
intervention, Gajda later became—in the Hitler period—the leader of a small Czech
fascist party which the Nazis toyed with—halfheartedly and unsuccessfully—as a
means of sowing dissension and gaining influence among the Czechs.

[34] P. N. Milyukov, *Rossiya na perelomye* (Russia at the Crossroads), Imprimerie
d'Art Voltaire, Paris, 1927, Vol. ii, *Anti-Bolshevik Movement*, p. 32.

at Novo-Nikolayevsk there seems to have been nothing at all that could be described as a "plot" between the Czechs and the Russian Whites. The situation was well described in an official Czech account of the origins of the uprising, drawn up during the immediate aftermath of these events by the Temporary Executive Committee of the Czechoslovak army, entrusted by the Chelyabinsk Congress with the further direction of the military operations and political negotiations of the Corps:

. . . the Czecho-Slovaks from their intimate knowledge of political conditions throughout Russia judged that the feeling against the Bolsheviks was strongest in the very regions where most of their eschelons were located, namely in the Urals and western Siberia. The executive committee, therefore, in planning their action, took cognizance of these facts, and planned to take advantage both of the weakness of the Red Army and of the strong popular feeling against the Bolsheviks to force their way through to the east. That their action would be accompanied by or followed by the overthrow of the Soviet Government and the establishment of a new government in western Siberia never entered into their calculations, although later when the fall of the Soviet government was an accomplished fact, the Czecho-Slovaks were the first to welcome the new government and to lend it their moral and armed support.[35]

All in all, therefore, one is reduced to the conclusion that external instigation or encouragement, either from the Allies or from the central headquarters of the underground Whites, played no significant part in the decision of the Czechs to take arms against Soviet power. The outbreak of these hostilities was a spontaneous occurrence, resulting from decisions and actions promulgated, respectively and almost simultaneously, by the Soviet authorities in Moscow and in Siberia and by the Czech commanders on the spot. It was a development desired by none of the parties concerned— neither by the Bolsheviki nor by the Allies, nor by the majority of the Czechs themselves.

It is idle to attempt to find in this occurrence the reflection of any deliberate conspiracy or of any special duplicity on one side or the other. Neither side was without provocation in the events that led to it, and neither was without blame. Its reasons must be sought primarily in the general climate of confusion and suspicion that

---

[35] Harris MSS, *op.cit.*, from an English translation of the paper in question, undated, entitled "The Czecho-Slovak Incident."

prevailed at this culminating moment of war and revolution; in the extremely complex situation in which the Czech Corps then found itself; in the complicating factor of the presence of large numbers of the war prisoners of the Central Powers, partly bol-shevized and partly not so, all along the Siberian line; in the abundant rumors of German instigation of Soviet actions; and in the inadequacy of the disciplinary bonds that ran both from the Allies to the Czechs and from the Soviet government in Moscow to the local soviets throughout Siberia.

Bearing in mind these factors it is easy to see that the Czech Corps, representing at the moment—as it did—the strongest compact and unified armed force in all of Siberia, could hardly fail to become, willingly or unwillingly, a factor in the state of smoldering civil conflict that had been brought into being throughout Siberia by the sudden communist seizure of power. Had the Corps succeeded in making its way peacefully through the vast tinderbox of central Siberia during the spring of 1918, striking no sparks and raising no crucial issues as it went along, this—rather than what actually oc-curred—would have been the true wonder.

CHAPTER VII

~~~~~~

ROBINS AND SUMMERS

~~~~~~

THE move of the Soviet government to Moscow, in the first part of March, increased greatly the burdens, responsibilities, and problems of Consul General Maddin Summers. The long Russian winter, the pressure of war work, and the excitements of the times, operating on a relentlessly conscientious nature, had undermined his health. In normal circumstances he would have been due, at this juncture, for a long vacation and recuperation. Instead of that, the city in which he functioned as senior representative of the United States government now suddenly became the political, as well as the economic, capital of the great Russian land; there was now a central, as well as a local, authority to be watched, dealt with, and reported on; a horde of new faces, many of them American, appeared on the local scene; the Consulate General's responsibilities for protection of American interests were suddenly engaged, as never before, by the harassment to which American business interests in Russia were being increasingly subjected at communist hands throughout Russia. Far from being able to take a vacation, Summers found himself inundated with new demands on his time, his attention, and his strength.

This situation was not eased by the appearance in Moscow of Raymond Robins and the other members of the Red Cross Commission. Summers had no high opinion of the Red Cross Commission. Like others of the official family, he had resented from the start its intrusion into matters that were normally the responsibility of the regular governmental representatives. He had unfavorable recollections (based on a most regrettable misunderstanding) of the behavior of those members of the Red Cross Commission who had found themselves in Moscow at the time of the heavy street fighting in November. He was familiar with Robins' general attitude towards the Soviet regime, disagreed violently with it, and considered the very expression of it to be a form of service to the Germans. So long as Robins had remained in Petrograd, Summers had been able to console himself with the reflection that the responsibility for tolerating Robins' activities was the Ambassador's, not his own. He was now forced to recognize, in the light of Robins' presence in Moscow and of his own new responsibility for reporting on the affairs of the central Soviet authority, that his reports and Robins' would henceforth be in direct competition. It would be up to him, now, to balance out and set to rights any misimpression that Robins might gather and convey to Washington.

As for Robins—he had been greatly disturbed, to be sure, at the time of his arrival in Moscow, by the failure of the United States government to reply to what he took to be a sincere Soviet offer of collaboration against Germany, as expressed in Trotsky's questions of March 5.[1] He continued to be worried by the hesitancy, if not downright opposition to his purposes, which that failure seemed to reveal. He felt that time was running out. Once the German representatives arrived in Moscow and began to cash in on the advantages of the Brest-Litovsk Treaty, it would be too late, he feared, to save Russia from German domination and exploitation. But he was heartened, upon Trotsky's arrival (March 18), by the abundant evidence that Trotsky continued to mistrust German intentions and was serious about exploring possibilities for military collaboration with the Allies. The news that it might be some time before the German representatives would reach Moscow, coupled with the realization that the rumors of Allied intervention in Siberia were at least premature, meant that the breathing-space Lenin had cited as justification for concluding the Brest-Litovsk Treaty might still be turned to Allied, as well as Soviet, advantage.

In these rather desperate hopes, Robins was supported, as we have seen, by his newly arrived British opposite number, Lockhart. And Robins' freedom to pursue these hopes was enhanced, as he saw it initially, by the removal of the Allied ambassadors to a spot in which it would be far more difficult for them to control, to participate in, or to interfere with, such contacts as he and Lockhart and Sadoul might maintain with the Soviet authorities. The situation was further aided by the good feeling which developed between Robins

[1] See Volume i, Chapter xxiv.

and Francis at the time of the removal of the Embassy to Vologda, and particularly by the extent to which Francis appeared to have accepted, and espoused, Robins' belief in the fatal folly of any Allied intervention that did not have Soviet approval. Thus Robins swallowed his disappointment over the failure of the United States government to respond to Trotsky's questions in time to affect, as he had hoped, the ratification of the Brest-Litovsk Treaty; [2] and he had set out, with the buoyant enthusiasm and mystical faith that were the marks of his character, to make one more try to prevent the threatened catastrophe: a try as gallant and sincere as it would be disastrous to himself and others.

Robins and Summers, it should be noted, did not disagree in their view of the danger to be combatted. Both feared an effective German conquest of Russia—economic, if not military—and both exaggerated the possibility of it. Both felt, with an intensity that speaks for their patriotic earnestness, that this German conquest must, at all costs, be prevented. But their respective views as to *how* this was to be accomplished clashed violently. Summers, believing the Bolsheviki to be German agents, felt that only the destruction of Bolshevik power could avert the danger. Robins was confident that the Soviet leaders were far from being German agents, and felt that the danger could be averted only by winning the confidence of the Soviet leaders and cultivating their collaboration. Both men, as it happened, were largely wrong in the premises underlying their respective convictions. Summers was wrong in believing the Bolsheviki to be German agents. Robins was wrong in supposing that they could be made, over a short time, into reliable and effective allies. Official Washington, with its belief that the decisive factor would not be the course of events in Russia but the happenings on the western front, where the last great German offensive was just beginning, was closer to the truth.

The troubles, as between Summers and Robins, were not long in beginning. Within a few days after Robins' move to Moscow, differences of opinion began to be evident in the reports of the two men. In each case, the wish was partially father to the thought.

[2] Robins did not know, and was never to learn, that the despatch of Trotsky's questions had been held up by the Military Attaché, Colonel Ruggles, and that the actual text of the document did not reach Washington until several days after the treaty was ratified.

Summers thought Soviet power was disintegrating; Robins thought it was being consolidated. Robins placed hopes on the development of Allied military collaboration with the Soviet government. Summers scoffed at the Soviet effort to re-create a fighting force, and stamped as "unpromising" any hopes of Allied collaboration in it.

This conflict of views tended to become increasingly irritating and worrisome to both men. Each felt that the public interest was importantly at stake, and saw in the other a danger to it. Both, in these circumstances, turned to Francis and sought his support. Robins, profiting from his excellent relations with the Soviet leaders, had arranged—soon after his arrival in Moscow—for use at a given hour each night of a direct telegraphic circuit with Francis at Vologda. (This arrangement, suggesting as it did that Robins was the senior American official in Moscow, can scarcely have failed to grate on the susceptibilities of Summers, who enjoyed no such facilities.) In the somewhat intensive exchanges he conducted with the Ambassador over this channel, Robins gave vent—tersely but with obvious seriousness—to the feelings he entertained for Summers' views and their effects. He bore, it should be said in justice to him, little personal rancor, if any. His eyes were fixed on higher things—to the point of impersonality—and one feels that he had as little personal hatred for Summers as he had sympathy for him in his trials and efforts. Summers, he said to Francis in one of their private telegraphic exchanges (on March 23), was "an able business man and delightful gentleman," but had, alas, no confidence in collaboration with the Soviet government. Why, he had even favored support of the Ukrainian Rada and the anti-Bolshevik Cossack general, Kaledin.[3]

Robins was particularly impatient and alarmed over the reports, which he knew to be supported by Summers, that the Bolsheviki were German agents. When he learned that the Department of State, pondering the various recommendations for military collaboration with the Bolsheviki, had suggested to Francis that the Soviet leaders

. . . must be suspected of acting on orders from German staff with a view to diverting Entente efforts from western front. . . .[4]

[3] Cumming & Pettit, *op.cit.*, p. 110.
[4] *Foreign Relations, 1918, Russia*, Vol. I, *op.cit.*, p. 486; March 23 telegram to Francis from SECSTATE.

his pot boiled over. The suggestion, he told Francis, was absurd and impossible. "If Washington credits this contention," he asked, "why are we wasting time here?" [5]

In vain Francis tried to explain that the Department hadn't *said* this; it merely stated that it had such a report. Robins returned repeatedly to the charge. He recognized the tenacity of the belief in Allied circles that the Bolsheviki were German agents, and was justifiably afraid of the damage it might do. He was convinced, he wired to his former aide Thacher (now in London) on March 27th, that the Soviet government was "hostile to Germany." [6] The Soviet government, he wired to Francis on April 4, following a conference with Lenin the previous evening,

. . . is eager to satisfy America of good faith and secure economic organization through American supervising skill, but, if every evil rumor becomes foundation for suspicion, co-operation will be impossible. . . . [7]

Never does it appear to have occurred to these Americans to sit down together and go over the evidence calmly and patiently in an attempt to arrive at a common outlook on this vital question. Summers, who had his information from the anti-Soviet opposition parties, no doubt feared that Robins—or Robins' personal aide, Alexander Gumberg—would, if made privy to this information, reveal the sources of it to the Bolsheviki; and he was not lacking in grounds for such suspicion. There was no reason to suppose that Robins had any secrets from Gumberg; and Gumberg was, after all, a Soviet citizen, the brother of one Soviet official, and the intimate of many others. Robins would almost surely have entertained the converse suspicion: he would have asked himself, that is, why he should jeopardize the priceless confidence he enjoyed with the Soviet leaders by revealing what they told him to Summers, who might only be expected to pass it on to the opposition parties. Thus the two men went their respective ways in bitterness and suspicion. And while Robins continued to pour in his bitter complaints over the credence given to the thesis of German control, Summers continued to assure the Department of State and Francis that all the opposition parties were persuaded that

[5] Cumming & Pettit, *op.cit.*, p. 114.
[6] *Ibid.*, p. 116.
[7] *Ibid.*, p. 130.

the policies of the Soviet regime were directed solely by the German General Staff.[8]

Throughout late March and April, the telegraphic correspondence between the American offices in Moscow, Vologda, and Washington was replete with reflections of the tension between these two leading American figures in Moscow. Today, the issues may look petty. One must make allowance for the extreme tensions, the wartime feelings, and the highly charged political atmosphere of the time —an atmosphere in which small things often seemed symbolic of bigger ones. When the Moscow press carried a curious report to the effect that the American Consul had said that United States government would resume commercial and industrial relations with Russia regardless of the repudiation of debts by the Soviet government, Robins joyfully relayed this item to Francis, with the insinuation that Summers had exceeded his competence.[9] When the ire of Summers and the other official Americans was aroused by the action of the Soviet municipal authorities in supporting an anarchist group against the American Military Attaché's office in a dispute over occupancy of some rather luxurious premises the latter had been using, Robins counterattacked vigorously. What was involved in the occupation of these premises by foreign diplomats was, he wired to Francis, an effort to protect the large palace and wine cellar of a Russian prince: he considered this a misuse of the American flag. The effort to make an international incident out of the occurrence was, he said, "entirely unwarranted by the facts." He was telling this to the Ambassador confidentially, he added; he had no desire to make trouble for anyone, but he would not

. . . allow stupid incident to be used against co-operation either here or in America, if I can help it, . . .[10]

Further trouble developed out of the attempts to aid a group of Serbian refugees who were stranded in central Siberia. The Y.M.C.A. representatives on the spot wanted the Red Cross Commission to help. Summers wanted to handle the matter himself, using funds

[8] *Foreign Relations, 1918, Russia*, Vol. I, *op.cit.*, pp. 501–502; Summers' telegram 367, April 17, 1 p.m.
[9] Cumming & Pettit, *op.cit.*, pp. 119–120; also Francis' telegram to SECSTATE March 29, 9 p.m., *Foreign Relations, 1918, Russia*, Vol. I, *op.cit.*, p. 488.
[10] Cumming & Pettit, *op.cit.*, pp. 131–132.

made available to him from private American sources for philan-thropic purposes. Confusion and cross-purposes developed. Francis tried, from his distance of 250 miles away, to straighten out the tangled lines of authority. His final decision was that this was proper Red Cross work; Summers had been wrong to get into it. Unfor-tunately, in apprising Robins of this decision, the Ambassador sug-gested a certain lack of confidence in Summers by asking Robins, over the telegraphic circuit, "What business relations has Summers with Soviet?" [11] With alacrity Robins took advantage of this open-ing. Summers' relations with the Soviet authorities, he hastened to assure Francis, were confined to the Moscow Soviet—i.e., the local municipal government. Summers was unknown to the national leaders. He had been unable even to obtain a correct copy of the Brest-Litovsk Treaty until Robins procured one for him. He was now trying to get a map of the boundaries prescribed in the treaty; but this, too, Robins would have to obtain for him. He had been unable to help the International Harvester Company in its dif-ficulties with the Soviet authorities; Robins had finally seen Lenin about it and had gotten the desired results.

Robins could not resist driving the nail home with reflections on the efficacy of Summers' attitude toward the Soviet authorities. Busi-ness relations, he pointed out, were not usually strengthened through a policy of "kicking people in the face." A constant desire for the overthrow of Soviet power, together with the expectation of it, was a poor foundation, Robins observed, for cooperation with it in practical matters.[12]

Francis was troubled by this friction between the two senior figures in the official American group at Moscow. He repeatedly brought it to the Department's attention,[13] but made no recommendations for resolving the unhappy situation. Summers he respected; and Summers was practically irreplaceable. But Robins was increasingly useful as a source of information; and Robins, too, had influence at home. So he vacillated again, as was his nature, and tried to patch things up on the spot. On March 20 he wired Robins, anxiously,

. . . Of course you are doing nothing to impair Summers' efficiency as consul. He is consul general. . . . Has extended experience, possesses

[11] *Ibid.*, p. 147.
[12] *Ibid.*, p. 149.
[13] *Foreign Relations, 1918, Russia,* Vol. I, *op.cit.*, p. 485, telegram of March 22; p. 487, telegram of March 26; p. 488, telegram of March 29, etc.

confidence of Department which has recently warmly commended his services.[14]

In early April Summers made a special trip to Vologda, apparently to carry to the Ambassador his complaints about Robins. Francis listened to him, and was almost moved to the point of asking for Robins' removal. But he could not quite make it.[15] He let Summers return with no clear answer, hoping—he later claimed—that he had him "reconciled to Robins' presence in Moscow."

Just at the time of Summers' visit two things occurred which greatly exacerbated Robins' already aroused feelings. First, there was the incident of the Japanese landing, for which—as we have seen— he was personally called to account by Chicherin. Robins, like the Soviet authorities, took this incident at the time as the probable precursor of full-fledged Allied intervention in Siberia, and received the news of it with much bitterness of feeling. The reader will recall (see Chapter IV) his statement to Francis to the effect that

. . . We are now at most dangerous crisis in Russian situation, and if colossal blunder of hostile Japanese intervention takes place all American advantages are confiscated.

On the heels of this came the news, relayed by Francis from the Department of State, that the Department forbade any extension to the Soviet government of military support. This put an end, as has been seen, to American participation in the talks looking toward military collaboration between the Allies and the Soviet authorities, and ruined one of Robins' fondest dreams. It is wholly possible that since the message bearing this bad news came from Vologda, he attributed it to the influence of Summers, who was then there, and supposed that Summers' journey had been for the purpose of spiking all progress toward military cooperation.

In the light of these reverses, Robins began to press vigorously for Francis' removal to Moscow and for the establishment of the Embassy in that city. In early March he had encouraged Francis to remain in Vologda; but by the beginning of April he had concluded that the Ambassador's presence in Moscow was necessary as a counterweight to the influence of Summers. He approached Francis

[14] Cumming & Pettit, *op.cit.*, p. 122.
[15] National Archives, State Department File 123 Su 61/121; telegram from Francis to SECSTATE, April 20.

several times with such suggestions. "Your coming," he wired on April 20, ". . . would greatly advantage American interests." If the Allies were to remain at Vologda while the Germans and Austrians opened embassies in Moscow, the Allies, he pointed out, would be at a great disadvantage. Unless there was to be organized opposition to the Soviet regime, there would have to be organized cooperation with it. The "micawber policy" that was being followed was becoming daily more impossible. The Soviet government was constantly requesting technical assistance of all kinds. The Russian economic system would have to be reorganized under either German or American supervision and support. This was the greatest economic and cultural enterprise left to accomplish in the world. In determining the outcome, Francis' position and his influence would be a decisive factor.[16]

These were powerful arguments, but Francis was unmoved. Washington had repeatedly approved his policy of watchful waiting. A move to Moscow would be hardly distinguishable from recognition. The State Department had wired him only recently (March 23) that while it relied on his discretion and judgment to determine his "movements and matters not affecting policy of this Government," it did not wish "to modify in any way previous instructions as to recognition of Soviet government." [17] And in the message disapproving military assistance (April 5) it had said:

. . . Department concurs in your general estimates of Bolsheviki, and approves your decision to feel your way to certainty before making positive recommendation.[18]

Thus Francis remained unreceptive to Robins' appeals; and this further frustration was added to those Robins was already experiencing.

❖

Shortly after Summers' visit to Vologda an incident took place which served to heighten greatly Robins' confidence both in the stability of Soviet power and the good faith of the Soviet leaders.

The Soviet leaders had been bedeviled, in the early months of their power, by anarchist factions which were not part of the Bolshevik

[16] Cumming & Pettit, *op.cit.*, pp. 152–153.
[17] *Foreign Relations, 1918, Russia*, Vol. I, *op.cit.*, p. 487.
[18] *Ibid.*, p. 495.

movement, were so undisciplined that they were difficult to control, and yet were close enough ideologically to the Bolshevik Revolution so that the Soviet authorities were at first inclined to tolerate them as harmless, if sometimes annoying, fellow-travelers. After the move to Moscow, the activities of the anarchists, combining disorder and brutality with a good deal of debauchery, began to get out of hand. Refusing, on principle, to submit to Soviet authority or to any other, they became increasingly a problem to the Bolsheviki. The latter worried over the possibility that the anarchists might adopt a hostile and provocative attitude toward the German diplomatic representative, due soon to arrive in the Soviet capital. Some of the Allied representatives, on the other hand, saw the anarchists as likely German agents, and pointed to their seemingly privileged position as proof of the German influence in Moscow.

On the evening of April 9 Robins' car was surrounded and sequestered by a group of these anarchists. A few days earlier, when the anarchists had invaded the premises of the Military Mission, Robins had shown little sympathy for the Americans whose interests were affected. Now, however, it was his own car that was gone. With the usual dramatization of his own position, he decided to view the incident, and to portray it to the Soviet authorities, as a test of Bolshevik authority within the country and freedom from German influence. It will be well to let him tell the rest in his own language:

. . . I went that afternoon to the foreign minister, Tchitcherin, and made a simple statement of the facts. I said, "I know this is a rough game, and this is probably just done for my comfort to make me quit the play, but I want that automobile, and I want a show of definite power in the situation. There are those who say that the power is over there at 9 Duvorskaya [undoubtedly this should have been "9 Povarskoye," one of the anarchist headquarters] and those who say that the power is in the Kremlin. I have been saying it is in the Kremlin, and I want to know where the power is."

I was promised my automobile that afternoon. The afternoon came, but not the automobile. I went to see Derjinski [Felix Dzerzhinski, new chief of the secret police] of the committee on counter revolution and sabotage. He said, "I will get your automobile." Later on he called up and said that he could not get it until the next day. There seemed to be backing and filling. I went to see Trotsky and talked with Trotsky about it. I went to see Lenine and talked to Lenine about it. I said, "Now, I do not give two raps about the automobile, but I want to know where the power is in Moscow. I have said it is in your hands. If it is over here with the anarchists, I know where that leads back to. It leads back to German control, and I am going to know." [19]

Robins' intensive complaints evidently caused considerable concern to the Soviet leaders. Their hopes depended, in many respects, on the creation of the impression with the Allied governments and elsewhere that their hold on Russia was firm and that it was idle for foreign governments to attempt to deal with other Russian factions. Robins had theretofore been the principal agency in relaying this impression to the United States. This is probably the reason why he received, on April 10, a personal note from Chicherin, handwritten in English, and reading in part as follows:

I am exceedingly sorry about the untoward event that has happened to you, and I am sure that very soon our friends will succeed in returning to you your automobile. You are aware how drastic the measures are, which our Government applies against robbers, marauders, etc. You know how many of these were shot down in Petrograd and are shot down in Moscow by order of the "Extraordinary Committee," but we are just going through the period of the sudden disappearance of the multi-secular system of universal despotism and blind obedience, and the stormy growth of the exuberant and buoyant new proletarian and peasant society cannot go on quite smoothly. At the present stage our Government is the only one which can afford to apply such violent measures against robberies. I await with confidence the early return to you of your machine, and I am sure that you will clearly discern the real position. Who knows who these aggressors were? And if by this opportunity you blame the physical feebleness of our Government (although it is the strongest one, possible in Russia now), the more clear is the moral power of a Government which, with such insufficient means of coercion, is so firmly established and deeply rooted. . . .[20]

The following day, apparently, Trotsky asked Robins to come to his office again, and explained the embarrassment of the Soviet government with regard to the anarchists. The latter, he said, had helped the Bolsheviki "in our hour of revolution" and there were those Bolsheviki who were reluctant to take action against them. Elections were being held just at this time in the various factories.

[19] *Bolshevik Propaganda, Hearings before a Subcommittee of the Committee on the Judiciary, United States Senate, Sixty-Fifth Congress,* Government Printing Office, Washington, 1919, p. 823.
[20] Raymond Robins MSS, Wisconsin State Historical Society, Madison.

The Mensheviki and the other opposition groups were charging the Soviet government with brutality. Therefore they did not wish to take armed action against the anarchists until after the elections.

"Well," said Robins (we are following here the oral account he gave to the investigating Senators in 1919),

. . . I do not care about a few days, but I want a definite expression of power in this situation, so we can know where we are, or I am going to cable my Government that there is a real question as to who is running this show."

Three days later, Robins continued,

. . . the last election having taken place, I was called up on the telephone, and he said: "At 2 o'clock to-morrow morning . . . we are going to move against the anarchist centers. . . ." . . . Every center was taken by about 6:30 in the morning. . . .

Now, this was another demonstration of power against what . . . I now believe to have been a definite German interest.

. . . I got my automobile, unscratched, . . .[21]

So far as the action of the Soviet government against the anarchists is concerned, Robins' account is substantially correct. On the 12th of April, a major action was undertaken to bring the anarchists under control. The action was mounted at 3:00 a.m. and led to hundreds of arrests as well as to a large number of casualties on the spot. Lockhart and Robins followed up the Soviet detachments in company with Dzerzhinski's assistant, Jacob Peters. The anarchists had made it a practice to commandeer for their own uses the palaces of the wealthiest merchants. Many of them were caught in the midst of their social debauches. In depicting the scenes resulting from the raid, Lockhart, a more sober and accurate chronicler than Robins, has given us one of his unforgettable descriptions:

. . . we entered house after house. The filth was indescribable. Broken bottles littered the floors. The magnificent ceilings were perforated with bullet-holes. Wine stains and human excrement blotched the Aubusson carpets. Priceless pictures had been slashed to strips. The dead still lay where they had fallen. They included officers in guards' uniform, students —young boys of twenty and men who belonged obviously to the criminal class and whom the revolution had released from prison. In the luxurious drawing-room of the House Gracheva the Anarchists had been surprised

[21] *Bolshevik Propaganda, Hearings . . . , op.cit.*, pp. 823–824.

in the middle of an orgy. The long table which had supported the feast had been overturned, and broken plates, glasses, champagne bottles, made unsavoury islands in a pool of blood and spilt wine. On the floor lay a young woman face downwards. Peters turned her over. Her hair was dishevelled. She had been shot through the neck, and the blood had congealed in a sinister purple clump. She could not have been more than twenty. Peters shrugged his shoulders. "Prostitutka," he said. "Perhaps it is for the best." [22]

Robins believed the anarchists to have been supported by German money. Summers, characteristically, saw it in precisely the opposite way and reported it to be understood that "Count Mirbach, the German Ambassador, who is expected in Moscow daily, warned the local authorities that anarchism must cease before he arrived." [23]

There is no ulterior evidence that either of these versions was right. The probabilities are that the Soviet leaders were simply fed up with the indiscipline of the anarchists, were beginning to find themselves embarrassed by them in many ways (the incident of Robins' car being only one), and felt that in view of the forthcoming arrival of the German Embassy they could not afford to permit these conditions to continue to exist.

Robins, however, in addition to being pleased at the recovery of his car, was elated at what he took to be a new demonstration of the reality of his own influence with the Soviet leaders, of the stability of their power in Moscow, and of their freedom from German control. But he was all the more convinced of the urgency of some conciliatory action from the Allied side. On the 15th, he sent a wire to Mr. Henry P. Davison, head of the American Red Cross, who was then in Paris. In this cable, Robins reaffirmed his recommendations for a constructive program of economic cooperation between the Soviet government and the United States, and argued that these recommendations had been reinforced by recent events. The complete wiping out of the organized anarchist force in Moscow represented, he said in this message, the final vindication of the reality of Soviet internal control. He could do no more than to repeat the cumulative conclusions he had been voicing for five months. Unless "cooperation" between the two governments could be arranged, use-

[22] Lockhart, *op.cit.*, p. 256.
[23] *Foreign Relations, 1918, Russia*, Vol. 1, *op.cit.*, p. 497.

ful work for the Red Cross Commission would be ended by May first.[24]

❖

Immediately after the anarchist affair another incident occurred which entered with shattering effect into the already painful situation as between Robins and Summers.

Among the American newspapermen in Russia at the time of the Bolshevik seizure of power was Mr. Louis Edgar Browne of the *Chicago Daily News.* Whatever Browne's views may have been, he appears to have enjoyed good relations both with the Soviet authorities and with Robins.[25]

It will be recalled (see Chapter xxii of Volume 1) that in February and March 1918 Mr. Edgar Sisson, chief of the Petrograd office of the Committee on Public Information, had procured through clandestine channels a series of documents purporting to prove that the Bolsheviki were German agents. To be sure, the documents were forgeries; but this was not known at the time either to Sisson (who confidently believed them genuine), to the Embassy, or to the government in Washington. Sisson supposed that his procurement of these documents had remained unknown to the Soviet government; he had taken great care, in removing them from Russia at the beginning of March, to do so in a manner which he thought would make them safe from detection and seizure by the Soviet authorities. He attached great significance to the documents and considered it of vital importance both that the Soviet government should not learn of their being in American hands and that nothing be revealed concerning them prior to their delivery to the United States government.

After leaving Petrograd on March 3, Sisson was held up in Finland by the vicissitudes of the Finnish Civil War and did not get through the battle lines to neutral Sweden until early April.

It was also related in Volume 1 that Sisson and Robins had dis-

---

[24] Cumming & Pettit, *op.cit.,* pp. 146–147.

[25] At the time of the Bolshevik seizure of power, Browne told Francis his despatches were the only telegrams leaving Russia, and he offered to help get the Embassy's messages through. (Francis mss, *op.cit*)

When Robins and Gumberg left Russia in May, Browne accompanied them to the United States.

agreed violently over the principle of seeking and acquiring documents of this sort. Sisson, probably suspecting Robins' discretion and Gumberg's intimacy with the Soviet authorities, had deliberately refrained from divulging to Robins anything concerning the main body of the materials he had collected, though it is clear that Robins was aware, from many indications, that something unusual was going on.

On April 11, Browne filed at the Moscow telegraph office, in plain English text, the following telegram to the *Chicago Daily News* correspondent in Stockholm:

Barwell Digby, care American Minister, Stockholm:
. . . Please cable me urgently care American Consulate, Moscow, what disposition Sisson made or intended making of certain material he collected regarding Soviet-German affiliation. This confidential.

Moscow was at that time honeycombed with intelligence operations of all sorts. A copy of this telegram—lifted, presumably, from the telegraph office—was made available to Sisson's successor, Arthur Bullard (now directing the informational work in Moscow), by an official of one of these agencies. Bullard was deeply shocked and disturbed at the revelation that Browne was aware of what Sisson was doing. He at once took the matter up with Summers. Browne was called to the Consulate General and an explanation was requested. He admitted despatching the telegram, and claimed that his motive for doing so was his interest in purchasing for publication the materials Sisson was suspected to be carrying. He divulged nothing, it appears, about the source of his information concerning these materials.

Bullard, more alarmed than ever by this reticence, immediately wired George Creel, the Chairman of the Committee on Public Information in Washington. "Do not know," he said in this telegram,

where Brown heard of what he calls 'material.' He is Annapolis man and cannot claim ignorance in seriousness of acquiescence of act. Fortunately Sisson was out of danger although that was not generally known here at the time. His papers went by another route and no one here knows where they are. Under the circumstances cannot consider Brown's act foolish remissness and recommend investigation. Publication Sisson's name as anti-Bolshevik endangers the work of the organization Sisson established.

Chicherin's letter to Robins, April 10, 1918

Left: Consul General Maddin Summers

Center: Aboard the *Alexander*, June 1918, in British naval uniforms
L-r: Otto T. Glaman, Graham R. Taylor, Arthur Bullard, Read Lewis, and George W. Bakeman

Bottom: The Red Cross car in the Moscow railroad yard
L-r: J. W. Andrews, Raymond Robins, Allen Wardwell, D. Heywood Hardy

. . . Gumberg also has tried to find out from me what papers Sisson had collected, what use he intended to make of them and whether he had them in his possession while in Finland. I claimed complete ignorance.

This message was sent by Summers, through State Department channels, at Bullard's request. It was accompanied by a statement from Summers that it should be brought to the attention of the Secretary of State.[26]

Summers must, of course, have put two and two together and concluded that if Gumberg had attempted to find out from Bullard what papers Sisson was carrying, he was also probably the source of Browne's curiosity. This cannot have failed to appear to Summers, as it obviously did to Bullard, as a probable bit of espionage by Gumberg on behalf of the Soviet authorities, directed against the Americans. If Gumberg had been just any Soviet citizen, this would not have been exceptional. But Gumberg was Robins' intimate aide and Man Friday. Was it possible that Robins was involved in this, too? Knowing what we do today, from a broader record of documentation, we may accept it as out of the question that Robins would have deliberately tried to gather, on behalf of the Soviet government, information about the doings of his own, though he may have reposed in Gumberg a confidence which took little account of the latter's status and obligations as a Soviet citizen. But to Summers the matter must have looked suspect. And to the extent that this suspicion was allowed to prevail, Robins had, of course, to be regarded as an out-and-out Soviet agent. As the full horror of this dawned on him, Summers' patience came to an end.

From this moment (April 19–20), things moved rapidly to a denouement. On the day Bullard's telegram was sent, Summers cabled to the Department of State a formal request that he be transferred from Moscow. Nothing had come of his appeal to Francis for Robins' removal. His request was now that he himself be removed. "There can be," he wired to Assistant Secretary of State Wilbur Carr, "no cooperation between Robins and myself." [27]

Francis, on being informed of Summers' step, immediately wired the Department in surprise and consternation (April 20). He hoped,

[26] National Archives, State Department File 861.00/1643; Summers' telegram 393, April 20 "from Bullard to Creel." The Department of State considered taking up Browne's passport, but thought it would stir up more trouble than it was worth.
[27] *Ibid.*, State Department File 123 Su 61/120.

he said, that the Department would not grant the request. It would be a great loss. Robins, he admitted, had been useful to him

. . . in keeping touch with British and French relations with Soviet government. . . .

Summers . . . bitterly hates Bolsheviks and perhaps justifiably but should conceal his feelings, which Robins claims Summers does not do. Suggest arbitration, you asking him to visit me again and that you refrain for the present from acting on his request. . . .[28]

But immediately after learning of Summers' wire, Francis delicately hinted to Robins that it might be best for him to leave. "Do not feel I should be justified," he wired to Robins on (or about) the 22nd,

in asking you to remain longer in Moscow to neglect of the prosecution of your Red Cross work, but this does not imply any want of appreciation of the service you have rendered me in keeping me advised concerning matters important for me to know, and giving suggestions and advice, as well as being a channel of unofficial communication with the Soviet government. . . .[29]

Robins was himself, by this time, coming to the view that there was no point in his remaining longer in Russia without greater support from Washington. To him, the arrival of the German Embassy had always seemed to be a sort of deadline. He had maintained for weeks that if "collaboration" could not be arranged by May 1, the immediate game was up. Now, on April 25—two days after the arrival of the new German Ambassador, Count Mirbach—he wired to Davison and to the Washington headquarters of the Red Cross:

. . . Liquidation American Red Cross supplies relief work Russia practically complete. Recommend return all members mission America. Planning departure about May fifteenth. . . .[30]

By sheer coincidence, both the Department of State and the American Red Cross headquarters had arrived, at precisely the same time but by wholly independent processes, at the very same conclusion—namely, that Robins must leave.

[28] *Ibid.*, State Department File 123 Su 61/121.
[29] Cumming & Pettit, *op.cit.*, p. 156.
[30] *Ibid.*, p. 202.

Even before this time, there had already been signs of some anxiety in the Department about Robins' position in Moscow. What brought this on is not clear. A suggestion contained in a note received by the Department from the British Embassy on April 19, to the effect that "Colonel Robins" be directed to state to the Soviet government an agreed Allied position on intervention and several other matters, may have come as a shock to the Secretary and his advisers, revealing as it did the extent to which Robins was already regarded in Allied circles as the official United States representative to the Soviet government. On the 23rd, furthermore, the Department had cabled to Francis that Robins was "cabling to Thompson and also Red Cross direct without Embassy's knowledge on matters of political policy," and had told Francis to see that such messages came in future only through the Embassy or the Moscow Consulate General. Now, on April 25, the Secretary of State, according to his desk diary, had an interview with the Counselor, Frank Polk, "on getting Raymond Robbins out of Russia thru Red Cross," and a second interview with Assistant Secretary of State Wilbur Carr "on Raymond Robbins and Summers." [31] The Secretary also had before him, at this time, Summers' request for a transfer and the aroused message from Bullard about the inquisitiveness of Browne and Gumberg with regard to Sisson and his documents. Sisson, furthermore, now in London en route to the United States, had just sent a telegram (April 24) to his principals in Washington recommending that all representatives of the Committee on Public Information and the Red Cross be ordered out of Russia within a fortnight. The reason for this recommendation was his assumption that his documents would be published by the American government immediately upon his own arrival in Washington, and that this would cause the Soviet government to take reprisals against the Americans in Russia. (Significantly, Sisson mentioned only the personnel of the Committee on Public Information and the Red Cross; he evidently viewed the State Department representatives as either uncompromised in the matter or expendable.)

Robins received on or about the 26th a message from Cornelius N. Bliss, the acting director of the Red Cross in Washington, implementing Sisson's recommendation and describing it as advisable

[31] Lansing MSS, *op.cit.*

In the light of information received here . . . that you and all members of your commission leave Russia immediately. This out of consideration your safety . . .[32]

This message crossed Robins' own announcement of his decision to leave. Actually, we may assume, in the light of what we know about Lansing's interest, that Bliss's message reflected not only Sisson's fears for the safety of the Red Cross personnel in Russia but also the Secretary of State's desire to terminate as soon as possible the curious semi-diplomatic status which Robins had occupied at the seat of the Soviet government since the departure of his predecessor, Mr. William Boyce Thompson, on November 29, 1917—a status which had now led to trouble within the Foreign Service family and was threatening to get out of hand, diplomatically.

On receipt of this message from the Red Cross, Robins at once made plans to liquidate his work in Moscow and to leave for Washington in the very first days of May.

❖

On the morning of April 26, the day of Robins' recall, the Moscow press appeared with stories to the effect that *Francis* had been recalled and that Robins was to become the first American Ambassador to the Soviet government. Robins immediately wired Francis about these reports, referring to them as "stupid stories" evidently prepared to produce dissension and suspicion among American representatives in Russia. "Your proved strength," he added, "sufficient guarantee against absurd stories both Washington, Russia." (What the absurd stories in Washington were, the record does not reveal.) Robins returned to the matter in a letter to Francis the same day:

. . . Evidently your management of the situation troubles our enemies and they would have you out of the way or get me out of the way or both if possible.

I have given no interviews and of course will not give any. I have seen no Russian newspaper men and will not see any.

These small matters I would not bring up at so critical a time were it not for the fact that they are sought to be used to confuse a delicate situation.[33]

[32] American National Red Cross Archives, Washington.
[33] Cumming & Pettit, *op.cit.*, pp. 157–158.

Nearly a year later, in the course of the senatorial hearings, Robins had the following to say about these reports:

Senators, it has been testified here by certain persons that I was seeking the office of American ambassador in Russia. No one who knows politics —and whatever else I may be, I am not supposed to be entirely ignorant or entirely a fool—would have entertained the idea for a moment. . . .

May it under oath be recorded that I never made a single public statement regarding my official position or unofficial service in any paper during my work in Russia. May it be recorded that I never at any time publicly in any wise pretended to represent the Government of the United States, but did only, in the matter intrusted to me, act quietly, and at most times secretly, to the end that we might handle the difficult situation that was there. I conceived the ambassador and myself as working . . . in entire harmony, with certain differences of judgment as to the actual facts and conditions that are reasonable and expected in honest and sincere men everywhere.[34]

The news of the Moscow rumors aroused in Francis, by way of reflex, that species of elaborate and acid courtesy that often comes into play in American domestic politics when the most deadly rivalries are involved: "You are correct," he replied to Robins in a letter on May 3,

in thinking that I was not at all disturbed by the newspaper surmise that I was to be succeeded by yourself, not that I think such suggestion absurd but I did not for a moment feel that you were a party to any such move. . . .[35]

It was noted above that a Cossack captain, Ilovaiski, who had served as interpreter for the American Red Cross Commission in Russia, admitted to the Vice Consul at Stockholm that he had on occasion distorted in translation, in a manner agreeable to the Soviet authorities, statements made by various officials of the Commission, and hinted that misinformation had been insinuated in this way into the Soviet press. The Vice Consul, in reporting on his conversation with Ilovaiski, had the following to say with relation to the rumors of Francis' recall:

"This Russian Captain further recounted to me several instances of his and Colonel Robins' use of the Bolshevik press, particularly in regard to the recall of the Ambassador, Mr. Francis, even stating that they had not been as scrupulous as exact honor might demand but that they had acted according to their ideas of right, regardless of how they might have conflicted with the policies of the accredited American representatives." (War Department Archives, Records Branch, report, September 13, 1918, of Vice Consul at Stockholm to the State Department, *op.cit.*)

That those in Robins' entourage might have spread misinformation in this manner would seem, in the light of Ilovaiski's own admission, not improbable. It is doubtful that Robins could have known of it and approved it. This was not in his character.

[34] *Bolshevik Propaganda, Hearings* . . . , *op.cit.*, p. 1019.
[35] Cumming & Pettit, *op.cit.*, pp. 161–163.

To the press at Vologda, the Ambassador issued the following statement, the text of which he reported to Washington on April 29:

I have paid no attention to the false rumors that have been circulating concerning the Embassy and myself for the past three weeks but have been curious to know their source and their object. I mean the reports concerning my differing with the Government at Washington and planning to return to America or quit Vologda. I have concluded that such rumors, false and utterly without foundation as they are, were not inspired by a friendly sentiment toward America or Russia, or for the promotions of friendly relations between these countries.

I only notice them now because the name of Colonel Robins has been mentioned in connection therewith. Colonel Robins and I are friends and understand each other thoroughly; we have the same object in view, which is to make the world safe for democracy, and we agree that such desirable end cannot be accomplished without the defeat of Germany.

It is necessary to state that the only authoritative expressions concerning American policy in Russia are given out by myself. . . . All other statements said to emanate from or be inspired by the American Embassy are wholly without foundation.[36]

The Department, meanwhile, aware that steps had now been taken by the Red Cross for Robins' recall, decided not to relieve Summers. Secretary Lansing wired to the latter on the 30th that while his request for a transfer had been given "careful and sympathetic consideration," the Department was convinced that he could be of greatest service to the government by remaining in Russia. "The conditions which have embarrassed you," the Secretary added significantly,

will unquestionably show early improvement. Meanwhile keep in close touch with Ambassador, visiting him whenever desirable and endeavoring to do your utmost in supporting the President's attitude towards Russia of utilizing every opportunity to secure for Russia freedom from autocratic government and complete sovereignty and independence in her own affairs.[37]

Summers was never to receive this message. On Friday, May 3, before the telegram had arrived in Moscow, he felt unwell in the

[36] *Foreign Relations, 1918, Russia*, Vol. I, *op.cit.*, pp. 508–509. (This telegram was not received in the Department until May 12.)
[37] National Archives, State Department File 123 Su 61/120.

office and went home to lie down.[38] The following day (May 4), at 5:30 in the afternoon, he died. He himself appears to have thought, in the hours preceding his death, that he had been, or might have been, poisoned by the Germans. There was every reason to believe that this thought was the product of a brain already disordered by illness. Although there was no autopsy, his second-in-command, Consul DeWitt C. Poole, after a thorough talk with the attending physicians, was satisfied, and so reported to the Department, that Summers' death was due to a brain hemorrhage—the result of overwork and worry.

Summers' death came as a tremendous shock not only to the American colony in Russia but to the many people in Washington and throughout the Foreign Service who were familiar with his personality and his work. The Washington correspondent of the *New York Times,* in reporting his death, observed that

As head of the American Consulate General at the Bolshevist capital, Mr. Summers had probably the most extraordinary and most exacting task of any man in the Consular service. He directed the activities of a great organization of Consular officers and agents extending throughout Eastern Russia, all the way to Vladivostok, and even before the Bolshevist Government moved to Moscow the work of the office there was vast.

Officials of the Department of State, the *Times* account continued, had spoken of Summers "in terms of almost unmeasured praise." Few men, it was said, had given such service to their country. He should be regarded as a war hero, "as truly as though he had lost his life in the trenches." [39]

The funeral took place on the 8th. The service was held in the little English Church, adjoining the premises of the Consulate General. It was the church in which Summers had been married, several years before. Now, on this last sad occasion, it was filled to capacity. The American colony and the members of the official Allied community were there in force. Francis, himself still weak from a violent ten-day illness (the long Russian winter had now begun to tell on everyone), had come down from Vologda to attend the funeral; and

[38] According to the impression held by one of the Foreign Service officers who was then in Russia, this attack of illness came immediately on the heels of a resounding altercation with Robins over the question of protection of the interests of the Irkutsk branch of the Singer Sewing Machine Company; but there is no confirmation of this from any other source.

[39] *New York Times,* May 6, 1918, p. 13.

together with Summers' successor, Consul DeWitt C. Poole, and the Allied consular colleagues, he served as pallbearer. The Soviet government was also represented, somewhat diffidently, by the Chief of the Far Eastern Section of the Commissariat for Foreign Affairs, Comrade Voznesenski (who took advantage of the occasion to get into touch with Francis and to press for a further interview, with a view to persuading the Ambassador to remove to Moscow).

Following the service at the church, the body was taken to the vestibule of the building, where speeches were made by the Italian Consul General as dean of the Consular Corps, by Francis, and even by Voznesenski.

Francis said:

He who gives his life for a cause can contribute no more. . . . Maddin Summers yielded his life in his country's service and did so as effectually as if he had been taken off by the enemy in ambush and as courageously as if he had fallen in attack on the enemy's works. . . .[40]

Voznesenski, speaking in English, said that the Commissariat for Foreign Affairs had authorized him to express its "profound sorrow" as well as "the warm sympathy and sincere friendliness of the people of Russia for the American people." He was certain, he added somewhat obliquely,

. . . that the mutual regard and hearty cooperation of both peoples will be an essential factor of future progress and development of the great popular masses of the world.[41]

After the speeches, the funeral procession moved from the church to the "Cemetery for Those of Other Faith," several miles distant at

[40] David R. Francis, *Russia from the American Embassy,* Charles Scribner's Sons, New York, 1921, pp. 238–239.

[41] National Archives, State Department Files 123 Su 61/38 to 123 Su 63/13. In these words, extraordinarily cordial by comparison with the tone customarily struck by Soviet statesmen and the Soviet press in references to the Allies, Voznesenski was only echoing a most curious telegram sent directly by Chicherin to Francis on this occasion. In this message "profound sorrow" was again expressed over Summers' death, and the American Consulate General in Moscow was described as a "link of first-rate importance" between the Russian Soviet Republic, the world's "most comprehensive democracy," and the United States, "land of puritan revolutionary pioneers, of Washington and Abraham Lincoln." All in all, it was clear that with Robins' departure impending, the Soviet government was prepared to forget the strongly negative attitude Summers had always taken toward the new Bolshevik power (after all, he was now dead) and to go the limit in an effort to exploit the occasion as a means of prying Francis loose from Vologda and inducing him to move to Moscow, thus splitting the united front of the Allies in their practice with regard to diplomatic representation in Russia.

the eastern edge of the city. The automobiles of the distinguished guests were hard put to it to observe the leisurely pace of the horse-drawn hearse, and the motor cavalcade advanced only in low gear, with many stops and starts, over the cobbles of the endless Pokrovka.

It was a raw, cold day, overcast but clear. The tall pines of the cemetery stood brooding and somber under the leaden sky, their trunks glistening with moisture; and no birds sang. Summers had died just too soon for the late Russian spring, and just too soon for his own tardy vindication.

CHAPTER VIII

ARTHUR BULLARD AND THE "COMPUB"

VOLUME I of this work dealt at length with the person and activities of Mr. Edgar Sisson, chief of the Russian branch of the American propaganda office of the First World War: the Committee on Public Information. It was noted above that Sisson, passing through London on his way home from Russia, wired to his principals in Washington on April 24, insisting that not only the members of the Red Cross Commission but also the personnel of the offices of the Committee on Public Information leave Russia within a fortnight. We have seen the effect this had on the Red Cross Commission. It now becomes necessary to observe the similar effect produced on the personnel of the Russian representation of the Committee on Public Information. And since the earlier portions of this narrative have afforded little occasion for noting generally the work of this interesting branch of America's representation in Russia in 1917-1918, this will be a convenient point to go back and review its activity in the months prior to May 1918.

The origins of the Russian operation of the Committee on Public Information—familiarly known in the governmentese of the time as "Compub"—were described in Volume I, Chapter II. It was related there, in particular, how Mr. Arthur Bullard—liberal socialist, free lance writer, and private eye of Colonel House—went to Russia in the summer of 1917, partly as an observer for House but partly also to explore, on behalf of the Committee on Public Information, the possibilities for the conduct in Russia of informational and propaganda activity in favor of America's war effort.

The very idea of the conduct by a government of a highly organized, long-term effort to affect public opinion in a foreign country by feeding material into its various media of information and communication was at that time something of an innovation in the techniques of American diplomacy. It reflected, of course, a whole series of changes that had come over the environment of international life: the growth of literacy in many countries, the spread of parliamentary democracy, the influence of telegraph and wireless on the daily press, and the growing belief (to which Americans were particularly susceptible) in the power of public opinion to affect governmental action. This new approach marked, in short, a stage in the transition from dynastic to national diplomacy. Whereas in the past it had been the function of diplomacy to influence royal personages and court circles, these latter being regarded as the driving power of governments, it was now becoming necessary to find means of influencing whole peoples—they being considered to have replaced the royal courts in this capacity.

If the approach to mass opinion was, then, to be regarded as a legitimate part of diplomacy, the question at once arose as to the proper mode of integration of this new type of effort with the traditional diplomatic process. Regular diplomatic officials tended everywhere to view propaganda with distaste and skepticism. The profession of diplomacy induces a weary detachment, foreign to all political enthusiasms and *ex parte* pleas. Propaganda smacked of overt interference in the domestic affairs of other countries—something that went strongly against the grain of diplomatic tradition. Most diplomatists were instinctively convinced that government was everywhere in some degree a conspiracy and that, whatever the outward trappings of democracy, it was always more important to influence a few select individuals than to appeal to the broad electorate. The professional diplomatist thus tended to shy off, temperamentally, from the very thought of distributing propaganda. And he was generally held, then as now, by the enthusiasts of the propagandistic approach, to be quite unqualified for this sort of work.

Where propaganda was systematically conducted by the European governments, up to and during World War I, this was generally done clandestinely and camouflaged as a private or semi-private operation. The United States government, uninhibited by any firm attachment to the traditional principles of diplomatic intercourse, appears to have been one of the first to embrace this new type of activity with breezy candor and to conduct it openly, as an avowed governmental operation. It was the American involvement in the First World War that brought this about.

Arthur Bullard and the "Compub"

In addition to embracing propaganda as a regular function of its diplomacy, the United States government in 1917 made another decision that was to have important significance as a precedent: namely, *not* to center this activity in the Department of State but to set up for this purpose a separate agency not under the control of the State Department and manned by people unaffected by any diplomatic experience of any sort. This system, centering the power of decision as to what was to be said to foreign *peoples* in a wholly different place from the power of decision as to what was to be said to foreign *governments,* and giving to each of these rival centers of decision a different outlook and spirit, obviously harbored major possibilities for confusion and incoherence in the governmental effort, both administratively and in substance. It was pursuant to this system that there was established in Russia, in 1917, a special Compub representation, parallel to that of the Department of State.

Bullard, on his arrival in Russia in the summer of 1917, found that the French and British were conducting small-scale clandestine or camouflaged propaganda efforts in Russia, and that a very modest amount of similar activity was being carried on, quite independently, by Americans in Petrograd and Moscow. The American operation in Petrograd was, like the French and British ones, ostensibly a private show, conducted by an American resident, Mr. Frederick M. Corse, long-term manager of the Russian division of the New York Life Insurance Company. In Moscow, the work was handled directly by Summers, as a side line to his regular consular activity. Of the two operations, Bullard was the more favorably impressed with that of Summers; and he spent the late summer and early fall in Moscow, helping Summers in the capacity of a volunteer.

After Sisson's arrival, following the November Revolution, efforts were made to organize the work on a wider and more regular basis. A Compub office was opened on the Gorokhovaya, in the very heart of Petrograd. Bullard, at Sisson's request, took charge of news distribution. Arrangements were made for the receipt of a wire news-service direct from Compub headquarters in Washington. The plan was that this material would be received and translated in Petrograd, made available there to the leading Russian newspapers through the governmental Petrograd Telegraph Agency, and distributed by mail to the provincial press from Moscow. In practice, the Petrograd Telegraph Agency, under Bolshevik control, proved either wholly inefficient or deliberately uncooperative (no one could determine which). Thus the burden of the news work fell to the Moscow branch.

By the end of the winter Bullard had assembled a first-rate staff for the Compub work. Mr. Malcolm W. Davis (later to be associated for many years with the Carnegie Endowment for International Peace) was drawn from the Y.M.C.A. staff in Russia. From the Embassy's former prisoner-of-war section the Compub recruited Mr. William Adams Brown, Jr. (subsequently professor at Brown University and internationally known economist), Mr. Graham R. Taylor (later Director of the Division of Publications of the Commonwealth Fund in New York), and Mr. Read Lewis (subsequently Executive Director of the Common Council for American Unity). Lewis was put in charge of the Moscow news work. Taylor acted as Bullard's deputy in Petrograd. From Summer's staff, Bullard drew Mr. George W. Bakeman (now Associate Dean of the Medical College of Virginia). All of these were men of unusual intelligence and ability.

Sisson himself gave relatively little attention, during his brief stay in Petrograd, to the regular Compub work, which he was content to leave to Bullard and Taylor. His passion, aside from the distribution of the President's Fourteen Points speech (see Volume I, Chapter XII), was the moving picture program.[1] This, too, as can readily be imagined, was an exciting innovation in the year 1918. Sisson had collected in the United States, prior to his departure, a whole series of documentaries which he thought would be interesting and useful in their impact on the Russian public. These were to be sent after him and brought to Russia by courier. Sisson took with him a moving picture operator, rented a separate office exclusively for this work, and hired an entire theater on the Nevski Prospekt for the demonstration of the films. Unfortunately, the main body of the films became stranded in Stockholm and never arrived in Petrograd. The somewhat elaborate preparations thus remained suspended in mid-air; and Sisson was obliged to content himself with the demonstration of two small documentaries the operator had brought along

---

[1] Excellent work was done by the Compub staff in Russia in getting the Fourteen Points speech infiltrated into the German and Austro-Hungarian forces along the old eastern front; and there is evidence that this may have had a palpable effect on their morale. Since this part of the Compub effort was not addressed to Russia, it is not further treated in this volume.

in his personal baggage. One of these was entitled "The Presidential Procession in Washington." The other was referred to as "the Uncle Sam Immigrant film." It bore the somewhat awkward caption "All for Peace through War"—awkward, that is, for use in Russia: because if there was anything on which the mass of the Russian people were united at this particular juncture it was the proposition that peace should be achieved, so far as Russia was concerned, by any means *except* more war. Sisson therefore deleted the last two words of this caption in the Petrograd showings of the film. "We left it to the audiences," he observed in his official report, "to find that out for themselves." [2]

A further and more serious informational effort of the Compub staff in Russia, during the winter of 1918, was the preparation by Bullard, and the distribution throughout Russia, of an anonymous pamphlet entitled "Letters from an American Friend." While anonymous in respect to authorship,[3] the pamphlet appeared under the imprimatur, and with the seal, of the Committee on Public Information; no attempt was made to disguise its semi-official character.

In this document, a work of some thirty pages, Bullard undertook to explain to the Russian people a number of things he thought they ought to know about the United States: its history, the origin and spirit of its institutions, the development of its relationship to the World War, the purposes of its war effort, and the factors that had underlain, in the past, the shaping of American opinion with respect to Russia. Particular emphasis was placed on correcting the impression just then gaining currency in Russia that there was a danger of America, together with the other Allies, making a compromise peace with Germany at Russia's expense. Extensive use was made of the President's Fourteen Points speech, introduced in full into the text of one of the letters.

The over-all purpose of this document was obviously to disarm a number of the more absurd rumors then circulating in Russia with regard to American policy and intentions, and to win confidence for America's war effort, as a means of combatting German influence

---

[2] Bullard MSS, *op.cit.,* Box 14, "Report on Installation of Committee on Public Information Service in Russia" by Edgar Sisson, May 29, 1918. The incident is also described in Edgar Sisson, *100 Red Days: A Personal Chronicle of the Bolshevik Revolution,* Yale University Press, New Haven, 1931, p. 181.

[3] It is characteristic of the fantastic lack of coordination among the American offices in Russia that even the Ambassador was not told who had written the document and had to make private inquiry, through Robins, to find out.

and stimulating resistance to the German demands at Brest-Litovsk. The issuance of the pamphlet was of course soon overtaken by the conclusion of the Brest-Litovsk Treaty; but fortunately its content was so broadly conceived, and had such historical depth, that its usefulness was not materially affected by Russia's final departure from the war. (Much of it, in fact, would be useful today.) Distribution was thus continued even after ratification of the treaty. More than 300,000 copies of the pamphlet were eventually distributed.

This document occupies a unique position in the record of the handling of the Russian problem by the United States government during the First World War. Amid all the frantic and expensive efforts put in hand by Americans to affect the Russian situation in those months, this was literally the only serious and competent attempt, based on knowledge and careful consideration of the real state of Russian opinion, to bridge the gap between the Russian and American outlooks and to explain America to the Russian people in terms that would have some real meaning for the latter. Bullard himself had, to be sure, a poor knowledge of the Russian language; the pamphlet had to be drafted in English and translated into Russian (a job, incidentally, that was not badly done). But as a man familiar with the socialist intellectual world, who had given long and thoughtful attention to the Russian revolutionary movement, Bullard had a fair idea of what sort of thing ought to be said, and how it ought to be said, if any real effect were to be achieved on the sections of public opinion now dominant in Russia. The Fourteen Points speech had had some elements that were helpful in their impact on Russian opinion; but its usefulness was weakened by the cumbersomeness of some of the language, by the ambiguity of Wilson's position with respect to Bolshevik power (one could not tell whether he realized that there was any distinction between the Soviet regime, on the one hand, and the liberal Russia of which he spoke so warmly, on the other), and by the free use of specifically American phraseology in entire disregard of the possibilities—and pitfalls—of translation into Russian. A great deal of the news material wired to Russia by the Committee on Public Information suffered from similar deficiencies, and proved so inapplicable to Russian needs that it could not be used at all. To Bullard alone must go the credit for a pioneering effort to shake off the subjectivism that so often tends to bedevil American governmental propaganda,

[195]

and to attempt to take seriously into account, in the approach to a foreign country, the pecularities of its psychology, its outlook, and its needs. It is sad to note that this effort was purely an individual one, the result of the initiative of one man acting without instructions or encouragement from Washington.

With Sisson's departure in early March, Bullard was left in charge of the whole Compub operation. For the first time the organization was set up to begin large-scale operation. The British operation had by this time been suppressed by the Soviet government. The French effort now amounted to very little. The American officials were thus left to represent, in large measure, the Allied community as a whole on the propaganda front.

In view of the fact that the capital had now moved to Moscow, Bullard moved the Compub office to that city in mid-March. The operation being now too large for accommodation on the Consulate General's premises, new quarters were found, after some difficulty, in a building of the Moscow University, adjoining the site on the Mokhovaya that was later to be, for so many years, the location of the post-1933 American Embassy.

The work in Moscow proceeded smoothly. Summers and Bullard saw eye to eye on the needs and methods of the undertaking. "I've had a unique relationship with Summers," Bullard wrote after Summers' death.

It has never been my chance before to work with a man quite like him. I never knew anyone who could really agree to disagree as he could. On a whole lot of important things we disagreed fundamentally. But he never let this interfere with the working agreement we had on the job. I feel that it has been a real privilege to have known him and his loss is a real personal pain.[4]

In the Moscow Compub office the news cables, now being received regularly from the Compub headquarters in Washington, were edited, translated, and brought together in a weekly bulletin which was mailed to Russian editors and other interested people all over the country. By the end of April the circulation of this bulletin had risen to 25,000 and was still increasing. Experience was being acquired; the new staff members were shaking down in their jobs. There was every prospect that the operation, if developed further

----

[4] Bullard MSS, *op.cit.,* Box 15, letter to DeWitt C. Poole, May 6, 1918.

consistently along the established lines, would soon be able to exert a palpable influence on Russian opinion.

Into this promising prospect the telegram ordering all American Compub personnel to be out of Russia by May 5 struck with shattering and agonizing effect. The matter was made still worse by the cryptic terms of the message, which gave no indication of the reason for the action, and by the fantastic series of confusions, to be described shortly, that attended its transmission to Bullard and his own efforts to comply with its terms. It turned out, as things developed, to have been wholly unnecessary. No publication of Sisson's documents occurred at that time. The lives and safety of Americans in Russia were in no way threatened. And while the departure of Bullard and his associates was quietly and discreetly accomplished, it is not to be assumed that it escaped notice by the Soviet government, which could only have been bewildered and misled by it.

The immediate sequence of events unleashed by the arrival of this message in Russia might well be noted as an example of the confusions that can occur when the representation of the United States government in a foreign country is so dispersed, administratively, as was the case in Russia in 1918.

The message was sent, on behalf of the Committee on Public Information, by the Department of State. For some reason, probably in order that Francis should be informed of the action, it was addressed not directly to Bullard but to the Embassy at Vologda. As received in Vologda on April 27, with the usual telegraphic garbles, it read as follows:

For Bullard from Irwin Compub.

On information and advice from Sisson who understands aspects of situation of which you are probably ignorant and with indorsement of Creel you and [garble] and with all possible secrecy to leave for the present all territory controlled by B[olsheviki]. Leave your Russian assistants in control of office for the present and report final whereabouts pending orders should by all means be out of B[olshevik] territory by about May fifth. . . . Where is Gumberg.[5]

It seems to have occurred to no one in Washington that Francis,

[5] *Ibid.*, Box 14, Bullard's report to George Creel of May 9. The complete text is in James R. Mock & Cedric Larson, *Words that Won the War, The Story of the Committee on Public Information 1917–1919*, Princeton University Press, 1939, p. 308. The passage garbled in transmission should read: ". . . you and *your American assistants ordered immediately* and with all possible secrecy to leave . . ."

knowing nothing of the reasons for this step, could only be puzzled and worried, rather than enlightened, by the receipt of this enigmatic communication.

Understandably persuaded that something was going on that he ought properly to know about before any action was taken, Francis, instead of transmitting the message at once, despatched a telegram to Summers asking that Bullard be sent to Vologda for a confidential conference with the Ambassador. When this was received in Moscow, Bullard's name was so garbled that no one could figure out who was meant by the telegram. The Assistant Military Attaché, Riggs, thinking it likely that the message was meant for him, rushed to the railway station and jumped on a train for Vologda. Not until Riggs' arrival in Vologda had cleared up the misunderstanding did Bullard learn, on April 30, that it was himself the Ambassador wanted to see.

On the same day (April 30), Francis, worried over the time that was being lost, sent the text of the message down from Vologda by a Y.M.C.A. man who happened to be making the trip. By the time this courier arrived, however, Bullard had just boarded the train and departed for Vologda, with a view to seeing the text of the message. Two more precious days were thus lost from the brief period remaining before the departure deadline.

In Vologda, Francis questioned Bullard sharply about the reasons for the message. Bullard knew nothing; and the two men found themselves equally at a loss to understand what could have occasioned it. They agreed that there was nothing to do, in the circumstances, but to comply.

This raised the question: where should Bullard and his associates go? Finland was a poor bet; Sisson himself had got stuck there for nearly a month. The Ukraine was in the hands of the Germans. Siberia was too far to permit of exit from Soviet-held territory within anywhere near the appointed time. Murmansk involved requests for permits from the Bolsheviki and passage over 800 miles of the most closely guarded railroad in Russia.

The decision finally fell on Archangel. The two food ships which the British government had despatched to that port early in the spring, somewhat hastily and against the advice of the British consul there (see above, page 20), had now arrived in Archangel, shepherded by an icebreaker of the Royal Navy, the *H.M.S. Alex-*

ander. No agreement having been achieved with the local Bolsheviki concerning release of any of the Bakaritsa supplies, and the ice still being thick in the inner harbor, there could as yet be no question of unloading the food. The three vessels were thus lying uneasily at anchor in the waters of the delta, some fifteen miles below the frozen port, where they could have some hope of defending themselves or of making a getaway in case of a raid by the Bolsheviki. It was decided that Bullard should return posthaste to Moscow, in order to close out his operation, and that he and his associates should then make their way to Archangel and seek asylum aboard one of the British vessels. Francis and the Embassy were to approach the British and do what they could to pave the way for this move.

It was now May 2. The order called for Bullard and his men to be out by the 5th. Bullard, anxious to make his position and plans understood in Washington, delayed his departure from Vologda in order to despatch some last minute telegrams from there. Several hours were expended on drafting and encoding these messages. The Soviet government happened to choose that day to prohibit telegraphic cipher communication by the Vologda missions (a measure that was rescinded some days later in response to Robins' vigorous representations in Moscow). Telegraphic communication being now impossible, Bullard might have left for Moscow that night. But by the time he learned of it, the daily Moscow train had left. Only three days now remained before the mysterious deadline. Frantic with exasperation, frustration, and concern for the safety of his men, Bullard was obliged to cool his heels in Vologda for another twenty-four hours before returning to Moscow to pack and make his departure.

He arrived in Moscow on the afternoon of May 4, just at the moment of Summers' death. During that one evening and the following day, with the help of a Consulate General badly shaken and confused by the sudden death of its chief, Bullard had to complete the arrangements (already instituted, fortunately, by his assistants) for closing out most of the activities of the office, arrange for a continued operation of the program by local Russian employees, and make personal preparations to leave for an indefinite period. The situation was made doubly difficult by the fact that his orders had given him no clear indication whether the measure was final or whether he should expect to return. The necessary arrangements were made, however, in one way or another; and by evening of May 5 Bullard and his American associates found themselves, weary and breathless, proceeding by *drozhki* to the Yaroslav Station in order to catch the train for Vologda and the north.

There, at the station, was enacted the last scene in the drama of the differences between the Compub group and the Red Cross Commission, dating from the break between Sisson and Robins in February. Bullard, paying off his *izvozchik* at the Yaroslav Station, saw the Red Cross Pierce Arrow driving up. Not wishing to see Robins (the two men had not been on speaking terms since the Robins-Sisson controversy), he dodged into the station buffet-restaurant and waited there, hoping Robins had come down only to visit the special Red Cross car, kept on a siding in the station yards, and would soon disappear again. But when he later went to the platform, there was Robins, "with Man Friday Gumberg at his heels," also bound for Vologda.

What was it that brought Robins to leave for Vologda on this same evening of May 5? He was not leaving Russia for good; he had, in fact just received messages from Paris and Washington requiring that he remain in Moscow for "some days longer." [6] He had been expecting, however, for two or three weeks, to pay a visit to Vologda. He had just received from Francis a long letter indicating that Francis wondered that he had not come sooner, and wanted to talk to him. This was presumably the main reason for his journey. He had armed himself, before leaving, with a letter from Lockhart, plainly designed to be shown to Francis, and dealing with the possibility of intervention by invitation.[7]

[6] This was presumably because Henry P. Davison was just sailing from Europe on his return to Washington, and it was thought wise to await his return before making a final decision.

[7] The text of this letter, written May 5, is worth noting in itself:

"I am afraid you will have left for Vologda before I have a chance of seeing you. Do let me, in support of my view of things here, put before you the following definite instances in which Trotsky has shown his willingness to work with the Allies.

"(1) He has invited Allied officers to co-operate in the re-organization of the New Army.

"(2) He invited us to send a commission of British Naval officers to save the Black Sea Fleet.

"(3) On every occasion when we have asked him for papers and assistance for our naval officers and our evacuation officers at Petrograd he has always given us exactly what we wanted.

"(4) He has given every facility so far for Allied Co-operation at Murmansk.

"(5) He has agreed to send the Czech Corps to Murmansk and Archangel.

All this would suggest that Robins expected simply to consult with Francis, at this critical moment, about intervention. But was this the sole motive of his trip? It was undertaken immediately after Summers' death. He must, one would think, have been aware that there was a question as to whether he himself, as the most prominent American in Moscow, ought not properly to be in attendance at the funeral. He knew that certain "information" had been received in Washington which had given the government concern for the safety of himself and his associates; and he had some knowledge that Bullard and the other Compub men had been ordered out by May 5th, i.e., this very day.

Actually, at the time Robins arrived at the station, Francis was already on a train bound for Moscow. (The two trains would be passing in the night.) Just before his departure, Francis had received Robins' message saying he was coming to Vologda, but had had no time to answer it before leaving. Now, on the train, he puzzled about Robins' decision to undertake this journey at this time. He thought it strange that Robins' telegram, sent subsequent to Summers' death, had made no mention of that tragic event. "It may be possible," Francis speculated in a report to the Department written on the train,

that his sudden departure was precipitated by Summers' death or that he had some message to convey from the Soviet Government. . . . It is barely possible that Robins had other motives for desiring to be out of Moscow, notably had heard of some action contemplated by the Soviet Government along the line of the cable sent by the Committee on Public Information. . . .[8]

Whatever the reason for Robins' journey, he and Bullard encountered each other, as noted above, on the station platform. They were two confused men: Robins setting out for Vologda in quest of an ambassador who was not there; Bullard departing, under instruc-

---

"(6) Finally, he has to-day come to a full agreement with us regarding the Allied stores at Archangel whereby we shall be allowed to retain those stores which we require for ourselves.

"You will agree that this does not look like the action of a pro-German agent, and that a policy of Allied intervention, with the co-operation and consent of the Bolshevik Government, is feasible and possible."
(Cumming & Pettit, *op.cit.*, pp. 202–203.)

[8] National Archives, State Department File 123 Su 61/154, Francis' despatch 1110 of May 6 and 14.

[201]

tions, to escape he knew not what. Bullard later described, in a letter to DeWitt Poole, the scene that ensued:

. . . "Oh!" says he [Robins], "Going away?" "No," says I, "I brought my bags down here to see if I could sell them. How much am I offered?" They walked away and then came back.

Gumberg: "You're taking a lot of baggage. Full of secret documents like those Sisson had?"

Me: "You seem to know a lot about those secret documents—we might almost call them famous, so many people have been told about them."

Robins: "They've been published in *Le Petit Parisien.*"

Me: "Is that so? I haven't seen a copy of the *Petit Parisien* since God knows when."

Gumberg: "Is Sisson still in London?"

Me: "I don't know. The last I heard from him, he was going to London, and I heard indirectly that he had got there. I don't know how long he will stay."

Robins: "You say you have not heard from Sisson from London?"

Me: "No, I haven't had a word from him direct since he left Finland. Smith cabled to me from Stockholm the date Sisson was due in London."

Robins: (fixing me with a "penetrating eye") "Somebody is lying."

Me: "I wouldn't put it a bit above two of the three here present."

Mutual scowls.

Curtain.

ACT II . . .

. . . (Scene: Station platform. Bullard and cohorts marshalled behind fortification of baggage, down stage right. Robins and cohorts, several Captains and Privates, also Gumberg. International Wagon-Lits in background. Temperature icy. Robins saunters out and indicates that he wishes to meet Bullard in single combat. The two champions meet down stage center. Robins swaggers, with the air "I-know-it-all-My-secret-service-have-told me-Je-sais-tout-beware.")

Robins, opening with heavy guns: "I've seen the despatch from Sisson, ordering you home."

Bullard, a bit nonplussed, but realizing that R[obins] was en route for Vologda—the source of all information: "I'm afraid you've been victimized, Colonel; I haven't been ordered home."

R.: "Well, ordered by Sisson to get out of Russia."

B.: "Wrong again. As I told you ten minutes ago, I have not received any direct word from Sisson since he left Finland."

(Once more the "penetrating glance.")

Curtain.

Arthur Bullard and the "Compub"

The last act turned out to be farce, as the Colonel did not have a place reserved and Gumberg slipped in ahead and tried to pinch one of our compartments. . . .

But the important thing, of course, is—How the Hell did the Colonel get the tip? He was lying when he said that he had seen the despatch, or he would not have insisted that it came from Sisson. I am morally certain that the leak was in Vologda. . . .[9]

Unsatisfied as to the sources of Robins' knowledge, Bullard proceeded on his journey to Vologda and thence, posthaste, to Archangel. There, after a delay of some days, for which they unjustly blamed the casualness of the Vologda Embassy, and during which they slept in the crowded premises of the British Shipping Office, he and his associates finally succeeded in being received—very kindly, in the circumstances—as guests aboard the *H.M.S. Alexander*. Somewhat ludicrously attired in the uniform of His Majesty's Navy ("like the male chorus in Pinafore," as Bullard put it), they passed several weeks of enforced idleness on board the icebreaker, before being finally evacuated on June 24 on one of the two food ships.[10]

Bullard's initial exasperation over this sudden termination of his work in Moscow knew no bounds. In a friendly letter to Sisson, written in Archangel, he poured out his grievances:

If ears burn because of what people think about one, yours must be pretty near ashes!

. . . Why in hell couldn't you send me some word from London as to your plans? . . .

. . . if there was any sense at all to your cryptic cable we are all in imminent danger of arrest. And every day that passes without any rumor of trouble from the police makes it harder to believe that the order of withdrawal was necessary.

[9] Bullard MSS, *op.cit.,* Box 15, Folder labelled "Robins & Gumberg in Russia."
Bullard was in error. Robins' subordinate, Wardwell, had learned of the directive from the Compub representative in Petrograd, and had passed the word on to Robins. That the message came not from Sisson personally, but from another subordinate of Creel, was of no consequence.

[10] Arrangements were finally made in Washington whereby one member of Bullard's staff, Read Lewis, was permitted to return to Moscow and to take charge of the residual work being carried on by the local Russian employees. Even during this period the Moscow Compub office was quite an organization, embracing some seventy employees. Publication of the weekly Bulletin was continued until August 24, the very eve of the final departure of the Moscow Americans. After the Mirbach murder non-communist newspapers ceased to appear in Moscow and the larger cities, but the communist papers took some material. Press material from the United States also ceased to come through by early July; so the Bulletin was subsequently made up of valuable background information.

What danger did we run that justified this ignominious flight? It seems to me poor generalship, when dealing with fairly intelligent men, to strain their blind obedience. . . .

You can't get men to work loyally on a job like this, if you treat them like school boys—or the lay characters in an Oppenheim diplomatic-detective story. . . .

. . . After all we are the only organized agency here which is getting before the Russian people the liberal democratic aspirations of our government. . . .

Perhaps we could rebuild the organization . . . but it will be a damn sight harder to rebuild the morale of these men. . . . If you had wanted to discourage them, take all pep and go out of them, you could not have done better than this treatment which seems to say: "Don't take yourselves seriously, my children, I used you as camouflage for my work, about which I do not care to trust you. Your job is over.". . .[11]

Sisson, in his reply, indicated that the action had been deliberate and that it had been done to attract the attention of official Washington to the importance of his documents. He voiced the opinion that the Americans on Soviet-held territory would thenceforth become in increasing measure hostages, and possibly even victims of retaliation, and that Bullard was better off outside the Soviet-held territory until he could go in from the east onto territory already anti-Bolshevik.[12]

Sisson was, of course, violently anti-Soviet and persuaded that the Bolsheviki were German agents. His language may well have reflected nothing more than belated rumors of successes by Semenov, in whose wake he pictured Bullard reentering Russia, and the anticipation of mounting anti-Soviet sentiment in the United States in connection with Kerensky's expected arrival in the country. Both these factors are referred to in the telegram. But his phrases will stand as evidence of the extent to which, within a few days after Robins' departure from Moscow, and just before the Czech uprising, sentiment in at least some Washington quarters had turned away from any possibility of any accommodation with the Bolsheviki and was already taking on a coloration which would help to alter the established position of the United States government in the matter of intervention.

[11] *Ibid.*, Box 14; letter of May 12, 1918, in folder "CPI, Russian Division, October 1917–May 1918."
[12] *Ibid.*, Box 1.

Bullard and those who accompanied him, incidentally, were not the only ones who had to make a dramatic and unusual exit from Bolshevik-held territory in response to Sisson's initiative. Brown and Davis were at that time in Siberia surveying the possibilities for extending Compub activities to that area. The Amur and Manchurian railways both being blocked at that moment by Semenov's activities, they were obliged to make their departure through Mongolia and across the Gobi Desert to China proper and thence to Harbin. This remarkable journey, performed partly by river transport, partly by horse and wagon, and finally by the Ford cars of the Chinese mail service from Urga (now Ulan Bator) across the desert to Kalgan, was an odyssey in itself.

❖

One cannot conclude this chapter without noting the ironic fact that America's only serious effort, in the wake of the Russian Revolution, to find intellectual contact with the more literate portion of Russian opinion on Soviet-held territory was largely halted, within a few months after its inception, by the actions of the man who was the first formal representative in Russia of the Committee on Public Information and whose responsibility it was—nominally, at least—to see that this work was put in hand and brought to successful fruition.[13] When one pursues the origins of this circumstance, one sees that it was occasioned by the fact that Sisson was confused by the competing demands of his dual competence as secret intelligence agent and as propagandist—also by the effects of the division of command as between the Committee on Public Information and the Department of State. If any single and dramatic example were needed of the damage that can be caused by the dissipation of the policymaking function in foreign affairs, the history of America's propaganda effort in Soviet Russia in 1918 would provide it.

There is a question as to what real possibilities existed for an American propaganda effort in Russia in the passion-ridden year of 1918. The non-Bolshevik elements were already favorably inclined

[13] It should be noted that the discussion of the Compub work in this volume relates only to that portion of the work performed on Bolshevik-held territory. Bullard, after his return to the United States, was again despatched to Russia in 1918, this time to organize propaganda work in the rear of the intervening Allied forces in Siberia. Here, valuable and interesting work was performed by the Compub organization; but the account of it does not belong in the present volume.

toward what they understood under the name of America. It is true that this understanding was vague in the extreme and wide of the mark in many respects. But the native subjectivity of the Russian intellectual, together with the extreme intensity of his preoccupation with Russia's own domestic struggle in the year 1918, rendered him at that time little susceptible to instruction about American realities. As for the Bolsheviki, they were already protected by seemingly insurmountable barricades against such suggestions as an American informational office might produce. There were those among them, to be sure, whose minds might perhaps have been affected over a longer period by a combination of persistent theoretical argument and the discipline of responsibility, had American policy been directed to these ends. But to the kind of material that was likely to emerge from an official American establishment—theoretically primitive, by necessity, and drawn up in terms which were either entirely unfamiliar to Russian-Marxist thought or had acquired outright negative associations in its lexicon of political concepts—the Bolsheviki were, as a group, quite impervious. Even the basic good will with which many Americans approached them could not readily dent the armor of their fanaticism.

The following passages from the memoirs of one of the members of Bullard's staff who looked coolly and attentively at Russian realities, Mr. William Adams Brown, Jr., will illustrate the deeper handicaps under which Bullard's efforts rested. Recounting his conversation at the Congress of Soviets in March 1918 with a radical Social-Democrat (in this instance not even a Bolshevik), Brown relates [14] that he asked this man whether a bourgeois person animated by a real dedication to the needs of the people was not to be respected or listened to in the counsels of the sort of government the Bolsheviki were now establishing.

. . . "Do you mean to say," I asked, "that, if for instance I, being a Burjúi [bourgeois], give all my life to a study of the needs of the people, and arrive at a conclusion different from that of this militant minority, I am not even to be heard or considered in any way?" "No," he replied, "for you cannot escape from the fact of class and you are not a real 'friend of the people.'" "Who is to judge," I asked, "whether or not I am a true

[14] William Adams Brown, Jr., *The Groping Giant: Revolutionary Russia as seen by an American Democrat*, Yale University Press, New Haven, 1920, pp. 116–117, and 123–124.

friend of the people?" His reply came with firmness and absolute conviction. *"We* shall judge."

I parted from this man, intelligent, forceful, even widely read in certain lines, and evidently capable, active and energetic, as one might part from an enemy after a truce, with a friendly shake of the hand, but with the consciousness of an unbridgeable gulf between him and me. The little pile of American literature on the table near which we were standing seemed quite overwhelmingly submerged amid the mass of Bolshevik pamphlets that surrounded it. I, too, felt overwhelmed among that great crowd of men who were acting, some consciously, others unknowingly, under the influence of the new dispensation to which I had just been given this key—"We shall judge.". . .

. . . wherever the cardinal doctrine of Bolshevism was not dominant in a man's mind, an American was accepted as an honest man and a friend, and found among the people a welcome and response that gladdened his heart. It was confirmation of the fact that only where the doctrine of my friendly enemy at the All-Russian Congress was accepted from conviction or swallowed as propaganda, was an almost insurmountable barrier erected between American and Russian.

CHAPTER IX

ROBINS' DEPARTURE

Colonel Robbins is not taken seriously here and will not be received by the President.—Message to the British Foreign Office, June 15, 1918, from Sir William Wiseman, special British diplomatic agent in the United States

AT the time of Summers' death, Robins was still in cable correspondence with his Washington principals about what was to happen to himself and his staff.

On May 9, the day after Summers' funeral, final instructions for the future of the Red Cross Commission were received from the Red Cross in Washington through the State Department. The other members of the Red Cross Commission, it was stated, might remain for the time being, if Robins approved. He himself was "under all circumstances" to come home at once for consultation.[1]

No information is available as to the background of this final telegram. There is every reason to suppose, though the message did not so indicate, that the Department of State had a voice in the framing of it and that it reflected accurately the Department's desires. Robins himself took it as an order from the State Department, and told Francis so.[2]

❖

[1] Cumming & Pettit, *op.cit.*, p. 203. On the night before his departure Robins received a further message from Thacher urging him to wait for a telegram despatched the previous evening in which, he said, the State Department, Red Cross officials, and Thompson all agreed. But Robins was by this time unwilling to change his plans and insisted on leaving as scheduled. (Wardwell MSS, Diary, *op.cit.*)

[2] *Foreign Relations, 1918, Russia*, Vol. I, *op.cit.*, p. 530. Five months later, a representative of the War Department, who had occasion to consult Basil Miles, on the Russian desk of the State Department, about the possibility of Robins' going abroad again, made the following confidential record of what Miles gave him to understand:

"Mr. R[obins] was sent to Russia with a Red Cross Mission the object of which was to study the conditions existing in that country. . . .

Robins' Departure

It is not possible to trace, in the confusing welter of telegrams of the last days of April and the first days of May, any clearly documented and direct relationship between Summers' death and Robins' departure. Nevertheless, it was the general intuitive feeling among the Americans in Russia that the one event had made the other inevitable. Summers' death somehow achieved, or marked, as nothing else could perhaps have done, the triumph among the Americans of the orientation which he had so stoutly represented. The image of Robins' high-powered operations, tinged as it was with the suspicion of an excessive intimacy with the Soviet leaders and of a personal ambition for the ambassadorship, contrasted unfavorably with that of the hard-working and self-effacing Consul General, who had been left—as many saw it—to bear in Moscow the burden of upholding the dignity of the world that both the Bolsheviki and the Germans were determined to destroy, and whose health had proved too fragile for the burden. Unjustly but perhaps—in the circumstances—inevitably, it became a common saying in the American colony, and soon thereafter in Washington, that "Robins killed him." The reaction was, in many instances, a certain revulsion for what Robins had stood for and for the manner in which he was reputed to have stood for it. Robins himself was unaware of this—perhaps he never understood it. But from the day of Summers' death the cause to which he had devoted such earnest effort was a lost cause in the minds and hearts of American officialdom.

And not of *American* officialdom alone . . . For quite other reasons, a similar crisis, with a similar denouement, was just then occurring in the French and British official colonies.

Here again, many factors were involved. The influence of the anti-Bolshevik opposition groups was now beginning to make itself felt. Untoward incidents, such as the Japanese landing at Vladivostok, had played a part. The arrival, on April 23, of the new German Ambassador had fanned Allied suspicions of the Soviet-German relationship. But it was the influence of French Ambassador Noulens that tipped the scales. Whether it was because his *amour propre*

"He then acted in such a way as to create the impression that he was an accredited agent of the U.S. and that his acts and statements were, so to speak, official. The State Department then notified the Red Cross to withdraw him from Russia, which was done. . . ." (War Department Archives, Records Branch, The Pentagon, *op.cit.*, memorandum of October 22, 1918 by Lt. L. W. Perce.)

had suffered in Russia's defection from the war and in his own ignominious peregrinations in Red Finland following his departure from Petrograd in February, or whether his conduct was motivated by more serious ideological reasons, Noulens' anti-Sovietism never wavered. Vain, politically adept, and persuasive, he was unquestionably the most formidable enemy the Bolsheviki had in the camp of the Allied representatives.

We have already noted the skillful manner in which Noulens sidetracked the discussions looking toward Allied military collaboration in early April. During the ensuing weeks, his efforts had not lagged. On April 23, the day of Mirbach's arrival in Moscow, Noulens gave an interview to the press which was no doubt calculated to stiffen the hands of the Soviet government in its dealings with the Germans but which actually served primarily to infuriate the Soviet leaders against Noulens himself. Defending the Japanese landing at Vladivostok, Noulens said that the question could be localized "provided that the Tokio Government is given the satisfaction which it has the right to demand," thus hinting broadly that it was up to the Soviet government to make concessions to Japanese aspirations in the Far East. He then turned to the situation in European Russia, particularly the Ukraine, where—he pointed out —the advance of the German forces was going far beyond the limits suggested by the Brest-Litovsk settlement. Charging the Germans with plans to establish economic domination over Russia and to "organize colonization centers in Siberia through their prisoners of war," he proceeded to threaten the Bolsheviki quite bluntly with a general Allied intervention:

. . . The Allies may be compelled to intervene in order to meet this menace, which is directed against them and, to a much greater extent, against the Russian people. Should the Allies at any time be forced to resort to military operations, they will act solely in the capacity of friends. . . . I have no data of any kind relative to the intentions of the governments in this question; but, no matter what happens, I feel confident in saying that should armed intervention take place in Siberia, it would have an Interallied and distinctly friendly character.[3]

The main effect of this interview—and it may have been the effect Noulens intended—was to inflame the violent suspicions that already wracked the Soviet mind in connection with the Japanese

[3] Bunyan, *op.cit.*, p. 71.

landing at Vladivostok and the intentions of the Allies generally, and to cause the Bolshevik leaders to adopt a new wariness and sharpness in their dealings with the Allied community. They at once demanded Noulens' recall—a demand which the French government, at Noulens' recommendation, simply ignored. They cracked down, for some days, on the telegraphic communications of the Allied representatives at Vologda, even going so far as to interdict Robins' direct channel to Francis—a development which the latter, to whom the intensity of the recent telegraphic intimacy with Robins had not been entirely comfortable, accepted with a certain sense of relief. In many ways, the Soviet attitude toward the Allies began to tighten up noticeably in the wake of Noulens' pronouncement.

Sadoul, who stood to lose most from this trend of developments, was in despair. Throughout the month of March, while Noulens was in Finland, the *rapprochement* of the Allies with the Soviet leaders had appeared to Sadoul to be making giant strides. At that time "one had seemed," he wrote some weeks later,

to be close to agreement. The return of our ambassador marked a palpable check to this new tendency, as did the non-execution or the half-hearted execution of obligation accepted by the United States and France for the promised collaboration by their engineers and military experts. Noulens' interview has given to Trotsky and Lenin the impression of a return to the old hostility, of a clear desire to compromise the English negotiations and in any case to put France in official opposition to England.[4]

Lockhart, well aware of this new trend, had the same impression as to its origin: ". . . in Vologda," he later wrote,

there was M. Noulens, the French Ambassador, intent only on one aim: to have no dealings with the cutthroats who had insulted him. On April 29th we had a meeting of the Allied representatives in my rooms. General Lavergne informed us that M. Noulens was in favour of intervention without Bolshevik consent and without asking for it.[5]

This last reference, and particularly the date to which it refers, holds special interest for the student of Soviet-American relations, for it was only three days after Lavergne made this statement to Lockhart that Francis, who since the end of February had con-

---

[4] Sadoul, *Notes* . . . , *op.cit.*, p. 320.
[5] Lockhart, *op.cit.*, p. 268.

sistently opposed every suggestion of Allied intervention without Soviet consent, now reversed his opinion and despatched to Washington a telegram in the opposite sense which was to have considerable importance in Allied counsels and to enter prominently into most of the historical records of the period.

What prompted Francis to send this message just at this time is not entirely clear. He himself attributed his change of heart primarily to his belief that the Germans were now beginning to put heavy pressure on the Bolsheviki over Murmansk.[6] Coupled with this, he indicated, was his growing realization of Lenin's dominant position and of the seriousness of Lenin's ideological purpose. But Noulens' personal influence was also certainly in the picture. The press reports of Francis' displacement by Robins had been coupled, in each case, with the parallel allegation that Sadoul was to replace Noulens. The sense of being the victims of a common intrigue can hardly have failed to bring the two ambassadors closer together. The French in Vologda, in any case, were not slow to exploit the advantage this incident gave them. They "put a spoke in Robins's wheel," as Lockhart put it,

by playing on the American Ambassador's vanity. In his presence a member of the French Embassy had asked who was the American Ambassador —Francis or Robins—because they always said the opposite of each other. As a result of these intrigues Robins's position became intolerable, . . .[7]

Whatever it was that tipped the scales of Francis' mind to the anti-Soviet side at the end of April—whether suspicion of Robins' ambitions, or shock at the breach created with Summers, the abundant rumors of German control that accompanied the arrival of the German diplomatic mission in Moscow, or the realization of Lenin's earnestness about world revolution—the message that Francis sent on May 2, two days before Summers' death, was a comprehensive one, the preparation of which had obviously taken several days. And it was also a decisive one; it fixed irrevocably the line that would now be taken to the bitter end by the American Embassy at Vologda. Summers would no doubt have died more easily had

[6] In a letter to Felix Cole of June 13, Francis stated: "The immediate occasion for my recommendation was that I heard the Soviet Government would demand the evacuation of Murmansk by the Allies." This statement was almost certainly connected with the rumors of increased German pressure which followed Mirbach's arrival in Moscow. (Francis MSS, *op.cit.*)
[7] Lockhart, *op.cit.*, p. 270.

he known the tenor of this message, sent on the eve of his own fatal illness; for it marked, in reality, the triumph in the Vologda Embassy of his own beliefs and the defeat of those of Robins.

Before we turn to the content of Francis' message, it might be well to note that the turning point that took place in Francis' thinking around the first of May was somewhat different in nature from that which took place in the counsels of the French and British. In the case of Britain and France, the choice was between a real military collaboration with the Soviet authorities, on the one hand, and a policy of encouragement of anti-Soviet forces, with a view to restoring an eastern front against Germany, on the other. The Americans —and this is most significant for the interpretation of the intervention as a whole—had no such thoughts of interference in Russian internal political life, nor were they ever really convinced of the reality of the French and British schemes for restoring an effective military opposition to the Germans in the east. Although Francis did not spell out clearly in his message of May 2 the purposes to which he conceived that intervention would be conducive, and did not define what sort of intervention he had in mind, we may infer from his message that he was thinking only of countering what he believed to be the growing German penetration of the country, protecting the military stores at Vladivostok and Archangel, maintaining the Murmansk base, and guarding against German exploitation of the Soviet weakness in the Russian Far East. His decision was based, of course, on a negative determination precisely counter to the views that Robins was advocating—a determination, that is, that the Soviet leaders could *not* be trusted, that their ideological preconceptions against the western countries were too deep, their cynicism about the war aims of the western governments too sweeping and appalling.

With these observations as an introduction, let us turn to the text of the message Francis sent on May 2. Despite its length, it deserves careful analysis and attention.

Francis began, bluntly and somewhat dramatically, with the flat assertion: "In my judgment, time for Allied intervention has arrived." He had been hoping, he went on to explain, that the Soviet government would request intervention. His course of action in recent weeks had been directed to that end. He proceeded to list the things he had done with a view to bringing the Soviet government to request intervention. He had remained in Russia, even when all his colleagues had departed. He had, despite "Summers's expressed humiliation," encouraged Robins to remain in Moscow and to cultivate close unofficial relations with the Bolsheviki. He had opposed unilateral Japanese intervention. He had encouraged, so far as he was able, the proffering of Allied military advice in the formation of a new army. He had tried to have American railroad men sent from the Far East to help the Soviet government. He had favored the revival of commercial exchanges. He had soothed the ruffled feelings of the Soviet leaders over the Chinese embargo on shipments to Siberia. He had turned the other cheek to the Soviet restrictions on American official telegraphic communications, to the Soviet demand for the recall of the American Consul at Vladivostok, to the complaints over the Japanese landing. Finally, although he had been seriously ill from April 19 to 28 and had been greatly weakened by his illness, he had "never ceased to work nor lost spirit." (We must remember here that Francis was now 67 years old.) All this he had done in the hopes that the Bolsheviki could be induced to request the intervention of the Allies. Yet they had not done so.

He knew, he went on to say, that the Secretary of State was opposed to an exclusive Japanese intervention. This position he earnestly approved. But he had no knowledge of the Secretary's attitude toward a *joint* Allied intervention. Nor did he have any up-to-date knowledge about Japanese policy.

His present recommendation, "the gravity of which I fully realize," was precipitated by the following conditions:

1. The new German Ambassador, Count Mirbach, was dominating the Soviet government and was "practically dictator in Moscow."

2. To the Soviet complaints over German violations of the Brest-Litovsk Treaty, Mirbach had replied that the German military advance onto Soviet territory would cease if the Allies would evacuate Murmansk and Archangel. Such evacuation he, Francis, thought would be exceedingly unwise.

Riggs, he went on to explain, still thought that the Soviet government would approve Allied intervention if it felt it to be inevitable and if the military representatives were in a position to give it advance notice of what was to be done. But "the longer we wait," Francis considered, "the stronger foothold Germany will secure."

Riggs also thought that either the Embassy ought to move to Moscow or the United States ought to have a diplomatic representative there. With this, too, Francis was unable to concur. It would lead, he observed shrewdly, either to recognition or to "emphasizing non-recognition." In the first case the United States would strengthen the Soviet government, and thus make itself guilty of a form of intervention in Russian internal affairs; in the second case, the existing tensions would only be increased. He had never, he reminded the Secretary, advocated recognition, though Robins and "probably" Lockhart favored it.

He had delayed making this recommendation for intervention, he said, not only in the hope that the Soviet government would request it but also in the hope that there would be some expression of Russian public opinion demanding it. But he now doubted that such popular sentiment as existed in Russia in favor of an Allied intervention would assume any "physical form." The Bolsheviki, he observed, "treat with severity every such movement, terming it counter-revolutionary." He had also expected that the Soviet government would yield to Allied demands that the military stores be kept out of German hands. But thus far, he inferred, no such assurances had been forthcoming.

What else then remained? Russia was passing through a "dream or orgy." She would awaken someday; but would it be in time? Lenin was dominant and Lenin was calling for world-wide social revolution. As late as April 28, Lenin had approved of the slaughter on the western front as something that would weaken the imperialist governments and bring the world nearer to the dictatorship of the proletariat. Francis doubted, as he observed in conclusion, "whether Allies can longer afford to overlook principles which Lenin is aggressively championing."

With these reflections, Francis dropped his voice and permitted his message to trail off to an unrhetorical conclusion. He would "patiently await," he said (somewhat wistfully), either instructions or information.[8]

❖

Robins, oblivious of the fact that his hopes had just received a severe blow in the form of Francis' telegram, was not downhearted

[8] *Foreign Relations, 1918, Russia*, Vol. 1, *op.cit.*, pp. 519–521.

as he set about his preparations for departure. His own hand was substantially played out in Moscow. It was just as well, he felt, that the scene of action should be shifted for the time being to Washington. There, he would be able to add his eloquent voice to those of Thompson and his other supporters at home. He would know how to carry his case to the American public. By operating in Washington, he would be able to by-pass the obstruction presented by Noulens and the other "indoor minds" (as he conceived them) in Russia, and to swing opinion in favor of "collaboration."

In departing, Robins did not abandon the hope that Francis might be persuaded to move to Moscow. This was a hope which he shared, quite obviously, with the Soviet leaders. Voznesenski, representing the Soviet government at Summers' funeral, had pressed Francis to grant him an interview during his visit to Moscow. This Francis reluctantly did on May 10. The Soviet official asked why he did not come and take a house there, instead of remaining in Vologda. Francis pointed out that the other Allied missions had joined him in Vologda; they felt safer there, he said, from possible German interference. The Soviet official pointed out that the German Ambassador was now in Moscow. To this Francis countered with the observation that the German was treated more considerately than the rest of them.[9]

Two days later the Commercial Attaché, Mr. Chapin Huntington, who had also come down to Moscow for the funeral, met Robins in his box at the opera. (This was only two nights before Robins' departure.)

"Why can't you persuade the Embassy to move down to Moscow?" Robins asked Huntington. "It's just as safe as Vologda."

Huntington said that it was beyond his competence. When, he countered, would the Germans occupy Moscow?

"When the Allies occupy Siberia and not until then," was Robins' answer.[10]

Among his other preparations for departure, Robins evidently wrote some sort of letter to Trotsky, expressing appreciation for the latter's kindness and attention. On the eve of his departure he received Trotsky's reply:

[9] *Ibid.*, p. 527.
[10] National Archives, State Department File 123 Su 61/127; letter, Huntington to Francis, May 17, 1918.

Permit me to express to you my most sincere gratitude for those words of greeting which you so kindly addressed to me on the occasion of your, I hope, temporary departure from Russia. Among the official representatives of foreign states, you were one of the few who cared to and who could impartially comprehend those immense difficulties under which the Soviet power had to labor. All the misfortunes, vices, crimes of the centuries-long despotism, increased by the war, had fallen upon the head of the revolutionary government, which with all of its energy is aspiring to elevate the life of the Russian people to the level of the principles and demands of the socialistic program. Now, as six months ago in the days of the October rebellion, when I had the honor to meet you for the first time, I thoroughly believe that the Russian people, under the leadership of the working class, will come out with honor from all difficulties, and that the Soviet Republic will not become a slave. Now, as six months ago, I have no doubt that the toiling masses of all countries will give us mighty support and will help to establish on this earth, steeped in crimes, a new system which will unite the humanity of both hemispheres into a single fraternal toiling family. . . .[11]

It was not from Trotsky alone that Robins received a parting attention. At some time on the eve of his departure Robins paid a farewell call on Lenin and received from the latter what, of all things in the world, he most wanted to receive. From what preliminary discussions, if any, it flowed is unclear. It was a document outlining Russia's economic needs and her possibilities for trade with the United States.[12]

The paper was itself unsigned; but it was submitted under the cover of a personal note from Lenin, in English and in his own hand, saying:

I enclose the preliminary plan of our economic relations with America. This preliminary plan was elaborated in the Council of Export Trade in our highest Council of National Economy.

I hope this preliminary can be useful for you in your conversation with the American Foreign Office and American Export Specialists.

The paper attached to Lenin's note was entitled: "Russian-American Commercial Relations." It consisted of three parts. In the first of these, figures were given to show the decline in Russian production and imports, and to make plain the extreme exhaustion

---

[11] Robins mss, *op.cit.* (The letter was in Russian; the translation is mine.)

[12] Cumming & Pettit, *op.cit.*, pp. 204–212. A photostat of the covering note is in the Robins mss, *op.cit.*

of the Russian economy. The claim was made, defensively and surely to some extent inaccurately, that the decline in Russian production was due to curtailment of imports of capital goods rather than to the decline in the productivity of labor.

In the second part statistics were cited to demonstrate Russia's extreme dependence, in the years just before the Revolution, on imports of capital goods from the leading western industrial countries, and to show the great increase of the share of the United States in total Russian trade in the period immediately preceding the Revolution.

In the third section, the point was first made that while Germany was indeed entitled to most-favored-nation treatment by the provisions of the Brest-Litovsk Treaty, her present wartime difficulties were such that she would not be able to take extensive advantage of this privilege. A comparative breakdown was then given, by main commodity groups, of American exports to Russia in 1916, and of German exports to Russia before the war, with a view to driving home the point that America ought, in view of Germany's exhaustion, to be able to become the supplier of many items previously supplied by Germany. A strong bait was offered to American capitalists in the statement:

. . . With the inability of Germany to exploit the Russian market for German industry during the next few years, it will be very difficult for her in the future to regain the leading part, if during that time America succeeds in taking advantage of the favorable circumstances created for her by events and establishes a working apparatus of commerce between the two countries.

A listing was then given of the commodities with which Russia had been in the habit of paying for German products. Hope was held out that the variety of these commodities could eventually be increased in exports to America. But it was hinted that full payment could not be expected until Russian productivity had been revived, and for this, of course, imports would have to come first. (Russia, in other words, would need credits.)

Russia's needs from the United States were defined by broad commodity groups—railroad supplies, agricultural machinery, electric power plant equipment, and mining machinery being the main items. Further studies were promised which would permit the drawing up of precise lists.

There followed, then, a paragraph on possible concessions, pregnant with prophetic suggestions both for future Soviet policy on concessions generally and for the future exploitation by the Soviet government of the monopoly of foreign trade which it had, at that time, just recently established. An unwillingness to grant exclusive concessions was justified by reference to the provisions of the Brest-Litovsk Treaty. But there were, the document suggested, other ways of skinning a cat. On the basis of "business arrangements" rather than of written concessions,

. . . America [could] participate actively in the exploitation of the marine riches of Eastern Siberia, of coal and other mines, as well as in the railroad and marine transportation construction in Siberia and northern European Russia. . . .

As security for payment for American economic assistance, the document then finally suggested the following: American participation in the construction of power stations on the Volkhov and Svir Rivers and in the "development of the water routes of the Donets Basin and the Volga-Don Canal," and likewise in the development of coal mines, in the sealing industry, in the lumber industry of southern Kamchatka, and in railway construction in the Soviet Far East. The suggestion was further made that Americans might help in the reconstruction of Soviet agriculture.

Russia was prepared, it was finally stated, to guarantee that the military stores on hand in Russia would not be sold to Germany and that all war materials manufactured in England and America would be restored to the United States.

It was with this remarkable document in his pocket that Robins made his departure the following day. In view of the importance it was to have henceforth in his own mind and in the minds of many who were influenced by him, it becomes necessary to inquire carefully into the motives which caused Lenin to present it to him.

We have already noted in Chapter v the basic outlines of Lenin's foreign policy in the weeks immediately following the Brest-Litovsk Treaty. In late April and early May, several things had occurred that caused deep alarm to the Bolsheviki and made them increasingly apprehensive that the breathing-space might soon be broken by Allied or German action against them.

First of all, Semenov had launched a new offensive, and launched it with Japanese support—of which the Soviet government was well aware.

Secondly, in some way or other the Soviet leaders received in the first days of May the impression that the Allies were about to present them with an ultimatum calling upon them either to resume the war against Germany or to submit to Japanese intervention. The origin of this impression is obscure. It may well have lain in the Soviet interpretation of statements made by Lockhart in connection with the Archangel war supplies, which subject he had discussed with Trotsky on the 5th.

Thirdly, as we shall see in a later chapter, the first reports from the newly appointed Soviet representative at Berlin, Adolf Joffe, had been interpreted in Moscow, incorrectly, to mean that the Germans were threatening to tear up the Brest-Litovsk Treaty and renew full-fledged hostilities against the Soviet republic. The Soviet leaders gained momentarily the impression that greater influence in German policy was now being, or was about to be, exercised by the military high command. All this caused great uneasiness to the Soviet leaders. They were already much disturbed by the fact that German military operations and intrigues in the south of Russia were depriving the Soviet republic of sorely needed food supplies and were giving aid and comfort to opposition groups.

In these alarming circumstances, the Soviet leaders began to give renewed attention to every conceivable possibility for increasing the divisions among the western powers generally and for preventing any of them from adopting any common course of action toward the Soviet republic. In a set of "Theses on the Present Political Situation," drafted on either the 12th or 13th of May (i.e., one or two days before the presentation of this document to Robins), Lenin repeated once again his injunction to his followers to "maneuver, retreat, and bide one's time." After pointing out that the aggressive tendencies of the German military party were still somewhat restrained by the general disinclination of the ruling German circles for a reopening of the war in the east, Lenin proceeded to say the following about the Japanese:

The Japanese inclination to move against Russia, on the other hand, is restrained, first, by the danger of unrest and uprisings in China; secondly, by a certain antagonism from the side of America, which fears the strengthening of Japan and *hopes with the conclusion of peace to find an easier way of acquiring raw materials from Russia.*

Of course it is entirely possible that in Japan and in Germany the extreme elements of the military party can gain ascendency at any minute. . . . The American *bourgeoisie* can make a dicker with the Japanese *bourgeoisie,* or the Japanese with the German. For this reason the most intensive military preparation is our unquestionable duty.[18]

On the evening of May 14, Lenin made a major statement on foreign policy at a combined session of the All-Russian Central Executive Committee and the Moscow Soviet. While this statement would be well worth noting in any case for its bearing on the general course of events described in this narrative, it is particularly interesting if it be recalled that it was uttered on the very day, apparently, of the delivery to Robins of the scheme for America's participation in Russian economic reconstruction.

The Soviet state, Lenin began by pointing out (with an uninhibited mixing of metaphors), was still "an oasis amid the raging sea of imperialist rapaciousness." The war had given birth to "such complicated, such sharp, such confused conflicts" that at every turn situations were arising where the decision as between war and peace, or in favor of this or that grouping, hung by a hair. "Just such a situation," Lenin said, "we have been experiencing in the last two days." The Soviet republic was being saved only by the fact that the waves of this raging sea of imperialist reaction were "cancelling each other out and sapping each other's strength before they reached the shores of the Soviet republic." The security of the Soviet republic hung on the existence of two conflicts in the capitalist camp. One was the World War in the west, dividing the Germans from the British. The other was the rivalry between Japan and America.

. . . The economic development of these countries [Japan and America] over the course of several decades has stored up a great mass of inflammable material which renders inevitable a desperate conflict between these two powers for mastery of the Pacific Ocean and its shores. The entire diplomatic and economic history of the Far East places it completely beyond the range of doubt that the fierce ripening conflict between Japan and America cannot possibly be prevented under conditions of capitalism.

[18] Lenin, Vol. 27, *op.cit.,* p. 326 (italics added).

It is this conflict, temporarily covered over at the present time by the alliance of Japan and America against Germany, which restrains the advance of Japanese imperialism against Russia. The campaign which was begun against the Soviet republic (the landing at Vladivostok, the support of Semenov's band) is being held back because it threatens to turn the concealed conflict between Japan and America into an open war. Of course it is entirely possible, and we must not forget it, that the groupings among the imperialist powers, however solid they may appear, might be turned upside down within a few days' time if the sacred interests of private property, the sacred rights to concessions, etc., should demand it. The tiniest sparks would perhaps suffice to explode the present groupings of the powers, and then these conflicts to which I have pointed could no longer serve for our protection.[14]

Lenin then went on to describe in greater detail the contrary possibility, equally threatening to Russia, that the Japanese might come to an agreement with the Germans. It was understandable, in view of these considerations, he said, why

. . . the situation in the Far East is an unstable one. One thing must be said: it is necessary to look clearly at these contradictions between the capitalist interests. . . .

Turning, in the latter part of his speech, to the question of what the Soviet government could do in this difficult situation, Lenin said they would do everything that lay within their power, everything within the possibilities of diplomatic tactics, to postpone the moment of a final capitalist attack against Russia:

. . . We will do everything in order to prolong this short and unstable breathing-space which we gained in March, because we are firmly convinced that we have behind us tens of millions of workers and peasants who know that with every week and with every month that this breathing-space lasts they are gaining new strength.

We say to ourselves . . . everything that our diplomacy can give to delay the moment of war, to prolong the intermission, we are obliged to do.

It was against this background of calculation that the document described above was sent, or handed, to Robins on May 14. The motivation is, in the light of Lenin's statements, not hard to discern. One must bear in mind here the total, sweeping cynicism by which the doctrinaire minds of these Russian Communists were

[14] *Ibid.*, p. 332.

guided in their assessment of the psychology of the governments of the great non-communist powers. It was a cardinal tenet of communist belief that these governments were only the spineless puppets and agents of their own financiers and manufacturers. The latter, in turn, were pictured as governed in all their actions by a voracious and consuming passion for profit—a passion overriding all forms of individual conscience, all natural feelings, all patriotism, in fact every other conceivable human impulse. Believing this, the Soviet leaders were convinced that the capitalist governments were always to be had by an appeal to the cupidity of the financiers who stood behind them.[15] Even in these years of the utmost patriotic dedication in the Allied countries, the Soviet leaders remained convinced that behind all the superhuman exertions of the western peoples in the war, behind all the sacrifices and sorrow and devotion that went into the respective war efforts, there lay, basically, only the calculations of sinister and unfeeling men whose sole goal in life was profit.

This being the case, it is only too clear that Lenin's aim, in giving the document to Robins, was to encourage American capitalists to hope that if only the Japanese could be kept out of Siberia there would be serious possibilities for a future preferential economic position of the United States in relation to that area and in the economic reconstruction of Russia generally. The suggested concessions with respect to mineral rights, to participation in electric power plant construction, to a part in the construction of the Russian railroads, etc.—all these were conceived by Lenin, in coldest cynicism and contempt, as baits to the American capitalists—irresistible baits, he thought, which would cause them to reject any possible immediate dickers with the "Japanese *bourgeoisie*" and to hold out for future deals with the Soviet government which, they were to be encouraged to believe, would relegate both the German and Japanese businessmen to a secondary place. The attachment to the "sacred right of concessions" was the handle by which, Lenin believed, the behavior of the American capitalists could be manipulated, even by those who themselves despised and abhorred this motivation.

[15] One is moved to recall, here, John Reed's naïve attempt (see Volume 1, p. 408) to interest American "bourgeois circles" in Russia, in the winter of 1918, by appealing to their hope of future profit.

This evidence of Lenin's motive finds confirmation in the fact that on this same day, May 14, Chicherin apprised the Germans that all was ready on the Soviet side for the inauguration of the work of the economic commission envisaged by the Brest-Litovsk Treaty; and on the following day he further revealed to the Germans instructions that were to be given to the Soviet representative on this commission.[16] These instructions held out the prospect of economic concessions to the Germans, paralleling the offer made simultaneously to the Americans through Robins. It was frankly admitted, in the instructions governing negotiations with the Germans, that the reconstruction of Russian economy would necessitate "the continuation and possible expansion of commercial relations with the Entente." Actually, there was little direct conflict in the possible concessions dangled, respectively, before the Germans and the Americans. The latter were mostly specific, and related primarily to the Siberian and North Russian areas to which Americans might reasonably expect to have access. The concessions suggested in the case of the Germans were general, the references being to the production of oil and artificial fertilizers, to gold mining, and to railway construction generally. Only in one point were the offers identical: namely, in the reference to possible German or American participation (as the case might be) in the development of large agricultural tracts by modern methods, against compensation in the form of a share in the profits.[17]

The fact that these instructions for the Soviet negotiators were handed to Mirbach, for transmission to Joffe, may be taken as a clear indication of the fact that they were intended as a means of exciting German hopes and interest, rather than as a serious basis for negotiation. A similar motive most certainly underlay the communication handed, simultaneously, to Robins.

In making these suggestions to Robins, Lenin did not need to be too worried about the possibility that he might some day be seriously held to the offer. The position of the Soviet regime, as we have seen, was viewed by him as desperate. The main and overriding objective was to prolong, at all costs, the breathing-space. This,

---

[16] National Archives, Foreign Affairs Branch, German Foreign Ministry Archives; St. Antony's Box 83, Deutschland 131, telegrams 105 and 113 of May 14 and 15, respectively, Mirbach to Foreign Office.

[17] In the case of the Germans, this dream materialized some years later (not too happily) in the form of the large Krupp concessions on the Manych River.

in terms of the Far East, meant to prevent any sort of dicker between the Japanese and the Americans. What better means could there be of doing this than to hold out to the Americans the hope of a favored commercial position in Siberia and European Russia on the basis of an agreement with the Soviet government? It would be weeks and months before one could conceivably get down to any detailed and businesslike discussion of any of these vaguely delineated projects. But even a few weeks of further respite from intervention—a few weeks more of the breathing-space—represented in Lenin's eyes the greatest and most precious of all treasures. This present gain would be worth a thousand minor embarrassments in the more distant future. If the time should ever come when one would be asked to make good on these promises, there would still be infinite opportunity for maneuver, for evasion, for argument. There was no reason why anything should have to be accepted, in the final analysis, that appeared really to threaten the interests of the Soviet state.

It was advantageous, then, to let Robins disappear from the Moscow scene with this document in his pocket. If it postponed for even a few days the threatened dicker of the Japanese and American capitalists, it would have served its purpose. If it did not, then nothing, at any rate, was lost; the catastrophe would then already be at hand.

❖

Wardwell, who had been called to Moscow from Petrograd to take over what was left of the Red Cross operations (he arrived in Moscow May 10), had several occasions to talk with Robins just before the latter's departure. If Robins said anything of the communication from Lenin, Wardwell was too discreet to mention it in his diary. Robins did say that he thought his situation in Moscow had become quite impossible. He told of the constant difficulty he had had with Summers. He complained of the Ambassador's impossible "wobbling" between the two points of view: his and Summers'. As a result, he said, no decision was being taken at all on the great questions of policy, and the danger of German influence and control was becoming constantly greater.

Lockhart also had opportunity to talk with Robins on the eve of the latter's departure. Robins dined with him on his last evening in Moscow. On this, as on many other occasions, Robins talked with enthusiasm about his idol Cecil Rhodes; and again Lockhart was impressed with his eloquence and force of personality. He later recorded, in connection with this occasion, that Robins

possessed in a remarkable degree the talent of extracting exactly what he wanted from everything he read, and dramatising it afterwards in his conversation. He was a great personality and a man of sterling character and iron determination. His departure was a great loss to me. In the almost lone hand I was playing his moral courage had been an immense support.[18]

❖

On the evening of May 14, Robins left in his special car on the night train for Vologda, Siberia, and Vladivostok. He was accompanied by one of his own Red Cross assistants, Captain D. Heywood Hardy, by the *Chicago Daily News* correspondent Louis Edgar Browne (the same who had tried to find out about Sisson's activities), and by the faithful Alexander Gumberg.

Gumberg, incidentally, facing an uncertain future, had contrived in the final days before departure to obtain authority to represent in the United States the interests of the Petrograd Telegraph Agency, at that time the official Soviet news-gathering and distributing agency, comparable to the TASS of a later day. Gumberg had continued, up to the moment of his departure, to maintain intimate relations with the highest Soviet leaders and to enjoy a most unusual confidence on their part. The precise nature of the hopes placed by himself and by the Soviet leaders on his future activity as representative in America of the Petrograd Telegraph Agency is not wholly clear; but it is evident that his role was conceived as that of a major propaganda and public relations agent for the Soviet government, with functions far surpassing in importance those of a mere head of a wire service. In the Gumberg papers, in the Wisconsin State Historical Society, there is an original note written by Lenin in his own hand, on April 27, 1918, to Axelrod, head of the governmental press bureau.[19] The note read as follows:

Comrade Axelrod!

I earnestly request you to help the bearer, Comrade Gumberg, to

[18] Lockhart, *op.cit.*, p. 270.
[19] The reference is to Pavel Borisovich Axelrod, a prominent Menshevik and old-revolutionary, who shortly thereafter went into the emigration and attached himself to the moderate socialist movement.

collect all materials (printed) concerning our revolution. This matter is without doubt of major public significance because on it depends the informing of America and of the entire world.

Greetings!

[signed] Lenin

Both authorship and tenor of this chit make it evident that Gumberg's mission, like that of Robins himself, was no minor matter in Soviet eyes.

On the day after his departure from Moscow, Robins' train passed through Vologda. The Ambassador came down to meet him and talked with him for a time on the station platform. It was their last meeting in Russia, and apparently the last they were ever to have. Robins said nothing to Francis about the document he had in his pocket from Lenin. Francis said nothing about the telegram he had just sent recommending intervention. They discussed Robins' recall. Robins professed to have been surprised by it. When Francis asked him to what he attributed it, Robins replied, "To Summers' suggestion."

"We had," Francis subsequently told an investigating senatorial subcommittee,

a private conversation of about 20 minutes—the train was there 50 minutes —and I turned away from him, or he turned away from me; I have forgotten which—not in any unfriendly spirit, . . .[20]

Though saying nothing to Francis about Lenin's communication or about his own future plans, Robins was indiscreet enough, after Francis departed, to tell the Associated Press correspondent and an embassy clerk who had remained on the station platform that he had with him a definite proposition from the Soviet government to the United States and was hastening to America in expectation of receiving a favorable reply, after which he expected to return promptly to Russia. ("I have the goods on my person," Francis later quoted him to the Senators as having said on this occasion.[21])

[20] *Bolshevik Propaganda, Hearings . . . , op.cit.*, p. 965.
[21] *Loc.cit.* From Omsk to Irkutsk, Robins had as a fellow passenger on the same train the new Consul General in Irkutsk, Mr. Ernest L. Harris, who was proceeding to his post from Central Asia. Nearly a year later Harris, queried about his recollections of this experience, told the Department: "[Robins] stated to me that he was returning to the U.S. for the purpose of attempting [to] induce President Wilson to recognize Bolsheviks. He carried with him an autograph letter addressed to him from Lenin. . . ." (War Department Archives, Records Branch, The Pentagon, *op.cit.*, telegram 202 of March 27, 1919 from Vladivostok.)

Francis, to whom this fascinating item of news was promptly re-layed, was deeply and understandably offended by Robins' failure to tell him any of this. "I do not understand Robins's failure to inform me of his plans," he wired the Department,

as he has continuously . . . expressed friendliness and admiration of my course. . . . Of course have no fear of Department's recognizing Soviet government if it should [last] until Robins's arrival Washington, which I doubt. Bolshevik press states Robins going to America and will return soon, while opposition press claims his final recall.[22]

At Vologda, Robins' special car was attached to the regular Siberian Express for Vladivostok. He carried a pass addressed by Lenin personally to all the soviets on the route, requiring them to "give every kind of assistance to Colonel Robins and other members of the American Red Cross Mission for an unhindered and speediest journey from Moscow to Vladivostok." [23] He had been permitted, furthermore, by special permission of the Soviet government, to take five rifles and 150 rounds of ammunition in his car.

These last, fortunately, were not needed. The journey proceeded smoothly. The pass disarmed all attempts at harassment or efforts to satisfy curiosity on the part of the local authorities. In Khabarovsk the leading Bolshevik official, Krasnoshchekov, even took Robins as a guest to a meeting of the local Soviet. The train reached Vladivostok only a few hours behind the normal peacetime schedule.

Robins was very pleased by this rapid and peaceful passage to Vladivostok. He took it as a proof of the solidity of Bolshevik control in Siberia. On arrival in Tokyo, he sent a telegram to Davison announcing his forthcoming arrival in the United States, and adding, proudly, that the Soviet government was in complete control from Moscow to Vladivostok.

Little did Robins realize that as his special car, with its eager, hopeful occupants, clicked day after day over the endless reaches of eastern Siberia, the final defeat of his purposes was following closely

---

Robins, incidentally, refused to accommodate Harris in his private car, with the result that the latter had to accept the hospitality of English travelers, already crowded in their own car. This sort of thing obviously did not endear Robins to the members of the Foreign Service.

[22] *Foreign Relations, 1918, Russia*, Vol. I, *op.cit.*, p. 531; from Francis' telegram to SECSTATE of May 16, 9 p.m.

[23] William Hard, *Raymond Robins' Own Story*, Harper & Brothers, New York, 1920, p. 191.

on his heels. At the time he sent his telegram from Tokyo the major portion of the Siberian railroad over which he had just passed, including practically the entire section from Omsk to Irkutsk, had actually already been seized by the Czechs and various anti-communist Russian elements in the course of the Czech uprising. In some instances, the transfer of power had occurred even before Robins' train had reached Vladivostok (in Irkutsk it took place only four days after he passed through).

There was of course no reason why Robins should have anticipated this; the development came unexpectedly for everyone concerned. But it is in keeping with the irony of the time, and of Robins' experiences in particular, that his gratified deduction about the firmness of power in Siberia had actually been rendered quite inaccurate by the time he was able to report it to Washington. Had he known at that time that these things had happened, and had he understood the full import of the Czech uprising and the effect it was to have for his own purposes, his disturbance would have been profound; for this event, more than any other, would serve to put the final seal of frustration on precisely those tendencies in Allied diplomacy which he had supported with such unbending enthusiasm and determination.

❖

If the circumstances of Robins' departure from Russia were tragic, what awaited him in the United States was no less so. Unbeknownst to him, the temper of official Washington had already been decisively inclined in his disfavor by Sisson's agitation, by Summers' death and the circumstances attending it, and by the influence of the Russian Embassy and members of the Root Mission, already alarmed by William B. Thompson's expansive and undiscriminating advocacy of what was now taken to be the "Red Cross" line.[24] Lansing and his senior associates in the State Department, in particular, had been brought to a state of high suspicion of Robins' integrity and motives.

[24] The British Embassy at Tokyo, somewhat startled by the impression of mystery, authority, and pro-Sovietism created by Robins in the Japanese capital as he passed through there on his way home, made inquiries of the Foreign Office in London as to Robins' real status and significance. These were passed on to Sir William Wiseman, in New York, who replied on June 15, just prior to Robins' arrival in Washington: "Colonel Robbins is not taken seriously here and will not be received by the President." (House MSS, *op.cit.,* Wiseman Correspondence folder.)

The results of this unhappy state of affairs began to affect Robins even before he reached Washington. At Vladivostok, Tokyo, and Seattle, messages reached him warning him not to talk for publication.[25] At Seattle he and Gumberg were subjected, at the request of the State Department, to a humiliating search of their persons by the immigration authorities—a procedure which apparently revealed nothing in any way sinister.

Robins' friends did, from the moment of his arrival, the best they could for him. Thompson and Thacher met him at Chicago and accompanied him to Washington. There others joined in the cause, and every effort was made to get his views before the government. He was received on June 26 by Lansing, to whom he transmitted Lenin's communication. Lansing asked him to put his own views in writing, and referred him (with a certain malicious pleasure, one suspects) to Lord Reading and Henri Bergson (the noted French philosopher who, as will be seen below, had been sent to the United States to influence Wilson in favor of the intervention).

Robins' written views were handed to Lansing on July 1 in the form of a long memorandum, setting forth his ideas on the organization and mode of operation of a proposed economic aid commission for Russia, emphasizing that nothing constructive could be accomplished without the cooperation of the Soviet authorities, holding out the hope that once the work of the commission had begun to bear fruit Allied military assistance would be "gladly accepted by the Soviet power," but warning that the Soviet government could not be expected "to countenance Allied intervention until convinced that the intervening force will not be used to destroy it." [26] The memorandum was passed on by Lansing to the President, whose reaction, in this particular case, was as ambiguous as it was in many other matters. Robins' suggestions, he replied to Lansing (July 3) were "certainly much more sensible than I thought the author of them capable of. I differ from them only in practical details." [27] Yet, as will be seen below, the President never did anything to implement in any way the recommendations of the Robins report, nor

[25] Hard, *op.cit.*, p. 204.

[26] *Foreign Relations, The Lansing Papers*, Vol. II, *op.cit.*, pp. 365-372. Also Cumming & Pettit, *op.cit.*, pp. 212-219. In order that full justice may be done to Robins' views, the text of this memorandum is reproduced in full in the Appendix.

[27] Wilson MSS, Series II, *op.cit.*

did he ever do Robins the courtesy of receiving him and permitting him to present his views in person.

It is true that Robins' arrival in Washington coincided with the final period of Wilson's decision in the matter of the intervention. It was known to Lansing and other highly placed persons that the President had the whole matter under advisement. These people were well aware that the President's decision could easily be adversely affected by any leaks or appearances of outside pressure just at that moment. These circumstances sufficed, perhaps, to explain why it would have been difficult for them, in any case, to have talked the whole problem over with Robins and made him privy, just at that time, to governmental thinking.

But beyond that there was also, in the official milieu, a suspicion and hostility toward Robins that continued to make itself felt in many ways. The ban on public statements by him was evidently not rescinded, and he obeyed it faithfully until summoned, in February 1919, by the Overman Committee of the Senate,[28] to testify on his experiences in Russia. How hard it must have been for him, bursting as he was with the story of his Russian experience, to observe this restraint, we can well imagine. He did find a sympathetic hearing with some of the Progressive-Republican Senators—notably, William Borah and Hiram Johnson. On July 13, 1918, Borah delivered on the floor of the Senate a flowery speech on the significance of Bastille Day. Here he moved from the French Revolution to the Russian, and pleaded—in terms as high-minded and vague as any

[28] The body in question was, like the recent McCarran-Jenner Committee, a subcommittee of the Committee on the Judiciary of the United States Senate. It was set up in September 1918 to investigate charges that certain American brewers of German ancestry had endeavored to make their influence felt in a number of improper ways. The end of the war removed the main incentive to this investigation before it was fairly under way. But on February 4, 1919, the Senate passed a further resolution extending the investigatory authority of the Committee on the Judiciary in such a way as to give it "the power and duty to inquire concerning any efforts being made to propagate in this country the principles of any party exercising or claiming to exercise authority in Russia, . . ." (Senate Resolution 439, *Bolshevik Propaganda, Hearings* . . . , *op.cit.,* p. 6.) Pursuant to this resolution, the subcommittee proceeded to embark on what appears to have been a combined investigation both of the nature and purposes of the Soviet government and of the relation of individual Americans thereto. In the course of this investigation a number of persons who had served in Russia in 1917 and 1918, including both Ambassador Francis and Raymond Robins, were questioned at length. Robins' testimony comprised in all approximately two days of the hearings, and appears, *ibid.,* pp. 763-896 and pp. 1007-1032.

[231]

this period could show—for aid and counsel to the Russian people in their effort to find freedom. This unleashed, on the floor of the Senate, a sultry and hopelessly confused debate, in which the names of Robins and Thompson were repeatedly mentioned. It was evident from this that Robins' presence in Washington was not wholly without effect on congressional opinion. On a portion of the press, too, Robins must have had a palpable influence. But his counsel was simply brushed off by the government; the fateful decisions on the intervention were made either in total disregard or direct defiance of his stated views; and it is no exaggeration to say that no serious effort was ever made by the government to hear and to weigh on their merits the details of his Russian experience. The realization of this state of affairs, dawning gradually on him as the summer of 1918 went by and coming as it did on the heels of the huge excitement and hope of his months in Russia, constituted for him a major personal tragedy, from the effects of which—one suspects—he was never fully to recover.

The unhappy tale of Robins' reception in the United States would not be complete without a word about the similar fate of Gumberg. Here, we have only a cryptic statement by Sisson. After relating, in his memoirs, that Gumberg returned to this country "without objection of mine," Sisson continues:

. . . I let him come to see me one night afterward in a New York hotel, sat him down alongside me, told him that he was so close to Trotsky that he ought to have absorbed knowledge of the elaborate game of the winter, that I sought no admissions from him, had no threats for him, but would expect him, in Russian as well as American idiom, to "keep out of politics" while the war lasted. That pledge he smilingly gave. I hope he kept it, and never made any effort to find out if he did. A mighty man in Russia, he was powerless in America.[29]

Gumberg, more cynical and less emotionally engaged than Robins, accepted this rebuff with resignation and good humor. He kept quiet and disappeared amicably into obscurity, emerging only in later years to play a quiet but not ineffective role—again always in the background and always with discretion—as a middleman in the unfolding pattern of Soviet-American relations.

[29] Sisson, *op.cit.*, p. 95.

CHAPTER X

ıllıtıllıtıllıtıllıtıllıtıllıtıllıtıllıtıllıtıllıtıllıtıllıtıllıtıllıtıllıtıllıtıllıtıllıtıllıtıllıtıllıtıllıtıllıtıllıtıllıtıllıtıllıttıllıt

ENVOI TO ROBINS

The absolute issue was drawn between a betrayed state, a betrayed church, a betrayed social order that had brought injustice and oppression to folks' lives until they were ready to turn to this gospel of Marx, of this very materialistic economic gospel, believing that it was really greater than the Gospel of the Galilean, and I know of no single instance that affected me more with utter sorrow and regret, and the wonder of how far it would go, and the desire that we might not be permitted to develop that class cleavage in my own land.—*Raymond Robins, March 6, 1919*

It is impossible to dismiss Raymond Robins from the Russian scene without a retrospective glance at his personality and a word of appraisal for the totality of his contribution to the development of Soviet-American relations during these brief but crowded months he spent in Russia in 1917 and 1918. There was, after all, no one on the American side whose connection with this relationship was more intimate, and none who gave to the problem more of his strength and his sincerity.

We have seen that as Robins left Russia events were conspiring, unbeknownst to him, to frustrate completely the undertakings to which he had devoted himself. Within three months after his departure, there would be little to show for his efforts beyond a feeling of gratitude toward him (evidently quite sincere) on the part of the Soviet leaders. His life and thoughts had been, of course, for them an open book. They had taken the measure of his virtues and deficiencies and they were not long to remain ignorant of the extent of his failure. But they had recognized in him a man without guile who, though proceeding from premises they abhorred, had dealt with them openly and honorably, with his cards on the table, and had done them the compliment of taking them at their own worth, crediting them with a genuine revolutionary sincerity and with an essential, if misguided, decency of purpose. All this impressed itself on their elephantine memories; and they appear to have borne him an enduring feeling of appreciation.[1]

Certain of Robins' personal qualities and concepts contributed to his failure. Prominent among these was his extreme "ungovernmentalness"—his lack of understanding for, or patience with, the strictures of governmental operation; his failure to realize that in the last analysis things had to be done through government; his reluctance not only to go through "channels" but to recognize or pay any attention to them; his belief, common to many Americans of that day, that the lower echelons of the governmental apparatus were there only to be ignored and by-passed; his occasional secretiveness vis-à-vis the American officials in Russia about such of his own doings as affected the official interests. There was also, as was noted in Volume I, his failure to recognize that in the communication between governments precision is the first requirement of effectiveness. Robins' broader judgments on the nature and situation of the Soviet regime were, with certain exceptions, well taken; but in receiving and interpreting the stated positions of the Soviet leaders on specific matters at issue between his government and theirs, he was impulsive, hasty, careless, and repeatedly inaccurate. Here the lack of any sort of professional training for foreign affairs work made itself particularly painfully felt.

Added to this, there was a deplorable high-handedness, tactlessness, and personal insensitivity vis-à-vis the other Americans in Russia. One senses, in examining Robins' activity and his statements, that he was at that moment more interested in people in the mass than in people as individuals. In any case, his attitude toward other members of the American community was often marked by a remoteness that smacks of arrogance and contempt. His behavior to-

[1] In 1933, Robins returned (under arrangements made, once again, by the faithful Gumberg) to the Soviet Union as a tourist of sorts, and was permitted to make an extensive trip through the country. The treatment accorded him seems to have been that conceived appropriate for an honored friend; and there is no evidence that any effort was made to exploit his presence or his—by this time—quite uncritical predisposition toward Soviet power. The fact that this occurred at a time when both Lenin and Trotsky had passed from the scene is interesting as an indication that appreciation for Robins' attitude of 1917–1918 was not confined to the officials with whom he had dealt personally. It did presumably rest, however, on Gumberg's continued active support, and can scarcely have survived the purges, which cost Gumberg's brother (apparently) his life, and Gumberg his influence with the Kremlin.

ward Summers was, under the most charitable judgment, unfeeling; and not the least deplorable aspect of it was the fact that he was so little aware of the pain and disturbance he caused. With Bullard, too, he found no rapport. Despite the fact that the two men spent weeks together in Moscow, Robins (as a result, no doubt, of the Sisson episode) seems to have made no effort to compose differences and to tap Bullard's thoughtful and experienced judgment. (It is a question, admittedly, whether Bullard would have been receptive to any such advances.) With Francis, Robins' relations in the early months of 1918 were outwardly cordial; but prior to that time he had not treated the Ambassador with the entire respect and frankness due the latter's position as personal representative of the American President; and even in the happier period one senses an undercurrent of arrogance and condescension on Robins' part, of which Francis was never unaware. Robins' failure to apprise Francis of Lenin's final approach about economic collaboration was a grievous impropriety, which, coming on top of many smaller causes, permanently embittered the Ambassador against him. And as to the rumors that Robins was to replace Francis as ambassador: one may well accept his disclaimers that he was responsible for these rumors or that he deliberately and consciously sought the ambassadorial position at that time. But there is no evidence that he discouraged such talk in his entourage; the impression that he coveted this position was permitted to gain currency throughout the entire American and Allied communities in Russia; and when he left Russia—as he did in May 1918—expecting to return, it is difficult to imagine in what capacity he pictured himself as returning if not in that of the senior American representative in Russia. He had recognized, after all, that the Red Cross work no longer required his personal supervision.

Not all of these instances of tactlessness or discourtesy were serious lapses; and one must allow for the passions and excitements of the time. In the year 1918 many people had an intuitive feeling that they were living through one of the decisive moments of history; beliefs and convictions were put to the ultimate test; and the urge to action was permitted to override many normal inhibitions. But by his underestimation of his official associates in Russia, by his lack of interest in them—and consideration for them—as human beings, Robins cut himself off from sources of advice and information that might have deepened and modified his critical appraisal of the impressions that came his way. He was, after all, dependent, in most of his contacts with the Soviet scene and in many of his observations of it, on interpreters and advisers who had no reason to have the interests of the United States primarily at heart. His dependence on Gumberg, in particular, was a weakness insofar as (and this, in actuality, was quite far) it was allowed to go unbalanced by other influences and interpretations.

It would be wrong, incidentally, to allow Gumberg to appear as a sinister or anti-American character. He was neither. The line between allegiance to Soviet power and allegiance to the United States had not yet been drawn, in early 1918, with that terrible finality that was to become its mark in later decades. But Gumberg was, after all, a Soviet citizen, amenable to Soviet laws and to the pressures of Soviet power. In addition to that he was a radical socialist (of Menshevik leanings) whose ideological views were rooted in long conviction and long immersion in the personal atmosphere of Russian socialism. The record shows that if Robins viewed Francis as a political child, Gumberg regarded Robins (though with more affection) in precisely the same way. And Gumberg does not appear to have been at all times as frank with Robins as he was with the Soviet leaders to whom, at that time, he conceived his basic allegiance to lie.

Gumberg was a well-informed man, with unique contacts in the higher Soviet circles. Robins, and for that matter the other Americans as well, had a great deal to learn from him that they could learn from no other source. Corrected by competent and responsible critical appraisal and by careful checking with other information available, Gumberg's contribution could have been of prime value in enabling American officialdom to find its way through the crucial mazes of the first year of Soviet power. Lacking this corrective, it became at times a source of weakness and confusion. And the fact that it lacked that corrective must be attributed, in the main, to Robins' inexperience and lack of preparation for the political tasks so suddenly thrust upon him in Russia.

There were, moreover, certain broader deficiencies of understanding of the Russian scene which, though they probably did not enter into the actual causes of Robins' failure, heightened quite needlessly his enthusiasm for his undertakings and increased the cruelty of the disappointment he was destined to suffer. Like many other Americans, especially those who saw Russia only in the toils of war and revolution, he was not fully aware of the progress that had been made in many directions in the final decades of Tsardom. He exaggerated the severity of Tsarist power on the eve of the Revolution, and tended to ascribe the evils and resentments of the 1917–1918 period to previous political oppression even when they were primarily the reflections of the inadequacy of the Tsarist system to the strains of modern war. In this way Robins was carried into a somewhat uncritical acceptance of the Bolshevik thesis of the need and popular demand for violent revolution. This attitude did less than justice to the strength and intellectual legitimacy of the moderate-liberal opposition to Bolshevism, as also to the tragedy of its experience.

Robins failed, furthermore, to recognize the compulsions that would force a revolutionary regime, at least in its early stages, to seek a jealous and exclusive monopoly of all power. He failed to appreciate the power of the forces carrying Russia in the direction of civil war and terror, and the importance, within this pattern, of the undisciplined actions of local Bolshevik supporters in the early period. He had little idea of those weaknesses inherent in any violent and uninhibited revolutionary process that render it vulnerable to capture—as indeed this one was destined to be captured and held in bondage for decades—by totalitarian forces. Failing in this way to appreciate the extent to which the winds of Pandora's box had been released by the reckless extremism of the Bolsheviki, he placed unreal hopes on the possibility of moderating Soviet power and easing its relations with the United States by promoting economic reconstruction and development in Russia.

Robins shared with many troubled Americans of a later age the belief that "the best answer to Bolshevism is food." "I believe," he told the investigating Senators some months after his departure from Russia,

that the reorganization of Russian life economically, the beginning to give substantial hope here and there, beginning to recreate the property interest and the stake in life, would begin at once to disorganize Bolshevik power and the adherence to the formulas. . . . I believe that the best answer to Bolshevik Russia is economic cooperation, food, friendliness on the part of America, . . .

This, he thought, "would help us, help Russia, and operate in this country to weaken the authority and power of Bolshevism."[2]

These were vain hopes. In nurturing them, Robins was underestimating the ideological earnestness of his friends, the Soviet leaders, and their determination not to be caught, even in the moments of their greatest weakness, on the hook of any easy and agreeable commercial relations with the western capitalists. In this respect they even deceived him a little, deliberately, in the final weeks of his stay in Russia; for their situation, at that moment, was desperate, and their personal appreciation for him never reached the point of self-denial in political matters. Thus even had he found a receptive response and support for his views at home, Robins would surely sooner or later have faced, like many other foreign well-wishers of the Soviet regime, a heavy measure of frustration and disappointment in the ultimate reactions of the Soviet regime itself.

Despite all this, the principal elements of Robins' failure were not of his own making. It is doubtful that he ever fully understood the depth and power of the forces arrayed against him. He was fighting, whether he realized it or not, the powerful bitterness and suspicion aroused in the Allied countries by Russia's departure from the war. In the case of the French, in particular, but also of the other western powers to some degree, he was fighting the acute resentment provoked in influential circles by the Soviet government's abrupt repudiation of the financial obligations of former Russian governments. He was fighting the cautious but very real determination of influential circles in Japan to take advantage of Russia's moment of greatest weakness to improve Japan's position in east Asia—a determination which the Allies had no choice but to abet, outwardly, if they were to have any hope of influencing and moderating it. He was fighting, finally, the extensive social influence exercised by the Russian upper classes in the salons and chanceries of the western capitals, and the natural sympathies of the western world for the injuries done by the Soviet government to these classes in the name of a doctrine western society as a whole was completely unprepared to accept.

These powerful factors were always present in the background, even in the moments of Robins' most exciting experiences and most exalted hopes. He appears never to have realized their inevitability

[2] *Bolshevik Propaganda, Hearings* . . . , *op.cit.*, p. 856.

and their latent strength. It was from this—from the fact of the tremendous, heartbreaking odds against him—that his efforts, viewed from the perspective of nearly forty years, acquire their quixotic and tragic aspect—an adventure full of gallantry but also of unreality: dreamlike, moving, and futile.

It is impossible to say that Robins' presence and efforts in Russia had no effects at all. But it is hard to say with any precision what these effects were. His influence was undoubtedly predominant in causing the American Ambassador to withdraw and to withhold for a period of two months the recommendation in favor of intervention. His enthusiasm gave comfort and support to Lockhart and to those factions within the British government that opposed intervention. His friends in Washington, supported by his reports and recommendations, were not without influence in stiffening the resistance of Colonel House, and possibly of the President, to the pressures for intervention. He surely had some part, therefore, in delaying the intervention—a function for which some statesmen and historians would bear him no gratitude.[3] But no human hand will ever sort and weigh with any precision the ingredients of the complex mixture of causes and motives that governed the final measures of Allied policy in the year 1918; and the exact measure of Robins' influence on the development of this situation must remain a matter of speculation.

There was, however, a sense in which Robins' contribution to the Soviet-American relationship, though never well-known and now scarcely remembered, was of greater importance than any of his early dealings with the Soviet leaders. This was in his reaction, as a thinking and feeling person, to the phenomenon of Soviet power. For here, in the dilemmas he confronted and in his method of reaction to them, Robins was more prophetic and in certain respects more profound than any other of the American actors in the drama of 1917–1918. And his utterances on certain of these problems deserve to be recalled to memory today, as representing one of the first and most courageous of all attempts to penetrate the baffling

[3] Mr. Alfred James Balfour's biographer has pointed out, "It was partly due to the long wrangle with the United States Government that the Allied troops landed at Archangel and Murmansk only in August, when the German power was already cracking in the West and the original arguments for sending them were ceasing to be valid." Blanche E. C. Dugdale, *Arthur James Balfour, First Earl of Balfour, K.G., O.M., F.R.S.*, G. P. Putnam's Sons, New York, 1937, Vol. II, *1906–1930*, p. 191.

problem, so unfamiliar to Americans, of how to deal with a worldly power, ideologically hostile to American society, which could neither be forgiven, destroyed, nor ignored.

Since Robins was a man who seems to have had, despite much verbal eloquence, little inclination or ability to record his thoughts in writing (perhaps he lacked the patience for this humdrum and unstimulating exercise), we are compelled to seek them in the record of his verbal statements, and primarily in those which he made to the senatorial investigating committee in March 1919.[4]

It is important to note, first of all, that Robins' feelings with respect to the Soviet government did not rest on any partiality to socialism as a doctrine or on any lack of appreciation, or disrespect, for the values of the American social and economic system. "I am one," he told the Senators,

who, though a radical, believes that in feeding, clothing, and housing people you are doing a work of the very highest social consequence, and of great moral value, and I believe in the principle of private, and, if you please, capitalistic industry, and think it can defend itself on its own ground.

"I spoke," Robins said at another point, referring to the general tenor of his statements to the Soviet authorities,

the language of labor. I had been active in labor debate and controversy in America, always anti-socialist, as I then was and am yet, progressive, if you please, in mind, but a step at a time progressive—a very poor sort of progressive from the point of view of some people. . . .

. . . For years I have been in the open fighting socialist doctrines, and certain men said that I did not have intelligence enough to be a socialist, which may be true, . . .

Conversely, Robins' devotion to the American system was beyond question. One was obliged, he insisted, to take the ideological doctrines of the Russian leaders as the reflection of *their* particular national background and experience. If he had lived, he said, under the state of Tsardom then he, too, would have been opposed to church and state—would have been, in other words, a revolutionary. But the background and experience of the Soviet leaders were not his. "I thank God," he said,

[4] The subsequent citations are from the record of these hearings, *Bolshevik Propaganda, Hearings . . .* , *op.cit.,* pp. 771, 808, 817, 818, 826, 828, and 863 (not necessarily in that order).

that I knew the state where my little county could meet in convention, in democratic fashion, and run the show, for I live in that part of the country where possibly are preserved in their purity more than anywhere else Anglo-Saxon institutions, south of Mason and Dixon's line. I remember the church as the little white church on the hill, where we went to hear the man speak that the people chose to have there, who taught us the old simple doctrines of Christianity, and I believe he was highly serviceable and not a betrayer of liberty and justice, but rather the friend of both. . . .

Explaining, at another point, why he felt that America and America alone could meet the challenge of Bolshevism, he said:

. . . Behind the American democratic, political, social control there are enough men, women, and children who live a decent, contented, successful life to bind with power the institutions of our Government, so that whether it is a Wilson or a Taft or a Roosevelt that is President, there is a majority of such numbers and faith in support of our Government that there can not be any question of its genuine authority and sanction; the mass of the people will fight for it, suffer for it; if need be, die for it.

Far from entertaining any predilection for communist ideology, Robins had, surprising as this may seem in view of the general tendency of his activity, strong feelings about the threat which Bolshevist doctrines and the phenomenon of Soviet power held for the western world. The Bolsheviki, he said, were "terribly misguided people" who "believed the class struggle was the only struggle worth talking about." He had no illusions concerning the danger of such views. "Is there a menace in Russian Bolshevism?" he asked the Senators rhetorically; and his answer was:

A fundamental menace, gentlemen, in my judgment; a menace so much more far-reaching, going so much deeper, than has sometimes been suggested by its bitterest opponents, that I think it well that we should take high ground and really know the thing we deal with. For the first time in the history of the human race there has been a definite economic revolution, an attempt to realize the stock formulas of Marx in a socialist, economic materialist, class control by force.

In the light of these views, it would be wholly unjust to suggest that Robins was infected by communist ideas, lacking in appreciation for the values of his own society, or obtuse to the threat which Bolshevism presented for the liberal world of the West. On the other hand, his thoughts as to what could be done to counter the Soviet

[241]

challenge were, like those of many others who were to ponder these problems at a later date, rudimentary, fumbling, and not very precise. There were two elements of his thinking, however, on which he himself laid great weight and which he expressed with much eloquence. Both were destined to have most direct revelance to the problems of coming decades.

First of all, he did not believe that the hostility of the communist ideology to western systems of government and social organization constituted any reason why the phenomenon of communist power should not be studied with the greatest care and objectivity. Robins was not a party to that deep-seated trait of American psychology which tends to make an inscrutable devil out of any external adversary, to deny to him the quality of common humanity, to expect of him only the worst, and to question the value and propriety of occupying one's self seriously with the study of the adversary's motives, his point of view, and his personality. "I believe," he said, referring to the Russian Revolution:

that when we understand what it is, when we know the facts behind it, when we do not libel it nor slander it or do not lose our heads and become its advocates and defenders, and really know what the thing is, and then move forward to it, then we will serve our country and our time. . . .

When some of the Senators manifested a hopeless inability to understand this point of view and questioned in particular how Robins could consider Trotsky an able and highly educated man and an orator, and yet not believe in the system of government Trotsky represented, Robins, who had already suffered hours of goading on such points, burst out, in some despair:

He was all three of those things, but I have known men who were those three things, whose character and principles I would be bitterly opposed to. I would like to tell the truth about men, and about movements, without passion and without resentment, even though I differed from men and from movements. I think that that is the essential thing, if we are going to get the truth about it. And there is in this whole Russian situation so much partisan bias. If this will suit your thought of what I am meaning, I am perfectly willing that the Russian people should have the kind of government that the majority of the Russian people want, whether it suits me or whether it is in accord with my principles or not.

Time after time, he returned to his conviction that the first pre-requisite for dealing with the power of the Russian communist movement was the understanding of it. "I would like to have you really see the Russian situation," he assured the Senators at one point, "and understand the lines of this movement, so that we can combat it effectively and not on false grounds."

The second of the appreciations he brought to the handling of the problem of international communism was the recognition that a challenge so largely ideological and so intimately relevant to weaknesses within the fabric of western society could not be re-garded as entirely an external threat and could not be met solely by force. In a passage that could well have been spoken in 1953 instead of 1919 (expect that by 1953 this brand of impromptu eloquence had become a rare phenomenon in congressional hear-ings), Robins defined his views on this point:

Behind the Christian sanction and conscience in America there is an uncorrupted faith that still continues with abiding power. We can meet that [the communist] challenge. We can raise these [American] forces into united action. You [the Senators] can be instrumental in rallying these forces against the real challenge of the Russian situation, under-standable as it is in the light of Russian history, coming out of the Russian story, out of its terrible past. The evils here in our country most of us will acknowledge willingly, but we know there is energy enough in the institutions we have to meet them on the square. But, Senators, mere force is an old failure against ideas. I am one who would use the force of the public power to meet that man or that group of men who conspired by force and violence or sought by violence and force to overthrow our Government or to deprive others by these methods of legal rights or property. I would meet this challenge at all times and places with un-hesitating and sufficient force to maintain the public law. But I would never expect to stamp out ideas with bayonets. I would never expect, sirs, to suppress the desire for a better human life for men, women, and children, no matter how ill founded in political fact and political experience, with force. The only answer for the desire for a better human life is a better human life. I believe that our institutions furnish that better human life for more men, women, and children than any other institutions in the world. I believe that whatever is wrong can be ironed out within the Constitution and the law. I believe that we have the means of meeting this Russian challenge when it is really understood and known.

[243]

Envoi *to Robins*

These utterances lend to the pattern of Robins' dreams and strivings in Russia a dignity that does not flow from the bare record of his dealings with the Soviet authorities. We are safe in assuming that the qualities that brought Robins, albeit through grievous mistakes and many illusions, to perceptions of this order did not escape the notice of the Soviet leaders and could not have failed to affect—by and large favorably—their judgment of at least a portion of American society. Here, as so often, it was the totality of the human personality, rather than any of its partial manifestations, that was of greatest importance. In the light of these appreciations, Robins cannot be permitted to depart the scene of Moscow, 1918, without this word of recognition for the effort he put forth, with such unique dedication, to understand the phenomenon of Soviet power in its infancy; nor can one deny him, posthumously, a pang of sympathy for the unfeeling rejection to which these efforts were subjected by people who, had events taken a different turn, would surely not have been averse to sharing in the credit of his achievements. Among all the personal tragedies that attended the earlier period of American-Soviet relations, there was none, aside from that of Robins' adversary, Maddin Summers, that bore so great a poignancy and dignity as his.

CHAPTER XI

THE NORTH IN APRIL AND MAY

THE reader will recall from Chapter II the tenuous and unsettled state of affairs that prevailed in the Russian North as of the end of March. At Archangel, where the port was still tightly frozen up for the long Arctic winter, the Bolsheviki had effectively taken over, and an "Extraordinary Evacuation Commission," sent out from Petrograd, was busily removing to the interior the valuable war supplies which had been made available by the Allies from their own precious stocks and which were now no longer needed in Russia for any operations against Germany. In Murmansk, due partly to the confusion of the Brest-Litovsk crisis, an intimate military collaboration had developed between the Allies and the local Soviet authorities; three Allied war vessels—a British battleship and cruiser and a French cruiser—lay in the roadstead; a detachment of British marines had been put ashore. The Soviet leaders in Moscow, still not aware of the full extent of this collaboration, were already troubled by such reports of it as they received, and were beginning to view the Murmansk situation, from afar, with mixed and anxious feelings.

The American government, it will further be recalled, had been pressed by the British government, throughout the month of March, to send an American man-of-war to join the British and French vessels at Murmansk. At the beginning of April the President had been persuaded by these urgings to approve the despatch of a vessel; but the Navy at first insisted no ship could be spared. Only when Francis and Ruggles, acting on the basis of reports from Martin and Wardwell, supported the suggestion was the Navy's resistance overcome. By mid-April Captain Bierer of the *U.S.S. Olympia* had his orders to join the French and British vessels in the far northern port.

❖

The North in April and May

During the months of April and May there was very little change in the situation at Archangel. The port remained frozen during both those months. The removal of the military supplies was pressed forward by the Extraordinary Commission with vigor and with such despatch as the poor state of the railway would permit. The supplies were shipped, initially, to a point some twenty miles north of Vologda, from which they were redespatched to various destinations. The Allied representatives had no difficulty in tracing the shipments as far as Vologda, but found it hard to keep track of their further distribution. Bullard, who had a chance to observe something of this problem on his way north from Moscow to Archangel in early May, had the following to say about it in a paper written while still aboard the *Alexander* in the harbor of Archangel:

On the way North, I had stopped off at Vologda. . . . It was . . . an admirable point for checking up the movements of trains. Most of the railroad employees in the yards and shops of Vologda were anti-Bolshevik; they kept the Embassies informed of the trains coming down from Arkhangel, their bills of lading and their routing. Some of the munition shipments went on South to Moscow to be forwarded to the "Don Front," some went East for use in the Civil War in Siberia, but some turned West and there wasn't any "front" in that direction till you reached Flanders.

On the twenty-four hour trip from Vologda up to Arkhangel we rode into the very heart of the problem. On every side was visual evidence of the zeal this Extraordinary Evacuation Commission was displaying. In almost every siding we passed munition trains headed South.

As we approached the end of the journey, the "ammunition dumps" came into view.

I have never seen anything more desolate, more depressing—more maddening. Acres on acres of barbed wire, stands of small arms, cases of ammunition and pyramids of shells of all calibres; great parks of artillery, motor trucks, field kitchens, ambulances—thousands of them; railroad iron, wheels, axles, rails, coils of precious copper telegraph wire; most important of all, the regularly piled, interminable rows of metal pig—the alloys so essential for artillery production—and the sinister looking sheds where the T.N.T. was stored. It was all worth its weight in gold to Berlin. It was all so terribly needed by our friends before Amiens, on the Chemin des Dames. So much of it would be valuable to our own men when the time would come . . .

For hours we rode through this futile wilderness. It was altogether too sad a sight for tears. The wasted efforts of all the staunch citizens behind the lines in the factories of France and England and America to hurry the production of this material! The cool heroism of the sailor folks who had brought it here through mine fields and submarines!

It would have been cruel enough just to think of it lying there idle to deteriorate and waste—much of it doomed to be ruined by the flood when the ice broke. But this Extraordinary Evacuation Commission, sent by Lenin, was straining every effort to move it, to save it for another use— much more tragic than waste! [1]

The subject of the removal of the war supplies was evidently among the matters discussed by the Allied representatives in Vologda upon Noulens' arrival there; for on March 30, on the heels of his first conference with Noulens, Francis wired Robins in Moscow, requesting him to investigate the matter discreetly and to ascertain what was the policy of the Soviet government with regard to these shipments. Riggs, the Assistant Military Attaché, was asked by Robins to make inquiry of Trotsky. On April 4 Robins replied to Francis (presumably on the basis of Riggs's report) that the stores were being sent "to Moscow, the Urals and Siberian towns." The Soviet government, Robins added, desired to take up the matter of payment for these munitions, and expected to pay for them in raw materials, but asked for time to organize the economic resources of the country. All war materials in the Petrograd area were likewise being evacuated into the interior. Reports of delivery of war materials to the Germans were absurd. Who could seriously think

. . . that a government whose best soldiers have fought against German control in Ukraine and Finland can now be planning to furnish to Germany the power to enslave their own land? Nothing short of Japanese invasion can change the deep resentment all Russians feel against Germany's robber raid and shameful peace forced upon Russia at the point of the bayonet . . .[2]

Francis took note of what Robins had said, but was not reassured by it. He pointed out to Robins, in reply, that

. . . [this] is the first information I have had from any source as to plan of Soviet to compensate allies for supplies removed from Archangel, in face of protest from allied representatives.[3]

---

[1] Bullard MSS, *op.cit.*, Box 13, "Dealing with the Bolsheviki" in folder "Russia, 1917–1919."
[2] Cumming & Pettit, *op.cit.*, p. 130.
[3] *Ibid.*, p. 132.

Francis does not appear to have pursued this matter further with the Soviet authorities, or to have had any special correspondence with Washington about it. But it evidently continued to trouble him. When, on May 2nd, he finally was brought to a point where he felt himself obliged to recommend Allied intervention, the continued failure of the Soviet government to meet Allied requests with regard to the disposition of these supplies played a prominent part in his decision.

At the beginning of April, the Soviet government became alarmed over rumors then circulating in the northern ports concerning England's intentions with relation to Archangel. On April 2 Chicherin wrote to Lockhart asking him, "In view of the alarming reports which are being spread on our northern coast and of the apprehensions regarding England's intentions as far as Archangel is concerned," to give some explanation that could enable the Soviet government "to reassure our alarmed northern population and to dissipate its fears." [4] To this Lockhart, wholly without instructions, replied cautiously that "as far as I am aware, these rumors are devoid of all foundation." [5]

It is not known what the rumors were that led to this exchange. Among the official British personnel in Russia there were, from the time of the Brest-Litovsk crisis, strong protagonists of an occupation of both the northern ports. But in early April the British government still nurtured the hope that there would be a Soviet request for Allied assistance in the north, and it does not appear to have made, as yet, any specific plans for independent action in the event such a request should not be forthcoming.

Chicherin's exchange with Lockhart does, however, indicate the nervousness that existed in Soviet circles over the possibility of an extension of British operations in the north. It is fair to say that this nervousness was matched on the Allied side by the concern over the fate of the Archangel stores, indignation over the highhanded attitude and methods of the Extraordinary Commission, and a general feeling that if these removals continued some sort of effort would have to be made, with the opening of the navigation season at

---

[4] *Correspondance diplomatique se rapportant aux relations entre la République Russe et les Puissances de l'Entente, 1918,* Publié par le Commissariat du Peuple pour les Affaires Etrangères, 1919, p. 18. The translation of Chicherin's letter is that of *Correspondance diplomatique.* . . .
[5] *Loc.cit.*

Archangel, to bring the remaining supplies under Allied protection.

It was shortly after the middle of April that the two food ships despatched to Archangel by the British government (see Chapter 1, above), the *Egba* and the *Nascopie,* assisted and guarded by the Admiralty icebreaker, *H.M.S. Alexander,* arrived off the delta of the Northern Duna. It proved impossible to reach any agreement with the local authorities for the desired cessation of the removal of war supplies in exchange for the release of these cargoes of food. The population was naturally in favor of such an agreement, and the moderate elements in the city administration would certainly have welcomed it; but the members of the Extraordinary Commission were adamant. The war supplies must be moved inland, even if the population starved. The ships, as noted above, therefore proceeded only part way up the delta, anchored in the channel some fifteen miles below the city, and settled down to await further developments.

In view of the deadlock with the local authorities, Lockhart was asked to take the matter up with the Soviet authorities in Moscow, which he did. Initially, and in principle, the talks seemed to go well. In his letter to Robins of May 5 (see above, p. 200), Lockhart said that he had that day come to complete agreement on this subject with Trotsky "whereby we shall be allowed to retain those stores which we require for ourselves." Robins, as we have seen, was given a similar, though not identical, impression by Lenin in the communication of May 14, which included a guarantee that the stores would not be sold to Germany, and that all those manufactured in the United States and England would be turned over to the United States.

The British government appears, however, not to have been satisfied with the vague assurances given to Lockhart, and probably with good reason. A great portion of the stores had, after all, by now been removed, and would hardly be recoverable. There was no indication, furthermore, that Lenin's statements were followed by any slackening in the rate of removals from Archangel. The *Nascopie* remained there, without discharging, until the latter part of June, when she returned to England, her cargo still aboard.[6] The *Egba* remained until midsummer, by which time the last of the military stores had been removed. The release of her food finally occurred only on the eve of the Allied intervention, in return for the release by the Soviet

[6] Bullard and his party were evacuated to England on the *Nascopie.*

authorities of a large number of Allied nationals who had accumulated in Archangel seeking passage home.

❖

At Murmansk, in contrast to Archangel, the relative fluidity of the water in the harbor was matched by the fluidity of the political situation throughout these spring months. Here, matters moved with increasing speed toward a crisis in the conflicting interests of the Allies, the Germans, and the Soviet regime.

We have already noted the arrival in March in the zone of the Murmansk Railway near Kandalaksha of a fairly large detachment of Finnish Reds. It was apparently primarily lack of food, rather than any direct military action, which had moved these detachments to seek positions in the neighborhood of the railroad. A considerable portion of the men were afflicted with scurvy and other effects of malnutrition. The detachment, nevertheless, had retained some degree of combat potential; and the Finnish Whites plainly could not afford to ignore its presence on their northeastern flank.

While this detachment entered the area on its own initiative, with no forewarning to the Murmansk Soviet, and continued to retain a large measure of independence of action, it tacitly accepted the Murmansk Soviet and the associated British and French forces as allies in the struggle against the Finnish Whites; and the local Allied representatives, entertaining as they did an exaggerated idea of the degree of German involvement in the Finnish-White cause in that area, accepted the Red Finns in the same manner.

At the beginning of April, a small White detachment appeared in the same area. Only a short time remained now before the spring thaw would set in. It was evidently the aim of the Whites to make sure that the Red force should, at the least, be engaged and contained until its mobility was reduced by the thaw. (This marshy country, intersected by thousands of lakes and streams, was far more passable for military purposes in winter than in summer; and the melting snows, in particular, presented formidable obstacles to military mobility.) Skirmishes began between the two forces on April 5 and continued for about a fortnight, when the thaw put a stop to further fighting. They took place thirty or forty miles west of the town of Kandalaksha, some eighty miles south of Murmansk.

At about the same time other White Finnish detachments entered the Ukhta area, farther south. They were received with political enthusiasm by the non-communist portion of the population, a circumstance that further complicated an already complex situation. From among their number a reconnaissance force of something under five hundred men was sent farther east, to the outskirts of the port and railway center of Kem, on the White Sea.

Reports of these activities, inflated in transmission and superimposed at the receiving end on the general assumption that the Finnish Whites were operating under German command, caused perturbation among both Allies and Russians in Murmansk. There was a general belief in Murmansk that these penetrations were only a prelude to a general German attack, or German-commanded attack, on the railroad and the Murmansk area.[7] The Murmansk Russians, desiring to get help to the Finnish Red contingent near Kandalaksha, but lacking any forces or facilities of their own, appealed to the local Allied commanders. The latter, equally worried over the Finnish White incursion and chafing under the long months of inactivity, were glad to have something to do, and responded with enthusiasm. By the combined efforts of the Russian repair ship *Kseniya* and the British and French naval forces, an armored train was rigged and fitted with artillery pieces from the *Glory*. A crew was selected from among the British marines and some of the French artillery men who had been held up in Murmansk on their evacuation from Rumania. Commanded by a French officer, Lieutenant Colonel Moliére, the train was despatched to Kandalaksha. Moliére was entrusted by the People's Collegium with the defense of the entire Kandalaksha area. The train remained there for some weeks, guarding the Kandalaksha station and, in effect, the town and its environs. The mere presence of the train there was sufficient to the purpose involved, and no extensive armed action was necessary. This extended the Allied military commitment to a considerable distance inland.

[7] Actually, it is not at all certain that even the Finnish government, much less the Germans, had anything to do with these incursions. On April 14 the White-Finnish government informed the British government that while it sympathized with the local White Guard detachments in Karelia, it did not find it possible to give them any effective help; volunteers from Finland proper, it was said, had joined them, but no officers had been sent; the Finnish government "would do all in its power to keep the Murman open for international traffic." (*Foreign Relations, 1918, Russia,* Vol. ii, *op.cit.,* p. 792.) There is no evidence that these reassurances ever percolated to the British naval and military authorities at Murmansk. Perhaps no credence was given to them.

The White-Finnish incursion in the neighborhood of Kem, being somewhat nearer to Archangel than to Murmansk and accessible to forces operating from the White Sea, was met by a small expedition despatched on an icebreaker from Archangel by the Bolshevik regional authorities there. In a hastily improvised and highly amateur military action this little force, cooperating with the local Bolshevik element in Kem, succeeded in holding off the White Finns until, once more, the thaw compelled the withdrawal of the latter. One of the commanders of this Soviet force at Kem got through by telephone on April 8 to Vesselago at Murmansk and inquired about possible help from the Murmansk Soviet. Vesselago's reply was revealing. He would at once get into touch by telephone with the Soviet of People's Commissars in Moscow, he said,

. . . since in the interests of avoiding confusion the British and French do not consider it possible to send their detachments so far into the interior to the assistance of our Red Army without the direct agreement of the central government.[8]

The Soviet historian Kedrov was at some difficulty to explain this reaction of the Murmansk Soviet, so little compatible with the Soviet thesis that all the reactions of the Murmansk leaders, even at that time, were dictated by a deep-laid plot between them and the Allies to overthrow the Soviet government. Had the British and French authorities at Murmansk been seeking a pretext for intervention into the interior of Russia, what better one could they have had than this direct appeal for aid from an authority completely loyal to, and in good standing with, the central Soviet authorities. Kedrov sought to extricate himself from this difficulty by charging that Vesselago's reply was a ruse, designed to cause the central Soviet authorities to take a position which would involve violation of the Brest-Litovsk Treaty and would thus embroil them with the Germans. Plainly, under the lens of Stalinist historiography the Allies could do no right: if they took action without approval of the central Soviet authorities, this was intervention; if they solicited the consent of Moscow, this was an attempt to involve Moscow in difficulties with the Germans.

Vesselago seems never to have gotten through to Moscow with this request. The Kem situation, in any case, continued to be handled by

[8] Kedrov, *Bez bolshevistskogo rukovodstva, op.cit.,* p. 65.

the local forces and those sent from Archangel. With the advent of the spring thaw, the whole question became no longer serious.

The extension of the radius of operation of the People's Collegium that was involved in the Kandalaksha operation, as also the confusion as to who had the military responsibility at Kem, emphasized the need of a widening of the political basis of the Murmansk regime. It was becoming increasingly clear that the basic design of defending the entire northern area from the Germans could not be carried out unless the collaboration of other local authorities throughout the entire Murmansk and Karelian areas could be assured. At the end of March and beginning of April the Murmansk Soviet repeatedly pressed the central authorities in Moscow to agree to such an extension. In the absence of any positive reaction from Moscow, the Murmansk Soviet finally decided to proceed on its own responsibility.[9] On April 18, accordingly, there was formally brought into existence a body called the "Murmansk Regional Soviet of Workers' and Peasants' Deputies," in which there were some representatives of neighboring communities in addition to those from Murmansk itself. Yuryev became its first chairman; and Vesselago, who was the driving force behind the entire development, became here, too, the executive secretary.[10] This development was viewed with deep suspicion not only by Moscow but also by the strongly Bolshevik Soviets in Archangel and Petrozavodsk. It probably did more than any other factor to arouse suspicion in Moscow as well as a determination, on the part of the Moscow Party authorities, to bring the local political situation in Murmansk back under their own control.

The senior Allied representatives attended the opening of the new body and were asked to make speeches of greeting.[11] Admiral Kemp and Captain Petit (for the French) both took occasion to deny categorically that their respective governments had any annexationist aims with respect to the Murmansk area. Martin also spoke, and it is perhaps of interest to note some of his remarks on this occasion.

We are with you today in order to assure you of the aid of the Allies. Rest assured that we will not abandon you in this crucial moment. When you were in good health—we were your friends. You may be sure that we will be your friends in sickness as well. At this moment America has

[9] *Ibid.,* pp. 70–75.
[10] In Russian: *upravlyayushchi delami.*
[11] Full texts of all the speeches by the Allied representatives are given in Kedrov, *op.cit.,* pp. 75–80.

no land or sea forces in the Murmansk region. But if there should be such forces here in future, as you have requested and as I very much hope, then I can assure you in the name of America that these forces will be here for only one purpose: to help Russia free herself from the clutches of Germany, who wishes to strangle her freedom. There will be people who will try to persuade you that we have come here with the ulterior motive of seizing your territory. My friends! Such thoughts are far from our minds. As soón as the need for our help has passed, we shall leave again and we shall not make the slightest effort to seize your territory . . .[12]

Considering that Martin was not only without previous diplomatic experience but also without any instructions or guidance as to his own government's views and intentions, one must concede that this was a creditable effort, and one that kept him on fairly safe ground throughout.

❖

During the entire month of April, there was much discussion among the Allied representatives at Murmansk, and between them and the local Russian leaders, of the possibility of a more extensive and ambitious Allied military commitment to the defense of the area. This thought accorded with the natural feelings of most of the Allied representatives. It appears to have been stimulated by the passage through Murmansk, in late March, of the outgoing head of the French Military Mission to Russia, General Niessel, and his colleague, General Berthelot, who had similarly headed the French Military Mission to Rumania. Niessel, in particular, was strongly anti-Bolshevik and convinced of the necessity of early intervention. The idea of Allied intervention gained impetus in mid-April, it should be noted, as news from the western front indicated that the German offensive there would probably be held, and that the war could thus be expected to go into another season. This accentuated the importance of the re-creation of some sort of eastern front.

Around the time of the establishment of the new Regional Soviet, the Russian leaders Yuryev, Vesselago, and Zvegintsev worked out a contingent plan for future intervention which envisaged the use of American forces on a large scale.[13] This, it should be noted, was only

[12] Vesselago, *op.cit.,* Chapter 4. The above is only an excerpt from Martin's statements.
[13] Strakhovsky, *op.cit.,* p. 37.

a local initiative. There is no evidence that any of the Allied governments had encouraged it. The scheme, whatever it was, evidently
reflected among other things a distrust of the British on the part of
the Murmansk Russian leaders, and a desire to engage the United
States more prominently as a counterbalance to British influence.

On April 25, Martin left Murmansk for Vologda, in order to report to Ambassador Francis. He left Halsey as his informal deputy
in Murmansk—a somewhat unusual position for a pastor, to be sure,
but one which appears to have been accepted without question by the
local Russian authorities.

Whether Martin took with him on his journey to Vologda any
written document agreed upon with the leaders of the Murmansk
Regional Soviet is uncertain. Strakhovsky, citing certain personal
papers of Vesselago to which he had access, says that Martin, on
arrival in Vologda, recommended to Francis a plan for immediate
despatch of an American warship to Murmansk

. . . to be followed by a large American military force, which was to have
been speedily increased to the size of an army corps to operate in conjunction with forces of comparable strength from other allied powers.[14]

Strakhovsky conveys the impression that this was the plan previously
elaborated by the Russian leaders in Murmansk.

Vesselago, in his "Digest," merely gives the text of a memorandum
he says he wrote at some time in April and meant to send to the
Allied representatives in the form of a circular letter. He never did
send the memorandum, he explained, because when he expounded
its contents orally to the Allied representatives he

. . . met with complete understanding and sympathy, on the part of
Berthelot, who was leaving for France with these same thoughts, as well
as of . . . Kemp, . . . de Lagatinerie and the American Lt. Martin. The
latter, being a convinced protagonist of this idea, left on April 25, to make
a corresponding report in Vologda.[15]

The undelivered memorandum to which Vesselago here referred
will be found in his "Digest." It set forth no actual plan for intervention, but spoke of the need for the creation of a new eastern front
as essential to winning the war. For this, Vesselago argued, it was

[14] *Ibid.*, p. 38. Martin had been urging despatch of an American warship ever
since the end of March.
[15] Vesselago, *op.cit.*, pp. 66–73.

necessary to create at this time an organizational basis both in Siberia and in the Russian North, in order that one should be in a position to act in the autumn, when the Russian people would—as he thought —have their bellyful of German domination. The memorandum said nothing about any specific employment of American forces.

Martin's journey to Vologda was, as it turned out, a long and eventful one. Just at this time the commander of the immobilized Russian cruiser *Askold,* Shaikovski, had found himself the object of the same threats and harassments from the communist faction among the naval sailors that had already culminated in so many lynchings and murders of officers, including his own predecessor, Kyetlinski. Convinced that his usefulness was at an end and desirous of escaping to the interior, where he could elude the animosity of the sailors, Shaikovski sought asylum in Martin's private railway car and asked to be taken along.[16] Martin obtained from the well-disposed Murmansk Soviet a pass authorizing him to accommodate Shaikovski as a passenger. Nevertheless, when the train came to leave, the car was surrounded by a mob of sailors, who demanded Shaikovski's blood. Martin stood them off successfully with a revolver at the door of the car, and the train departed with the intended victim still aboard, the mob shouting after it: "We'll get you, Shaikovski, before you reach Petrograd." In view of the sympathy which the sailors enjoyed among the members of the violently pro-Bolshevik railwaymen's union, this was no idle threat. The following morning, the train struck a pile of ties laid across the track, and was wrecked. Six peasants were killed in the car adjoining that of Martin. Martin's own car was turned over, ending up on its roof. Martin and Shaikovski both escaped fatal injury; but Martin was obliged to lay up for some days in Kandalaksha, under the care of a French army doctor. On the rest of the journey several further attempts at sabotage were made, Martin's car being even uncoupled on one occasion, while in motion, and left to its fate on the right of way.

In the face of these adversities, it was not until May 8 that Martin

[16] For the account of this journey, see the long story in the *New York World* of June 26, 1918, by the French correspondent Arno Dosch-Fleurot. He obviously had it from Martin, who, great raconteur that he was, was not above the occasional minor embroidering of a tale for greater clarity and effectiveness. But the main circumstances—Shaikovski's presence in the car, and the wreck—were also mentioned by Wardwell in his diary, *op.cit.*

arrived in Vologda. Francis was at that time in Moscow, attending Summers' funeral. Martin, in Francis' absence, drew up a written report to the Embassy about the situation in Murmansk. Here he stressed the extent to which the British and French were already involved in that situation, noted the sanction for this commitment in Trotsky's telegram of March 1, and pointed out that the leaders of the Murmansk Regional Soviet all wished for American assistance and would be glad to request it in writing.[17] No specific plan of intervention was presented. Francis, having by this time himself recommended intervention, appears to have made no further use of Martin's report.

❖

Meanwhile, the entire Murmansk situation had received a new dimension of seriousness by the self-interjection of the Germans into the picture. On April 22, the day before the arrival of the German Embassy in Moscow, the Soviet government received from the German Foreign Office, through open telegraphic channels, a protest based on Norwegian press reports to the effect that 6,000 French and English troops had been landed at Murmansk.

On May 2, Chicherin instructed Joffe, the newly arrived Soviet representative in Berlin, to tell the Foreign Office there that these reports were false—the Soviet government had arrested the editors of Russian papers who had reproduced them. "In reality," Chicherin wired,

there was no landing of troops in Murmansk at all. The evacuation of a number of French and British military specialists, that were in Russia, could not have been carried out right away. When the White Guards started their operations against the Murmansk region, almost completely devoid of defense, the German government answered our note by stating that these operations were conducted by irregulars, not forming a part of Mannerheim's army, and that the German government could not be held responsible. It should not be surprising that, under the circumstances, the local Soviet has turned to the British and French who had not yet left Murmansk in order to obtain their help against bands, the responsibility for which the German government denied. We did not protest then against this temporary help extended for purposes of self-defense

[17] National Archives, Petrograd Embassy File "Miscellaneous Confidential Information, 1918," *op.cit.*

to the Soviets by the British and French, but now we are protesting against the prolonged stay of the British in Murmansk.[18]

On May 8, DeWitt C. Poole, who had just taken over the Consulate General in Moscow as Summers' successor, reported to the Department of State that it had been learned from a source considered reliable

. . . that Count Mirbach has presented an ultimatum to the Soviet authorities stating that if British and French troops do not at once evacuate Murman Peninsula the consequence will be most grave and it will be necessary for Germany to undertake military operations occupying further territory either in the direction of Murmansk or elsewhere.[19]

The following day Poole reported that new information "practically" confirmed this rumor. According to the latest information, he added, the ultimatum demanded immediate departure of the British and French troops from Murmansk, as well as occupation by the Germans of Fort Ino, near Petrograd, and the disarming of the Lettish regiment which was used by the Soviet leaders as personal bodyguards.[20]

This was not entirely correct. There is nothing in Mirbach's despatches to indicate that he had as yet discussed these matters with the Soviet government; the Germans had presented no ultimata. But the rumors were not wholly devoid of substance. The Soviet leaders had now received the first reports from Joffe about his discussions in Berlin. When he complained to the German military authorities about the continuation of German hostilities against Soviet forces in the Ukraine, the Germans countered with complaints concerning the continued occupation of Fort Ino on Finnish territory on the Gulf of Kronstadt by a Soviet garrison, and the use by the Bolshevik leaders of the Lettish regiment, composed as it was of men whose home land was under German control. These situations, the Germans argued, represented violations of the Brest-Litovsk Treaty. It was implied that if the Soviet leaders really wished operations in the Ukraine to cease, they should themselves stop violating the treaty.[21]

[18] The above translation is that of Strakhovsky, *op.cit.*, p. 22, who took it from *Izvestiya*, No. 88 (352), May 3, 1918. The Russian text is also reproduced in Kedrov, *op.cit.*

[19] *Foreign Relations, 1918, Russia*, Vol. II, *op.cit.*, p. 472.

[20] *Ibid.*, p. 473.

[21] National Archives, German Foreign Ministry Archives, *op.cit.*, St. Antony's Reels Nos. 83 and 147.

The German documents do not specifically mention Murmansk as having been discussed on this occasion; but it is quite probable, in view of the recent German protest about Murmansk and the fact that Lenin (as will be seen shortly) mentioned the problems of Murmansk and Fort Ino in the same breath, that this matter was also raised with Joffe, and perhaps brought up informally by members of Mirbach's entourage.

The German desiderata were considered at a meeting of the Soviet of People's Commissars on May 8. This was no doubt the source of the rumors Poole had picked up. Lenin made reference to them again in his report on foreign policy at a joint session of the All-Russian Central Executive Committee and the Moscow Soviet on May 14. Admitting that the international situation of the Soviet government had "become in many respects more complicated during the last few days," he said that the entire question of the preservation of peace with the Germans boiled down to Fort Ino and Murmansk. He then addressed the following words particularly to the Murmansk situation:

The question of Murmansk has been the source of even greater friction. The British and French have raised claims concerning Murmansk because they have invested tens of millions on the construction of the port in order to secure their military supply line in the imperialist war against Germany. They have such a wonderful respect for neutrality that they make free use of everything that is not nailed down. And the fact that they have an armored vessel and we have nothing with which to drive it away serves as sufficient grounds for seizures. Now there is an external wrapping, a juridical expression, called into being by the international situation of the Soviet Republic, which postulates that no armed force of a warring power may enter neutral territory without being disarmed. The English landed their armed forces at Murmansk, and we had no possibility of preventing this by armed force. In consequence we find ourselves faced with demands bearing a character close to that of an ultimatum: if you cannot protect your neutrality, then we will fight on your territory.[22]

It will be noted that here the term "ultimatum" was used to refer to the British position at Murmansk, whereas in Poole's messages it had referred to the desiderata voiced by the Germans. In neither case had there been anything in the nature of an ultimatum in the west-

[22] Lenin, Vol. 27, *op.cit.*, p. 344.

ern sense (in the case of the British there had been no communication at all on this subject). It is probable that the term "ultimatum" had quite a different meaning in Soviet usage from that which is customarily attached to it in western countries. The Bolsheviki evidently considered that any desiderata voiced, or even actions performed, by a more powerful adversary that were disagreeable to one's own interests could properly be described as "ultimata," whether or not there had been any threats, any time limits, or indeed any communication at all.

Lenin, in the speech just cited, was probably deliberately exaggerating the severity of British pressure, with a view to strengthening the Soviet position against the Germans.

Despite this new show of interest from the German side, the Soviet government continued to temporize with the Murmansk situation, and made no actual demand of the Allied governments, at this stage, for evacuation of the port. But the fact of increased German interest in Murmansk did not remain concealed from Allied representatives or the officials of the Murmansk Soviet; and the somewhat inaccurate reports received of the details of the German-Soviet exchanges naturally greatly increased the nervousness in both quarters. On May 14 Vesselago addressed to Admiral Kemp a letter which revealed acute anxiety as to the effect on local opinion of what he took to be a hardening of the attitude of the Moscow authorities under German pressure. As examples of this he cited the despatch by Moscow to the Murmansk Railway zone of a detachment of several hundred communist railway guards, extremely hostile to the Allies,[23] a demand of the Kandalaksha railwaymen for the withdrawal of the Allied detachment there, similar demands from groups in Petrozavodsk and Kem, and renewed manifestations of hostility by the Murmansk naval garrison. Vesselago went on to plead for a more decisive and energetic policy on the part of the Allied governments as a means of combatting this threatened disintegration of the political position of the Murmansk Soviet.

Whatever impression this made on the British and French governments must have been heightened by two other developments that occurred in rapid succession in the first part of May.

[23] These were special troops of the Cheka, the forerunner of the G.P.U.-N.K.V.D. forces, selected for their reliability to the central Soviet authority, and obviously sent to the Murmansk region with a view to taking the local political situation more directly under Moscow's control.

First of all, at the beginning of the month, another detachment of Finnish Whites, stationed near the Russian-Finnish-Norwegian frontier junction, went over to the attack in the Petsamo area and pushed back the Murmansk border guards near the fishing village of Pechenga (Petsamo), forty or fifty miles from Murmansk. Its objective appeared to be to seize that point. This immediately raised in the minds of the local Allied commanders the specter of the Germans gaining a foothold, and eventually a naval base, in the immediate vicinity of Murmansk.[24] Acting—once more—on the request of the Murmansk Soviet, Admiral Kemp embarked some of the Royal Marines, accompanied by a party of Red Guards, in the cruiser *Cochrane* and sent the ship to Pechenga, where she arrived on May 3. Both the marines and the Russians were put ashore. The former fought a small defensive engagement on May 10 against sixty or seventy Finns. (In this engagement, the British found themselves embarrassed by the fact that the Finns were on skis whereas their own men were floundering in the deep snow—a situation prophetic of that in which the British units would find themselves on their landing in northern Norway in 1940.) The Finns did not press the attack; and here, again, the advent of the thaw (somewhat later than in the Kandalaksha region) soon put an end to any serious threat from the White Finnish side.

The second development was a more serious one. In the middle of May a German submarine began operating off Vardö, at the entrance of the bay on which Pechenga is situated. It sank three small Russian steamers, one of them on the Russian side of the fjord, and bombarded a Russian signal station. On May 17 Chicherin protested to Mirbach about this, only to be told (May 21) by Mirbach that "under the terms of the Brest Treaty the Arctic Ocean remains in the forbidden zone and these operations may therefore be expected to continue."[25]

Chicherin described this exchange, quite accurately, to DeWitt

[24] This fear was grotesquely exaggerated. Major General Sir C. Maynard, late commander of the Allied ground force in the Murmansk area, a man not given to underrating the German threat, disposed very effectively, in his memoirs (*The Murmansk Venture*, Hodder & Stoughton, London, no date, pp. 66–68), of the suggestion that the Germans could conceivably have used Pechenga as a submarine base. Their submarines could have taken shelter in the bay; but they could not have made a real base out of the inlet, which was shallow near the shores and contained not even the rudiments of a modern port.

[25] *Foreign Relations, 1918, Russia*, Vol. 1, *op.cit.*, p. 541, telegram from Poole to SECSTATE, May 24, 8 p.m.

Poole in a discussion on the 23rd. Poole asked whether the Germans had offered to cease their operations if the Allies would withdraw from Murmansk. Chicherin replied, "Not yet." Poole pointed out that in these circumstances Murmansk, in the absence of Allied protection, would certainly become a German submarine base, in which case Archangel, too, would become a blocked port, cut off from access to the outside world. In this conclusion Chicherin unhappily acquiesced, and he conjured up a gloomy picture of the starvation that would prevail in the northern area if all this were to occur.

"It is clearly Bolshevik policy," Poole concluded after this conversation with Chicherin, "to avoid a break with either Germany or the Allies and they will certainly do their best to escape a definite issue on the present question." [26]

This was an accurate description of the situation, so far as it went. Chicherin, then and later, repeatedly gave to Allied representatives the impression that the Soviet authorities were at least tolerant of the Allied position there and would make no trouble over it. In this respect, he went further than Lenin or Trotsky (after his telegram of March 1) ever did; and it is probable that, in addition to being somewhat sympathetic himself to the Allied situation there, he was deliberately permitted by Lenin to take this reassuring position in order to avoid giving provocation for an actual increase in the Allied involvement.[27] On the other hand, there is ample evidence of a strong determination on the part of the central Party authorities, throughout May and June, to bring the local political situation at Murmansk under their own complete control. On the foreign-political plane, in other words, they were not inclined to make an immediate formal issue of the presence of the Allied forces at Murmansk; but they were determined to take charge of the local situation on the domestic-political plane: a purpose which, if successfully concluded, would have meant eventually the elimination of most of the Russians then

[26] Francis MSS, *op.cit.*, letter, Poole to Francis, May 24, 1918.

[27] In his *The Soviets in World Affairs: A History of the Relations between the Soviet Union and the Rest of the World 1917–1929* (Second Edition, Princeton University Press, 1951) Mr. Louis Fischer stated (Vol. I, p. 126) that Chicherin told the Allied representatives at this time that the Bolsheviki would resist foreign landings in the northern ports "only in case they were directed against the Communist government." He cited in proof of this Chicherin's oral statement to himself that Voznesenski had been instructed to tell this to the Allied representatives at Vologda. In another book (*Men and Politics: An Autobiography,* Duell, Sloan and Pearce, 1941, p. 146) Mr. Fischer has described Chicherin's anguish over the appearance of this passage, which he was sure would ruin him in Russia.

prominent on the Murmansk scene and their replacement with trusted Bolshevik Party figures. Had the central Soviet authorities succeeded in this purpose, the move would unquestionably have been followed by demands for a revision, in favor of the Russian side, of the defense agreement with the Allied forces. The internal-political purpose of the Bolsheviki with respect to Murmansk was thus actually more in conflict with Allied interests than Soviet statements on the diplomatic level would suggest. This distinction, not generally apparent to Allied observers, was the source of much confusion.

❖

At what points the reports of these various developments entered into the calculations of the Allied chanceries, and affected their decisions, it is difficult to say. But during the period in which these things were occurring, the British government, in particular, began to take a more serious view of the Murmansk situation.

In London, some far-reaching measures were put in hand. It will be recalled that the Supreme War Council, at its Fifth Session held in Abbeville (see above, Chapter VI), had decided (May 2) that all those Czechoslovak forces that had not passed the Urals should be despatched "with the greatest rapidity" to Archangel and Murmansk, where, pending evacuation, they might be "profitably employed in defending Archangel and Murmansk and in guarding and protecting the Murmansk railway." Throughout the month of May, the British and French governments faithfully believed this plan to be in process of implementation. Now, in the light of the disturbing reports of German pressure on the Soviet government and of German submarine activity in the Murmansk area, the British military authorities made up their minds to hasten preparations for the reception and training of these Czechs. It was decided to despatch to the North Russian ports without further ado a strong military training mission and a small expeditionary force. As described in retrospect by Major General Sir C. Maynard, who was selected to command the expeditionary force (the entire operation was to be under the over-all command of Major General F. C. Poole), the mission and strength of these detachments were to be as follows:

The Mission was to consist mainly of officers and non-commissioned officers selected as instructors from combatant and administrative branches, and thus could not be regarded primarily as a fighting unit. It was to proceed to Archangel as soon as the White Sea was ice-free, in order to equip and train such Czecho-Slovaks as should find their way to that port, and also to take in hand the organization, equipment, and training of a local Russian contingent, which it was anticipated confidently would reach a strength of at least 30,000.

When ready to take the field, the whole force was to endeavour to join hands with the pro-Ally forces in Siberia, and then to assist in opening up a new front against Germany. . . .

The expeditionary force was destined for Murmansk, . . . Its immediate task was to prevent the occupation of Murmansk and Petchenga [Petsamo] by the Germans, or by the Finnish troops cooperating with them. . . .

A further task of the Murmansk force was to pin down the German army in Finland for as long a period as possible, and thus prevent reinforcements being sent from it to the Western front. Little success could be hoped for, however, in this respect, without the raising of local forces. It was therefore part of the duty of the commander at Murmansk to organize and train local troops to supplement the expeditionary force. . . .

The expeditionary force was to consist of a meagre 600 men, almost all of whom would be of a physical category so low as to render them unfit for duty in France; whilst 400 Royal Marines, a few Royal Engineers, a battalion of Serbian infantry, and some French artillery would come under my command on arrival.[28]

It will be noted that this British scheme, the implementation of which was at once put in hand, amounted now to a full-fledged though very limited intervention, despite the absence of any express statement of Soviet consent. It envisaged military cooperation with "the anti-Bolshevik forces" (it was probably Semenov who was envisaged) understood to be operating in Siberia. Nothing seems to have been said about this scheme, at the time of its adoption, to Lockhart in Moscow, who was still faithfully endeavoring to obtain Soviet consent to Allied intervention. He learned of these new plans only after General Poole's arrival in Murmansk (he took passage as a guest on the *Olympia*) on May 24. The implementation of these plans, at a time when Lockhart was continuing to conduct his discussions in Moscow, could hardly fail to create on the Soviet leaders, as it gradually became known, an impression of deep duplicity.

[28] Maynard, *op.cit.,* pp. 12–14. Maynard does not indicate exactly when this plan was adopted. General Poole was despatched to Russia May 17. Presumably, the decisions had been made in the immediately preceding days.

This British scheme may stand as a good example of the inadequacy of information and poor coordination that marked generally the actions of the war-weary governments in London and Washington as they addressed themselves to the Russian problem in the spring of 1918. As we have already seen, the scheme to divide the Czech Corps and to bring part of it to the northern ports was abortive; no Czechs were ever recalled to the Northern Region.[29] The idea that Semenov's tiny force, then numbering at the most some five to six hundred men, would reach out across some 5,000 miles of northern Siberia and Russia to join forces with the Russian and Czech units to be trained near Archangel was again one which reflected little understanding of the realities of Semenov's position or of the Russian situation generally. The same may be said of the implicit assumption that Semenov's purposes would have had something in common with those of the Allies. Finally, the British government seems to have distinguished very poorly between the situation in Murmansk, where a relatively friendly Soviet, bound to Moscow only by the most tenuous of bonds, was in control, and that in Archangel, where the dominant force in the city was still wholly and defiantly Bolshevik, under strictest Moscow discipline and deeply hostile to the Allies. The scheme appeared, after all, to envisage disposing of Archangel as though it were an Allied port, in friendly, welcoming hands. But Bullard has well described the extremely tense and dangerous situation in which the officers and men of the British naval icebreaker *Alexander* and the two food ships actually found themselves at Archangel in late May and early June. The local Bolshevik authorities were suspicious and hostile in the extreme. The officers of the British vessels, anchored in midstream, half expected to be the victims at any time of sabotage or outright attack. When an attempt was trustingly made in mid-June to send the French battleship, the *Amiral Aube,* to Archangel, presumably with the members of the training mission, only the fact that the vessel was unable to make her way through the ice and had to return to Murmansk for repairs prevented the creation of what would unquestionably have been an extremely tense situation, with a strong probability of the outbreak of open hostilities. Of this vital difference in

---

[29] The historian of British naval operations in World War I, Newbolt (Vol. v, *op.cit.,* pp. 318–319), records that on Poole's arrival in Murmansk, "It was not known . . . where exactly were the Czechs he had come to train; . . ."

the situations at Murmansk and Archangel the British planners seem to have taken no account at all.

❖

There is no evidence that the full nature of these British dispositions —particularly those relating to the training mission—was ever made plain to President Wilson and Secretary of State Lansing. The arrangements were presumably arrived at by the War Office; perhaps the Foreign Office was itself not fully informed. But the Foreign Office did keep in touch with Washington concerning the Murmansk problem, and continued to press the President for agreement to the general principle of Allied action to keep the port out of German hands. On May 11 and again on May 15, Lord Reading, in the course of oral discussions with Lansing about the problem of intervention generally, mentioned Murmansk as well as Siberia. After the discussion on the 11th, Lansing made the following significant written report to the President:

Lord Reading called again this morning and presented me with the enclosed telegrams which he had received from Mr. Balfour in relation to intervention in Russia.

I pointed out to Lord Reading that the problem had really become two problems in that intervention in western Russia in no way involved the racial difficulty which had to be considered in regard to Siberia. I further told him that intervention at Murmansk and Archangel would receive far more favorable consideration on our part than intervention in Siberia, for the reason that we could understand the military advantage of the former but had been unable, thus far, to find any advantage in sending troops into Siberia. I also said that the communications which had been received from Trotsky as to his favorable attitude toward intervention might apply only to the northern part and not the Far East and that I had some doubts as to how far the reported invitation for intervention would go even if it was made by the Bolsheviks, and, therefore, it seemed to me advisable that that should be thoroughly understood in case the purpose of inducing an invitation persisted.

He asked me if you would not express your views as to whether it was not advisable, in any event, to secure an invitation from Trotsky or from the Bolshevik authorities and I told him I would ask you.[30]

This statement by Lansing is of great importance, for it indicates that as early as May 11 the United States government drew a sharp

[30] *Foreign Relations, 1918, Russia*, Vol. II, *op.cit.*, p. 160.

distinction between the Northern Region and Siberia, from the stand-point of possible Allied action. It accepted the possibility that there might be adequate necessity, from the standpoint of the prosecution of the war against Germany, for intervention in the Russian North. Finally, it accepted the somewhat dubious thesis that Trotsky had actually invited, and continued to approve, the Allied activity at Murmansk.

Lansing followed up on this communication, after his second conversation with Lord Reading on the 15th, with a further letter to the President (May 16). Here he told the President that Reading was insisting on a joint Allied effort to elicit from Trotsky a Soviet request for intervention in Siberia. Again he, Lansing, had argued that the two problems had nothing to do with each other, and should be treated separately:

I told him that I could see no objection to securing a request from Trotsky that we should intervene via Murmansk, but that I was not at all sure we would gain anything by a request as to a conditional Japanese intervention in Siberia . . .

In view of the present situation do you think it wise to advise Francis to unite through unofficial channels in obtaining from Trotsky a request for us to intervene by way of Murmansk? I do not feel that we should go further than this at the present time and I am not sure that this is expedient in view of the uncertainty of Trotsky's power. . . .

Will you please give me your opinion as to the course which should be taken? . . .[31]

To these communications, the President replied on May 20:

I do not know what to say by way of comment on these papers that I have not already said repeatedly. The two parts of this question (as you properly discriminate them) must not and cannot be confused and dis-cussed together. Semenoff is changing the situation in Siberia very rapidly, apparently; and General March and the Staff are clear and decided in their opinion that (1) no strong enough force to amount to anything can be sent to Murmansk without subtracting just that much shipping and man power from the western front, and (2) that such a subtraction at the present crisis would be most unwise . . .[32]

Lansing, dining that evening (May 20) at the British Embassy, took the opportunity to tell Reading that the President's views on

[31] *Foreign Relations, The Lansing Papers,* Vol. II, *op.cit.,* p. 361.
[32] *Ibid.,* p. 361.

intervention, which had been expressed on a number of occasions, remained unchanged.[33]

There is nothing in these interviews between Reading and Lansing to suggest that either man had, at that time, any knowledge either of the decisions of the Abbeville meeting of the Supreme War Council, concerning the routing of a portion of the Czechs to the northern ports, or of the British military plan—then in process of adoption—that flowed from the Abbeville decision.

The President's views on the Murmansk problem were spelled out further in a message despatched by the War Department on May 28 to General Bliss, who was asking for instructions as to the position he should adopt in the problem of intervention at the forthcoming meeting of the Military Representatives at the Supreme War Council. "The President," General Bliss was told,

is heartily in sympathy with any practical military effort which can be made at and from Murmansk or Archangel, but such efforts should proceed, if at all, upon the sure sympathy of the Russian people and should not have as their ultimate object any restoration of the ancient regime or any other interference with the political liberty of the Russian people.[34]

On May 28 Balfour returned to the matter once more in a telegram to Lord Reading (a paraphrase was handed to Lansing the following day) in which, apparently for the first time, something of the British dispositions was revealed:

. . . On the Murmansk coast assistance from America is badly required and is, in fact, essential. Every day the position of Murmansk is more seriously endangered and, as the United States Government will of course be aware, it is of vital importance to us to retain Murmansk, if we desire to retain any possibility at all of entering Russia.

This danger has become so extreme that we are sending to Murmansk such small marine and military forces as we are able to spare during the present crisis in France. These forces will, however, clearly not be enough to resist the further efforts which the enemy are certain to put forward on this coast. The despatch of additional French or British reinforcements is impossible and it is therefore essential that America should help by sending a brigade, to which a few guns should be added. It is not necessary that the troops sent should be completely trained, as we anticipate

[33] Lansing mss, *op.cit.*, Desk Diary.
[34] Ray Stannard Baker, *Woodrow Wilson, Life and Letters*, Doubleday, Doran & Co., Inc., New York, 1939, Vol. viii, *Armistice, March 1–November 11, 1918*, p. 175.

that military operations in this region will only be of irregular character.
... There is a further consideration which is worthy of careful consideration by the President. Great use has been made already of the divergence of view among the Allied countries with regard to the Russian situation, and for this reason it is of great importance that the United States should show their agreement with us on this matter by taking part in the steps adopted for preventing the closing of the only remaining door through which assistance can be given to Russia in her hour of need.[35]

On the 29th and 30th, on the heels of Balfour's approach, alarming reports about the Murmansk situation were received in Washington from Francis: the Murmansk Railway had been cut on the northern stretch by the Finns (this was actually quite erroneous); German submarines were doing damage in the adjacent waters; the Germans planned to capture the Murmansk line and Murmansk itself. It was highly important, Francis stated, that the Allies "should retain Murman as its capture by the Germans would sever Archangel and result in Russian-American communication's being confined to Pacific." [36]

These messages were supplemented by the receipt, on the morning of June 1, of another one from Poole in Moscow (sent May 28), reporting—on the impeccable authority of Chicherin himself—that the Soviet government had decided, under German pressure, to cede the Petsamo area, just west of Murmansk, to Finland—which meant, in the circumstances, to the Finnish Whites.[37] The cession of this territory was a Soviet promise of long standing to the *Red* Finnish government; but the Allied authorities in Murmansk had been repeatedly assured that any such cession to the *White* Finns was out of the question. The fact that the Soviet government now agreed to such a step, and did so under German pressure, appeared indeed to be a development of high strategic importance. It was assumed that with Petsamo in White Finnish hands, the bay, at least, would provide a haven for German submarines, already operating within a few miles of the point. Of all the factors that led the Allies to fear German encroachments in the Murmansk area this development was, in fact, the most real and the most serious.

---

[35] *Foreign Relations, 1918, Russia,* Vol. II, *op.cit.,* p. 476.
[36] *Ibid.,* p. 475, from telegram of May 26, 8 p.m.
[37] *Ibid.,* p. 790, telegram, Poole to SECSTATE, May 28, noon. Actually, Poole had wired the preceding day reporting an official Soviet communiqué to this effect; but this first message was not received in Washington until June 3.

Whether or not these reports had anything to do with the President's reaction to Balfour's requests for American forces, is not clear. It would seem very probable that they did. In any case, on Saturday, June 1, the President telephoned Lansing and asked him to come to the White House at 2:00 p.m. The result of this conference, and its consequences, was summed up by Lansing in the following memoandum (June 3):

After conference with the President on Saturday, June 1, it was agreed that I should say to Lord Reading that this Government was entirely willing to send troops to Murmansk provided General Foch approved the diversion of troops and the necessary shipping for that purpose from those now going to France. Before doing this I saw Secretary Baker who entirely agreed with this action and to-day I saw Lord Reading and told him of our attitude. He made notes and said he would inform his Government.[38]

As of the beginning of June, therefore, the American position with regard to Murmansk might be summed up as follows. The United States government recognized the military necessity, from the standpoint of the prosecution of the war against Germany, of continued Allied strategic control of Murmansk and its immediate environs. It believed this control to be seriously threatened, at that point, by German activities. It believed that the Soviet government was favorable to the idea of Allied assistance in the defense of the region against the Germans. In response to recommendations by its military and diplomatic representatives in Russia, the United States government had already sent a cruiser to Murmansk, the commanding officer of which had instructions to place himself under the orders of the senior Allied commander (at that time, the British Admiral) in that port and to cooperate with him in protecting and furthering Allied interests generally and in efforts to recover the Allied stores at Archangel. Pressed by the British government to make available, in addition, land forces for service at Murmansk, the United States government had indicated that in its view this question was entirely dependent on the military availability of the forces in question in the light of general Allied war plans; and it had, accordingly, passed the question to General Foch. American military authorities did not consider that the forces in question were more needed at Murmansk than on the western front; but if Foch

[38] *Ibid.*, pp. 484–485.

thought otherwise, the United States government would abide by his opinion. In arriving at this decision, the senior officials of the United States government were either wholly unaware of the British scheme to link the northern expedition with a similar action in Siberia or they considered this idea to have been dropped, pursuant to their own insistence that the two situations must be treated separately.

Balfour had motivated his written request for American forces at Murmansk by the bald contention that "every day the position of Murmansk is more seriously endangered." He did not spell out the nature of this danger, as the British government saw it. Presumably the British government had in mind the operations by the White Finns (of which the Allied chanceries had received such misleading reports), the German pressure on the Soviet government to demand the departure of the Allied forces, the German submarine operations off the Murmansk coast, and possibly the recent Soviet decision to cede Petsamo to the Finnish Whites. It is permissible to conclude that the mission conceived by the American governmental leaders for any such American forces as might be sent to Murmansk, in the event of Foch's approval, was primarily to participate in the defense of the port of Murmansk and its environs against possible German, or German-inspired, encroachments, the danger of which seemed now, for the first time, to be quite serious. Nothing in the record suggests that the President, in giving his conditional assent to the despatch of American forces, had any other thought in mind. There is abundant evidence, in particular, that he would have deplored the suggestion that these forces should intervene in any way in Russian internal affairs.

❖

The last days of May, precisely those same days that saw the outbreak of the Czech uprising in western Siberia, also marked the beginning of the final internal-political crisis at Murmansk.

In early May Yuryev, in an effort to clarify matters with the central Soviet authorities, had gone to Moscow in person. There he was taken severely over the coals for his failure to show sufficient firmness vis-à-vis the Allied contingents in the port. He was regarded by the Moscow leaders as a political child, not up to the demands of the delicate situation into which he had been thrust. On the other hand, the key position that he occupied in that situation was appreciated in Moscow, and it was recognized that he could not be simply removed. The decision was therefore taken to send him back in the company of a suitable Party mentor, described as a "special commissar," who could take charge of the situation behind the scenes. The man chosen for this task was a Lithuanian Communist, one S. P. Natsarenus. Kedrov's description of Natsarenus' status, and the circumstances surrounding his appointment, is worth noting:

As early as the end of April the *Sovnarkom* took account of the full seriousness of the situation that had been created in Murmansk and the weakness and incorrectness of the regional leadership.

The result of this was the appointment by the central authorities, in agreement with the Regional Soviet, of the Special Commissar for the Murmansk Region, S. P. Natsarenus, who left for Murmansk in the beginning of May. His mission was uniquely difficult. He was supposed to reorganize completely the entire work of the Murmansk Soviet and to alter the nature of its relations with the "Allies." It was likewise necessary to dispel the illusions that had grown up among the population about the help and aid of the Allies and to explain that for Soviet power the Entente and German imperialism were equally dangerous and hostile.

All this had to be done in such a way as to preserve official etiquette and not give the "Allies" any formal grounds for breaking relations and for aggressive measures against Russia. . . .[39]

This *ex post facto* definition of Natsarenus' mission must be taken with some reserve. It was true that Moscow wished to take the Murmansk Soviet under a closer control and to combat pro-Allied sentiment among the population. But it also wished to continue to use the Allied activities in Murmansk as a counter to German influence. It was precisely this delicate and contradictory policy that Natsarenus was supposed to find means of conducting.

Yuryev and Natsarenus arrived in Murmansk on May 25, one day after the arrival of General Poole in the *Olympia*. On the very eve of these various arrivals (May 23), a telegraphic instruction was received by the Murmansk Soviet from Chicherin. It reflected a final clarification of the policy of the central authorities in the light of the discussions which had been taking place between Mirbach and Chicherin. It was as follows:

[39] Kedrov, *Bez bolshevistskogo rukovodstva, op.cit.*, p. 86.

No local Soviet organization should appeal for aid to one of the imperialist coalitions against the other. In case of an offensive by the Germans or their allies we shall protest and resist to the limit of our strength. We shall likewise protest against the presence of the Allies at Murmansk. In view of the general political situation, any appeal to the English for help is quite impermissible. Such a policy must be most decisively combatted. It is possible that the English will themselves fight against the advancing White Finns, but we must not join them as allies, and we shall protest against their actions on our territory.[40]

This message reached Murmansk just before Natsarenus' arrival; and it probably represented a certain tightening of the instructions he was bearing with him. Obviously, it was intended only for Soviet eyes. Vesselago hastened, nevertheless, to transmit it to Kemp, Petit, and Halsey, with a long covering letter assuring the Allied officials that the friendly policy of the Murmansk Regional Soviet would remain unchanged and that in case of a German attack the Allies could depend on receiving a formal request from that Soviet for Allied assistance.[41] This all represented, of course, a direct defiance of the instruction.

It is not surprising that the simultaneous arrival of an English "supreme commander," expecting to command an Allied expeditionary force and training mission, and of a high-powered Moscow envoy, commissioned to combat pro-Allied sentiment among the population and to reestablish Moscow's control over the local Soviet, produced a most delicate and confusing situation.

Just what occurred in the ensuing days is not wholly clear. Natsarenus' first task was to straighten out the complicated question of the degree to which the local Russian naval forces should be permitted to operate, in collaboration with the Allies, to defend Russian commercial and fishing vessels from German attack. Ever since the submarine sinkings, earlier in the month, this question had been the subject of agitated exchanges between the Russian naval authorities in Murmansk, who were anxious to engage in such operations, and those in Archangel and Petrograd, who opposed it for political reasons. The matter had finally been appealed to Trotsky; and on the day following Natsarenus' arrival instructions were received from Trotsky through naval channels to the effect that the Murmansk

[40] Vesselago, *op.cit.* The date of despatch of this message was May 22.
[41] *Ibid.*

naval forces were to refrain from any steps which "could be interpreted by the Germans as a renewal by us of military operations." [42] Natsarenus at once supported this instruction by a similar directive of his own, forbidding Soviet naval vessels to put to sea at all, but permitting acceptance of Allied assistance in making the vessels operable for future eventualities. Commercial vessels and the fishing vessels might, he conceded, put to sea, but only at their own risk and without naval protection.

This directive was protested by the Russian sailors in Murmansk, who had no desire to expose themselves without naval protection to the depredations of the German U-boats. Natsarenus then reconsidered and issued a supplementary directive (June 1) permitting Russian naval vessels to do convoy duty, but without flying the Russian naval flag. In such convoy operations, Natsarenus agreed that the Soviet naval authorities might accept the collaboration of the local Allied naval command; but he asked them to

. . . bear in mind that these instructions were in contradiction to the Brest treaty; therefore they must be kept secret; the most complete caution must be shown in implementing them, for which purpose it was also necessary to see that actions were "concerted with the general line of local policy with respect to foreigners." [43]

After thus laying down the law to the local Russian officials, Natsarenus entered into contact with the Allied commanders. A meeting took place, apparently on May 31, between him, General Poole, and Admiral Kemp. Vesselago, who was not present and had his information only secondhand, gathered that the talk had turned on the broad question of Anglo-Soviet relations and Natsarenus had indicated that there could be no acceptance of Allied aid by the Bolsheviki unless the Soviet government were accorded formal recognition. This was generally confirmed by the subsequent report of General Poole to his government:

. . . We have also seen Mr. Nazarenus who has arrived from Moscow as a special commissioner to organize defense. He would at our interview give us no official information but unofficially said that government intended fighting. He laid great stress on the necessity for Allies to recognize the government before he would discuss anything officially with us.

[42] *Ibid.*, p. 92.
[43] *Ibid.*, p. 93. (In this transitional period, the Russian naval vessels still flew the old Andreyev flag of the former Tsarist navy.)

We said that this question was outside the scope of our power but there was much more chance of obtaining recognition if they gave clear proof to us that they intended to throw in their lot with us and fight the Germans.[44]

It is interesting to note that Kedrov, in his book on the Murmansk situation, makes no mention of this discussion between Natsarenus and the Allied commanders, further than to cite a statement made by Natsarenus in the course of his subsequent testimony at the trial of Yuryev (in 1920) to the effect that

Immediately upon arrival I presented to Admiral Kemp a protest over the presence of their ships and in general their armed forces in the port . . . but up to my departure from Murmansk I had no definite answer from the Allies.[45]

Kedrov's reticence on this score may reasonably be taken as an indication that the Soviet government was, in 1930 at any rate, reluctant to admit that amicable discussion was possible at so late a date between a trusted representative of the central Soviet authorities and the Allied naval commanders against whose presence in Murmansk the Soviet government was ostensibly protesting.

The impressions of this week in Murmansk evidently served to convince Natsarenus that the situation was more difficult and more complicated than had been supposed in Moscow. On June 2, after a very brief stay, he left again for Moscow—a move he would scarcely have made had he felt his existing instructions to be adequate to the situation. By the time he reached Moscow, the shock of the Czech uprising had wholly undermined Soviet-Allied relations. There was now no question of Moscow's assenting further to the development of Allied activity at Murmansk. Natsarenus, after reporting to his superiors in Moscow, was sent back to the North—but this time at the head of armed Soviet detachments with whose aid he was now to assail the position of the Murmansk Soviet and take charge, by brute force, of the local political situation.

❖

Meanwhile, Martin, who had been absent since the end of April, had returned to Murmansk, arriving there at the beginning of June.

[44] Strakhovsky, *op.cit.*, p. 49, cited this telegram from the American Navy Department archives.
[45] Kedrov, *Bez bolshevistskogo rukovodstva, op.cit.*, p. 87.

[275]

He carried with him an oral message from Francis to Captain Bierer of the *Olympia*, encouraging the latter to land marines, as the British and French had done, if so requested by the local Soviet. "Tell Captain Bierer," Francis had said,

. . . that I do not assume authority to command him to land his marines, but if I were called upon to give advice, I should want American marines to land, provided the British and French and Italian troops were landed.[46]

Whether Captain Bierer was influenced by this suggestion is unclear. He was, after all, subject to the orders of Admiral Kemp and not of the American Ambassador.[47] However that may be, on June 11, according to Strakhovsky, 150 American marines were put ashore. Francis no doubt attributed this to his authorization. But Strakhovsky, citing the Navy Department archives, indicates that the landing occurred because some of the British and French marines already ashore had been sent down the railway, just at that time, to cope with another reported invasion by the Finnish Whites, and Americans were needed to replace them. This seems more probable.

As of June 11, at any rate, American armed forces were now, for the first time, on Russian soil. Their presence there was the result of a local decision, taken under general authorization granted by Washington. It is important to remember that Washington, in granting this general authority, had no idea that it was authorizing anything other than a defensive action against the Germans at a remote but strategic point where the Soviet government was quite powerless to prevent German encroachment on Allied military interests and where the local Soviet authority had, thus far, taken a benevolent attitude toward Allied military operations. It was also, in granting this authorization, relying—pursuant to Admiral Sims's recommendation—on the good judgment of an Allied official. If the British and French governments had more far-reaching and ambitious plans in connection with these activities at Murmansk, there is nothing in the record to indicate that President Wilson or Secretary Lansing had knowledge of them at the time of this landing, or would have approved them if the question had come before them.

---

[46] Francis, *op.cit.*, p. 265.

[47] Francis says (*loc.cit.*) that Assistant Secretary of the Navy Franklin D. Roosevelt later assured him to the contrary—that Captain Bierer had been instructed to abide by Francis' orders. One suspects that this was a bit of *ex post facto* politeness on Roosevelt's part. Bierer was no doubt pleased to have Francis' approval, but would hardly have acted on this basis alone.

CHAPTER XII

THE AMERICANS AND THE CZECH UPRISING

As was noted in Chapter VI, the hostilities between the Czechs and the Bolsheviki broke out in full force following the despatch on May 25 of Trotsky's telegram to the local soviets along the Trans-Siberian Railway telling them to disarm and detrain the Czech forces at once. Trotsky's telegram brought into being a situation which had already been anticipated on the Czech side by the decisions of the Chelyabinsk Congress some days earlier. It reached the Siberian soviets almost simultaneously with the return to their units of the Czech officers, determined—now—to shoot their way through.

The American or English reader will scarcely wish to be burdened with the details and chronology of the complicated happenings that took place at various points along the Trans-Siberian Railway in the ensuing days. Suffice it to say that in the course of the fortnight following Sunday, May 26, the greater portion of the stretch of railway from a point west of Samara, on the Volga, to one somewhat west of Irkutsk—a distance of about 2,500 miles—was wrested from Bolshevik hands either by Czech forces strung out along the railway or by anti-communist Russian groups who took advantage of the Czech action to seize points independently and to set up a new civil authority. By mid-June pockets of Soviet resistance remained, preventing as yet the complete union of the various Czech detachments; but most of the rail line across this great region was already in the hands of the Czechs or the Whites. The 15,000 Czechs who had already reached Vladivostok were not, as yet, involved.

While Americans had no part in the origin of this extraordinary series of events, they did play a certain part in the course of events once hostilities had begun. Without taking account of their role in the development of the Czech action it is not possible to understand fully either the measure of American responsibility for the turn of events in the summer of 1918 or the pattern of information and pres-

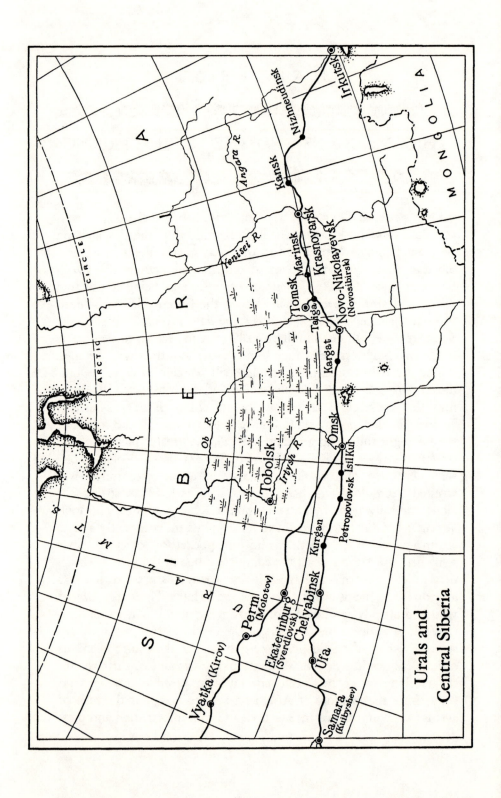

Urals and
Central Siberia

sures against which President Wilson was obliged to weigh the problem of intervention in the crucial months of June and July. It now becomes necessary, therefore, to have a glance at the way in which various Americans found themselves involved in the matter of the Czech uprising.

❖

At the time of the Brest-Litovsk crisis, Consul General Summers, sharing in the general fear that not only Petrograd but also Moscow might be seized by the Germans and anticipating the possibility that Siberia might become a major center of Allied interest in Russia, took steps, with the approval of the Department of State, to reinforce the American consular representation in Siberia. To this purpose he recruited and assigned to Siberian cities a number of Americans who had been engaged in private activity of one sort or another in Russia. Some of these men were drawn from the Y.M.C.A. contingent, others from the Russian branch offices of American firms. The most prominent of them was Mr. Ernest L. Harris, who had previously been a member of the consular service for many years and had left it only in June 1916 to take a position with the National City Bank of New York. Serving in the bank's Petrograd office at the time of the Bolshevik seizure of power, Harris was induced by Summers (in March 1918) to accept reappointment in the Consular Service. He was assigned as Consul General at Irkutsk. Just prior to his entry onto the assignment, he made a trip to Russian Turkestan, where he conducted a survey of the cotton situation—presumably (this is not entirely clear from the records) on behalf of the United States government, which was interested in seeing what could be done to keep the export surplus of cotton out of German hands. From Central Asia he proceeded to Irkutsk, completing the last part of his journey on one of the Czech troop trains. He reached Irkutsk on or about May 23, and thus assumed charge of the new Consulate General only two or three days before the serious trouble began.

Summers' action in strengthening the consular representation in Siberia was, as it turned out, a wise move, despite the fact that Moscow was not overrun. Very shortly, just after Summers' own death, the Czech uprising severed communications generally between European Russia and Siberia, leaving the consular officers throughout Siberia deprived of all direction from Moscow. As a result of

Summers' action the United States government had, at the time of the outbreak of hostilities between Czechs and Bolsheviki, in addition to the Consulate General in Irkutsk, consular officers at Chita, Krasnoyarsk, Tomsk, Novo-Nikolayevsk, Omsk, Ekaterinburg, and Samara (now Kuibyshev). In view of the importance of America's wartime position, and the high degree of confidence with which Americans were initially viewed by all the parties to the Siberian drama, it is not surprising that, once hostilities had begun between Czechs and Bolsheviki, these men immediately found themselves the object of approaches, entreaties, and pressures from many sides.

In addition to the regular consular officers involved in these happenings, the United States government had, by accident rather than by design, a further representative in this area in the person of Colonel George H. Emerson, the commander of the Russian Railway Service Corps, now stationed in Manchuria. A word of explanation is also in order as to the processes by which Colonel Emerson, in normal circumstances General Manager of the Great Northern Railroad, found himself involved in these remote and complicated happenings.

It will be recalled (Chapter v) that Trotsky had, in his first exchanges with Robins and Riggs after the removal of the Soviet government to Moscow, requested (March 21) the assignment of a group of American railway experts to aid the Soviet government in the restoration of the operating efficiency of the Russian railways. This request, strongly supported by Robins, had been relayed to Francis, who had endeavored unsuccessfully to induce the Department of State to authorize the despatch of a group of engineers from Emerson's contingent. Immediately after the Japanese landing at Vladivostok, Francis himself had come to the conclusion that the matter had best be deferred for the time being, in view of the unsettled situation in Siberia, and told the Department so.

By mid-April, excitement over the Japanese landing had quieted down; and Francis again approached the Department of State, asking that Emerson, together with two to five engineers, be sent to Vologda to confer with him about the response to the Soviet request. This time the Department responded favorably. But when the ensuing order finally reached Stevens, in Harbin, to whose over-all guidance the Emerson mission was still subordinate, it caused him great anguish. He received it on April 28 or 29. Horvat, as it happened, had just announced (April 27) the establishment of a new board of directors of the Chinese Eastern Railway. This move, the product of long and involved political negotiations among the leading non-communist Russian figures in the Far East, was designed to free the railroad from the influence both of the Soviet and the Chinese governments and to lay the groundwork for a future anti-communist government in Siberia. Stevens, after weeks of delay, was at that time just finally completing arrangements for the employment of Emerson's engineers on the Chinese Eastern. He feared, not without reason, that any attempt to employ a portion of this force in Soviet service would infuriate Horvat, would render him suspicious of the entire Railway Corps, and would put an end to all hope of employment of the Corps in the area under Horvat's authority. He therefore protested the order. To antagonize Horvat in this manner, he told the Department, would be

. . . to play directly into the hands of Japan, which is opposing us all the time undoubtedly with the view of controlling entire transportation systems of Manchuria. . . .[1]

The Department explained, in reply, that the desire to improve the Soviet-controlled railway system had arisen from considerations connected with the military effort against Germany—an angle that had apparently been quite lost sight of in the local complexities of the Far East. Disturbed by the reports of Horvat's obviously political purpose, and bearing in mind that the railwaymen were to work in Horvat's domain, the Department went on to warn Emerson that the Corps must not be employed, even in Manchuria, in any way that would have an appearance of supporting one faction or another in a Russian civil war. Most reluctantly, Stevens yielded to the Department's arguments for despatch of Emerson to European Russia; but he did so only after endeavoring unsuccessfully to get the government to accept his own resignation.[2] It was apparent that with the coming-apart of Russia herself, the views and recommendations reaching the American government about Russian matters were also now beginning to show great divergencies of outlook, depending on the region from which they emerged.

[1] *Foreign Relations, 1918, Russia,* Vol. III, *op.cit.,* p. 231.
[2] Francis was hurt by Stevens' reaction in this instance, as he had been by others of Stevens' acts. There seems to have been a complete lack of rapport between the two men.

The Czech Uprising

On May 6 Emerson proceeded to Vladivostok. After a delay occasioned by the effort to get a private railway car from the Soviet authorities (the Chinese Eastern, its nose out of joint, had refused to give him one), he and his party of several engineers finally left Vladivostok for European Russia via the Amur line on May 19. He was accompanied by three or four of his engineers, and one American officer, Major Homer H. Slaughter, who was under orders to join the staff of the United States Military Attaché in Vologda, and was trying to make his way there. The poverty of communications within the American governmental establishment at that moment, as well as the general absence of rapport between the Americans in the Far East and those in European Russia, is well-illustrated by Emerson's statement, in a letter written some years later, that his purpose was "to connect up with Ambassador Francis, who was supposed to be located somewhere in the vicinity of the Volga River." [3]

Colonel Emerson, it may be added, was an eminent and competent engineer. His knowledge of Russian politics could at best be described as rudimentary. He was definitely not a person prepared, either by interest or experience, to unravel the tangled skeins of the Czechoslovak uprising.

Colonel Emerson and his party reached Irkutsk on the late morning of May 26. Nothing untoward had as yet occurred at that point, and there was no knowledge in local Allied circles of any trouble farther afield. Consul General Harris came down to greet Emerson and his associates at the station and to wish them a successful journey westward. The deputy agent in Irkutsk of the Moscow Commissariat for Foreign Affairs, Geitzman, also appeared to pay respects on behalf of the local Soviet authorities. It was a balmy May morning. The long Siberian winter was at last yielding to the lateness of the season. Ten days earlier, as Harris crossed western Siberia en route to his new post, snowstorms were raging, and the rivers were still cluttered with ice jams. Now, a warm, welcome sunshine flooded the station platform. There was a general feeling of hope that summer would bring release from the tensions of the long, hard winter, and that somehow or other a reconciliation would be found between the aspirations of the Bolsheviki and those of the population and the

[3] Letter, George H. Emerson to H. H. Fisher, May 13, 1932; in the manuscript collection of John Frank Stevens, Papers on the American Railway Mission to Russia, Hoover Institute & Library, Stanford.

Allied powers. Geitzman—like many another of the early Bolsheviki a warm and even sentimental man in personal life, heartless only when it came to politics—had enjoyed pleasant relations with the Americans.[4] He had, Harris later recalled, donned a resplendent new peasant blouse for this agreeable occasion.

All in all, the atmosphere was relaxed and unsuspecting. The various official welcomers chatted amiably with the members of the Emerson group on the station platform. The train got off at two p.m. Harris and Geitzman continued, after it had gone, to converse for a time about this and that. There was still no intimation of troubles ahead.

An hour or so later, Harris happened to be strolling in the public park along the bank of the Angara River, directly across from the railway station. He saw a Czech troop train, occupied by what he estimated to be some 500 men, pull into the station and stop. Before the Czechs had left the train Harris heard a loud command given—in German, he thought—to open fire.[5] A Soviet detachment, heretofore concealed at various points around the station, at once fired on the Czechs. A sharp engagement followed.

What Harris was witnessing was the outbreak of one of the initial encounters between Czechs and Bolsheviki. The Czechs, here as in most other instances, came out on top. In a short time they succeeded in clearing and capturing the station. They then forced the railway officials to permit their train to proceed and departed southward on the line around Lake Baikal to the Far East.

A communiqué later issued by the communist authorities in Irkutsk claimed that they mounted this ambush against the Czechs because they had just learned of the seizure of the stations at Verkhneudinsk (now Ulan Ude) and Novo-Nikolayevsk (Novosibirsk), to the west, by Czech units. It described the bloodshed at the Irkutsk station as being due to a misunderstanding or provocation.[6]

That same evening, about ten p.m., two more Czech trains, bearing the members of the Second Artillery Brigade (devoid now of

[4] Geitzman was captured and shot by the Whites later that summer.
[5] Harris should have been able to distinguish the language: he had taken his doctor's degree at Heidelberg many years before. There is no question but that at Irkutsk, in particular, the local Soviet—its own forces being then committed on the front against Semenov—made use extensively of Internationalist prisoners as a local security force. This was probably the explanation for the German command.
[6] *Foreign Relations, 1918, Russia*, Vol. II, *op.cit.*, pp. 196–197.

their artillery), halted for some reason at a point some three miles west of Irkutsk, in the immediate vicinity of a prisoner-of-war camp. Here they at once became involved in a skirmish with war prisoners who were guarding the camp stores. Reinforcements were brought in on the Soviet side. These reinforcements appear to have included both Internationalist war prisoners and Russian Red Guards. The firing continued, in pitch darkness, into the late hours of the night.

It is not at all clear who was to blame for this particular incident. Information based on the Swedish Red Cross records would indicate that it was the Czechs, this time, who started the trouble and the Communists who reacted in self-defense. These Czechs had by now learned of the trouble that had befallen their comrades earlier that day, at the Irkutsk station. They were no doubt anxious to seize further arms before attempting the passage through Irkutsk, and saw the prisoner-of-war camp as a likely place to find them.

There was a good deal of confusion in the night as to who was who. According to best available evidence,[7] the Czechs shot in cold blood the captured camp guards, who were not Internationalists at all but innocent non-communist prisoners posted by the Swedish Red Cross, and allowed the actual Internationalist prisoners to depart unscathed.

At midnight, while the fighting was still in progress, Harris received at his home an unexpected visit from Geitzman and the chairman of the Irkutsk Soviet, Yansen. The two men seemed very agitated. They informed Harris of the outbreak of hostilities near the city and asked him to go with them in order to mediate and to induce the Czechs to move on. Knowing that the Czechs were supposed to be under French command, Harris told the Soviet officials that they should address themselves to the French Consul General, M. Bourgois. Geitzman and Yansen, suspecting the French (quite unjustly) of being the instigators of the trouble, were reluctant to do this; but Harris insisted; and the two communist officials finally agreed to go if Harris would accompany them. Together they proceeded to the French Consulate General, aroused the unfortunate Bourgois from his slumbers, and persuaded him to join them in proceeding to the scene of the trouble. Harris' assistant, Consul David B. Macgowan, likewise joined the party.

---

[7] Klante, *op.cit.*, who drew her findings from the Swedish Red Cross records and the Prague Archive of the Czechoslovak Legion.

The little group proceeded first to the railway station, where they telephoned up the line to find out where the fighting was in progress. The answer from the next stationmaster was that it was too dark to see anything. In the face of this uncertainty, it was decided to wait for the early summer dawn. Given a bedroom over the stationmaster's office, Harris tossed uncomfortably through the remaining hours of darkness, listening to the distant rifle fire and fighting a desultory battle of his own against attacking detachments of bedbugs. At dawn the party installed itself in an open touring car and proceeded out along the right of way, bumping along the ties, waving overhead French and American flags and a large bed sheet. After overcoming the suspicions of a trigger-happy Czech patrol, they got through to Czech headquarters, where the Czech commander gave them his account—highly colored, by all ulterior evidence—of what had transpired during the night.

Long negotiations ensued, lasting into the afternoon. The Czechs were finally persuaded to part with their newly captured arms, beyond an agreed thirty rifles per train, in return for which the communist officials promised them safe passage eastward. There and then Harris put Macgowan on one of the Czech trains to accompany them on their eastward journey and to see that no further difficulties arose. (The trains did indeed get through, without further difficulty, to Vladivostok.)

Harris and Bourgois knew nothing of the new orders that had been received, respectively, by the Czechs and the local Soviet authorities. They faithfully believed the incident to be the result of a misunderstanding, and deemed it their earnest duty to see that the passage of the Czechs to Vladivostok, and thus to the western front, was expedited. Impressed, however, by the professions of innocence on the part of the Czech commander, Harris, whose relations with the local Bolsheviki had thus far been excellent, now began to suspect the latter of double-dealing. He recalled Geitzman's relaxed normality on the station platform the preceding morning, as contrasted with the evidence of Soviet initiative in the afternoon attack at the Irkutsk station. "I refrained," he related in his official report, "from asking the wily gentlemen if these attacks at Irkutsk had been made with their knowledge and consent." [8]

Harris' action in expediting the passage of these first Czech trains

[8] Harris MSS, *op.cit.*, draft of Harris' official report.

through Irkutsk had consequences he could certainly neither have foreseen nor intended. Once the Czech units had thus passed through the city, Soviet control there was again unchallenged. By relieving the Irkutsk communist authorities of the presence of the Czech trains that were in that vicinity at the time of the uprising, Harris made possible the survival of Soviet power in that city for an entire month after thousands of miles of the railway to the westward had fallen into non-communist hands. His action may, in this way, even have been a determining factor in creating the greatest break—between Irkutsk and Vladivostok—in the initial Czech seizure of the railroad, a circumstance which, as we shall see shortly, had considerable influence on the future course of the uprising and was not without significance in connection with President Wilson's final decision in the question of intervention. The Czech general, Gajda, in command of the central Siberian group of Czechs, was furious when he learned of what had occurred at Irkutsk, and told the Americans if he ever caught up with the officers of these first trains he would have them court-martialed for accepting the mediation and consenting to proceed.

While these things were happening in Irkutsk, Emerson and his party, still innocent of any knowledge of them, were peacefully rolling westward along the main line of the Trans-Siberian. They had left Irkutsk an hour or so before the first incident, and learned nothing about it. Although they passed, during the night, through one station where a skirmish between the Communists and the Czechs had just taken place, they apparently knew nothing of any of these difficulties until they arrived at Krasnoyarsk, in the early morning of the 27th. There they were informed that they could proceed no farther: trouble had broken out between the Czechs and Communists at Marinsk, some 200 miles farther west, and the line was blocked. They sought out the American Vice Consul, Mr. Edward B. Thomas, who arranged for Emerson a meeting the following morning with the chairman of the Krasnoyarsk Soviet, Weinbaum. The latter confirmed the report of trouble at Marinsk, and said he was sending troops with a view to ending the incident and getting the Czechs to move on. Emerson, overriding the disapproval of Vice Consul Thomas, offered his services to help compose the difficulties, and left that evening for Marinsk. There, on the following day (May 29), he conferred with the Czech commander, Captain Kad-

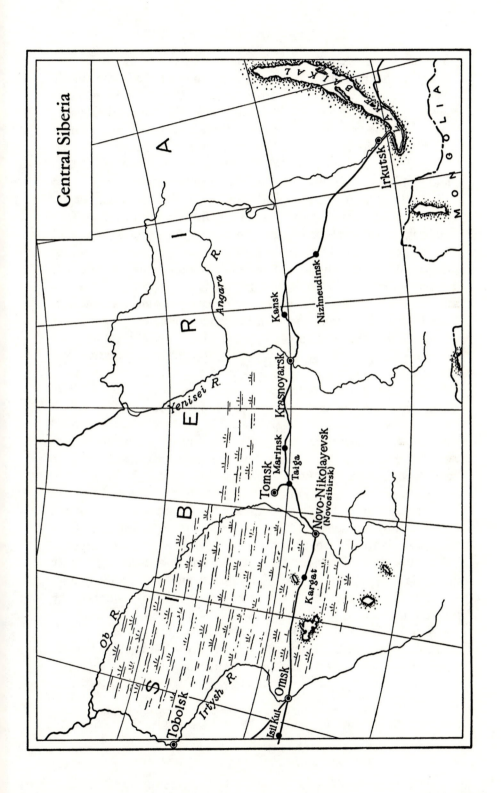

Central Siberia

lets. He was shocked to learn that Kadlets had acted on orders from above, envisaging the seizure of the stations all along the line by the Czech detachments. When he relayed this news to the local Soviet commander, the latter, imbued with the characteristic Soviet suspicion of the Allies, reacted by observing that France, through the Czech action, had "taken Siberia in twenty-four hours." [9]

Reminded in this way of the French connection with the Czechs, and finding the positions of the two commanders as yet unreconcilable (the Soviet commander insisted on the disarming of the Czechs; Kadlets would not hear of it), Emerson returned to Krasnoyarsk and telegraphed Harris, in the hope of getting a French representative despatched from Irkutsk to exert an influence on the Czechs. After learning from Harris of the success of the joint French-American effort at Irkutsk, and getting Harris' approval for a continuation of his mediatory efforts, he returned to Marinsk, where he met both with Kadlets and with the latter's superior officer, Gajda, who was in over-all command of the Czech detachments in that section of Siberia. After many hours of negotiation Emerson succeeded (June 3) in getting both sides to sign an armistice arrangement, ostensibly inhibiting hostilities in that area for a period of some days (neither side observed it completely). Assuring in this way his own passage through Marinsk, Emerson then continued westward, conducting at various points further mediatory efforts which carried him, in the ensuing days, as far west as Kargat, in the Barabinsk Steppes, west of Novo-Nikolayevsk.

Emerson's principal motive in these efforts was, it may be noted, the preservation of the physical intactness of the railway, for which he—recalling no doubt the original reason for the despatch of his engineers to Russia—seems to have felt a sense of personal responsibility. In this respect his attitude typified the unquestioning fidelity to technical purposes and the high-minded impatience with the domestic-political conflicts of other nations which have marked the American mind in all ages and which often made it difficult for Americans and Russians, in particular, to understand each other's preoccupations in the distracted year of 1918. General William S. Graves, who was later to lead the American Siberian Expedition and

[9] William S. Graves, *America's Siberian Adventure, 1918–1920*, Jonathan Cape and Harrison Smith, New York, 1931, p. 43. Graves had evidently had access, in preparing his book, to an official report of the Emerson Mission which my own researches into the governmental papers have failed to reveal.

who was himself the embodiment of these sterling but—to non-Americans—frequently puzzling qualities, naturally respected Emerson precisely for this refusal to take cognizance of the political struggles and passions raging around him. "Colonel Emerson," he wrote approvingly in his memoirs,

was as disinterested in the political squabbles of the Russian factions as any man I saw in Siberia. He was in Russia for the sole purpose of helping the Russians operate the railroad and took no interest in any other activity.[10]

Harris, meanwhile, was asked by the Bolshevik leaders in Irkutsk to add his efforts to the task of mediation farther down the line. He was already becoming disturbed by the reports now reaching him of further incidents at other points, and nervous about the activities and fate of the Emerson party, with which his communication was very unsatisfactory. He therefore consented to undertake the journey westward, accepted the proffered private railway car, and set out to see for himself what was doing. Accompanied by Major Drysdale, who had by this time arrived on his third journey to Irkutsk from the Far East, Harris left Irkutsk on June 3rd in Emerson's path. He took with him two representatives of the Irkutsk Soviet, assuming that the presence and authority of these officials would be useful in dealing with other local Soviet authorities.

To Harris' surprise and consternation, he found nearly all the stations west of Krasnoyarsk safely in the hands of the Czechs and White (i.e. anti-communist) Russians. The latter professed great friendship for America and claimed that one of their earliest acts, as soon as their governmental power was consolidated, would be to denounce the Brest-Litovsk Treaty and resume the war against Germany. All were highly imbued, or professed to be, with the belief that the Internationalist war prisoners were operating under the inspiration of, and with the blessing of, the governments of the Central Powers. They, like the Czech commanders, professed certainty that Trotsky's order for the disarming of the Czechs (now common knowledge) had been issued by direct order of the German Ambassador, Count Mirbach.

When Harris asked the Czech commanders what their intentions were with regard to their further eastward movement, he found

[10] *Ibid.*, p. 53.

them hesitant to commit themselves. Several of them pointed out that they felt a responsibility toward the Russian Whites who had cooperated in the overthrow of Soviet power and did not feel that they could simply move on and abandon these recent allies before the latter had had sufficient time to consolidate their power.

As Harris and his party moved farther west, the realization grew upon them that this was not only a conflict between Czechs and Communists but also a virtual Russian civil war, and that any form of mediation by Americans could not fail to have the effect of interference in an internal Russian conflict.

By June 8, Harris had succeeded in stopping Emerson and catching up with him at Kargat. Here the two men conferred. They agreed that, in view of the evidence that what was in progress was not a series of misunderstandings but a full-scale civil war, they had no choice but to desist from further efforts to compose the incidents. Their decision was at once communicated to both parties. Addressing the various Soviet emissaries who had accompanied him and Emerson (the latter had picked up four of his own along the way), Harris said:

When we left Irkutsk, nothing was known to me concerning any new political movement whatsoever along the Siberian Railway Line. Had I been aware of such disturbance, I would have refused to come. If I had been aware of such disturbances, I would not have instructed Colonel Emerson to enter into any peace negotiations whatsoever. The counter-Bolshevik movement, if I may call it so, introduced a new factor into this proposition with which America can have nothing to do. All Consular and Diplomatic officials of the United States in Russia and Siberia have direct instructions from the President of the United States to refrain from mixing up in any partisan or factional politics whatsoever. It is the business of the official representatives of the United States in this country to observe an absolute neutrality.[11]

Thus ended the mediatory efforts of Harris and Emerson. Harris returned to Irkutsk. Emerson pressed on in the hope—futile, as it turned out—of getting through to Francis.

These were not the only instances in which American officials were involved in the initial phases of the uprising. The Allied consular

[11] Harris MSS, *op.cit.,* memorandum entitled "Conference with Four Representatives of the Soviet who Accompanied Colonel Emerson and Two Representatives who Accompanied Consul General Harris at Kargat, Siberia, June 8, 1918."

officers at Omsk likewise endeavored, in company with the French liaison officer at that point, Major Guinet, to mediate the initial conflict between the Czechs and Bolsheviki to the west of that city. At Samara, the American Vice Consul, Mr. George W. Williams, received a visit from the Czech commander, Čeček, on the day after the fall of the city, and was asked to forward to Ambassador Francis certain documents presented to him by Čeček explaining the background of the Czech action and the official position of the Czech military authorities. There were doubtless other contacts of this nature. All available records of these meetings, without exception, show the Americans to have been scrupulously concerned to avoid taking sides in the controversy and inclined to reiterate on every occasion that their government did not wish them to become involved in any domestic-political quarrels.

❖

During the first month following the outbreak of hostilities between the Czechs and Bolsheviki, there could no longer be any question of the Czech Corps' attempting to continue its eastward movement toward Vladivostok. While most of the points along the Trans-Siberian Railway west of Irkutsk had been seized with surprising ease and speed, a few held out for longer periods. It was several weeks before all the various gaps in Czech control of the line could be closed and all Czech units west of Irkutsk brought into contact with one another. Krasnoyarsk did not fall until June 16. It was only four days later that the easternmost detachment of the embattled Czechs, a shock battalion caught between the Bolshevik forces at Irkutsk and those at Krasnoyarsk, was able to establish contact with the other Czech forces farther to the west. At the opposite end of the area of hostilities, a group of some 8,000 Czechs were still in European Russia, faced with the necessity of fighting their way eastward to join the other Czech forces in the Urals and Siberia. This group, under the command of Čeček, was in the area of Penza-Rtishchevo when the uprising began. To effect its reunion with the main body of the Corps, it was obliged to move through Syzran, cross the Volga, take Samara, and fight its way up the railway line toward Ufa. It was not until July 6 that this group succeeded in establishing contact with the main body of the Corps to the east.

Finally, at Irkutsk, which was the main Bolshevik military center in Siberia, and which—in consequence of Harris' successful effort at mediation—had remained in Bolshevik hands, the Communists now had ample opportunity to make military preparations and to mount more serious operations against the Czechs. They were in a position, moreover, to fall back, if pressed from the west, on the formidable strategic barrier of Lake Baikal, along the proclivitous southern coast of which the railway wound its way in a long series of bridges and tunnels, easily defended and easily blocked if defense became impossible. Before there could be any hope for the Czechs in central Siberia of opening up the path to Vladivostok, Irkutsk had to be taken and the Baikal barrier passed. The attack on Irkutsk began June 21; the city was occupied July 11. Several more weeks passed before the entire line around Lake Baikal was in Czech hands. It was not until August 31 that the Czechs moving from the west met up, in the Chita region, with others from the group that had reached Vladivostok prior to the uprising.

Throughout June, July, and August, therefore, the basic military task of the Czechs was to unite the various elements of their divided force. During these weeks their efforts would have had to be addressed primarily to this end rather than to a general movement eastward, even had there never been any question of their abandoning their purpose to get to France. In the month of June, in particular, there could be no question of any general movement eastward in the Urals and central Siberian area, for the Čeček group had not yet established contact from the west, and it was unthinkable that the others should move away from them. Thus during this entire period the Corps had to remain generally in the area between Samara and Irkutsk; some of its heaviest and most difficult military operations had to be directed against Bolshevik forces in the Volga and Urals regions.

But throughout this entire period, the Czechs found themselves subjected increasingly to the suggestion that they should not persist at all in their ultimate intention of proceeding to Vladivostok but should embrace the situation in which their operations had already involved them and should continue, even after the reunification of the Corps, to devote their main effort to fighting the Bolsheviki. It is idle to seek any single source for this suggestion. It arose—if the preponderance of evidence may be believed—in a thousand minds at once: some of them Czech, some of them Allied, most of them Rus-

Consul Embry, Consul General Harris, and Vice Consul Gray at Omsk

John F. Stevens, chairman of the Advisory Commission of Railway Experts

Colonel George H. Emerson, head of the Russian Railway Corps

George Chicherin

Sketch from Musacchio, *I Responsabili della Pace*

STATE HISTORICAL SOCIETY OF WISCONSIN

Lenin's letter to Axelrod requesting assistance for Gumberg, April 27, 1918

War supplies on icebound barges, Vladivostok, 1918

The Trans-Siberian Railway's eastern terminus, Vladivostok, 1918

Vladivostok street scene, 1918

John K. Caldwell, American
Consul, Vladivostok

U.S.S. Brooklyn arriving in Golden Horn Bay, Vladivostok,
with *H.M.S. Suffolk* in foreground

sian. A portion of the Czechs, with General Gajda in the lead, fervently aspired to take part in the overthrow of Soviet power, and were thus already predisposed to abandonment of the idea of proceeding to France. In Allied circles, as we shall see shortly, the news of the uprising decisively tipped the scales in favor of those who desired intervention. All sorts of schemes at once arose in the minds of Allied officials for combining the now-proven fighting power of the Czechs with that of the Allied forces whose intervention was now expected at an early date. As for the White Russians, their reasons for attempting to persuade the Czechs to desist from their purpose of moving eastward and, instead, to continue hostilities against the Bolsheviki in the Volga and Ural regions, were only too obvious. They had ridden into power on the Czech coattails; whatever the hopes for consolidation of their power in the more distant future, it was quite evident that if the Czechs were to leave the area at this time, the prospects of the Whites for holding out against the Bolsheviki were, to say the least, not bright.

It should be noted that there were several reasons why suggestions for the retention of the Czech Corps in Russia appealed even to those Czechs who did not share Gajda's enthusiasm for the anti-Bolshevik cause. In the first place, a great many of them firmly believed that the Bolsheviki, in their effort to disarm the Corps, had been acting on German orders, and that the development represented only the first move in a German attempt to seize Siberia.[12] They disliked to abandon the Siberian territory to the real and unquestionable enemy.

---

[12] This belief was entirely erroneous. The captured German Foreign Office documents make it clear that the Germans knew very little about the Czech Corps and did not take any serious interest in it before the end of May, when they picked up highly erroneous reports about its being evacuated to France via Murmansk and Archangel. It was not until the first days of June that the matter was taken up with the Soviet government, both through Joffe in Berlin and through Mirbach in Moscow. By this time the Soviet government was already doing everything in its power to disarm the Czechs, and German pressure could have no further effect in this direction. (National Archives, German Foreign Ministry Archives, *op.cit.*, University of California Box No. 147 [Russland 61]. See particularly Berckheim's telegrams of May 28 and June 4 from the *Grosses Hauptquartier,* Kühlmann's telegram to Mirbach of June 1, Mirbach's telegram to the Foreign Office of June 4, and a Foreign Office memorandum of June 7, concerning a discussion with Joffe.)

The German documents confirm in this respect the interesting observations of Klante, who had also derived from the Swedish Red Cross records the impression that the Germans knew very little about the situation of the Czechs prior to the uprising, and made no protests about their activity at that time. (Klante, *op.cit.,* p. 110.)

Many of them were also convinced that the German and Austrian governments were behind the arming of the Internationalist war prisoners.[13] They felt, accordingly, that by fighting to keep Siberia out of Bolshevik hands they were actually keeping it out of the hands of the Central Powers and rendering an important service to the cause of the Allies. Beyond this, they felt—as was noted above—a responsibility to the White Russian faction which had aided them in their uprising and with which they were now fighting hand in hand. They were reluctant to abandon these White Russian comrades, who had not yet had time to organize any serious armed force, to the reprisals of the vengeful Bolsheviki. Finally, the Czechs were well aware that the Allied governments had made no practical preparations for removing them from Vladivostok, even if they could get there. No ships had yet been sent. The Czechs who had reached Vladivostok at the beginning of May were still there and had no idea when, if ever, they would be evacuated.[14]

For all these reasons, together with the fact that in these early weeks after the outbreak of hostilities they were unable anyway to continue their progress toward the east, the suggestions that the Czechs direct their efforts against the Bolsheviki in the Ural and Volga areas, rather than persist in their purpose to leave Russia via the Far East, fell on ready ears.

Up to the latter part of June, however, the pressures along this line, while many and persuasive, had not yet come from any authoritative Allied quarter. It was generally understood that in the last analysis it would be the Allied attitude that would be the decisive factor in the decision. Considerable importance attaches, therefore, to two messages despatched to the Czech commanders in the latter part of June—one from American Consul DeWitt C. Poole, at Moscow; and the other from Ambassador Noulens in Vologda—both urging them not to endeavor to proceed eastward but to remain where they were and direct their military efforts against the Bolsheviki.

Poole's message, despatched from Moscow on June 18, and addressed to the American Vice Consul at Samara, read as follows:

You may inform the Czecho-Slovak leaders confidentially that pending further notice the Allies will be glad from a political point of view

---

[13] This was likewise wholly incorrect. See above, Chapter III.

[14] The Soviet authorities in Irkutsk told Harris, at the end of May, that they thought this was one of the reasons for the uprising. *Foreign Relations, 1918, Russia*, Vol. II, *op.cit.*, p. 182.

to have them hold their present positions. On the other hand, they should not be hampered in meeting the military exigencies of the situation. It is desirable first of all that they should secure control of the Trans-Siberian railroad, and second, if this is assumed at the same time possible, retain control over the territory where they now dominate. Inform the French representative that the French Consul General joins in these instructions.[15]

Noulens' message, despatched (evidently) about the same time to Guinet, then at Chelyabinsk, read substantially as follows:

The French Ambassador informs Major Guinet he can thank the Czecho-Slovaks for their action, this in the name of all the Allies, who have decided to intervene the end of June, and the Czech army and French Mission form the advance guard of the Allied army. Recommendations will follow concerning political and military points with respect to occupation and organization.[16]

In view of the obvious importance of these messages for the decisions and dispositions of the Czech commanders, and their peculiar chronological relationship to Wilson's final decision concerning the intervention, it becomes necessary at this point to reach ahead a bit and to examine the curious processes by which the two messages, particularly that of Poole, came to be sent.

[15] Harris MSS, *op.cit.* This text is taken from the report of American Consul Gray at Omsk, dated November 10, 1918. The message was forwarded by the Consulate at Samara on July 22 to the Consulate at Omsk, and repeated by the latter office to Harris.

[16] *Ibid.* Gray, in the report cited above, states that this message was received by Guinet on June 22; that it was brought by courier; "and dated Perm, May 18th." This last was obviously an error; probably the date should have been June 18.

CHAPTER XIII

CONSUL POOLE AND THE FUTURE OF

THE CZECHS

With Summers' death and Robins' departure, contacts between the Soviet government and the American representation in Moscow acquired a new atmosphere. Summers, as he himself frankly admitted, had been too uncompromising in his abhorrence of the Communists to provide a suitable medium for the discussion of those practical problems which, in an imperfect world, have to be discussed even between ideological adversaries. Robins, on the other hand, had been too fascinated by his Soviet counterparts, and had taken too dramatic a view of his own dealings with them, to be an effective mediator between his own government and theirs. Now both of these men were absent.

Consul DeWitt C. Poole, who took over Summers' responsibilities, was young, energetic, cheerful, and likeable. He had succeeded in remaining aloof from the suspicions and controversies that had wracked the American community in earlier months and had ended so tragically. With Robins' successor, Allen Wardwell, as well as with the American military officers in Moscow, Poole got on well. There was now unity in the American camp there. Above all, both Poole and Wardwell, younger and more adaptable to the new age than the men who had gone before them, soon developed that peculiar brand of toughness—a combination of humor, skepticism, bluntness, patience, dominant despair and subdued hope—which is most useful for those who have to effect communication between great political entities theoretically desirous of witnessing each other's ultimate destruction but obliged nevertheless to communicate with one another over mundane problems of the present.

For Francis, Poole's new status in Moscow was in many ways a relief. There at once grew up between the two men a relationship more cordial and less defensive, all around, than any Francis had had with Summers or Robins. For one of Francis' temperament, Summers had been too upright; Robins, too much of an idealist. Francis, with his more earthy nature and less agitated conscience, had felt vaguely uneasy in the presence of both. Poole, to be sure, was neither a reprobate nor a cynic; but he was worldly, had a sense of humor, and handled Francis with a shrewd deference. There was something about Poole's cheerful skepticism regarding human nature and his easy acceptance of political realities that put Francis at his ease. He felt, in Poole's company, that peculiar sense of security experienced by sinners in the presence of others who may at least be presumed to have sinned.

With Robins' departure both Lenin and Trotsky, on the Soviet side, dropped out of the picture, except for rare occasions, so far as contacts with the Americans were concerned. From this time on the more important discussions with American representatives in Moscow were conducted by Chicherin, who had succeeded Trotsky as Foreign Minister in March. Karakhan, then a junior Foreign Office official, an Armenian, who had previously worked in the Far Eastern office of the Party organization and had been included in the delegation that finally signed the German terms at Brest-Litovsk, functioned nominally as an assistant to Chicherin (more likely his real position was that of a Party "eye" on Chicherin's activity). He also occasionally conducted, or took part in, discussions with American and other Allied officials. Voznesenski, nominally head of the Far Eastern Section of the People's Commissariat for Foreign Affairs, was used to maintain some sort of contact with Francis and the other diplomatic representatives, and paid at least one visit to Vologda for this purpose.

Chicherin [1] has been the subject of so many excellent pen portraits by those who knew him that one hesitates to add another. He was, however, a striking figure, both outwardly and as a political personality; and the real flavor of the events of May to August 1918, with respect to Soviet-American relations, would be partially lost if his image as a human being were omitted.

Of gentle birth and superior education, Chicherin could stand as an example of that strain of deep idealism, composed of a sense of

[1] His full name was Georgi V. Chicherin, but he has always been known to individual foreigners and to the world at large by his last name.

social guilt superimposed on an intense fidelity to philosophic deduction, that occasionally cropped up in members of the Russian upper class of the nineteenth century and drove men either to produce, like Tolstoy, important works of literature, or to throw themselves into the extremism of the revolutionary movement, or both. The son of a landowner and diplomat, Chicherin received an excellent university education and worked at one time in the Tsarist Foreign Office, as archivist and research historian. He then returned to private life, became a socialist, and joined the emigration in western Europe. In London at the time of the revolution, he was first arrested by the British and then repatriated to Russia, in January 1918, under the terms of a rather tortured deal between British and Bolsheviki for the settlement of various difficulties that had arisen with regard to diplomatic couriers and detained persons. Up to this time, Chicherin had been affiliated with the Menshevik wing of the Russian Social-Democratic Party. Not until his arrival in Russia, at the end of January 1918, did he join the Bolsheviki. In view of his educational qualifications, his knowledge of the world, and his familiarity with diplomatic forms, he was at once taken into the Foreign Office, and was soon given the post of Commissar for Foreign Affairs. He was valued, for this work, as a technician. As a Party member and a voice in the counsels of the ruling group, he was of minor significance.

Many of those who dealt with Chicherin as Commissar for Foreign Affairs have left accounts of his eccentric and unforgettable personality: the gigantic disorder of his office, his apparel, and his working habits; his near-sightedness; his ill health and hypochondria; his aversion to daylight and fresh air; his limitless pedantry and inability to delegate detail; his love of music in general and Mozart in particular. Aesthete and bookworm turned revolutionary, animated by a faith always close to despair, slaving day and night to execute the hectic diplomacy of the young revolutionary state, Chicherin is one of the most appealing and tragic figures of early Bolshevism.

Louis Fischer, in his autobiography,[2] has given a fascinating picture of Chicherin's personality as he observed it over the course of several years. For his outward appearance in the spring of 1918 we may fall back on Lockhart's talent for vivid description:

[2] *Men and Politics: An Autobiography, op.cit.*

. . . He was dressed in a hideous yellow-brown tweed suit, which he had brought with him from England, and during the six months of our almost daily contact I never saw him in any other. With his sandy-coloured beard and hair and his sandy-coloured suit he looked like one of those grotesque figures made by children on the sea-shore. Only his eyes, small and red-rimmed like a ferret's, gave any sign of life. His narrow shoulders were bent with much toiling over his desk. Among the group of men who worked for sixteen hours out of the twenty-four, he was the most indefatigable and relentless in his attention to his duties. . . .[3]

Chicherin was a socialist of profound sincerity; but his views, like those of most of the Russian socialists of that day, were oriented primarily to the Russian and western European societies with which he was personally acquainted. For reasons both of social ideology and of national feeling derived from earlier experiences, he was mistrustful of the British. The United States, which he had never visited, loomed only dimly—half hopefully, half dubiously—on his horizon. He was not quite certain whether it was foe or friend. In general, he liked Americans, and gave them a ready confidence not conceded to the representatives of western European "imperialism." He was, moreover, open-minded generally to a far greater degree than were the more influential members of the Bolshevik hierarchy. One cannot avoid the feeling that with Chicherin, from the American standpoint at least, things might have been eventually "talked out" to a point where his beliefs and those of responsible Americans could be, if not reconciled, at least brought under the roof of a mutual tolerance and respect. With Lenin and Trotsky, this would have been far more difficult—with Stalin, impossible.

❖

The new era was not long in making itself felt. On May 14, the day of Robins' departure, Poole, accompanied by the Commercial Attaché, Mr. Chapin Huntington[4] and Mr. John Lehrs,[5] paid a

[3] Lockhart, *op.cit.,* pp. 218–219.

[4] Huntington, formerly Commercial Attaché at the Embassy in Petrograd, had left there at the end of February on the first of the two trains bearing the American Embassy party. On Francis' orders, he had left the train at Irkutsk and remained there on temporary detail until the end of April. Ordered back to service in European Russia, he arrived in Moscow only at the time of Summers' death.

[5] Lehrs, who had been serving as Vice Consul and Summers' liaison man with the local Soviet authorities, was the son of a local American resident. He had been born and brought up in Russia, and educated in Germany. He joined the consular establishment at Summers' request, in view of the special wartime burdens with

courtesy call on Chicherin and had a cordial talk with him. Poole explained that Francis desired that the Consulate General should henceforth be the channel of communication between the Embassy and the Soviet authorities. Arrangements were made for a regular bi-weekly meeting.

In minor ways, the improvement in the atmosphere showed immediate practical results. At the beginning of May, the Soviet government had put a ban on cipher communications at the Allied offices, probably as a result of their irritation over Noulens' provocative statements. This was now removed. Poole called on Chicherin on May 23 and expressed appreciation for the removal of the ban. Chicherin admitted that the whole episode had been "stupid and unfortunate." [6]

From this the talk turned to more important matters. The Murmansk situation was aired, as related above (Chapter XI). Chicherin read to Poole a despatch from the Petrograd Telegraph Agency's correspondent at Washington indicating that there was growing feeling in the United States in favor of intervention. He found this, Chicherin said, very disquieting.

Poole replied by first reading him the text of a telegram the Department had sent to Francis—perforce, *en clair*—during the period when cipher communication was interrupted. In this message the Department, referring to Moscow's protest about the behavior of the American Consul at Vladivostok, denied that American representatives had assisted any anti-Soviet movement. The friendly purpose of the United States toward Russia, it was said, had been made clear in the President's Fourteen Points speech. It would not be modified "so long as Russia does not willingly accept the autocratic domination of the Central powers." [7]

In addition to reading this telegram, Poole pointed out to Chicherin that

. . . he must bear in mind the attitude of the ordinary citizen in the United States who believes that the war has been prolonged by events in

---

which it was then being saddled. He subsequently continued on in the governmental service, rendering valuable service down to the present day at a number of posts in the Baltic countries and in western Europe.

[6] Francis MSS, *op.cit.;* two letters from Poole to Francis of May 24, 1918 relate the course of this conversation.

[7] *Foreign Relations, 1918, Russia,* Vol. I, *op.cit.,* pp. 525-526. Poole properly assumed that the Department had meant this message to be seen by the Soviet authorities—otherwise it would not have been sent *en clair.*

Russia, that many more American lives will be lost on this account, that the war might even be lost and the development of all liberal ideas and institutions thereby seriously set back as a result of the Russian collapse. In view of this it would not be surprising if there were a growing feeling in the United States requiring a more active policy in Russia. . . .

There could be, Poole continued, only one objective for all liberal and advanced people: the defeat of Germany. If the Allies were willing to undertake military operations in Russia, this ought to be welcomed by the Russian people "as an evidence of the Allies friendship in helping them to throw off the German yoke."

Chicherin countered by saying that he doubted that any force sent in over the Trans-Siberian Railway would be enough to embarrass the Germans seriously, and that the action would only give the Germans an excuse "for gobbling up what remains of Russia." If the Germans should later advance and take Moscow, then the Bolsheviki would ask for intervention.

This, Poole replied, might be too late; America was not anxious to intervene; she would do so only under pressing military necessity; perhaps this necessity might not exist at the later date Chicherin had in mind.

In the end, Chicherin summed up Bolshevik policy (the words are Poole's) as being designed

. . . to maintain equilibrium and an equal contact with the Allies and with the Germans, commercial as well as political, and to put off to the last possible moment any active military operations.

This discussion, friendly but frank throughout, represented a new departure in Soviet-American relations. No one on the American side had ever talked this way to the Soviet leaders before. Francis and Summers had not done so because with rare and insignificant exceptions they had not talked with the Soviet leaders at all. Robins had not done so because his sympathies had been too deeply engaged by the personalities of those with whom he talked. Poole, in faithfully reiterating the line of the President's Fourteen Points speech, was to be sure reviving the same ambiguities that characterized that address, but he was saying, at any rate, precisely what his government felt. This was his duty, and it represented the most useful thing he could do. For the first time in the brief but intensive history of this tangled relationship, a Soviet official modest and reasonable enough to listen was given a faithful statement of American views by an American who, though speaking on this occasion without instructions, was properly qualified to speak for his government. This was, in short, the first proper political discussion between the two governments.

One can conceive that had the American position in the matter of intervention remained what it had been up to that point—had it been possible, in other words, to wait out the very few remaining months of the World War without proceeding to the despatch of any American forces to Russia—the entire subsequent course of Soviet-American relations might have been materially changed. The exchanges between Poole and Chicherin might have developed into an orderly process of communication between the two governments; the peculiar position of the Consulate General in Moscow might have evolved, almost imperceptibly, into that of a diplomatic mission under some species of *de facto* recognition. Above all, a long series of blunt and frank discussions, conducted by men prepared to keep personal feelings apart from the useful function they were fulfilling and enjoying some measure of detachment vis-à-vis the governments they represented, might really—over the course of time—have forced both of those governments into a somewhat more realistic understanding of the mental world and problems of the other.

But all this was not to be. The date of this conversation between Poole and Chicherin—May 23, 1918—was already two minutes before midnight in its relationship to the deterioration of the situation as between the Allies and the Soviet government. The Czech uprising, occurring three days later, would constitute the crucial point, beyond which even those few people who still hoped to stem the tide of conflict would be playing a losing game. From May 26 on, no conversations between American and Soviet representatives could do more than to mitigate the worst consequences of the stream of events in which both were caught up.

✧

The position of Bruce Lockhart had already been deeply shaken, even before the Czech uprising, by Robins' failure, by the growing influence of Noulens in the Allied camp, and by the repercussions of Mirbach's presence and activity in Moscow, bound as this was to fan the ready suspicions of the Allied governments. From the time of

Robins' departure, Lockhart knew he was fighting a losing battle. At the end of May, he proceeded, together with the senior officers of the French Military Mission in Moscow, to Vologda for conferences with Noulens and Francis. It must be borne in mind that the British Chargé d'Affaires, F. O. Lindley, had not yet returned to Vologda. There was, therefore, no British representative in Russia of major diplomatic rank—a situation which placed Lockhart somewhat at a disadvantage vis-à-vis the French and Americans.

The atmosphere in Vologda was by this time strongly pro-interventionist. Francis, as we have seen, had made his switch at the beginning of May. Noulens had sent a similar telegram to his government, strongly urging intervention, on the 14th.[8] The Italian had sent similar recommendations. Lockhart was faced, in the Allied camp, with a united front.

Arriving in Vologda on May 28, Lockhart dined that evening at the clubhouse with Francis. Of this event, the only political entry in his diary was that "Old Francis doesn't know a Left Social-Revolutionary from a potato."[9] But he found the American Ambassador a charming host, and the evening amusing as well as instructive. As soon as dinner was over, he later recalled,

. . . Francis began to fidgit like a child who wishes to return to its toys. His rattle, however, was a deck of cards, and without loss of time they were produced. The old gentleman was no child at poker. We played late, and, as usually happens when I play with the Americans, he took my money.[10]

The following day Lockhart lunched with Noulens and was given what would be called, in the jargon of a later day, "the full treatment." The views of the two men were divided at this late date on only one serious point: whether intervention should be carried out even in the absence of Bolshevik consent. In urging that it should, Noulens pulled all the stops. He talked about the critical situation on the western front. He produced anxious messages from the French General Staff insisting on "the necessity of some diversion in Russia, which would prevent the Germans from transferring more troops from the East." It was impossible, he maintained, to wait for a ques-

---

[8] *Foreign Relations, 1918, Russia*, Vol. II, *op.cit.*, p. 173, from telegram to SECSTATE from Sharp (in Paris), May 26, 11 p.m.
[9] Lockhart, *op.cit.*, p. 279.
[10] *Ibid.*, p. 280.

tionable Bolshevik consent, which might come too late, or might never come at all.[11]

In the end, Lockhart capitulated. He felt it useless to argue further. He retired and drew up, apparently that same afternoon, a telegram to London joining, for the first time, in the general appeal for intervention regardless of the Soviet attitude.

A meeting of the three ambassadors and the officials from Moscow took place later that afternoon in Francis' office. Lockhart having been swung into line, it was a pleasant and harmonious occasion. The big double windows, unsealed after the long winter, were now thrown open. The strong spring sunshine beat down on the little garden, the budding lilac bushes, the high board fence, and beyond it the cobbled street, already turning dusty with the advent of summer. The situation was discussed up and down. Noulens stressed the importance of the recommendations of the group in view of the forthcoming meeting of the Supreme War Council at Paris, where, he thought, the decision to intervene would be taken. There was little disagreement. Lockhart went along with the others, and showed them the cable he had sent. The other ambassadors asked Francis to associate himself with a joint telegram urging, once more, intervention in the north. Francis said he preferred to cable separately. This was agreed.

The situation of the Czechs was also discussed. The first reports of further trouble between the Czechs and Bolsheviki had just been received. But it was not known, as yet, whether this was a general uprising or just another series of incidents similar to the recent one in Chelyabinsk. It was agreed that the passage of the Czechs to Vladivostok should be expedited in every way, though Noulens and Francis insisted they must not be required to submit to disarmament.

The meeting broke up in general accord and good feeling. At long last, the Allied community in Russia, at least, was united in its views on intervention.

❖

While these things were happening in Vologda, there was taking place in Washington the final phase of the process by which the United States government moved, during World War I, from an initial position of reserve with respect to the national aspirations of

[11] *Ibid.*, pp. 280–281.

the subject nations of the Austro-Hungarian Empire to one of outright support for the breakup of the Empire. A consequence of this development was the despatch by the Department of State on May 29 of the following circular telegram to a number of diplomatic missions, including Vologda:

The Secretary of State desires to announce that the proceedings of the congress of oppressed races of Austria-Hungary, which was held in Rome in April, have been followed with great interest by the Government of the United States, and that the nationalistic aspirations of the Czecho-Slovaks and the Jugo-Slavs for freedom have the earnest sympathy of this Government.[12]

Francis, on receipt of this telegram (May 31), sent it on to Poole, instructing him to advise Chicherin informally of its contents. This Poole did, telling Chicherin

. . . that as these troops [i.e. the Czech Corps] were very much disposed to fight against Germany, our sympathies were very much with them and that in any controversy which might arise we would be disposed to regard their side with favor. . . .[13]

Neither Francis nor Poole had authority to take these steps; but both, being almost wholly ignorant of the thinking of their superiors in Washington, felt it necessary to use their discretion in promoting Allied war interests, as they saw them. Francis understood that the Allies desired to get the Czechs to the western front as rapidly as possible. He obviously thought that if the Soviet government were aware of the American support for the political independence of Czechoslovakia the prestige of the Czech Corps, as an Allied force, would be enhanced in Soviet eyes, and the chances for passage of the Corps through Siberia would be improved. As for Poole, he had had long talks with Lockhart and General Lavergne, after their return from Vologda; he had learned from them of the unanimity achieved among the Allied representatives at Vologda in the matter of intervention; he had gained from them the impression—already current in French and British circles—that intervention in Siberia was inevitable, and would probably take place in the near future. Persuaded, now, that intervention was in the cards but having no idea whatsoever of the details of Allied plans, Poole naturally began to wonder

[12] *Foreign Relations, 1918, Russia,* Vol. II, *op.cit.,* p. 183, footnote 1.
[13] Francis MSS, *op.cit.,* Poole to Francis, June 3, 1918.

whether the Allied governments would not wish to make use of the Czech Corps in one way or another in connection with Allied operations in Siberia. This possibility, suggested by the first reports of the uprising, just then reaching Moscow, was now beginning to be earnestly discussed among the Allied representatives there. At the same time, Poole was disturbed by the view expressed to him by Allied military officers in Moscow to the effect that if the Czechs received no assurances of Allied support they would probably be constrained to capitulate. No one in the Allied camp foresaw, at that early moment, the ease with which the Czechs would seize the railway line or the initial *élan* the Russian Whites would develop in supporting the Czech action.

Poole wired these misgivings to Francis. The latter, now aware for the first time that the conflict between Czechs and Communists was of major dimensions, also became alarmed at the prospect of the Czechs' being defeated and disarmed. Realizing that time was of the essence and that an attempt to elicit instructions from Washington would not be likely to lead either to prompt or to satisfactory results, he decided to act on his own responsibility. He wired Poole (June 3) to inform the Soviet government that if the Soviet government were to treat the Czechs severely and to disarm them the Allies would consider this "as inspired by Germany or certainly by hostile sentiment toward the Allies." [14]

In a letter to his son Perry, written the following day, Francis referred as follows to the action he had taken:

. . . I have no instructions or authority from Washington to encourage these men to disobey the orders of the Soviet Government, except an expression of sympathy with the Checko-Slovaks sent out by the Department of State. I have taken chances before however and another little chance will do me no harm.[15]

Actually, the Department of State was shocked to learn of Francis' initiative. It rebuked him several days later (June 10), admonishing him that any instructions he might issue to the Consul in Moscow to communicate to the Soviet government "should, so far as practicable, be limited to matters affecting American interests." [16] Francis

[14] *Foreign Relations, 1918, Russia*, Vol. ii, *op.cit.*, p. 188; Francis to SECSTATE, June 3, 7 p.m.
[15] Francis MSS, *op.cit.*
[16] *Foreign Relations, 1918, Russia*, Vol. ii, *op.cit.*, p. 201.

was much put out by this reprimand, and explained to the Department, in a telegraphic reply, that he thought the United States had a very definite interest in the fate of the Czechs.

Meanwhile, however, the other chiefs of mission in Vologda, inspired by Francis' initiative, had sent similar instructions to their representatives in Moscow, and the respective approaches to Chicherin had already taken place. Poole made his *démarche* on June 4. First he went alone and transmitted Francis' message. Later in the day, when the other Allied representatives had received their instructions, he also accompanied them on a joint visit, to emphasize Allied solidarity.[17] Lockhart has given us an account of this meeting. The four Allied representatives were received not in Chicherin's crowded study but in a large barren room with a single desk. The visitors lined up on wooden chairs on one side of the desk; Chicherin and Karakhan, wondering what had caused this invasion, on the other. The French Consul General spoke first for the Allied side. He reviewed the status of the Czech Corps in French eyes, and reiterated the familiar bill of complaints about the treatment of the Corps at the hands of the Soviet authorities. He voiced the prevalent Allied suspicion that the difficulties placed in the path of the Czechs had been inspired by Germany. He denied that the Czechs had been implicated in any counterrevolutionary activity. If they were now supporting counterrevolutionaries at Novo-Nikolayevsk, this, he said, was because of their intense exasperation with the Soviet authorities and the necessity of covering their retreat through Siberia. Lockhart then reinforced these assertions, pointing out that the Czechs were anything but counterrevolutionary in their sentiments and had, on the contrary, sympathized overwhelmingly with the Russian Revolution. He reiterated Poole's earlier assertion that any attempt to interfere with the progress of the Czech Corps, or to subject them to complete disarmament, would be regarded by the Allies as a hostile act.

Chicherin and Karakhan, desperately concerned just at that moment to avoid any conflicts with the Allies that might provoke or hasten intervention, listened in glum silence. Lockhart recalls in his memoirs that Chicherin,

[17] The Russians, unaware previously of Lockhart's change of front, were amazed to find him coming in such company and for such purpose. He later believed that their ill-disposition toward him, which was eventually to lead to his long imprisonment and very nearly to his death, dated from that moment.

. . . looking more like a drowned rat than ever, stared at us with mournful eyes. Karachan seemed stupidly bewildered. . . .[18]

In the end, Chicherin undertook merely to communicate the statements to his government and to let the Allied representatives know, at a later time, if there was any reply.

In reporting to Francis the exchange with Chicherin, Poole expressed (June 5) some concern at the brusqueness of the French and Italians in the presentation of their case. He, Lockhart, and Riggs were agreed, he said:

. . . that, in view of the fact that intervention is apparently not yet decided upon and in any case cannot be prepared for several weeks, we should pursue a more moderate course, *endeavoring to hold the Czecho-Slovaks available for possible subsequent use* and, at the same time, avoiding anything like a definite and final issue with the Soviet. . . .[19]

Chicherin's reply to Poole was made on June 12. It was apparently identical with that given the other Allied representatives. It denied that the measures taken against the Czechoslovaks had an anti-Allied character, blamed the Czechs for the initial complications that had ensued, and maintained that the Soviet government had been forced by the "direct counter-revolutionary armed rebellion" of the Czechs to "adopt the course of severe armed suppression of the rebels." The Czechs were acting everywhere, Chicherin wrote, in alliance with the White Guards and Russian counterrevolutionary officers. "In some places there are French officers among them." The Commissariat for Foreign Affairs was sure that the Allied governments could not take the disarmament of the Czech detachments as

---

[18] Lockhart, *op.cit.*, p. 284. The Soviet reaction to this approach was not quite so sluggish, or devoid of resource, as Lockhart's impression suggested. The Allied representatives never knew it, but Chicherin made adroit use of the incident the following day in a talk with the German Ambassador. He informed Mirbach in detail about the Allied approach and pointed out to him that Russia could act incisively in the Czechoslovak question only if it could have its hands freed so that it could address itself exclusively to this problem. This could be achieved, Chicherin pointed out, only if hostilities ceased on the Finnish, Ukrainian, and Caucasian fronts where, in each case, Soviet forces were still engaged in military operations against non-communist elements over which the Germans had some influence. Mirbach recognized, with a grudging admiration, the Soviet talent for turning adversity to advantage in a complicated situation. (National Archives, German Foreign Ministry Archives, *op.cit.*, University of California Box No. 147; telegram 247, Mirbach to Foreign Office, June 5, 1918.)

[19] Francis MSS, *op.cit.*, Poole to Francis on June 5 (italics added).

an unfriendly act, and hoped that on the contrary they would express their disapproval for this patent intervention in Russian domestic affairs.[20]

During these same days Poole was in touch with officials of the powerful Russian cooperative organizations. It will be recalled that the cooperative movement was particularly strong throughout Siberia; that it was closely associated with the S-R's, who were prominent in the Derber government; and that its leaders had extensive dealings with the Czech force. The leaders of the cooperatives were almost universally pro-Ally, and maintained fairly close liaison with Allied officials throughout this period. The Department of State had by this time become aware of the inclinations of this group and interested in the possibilities it presented as a channel for American aid. On June 5, Counselor Polk wired Poole asking him to ascertain the views of the Union of Siberian Cooperative Societies and the Moscow Cooperative Societies as to how resistance might be maintained against Germany.[21] On June 12, Poole responded by telegraphing a statement made by Alexander Birkenheim, a member of the All-Russian Union of Cooperatives, embracing both groups. The statement began by stressing the non-political character of the organization—a point which could not have been better selected to predispose Washington officialdom in favor of its further tenor. Direct military aid from the Allies was the only means, it was said, of stopping the German advance in Siberia. The usual warning was included against unilateral Japanese action. Speed, it was emphasized, was of the essence. In short, Allied intervention would be welcome.[22]

This query from the Department, and the reply it evoked, must have served further to convince Poole not only that the question of intervention was very close to decision, but that the action to be taken in Siberia would probably be based on the S-R's and the Czechs, with whom they were now so closely leagued.

❖

[20] *Ibid.* (A portion of the text of this message will be found in *Foreign Relations, 1918, Russia,* Vol. II, *op.cit.,* p. 211.)

[21] *Foreign Relations, 1918, Russia,* Vol. II, *op.cit.,* p. 190.

[22] *Ibid.,* pp. 205–206. (The name of Poole's informant is supplied in National Archives, State Department File 861.00/2053.)

Meanwhile, unbeknownst, as yet, to the American representatives in Russia, the fate of the Czechs had been the subject of renewed discussion in Paris and London.

The Sixth Session of the Supreme War Council had been scheduled to begin at Versailles on June 1. It was decided that it should be preceded, this time, by political discussions between the French and British governments. These preliminary discussions took place in London on May 26–28. The participants included, on the British side, Lloyd George, Balfour, Lord Robert Cecil, and General (later Field Marshal) Wilson; on the French, Foreign Minister Pichon, Ambassador Paul Cambon, and a number of military representatives. We have no direct record of the results of this conference. Beneš says in his memoirs that it was agreed that

. . . on the subject of our army the resolutions of the Abbeville conference should, on principle, be adhered to, i.e. our troops were to be transferred as soon as possible from Russia to the Western front, while in the Far East the Allies would make common cause with them, and co-operate with them as necessity arose. The transport was to be effected partly by way of Vladivostok and America, partly by way of Archangelsk. If necessary a portion of the army would remain in Russia to hold the Archangelsk base. These questions were to be discussed at the forthcoming meeting of the Supreme Military Council at Versailles.[23]

Of the discussions at the meeting of the Supreme War Council we have more detailed information. The discussions relating to Russia took place on June 3rd. They were preceded by deliberations of the Permanent Military Representatives, who addressed themselves to the problem of the northern ports and produced a Joint Note, No. 31, on this subject (which Bliss also signed). In this Joint Note the Military Representatives stated that it was hoped that the Serbian and Czech units in Russia could do the necessary work of occupation of the northern ports "without the transport of any considerable expeditionary force." The Serbian and Czech units could not in any case be immediately convoyed to France. For these reasons the Permanent Military Representatives considered that the agreement of the Czechs should be sought "to the maintenance of a portion of their forces in those regions." It recommended that an appropriate approach be made to the Czechoslovak National Council, asking its

[23] Beneš, *op.cit.*, p. 378.

. . . approval of the principle of retaining in these regions during the necessary time some Czech units, it being understood that the number of these units would be reduced to the minimum necessary and that the remainder would be sent to France as previously agreed.

It further recommended that, in addition to the Czechs, there be sent to the Russian Arctic ports: (a) "some English, French, American or Italian battalions, four to six in all"; (b) officers and specialists for the training of the Czech troops; and (c) materials and supplies.[24]

At the plenary session of the Supreme War Council on that same day, June 3, these recommendations of the Military Representatives, relating to the northern ports and to that portion of the Czech Corps which the Allied statesmen still conceived—erroneously—as being on its way to those ports, if not already there, were approved without question by the senior statesmen. But there was further discusssion on this occasion of the fate of those other Czechs who, in the plans of the Allied chancelleries, were to continue on through Siberia. The British, who had received reports (for which there seems to have been no substantiation) that German forces were about to ascend the Volga and invade the grain growing districts of the Volga basin in western and central Siberia, were anxious that the Czechs east of the Urals (other than those supposed already to be on their way to Archangel) should be held where they were, in order that they might defend this area against the Germans. Clemenceau, more interested, as always, in the western front, still favored the removal of this portion of the Corps to western Europe. An inconclusive and hasty discussion ensued. It was finally agreed, other Allied shipping being unavailable, to ask the Japanese to provide shipping for the removal of as many as possible of the Czechs. Specifically, the Japanese were to be asked to divert for this purpose certain shipping which they had previously been requested to make available for the removal of German citizens from China to Australia, for internment there.

[24] *Foreign Relations, The Lansing Papers,* Vol. ii, *op.cit.,* pp. 273–275, from General Bliss's report to Secretary of State of February 19, 1920.

The records of the Supreme War Council are in the War Records Division of the National Archives.

It will be noted that the British had not waited for the approval of the Supreme War Council to take action along these lines. As noted above, Chapter xi, General Poole had already been despatched to Russia on May 17 as head of a mission for just these training purposes.

These Germans, it may be noted, were not very numerous, and the shipping the Japanese were to have made available for their removal was obviously not extensive. If diverted to Vladivostok, it could have been expected to remove only a small portion of the Czech Corps—Mr. Balfour's biographer mentions 5,000.[25]

Thus the upshot of the Supreme War Council meeting, so far as the Czechs in Siberia were concerned, was one of those curious and ineffective compromises to which busy governments are addicted: the agreement of the Czechoslovak National Council would be sought to an arrangement whereby those Czechs who—it was thought—were being sent to Murmansk and Archangel would be detained there in order to cooperate with "some English, French, American and Italian battalions" in the occupation of these ports; the remainder of the Corps was to proceed on its way through Siberia to Vladivostok, theoretically for evacuation to France. At the same time arrangements were put in hand which, if successful (and even this depended on the attitude of the Japanese government), would achieve the removal of only a small portion of the Siberian contingent. No other arrangements were envisaged. From this it could be inferred that the others would have to remain in Siberia for the time being, though this was not specifically stated. In this way, both sides—presumably—were satisfied.[26]

❖

The repercussions of these meetings reached Francis and Poole in mid-June, not long after the protest of the Allied representatives in Moscow. It is instructive, for its bearing on the dangers of imprecision in the processes of diplomacy, to observe the manner and phraseology in which the reports of these Allied discussions reached the American representatives in Russia.

At some time just prior to June 13 Francis gained from Noulens the understanding that the French Embassy in Vologda had received word from Paris

---

[25] Dugdale, Vol. II, *op.cit.*, p. 190.

[26] In its memorandum of June 10th to the State Department apprising it of this decision, the British government said nothing to suggest that any portion of the force was to be left in Siberia; but they must have been aware of the insufficiency of the shipping envisaged. (*Foreign Relations, 1918, Russia*, Vol. II, *op.cit.*, pp. 199–200.)

. . . that the Allied Military Conference in Paris had agreed upon Russian intervention but of course this is very secret; it contemplated landing of several battalions each of American British French and Italian troops at Archangel. . . .[27]

Francis at once forwarded this information to Poole in a letter of June 13.

Secondly, on June 15 Francis learned of another cable received by Noulens from the French Foreign Minister confirming that a military conference had been held in Paris on June 3 at which it had been "decided" to land British, French, Italian, and American forces in the north, in addition to which it had been agreed that the Czechs should remain in Russia for the present with the approval of the Czechoslovak National Council. Francis wired this to Poole the same day stating

. . . The Military Conference in Paris mentioned in my letter of June 13th made specific mention of the Czecho-Slovak troops in Russia *and provided for their retention here for the present* . . .[28]

Let us now note the inaccuracies embraced in these messages, as received by Poole.

1. The statement that the "Allied Military Conference in Paris had agreed upon Russian intervention" was quite misleading. The note of the Permanent Military Representatives had dealt only with the situation in the northern ports—in one of which Allied marines were already ashore—and had envisaged only the *occupation* of these ports by the Allies, a step which did not go far beyond the situation already existing and should certainly have been distinguished from a full-fledged general intervention in Russia. The approval by the Supreme War Council of this Note by the Military Representatives also did not include approval by the United States government; this was not, therefore, as yet a fully concerted Allied decision.

2. The statement that it had been agreed that the Czechs should remain in Russia "for the present" made no distinction as between those supposed to depart via Vladivostok and those supposed to depart via the northern ports. It gave the impression that the entire Corps was to be held in its positions of the moment. Poole, being

[27] Francis MSS, *op.cit.*, Francis to Poole, June 13.
[28] *Ibid.*, Francis to Poole, June 15 (italics added).

[313]

aware—as the chancelleries in Paris and London were not—that nothing had come of the plan for the removal of a portion of the Corps via the northern ports, could only conclude that this passage referred to the bulk of the Corps in Siberia. This was of course a grievous distortion of the actual decision of the Supreme War Council which had, after all, reiterated that it was desirable as a matter of principle to "expedite the transport of Czechoslovak troops from Vladivostok to France, as agreed at Abbeville." [29]

3. The decision concerning retention of the Czechs in Russia was portrayed as a firm and final one. Actually, what had been decided was only to seek the approval of the Czechoslovak National Council to such an arrangement.

Just where this distortion occurred does not appear from the available record. It is improbable that the French Foreign Office failed to give its ambassador an accurate account of the Supreme War Council decisions. The likelihood is that Francis, hearing all of this orally from Noulens, and at that through an interpreter, gained a very imprecise idea of what Noulens had really heard from Paris. Poole, in any case, could only take the messages at their face value; and it is clear that to him they could only mean that the Allies had finally decided to intervene and desired, in the face of this decision, that in the Urals and Siberia the Czechs should remain roughly in the positions they occupied at that moment.

As luck would have it, on the same day that this second French report reached Poole, information was also received from some sort of Allied intelligence channel in Moscow to the effect that the Germans were planning, as a reaction to the Czech uprising, to seize Moscow on June 21. To this report, Poole was inclined to attach some weight.[30]

[29] National Archives, War Records Division, R.G. 120, *op.cit.;* Resolution No. 4, Sixth Session, June 1918.

[30] Francis MSS, *op.cit.,* Poole to Francis, June 15. Poole was not wholly wrong in attaching weight to these reports. There was some substance behind them. The news of the success of the Czech uprising had by this time unleashed feverish activity among the Russian opposition groups, all of whom thought the end of Soviet power to be near and were struggling to assure themselves of the succession. The German Foreign Office documents reveal that one faction from the right wing of the Kadet Party (the so-called Center of the Right) headed by the former Minister of Agriculture, Krivoshein, did indeed approach the Germans just at this time, holding out the prospect of a seizure of Petrograd by the oppositionists and asking for German military support. What had been reported to Poole as promises made by the Germans to this group appear actually to have been rather a description of the aid requested by the Russians. There is no evidence that the Germans promised them

Two days later (June 17) Poole received from Vice Consul Williams in Samara the communication from the Czech leaders handed to the Vice Consul by the Czech commander Čeček (see above, p. 291). The communication had been intended by the Czechs for Francis, but Williams, having no direct communication with Francis, had sent it to Poole. In transmitting this document, which merely reiterated the well-known Czech position of eagerness to get through to Vladivostok at all costs, Williams gave it as his conclusion, on the basis of his own personal observation,

. . . that it is indifferent to Czechs where they are to fight and that if the Allies so direct they will gladly remain in present position establishing new anti-German front along Volga. However, in the absence of other instructions, they will resume movement east as soon as railroad repaired which should be in a few days.[31]

This message can only have served to convince Poole, who was ignorant of the actual military situation of the Corps, that if some Allied guidance were not given to the Czechs immediately, they would leave their present positions in the Volga-Urals area and continue on their way eastward, in which case much of their usefulness to a future Allied expeditionary force might be lost.

What, in the light of these various messages, was Poole to do? The war in the west was, to all reports, at a most crucial pass. The Allies, as he had been given to understand, were about to intervene in Siberia in order to restore the eastern front against the Germans. The Czechs would be a useful adjunct to any Allied expeditionary force; and he now had serious confirmation that the Allies wished them to remain in Siberia for just this purpose. Yet Williams had warned that unless the Czechs received some immediate guidance they would probably continue their passage eastward. And evidence

---

any such military aid, though they did give them moderate encouragement, primarily to keep them from going over to a pro-Entente orientation. The Germans were likewise inclined to believe, at this time, that Soviet power was on the way out, and naturally did not want opposition groups under Entente influence to be the successors. (National Archives, German Foreign Ministry Archives, *op.cit.*, St. Antony's Reel No. 84, Deutschland 131; see particularly letter, Mirbach to Hertling, no. 152, June 13.)

Who was responsible for the misrepresentation of this situation to Poole is unclear. It was of course to Bolshevik interest that the Allies should believe the Germans were interested in overthrowing Soviet power.

[31] *Foreign Relations, 1918, Russia,* Vol. II, *op.cit.*, p. 215, from Poole telegram to SECSTATE, June 17, 9 p.m.

suggested that within a few days Moscow itself might be occupied by the Germans, with incalculable consequences to Poole himself, his files, and his office. Clearly, there was now no time for consultation with Washington. Any attempt at prior consultation with the Embassy at Vologda might only lose further precious days. Francis was not in direct communication with the consuls in Siberia, anyway. Besides, the old gentleman might well develop doubts and hesitations and bar the action entirely. Poole had no reason to suppose, moreover, that the Czechs in Siberia would necessarily learn of the position of the Allied governments from any other source but himself. It was not at all certain that Noulens could get through to them over the northern branch of the Trans-Siberian. Unless he, Poole, relayed the message to them at once, they might never learn of it at all before they had abandoned the Urals and western Siberia, leaving these areas open to the reprisals of the Bolsheviki and to military penetration by the Germans.

It was in these circumstances that Poole, after consultation with the French Consul General in Moscow, despatched on June 18 his message to Vice Consul Williams at Samara, directing the latter to inform the Czechoslovak leaders confidentially that the Allies would be glad, from a political point of view, to have them hold their present positions. He asked Williams to inform the French liaison officer that the French Consul General joined in these instructions.

At about the same time—possibly a day or so earlier—Noulens sent a similar message to the French liaison officer Guinet, then at Chelyabinsk. It was no doubt based on the same telegrams from Paris as those communicated to Francis, and through him to Poole. Guinet received it, apparently, on June 22.

Francis was amazed but not displeased to learn from Poole, on June 19, of the step the latter had taken. He strongly sympathized, personally, with Poole's motives and with the initiative Poole had taken. By this time he had received his reprimand from the Department for the earlier and less far-reaching initiative he himself had taken in the Czech matter. He realized that the Department would certainly not approve Poole's action, if it learned of it. But this time, he reflected (with a chuckle, one suspects), he himself could not be held responsible. He had not sanctioned the step; nor had he had prior knowledge of it. "I have not yet cabled the Department," he wrote to Poole on June 20:

the instructions you gave . . . concerning the Czecho-Slovaks. Hope they will not say anything about such instructions but if they do or in any way the instructions become public, I shall do all I can to protect you. In fact think your instructions were excellent and if I had had the authority to give instructions could not have improved thereon. This letter is written not to disturb you but merely for your information.[32]

There can be no question but that these messages from Noulens and Poole were taken by the Czechs as authoritative evidences of a considered Allied desire with respect to their further dispositions, and were of importance in encouraging them to give up the thought of proceeding to the western front via Vladivostok and to throw in their lot with the Russian Whites. But of the two messages it may safely be assumed that it was the French one that had the greater effect. For one thing, it reached the Czech military leaders well in advance of the other.[33] But beyond that, it was followed up very shortly by another and much more explicit instruction sent by the Military Attaché of the French Legation at Peking to Guinet. The American Legation at Peking and the American Consulate General at Irkutsk served as the forwarding channel for this message. Here it was stated, on the authority of the French government:

. . . Temporary retention of the Czech divisions in the present zone should be made use of with a view to

1) developing centers of resistance constituted by those divisions and grouping around them the Siberian and Cossack elements favorable to the reestablishment of order;

2) completing the possession of the Trans-Siberian, and

3) preparing for and covering eventual Allied intervention from the East.

For this purpose it is necessary to oppose energetically the possible disarming of Czechs and endeavor to keep them in organized units so as not to permit of their cohesion being impaired.

Categorical instructions in this sense should be given to all French officers on mission with the Czechs. . . .[34]

This message, wired from Peking to Irkutsk on July 2, and relayed from there by Harris, must be presumed also to have reached the

[32] Francis MSS, *op.cit.*

[33] The copy of Gray's report of November 10, 1918 in the Harris MSS, *op.cit.*, indicates that Poole's message, which had to be forwarded from Samara to Omsk, did not reach Gray until after July 22. The French message, on the other hand, was received by Guinet at Chelyabinsk on June 22.

[34] *Ibid.*, folder marked "Graves."

Czechs before Poole's did. Thus before the Czechs ever learned of Poole's message, they had received much more explicit instructions, of the same tenor, from other and—for them—more authoritative channels.

General Graves, who learned of Poole's message from a book by Professor F. L. Schuman,[35] attacked Poole most bitterly for this action in his own book (*America's Siberian Adventure, 1918–1920*) and apparently carried to his dying day the belief that Poole, in sending his message, had deliberately and inexcusably acted in violation of his government's instructions not to take sides in Russian internal conflicts. General Graves based this judgment on the tenor of his own subsequent instructions, which appeared to be in conflict with the sense of Poole's telegram, and on Harris' numerous statements to the effect that official representatives of the United States were instructed not to meddle in internal Russian affairs. While Graves took note in his book of the two French instructions, it is understandable that to his strict military mind, decidedly disinclined to accept any guidance or suggestion from anyone except his own immediate military superiors, these foreign messages could have no validity for American officials. He charged that the conflicting policies followed by the American representatives in European Russia and by himself "unfortunately create a justifiable belief that the United States was not entirely frank and candid in its dealings with the Russian people."[36] He took particular exception to the suggestion, contained in Poole's telegram, that the Czechs "should not be hampered in meeting the military exigencies of the situation." This, he said,

. . . had the appearance of containing intended and carefully prepared subtleties. If I had to determine the meaning of this sentence, I should unhesitatingly say it was a subtle suggestion to the Czechs that the Allies would not object to their beginning military operations against the Soviets. I realize, however, that the sentence is so worded that Mr. Poole, if the occasion arose, could deny that he had such an idea.[37]

To the civilian mind it is not easy to see how Poole could have dispensed with this *caveat* about the "military exigencies" without

[35] Frederick Lewis Schuman, *American Policy Toward Russia Since 1917: A Study of Diplomatic History, International Law, and Public Opinion*, International Publishers, New York, 1928.
[36] Graves, *op.cit.*, p. 71.
[37] *Ibid.*, p. 72.

laying himself open to charges that he, a civilian understanding nothing of military matters, had hampered the Czech commanders in their freedom to assure the military security of the Corps and was thus personally responsible for any and all military reverses they might henceforth suffer.

Graves went on to say that Poole, by this action, had greatly embittered the Czechs, because he had led them, or helped to lead them, to the belief that the United States and the Allies were going to intervene in Siberia, and thus brought them to cling to their existing positions in the unwarranted confidence that Allied troops would soon come to their assistance there.

Even if Poole's message had reached the Czechs before those from the French, it would be difficult to accept this thesis. It was, as we have seen, the end of August before the Baikal barrier was passed and a possibility existed for removing the body of the Czech Corps to Vladivostok. By this time, the despatch of American troops to Siberia had already taken place and the United States government had published a formal authoritative statement of its reasons for sending them there. This was the statement on which General Graves' instructions were based. Up to the end of August, the Czechs could not have left Siberia had they wished to. After that time, they had no excuse for not being aware of the definitive position of the United States government as expressed in early August in a solemn governmental communiqué which gave no grounds for hope that American forces would join them in fighting the Bolsheviki in western Siberia. They also had no justification for not recognizing this communiqué as more authoritative than a message despatched by the American Consul in Moscow two and a half months earlier and no reason to forget that it was the French army, not the American, of which they were a part and to the High Command of which they were subordinate.

Technically speaking, General Graves was correct. Poole was acting without instructions; he exceeded his competence. If this was reprehensible, so—then—was the action of thousands of other American officers, both military and civilian, who, over the course of our history, under the stresses of war and in the face of inadequate or senseless instructions, have taken it upon themselves to act on their own best judgment. If this had not been the final year of a long and fearfully exhausting war; if people all along the line had not been desperately tired; if the entire machinery for coordinating Allied policies and actions had not been coming badly apart at the seams; if there had existed clear channels of command and a rapid, effective system of communication; if intelligence on German movements had been authoritative and correct; and if no allowance was to be made for such human qualities as youth, wartime enthusiasm, eagerness to make a contribution, and a willingness to risk the displeasure of one's superiors if only the war effort could be thereby promoted —if all these conditions had been met, then it might be possible to concede to General Graves's opinion, in that species of equity that must govern the judgment of history, the same logic and force it no doubt had in the letter of the Infantry Regulations.

Poole himself, in any case, remained unrepentant. To a scholar who wrote to him thirty years later, inquring his motives for the despatch of this message, he replied that his action

. . . was inspired by the extreme anxiety then felt over the progress of German arms. It seemed that if only the smallest pressure could be added at any point it must be done regardless. . . . Graves' interpretation of my message . . . reflects his inability to project his thought beyond Siberia. . . . I acted without instructions, and I think I can add becomingly after thirty years that the message took some moral courage on the part of a youngster. I had no means of learning the practical consequences which Graves deplores. . . .[38]

Actually, the greatest damage, in this case, resulted not from Poole's action but from the failure of himself and Francis to report it to Washington. As will be seen in another chapter, the President appears to have remained for a long time ignorant of the dispositions which had been made by the French, supported by Poole's message, for the retention of the Czech Corps in their positions as of the end of June and for the dropping of the intention that the Corps should make its way eastward as soon as possible. This ignorance on the President's part was, as we shall see, to have serious consequences. It was not, to be sure, the primary responsibility of Francis and Poole to set him right on this point. It was the French government that should have informed the United States government of these dispositions, particularly at a moment when the President had the whole question of intervention in Siberia under most intensive con-

[38] DeWitt C. Poole MSS, Wisconsin State Historical Society, Madison; Poole to David Otto Tyson, March 10, 1948.

sideration. But in failing to report Poole's action, Francis and Poole unwittingly neglected an opportunity to provide the President with information intimately germane and important to the heavy decision with which he was faced. Had he known of these circumstances, it is possible that American intervention in Siberia might never have assumed the form it did.

This, of course, Francis and Poole could not know. And the pattern of responsibility is not fully clear unless we bear in mind the paucity of Washington's guidance to Francis over the whole course of the preceding months, the President's failure to send him a single word of interest or encouragement throughout the entire ordeal of his experience with the Russian Revolution, and the fact that only a week earlier the Department of State had delivered to him a cryptic and harsh rebuke for a relatively innocuous step which was—in the circumstances—not at all unreasonable.

CHAPTER XIV

PRIVATE AMERICAN INFLUENCES

INSOFAR as this narrative has dealt with influences brought to bear on the American policymakers in matters of Russian policy, the influences mentioned have been primarily the official ones, arising either from other governments or from the calculations of advisers within the United States governmental establishment. But these people did not, of course, live in a vacuum; and as one approaches the final weeks of decision in the matter of the intervention, it might be well to take brief note of the climate of private opinion by which they were surrounded.

It will be useful to observe, at the outset, the main sources of external influence on the government in its Russian policies at the time of the Bolshevik seizure of power.

The first of these was the Russian Embassy in Washington, ably headed by Mr. Boris Bakhmeteff. An engineer by training and profession and a man of wide cultural interests and mature political judgment, Bakhmeteff had excellent connections in Washington and in the American business world and was able to make his influence felt in a number of ways. In addition to his own circle of acquaintances and those of his leading associates in Washington, he had at his disposal a full-fledged and strategically placed propaganda agency, in the form of the Russian Information Bureau, with offices in the Woolworth Building in New York City. This institution, founded in 1916 as a semi-official agency of the Russian government of that day, was headed by a Russian citizen of excellent connections and some literary ability: Mr. A. J. Sack, formerly staff correspondent of the official publications of the Russian Ministry of Finance. The Bureau evidently had as its original purpose the promotion of a climate of opinion favorable to the expansion of trade between Russia and America. Its list of honorary advisers included—in addition to such distinguished names as those of ex-President Theodore Roosevelt, Mr. Edward N. Hurley (chairman of the United States Shipping Board), Dr. Nicholas Murray Butler, and Mr. Lawrence F. Abbott (editor of *The Outlook*)—a number of prominent figures from the business world, including Mr. C. A. Coffin (head of the General Electric Company), Mr. Darwin P. Kingsley (president of the New York Life Insurance Company), Mr. Samuel McRoberts (executive manager of the National City Bank), Mr. Charles H. Sabin (president of the Guaranty Trust Company), Mr. Jacob Schiff, and Mr. Oscar Straus (then chairman of the New York Public Service Commission). It also included certain Russian governmental officials and representatives of the All-Zemstvos Union, an association of local governmental advisory bodies established in Russia in the later years of Tsarist power.

The political coloration of the influence exercised by the Russian Embassy flowed logically and naturally from the position in which it found itself. It naturally opposed any form of recognition of the Bolsheviki; endeavored to prove the likelihood of the early overthrow of communist power in Russia; and encouraged Washington to look to the Russian moderates, particularly the Constitutional-Democrats (Kadets), as the most promising Russian political faction. Supported as it was by powerful American allies, the Russian Embassy played an important part in shaping the initial American response to the Bolshevik seizure of power.

Closely associated with the Russian Information Bureau, though not under Russian governmental control, was the organization known as the American-Russian Chamber of Commerce. This organization, like the Information Bureau, was a reflection of new interest aroused by the enormous increase in American-Russian trade—particularly in American exports to Russia—that took place in the first years of the World War. It was the counterpart of a corresponding organization—the *Russian-American* Chamber of Commerce—established in Moscow under the chairmanship of a prominent Russian industrialist, N. I. Guchkov. The American Chamber was headed by Mr. Charles H. Boynton, president of the banking firm of that name and of the Consolidated Coppermines Company. The executive secretary was Mr. E. Chappell Porter, formerly director of the New York office of the Federal Bureau of Foreign and Domestic Commerce. The directors included, in ad-

dition to Messrs. McRoberts, Kingsley, and Sabin, mentioned above:
Mr. A. Barton Hepburn (chairman of the board of directors of
the Chase National Bank); Mr. Donald G. Wing (president of the
First National Bank of Boston); and representatives of a number
of other firms interested in Russian trade, including Kidder, Pea-
body & Company, Deere & Company, the National Carbon Company; the Shawmut National Bank; the Guaranty Trust Company,
etc. Thirty or forty other firms interested in Russian trade made up
the membership.

With the Chamber, too, the Russian Embassy had a considerable
influence, due to the importance of the Provisional Government as
the leading purchaser of American goods in the immediately preceding period, and the fact that it still disposed, nominally, over
unexpended American governmental credit, running into many millions of dollars. But the businessmen represented in the Chamber
were, for the most part, realists; sooner than anyone else, they
recognized the hopelessness of the emerging situation in Russia,
from the standpoint of American business; and they generally refrained from lobbying or the promotion of schemes and causes designed to remedy the unhappy situation.

A third organization with exclusive interest in Russian matters—
this time one that was entirely American in its connections and quite
non-commercial—was The Society of the Friends of Russian Freedom. This organization, established in the 1890's by a group that
included Samuel Clemens, William Lloyd Garrison, and George
Kennan, had as its purpose the expression of American support for
the liberal and democratic tendencies in Russian life (see Vol. 1,
pp. 12–13). The Society was headed, in 1917–1918, by Mr. Herbert
Parsons, a prominent and respected New York lawyer who had at
one time been a member of Congress. Kennan, although he still
functioned as one of the vice presidents, no longer took a prominent
part in its affairs. Mr. Louis Marshall, a prominent lawyer who had
taken a leading part in the American protest against the treatment
of the Jews in Russia, was another of the vice presidents. The third
was the Right Reverend David H. Greer, Episcopal Bishop of New
York. The organization thus embraced what were perhaps the three
major sources of American interest in Russia outside the commercial
field: the sympathy of American liberals for what they considered
to be the liberal-democratic political tendencies in Russia; the feel-

ings of American Jews, aroused by the treatment of the Jewish population in the Russian Empire, where so many of them had their family origins; and, finally, the traditional interest of the Episcopal Church in the Russian Orthodox Church, whose history and outlook had, along with great differences, certain important similarities with its own.

At the time of the Revolution, the Society of the Friends of Russian Freedom was no longer very active. Some differences of opinion had already developed among the rather disparate elements it now embraced. Its function, at the time of the Revolution, consisted primarily of the discreet dispensing of modest stipends to some of the older and less radical members of the Social-Revolutionary Party in Russia, who had maintained friendly connections with the American liberal world. But the stationery of the Society still showed, as members of the National Committee, the names of a number of distinguished Americans from all walks of life, including for example, Dr. Lyman Abbott, editor-emeritus of *The Outlook;* Miss Jane Addams; Mr. Samuel Gompers; Mr. Norman Hapgood; Senator Robert M. LaFollette; Julius Rosenwald, vice president of Sears Roebuck & Company; Mr. Jacob Schiff; Mr. Cyrus L. Sulzberger; Miss Ida Tarbell; Mr. Oswald Garrison Villard, then editor of the *New York Evening Post;* and Rabbi Stephen S. Wise. Its influence was of a moderate-liberal nature; and the target of its interest, at the Russian end, lay somewhere between the Right S-R's and the liberal wing of the Kadet Party.

To these three organizations there was added, in the late spring of 1917, another group—made up of some of the leading members of the Root Commission (see Volume 1, Chapter 1), notably Senator Root himself; Mr. John R. Mott, head of the Y.M.C.A.; Mr. Samuel Bertron, New York banker; Mr. Cyrus McCormick, head of the International Harvester Company; and—last but not least—Mr. Charles R. Crane, industrialist, philanthropist, world traveler, friend of Wilson, and patron of Russian studies. The Mission also embraced, in the persons of Mr. Charles Edward Russell, a moderate socialist, and Mr. James Duncan, vice president of the American Federation of Labor, what might be called a socialist-labor wing; but these two men were neither as active nor as influential as the others in the group's activities, and the tone was set, throughout, by Crane, Mott, and McCormick. Crane and Mott, in particular, were strong partisans of the Kadet orientation, and very close to the Bakhmeteff Embassy in their view on the problems that flowed from the Bolshevik seizure of power.

When the members of the Mission returned from Russia, in August 1917, and presented their report to the President, their task would seem to have been completed and their official status exhausted. This was certainly the President's view. But Root himself thought otherwise. As late as March 1918, he still considered, according to his biographer, Mr. Philip C. Jessup, that:

. . . while he was of course not acting in any official capacity, everybody assumed that he was and he was more or less forced into a position of acquiescence, because the only possible reason which would have justified the President in sending him to Russia was to use him afterwards as an adviser on Russian matters. He said that any man properly qualified to be President would have sent a commission qualified to become experts on Russian affairs and would have retained them in that relation to the Administration on their return. President Wilson had not in fact consulted him or any member of the Mission since their return (although the question of the Allied intervention in Russia would have given an occasion for such consultation) but everybody else was consulting him about Russian affairs all the time. He felt sufficiently strongly on the subject to refuse to accept any employment, such as representing foreign governments and claimants, which would be inconsistent with the position of an official of the government. . . .[1]

In the weeks immediately following the November Revolution, persons close to the Russian Embassy in Washington, anxious to find means for using the unexhausted portion of the American credits previously extended to the Provisional Government, attempted to draw on the authority of the Root Mission as a means of influencing the Administration. They drew up a plan (very skillfully designed to appeal to the various interests of the members of the Mission) for a program designed to assist "in the process of consolidating the Russian democracy." [2] It was a three-point program, involving propaganda, aid in rehabilitation of Russian transport and agriculture, and shipments of consumer goods. It was to be financed

[1] Philip C. Jessup, *Elihu Root,* Dodd, Mead & Co., New York, 1938, Vol. II, *1905–1937,* p. 368.
[2] Copies of this document will be found in the Wilson MSS, Series II, *op.cit.,* and in Elihu Root MSS, Library of Congress. It is unsigned; but a covering letter, from a State Department official, attached to the copy in the Root MSS, states that it "emanates unofficially from the Russian Embassy."

by the United States government and administered by a special committee, appointed by the government, but made up of representatives
of the "different factions of public thought and activity." The function of the committee should be "to deal with the whole of the
Russian situation." The committee, the Embassy thought,

should inherit the whole complex of orders actually executed or contemplated on behalf of the Russian Government. It should decide which of
these orders should be executed and which not. It should take charge of
goods delivered and see to their disposition.

Copies of a memorandum embodying this plan were sent to members
of the Root Mission as well as to Lansing and to the Secretary of
the Treasury.

This scheme obviously implied the removal of the control of policy
toward Russia from the Department of State and its assignment to
an outside committee. The Root Mission was the body that would
normally have suggested itself as the nucleus of such a committee.
The plan thus amounted, by implication, to a proposal that the
President consign the entire problem of Russia to the Root Mission
and place in the Mission's hands funds adequate for a large-scale
program of aid and propaganda.

In the first days of December 1917, members of the Root Mission
made a vigorous effort to get a hearing in highest governmental
circles for the Russian Embassy scheme. Root, Crane, and Bertron
called separately on Lansing, for this purpose, in the week beginning
December 7. Not unnaturally, they found the Secretary of State
distinctly cool to the suggestion. An effort was then made, through
Bertron, to reach the President, but without success: Wilson merely
referred Bertron back to the Secretary of State, and the matter was
dropped.

On January 17, 1918, Mott saw the President and apparently
wheedled out of him a grudging admission that no harm would be
done if some of the members of the Root Mission were to meet and
to reexamine the problem of the American government's propaganda effort in Russia—a matter to which they had given considerable attention in their original report. A meeting accordingly
took place on February 9 in Root's apartment in New York. Mc-
Cormick, Mott, and Bertron attended, and Basil Miles came up from
Washington to brief the members of the Mission on what had been

occurring within the walls of government. The consensus of the meeting was that the Committee on Public Information had the matter as well in hand as could be expected and that there was, for the moment, nothing further for the members of the Mission to do.[3]

This appears to have been the last occasion when the Root Mission functioned as a body. Mott continued to see the President from time to time and to discuss Russian matters with him; and Crane, who saw him less frequently, continued to enjoy his friendly disposition and confidence. But Root himself was quite cut off; and the members of the Mission evidently got the idea that the Department of State opposed their taking any part even in private activities relating to Russia. On April 5, Russell wrote to Cyrus McCormick:

I do not understand that this government takes the position that nothing whatsoever must be done in this country to assist Russia. Secretary Lansing is opposed to members of the Commission having any conspicuous part in such activities and the President told Bertron that the government itself had certain limitations that you doubtless understand perfectly, . . .

I am very much in favor of your suggestion of an occasional meeting [of the Root Commission], keeping in touch with one another. . . . I am convinced for my part that if anything is going to be done for Russia we shall have to do it. In spite of Mr. Lansing's notion that we ought to retire and keep still, . . . we are closer to the Russian situation than anybody else; . . . nobody else will ever make a move.[4]

While the senior officials of the Department of State were naturally lacking in enthusiasm for tendencies which they felt would eventually result in the removal of the delicate Russian problem altogether from their control, the members of the Root Mission were probably wrong in blaming Lansing personally for their exclusion, as a body, from any further part in the handling of Russian matters. The main difficulty lay, unquestionably, in Wilson's own dislike of Root and his belief that he represented precisely those reactionary tendencies which he was determined to exclude—especially now that the Russian Revolution had taken this unfortunate turn—from the handling of the Russian problem in Washington.

In addition to these various groups, all in existence at the time of

[3] Samuel N. Harper MSS, University of Chicago Library, memoir material.
[4] *Ibid.*, correspondence file.

the November Revolution in Russia, there were two individuals—
both connected, to be sure, with one or another of them, whose
personal positions deserve special mention. These were Mr. George
Kennan and Professor Samuel N. Harper, of the University of
Chicago.

Kennan, then seventy-two years of age, residing at his home in
Medina, New York, and restricting his connection with public affairs to an occasional letter or article, was still a force to be reckoned
with in the development of American opinion on Russia. His knowledge of Russia had been gained from extensive exploration in eastern
Siberia, residence in St. Petersburg, and travels in the mountains of
the Caucasus, all in the period 1865–1870, and then later, in the
1880's, from a two-year study of the political exile system in Siberia.
The accounts of this latter expedition, first carried serially in *The
Century* in 1888, and subsequently republished in book form, had
made a profound impression on educated American opinion of that
day. This impression had been reinforced and kept alive by Kennan's
extensive activity as a lecturer and by the vigorous support his writ-
ings received from the best liberal elements in Russia.

Quiet, gentlemanly, moderate but always clear and forceful in his
language, conservative as an American though a friend of liberalism
in Russia, the protagonist of no particular ideology but merely the
advocate of compassion, decency, and tolerance in the adjustment of
political differences within Russia, Kennan enjoyed a position of
unique authority and respectability in all sections of American
opinion, but particularly among the members of the educated, well-
bred, old-American upper class. In 1903, on the occasion of a further
visit to Russia, he had been expelled by the Tsarist government, and
was never to return there; but his status as America's leading authority on that country remained unimpaired. In 1917–1918, his
measured comments on contemporary developments in Russia and
on the attendant problems of public policy still appeared, from
time to time, in *The Outlook,* where they plainly did much to shape
the editorial line of that journal and to influence its readers. In
addition to this, he was one of the few men who could be certain
that personal letters from their hand would be read with respect and
attention both by the Secretary of State and by the President himself; and of this advantage he availed himself, rarely but effectively.

As for Harper, his position was in many respects the opposite of

Kennan's. If Kennan was already too old to be a participant in the unfolding of the drama of incipient Soviet-American relations in 1918, Harper was still too young and obscure to take a conspicuous place in it. If Kennan's views had been forged in the lonely austerity of his nineteenth-century struggles with the Arctic wastes of Siberia, Harper's were the product of immersion of a highly gregarious nature in the excitements of two Russian revolutions of the twentieth century and in the fevered activity of American governmental and academic life during the World War.

Samuel Northrup Harper was the son of the former president of the University of Chicago, Dr. William Raney Harper. The elder Harper was a friend of Charles Crane and had visited Russia in Crane's company in 1900. It was this interest in Russia on the part of his father and Crane which brought Samuel Harper to take up, in 1902, at the Ecole Libre des Langues Orientales in Paris, the study of the Russian language and institutions. From 1904 to 1917 he interspersed visits to Russia with teaching at the University of Chicago, Columbia University, and the University of Liverpool, where he was closely associated with Bernard Pares in the university's new School of Russian Studies (1911–1913). At the beginning of the First World War he went back to his teaching at Chicago; but he was called away from his academic studies in the summers of 1916 and 1917 to serve as temporary aide and adviser to Ambassador Francis in Petrograd. Returning to Chicago in September 1917, he remained in the United States throughout the year 1918. By this time Charles Crane's son, Richard Crane, had taken a position in the Department of State as personal assistant to the Secretary. By virtue of this fact, as well as through his own experience with the Petrograd Embassy and his wide acquaintance among other persons now connected with other offices of the government, Harper was in close touch throughout the 1918 period with persons in Washington interested in governmental affairs. In this way, his person became a central point of contact and liaison for almost all the major American elements interested in the Russian problem: the government itself, for the reasons just named; academic circles, by reason of his own major occupation and interests; commercial circles interested in Russia, by virtue of his long acquaintance with their representatives in Russia (he was an intimate friend, for example, of Mr.

Frederick M. Corse, the Petrograd representative of the New York Life Insurance Company); and the Root Mission, again through the Crane connection, as well as through his direct acquaintance with John R. Mott and Cyrus McCormick.

Harper, a perennial bachelor with a yearning to be connected with many things and a fear of being wholly committed to any of them, lived for his interest in Russia, and was indefatigable in the cultivation of his contacts with others who shared that interest. He conducted, in just these years, a huge correspondence (his personal correspondence file contains over 1,600 items from the year 1918 alone); and wherever he was—in Chicago, in Washington, or in various other points to which his frequent lecturing engagements took him—he invariably threw himself into an intensive round of interviews and meetings with all sorts of people. Throughout the wartime period his travel and personal activity, like his work at the University, continued to be subsidized by Crane—an arrangement which probably alone made possible the stupendous dispersal of energies that was the mark of his life. Endlessly torn between his academic obligations and his interest in public affairs but unable to renounce either one or the other, Harper managed to remain in contact with all aspects of Russian matters, giving himself entirely to none. His reluctance to abandon academic work was such that he never took a responsible position in government. For years he hovered on the fringes of governmental activity, serving from time to time as an adviser to those charged with the conduct of American policies, sharing avidly in the gossip and intrigue surrounding the lives of his friends in government, fearing always to be wholly left out, fearing even more to be wholly included. On the other hand, the drain on his time and energies exerted by non-academic interests was such as to cause constant complaints from his academic superiors and to reduce his output of published scholarly inquiry to slender dimensions.[5]

Despite this dissipation of energy, Harper's contributions in both of these conflicting fields were appreciable. In the shaping of the attitudes and atmosphere of the American governmental circles

[5] Professor Harper's main published works included: *The New Electoral Law for the Russian Duma* (1908), *Civic Training in Soviet Russia* (1929), *Making Bolsheviks* (1931), and *The Government of the Soviet Union* (1938).

concerned with Russian policy, a unique and—for those who knew it—unforgettable part was played by his breathless, loquacious, and intensely sociable personality. In his relation to the academic world, he deserves to be recognized as one of the founders of Russian studies in the United States, and as one who provided indispensable stimulus and example for a large number of younger scholars. In 1918, in particular, he played—with his manifold connections and his taste for operating on the fringes, rather than at the center, of all streams of activity—a role that could have been played by no one else in the effort to unify the various elements of American opinion concerning Russia and to channel them into a single effort.

This discussion would not be complete without a mention of the American press of the period. It is impossible to speak of any influence exercised by the press, as a whole, on the government's Russian policy. In general, the editors of the daily press walked gingerly around the Russian problem in the 1917–1918 period, as bewildered as anyone else—concerned, like the government, primarily with the winning of the war and only secondarily with Russia for its own sake—unwilling to make the problems of policy toward Russia into a major issue of difference with the government. The more important contributions to thinking about Russian matters, on the pages of the periodical press, tended to be, not those of the editors, but rather of individuals who enjoyed some special knowledge of Russian conditions.

Some of these were correspondents in Russia, notably Mr. Harold Williams, correspondent for the *New York Times,* and Mr. Louis Edgar Browne of the *Chicago Daily News.* These two varied greatly in their interpretation of the situation, Williams being closely connected—through his Russian wife, Ariadna Tyrkova—with the relatively conservative Kadet Party, and therefore strongly inclined toward intervention. Browne, on the other hand, fell increasingly under the sway of Robins and Gumberg in Moscow, and repudiated with no less vigor the possibility of intervention without Soviet consent.

Harper's own articles appeared, anonymously, in the *Christian Science Monitor,* where he cautiously, and with evidence of some torture of spirit, pleaded generally for economic aid and moral support to the Russian people as a matter of first priority, admitting —more and more freely as time went on—that if a few soldiers were necessary to assure the proper distribution of these expressions of friendship, they could of course be sent for that purpose.

Kennan, as noted above, continued to write for the *Outlook,* advocating a cautious intervention in Siberia—not in European Russia —and taking a line that was, generally speaking, ahead of the Administration simply in point of time. This, in essence, was also the editorial policy of the paper.

In the other journals, similarly, opinion more or less cancelled out. In the *North American Review's War Weekly,* Colonel George Harvey, former Ambassador to the Court of St. James, carried what was essentially Balfour's case, urging United States agreement to the British and French desire for a largely Japanese expedition, and pleading for confidence in the honorable intentions of the Japanese. He was not, however, sharply critical of the Administration. He admitted freely the complexity of the problem and the contradictions involved in it from the standpoint of American national interest.

At the opposite end of the spectrum, but also by no means unsympathetic to the President, stood *The Liberator,* founded in March 1918 by Mr. and Mrs. Max Eastman. *The Liberator* favored recognition of the Soviet government, but found it possible, up to the time of the intervention, to interpret its position as merely a correct application of the sentiments Wilson had expressed in the Fourteen Points speech. *The Nation,* of which Oswald Garrison Villard was just assuming the editorship, took a similar line, favoring recognition of the Soviet regime, and opposing intervention on grounds which— as the future was to show—were very cogent ones indeed.

Also on the liberal side, though much more moderate and reserved in its view of Soviet power, was the *New Republic,* then edited by Mr. Walter Lippmann. The *New Republic* adhered throughout to Wilson's original position of "no interference in Russia's internal affairs" and consistently opposed military intervention on this ground. It, too, found support for its position toward Russia in the President's own general and ambiguous phrases, and was therefore not sharply critical of his Russian policy.

Generally speaking, press reaction on the Russian problem was too hesitant and troubled, and too nicely balanced to the right and left of the President's Fourteen Points position, to have any strong influence on governmental action with regard to Russia during the last year of the war. The government had little to fear from the press, in which it found—for the most part—only the reflection of its own dilemmas and hesitations.

❖

None of the groups mentioned above was so constituted as to tap public interest in the Russian problem on a wide scale. In the winter and spring of 1918 an abortive effort was made to create a broader organization of this nature, in the form of an "American League to Aid and Cooperate with Russia." The precise origins of this undertaking remain to this day surrounded by some obscurity. The aim was obviously to bring together under a single roof all the various American elements interested in the Russian question. Representatives of the American-Russian Chamber of Commerce and of the American Friends of Russian Freedom attended the organizational meeting in January 1918, as did Harper, and gave the organization at least their nominal initial support; but none of them seems to have been among the initiators or moving spirits. The organization appears to have taken its departure from an article in the *New York Times* of December 2, 1917, by Senator William Borah, entitled "Shall We Abandon Russia?" in which the Senator called for an aid program to demonstrate America's friendship for the Russian people. He and three other legislators [6]—a bipartisan group—gave the organization their support. Theodore Roosevelt is also said to have been initially interested in it and even to have been dissuaded with difficulty (by friends who knew this would be the kiss of death for the undertaking) from attending the initial organizational meeting. But the moving spirit, in initiating the undertaking and in carrying it forward, was a young New York businessman, Mr. Herbert L. Carpenter, who seems to have had no previous connection with Russia or the handling of Russian matters in America and whose interest flowed—if available evidence may be credited—solely from acquaintance with Senator Borah and respect for his views, together with a common citizen's concern over the defection of Russia from the Allied side during the war.

The project encountered difficulty from the beginning in the

[6] The others were: Senator Robert L. Owen, Democrat, of Oklahoma, chairman of the Banking and Currency Committee and member of the Democratic National Committee; Senator William N. Calder, Republican, of New York; and Representative Henry D. Flood, Democrat, of Virginia, and chairman of the Foreign Affairs Committee.

jealousies and differences among the various factions it attempted
to unite. The Russian Embassy, made suspicious by William Boyce
Thompson's association with the initial organizational committee,
opposed the enterprise from the start; and no member of the Root
Mission could be induced to join it. Things moved slowly. It was
not until April 1918 that an appeal was launched for membership
in a "General Committee"; and only in May did the Executive
Committee meet for the first time. Vigorous efforts were made by
Carpenter to cultivate governmental support. He called repeatedly
on State Department officials, and on May 14 he saw Colonel House.
In early June he succeeded in worming out of Lansing a guarded
official letter, stating that he had no objection to the League's launching a national publicity and membership campaign to stimulate and
direct public support for the government's program of aid and cooperation with Russia. But the State Department, having no clear
and reassuring picture of the origins or motives of the project, was
puzzled by it and a bit leery.[7] It feared, furthermore, that the
launching, or even airing, of any independent program might cause
the President to feel that pressure was being brought to bear on
him, and would thus frighten him out of making any decisions at
all on the Russian question. It therefore held Carpenter at arm's
length and did what it could to delay his organizational efforts—
first on the grounds, in June, that the President had the whole matter of Russian policy intimately under advisement; then, later, on
the grounds that all such efforts must be coordinated with the official
action now launched in Siberia. Thus the League project, which remained throughout a one-man show, marked time throughout the
summer of 1918; the considerable number of prominent people who
had been induced to lend their names to the undertaking gradually
melted away; and within a few months the enterprise died a listless
and ignominious death.

Of this, the first and only effort to mobilize wide popular support

[7] On May 21, 1918, Assistant Secretary of State William Phillips wrote to Charles
Crane, asking him what he knew about the League, observing that no member of
the Root Mission was included in its membership, and adding: "We do not want
to stir up trouble by refusing to cooperate with them. On the other hand, it is a
queer committee, and I don't quite get it." Crane replied (May 24), tactfully, that
he was "loathe to criticize any organization that really has at heart the welfare
of the Russian people," but admitted that he did not have "much confidence in
the profundity or special talents of the new organization." (National Archives,
State Department File 861.00/1938.)

for an aid program addressed to the Russian people, it can only be said that the impetus did not emanate from any of the groups and individuals that were known as having a normal interest in Russian matters; the State Department remained as puzzled about what was really behind it as is the historian of a later date; and while interest in Russia was then so keen that a number of well-known people were willing to lend their names in order to give the effort a chance, it never got off the ground. Its experience was, for various reasons, not a fair test of the interest taken by influential private circles in the possibility of bringing economic aid, and every other evidence of good will, to the people of Russia.[8]

❖

It is worth noting that none of these outside groups interested in the Russian problem pressed for a purely military intervention in Russia. There were two themes on which all were, in one way or another, agreed. One was the mounting of a program of economic and psychological assistance, designed to persuade the Russian people of America's friendship and to "reeducate" them in the direction of American democratic ideals. The other was the creation of a "commission" or "committee"—either wholly independent or subject only to the President's authority—which would "take charge of" all aspects of the Russian problem and would administer the program of aid and enlightenment. This meant, of course, however you looked at it, the removal of the control of Russian policy from the hands of the Department of State. These ideas may be said to have been, in fact, the central feature of influential private opinion on the Russian problem in the winter and spring of 1918. In one form or another, they dominated the thinking of Bakhmeteff, of Borah, of Carpenter, of Harper, of the American-Russian Chamber of Commerce, of the members of the Root Mission (who saw themselves as already cast in this role), and of a large portion of the press.

There can be no question but that these currents of thought were

---

[8] The nominal head of the "League" was no less eminent a person than Dr. Frank Goodnow, then president of Johns Hopkins University. A perusal of the file on this subject contained in his personal correspondence (I am indebted to Johns Hopkins University for the privilege of seeing this material) does not indicate that Dr. Goodnow had any lively interest in the project, or that he was animated, in giving his name to it, by anything more than the vague and somewhat trusting good will that brought so many other well-known names to the League's letterhead.

greatly influenced by the tremendous impression only recently made on the American public by the success of Herbert Hoover's Commission for Relief in Belgium. It is in the pragmatic and competitive nature of American society that every success attracts a host of emulators. Americans tend to assume that what has worked once will work again—an assumption natural enough in many circumstances but usually dangerous when it comes to operations in the foreign field, where the specifics of time and circumstance are vital.

There were a number of reasons why the experience of the Hoover Commission in Belgium could not be repeated in the Russia of 1918. The action in Belgium was wholly non-political in concept, conceived as such by its authors and accepted as such, in the main, even by the warring powers, including the Germans, who were then the masters of Belgium. It was not designed, as was the proposed action in Russia, to bring about a change in the governmental realities. Sensing the awkwardness of this distinction, the proponents of an economic relief program for Russia generally tended, just as Wilson did, to slide over the fact of Bolshevik power, as though it were something unimportant or irrelevant to the question at hand, and to convey the impression that there was some way in which relief and assistance could be brought directly to the Russian people over the head of the governmental authority. The latter—it was vaguely implied—would eventually be shamed or pressed by public opinion, precisely as a result of the success of the aid program, into falling in line with a new pro-Ally, democratic spirit or disappearing from the scene entirely. In this convenient assumption, both the misleading experience in Belgium (for there the aid had indeed been extended over the head of the governmental power) and the general belief in the impermanence of Soviet rule played a part.

Kennan alone, of American commentators, appears to have noted the unsoundness of these assumptions and the dangers they involved. In an article which appeared in the *Outlook* (May 22, 1918) he wrote:

The first difficulty that we should encounter in an attempt to furnish help by these methods would be a conflict with the power and authority of the Bolsheviki. Suppose that we send engineers. . . . Under whose direction will they work? Suppose that we furnish unlimited supplies in the shape of cars, locomotives, foodstuffs, clothes, shoes, etc. Into whose hands will they fall, and who will manage the sale or distribution of

[337]

them? Unquestionably they will be controlled by the *de facto* Government of Lenine, Trotsky, and the Soviets. . . . It comes, then, to a question of helping a majority of the Russian people against the Bolshevik minority, and that might compel us to take part in a civil war, with all the Bolsheviki and probably all the Germans against us.[9]

The reality of these observations is apparent in Lenin's curt reaction when the suggestion was first made to him that Allied circles were interested in sending economic help to the Russians. "What Russians?" Lenin immediately asked. The whole idea that an external action in a matter so intimately connected with governmental responsibility as the supply of food could remain without political intent or political consequences was quite foreign to the Russian mind. In Russian terms, food—as Litvinov was later known to observe—"is a weapon."

The thought of removing Russian policy from the State Department and placing it under an independent commission was also in large measure the reflection of Hoover's experience. Freed of governmental restrictions as to employment practices, having essentially a technical task to perform, able to draw on business staffs displaced by the European war, Hoover had succeeded in surrounding himself with a group of able and energetic men, who surely contrasted favorably with the regular diplomatic staffs in Europe, weighed down as they were by the routine pressures of war work and oppressed, as always, by the strictures of governmental routine. Hoover, furthermore, operated in a region where linguistic differences were not a serious barrier to the accomplishment of his work and where the entire substructure of custom and tradition was sufficiently familiar to make possible an appeal at almost every point to common standards of decency and propriety. In Russia, none of this would have applied. One shudders, in fact, to think what would have been the result had the American government's responsibilities in the Russian problem in 1918, intricately intermeshed as they were with the interests of the European Allies and with America's war policy as a whole, been turned over to a commission of this sort and had the commission, unprepared for the delicate political problems in-

[9] Article in *The Outlook*, May 22, 1918, "Can We Help Russia?" Kennan was dealing here with a statement by A. J. Sack, head of the Russian Information Bureau, in which the latter urged a program of shipment of American consumers' goods to Russia, as well as the despatch of military instructors to reorganize such military units as were willing to fight Germany.

volved and amenable only in small and tenuous degree to governmental discipline, been injected into the existing confusions of the Siberian situation.

This thought, nevertheless, came to dominate more and more the discussion of the intervention problem in America in the first months of 1918; and it absorbed—as we shall see presently—not just outside opinion but to a very considerable extent that of the President's entourage as well.

CHAPTER XV

THE RIPENING OF THE SIBERIAN QUESTION

In Chapter IV, above, we followed up to mid-April the exchanges between the Allied powers on the subject of a possible intervention in Siberia by Japan, as mandatory for the Allies.

The remainder of the month of April brought little basic change in the situation, from the standpoint of the United States government. The replacement of the Japanese Foreign Minister, Motono, by Baron Goto, on April 24, merely confirmed the policy on which the Japanese government had settled at the time of the Brest-Litovsk crisis: refusal to intervene *as a mandatory for the Allies* without American request and assurances of American material support; but retention of full freedom to take independent action if and when the situation might warrant such action from the standpoint of Japan's national interests.

In Manchuria, the month of April was dominated by Horvat's efforts to form a nucleus of a new non-communist Russian government under the guise of the establishment of a new board of directors of the Chinese Eastern Railway. This project, first launched in discussions between Horvat, Prince Kudashev (the Russian Minister at Peking), and Admiral Kolchak at the beginning of April, was not brought to a conclusion until April 27, when the new board was formally established. The project caused anxiety both to the Chinese and to at least some sections of the Japanese government, and led to some complex intriguing on the part of the Japanese with Horvat, Derber, Kolchak, and Semenov. This, in turn, caused one or the other of these elements, worried by the Japanese vacillations, to make approaches to the United States representatives from time to time. Members of the Derber group appealed to the American Consul in Harbin, Mr. Charles K. Moser, early in April for American support; and soon thereafter they published a similar appeal to the Allies generally. About the same time Horvat, in a moment of what must have been special desperation, offered to Moser, as a *quid pro quo* for United States support, the transfer to United States operation of the Manchurian and Siberian railways for the duration of the war.[1] These approaches were of course reported to Washington. Moser himself favored an American effort to promote a compromise between the Horvat and Derber factions, with a view to ultimate establishment of a coalition government. But the Department of State remained cold to all these urgings. It evinced, from time to time, interest in learning what it could about these schemes and plans; but it informed the Minister in China, Mr. Paul S. Reinsch, on May 1 that

. . . This Government is not prepared at this time to support any of the movements for a government of Siberia, so far as reported. . . .[2]

This instruction accorded generally with Reinsch's own recommendations. He was suspicious of Kudashev and Horvat, considering them reactionaries and "imperialists." He had, by this time, become skeptical of reports flowing from Japanese and other Allied circles about the alleged danger to Siberia from the Germans. For these reasons, he urged caution in the face of the continued Allied suggestions for intervention. "Intervention in support of a group superimposed from above," he wired on April 10, "would badly upset things for the Allies." By a "group superimposed from above" he had in mind Horvat, whose popular support in Russia was minimal. Reinsch came, therefore, to the conclusion—already so widely held in private circles in the United States—that economic, rather than military, action was what was required. He envisaged the creation of a Russian trading corporation, backed in particular by the United States and Japan. This, together with the restoration of railway traffic, ought to be put in the foreground, military intervention in the background. "Economic support as primary action, military assistance in the background made effective where local anarchy requires . . ."—these, he urged, would constitute the "safe policy." [3]

Meanwhile, Stevens, after a month of "exasperating unnecessary delays," reported on April 10 that he had finally succeeded, after

[1] *Foreign Relations, 1918, Russia,* Vol. II, *op.cit.,* p. 99; from Moser's telegram of April 4, 11 p.m.

[2] *Ibid.,* p. 150.

[3] *Ibid.,* pp. 117–118.

many last-minute hitches, in making detailed arrangements whereby his engineers were to be put to work on the entire line of the Chinese Eastern Railway, with a view to assisting in the restoration of its full operating efficiency.[4] The first of the men left for their posts along the line in mid-April.[5]

Stevens' negotiations had unquestionably been hampered by the misgivings and covert opposition of the Japanese, to whom the presence of these American engineers came as a distinctly jarring embarrassment. This hindrance had now been finally overcome, at least to the point of the procurement of formal Chinese consent to the arrangement. But the significance of the achievement was somewhat reduced by the fact that the connection between the Chinese Eastern and the Trans-Siberian to the west had now been broken by Semenov's operations. So long as this condition endured, improvements in the operation of the Chinese Eastern could have no useful effect on the situation in Russia itself.

A minor unpleasantness arose at the end of April, when Robins, in Moscow, was called in by Chicherin (April 26) and presented with a written protest over alleged connections between Caldwell and the Legation at Peking, on the one hand, and members of the Derber government, on the other. The note of protest called upon the United States government to remove Caldwell without delay, to investigate the possible complicity of the American Legation in Peking in the matter, and to

. . . declare definitely and unequivocally the policy of the Government of the United States towards the Soviet government and toward all attempts of its representatives to interfere in the internal affairs of Russia.[6]

Similar protests were addressed to the French and Japanese governments.

This complaint was based on four documents alleged (probably correctly) to have been picked up by the Soviet police in Vladivostok on the occasion of a raid on the apartment of one Kolobov, who figured as a "minister" of the Derber government.[7] Copies of these

---

[4] *Foreign Relations, 1918, Russia*, Vol. III, *op.cit.*, p. 229, telegram, Stevens to SECSTATE, April 10, 11 a.m.

[5] *New York Times*, April 21, p. 1.

[6] *Foreign Relations, 1918, Russia*, Vol. II, *op.cit.*, p. 139.

[7] Kolobov is described by Horvat, in the manuscript of his unpublished *Memoirs, op.cit.*, as "a former priest and teacher of religion, who had been dismissed from his school in Harbin for his intractable temper, his noxious teachings, and other

documents were handed to Robins in support of the protest. They were not very convincing. One sees in this episode, in fact, the precursor of many subsequent instances in which, over the course of the decades, the inordinate suspiciousness of Soviet officialdom, coupled with the desire of the Soviet government to portray itself as the innocent object of sinister imperialist plots, would operate to inflate out of all reasonable proportion minor actions of foreign representatives in Russia. The seized documents suggested, at the worst, only that the Derber group was interested in enlisting American support (a fact which was in no way surprising and reflected no particular discredit on the American representatives); that Derber and his associates had been appealing to the Allied Ministers in Peking as well as to Admiral Knight for such support; that they hoped at one time to use the official American telegraph channels between Peking and Vladivostok as a means of communication (there was no evidence that they ever did); and that two Russian political figures, Ustrugov and Staal, had conferred on April 8, with the knowledge of the Derber group, with the American and French Ministers in Peking, who had discouraged them from making any political declaration or appealing formally to the Allies for support.[8]

The Department at once recognized this evidence as "inconclusive and unconvincing." It did call for reports from the representatives in question, who had little difficulty explaining their actions. It also admonished them once more to maintain strict neutrality in their attitude toward the various Russian factions and to make "no commitment as to policy, no matter how slight, . . . except under instruction from the Department."[9] But it did not think of with-

---

shortcomings." He was evidently serving in Vladivostok in April as the underground representative of the Derber government. The search of his apartment occurred on April 21.

[8] L. A. Ustrugov, former Assistant Minister of Ways of Communication in the Provisional Government, had found his name included, without his knowledge or consent, in the list of the members of the Derber "government," when the latter appointed itself in February 1918. He soon broke his connections with Derber and became a supporter of Horvat, serving as a member of the latter's "Business Cabinet."

Aleksei Fedorovich Staal, a liberal lawyer (S-R), former Public Prosecutor in Moscow under the Provisional Government, was well acquainted with Crane and Harper. He, too, seems to have had very little to do, subsequently, with the Derber group.

[9] *Foreign Relations, 1918, Russia*, Vol. ii, *op.cit.*, pp. 153–154; telegram SECSTATE to Reinsch in Peking, May 6, 6 p.m.

drawing Caldwell. The press in Washington was told on May 7 that Caldwell had done nothing improper. "Of course," the Department's spokesman said, "all the warring factions come to him, and it is his duty to report." [10] Francis was instructed to communicate this reply informally to the Soviet officials.

This incident stimulated the Department to make further inquiries about Horvat and the Russian political developments in Manchuria, concerning which Washington plainly knew very little. "The scene of these operations seems," the Department wired to Reinsch on May 6, "to be on the line of the Chinese Eastern Railway. Has not the Chinese Government occupied this line with its troops?" [11] It is evident that Washington could not, even at this moment of peculiar Chinese weakness, bring itself to realize that China played very little part in the affairs of northern Manchuria and that the three poorly disciplined and ineffectual Chinese garrisons that had been placed along the line—one at Harbin and one at each end of the line—were a bit of face-saving, designed to maintain the pretense of Chinese sovereignty in a situation where that sovereignty had little other real content.

The Department's naïve inquiry evoked a flock of explanations from the representatives in the Far East, the implications of which were not very comforting. Moser reported from Harbin that Horvat had been receiving some support from the other Allies. He was not relying upon support from the United States, Moser indicated, but he still hoped for it. If the support of the other Allies should be withdrawn, as was now possible, the new railway board would have no choice, in the absence of American support, but to "accept Japan's sole support and accede to her conditions." [12]

Reinsch, for his part, replied similarly (May 10) with a long résumé of the situation, adding a paragraph expressing his conviction that the Siberian problem was susceptible of solution from the Allied standpoint, if treated separately from that of European Russia. He urged once more the establishment of an Allied commission. [13]

On May 23 Moser reported local concern over Emerson's trip to Vologda; that he had interviewed Horvat, in company with Stevens;

[10] As reported in *New York Times*, May 7, p. 3.
[11] *Foreign Relations, 1918, Russia*, Vol. II, *op.cit.*, p. 153.
[12] *Ibid.*, p. 156, from telegram of May 8, Moser to SECSTATE.
[13] *Ibid.*, p. 159.

and that he had also talked with Kolchak. Both Horvat and Kolchak had reiterated their desire for American support, but had stated frankly that in its absence they would not hesitate to take support from the Germans or Japanese, since they did not consider any successful effort in Siberia possible without outside assistance.[14]

❖

Meanwhile, the French and British had not ceased their efforts to overcome Wilson's resistance to the thought of an Allied intervention.

The French, undismayed by previous rebuffs, continued throughout April their approaches on the formal level. On April 8 the French Ambassador, Jusserand, relayed to the Department of State a hodgepodge of information on the Siberian situation, including Noulens' account of the meeting of the Allied envoys at Vologda in the beginning of April, and once more asked that the President reexamine his position.[15] On the 23rd, the Embassy transmitted the text of a further message from Noulens averring, for the *n*th time, that only military action by Japan could thwart the schemes of the German government in eastern Siberia.[16]

The President remained deaf to all these entreaties.[17] On May 7 Lansing was permitted to reply to Jusserand, politely but uncompromisingly—in the usual vein. The French communications, the Secretary stated, had received serious consideration, but the United States government had been unable

. . . to find therein any reason to change the view it entertains that any action in the way of intervention in Siberia would now be inopportune . . .[18]

This was, be it noted, the sixth occasion in four months on which the United States government had found itself obliged to make formal reply rejecting Allied urgings looking toward intervention

[14] *Ibid.*, p. 168.
[15] *Ibid.*, pp. 109–112.
[16] *Ibid.*, p. 132.
[17] To a correspondent who had written him in mid-April relaying a plea by Count Ilya Tolstoi for despatch of American troops to Siberia, Wilson had replied (April 17): "Unfortunately we have no 'troops' which we can land at Vladivostok, and the whole state of sentiment in Russia is so confused and even problematical that I have found nothing more difficult than determining what course would be the best to pursue." Baker, Vol. VIII, *op.cit.*, p. 95.
[18] *Foreign Relations, 1918, Russia*, Vol. II, *op.cit.*, p. 154.

in Siberia. (The others were on January 16, February 8, February 13, March 5, and March 18.)

The British, similarly, continued to press, throughout April, for an alteration of the American governmental position, but they did this in a much less formal and more effective—though still not successful—manner. After the President's uncompromising reply ("I have not changed my mind.") to the approach flowing from the Allied Diplomatic Conference in mid-March, an approach which still envisaged an appeal to the Japanese to enter Siberia as mandatory for the Allies, the British reviewed the strategy of their siege of Wilson's mind and decided to try another attack. Balfour's outlook had now been affected by the first of Lockhart's messages suggesting that Trotsky might be prevailed upon to ask for intervention. This possibility, as seen above in Chapter v, was to dominate British Foreign Office thought over a period of several weeks.

On March 26, Wiseman was asked by the Foreign Office to ascertain from House whether it would be embarrassing to Washington if the possibility of a *joint* (not unilateral Japanese) Allied intervention, by invitation of the Soviet government, were to be explored with the Japanese. House thought *both* of the innovations in this proposal—the multilateral character of the proposed move and the provision for Soviet invitation—were helpful, and considered that the suggestion had possibilities. But it was evidently agreed that it would be premature to approach the President about it at that time. In mid-April, at the urging of House, Wiseman left for a short visit to England. There is no evidence, or reason to believe, that this visit was occasioned solely, or even mainly, by the Russian question; but we may assume that this was one of the matters he took up with the British government upon his arrival in England on April 20.

On April 25, presumably as a result of Wiseman's efforts, Reading received from Balfour a long cable designed to provide the basis for another approach to the President.[19] In this message Balfour elaborated the project of a joint Allied intervention in concert with the Soviet government, and described the encouraging reports he had of Trotsky's attitude. He admitted now, contrary to the earlier British position, that unilateral intervention by Japan would throw a large

[19] *Ibid.*, pp. 135–136. The message is also printed in Charles Seymour, *Intimate Papers of Colonel House*, Houghton, Mifflin Co., New York, 1928, Vol. III, *Into the World War*, pp. 403–407.

proportion of the Russians into the arms of Germany; and justified on this ground the concept of a joint expedition. The American component of such an expedition might be composed, he thought, "mainly of technical corps, especially mechanical transports, signal units, railway troops, and medical units, and also one complete division." The offer of Allied cooperation, it was suggested, ought at least to be made to the Bolsheviki; if it was accepted, "the whole position might be transformed"; if refused, then "the position of the Bolshevist Government would at least be defined." The British War Cabinet, it was stated, was anxious to learn whether the President would be disposed to agree (1) to a simultaneous British-American approach to the Soviet government for such an expedition —"an undertaking to be given for the withdrawal of all Allied forces at the conclusion of hostilities"; and (2) to the despatch of an American force, composed as suggested above.

Before broaching this scheme in Washington, Reading took it up to New York and showed it to House. He was delighted to find that it met with House's complete approval.[20] Here, finally, was a turning point; House, at least, appeared to be now on the British side. With high hopes, Reading returned to Washington and delivered the message to Wilson on the 25th. The President did not reject the proposal forthwith, but suggested that Reading, Lansing, Secretary of War Baker, and the new Japanese Ambassador-designate (Ishii) might meet to discuss the matter. The Secretary of State, to whose office Reading repaired after seeing the President, thought it would be better if he, Lansing, saw Ishii first, and this was agreed.[21]

The meeting with Ishii took place at Lansing's home on Sunday afternoon, April 28. The project for a joint expedition was thoroughly canvassed. The Secretary was pleased to gain from Ishii the impression

. . . that the Japanese Government agree fully with our point of view and that they do not see at present the military compensation for the dan-

[20] House himself wrote: "He seemed gratified to learn that I thoroughly endorsed the plan . . ." (*Ibid.*, p. 403.)

[21] The British proposal was reinforced the following day (April 27) by delivery to the Department of State of another telegram from Balfour, relaying the most optimistic and far-reaching of all of Lockhart's reports on this subject. The government at Moscow, Lockhart reported, was "no longer unwilling to see action by an Allied force in Russia operating through Vladivostok and under Japanese command, subject to the provision that the integrity and independence of Russia are properly guaranteed." (*Foreign Relations, 1918, Russia*, Vol. II, *op.cit.*, p. 140.)

ger of uniting the Russian factions to resist intervention and of throwing them into the arms of Germany.[22]

Intervention, Ishii thought, might increase rather than decrease the menace of a Germanized Russia.

The extract of Lansing's report to the President on this talk with Ishii does not indicate that Lansing brought up the main British argument: namely, that there was now believed to be a possibility of intervening by invitation of the Soviet government. This must, however, have been discussed at some time, in those last days of April, with the British; and the view was evidently put forward on the American side that Trotsky's statements could not be trusted, owing to the evidence of complicity between the Soviet leaders and the Germans. For on May 1 another message arrived from Balfour, freely admitting the difficulty of forming a correct estimate of Trotsky's reliability and conceding that the policy of working with him was not free from danger. Cooperation with him would admittedly antagonize other Russian political factions; and although this danger could perhaps be mitigated by a continued policy of non-recognition, he had no desire to minimize the risks involved. But he saw no other favorable alternative. The danger of the Germans obtaining a complete grip on Russia was real. "I am very apprehensive," Balfour stated, "that we are now allowing critical moments to go by without making full use of them."[23]

On the same day that Reading left this message with Lansing, Wiseman, still in London, sent a parallel cable to Colonel House which considerably weakened the British suggestion. He admitted in this message, in terms that sharply conflicted with Lockhart's very recent optimism, that he was beginning to doubt whether an invitation from Trotsky was feasible. "If Trotzky invites Allied intervention," he stated, quite correctly,

the Germans would regard it as a hostile act and probably turn his Government out of Moscow and Petrograd. With this centre lost the best opinion considers that the whole Bolshevik influence in Russia would collapse. No one knows this better than Trotsky and for this reason he probably hesitates. . . .[24]

[22] *Ibid.*, pp. 144–145.
[23] *Ibid.*, p. 149, from Balfour's telegram to Reading of April 29, handed to Lansing on May 1.
[24] Seymour, Vol. III, *op.cit.*, p. 421; from Wiseman's telegram to House of May 1.

Wiseman went ahead to outline the alternatives—none of them very hopeful—to a Soviet invitation to intervene. The best chance seemed to be, after all, the old and familiar project of an Allied expedition into Siberia regardless of Soviet feelings.

Although no formal answer seems ever to have been made to the British approach of April 25, Lansing continued to discuss the whole Siberian problem with Lord Reading at frequent intervals. Such conferences took place on the 6th, the 11th, and the 15th of May. In these discussions, the Secretary of State continued to stress the distinction between the situation in the northern ports, on the one hand, and in Siberia, on the other. Intervention in the north, he said to Reading on the 11th,

. . . would receive far more favorable consideration on our part than intervention in Siberia, for the reason that we could understand the advantage of the former but had been unable, thus far, to find any advantage in sending troops into Siberia. . . .

Lansing considered, furthermore, that Trotsky's allegedly favorable attitude toward intervention, if it had any reality at all, applied precisely to the northern ports, not to Siberia. He doubted that any invitation which might be forthcoming from the Bolsheviki for Allied action in Siberia would go far enough in its scope to answer the requirements of the situation.[25] This view, so far as it went, could not have been more accurate.

Lansing drove these opinions home once more in the interview of May 15th. Again, he argued that the British were confusing the two problems. He could not see that the two had anything to do with each other. Intervention in the north "might be desirable"; intervention in Siberia was questionable in view of the "inexpediency, if not the impossibility," of the Japanese moving farther west than Irkutsk.[26]

By this time, it should be noted, Semenov was at the high water mark of his second advance (begun in late April) into the transBaikal country. Actually, he had now reached the end of his punch; but roseate reports of his progress were now just reaching Washington, and the impression gained was that his fortunes would probably

---

[25] *Foreign Relations, 1918, Russia,* Vol. II, *op.cit.,* p. 160; letter of May 11, Lansing to Wilson. See above, p. 266.

[26] For the account of the meeting of May 15, see *Foreign Relations, The Lansing Papers,* Vol. II, *op.cit.,* pp. 360–361, Lansing's letter to the President of May 16.

continue to prosper. Lansing now argued that intervention in Siberia by Soviet request "would array us against Semenoff and the elements antagonistic to the Soviets."

The point was a strong one. Only a few weeks earlier it had been the British military authorities who were talking enthusiastically of making Semenov the spearhead of the Allied advance into Siberia. Closer acquaintance with his methods of warfare and with the wildness of his boasting, together with the recent hope of a Soviet invitation to intervene, had now cooled this ardor on the British part.[27] But Washington found it hard to follow these rapid shifts of view. Impressed by Semenov's success and jolted by the implications of the Sisson documents, the State Department was beginning to warm to Semenov's cause—at least to the extent of a certain wariness about antagonizing him. Not that Washington had yet gone to extremes in the hardening of its attitude toward the Bolsheviki. The fear of antagonizing them, too, and of driving them into the arms of the Germans, was not fully overcome. The problem was, as Lansing confessed to Reading on the 16th in an eloquent mixing of metaphors, a dilemma: "If we took hold of either one or the other horns . . . we would probably find ourselves in hot water."

✧

On Saturday, May 18, two days after this talk between Reading and Lansing, the President lent his presence to the gala opening in New York City of the great war drive of the American Red Cross. In the morning, ignoring the warnings of his secret service men, he marched two miles down Fifth Avenue in the warm May sunshine, at the head of the parade. In the evening he attended the formal opening ceremonies in the Metropolitan Opera House. Speaking extemporaneously on this occasion, the President gave attention to the international situation, and particularly to the attitude of the Central Powers in the matter of peace terms. Having in mind, apparently, the speech of German Chancellor Hertling of January 24, in which the latter had maintained that the peace settlement with Russia and Poland was something that concerned only the Central Powers, the President expressed his determination "not to be diverted from the grim purpose of winning the war by any insincere approaches upon the subject of peace." Every proposal with regard

[27] See above, p. 69.

to possible accommodation with the West seemed to involve, he observed, a reservation with regard to the East. He recognized these proposals for what they were: "an opportunity to have a free hand, particularly in the East, to carry out purposes of conquest and exploitation."

The reasons for Wilson's intense resentment of the position Hertling had taken were understandable. His hopes and his wartime policies were predicated on the prospect of a general peace settlement in which his ideals would find universal application. The thought that the final peace negotiations should be confined in their scope to the problems of western Europe alone was anathema to him. Such an arrangement would even knock the props from under his policy toward Siberia, which included the insistence that the Japanese agree to leave the settlement of all long-term problems to the peace conference. He therefore reacted with violent aversion to any suggestion that the Allies should ease their position in the West by permitting Germany to make peace independently, on her own terms, in the East.

It was for these reasons that Wilson, discussing the problem of peace feelers in the Metropolitan Opera House, was moved to throw in, at the conclusion of his observations on this point, a wholly unpremeditated but ringing declaration: "Now, as far as I am concerned, I intend to stand by Russia as well as France." [28] To his own amazement, this statement was greeted by a tremendous outburst of enthusiasm, a standing ovation, in fact—a reaction not accorded to anything else that he had occasion to say that evening. What most surprised him was that this reaction should have come from so prosperous and influential an audience. "It was," he later observed,

rather too well dressed. It was not an audience, in other words, made of the class of people whom you would suppose to have the most intimate feeling for the sufferings of the ordinary man in Russia, . . .[29]

How Wilsonian all this was, and how reminiscent of the Fourteen Points speech! Here, in this impromptu statement, was still the favored image of the Russians as a simple people, clothed in a peculiar virtue compiled of poverty, helplessness, and remoteness from worldly success—a mass of mute, suppressed idealists, languish-

[28] Baker, Vol. viii, *op.cit.*, p. 149.
[29] *Ibid.*, p. 149, footnote 1.

ing beneath the boot of the German captor, yearning for justice, freedom, and union with spiritual brothers in the West—sure to respond to the distant voice of sympathy and understanding. Wilson assumed that his feelings for such a people would be comprehensible only to those in America whose virtues were similarly rooted in modesty of status and lack of worldly success and whose aspirations might be expected to run in similar directions. It was clear that for all the immensity of disagreement between the two men about the remedies, Wilson shared something of Lenin's romantic image of class antagonism as the deepest reality of social and political feeling, and of Lenin's illusions about the force of working-class solidarity. In this respect the expectations of both were to be shattered by the experience of the succeeding decades, in which nationalism would emerge, to the surprise of a great many people, as a political force far stronger than class feeling.

Beyond this, there was also, in Wilson's words at the Metropolitan Opera House, that same convenient vagueness about the connection between the governmental situation in Russia and the manifestations of American support that was noted in the last chapter. Implicit in the President's words, once again, was the assumption that the realities of governmental power in Russia were something irrelevant to America's assistance and support—that these benefits could in some way be made to flow directly to the Russian people, by-passing all governmental arrangements.

The President's words were wholly sincere, and not devoid of practical meaning. When he said that the United States would not settle for peace negotiations affecting the West alone, he meant it. The Allies, with his blessing, did indeed insist, after Germany's defeat, on the annulment of the Treaty of Brest-Litovsk (though this insistence was somewhat redundant since the treaty became inoperative anyway, when the Germans lost the power to enforce it). The President also later made efforts to bring a strife-wracked Russia to the peace table and to see that some account was taken of its interests, though some would say he could have done much more than he actually did, in this respect.

But all this had little meaning to the Russian people. The predominant reality of their lives, then as later, was Soviet power. No manifestation of friendliness and sympathy from the United States could have real meaning to the Russians if they failed—as did

Wilson's attitude in the early months of 1918—to take account of, and to deal with, this awkward reality.

❖

When he returned to his desk on Monday morning after the weekend in New York, the President found Lansing's note reporting the latest discussions with the British Ambassador. The Secretary questioned, as was seen above (Chapter xi), whether one ought not, in deference to the strong British feelings, to join in asking Soviet permission for the intervention in the north; he did not even entertain the possibility of such an approach with respect to Siberia.

The President's reply to this note was uncompromising. He agreed fully that the two situations must not be confused. Semenov was changing the situation in Siberia very rapidly, "apparently." The Chief of Staff, General Peyton C. March and his associates were "clear and decided in their opinion that . . . there is no sufficient military force, in Japan or elsewhere, to do anything effective in Siberia." [30]

On the day after this reply was made (May 21), the *New York Times* correspondent in Washington succeeded in getting someone in the Department of State to talk to him about the problem of intervention. The pickings were lean. "All that can be learned here concerning the position of the Washington Government," he reported to his paper,

indicates that it has not been moved by the desire of Great Britain and France for quick action, having the double purpose of saving Russia and bringing her back as a strong nation into the Entente. The officials concerned are said to believe that it would be a grave error for any of the allied nations to send troops into Russian territory . . .

❖

All this would seem to suggest that up to the end of May—up to the time, that is, of the Czech uprising—there had been no change whatsoever in the attitude of the United States government toward the Siberian intervention. Such was the impression conveyed, on the formal level at least, to the British and French governments. Such was the impression conveyed to the press and public. Such was, certainly, the official position.

[30] *Foreign Relations, The Lansing Papers*, Vol. ii, *op.cit.*, p. 361.

Yet behind the scenes there were already hints of other things. We have noted Lansing's vacillations at earlier stages—once in late February, and again a month later, when he was shaken by incorrect reports about the alleged danger to Siberia from German prisoners-of-war. Even the President, it will be recalled, had been rendered momentarily uncertain on the first of these occasions. Now, in late April and May, there were again faint, but interesting, signs that in both cases the stone was beginning to wear away under the incessant and growing impact of the drops that were striking it.

The President, first of all, was beginning to evince something more than a detached curiosity about the situation in the Russian Far East. The considerable number of inquiries about Manchuria and Siberia sent out by the Department of State to representatives in the Far East in April and May certainly reflected in part his curiosity as well as that of the Secretary of State. A man not particularly given to soliciting from his juniors information on matters of high policy, Wilson addressed to Lansing on April 18 a note saying he would greatly value

. . . a memorandum containing *all* that we know about these several *nuclei* of self-governing authority that seem to be springing up in Siberia. It would afford me a great deal of satisfaction to get behind the most nearly representative of them if it can indeed draw leadership and control to itself. . . .[31]

To direct inquiries about America's Russian policy, Lansing, discreet man that he was, gave only the President's line. But when, in late April, a question arose of providing American shipping for removal from Nagasaki and Vladivostok of certain small detachments of Italian and Belgian troops whom the fortunes of war had tossed up in those harbors, his inner doubts were reflected in his answer. It seemed inadvisable, he thought, to bring these troops away from the Far East "when it might be embarrassing to send back there other such troops"; and he admitted that this position was "predicated upon the possibility of intervention in Siberia."[32] This was officially communicated to the governments concerned, as the American governmental position.

[31] *Ibid.*, p. 360.
[32] *Foreign Relations, 1918, Russia*, Vol. II, *op. cit.*, pp. 134–135; from telegram of April 23, 3 p.m. to Paris.

A further and most curious light is shed on Lansing's views by his report to the President of his talk with Ishii on April 28. Although he quoted Ishii as agreeing with him at the outset on the inadvisability of intervention, it is clear that the two men then proceeded to discuss the ins and outs of a possible Siberian expedition, and to do so with a seriousness and intensity not at all suggestive of the conclusion that they regarded such a thing as out of the question. Lansing inquired Ishii's views about the desirability of American and other Allied participation in a possible expedition. Ishii thought personally that American participation, in particular, would be most welcome to the Japanese government, and he suggested that an expedition composed of Japanese, Chinese, and Americans would go far to remove Russian suspicions. Lansing suggested to him that he obtain his government's authority to make this statement, which Ishii undertook to do. The talk then turned on the number of troops required, and how far an expedition should advance. Lansing ended by impressing on his visitor the need for holding German forces in the East, and painted a vivid picture of the danger, in the event of a German victory in France, of Germany's turning eastward and becoming the mistress of Siberia.[33] All this was put forward in terms that would have sounded nothing but familiar had they issued, at that juncture, from the lips of Balfour himself.

Lansing and the President saw Ishii on several occasions in the ensuing days. The notations on the latter's visits to Lansing's office, as recorded on the Secretary's desk calendar, indicate the subject of discussion (on May 6) as "his Gov[ernmen]t's desire to control any military movement in Siberia," and (on May 11) "impossibility of Japan supplying tonnage to transport our troops to Siberia."[34] On May 16 the American Ambassador in Tokyo, Mr. Roland S. Morris, was able to report back to Washington that discussion of the entire question of intervention had been revived very actively in Tokyo within the past fortnight owing—among other things—to a "report from Ishii to his Government that the President was now prepared to reconsider the entire question."[35] If the Secretary of State ex-

[33] *Ibid.*, pp. 144–145; from Lansing's letter to Wilson of April 29.
[34] Lansing MSS, *op.cit.*, Desk Diary.
[35] *Foreign Relations, 1918, Russia*, Vol. II, *op.cit.*, pp. 162–163.

pressed any surprise at the receipt of this report, the written record does not indicate it.

There was surely some measure of misunderstanding involved in this report from Tokyo. Nothing in the internal correspondence of the United States government would suggest that the President had been, as yet, in any way shaken in his disbelief in the efficacy of intervention in Siberia, along the lines suggested by the British and the French, and as an attempt to create a new eastern front. But what was happening—and what may have led the sensitive antennae of the Japanese to receive a somewhat inaccurate impulse—was that the President was now sufficiently interested in the Siberian problem, and impressed with its urgency, to feel that *some* sort of action was indeed necessary. Military force, as proposed by the French and British, was certainly not the answer; but something else might be.

The direction in which the President's mind was moving was indicated by his reaction to a telegram of May 16 from Reinsch, in which he recommended establishment of an Allied commission "to reconstruct Siberia." A fortnight earlier Lansing had told Reinsch (May 8), "No Allied commission for organizing representative or other government in Siberia is deemed advisable." [36] Now, on May 20, still glowing from the enthusiasm evoked in New York by his declaration of resolve to "stand by Russia," the President went to his typewriter and wrote out a brief instruction to the Secretary of State:

I would be very much obliged if you would let me have your comments and judgment on the suggestion with which this despatch from Reinsch closes.[37]

And on the same day he also asked Lansing to

. . . follow very attentively what Semenov is accomplishing and whether there is any legitimate way in which we can assist.

Plainly, despite the disclaimers to London and Paris, a new wind was now blowing in the inner counsels of the United States government. Just at the time when the Czech uprising was basically changing the situation in Siberia and European Russia, President Wilson—although still oblivious of that particular event—was ap-

[36] *Ibid.*, p. 157.
[37] Baker, Vol. viii, *op.cit.*, pp. 152, 153.

proaching slowly, and in the eyes of his European Allies belatedly, the point where he was prepared to accept the necessity of *some* American action with respect to Siberia.

✧

Before leaving this subject of the erosion of Wilson's resistance to the pressures for action in Siberia, it might be well to note certain of the influences that were now coming to bear, profusely and intensely, on both the President and Secretary of State in this tangled question.

There was, first of all, and underlying all the other factors, the situation on the western front. The German spring offensives of late March and April had failed of their main strategic objectives; but they had cost the Allies dearly and they had dented the Allied lines at two points. The Allied public as a whole was not aware— and could not be—of the degree to which these efforts had actually exhausted German resources. It was recognized that the Germans, aided by the immense transfers of manpower from the eastern front, still had important numerical superiority in France, and that in the interval that remained to be lived through until American forces might arrive in strength, further German attacks of dangerous power were to be expected. Throughout early May the British forces, fearfully decimated by their recent efforts, clung only precariously to the lines established by the earlier German offensives. And when, toward the end of the month, the Germans unleashed the highly effective offensive against Chemin des Dames (May 27) and advanced in less than a week all the way to Château Thierry on the Marne in one of the most spectacular break-throughs of the war, the concern on the Allied side was naturally extreme. The ensuing days, marked by actual preparations for the abandonment of Paris by the French government, were to be among the most anxious times of the entire war for both statesmen and public in the Allied countries.

In these circumstances, the reality of the advantage derived by Germany from Russia's departure from the war began to assume an undeniable clarity for everyone; and the somewhat frantic and fantastic character of French and British schemes for restoration of the eastern front did not seem so unwarranted or so out of place as they might previously have appeared.

The logic of this military situation cannot have been lost on the

President. His military advisers, to be sure, derived from it only a heightened conviction that where American forces were needed was on the western front—and as fast as possible—and that it was folly to think of diverting any portion of them, or of any other Allied forces, to any other places, particularly ones so remote from the central theater of war as Vladivostok or Archangel. But that everything possible should be done, in these desperate circumstances, to divert German attention from the west and to prevent the further exploitation by the German High Command of Russia and Siberia seemed now incontrovertible. Action of some sort was becoming a psychological and political necessity.

This reality was borne out, and reinforced, by the temper of American opinion. The press, as noted above, was not hostile; yet there could be no doubt that influential opinion was gravitating strongly, and with increasing impatience, toward recognition of a need for some sort of action in Siberia. Harper, in full accord with Crane and other members of the Root Mission and with a considerable section of the press, was urging an economic aid and friendship program for Siberia, to be backed up if necessary with armed force. Kennan went even further. He wrote to Lansing on May 26, enclosing a copy of his latest piece for *The Outlook* and expounding his views at length. He took an uncompromisingly anti-Bolshevik position. He disapproved of recognition. He thought America had nothing to hope from the Bolsheviki and should have no compunctions about antagonizing them. There was no need to worry, now, about driving them into the arms of the Germans.

. . . I doubt whether they could have done us much more harm if they had united against us three months ago. . . . A majority of the people would still be anti-Bolshevik and anti-German. . . .

Eastern Siberia—up to Irkutsk—was the area that could be saved for the Allies, and it was here that Kennan vigorously recommended the hand be applied.

. . . The best part of European Russia is already lost. . . . Why not save Siberia? With the aid of the Japanese and the sane and patriotic Russians we could certainly hold eastern Siberia. . . .

It is worth noting, for its bearing on later events, that this letter, like the record of Lansing's recent talk with Ishii, made no mention of any participation by the British or the French in such an undertaking.

After sending the letter on to the President, Lansing replied to Kennan that he, Lansing, had read it with special interest "because it comes from the highest authority in America on Russia." He was not sure, he said, of the wisdom of intervention in Siberia, but he was gratified to find "that your reaction to the confusion of the situation is very similar to my own. . . ." He could assure Kennan

. . . that the subject is receiving very careful consideration both as to the policy and as to the physical difficulties of transportation, which on account of lack of ships in the Pacific are very great.[38]

In the particular matter of a possible economic commission, pressure on the Administration was now beginning to go beyond mere expressions of opinion and to assume organizational forms. We have already noted that the end of May was precisely the time when the League to Aid and Cooperate with Russia was threatening most seriously to become active and to generate ideas and proposals of its own—a prospect always alarming to the men around Wilson. In addition to this the War Trade Board, under the able management of Mr. Vance McCormick, appointed on May 21 a three-man committee (one of the members was Mr. John Foster Dulles) to chart out a program for the resumption of economic dealings with Russia.[39] The deliberations of this body, involving as they did consultations with other persons having an interest in the Russian problem, could not fail to stir up new speculation and impatience with regard to possible aid programs in Russia. It was plain, in short, that the President, with his rousing announcement of intention to "stand by Russia," had kicked a pebble off the cliff; things were now in motion here; they would not be easily halted again.

Finally, there was the situation of the Czechs in Siberia and the personal influence of Masaryk, who, having left Moscow in early March (see above, Chapter vi), had arrived in Washington on May 9.

Wilson had never met Masaryk. He had heard of him, through Crane and others; and all he heard had inclined him favorably.

[38] George Kennan mss, Library of Congress, Box 8.

[39] National Archives, State Department File 861.00/2085½. It is not intended to suggest that this move on the part of the War Trade Board was in any way disagreeable to the Administration; on the contrary, it may well have been inspired by it. But it brought everyone a step nearer to the necessity of some decision.

Masaryk was, after all, a professor, not a businessman. He was the representative of a small and humble people, not a great one. In every way, he fitted Wilson's image of the positive and constructive political figure.

Something of the anticipation which preceded Masaryk's arrival may be gathered from a message sent by Lansing to the Embassy at Tokyo in March, at the time of Masaryk's passage through that capital. The Secretary instructed Morris to get into touch with Masaryk and to advise the Department fully of the latter's views on the situation in Russia and the possibility of organizing within Russia any effective resistance to the Central Powers.[40] Morris persuaded Masaryk to draw up a memorandum of his views, which was promptly forwarded to Washington and laid before the President. In relation to a possible intervention, the document was unclear. Masaryk recommended *de facto* recognition of the Bolsheviki, whom he thought would remain in power much longer than was generally supposed. But he stressed the danger of German domination, and pleaded for an Allied "plan"—for some joint Allied action to combat German influence. The recommendation was phrased in terms that were as vague—particularly about the relation of all this to the Soviet government—as was much similar talk in America. One can only conclude that its author had in mind something like the idea of intervention-by-agreement-with-the-Bolsheviki that preoccupied Lockhart and the British. But the news of the uprising of the Czechoslovak force in Russia naturally modified these views. Eventually it transformed the Czechs in America, including Masaryk, into strong partisans of an Allied action designed to restore the lost connection between Irkutsk and Vladivostok and to make possible the evacuation of the large body of the Corps that had not yet passed Irkutsk. The end of May and the beginning of June—a period in which the first reports of the difficulties of the Czechs in Siberia were just reaching the United States—marked the beginning of this transformation.

Masaryk's role in the United States was, in the fullest sense of the word, that of a lobbyist for the recognition of the independence of his people. This lobbying effort was one which the Czechs had al-

[40] *Foreign Relations, 1918, Russia,* Vol. II, *op.cit.,* p. 92; Lansing's telegram of March 29, 4 p.m.

ready been conducting for some time with much success. They had already made themselves useful to the Allied wartime intelligence services by assistance in espionage against the Austrians, and had won in this peculiar manner a confidence, particularly in Washington, that would not have been easily acquired in any other way. Their influence, consequently, was not negligible even prior to Masaryk's arrival. But with his appearance on the scene, the Czechoslovak lobby went into high gear. Masaryk immediately began with the systematic cultivation of a wide set of contacts within the government. Crane arranged meetings with various members of the State Department and with other officials of the government. There was a lunch with Lansing, and again, in New York (on June 12) with Colonel House. Crane's son, in the Department, saw to it that there was a steady contact with the higher Department officials.

With the President himself there was some initial difficulty. Even Crane was not able to break down at once the curious aversion Wilson appears to have had to receiving anyone who had come from Russia.[41] Crane had already been busy, soliciting an appointment, even prior to Masaryk's arrival; but the President put him off by saying he had read the memorandum Masaryk had prepared in Tokyo and that he did not think he ought to attempt an interview "unless something material can be added to what the memorandum contained." Crane sent back word that the situation *had* changed— the memorandum was outdated. The President remained adamant. "I am so pressed just now that I *must* postpone it." [42]

It was not until June 19 that Masaryk was finally received by the President. The delay, actually, had implied no disrespect. Wilson was a man who read more gladly than he listened; and he read with greatest receptivity all that which was not addressed directly to him. In May and early June Masaryk's views reached him through a number of channels, and there is every reason to suppose that he had noted them with respect and attention. Within a few days after

[41] It may be recalled that neither W. B. Thompson, nor General William V. Judson, nor Edgar Sisson, nor Thomas D. Thacher, nor Raymond Robins, nor Samuel Harper ever "got through" to the President, and the members of the Root Commission were received only with signs of great inner reluctance on his part. Even Francis, after his years of tribulation in Russia, was able to achieve no more than a single reception on the *S.S. George Washington*, while the President was returning from the Peace Conference.

[42] Wilson MSS, Series II, *op.cit.*

Masaryk's arrival in May the relationship of the position of the Czechs in Siberia to the problem of Allied intervention was already receiving the eager attention of senior State Department officials. It could not have been much later (certainly it was prior to mid-June) that the same thought occurred to the President.

CHAPTER XVI

DECISION ON MURMANSK AND ARCHANGEL

... the Government of the United States ... yields, also, to the judgment of the Supreme Command in the matter of establishing a small force at Murmansk, to guard the military stores at Kola, and to make it safe for Russian forces to come together in organized bodies in the north. But ... it can go no further ... —*American Aide-Mémoire, July 17, 1918, to Allied Ambassadors*

I convinced him [the President] that it was unwise, but he told me that he felt obliged to do it anyhow because the British and French were pressing it on his attention so hard and he had refused so many of their requests that they were beginning to feel that he was not a good associate, much less a good ally ... —*Statement by Newton D. Baker, former Secretary of War, December 24, 1929*

AT the end of May, Vice Consul Felix Cole, at Archangel, sat down to spell out for the Department of State, in a long despatch, his feelings about a possible Allied intervention in the Russian North. He could not, of course, know what was afoot in the Allied chanceries. But he could sense something of what was being thought about. Disturbed at the implications of what he felt to be in the wind, he produced, and sent off on June 1 to the State Department, what has subsequently proved to be the most penetrating and prophetic of all statements by western observers on the prospects for Allied intervention in Russia. The full measure of its soundness becomes apparent only when it is compared with the actual consequences of the intervention, of which it is not the intention to treat in the present volume. This is not, therefore, the place to describe its content in full. It will suffice merely to note the leading statements of certain of its paragraphs:

1. Intervention will begin on a small scale but with each step forward will grow in scope and in its demands for ships, men, money and materials. ...

2. The ground for landing an interventionary force has not been properly prepared. The north of Russia is nowhere near as pro-Ally as it might be. . . .

3. Intervention in the north of Russia will mean that we must feed the entire north of Russia containing from 500,000 to 1,500,000 population, . . .

4. Intervention can not reckon on active support from Russians. All the fight is out of Russia. . . .

5. The Socialist Revolutionists, Mensheviks, and Cadets who now advocate intervention are discredited officeholders seeking to regain power. They were only able to "lead" the people when they advocated peace . . . , anti-imperialism . . . , and socialism. . . .

6. On the other hand, the men who do rule Russia, however badly it is done, are the small Bolshevik leaders, who will always and everywhere oppose intervention. These men, not the "intellectuals," will direct Russian public opinion. . . .

7. No child can ever be convinced that it is spanked for its own benefit. . . . Intervention will alienate thousands of anti-German Bolsheviks. . . .

8. Every foreign invasion that has gone deep into Russia has been swallowed up. . . .

9. I can not see that the fundamental situation in Russia is changed even if it were proven that Lenin, Trotsky, Sverdlov, etc., drew monthly pay checks from the Berlin treasury. . . .

10. Intervention will not engage three Germans in Russia to every one Ally. . . .

11. Intervention will belie all our promises to the Russian people made since October 26, 1917.

12. We will lose that moral superiority over Germany which is a tower of strength to us everywhere, . . .

13. We shall have sold our birthright in Russia for a mess of pottage. . . .

And after all, unless we are to invade the whole of Russia, we shall not have affected that part of Russia where the population is massed, namely the center and the south where the industrial, mining and agricultural strength of Russia lies. . . .[1]

A copy of the despatch went to Francis. He did not think much of it. It ran counter, of course, to the recommendation he had already made.[2] He therefore made no effort to relay any of the recommendation to the Department by wire. This was a pity, for the despatch constituted a useful contribution to the picture of the problem then

[1] *Foreign Relations, 1918, Russia,* Vol. ii, *op.cit.,* pp. 477–484.
[2] Francis MSS, *op.cit.;* letter, Francis to Cole, June 13, 1918.

available to the United States government. Continuing its course by courier mail, it did not reach Washington until July 19, at which time the final decision in the matter of the northern intervention had already been taken. Thus the document had no influence over the course of events to be described in this chapter. But justice to Cole requires that it be mentioned here; and we may note, from the fact of its existence, that had the United States government been more inclined, at this juncture, to consult the judgment of the "man on the spot," it would have been better advised and better equipped to take the decision that was now looming before it.

❖

When Secretary of State Lansing pointed out to Lord Reading in May that Siberia and the northern ports were two separate problems and should not be confused, he was reflecting a most fundamental distinction in American policy. Stubborn as were Lansing and the President in their opposition to Allied pressures in the matter of intervention in Siberia, an area remote from the European theater of war, they showed no comparable resistance to Anglo-French suggestions concerning Murmansk and Archangel—in fact they never flatly declined any. When the request was made, in March, that an American warship be sent to Murmansk, one was sent, albeit after initial hesitations. When, at the end of May, Balfour sent a personal message to Wilson describing the Murmansk situation as extremely dangerous and begging for American military assistance—"a brigade to which a few guns should be added"—the President, as was seen in Chapter xi, did not turn this down, but authorized Lansing to reply that the United States government was prepared to send troops if General Foch approved the implied diversion of men and ships. This reply, it will be recalled, was given to Reading on June 3.

The third of June was, as it happened, also the day on which the Murmansk situation received detailed consideration at the Sixth Session of the Supreme War Council at Versailles. It was presumably partly in preparation for this meeting that Balfour had made the effort, one week earlier, to ascertain Wilson's readiness to send an American force.

We have already noted, in Chapter xiii, those of the deliberations of this War Council session that dealt with the fate of the Czechs. But the situation of the northern ports was also given attention.

Here the discussion centered around a lengthy Joint Note, No. 31, prepared by the Permanent Military Representatives, and dealing with Murmansk and Archangel. In this paper, the Military Representatives reviewed the situation in detail and outlined their recommendations.

The description of the existing situation, contained in Joint Note No. 31, can be seen now to have contained certain errors of fact, together with the usual exaggerations of the German threat to Murmansk, of Finnish designs on the Murmansk Railway, of Finnish subservience to Germany. It continued to postulate the availability for service in the north of a portion of the Czech Corps—a circumstance which, as we have seen, never at any time had reality outside the minds of the Allied military planners themselves. It also took account of the possibility of the Murmansk region being used, in the absence of firm Allied protection, as a German submarine base—a danger which, in the light of the recently expressed Soviet intention of ceding Petsamo to the White Finns and also of the recent German submarine activity along that coast, seemed now quite serious.

It was on these appreciations—plus the reflection that the two northern ports might serve, in Allied hands, to protect the flanks of a possible future Allied expedition into Siberia—that the Permanent Military Representatives postulated their belief that the ports must be kept out of German control and that a considerably heightened Allied effort should be mounted for this purpose. In order to limit the effort required from the western side, the Czechs were to be asked to make available that part of the force which was supposed to be on its way to Archangel. On the assumption that this Czech assistance would not be denied, the western powers—England, France, Italy, and the United States—were to make available some four to six battalions, in all, with necessary supplies, and officers for the training of the Czechs. The entire expedition was to be under British command.

The United States Military Representative, General Tasker H. Bliss, concurred in this paper. He did so on the understanding, derived from his own exchanges with the War Department and the President, that the United States government approved occupation of the northern ports for purposes of keeping them out of German hands and of securing the Allied war supplies understood to have accumulated in them. Like the others, he supposed that the Czech force would be available. He had no idea that there was any thought of conducting operations from these ports into the interior of the country, particularly in the face of any appreciable military opposition. It was his understanding, furthermore, that the participation of the various western governments in the proposed action would be approximately equal, so that the United States contribution would not be more than one to two battalions.

General Bliss, it should be noted, was in a difficult position when it came to such discussions. Although the United States theoretically participated at the senior political level of the Supreme War Council, the President steadfastly refused to be personally represented there after the First Session, in November 1917, when House had served as his representative. The discussions of the Prime Ministers had therefore to be sent to Washington for Wilson's approval after their adoption by the others—an arrangement which was not only offensive to the Europeans but also meant that General Bliss had no senior political representative of his country at the Council with whom he could consult on matters having political import. Not being in direct touch with the State Department, he also had no access to any independent source of official information other than the War Department. In purely military questions, this sufficed. In semi-political matters, it was neither adequate nor disinterested; and Bliss was obliged to make do with such data and reports as he could derive from his Allied colleagues. Surely only the United States government, with its peculiar and congenital aversion to dealing with political questions in multilateral bodies in wartime, would have tolerated arrangements so pregnant with possibilities for confusion and so unfair to the representative in question. Even the President's high regard for Bliss [3] and the marked degree to which the two men saw eye to eye on matters of substance could not fully compensate for the unsoundness of these arrangements.

The Supreme War Council ended its deliberations by approving Joint Note No. 31.

Shortly thereafter Lord Milner, then Secretary of State for War in the British government, sent a further communication to the President. He told of the decisions of the War Council, of which—for

---

[3] "Bliss," Wilson wrote to the Secretary of War on June 19, "is a remarkable man. Every word he writes strengthens my impression that he is a real thinking man, who takes the pains to think straight." Baker, Vol. VIII, *op.cit.*, p. 220.

some reason—neither the President nor the War Department appears to have been as yet fully informed. Reverting to Wilson's expressed willingness that United States forces might be sent to the north if Foch agreed, Lord Milner stated that he had talked with Foch and had found him aware of the importance of the matter and persuaded that the despatch of American forces was most advantageous. Milner asked that an American force consisting of three battalions of infantry and machine guns, two batteries of field artillery, three companies of engineers, and the necessary administrative and medical services be sent.[4]

Lansing discussed Milner's request on June 14 with Secretary of War Baker and the Chief of Staff, General March. Both of the latter were strongly averse to any such employment of American forces. They considered that it would constitute an unprofitable diversion of strength from the western front. It now occurred to them, on reading Milner's message, that perhaps it had been unwise to leave the consulting of Foch to the British. They found themselves wondering whether the matter had been adequately presented to the Supreme Commander by persons so opposed to the American view. They were also startled at the revelation that the War Council had made provision for British command of the expedition. They were not sure that this decision really represented Bliss's private opinion.

After checking with the President, Baker therefore despatched a message to Bliss (June 15) telling him of Milner's request, asking his opinion about the matter of command, and instructing him to see Foch himself and to explain to him that any such American undertaking must be at the expense of the effort in France.[5]

Bliss was indignant to learn from Baker's telegram that the British had boosted the level of American forces requested—from the one to two battalions envisaged at the War Council meeting to three, plus artillery and engineers. He saw Foch, as instructed, on the 20th. By this time, the general military situation was much improved over that of the beginning of June. The fourth German offensive had been stopped on the western front. Austria was in obvious difficulties. Foch, now relatively relaxed, sent for his Chief of Staff, General

---

[4] For the general tenor of Milner's message, see *ibid.*, p. 214.

Details of the force requested are mentioned in Bliss's report on the Supreme War Council, of February 6, 1920 (*Foreign Relations, The Lansing Papers*, Vol. II, *op.cit.*, p. 275).

[5] Baker, Vol. VIII, *op.cit.*, p. 214.

Weygand, and the files on Murmansk, went through the papers, came to the conclusion that the value of Murmansk was undisputable, and expressed approval of a small diversion of forces. The despatch of "one or two battalions" would not, he thought, materially affect the American effort in France.[6]

Bliss reported this to Washington on the 22nd, in a long cable which treated the entire subject of the Russian North as a problem in Allied military plans. He felt that only if the aid of the Czechs or of other Russian forces could be obtained would it be possible to hold Murmansk and Archangel "without an unwise expenditure of military effort." Meanwhile, the Allied forces maintained there should be "sufficient only for defense against small enemy operations," or—if the enemy should attack in strength—for the necessary demolitions. (Since the Czechs never did arrive, and since no Russian forces of any consequence ever became available, it will be seen that this amounted to a recommendation that no major reinforcement of the units already at Murmansk should be undertaken at all.)

In the light of Bliss's report, Washington went back at the British for an explanation of the discrepancy concerning the size of the American force requested, and the discussion continued inconclusively. Foch's statement to Bliss, approving the diversion of forces, seems not to have registered with the President. When, shortly thereafter, Jusserand brought in a message from Foch to the President, pointing out that the military situation had improved and asserting that this was a decisive argument in favor of intervention in Russia, Wilson, ignoring the report of Bliss's talk with the Supreme Commander, replied sourly to the French Ambassador:

> I am sorry that he [Foch] does not explicitly say whether he thinks we would be justified in sending troops . . . to Russia if there were involved in doing so a subtraction of that number of men from those whom we could send to France. . . .[7]

This was, as we have seen, precisely what Foch *had* already said in his talk with Bliss.

❖

[6] Frederick Palmer, *Newton D. Baker: America at War*, Dodd, Mead & Co., New York, 1931, Vol. II, p. 317.

[7] Baker, Vol. VIII, *op.cit.*, p. 232.

While these exchanges were taking place between Washington, London, and Paris, the entire Murmansk situation—as between Moscow, Berlin, the Murmansk Soviet, and the Allied forces in the port—was becoming increasingly tense.

The Germans, in the first place, were now becoming seriously worried about the situation in the Russian North. Their information about it showed approximately the same degree of distortion and exaggeration as that reaching the Entente with respect to German plans for action in this region. They consequently had a greatly exaggerated picture of what the Entente was up to. By the end of May they had become distinctly uneasy. Ludendorff wired the Foreign Office on May 28 asking that the Murmansk-Archangel situation be taken up in the forthcoming sessions of the Soviet-German Commission that was to examine difficulties growing out of the Brest-Litovsk Treaty. He described it as "an intolerable condition" that English warships should be permanently in Archangel (actually, there was none there but one icebreaker, guarding the two food ships) and that English troops should be stationed along the Murmansk Railway (these actually amounted, at that time, to a handful of men with an armored train at Kandalaksha).

We cannot tolerate this supporting of the Entente by Russia, and we shall be forced to move against the Murmansk Railway if the Russian government does not give guarantees that it will in future definitely refrain from such unneutral acts and grant us a certain control over the railway. . . . [8]

The German Foreign Minister softened this language somewhat in his instruction to Mirbach; but the instruction did go out, and in the ensuing days the matter was indeed taken up with the Soviet government. The Soviet reply was to the effect that the reports of Allied activity were exaggerated, and that the German submarine blockade, cutting off—as it did—fishing activity and normal overseas connections, had forced the population of Murmansk to seek the protection of the Allies. Would the Germans not put a stop to the submarine activity?

This last the Germans refused to do, so long as the English ships

[8] These passages are taken from two communications of Ludendorff to the Foreign Office of May 28. National Archives, German Foreign Office Archives, *op.cit.,* one in Box 147 (University of California group), the other (signed by Berckheim) in the series *Weltkrieg 29, Druck der Entente auf Russland,* Box 117.

were there. Instead, they urged the Soviet government to join with the White Finns in an attack on the Murmansk-Petsamo region— a fantastic idea of which, quite naturally, nothing came.[9]

It was partly to ease their position in the face of these German pressures that the Soviet government hardened its position, in June, toward the activities of the Allies at Murmansk and toward the intimacy between the Allies and the Murmansk Regional Soviet. At first, the protests made were still perfunctory. On June 7 a cryptic message was sent by Trotsky to the Regional Soviet, warning that "conniving with unknown foreigners is contradictory to the interests of the country and certainly not permissible."[10] A few days later, Chicherin handed to the Allied representatives at Moscow notes, largely identical, protesting against "the presence of military vessels belonging to the belligerent powers in the ports of the Russian Republic, with the possibility of their leaving for the open sea at any time. . . ." The hope was expressed, in the note to Poole, that the United States government, "which has given so many proofs of its friendly attitude toward the Russian Republic," would give consideration to "this stipulation which is obligatory on Russia. . . ."[11] In the notes to the British and French, less cordial language was used. Francis was told by Voznesenski, who visited Vologda in mid-June, that Chicherin had authorized him to say that this note was *pro forma*. Similar intimations were no doubt given to Lockhart.[12]

In the days immediately following despatch of this note, however, the Soviet attitude began to change. The anger and suspicion occasioned in Soviet circles by the reports of the Czechoslovak uprising were now beginning to affect the entire Soviet outlook on the Allies and to find reflection in the Soviet view of the Murmansk situation. A communication addressed to the Regional Soviet on June 16, demanding the departure of the Allied vessels, already revealed this change. Its tone was harder. There was, it was explained, "A possibility of belligerent action on the part of the British and their Allies in connection with the Czechoslovak movement."[13] This, in Moscow's eyes, was no laughing matter. From now on there would be no

[9] Protocol of a Crown Council at Spa, July 2, 1918. *Ibid., Weltkrieg 15 geh.*, serial 1500, frames 628482ff.

[10] Strakhovsky, *op.cit.*, p. 51.

[11] *Foreign Relations, 1918, Russia*, Vol. II, *op.cit.*, p. 486.

[12] Francis MSS, *op.cit.*, Francis to Poole, June 19. This note was forwarded by Poole to Washington, which paid no attention whatsoever to it.

[13] Strakhovsky, *op.cit.*, p. 56.

more temporizing on the Soviet side with the Allied position at Murmansk.

The telegram to the Murmansk Soviet unleashed a violent exchange between Moscow and Murmansk.[14] The first reply of Yuryev was characteristic of the Murmansk view:

> . . . It is obvious that 1) the Allies will not depart from Murmansk; 2) they will defend the region from the Germans and the Finns; 3) they will extend every aid to the local population and to all those who will fight the Germans; 4) they will support the authority of the Regional Soviet, . . . All sympathies of the population are with the Allies. . . . An anti-Allies policy of the Soviet is impossible. It is equally impossible to force the Allies to depart. They have the advantage of superior forces. Such telegrams as that of Cicherin . . . may raise agitation, but they are impotent to oblige us to forceful acts. . . .[15]

The Moscow reaction was sharpened not only by Yuryev's independent and even brazen tone, not usual in the correspondence of so disciplined a movement as that of the Russian Communists, but also by the fact—clearly reflected in the cables from Moscow—that the Soviet leaders had now gotten wind of the British scheme for linking a northern intervention with one from Siberia, and were extremely, and justifiably, suspicious.

The English at Murmansk, meanwhile, had become no less wary of Bolshevik intentions. They were worried, in particular, about the pending despatch (of which they had been forewarned by Natsarenus) of Red Guard detachments to Murmansk. Natsarenus had claimed that the mission of these detachments would be to participate in the defense of the port, if need be, against the Germans. (The actual purpose was to reinforce the pro-Bolshevik contingent in Murmansk to the point where it would be possible to unseat Yuryev and Vesselago and replace them with reliable Bolsheviki.) The British feared that once this force arrived, it would join the local naval garrison in the adoption of a hostile and menacing attitude toward the Allied forces in the port. Anxiety on this score among the Allied officials had been increased by the sharpness of Moscow's recent protests against the Allied presence there.

[14] *Ibid.*, pp. 57-68, presents an excellent summary of the ensuing exchanges between Moscow and the Murmansk Soviet.

[15] *Ibid.*, pp. 57-58.

Major General Sir C. Maynard, assigned to command the British expeditionary force at Murmansk, arrived there on June 23, bringing with him his tiny force of 600 men ("almost all . . . of a physical category so low as to render them unfit for duty in France") as well as the training mission, supposed to undertake the training—at an Archangel still icebound and in hostile hands—of a party of Czechs which would never arrive.[16] Maynard's superior officer, Major General F. C. Poole, had already been in Murmansk a month, having arrived, it will be recalled, on the *Olympia* in late May. From his initial discussions with Poole, Maynard derived, as will be seen from his memoirs,[17] a wildly distorted picture of the situation, including the impression that 15,000 White Finns, in German service, were already on the march against the Murmansk Railway. Deciding, for strategic reasons which—against this background of information —were sound enough, to defend the line at the points of Kandalaksha and Kem, rather than in the immediate vicinity of Murmansk, Maynard set forth on June 27th on a personal survey of the line to the south. Even before reaching Kandalaksha he was forced to realize that the attitude of the Soviet railwaymen toward him and his party was hostile, secretive, and quite unreliable. At Kandalaksha, as luck would have it, he encountered the first echelon of Natsarenus' Red Guards, moving northward. Its commander, obviously in his cups, proved sullen, abusive, and disinclined to amicable discussion. Maynard's train had been brought into the Kandalaksha station by the local railwaymen in such a way as to clear the line for departure of the Soviet train northward, and the latter was obviously about to proceed. It was plain that if the Soviet train once started, there would be no stopping it before it reached Murmansk, nor any predicting what effect its arrival would have on the situation there. Maynard decided he could not take the risk of letting it proceed. He mounted machine gun posts and gave orders that the train was not to move. He then continued his own journey southward. At Kem, where a British warship was stationed and where the situation was firmly in Allied hands, he found two more trainloads of Red Guards, proceeding northward. He learned that more, including an armored train, were following. From his own intelligence officers

[16] Maynard's force consisted of one company of the 29th London Regiment, the 253rd Machine Gun Company, and two sections of the 584th Field Company of Royal Engineers. Maynard, *op.cit.*, p. 15, footnote.

[17] *Ibid.*, pp. 25–29.

he now heard that there was definite information that these units were being despatched "with the express object of attacking the Allies and driving them from Murmansk." [18] He therefore took the bit in his teeth, summoned reinforcements from Murmansk, and issued orders that the Soviet units already at Kem and Kandalaksha were to be disarmed and the others were to be prevented from coming up the line into Kem. These orders were carried out, and the disarmed Red Guards were shipped back southward, most ignominiously, into the hands of their waiting comrades.

While these things were occurring—all in the last days of June —at the military level, relations between Moscow and the Murmansk Soviet suffered a rapid and final deterioration. If Maynard's information about German and White Finn intentions and capabilities was distorted, the reports reaching Moscow about Maynard's arrival, his intentions, and the size of his expeditionary force, were no less so.[19] No sooner had the first of these reports been received (about June 27) than a peremptory summons went forward from Moscow to the Murmansk Soviet to cease, at last, the pro-Allied policy and to fall into line at once with the policies and orders of the central Soviet authority.

Last-minute attempts by Chicherin to moderate the conflict were unsuccessful. On June 28 a violent altercation took place over the long distance telegraph between Yuryev and Lenin, which the latter finally attempted to terminate by the warning: "If you still refuse to understand Soviet policy—a policy equally hostile to the English and to the Germans—you have yourself to blame." [20] To this Yuryev, quite unabashed, replied: "It is all very well for you to talk that way, sitting there in Moscow." [21]

Things came to a head on June 30. It was decided that day, at a combined public session of the Regional Soviet, the *Tsentromur* and the *Sovzheldor,* to defy Moscow's demands, to support the continuance of the relationship with the Allies, and to strengthen that relationship by reducing it to a written, contractual basis.

This was too much for Moscow. The following day the Moscow *Izvestiya* published a decree, signed by Lenin and Trotsky, outlaw-

[18] *Ibid.,* p. 50.
[19] Sadoul reported that by June 27 Trotsky had already learned of Maynard's arrival with 2,500 (sic) men, and was furious. Sadoul, *Notes . . . , op.cit.,* p. 238.
[20] *Pravda,* February 21, 1935.
[21] Kedrov, *Bez bolshevistskogo rukovodstva, op.cit.,* p. 119.

ing Yuryev and proclaiming him an enemy of the people.[22] That evening Yuryev and Chicherin had a final altercation, over the 1,200 miles of primitive telegraph line. Chicherin told Yuryev that Lenin refused to speak with him—that he could expect to be denounced as a traitor. The Soviet government would fight against any imperialist invasion—German or Allied. They had not asked the British in; they rejected British aid.

"Comrade," Yuryev replied, in what was surely one of the most stinging reproaches ever to be levied by a junior Soviet official at a senior one,

has life not taught you to view things soberly? You constantly utter beautiful phrases but not once have you told how to go about realizing them. Russia has been reduced to a mere shadow as a result of these phrases. . . . The Germans are strangling us and you go on hoping that they will become magnanimous. If you know a way out of our condition please tell it to us. . . . We ourselves know that the Germans and the Allies are imperialists, but of two evils we have chosen the lesser. . . .[23]

"Tell the admirals who put you up to this," Chicherin replied, now obviously beside himself, and having in mind, of course, the Allied officers at Murmansk,

Tell the admirals who put you up to this that in the event of an armed intervention onto the territory of revolutionary Russia, they will encounter a popular uprising just as this has been encountered by those who have intervened in the Ukraine.

To this the doughty Yuryev gave blow for blow. "Comrade Chicherin," he replied,

you said that some sort of admirals put me up to this, but this is not true—they did nothing of the sort . . . and if you persist in thinking of me in this way, then I can say that I have the impression that Count Mirbach is standing behind *your* back and suggesting these thoughts to you. . . .[24]

This was the end. "In the name of the Soviets and Comrade Lenin," Chicherin stated, "I proclaim you and all who share your point of view to be outlaws."[25] He then broke off the conversation.

On July 5, Natsarenus, faced with Maynard's actions against his

[22] Strakhovsky, *op.cit.,* p. 67.
[23] Bunyan, *op.cit.,* pp. 133-134.
[24] Kedrov, *op.cit.,* pp. 130-132.
[25] Strakhovsky, *op.cit.,* p. 68.

units and acting no doubt under direct orders from Moscow, cut the telegraph wires and blew up a number of bridges on the sector of the railway between Soroka (now Byelomorsk) and Kem, thus severing all connections between Murmansk and the interior. The break between Moscow and Murmansk was now final and complete.

On July 6, the new agreement, rightly described by Strakhovsky as unique in international practice, was concluded between the Murmansk Regional Soviet and the representatives of the three main Allied powers. It recognized the Regional Soviet as the supreme authority in the region and established a common obligation for the defense of the area. It included a disclaimer, on the Allied part, of any desire to separate the region from Russia. The sole reason for concluding the agreement, it was stated, was to preserve the region for the "great undivided Russia" of the future.

This agreement, formally approved by the United States government in October 1918,[26] provided the legal basis for the intervention in the Murmansk region itself.

Thus just as the statesmen in Washington approached the final stages of their consideration of the question of sending an American force to Murmansk, that port and the surrounding region slipped— for reasons practically unavoidable—out of the control of the central Soviet authorities in Moscow and completely into the hands of an authority friendly to the Allied military purposes. This had great advantages, for the moment. But it also had disadvantages which almost no one then perceived; for it meant that the Allies were assuming a weighty responsibility toward these Murmansk Russians who had defied the fury of Moscow in favor of the Allied tie—a responsibility which, as time would show, the Allies had neither the steadfastness of purpose nor the resources to discharge to the full.

❖

The governmental leaders in Washington appear to have remained, for the time, quite oblivious of these happenings in the remote Arctic port (Lansing did not see a text of the agreement until August 20). They manifested generally, it must be said, a minimum of curiosity as to what was occurring "on the spot." But they continued to give their attention to the British request.

[26] The text of this document will be found in *Foreign Relations, 1918, Russia*, Vol. II, *op.cit.*, pp. 492-495; and the text of Lansing's letter to the Secretary of the Navy, approving the agreement, in the same volume, pp. 556-557.

The argument with the British about the size of the American contingent continued through the last days of June. It was still in progress when the Supreme War Council met again at Versailles, July 2 to 4. On the 2nd, Sir Eric Geddes, First Lord of the Admiralty, himself just back from a personal visit to Murmansk, presented to the Council the views of General Poole, favoring a broadening of the entire plan for intervention in the north. The Council then agreed on a lengthy document, presented by Lloyd George, treating the entire intervention problem and constituting the last of many appeals to President Wilson to approve a policy of intervention. Although addressed primarily to the Siberian problem, this document also touched on the northern ports. Their occupation was described as necessary in order that the Allies might retain "bridgeheads into Russia from the north from which forces can eventually advance rapidly to the center of Russia, . . ." Intervention in Russia should therefore include, it was stated, "Such developments of the Allied forces in Murmansk and Archangel as the military advisers of the Allies may recommend." [27]

There can be no question but that this recommendation was based precisely on the British idea—of which Bliss was so mistrustful—of a deeper intervention into the Russian interior, directed not only to securing the two ports but also to linking up with the effort to be made from the Siberian side. The American military authorities were right to be suspicious of this vague project; for it took little account —as the future was to show—of the geographic and climatic realities of Russia and involved a serious misjudgment of the political ones. For assurance of successful execution it would have required, as Bliss correctly perceived, a commitment of military strength much greater than anything the British were then talking about, and one which could not fail to constitute a serious diversion of effort from the western front.

Secretary of War Baker, whose misgivings had been in no way relieved by the Supreme War Council paper, wrote Bliss on July 8, asking his opinion.[28]

Bliss, in reply, reiterated the view that the British project was too sweeping to be carried out by such Allied forces as could conceivably be made available. The best a small Allied force could do would be

[27] *Ibid.,* pp. 243, 246, from Frazier's telegram to secstate, July 2.
[28] Palmer, Vol. ii, *op.cit.,* p. 318.

to hold the ports during the winter, secure the stores, and perhaps give comfort to the population by welfare activities. He adhered, therefore, to the earlier proposal for a total Allied reinforcement of only four to six battalions. Even this, he stressed, was a compromise, as any Allied military effort must be. His own aversion to the entire project remained unchanged. "It seems to me," he stated,

that our Allies want the United States to commit itself to expeditions to various places where, after the War, they alone will have any special interests. . . . We must fight somewhere, and originally we selected France and at the request of the Allies themselves.[29]

The senior officials in the War Department remained, throughout, of the same opinion as Bliss. "General March and I," Baker had stated in his cable of July 8,

have been in conference with the President about the Murmansk expedition. . . . None of us can see the military value of the proposal . . .[30]

Bliss's reply did not reassure them.

The President nevertheless decided, in the ensuing days, to accede to the British request—and for the full three battalions, at that. It was his own decision. Baker and March remained firmly averse. It was, Baker later recorded, the only disagreement he ever had with the President. "I . . . convinced him," he wrote,

that it was unwise, but he told me that he felt obliged to do it anyhow because the British and French were pressing it upon his attention so hard and he had refused so many of their requests that they were beginning to feel that he was not a good associate, much less a good ally. . . .

The primary responsibility rests upon the British and French, and particularly, I believe, in that question on the British. . . . The expedition was nonsense from the beginning and always seemed to me to be one of those side shows born of desperation and organized for the purpose of keeping up home morale. . . .[31]

The President's decision was made known to the Allied governments in the memorandum of July 17 (to be discussed in greater detail below) in which his views on the entire intervention problem were set forth. The United States government, it was stated here,

[29] *Ibid.,* p. 319.
[30] *Loc.cit.*
[31] Baker, Vol. VIII, *op.cit.,* p. 284, footnote (letter, Newton D. Baker to Ralph Hayes, December 24, 1929).

. . . yields, also, to the judgment of the Supreme Command in the matter of establishing a small force at Murmansk, to guard the military stores at Kola, and to make it safe for Russian forces to come together in organized bodies in the north. But . . . it can go no further. . . . It is not in a position, and has no expectation of being in a position, to take part in organized intervention in adequate force from . . . Murmansk and Archangel. It . . . will . . . feel obliged to withdraw these forces, in order to add them to the forces at the western front, if the plans . . . should develop into others inconsistent with the policy to which the Government of the United States feels constrained to restrict itself.[32]

Accordingly, General Bliss records, the American Section of the Supreme War Council was advised from Washington "that the President had decided to permit three battalions of infantry and three companies of engineers to participate in the Murmansk Expedition." The final arrangements were still to be subject to the specific approval of Foch, in the case of the infantry, and of Pershing, in the case of the engineers.[33]

❖

This is how it came about that some 4,500 young Americans, men of the 339th Infantry Regiment, the 337th Field Hospital Company, and the 310th Engineers Battalion, little suspecting what ordeals lay before them, went ashore at Archangel on September 4, 1918, to participate, under British command, in one of the most futile and luckless of military undertakings. They were sent against the better judgment of their own government, in deference to the pressure of the Allies and the express wish of Foch. The government which sent them entertained a concept of the purpose for which they were being sent wholly different from that of the British general who led them. The bewildering and trying situation in which they found themselves, as well as the subsequent public confusion and altercation about the wisdom of the action, must be laid in the first instance to the lack of effective communication among the Allied governments. And here one knows not who deserves the greater share of the blame—the British, who never dealt seriously with the sound counterarguments put up by the American military authorities but went over their heads to extort Wilson's assent to a proposition he

---

[32] *Foreign Relations, 1918, Russia*, Vol. II, *op.cit.*, pp. 287–290.
[33] *Foreign Relations, The Lansing Papers*, Vol. II, *op.cit.*, p. 278.

never fully understood or approved; or Wilson himself, who by his secretiveness, his tendency to paralyze the regular channels of intercourse by ignoring them, and his unwillingness really to talk things out with foreign governments in any normal way, made it possible for such misunderstandings to arise and to endure.

CHAPTER XVII

━━━

THE DECISION ON SIBERIA

. . . I have been sweating blood over the question what is right and feasible (*possible*) to do in Russia. It goes to pieces like quicksilver under my touch, . . . —*Woodrow Wilson, July 8, 1918*

━━━

THE beginning of June found the senior officials in Washington, for the first time, somewhat divided in their feelings about the various proposals for action in Siberia.

The War Department, in the persons of General March and Secretary Baker, remained consistently scornful of the Anglo-French schemes. "Intervention via Vladivostok," Baker wired to Bliss on May 28,

is deemed impracticable because of the vast distances involved and the size of the force necessary to be effective. The expedition could serve no military purpose . . .[1]

In the State Department, at the level just under the Secretary, opinion had swung—to the indignation of the War Department—in the direction of acceptance of the Anglo-French pressures. Lansing himself had been considerably affected by this prevailing sentiment. He went to some lengths, in late May and early June, to explore the availability of shipping, both Japanese and American, for a possible Siberian expedition; but the results of this exploration were so negative that he came away from the inquiry as frustrated as ever, convinced only that *something* ought to be done.

This last was also, in increasing degree, the feeling of House. Now officially vacationing at his home in Magnolia, Massachusetts, House nevertheless kept in close touch, by mail, telegraph, and telephone, with developments in Washington, and received a steady stream of visitors who made the pilgrimage to Magnolia to gain his

[1] Palmer, Vol. ii, *op.cit.*, p. 314.

ear for their views on the Russian problem. As the month of June progressed, and particularly the first fortnight with its alarming reports of the situation on the western front, House's conviction that *some* action must be taken, if only for action's sake, became overpowering.

As for Wilson, he continued to vacillate between conflicting impulses. He accepted entirely the views of his military advisers on the military absurdity of the Anglo-French schemes. Yet he, too, as was seen above, had at last been persuaded of the need for some sort of action. He took no one fully into his confidence; but there is every indication that his mind was incessantly occupied at this time by the anxious search for some expedient that would demonstrate America's friendship for the Russian people, give them the needed reassurance, and strengthen the anti-German forces in Russia, without committing the United States to pretentious military adventures or linking it to the ulterior political designs of the other Allies. His correspondence contains repeated reflections of the anguish of this quest for the correct solution.

In this month of June the reports, stimuli, suggestions, and pressures coming to the Administration in connection with the Russian question assumed formidable proportions. The matter had now become the dominant problem of American foreign policy. The heavy German pressure on the western front had thrown all hopes to the east; and Washington's long vacillation in its Russian policy had now drawn down upon its head the multitudinous pleas and pressures of a desperate and slightly hysterical Allied world. The telegraph tapes in the State and War Departments poured out a bewildering plethora of reports, information, misinformation, and recommendations about Russia—from Vologda, Moscow, Stockholm, Paris, London, Tokyo, Peking, Harbin, and Vladivostok. Along with this there came a veritable inundation of influential visitors, endeavoring to accomplish by personal suasion what could not be accomplished by the cables and letters. "We have been literally beset," Baker complained in early July, "with the Russian question in its various forms." More people had come from Russia in that one month, he thought, than in the entire previous year. "Each one's solution is dictated by the occurrences which he saw in the little corner of Russia in which he happened to be stationed." [2] For-

[2] *Ibid.*, p. 317.

mer officials of the Tsarist and Provisional Governments were now beginning to appear in numbers. Masaryk was in full circulation. To these were added a bevy of unofficial envoys whom the French—in their desperation—had sent over. General H. M. Berthelot, former head of the French Military Mission in Rumania, who had passed through Moscow and Murmansk on his way home, was despatched to Washington in the evident hope that his prestige and authority in the technical-military field could shake the obdurate skepticism of the President and his military advisers as to the strategic merits of a possible Siberian expedition. Professor Henri Bergson, noted philosopher and world figure, was also despatched—presumably to exploit Wilson's known weakness for the academic world. The newly appointed French Ambassador to Japan, Marcel Delanney, appeared en route to his new post, obviously instructed not to hasten on to his new job but to see as many influential people as he could in the United States and thus to support the efforts of his colleague, Jusserand, on behalf of Siberian intervention. He came armed with a desperate personal plea to Wilson from Clemenceau. On the British side, the incessant efforts of Reading continued to be supplemented by those of Sir William Wiseman, now back from England and in close touch, as always, with House and other influential figures.

The historian might wish that time and space permitted him to disentangle the turmoil that resulted from the workings of these manifold influences, and to trace to their precise origins, in impulse and informational background, the various steps that led, during the month of June, to America's ultimate involvement in the Siberian venture. Unfortunately, this is not possible within the limits of a study intended to hold meaning for the general public as well as for the specialist. One encounters, at this point, the problem that is bound to beset diplomatic historians in increasing measure as they move into the effort to recount the course of the international life of the present century: the huge number and complexity of contacts between the bloated governmental bureaucracies and the stupendous volume of the written record to which they have given rise. In these circumstances it becomes simply unfeasible to attempt to permit the sources to tell their own story. The historian has no choice but to simplify, to generalize, and to ask the reader to lean on his judgment. This means, in the present instance, that the processes by which the United States government finally clarified its attitude in the Siberian question in June and July 1918 can be only roughly summarized here. A great many individual communications, visits, and other events, each no doubt of some importance, must be left without specific mention.[3]

❖

When the Supreme War Council met on June 3 at Versailles, the sound of the German guns could be heard in the distance. Preparations, as noted above, were under way for the possible evacuation of Paris. Siberia appeared as almost the only hope. But Wilson was still the stumbling block. Considering that the chances for overcoming his opposition might be best if the Japanese could be induced first to give the necessary assurances, the three Allied Foreign Ministers decided at Versailles to ask the Japanese whether, in the event that the President's consent was forthcoming, Japan would be prepared to intervene under the following conditions:

(a) that she should promise to respect the territorial integrity of Russia;

(b) that she should take no side in the internal politics of Russia; and

(c) that she should advance as far west as possible "for the purpose of encountering the Germans." [4]

In the ensuing days a joint note was drawn up accordingly and despatched to Tokyo. There it unleashed a new and lively debate in governmental circles over the course Japan should take. The prospect of being pressed into an involvement with the western powers in a joint Siberian venture was always an alarming one to many Japanese. The new Allied step must surely have aroused the feelings of those who wished to see Japan, relying on the agreement recently concluded with the Chinese, "go it alone" in an effort to gain exclusive control not only of eastern Siberia but of northern Manchuria as well.

❖

Washington, promptly informed of this Allied step, viewed it with a skepticism bordering on contempt, and awaited without inordinate

[3] The interested reader will find a useful and balanced summary of these events in Betty Miller Unterberger, *America's Siberian Expedition, 1918–1920; A Study of National Policy*, Duke University Press, Durham, 1956.

[4] National Archives, War Records Division, R.G. 120, *op.cit.*

anxiety the Japanese reply. The minds of the men around Wilson were preoccupied, just in those days, with a sudden flurry of discussion and maneuvering over the question of a possible Russian commission. What brought this question to the fore just at that time is not wholly clear; presumably it was the combined impact of a report written (June 4) by Mr. Thomas D. Thacher, who had just reached Washington and had seen Lansing on May 28, and of the findings of the three-man committee appointed by the War Trade Board to look into the problem of the resumption of economic relations with Russia (see above, Chapter XIII). Thacher, stressing vigorously the need for working through the Soviet government, urged the establishment of "a commission equipped with financial support and personnel sufficient to render assistance to the Russian people," to be sent to Russia at once.[5] Thacher's well-written and effective report was given circulation among a number of influential people. The War Trade Board committee recommended (June 5) that the President appoint a "Russian Commissioner" whose function it would be to "take charge of all matters pertaining to Russia." The Commissioner, it was suggested, should enter Russia via Siberia and should coordinate his work with the activities of the Russian cooperatives.[6] In addition to these recommendations, the activity of Carpenter, engaged in just those days in the effort to extract from the President an official blessing for the League to Aid and Cooperate with Russia, may have contributed to the agitation of this question.

The suggestion of a Russian commission, in any case, set a number of wheels to spinning furiously. The Department of State was naturally worried at the danger, now threatening from several quarters, to its control of Russian affairs. A rivalry was immediately stimulated, as between the Red Cross faction headed by Thompson and the more conservative entourage of the Root Commission, supported by the Russian Embassy, for control of any commission that might be established. Finally, most important of all, the matter threatened, for a moment, to become the subject of partisan politics. At some time in the first week of June, ex-President William Howard Taft published in the Philadelphia *Public Ledger* an article calling for immediate action in Russia, along lines to be agreed with the Allies.

[5] A copy of Thacher's report will be found in the Manuscripts Collection of the New York Public Library; also in the Francis MSS, *op.cit.*

[6] National Archives, State Department File 861.00/2085½.

On June 6, Senator James W. Wadsworth, speaking at a Republican Party dinner in New York (Theodore Roosevelt was also a speaker) voiced similar sentiments.

These developments caused consternation in the Administration.[7] There was a general feeling that some initiative must be taken immediately if the Republicans were to be headed off from a partisan exploitation of the intervention issue. The ensuing days, particularly the 12th and 13th, witnessed a crescendo of high-level communication over the question of a commission for Russia and who should head it. Communications on this topic flew thick and fast between the State Department, the White House, the British Embassy, Wiseman in New York, and Colonel House in Magnolia. Although Mott's name had previously been mentioned in this connection (on June 4, by William Phillips to Lansing) it was now Herbert Hoover on whom all hopes centered. His appointment in this capacity commended itself to everyone as an answer to the Republican threat. The suggestion apparently originated with House, or in his entourage. It met with the enthusiastic approval of House, Auchincloss, Polk, Reading, and Wiseman. Lansing wrote personally to the President on the 13th, warmly urging the establishment of a commission "along the same lines as the 'Commission for the Relief of Belgium,'" to be headed by Hoover. The move, he thought, "would, for the time being, dispose of the proposal for armed intervention."[8] His letter was supported by one from House, of the same date.[9]

Through Auchincloss, House sounded out Hoover. The latter responded favorably, but left it up to the President to decide. At

---

[7] On Monday, June 10, whether on his own initiative or at the instigation of the Administration, Senator W. H. King, of Utah, a Democrat and a firm supporter of the President, introduced a resolution on the floor of the Senate, declaring it to be the sense of the Senate ". . . that a military expedition be organized and sent by the United States of America in conjunction with its allies, including Japan and China, to cooperate with the armies of the Russian people to repel the advance of German arms and to expel from Russia German military power and establish therein the authority of the people and Government of Russia." (*Congressional Record, Second Session, Sixty-Fifth Congress* [VOL. LVI], Senate, June 10, 1918 [Senate Resolution 262], p. 7557.)

This resolution, which was referred to the Foreign Relations Committee and on which no further action was taken, appears to have been an initial attempt by the Democrats in the Senate to prevent the intervention issue from being made into a political football by the Republicans.

[8] *Foreign Relations, The Lansing Papers*, Vol. II, *op.cit.*, pp. 362–363.

[9] Seymour, Vol. III, *op.cit.*, pp. 409–410.

some point, Wilson talked to Hoover about it. "I informed the President," Hoover relates in his memoirs,[10]

that I would serve anywhere, any time, but that to send an army to attack the Bolshevists' Eastern Front while extending kindness on their Western Front was not quite logical. In any event, our ideas of industrial organization would scarcely fit into the philosophy of Messrs. Lenin and Trotsky, even if they did not reject the plan utterly as an Allied Trojan horse. I heard nothing more of the matter.

This passage leaves room for question as to whether Hoover understood—or remembered—very well the proposal at issue. But it makes it clear that Wilson never definitely asked him to serve. The reason for this hesitation remains a matter of conjecture. It may have been that he felt that Hoover was still more needed as Food Commissioner.[11] It seems more likely that he realized that Hoover's appointment would mean that the Russian question would be, from that time forth, effectively out of his hands. For this, surely, he was not yet ready.

While not appointing Hoover, Wilson did not reject entirely the idea of a commission. On the contrary, he instructed the Secretary of Commerce to explore further the economic problems with which such a commission would have to cope, thus setting the wheels of government busily in motion. But plainly, the suggestion of a commission did not seem to him, even now, the entire solution of the problem. There was, after all, still the question as to how a commission could enter Siberia and function there without some sort of armed support and protection. The point Kennan had just recently raised (May 22)—that one must reckon with the existence of Soviet power—was an inexorable one; and however reluctant Wilson may have been to recognize it in his public statements, it is doubtful that it escaped his attention entirely. All of eastern Siberia, from and including Irkutsk to Vladivostok, was, after all, still in Soviet hands; and the reaction of the Soviet authorities to the Japanese landing of April 5 had shown that they would not take kindly to any Allied

[10] *The Memoirs of Herbert Hoover; Years of Adventure, 1874-1920*, The Macmillan Co., New York, 1951, p. 266.

[11] In July Wilson told Bernard Baruch, who was still pressing for Hoover's appointment to head a Russian commission, that he could not spare him from his present functions. Wilson MSS, Series II, *op.cit.*

incursion, be it even by a peaceful commission, on which they had not been consulted.

Thus Wilson, in principle not at all disinclined toward the idea of economic aid to Russia and prepared to see preliminary work along this line go forward, still could not find in the idea of a commission the answer to his problem. Aside from the fact that the staffing of such a body obviously involved awkward domestic-political problems, there was the unanswered question as to how it could function on territory held by the Bolsheviki.

The way out of these perplexities was then suddenly provided— or seemed to be provided—by the reports coming into Washington about the position and aspirations of the Czechs in Siberia. News of the Czech uprising reached Washington belatedly and in confusing driblets throughout the month of June. It was not until after the middle of the month that there was any reasonably intelligible picture of what had occurred, and even this was spotty and in many respects confusing. But in Washington, as in the Allied community in Russia, the dawning realization that the Czechs were in possession of a large portion of Siberia aroused a host of speculations as to their possible role in solving the dilemmas of Allied policy. Lansing's senior aides, notably Basil Miles and Butler Wright (himself recently back from a passage through Siberia), immediately became greatly excited over the possibility of using the Czechs on the spot. Their reaction was precisely that of Poole, in Moscow. And even the President, on reading (June 17) a telegram from Reinsch in Peking, urging that the Czechs be left in Siberia to "control" the region against the Germans, suddenly thought he saw in this suggestion "the shadow of a plan that might be worked, with Japanese and other assistance." The Czechs, after all, he observed to Lansing, were the cousins of the Russians.[12]

From this moment, things moved rapidly to a conclusion. Wilson had now found an approach that seemed to him really hopeful, although the outlines of the possible action were not yet wholly clear. The day after reading Reinsch's telegram (June 18) he told Delanney, who had come in to transmit Clemenceau's message, that he was "considering anew the entire situation" and would express his conclusions within ten days. Through Delanney this startling news was at once circulated throughout the entire Allied community. En-

[12] *Foreign Relations, The Lansing Papers,* Vol. II, *op.cit.,* p. 363.

couraging as it was in some respects to the British and the French, it also had disturbing possibilities from their standpoint; for the President's words were still wholly non-committal with relation to the Anglo-French proposals for a military intervention deep into Siberia. The possibility had to be faced that his decision might not be at all what was desired in London and Paris.

Consideration of the project for a commission, meanwhile, moved apace in the President's entourage. Washington buzzed with schemes and plans. The British and French received the impression that this was definitely the direction in which American policy was moving. House continued to press for a commission, with Hoover at its head. Robins' arrival, in mid-June, added to the intensity of the discussion. On the 25th Wilson met, in an unprecedented night session, with five of his Cabinet members: Lansing, Baker, Secretary of Commerce William C. Redfield, Secretary of Agriculture David F. Houston, and Secretary of Labor William B. Wilson.[13] The course of the preparatory work on the economic side, embracing both economic assistance and revival of commercial exchanges, was reviewed, and the President encouraged the others to press ahead vigorously with these studies.

All this had, from Wilson's standpoint, the advantage that it gave the others something to keep them busy, relieved him of the incessant pressure to "do something," and permitted him to address himself in privacy to the real decision which, under State Department encouragement, was ripening in his mind. The abundant documentation concerning the treatment of the Russian problem in Washington in June 1918 cannot—in fact—be understood unless it is realized that throughout the latter part of the month two things were happening simultaneously: almost everyone involved in the treatment of this problem, except the President himself, was busy working out schemes for the creation of some sort of high-powered commission, on the Belgian pattern; whereas the President himself, content that it should be this way, was pursuing in the quiet of his own mind a parallel, but wholly different, line of thought.

❖

On or about June 25, the Japanese reply was made to the French-British-Italian approach. Although the full text is not available, it is

13 Baker, Vol. viii, *op.cit.*, p. 231.

evident that the Japanese, while agreeing to respect Russia's territorial integrity and to refrain from interfering in her internal affairs, would make no promise to go beyond Irkutsk. And they clung to their insistence that they would take no action unless America joined in the request.

Something—not all—of this reply was revealed to the United States government by Ishii on June 26, when he handed Lansing a three-sentence telegram from his government on this subject. It was indicated here that the Japanese had told the Allies that they

. . . could not feel at liberty to express their decision before a complete and satisfactory understanding on the question was reached between the three Powers and the United States.[14]

Wilson was delighted. He had read Ishii's communication, he told Lansing, "with genuine pleasure." [15] The Japanese reaction took care of the Anglo-French initiative of early June and relieved him of the necessity of rejecting the proposal himself. In his relief, Wilson made the mistake of supposing that the Japanese reply reflected the same delicate sympathy in Tokyo for the American view that Ishii had manifested in Washington. The President failed to realize the depths of the differences within the Japanese government on these matters and the extent to which Japanese calculations were now coming to be influenced by the desire to pursue in Siberia an independent policy, having nothing to do either with American aspirations or with those of the French and British.

To the British, the Japanese reply brought consternation. They knew that the President had made up his mind to take some action. They had received no encouragement to believe that there had yet been any change of heart in the White House or the War Department about the military merits of the proposed expedition. The Japanese reaction, involving as it did a refusal to go beyond Irkutsk, was hardly likely to overcome the American inhibitions. The British now had all the more reason to fear that the President's mind might be moving in a direction undesirable from their standpoint.

The next meeting of the Supreme War Council was now only a few days off. It was decided in London to use this meeting for a last powerful effort to swing the President into line. A message was

---

[14] *Foreign Relations, The Lansing Papers,* Vol. II, *op.cit.,* p. 365.
[15] *Ibid.,* p. 365, footnote 55.

therefore sent to him (delivered personally by Reading on the 28th) from Lloyd George and the War Cabinet, saying that the British government would lay before the Supreme War Council at its coming meeting on July 2nd, "proposals for the assistance of the Russian people in their present unhappy situation," and expressing the hope that the President would refrain from a decision until the Supreme War Council's view had been communicated to him.[16] This was supported by an eloquent message from Foch (June 27) approving the despatch of American troops to Russia and stating that

. . . in the interests of military success in Europe, I consider the expedition to Siberia as a very important factor for victory, provided action be immediate, on account of the season being already advanced. I take the liberty of insisting on this last point.[17]

With these approaches, the French and British had introduced their largest guns. But it was now too late. It was the reports concerning the Czechoslovaks, not the arguments of the Allied chanceries, that were now determining Wilson's decision.

❖

From the moment of Masaryk's meeting with the President on the 19th, the American intimacy with the Czechoslovak cause grew apace. On the 23rd, the British Embassy sent over a paraphrase of a message from Lockhart, expressing apprehension over the possibility of a seizure of Moscow by the Germans and adding:

. . . if we leave the Czechs to their fate and if we fail to intervene now we shall suffer a blow to our prestige in Russia from which it will take us years to recover.[18]

Lansing at once sent this message to the President with an accompanying letter in which he wrote:

The situation of the Czecho-Slovak forces in western Siberia seems to me to create a new condition which should receive careful consideration. Prof. Masaryk assured me that these rebels against Austria-Hungary, collected from the Russian prison camps and from deserters, would not fight against the Russians, but only sought to pass via Vladivostok to the western front.

[16] Baker, Vol. VIII, *op.cit.*, p. 237.
[17] *Ibid.*, p. 235.
[18] National Archives, State Department File 861.00/2164½.

Now it appears that their efforts to reach Vladivostok being opposed by the Bolsheviks they are fighting the Red Guards along the Siberian line with more or less success. As these troops are most loyal to our cause and have been unjustly treated by the various Soviets ought we not to consider whether something cannot be done to support them?

. . . Is it not possible that in this body of capable and loyal troops may be found a nucleus for military occupation of the Siberian Railway? [19]

The following day there was received from Admiral Knight at Vladivostok the first of three messages concerning the Czechs which had a decisive influence on the thinking of the senior State Department officials and, directly or indirectly, of the President as well. After describing the military position of the Czechs, Knight reported the "seizure" of Irkutsk by German war prisoners,[20] and ascribed the obstruction of the Czech passage through Siberia to German influences. "It is believed," he stated,

that the Czech is now ready to cooperate with the Allied movements against German activities in Siberia and for reestablishment [of an] Eastern front . . . Czech situation and future movements have become dominating factor in Siberia and perhaps Russian situation.[21]

Knight's telegram was received with enthusiasm by the senior State Department officials, whose hopes had already been aroused by Lansing's letter to the President. "This is a 'God-send!' " Wright said to Miles, on a chit accompanying the message. "It is just the news we want. Masaryk is in town! Let's concentrate on this with all our power at once." [22]

And concentrate they did, with no small success. The following day (June 25) the State Department forwarded for Masaryk, through its official facilities, a long communication to Chicherin protesting

[19] *Loc.cit.*

[20] What Knight was referring to here was surely the fighting that took place at Irkutsk on June 14, when an underground force of Whites came into the open, liberated the political prisoners held by the Bolsheviki, and attempted to take the city. In repulsing this attack, which they finally succeeded in doing, the local Bolsheviki made extensive use of Internationalist war prisoners, as a result of which the latter acquired, for a time, a new prominence on the Irkutsk scene. The portrayal of this event as a "seizure" of Irkutsk by German prisoners was another example of Allied distortion of the war prisoner problem; but it was no doubt a wholly innocent error on the part of Admiral Knight, who was surely merely reflecting the information that had reached him from Allied representatives in Irkutsk.

[21] National Archives, State Department File 861.00/2165½. This was reinforced by a second message, received in Washington on the 26th, in which great stress was laid on the war prisoners, who were described as being quite out of Soviet control.

[22] *Loc.cit.*

the Soviet attitude toward the Czechs and reproaching the Soviet government for its failure to live up to the guarantee it had once given of free and unmolested passage of the Corps to France. The transmission of this message by the Department was a most unusual procedure. On the same day the Department wired Caldwell asking for a full report on the military situation of the Czechs.[23]

On the 26th, a telegram was received from Caldwell, relaying a request from the representatives of the Czechoslovak National Council in Vladivostok for military support. They had decided, the Czech representatives said, that the 15,000 Czech troops who had reached Vladivostok in early May, prior to the uprising, would have to turn westward once more and mount an operation to break through to Irkutsk and to reestablish communication with their compatriots in western Siberia. The Allied consuls agreed that this action was necessary; they recommended that both supplies and arms be sent and that an Allied armed force also be despatched to assist this Czech action.[24] The Czech request was also transmitted through Admiral Knight, whose report contained many more details, and also plainly favored acquiescence.[25]

The final determinant of the American decision was added when the Czechs, on the 29th, after delivery of an ultimatum to the local Soviet authorities, took armed action and seized the city of Vladivostok. This action was the culminating point of a long series of frictions between the Czechs and the local Soviet, in which the Czech hand was strengthened by encouragement from the local Allied representatives. But the action flowed automatically from the decision of the Vladivostok Czechs to move to the aid of their compatriots farther westward. This decision made it impossible for them to remain further in a state of nominal peace with the local Soviet authorities.

The Czech action was followed immediately by the landing of additional Japanese and British forces. Admiral Knight, too, now landed a small detachment of marines to guard the American Consulate. Caldwell reported that the entire development had been welcomed by the majority of the population.[26]

[23] *Foreign Relations, 1918, Russia*, Vol. ii, *op.cit.*, p. 224.
[24] *Ibid.*, p. 226.
[25] *Ibid.*, pp. 230–231. (The State Department received its copy from the Navy Department on June 29.)
[26] *Ibid.*, p. 235.

In this way, by a curious coincidence, the power of the central Soviet government came to an end in Vladivostok at precisely the same moment that the last vestiges of central Soviet authority similarly disappeared in Murmansk. Just at the time when Wilson was on the verge of decision with respect to the American action at both points, his problem was simplified, and his decision facilitated, by the fact that the respective ports suddenly gravitated into the hands of forces friendly to the Allies and eager for their intervention.

Official reports of the Czech seizure of Vladivostok began to come into the State Department on July 2nd, but it was not until the following morning that Lansing had a clear enough picture of what had happened to warrant his picking up the telephone and communicating this important news to the President.

Meanwhile, the Supreme War Council had met in Paris and approved a long document, prepared in advance by the British, going through the intervention question, once more, from beginnning to end. All the familiar arguments were repeated, in the light of the new situation, and the position of the Czechs was also brought in. A plan for an Allied military move into Siberia, to be accompanied— this time—by "relief expeditions under American direction and control to supply the wants and alleviate the sufferings of the Russian people," [27] was then elaborated in detail. The necessity of American support and encouragement for the military expedition was stressed. It was stated as the unanimous opinion of Foch and the military advisers that the immediate despatch of such an expedition was essential for the victory of the Allied army. In conclusion, the Council appealed to President Wilson "to approve the policy here recommended and thus to enable it to be carried into effect before it is too late." [28]

This final appeal from the Supreme War Council reached Washington, and was handed by Reading to the President, on the afternoon of July 3, shortly before Lansing's phone call about the Czech seizure of Vladivostok. The time of decision had now finally arrived. The choice—to the President, at least—now seemed reasonably clear.

The next day was the Fourth of July, and one of the hottest. There

[27] This reference was an obvious attempt to appeal to the American interest in the project for a commission, with which the President's mind was believed to be preoccupied.

[28] *Foreign Relations, 1918, Russia,* Vol. ii, *op.cit.,* p. 246; from Frazier's telegram to SECSTATE, July 2, midnight (pp. 241–246).

was an excursion to Mount Vernon on the Presidential yacht, *The Mayflower*. Both the President and Lansing were aboard. The other guests included a number of representatives of various foreign language groups in the United States. It was understood that the President would make a speech at Mount Vernon; and it was thought by many that he might use this as an occasion for announcing his decision with respect to Russia.

Wilson was courteous enough to his guests, and tried to make them feel at home in the face of the sweltering heat. But we may assume that both he and Lansing had their minds rather on Siberian matters than on the steaming banks of the Potomac past which they moved. At some time during the course of that day, whether before or after the excursion, Lansing found the leisure to draw up a memorandum for the President on the Siberian question. It was to prove a decisive recommendation. The seizure of Vladivostok by the Czechs, and their success in western Siberia, had "materially changed the situation," Lansing wrote, "by introducing a sentimental element into the question of our duty." There was now an American responsibility to aid them. He proposed that a supply of arms be sent to the Czech contingent in Vladivostok, and that "some" troops be sent to assist them in policing the railroad and in "disarming and dispersing" the German and Austrian prisoners-of-war who, he understood, were opposing them. Aiding the Czechs was, after all, an entirely different thing from intervening on other grounds. Even though some American forces were sent, one would have to rely on Japan to supply the bulk of the requisite forces. The announcement of the intention, and the readiness to refrain from interfering in Russian internal affairs, should be made at once. A peaceful commission of representatives of various phases of society, "to-wit, moral, industrial, commercial, financial and agricultural," should be sent and should "proceed westward from Vladivostok following as closely as possible, with due regard to safety, the Czecho-Slovaks." Its final destination and function should depend on its reception by the Russian people and on the military resistance encountered.[29]

Lansing's memorandum was presumably sent to the President on the morning of Friday, the 5th. Later that day the President phoned and said he wished to see Lansing, Baker, Secretary of Navy Josephus Daniels, and General March at two o'clock on the 6th.

[29] Lansing MSS, *op.cit.*, Diary Blue Boxes, Box 2.

The Decision on Siberia

The meeting took place that Saturday afternoon, as scheduled, in an upper room of the White House, with Admiral W. S. Benson (Chief of Naval Operations) also attending. "After we had . . . seated ourselves, somewhat in order of rank," General March later recorded, "the President entered the room with a pad in his hand, and taking a position standing and facing us, . . . read from his pad his views on the matter at issue." [30]

The views which the President set forth emerged, substantially unchanged, as the official record of the consensus of the gathering. Here is the text:

. . . After debating the whole subject of the present conditions in Siberia as affected by the taking of Vladivostok by the Czecho-Slovaks, the landing of American, British, French, and Japanese forces from the naval vessels in that port, and the occupation of the railroad through western Siberia by other Czecho-Slovaks with the reported taking of Irkutsk by these troops; and after reading and discussing the communication of the Supreme War Council favoring an attempt to restore an eastern front against the Central powers; and also a memorandum by the Secretary of State—

The following propositions and program were decided upon:

(1) That the establishment of an eastern front through a military expedition, even if it was wise to employ a large Japanese force, is physically impossible though the front was established east of the Ural Mountains;

(2) That under present conditions any advance westward of Irkutsk does not seem possible and needs no further consideration;

(3) That the present situation of the Czecho-Slovaks requires this Government and other governments to make an effort to aid those at Vladivostok in forming a junction with their compatriots in western Siberia; and that this Government on sentimental grounds and because of the effect upon the friendly Slavs everywhere would be subject to criticism if it did not make this effort and would doubtless be held responsible if they were defeated by lack of such effort;

(4) That in view of the inability of the United States to furnish any considerable force within a short time to assist the Czecho-Slovaks the following plan of operations should be adopted, provided the Japanese Government agrees to cooperate;

(a) The furnishing of small arms, machine guns, and ammunition to the Czecho-Slovaks at Vladivostok by the Japanese Govern-

[30] Peyton C. March, *The Nation at War,* Doubleday, Doran & Co., Inc., Garden City, N.Y., 1932, p. 124.

ment; this Government to share the expense and to supplement the supplies as rapidly as possible;

(b) The assembling of a military force at Vladivostok composed of approximately 7,000 Americans and 7,000 Japanese to guard the line of communication of the Czecho-Slovaks proceeding toward Irkutsk; the Japanese to send troops at once;

(c) The landing of available forces from the American and Allied naval vessels to hold possession of Vladivostok and cooperate with the Czecho-Slovaks;

(d) The public announcement by this and Japanese Governments that the purpose of landing troops is to aid Czecho-Slovaks against German and Austrian prisoners, that there is no purpose to interfere with internal affairs of Russia, and that they guarantee not to impair the political or territorial sovereignty of Russia; and

(e) To await further developments before taking further steps.[31]

When the President had finished reading the paper, General March recalled,

... he turned to Secretary Lansing, who agreed and commended the paper, Secretary Daniels also approved, and Secretary Baker nodded. Turning to me and finding me shaking my head vigorously, he said with some asperity, "Why are you shaking your head, General?" and instantly went on, "You are opposed to this because you do not think Japan will limit herself to 7,000 men, and that this decision will further her schemes for territorial aggrandizement." I have never been a "yes-yes" man, so I said in reply, "Just that, and for other military reasons which I have already told you." He replied, "Well, we will have to take that chance." [32]

The President's decision was subsequently restated, in his own words, in an *aide-mémoire* presented on July 17 to the Allied envoys in Washington. This was the only detailed statement Wilson ever made of his rationale for the actions undertaken in Siberia and the northern ports, and its importance for this study is basic. The document is too long for incorporation in the narrative in its entirety; the full text will be found in the Appendix. But it is necessary to take note here of those passages which deal specifically with the Siberian action; for Wilson's decision found expression in all three of these documents—Lansing's memorandum of July 4, the record

[31] *Foreign Relations, 1918, Russia,* Vol. II, *op.cit.,* pp. 262–263.
[32] March, *op.cit.,* p. 126.

of the decisions arrived at in the July 6 meeting, and the President's *aide-mémoire* of July 17. None of the documents suffices, alone, as an adequate basis for judgment.

The *aide-mémoire* included the following passages bearing on the Siberian action:

It is the clear and fixed judgment of the Government of the United States . . . that military intervention [in Russia] would add to the present sad confusion . . . rather than cure it, . . . It can not, therefore, take part in such intervention or sanction it in principle. . . . Military action is admissible in Russia . . . only to help the Czecho-Slovaks consolidate their forces and get into successful cooperation with their Slavic kinsmen and to steady any efforts at self-government or self-defense in which the Russians themselves may be willing to accept assistance. . . . the only legitimate object for which American or Allied troops can be employed, it submits, is to guard military stores which may subsequently be needed by Russian forces and to render such aid as may be acceptable to the Russians in the organization of their own self-defense. For helping the Czecho-Slovaks there is immediate necessity and sufficient justification. Recent developments have made it evident that that is in the interest of what the Russian people themselves desire, and the Government of the United States is glad to contribute the small force at its disposal for that purpose. . . . But it . . . can go no further. . . . It is not in a position, and has no expectation of being in a position, to take part in organized intervention in adequate force from . . . Vladivostok. . . . It . . . will feel at liberty to use the few troops it can spare only for the purposes here stated and shall feel obliged to withdraw those forces, . . . if the plans . . . should develop into others inconsistent with [this] policy. . . .

It hopes to carry out the plans for safeguarding the rear of the Czecho-Slovaks operating from Vladivostok in a way that will place it and keep it in close cooperation with a small military force like its own from Japan, and if necessary from the other Allies, and that will assure it of the cordial accord of all of the Allied powers . . .

It is the hope and purpose of the Government of the United States to take advantage of the earliest opportunity to send to Siberia a commission of merchants, agricultural experts, labor advisers, Red Cross representatives, and agents of the Young Men's Christian Association accustomed to organizing the best methods of spreading useful information and rendering educational help of a modest sort, in order . . . to relieve the immediate economic necessities of the people there. . . . The execution of this plan will follow and will not be permitted to embarrass the military assistance rendered in the rear of the westward-moving forces of the Czecho-Slovaks.

The nature of the President's decision flows plainly from these documents, and needs no extensive recapitulation. Small American and Japanese forces were to enter Siberia to facilitate the effecting of the junction of the Czech forces in Vladivostok with those west of Irkutsk. Later there might be an economic commission. This was all. But there are certain aspects of this decision that deserve special attention.

First, there was the question of the intended British-French relationship to the proposed action. Lansing, in his original memorandum, had suggested that "Allied" as well as American forces might be included, together with the Japanese. This suggestion was dropped entirely in the record of the July 6 decision. It reappeared, but only in a very cursory and off-hand form (". . . a small military force . . . from Japan, and if necessary from the other Allies . . .") in the *aide-mémoire*. As the ensuing discussions with the Allied governments would show, Wilson and Lansing would have been quite content to see the action limited to American and Japanese forces alone, and hoped this would prove to be the case. The July 6 decision represented, in fact, a flat rejection of the Supreme War Council's appeal of July 3 and the selection of a contrary course, in no way responsive to the proposals the Supreme War Council had advanced. In Wilson's concept the British and French would have had, initially at least, no appreciable part to play at all.

Secondly, there was the question of a commission. The suggestion for a commission appeared, albeit in last place and obviously as an afterthought, in Lansing's memorandum. In the July 6 decision, drafted personally by Wilson, it was absent entirely. It reappeared—again at the end and only as something the United States government "hoped . . . at the earliest opportunity" to get on with—in the *aide-mémoire*—only to be, in fact, never implemented at all.[33] What had happened?

---

[33] On August 17, when Wilson visited House at Magnolia, the latter was surprised to find that the President still had no one in mind to head a commission of this sort. In reply to House's query, Wilson said that there was no reason for haste—let the military forces go in first. (House MSS, *op.cit.,* Diary.)

The study of the possibilities for the work of a commission had led, in the final days of June, to sharp rivalries and differences among the various governmental entities involved. The State Department, in particular, had justifiable fears that the arrangements for a commission would be devised in such a way as to extract the entire subject of policy toward Russia from its competence. In the last days of June Lansing had complained bitterly to the President, by phone and by letter, against the obvious efforts of the Commerce Department to seize control of the work of the proposed commission, and against the employment of calculated leaks to the press as a means of drumming up sentiment in favor of such an arrangement.[34] To the President's mind, the idea of a commission must thus have conjured up, by early July, not only the specter of internal political problems in Washington but also the prospect of embarrassing differences among the members of his own Cabinet. One senses that he laid the idea aside primarily for these reasons, but also partly in the feeling that the possibilities for the functioning of a commission would not really be ascertainable until the results of the military expedition were known.

Thirdly, there was the question of the relationship of the proposed action to the internal-political realities of Russia. The *aide-mémoire* went further, in this respect, than the July 6 decision. The latter had mentioned only the negative proposition that there should be no interference in Russian internal affairs. The *aide-mémoire* now spoke, in the case of Siberia, of "steadying" Russian efforts at self-government or self-defense. But neither document mentioned the Soviet government or even hinted that there might be such a thing as Bolshevik power, or indeed any Russian political elements hostile to the American incursion.

Closely connected with this omission were the frequent references, in the July 6 decision and in subsequent discussions of the American plan, to the German and Austrian war prisoners. These, it was to be inferred from the American documents, were the only opponents by whom the Czechs were confronted. The July 6 decision described the purpose of the proposed American-Japanese landing as aid to the Czechoslovaks "against German and Austrian prisoners." The *aide-mémoire* simply ignored the question of the identity of the opponents against whom the Czechoslovaks were supposed to need

[34] National Archives, State Department File 861.00/2219½ B.

assistance. But when, as will be seen below, a paraphrase of a portion of the *aide-mémoire* was published on August 3 as an official communiqué, making known the American decision to the world public, the war-prisoner theme crept back in, and the world was told that the purpose of the military action in Siberia was "to render such protection and help as is possible to the Czecho-Slovaks against the armed Austrian and German prisoners who are attacking them . . ." [35]

It will be readily observed that in this formula the entire complexity of the war prisoner problem, as it had been exposed to the United States government in a number of reports over the course of the first months of 1918, was ignored. Nothing was said to suggest that these prisoners might be fighting in a cause, and under a command, entirely different from—and even hostile to—that of the Central Powers in the European war. Nothing was said to suggest that they were not the only forces opposing the Czechs.

In this way the United States government, disregarding the many reports in its possession that threw doubt on the validity of such a thesis, ultimately sponsored by implication the wildest and most alarmist image of a Siberia threatened with seizure by armed detachments of the Central Powers and saved from this fate, for the moment, only by the heroic Czechs. In this dramatic image there was no room either for the Bolsheviki, who were the real opponents of the Czechs in Siberia, nor the Russian Whites, who were their real allies.

As we have seen, official Washington was fortified in these delusions, at the last minute, by despatches from Admiral Knight; and the Admiral himself was the victim of misimpressions from a number of quarters. The Czechs themselves deliberately propagated these impressions, as did the Japanese, the French, and the Russian Whites. The S-R leaders of the Siberian cooperative movement, whose statements found so sympathetic an ear in Washington, did likewise. Sustenance was lent to these suggestions, furthermore, by the effects of the Czechoslovak uprising. The Czechs, animated by national animosities, took a hostile and in many instances even provocative attitude toward such Hungarian and Austrian prisoners as they found on their path; and there can be little doubt that the latter resorted to armed defense, in some instances, in a spirit of

[35] *Foreign Relations, 1918, Russia,* Vol. ii, *op.cit.,* p. 328.

self-defense. The cutting of the Trans-Siberian by the Czech action had the effect of penning up in eastern Siberia numbers of prisoners then in process of being moved westward for their repatriation. To the national animosities there was thus now added, in the case of the prisoners, the natural desire to get home. Just as the Czechs had initially attempted to fight their way out to the east, many Hungarian and Austrian prisoners were tempted to take up arms in the effort to fight their way out in the opposite direction; it was, of course, the Czechs who stood in their path; and the national animosities already present only exacerbated the resulting clashes. Finally, the Bolshevik military authorities in eastern Siberia, finding themselves now assailed or threatened on all sides—from the west by the Czechs in central and western Siberia, from Manchuria by Semenov, and from Vladivostok by the Japanese and the Czechs accumulated there—and being thus cut off from any source of Russian reinforcement, redoubled their efforts to enlist in their military effort the war prisoners already present in that area, and had some success in the undertaking.

Nevertheless, to picture the opposition by which the Czechs were faced in Siberia as consisting primarily of German and Austrian prisoners, instigated by their governments and fighting in the cause of their governments, was at all times a grievous distortion. (Germans, incidentally, were scarcely present among the prisoners in eastern Siberia.) Reinsch, whose messages seem first to have suggested to Wilson the outlines of the course finally adopted, did not believe in this thesis at all. Neither did Masaryk. Robins, now recently back from Russia, was available for consultation, had anyone wished to consult him. He would have challenged this thesis with utmost sharpness. Altogether, there was a sufficient weight of opinion and information available in Washington to make it quite clear that the thesis implied by the wording of the July 6 decision, and later conveyed to the world public, was at best a highly doubtful one.

If, as was plainly the case, Lansing and the President were partly the victims of misinformation—much of it deliberate—one senses that their vulnerability to this information was enhanced by the difficult position in which they found themselves. For men unwilling to face up to the awkward reality of Soviet power but desperately anxious to find a means of escape from the endless importunities of the Allied governments and of public opinion that they "do something" about Russia, the thesis that the Czechs, an Allied force, found themselves opposed in Siberia by the armed forces of the German and Austrian governments came as the perfect answer to all perplexities. It was human—if not entirely justifiable—that they should have allowed themselves to be convinced of the validity of this thesis, and should have sponsored it before the world.

A no less glaring ambiguity prevailed with regard to the purpose of the Czechoslovak action which the Americans and Japanese, in Wilson's view, were to support. Lansing's memorandum spoke of assisting the Czechs in policing the railroad and disarming and dispersing the German and Austrian prisoners. The July 6 decision spoke of assisting the Czechs at Vladivostok to form "a junction with their compatriots in western Siberia" and of guarding "the line of communication of the Czecho-Slovaks proceeding toward Irkutsk." The *aide-mémoire* spoke of helping the Czechoslovaks to "consolidate their forces and get into successful cooperation with their Slavic kinsmen," and of "safeguarding the rear of the Czecho-Slovaks operating from Vladivostok."

But to what end were the Czech forces to be consolidated? Was it to enable them to make their way to France? Or was it to enable them to participate in a Russian civil war (which, incidentally, at the time of Wilson's decision, they were already enthusiastically doing)?

Nothing in the official American documents throws any light on this question. Admiral Knight was instructed on July 6 by the Secretary of the Navy, who attended the White House conference that same day, that the American government wished Vladivostok to be kept open "as a base for the safety of [the] Czechs and as a means of egress for them *should the necessity arise.*" [36]—a phraseology which only heightens the ambiguity.

That subordinate officials knew of the plan for the Czechs to concentrate on the overthrow of the Bolsheviki and sympathized with it, seems beyond question. But what did Wilson know, and what did he have in mind? We must recall (see above, p. 388) that it was in Reinsch's suggestion about the Czechs being left in Siberia to "control" the region against the Germans that the President first thought he "saw the shadow of a plan." But was it his intention

[36] *Ibid.*, p. 263. Italics are mine.

that the Czechs should serve as a spearhead for action against the Bolsheviki?

The most likely answer to this question is that both Lansing and the President secretly hoped that the arrival of American and Japanese forces would elicit so powerful and friendly a reaction among the population that a pro-Allied political authority would be instituted throughout Siberia by spontaneous, democratic action. This might, in turn, lead to the prevalence of a new pro-Allied spirit in Russia proper, which in turn would either come to permeate the policies of the Bolsheviki or cause them to yield to other political forces more responsive to the political will. With all this, of course, the American forces would have had, under Wilson's plan, no direct connection. Their only ostensible purpose would have been to help their Czech allies and to bring friendly aid to any sincere Russian efforts at self-government. They would thus not be vulnerable to the charge of having intervened in Russian affairs. The decision on the ultimate disposition of the Czechs—whether evacuation to the western front or employment in European Russia on a reconstituted eastern front—could be left for later decision in the light of developments.

❖

It would be a mistake to conclude that in making the decision of July 6 Wilson thought that he had found the perfect or final solution to this problem. This was a troubled decision on a problem which had baffled him up to this time and would continue to baffle him in the future.

It is an interesting fact that Wilson took his decision without consulting House. From the moment in late April when House had been won over to an acceptance of the British view of that time, he occasionally wrote to the President about Russian matters but there seems to be no record of the President having consulted him further on this painful subject. Plainly, Russia was, in the President's mind, a subject of the utmost delicacy, and connected in some deep and curious way with his own *amour propre*.

CHAPTER XVIII

THE DESPATCH OF AMERICAN FORCES

TO RUSSIA

... Mr. Wilson ... should be judged by what he was and did prior to August 4th, 1918, the date of the paper justifying the attack on Russia. That was the first of his acts which was unlike him; and I am sure the beginning of the sad end.—*Justice Louis D. Brandeis, May 11, 1924, to the President of the University of Virginia, Edwin A. Alderman*

THE story of the actual course of the Allied intervention in Siberia and North Russia lies beyond the scope of this volume. For this reason it is not the intention here to follow in detail the tangled progress of Allied diplomacy in the Russian question through the remainder of the summer of 1918. But it does become necessary, if the events leading to the final withdrawal of the American official colony from Soviet-held territory are to be understood (and it is to this termination that the present volume is pressing), to note a few of the events that intervened, on the Allied side, between the time of Wilson's decision of July 6 and the actual landing of the American forces in the two theaters of action.

SIBERIA

The French and British governments were given no forewarning of the decision of July 6, and—by the same token—no opportunity to comment on it. Since it came just in the wake of the Supreme War Council's action on the same question—at a moment, in fact, when the Council's appeal was lying fresh on the President's desk—this was a flagrant discourtesy. The participants in the White House meeting on Saturday, July 6, seem not even to have considered the question as to how and when the western Allied governments should be informed—to say nothing of the question as to whether any answer, and if so what, should be made to the War Council's appeal.

It *was* agreed, however, that the Japanese would have to be consulted at once. The Japanese Ambassador, Ishii, was accordingly summoned to appear at Lansing's office early Monday morning.

Ishii took note—with intense interest and with a cautious amiability—of Lansing's description of the American proposal. He undertook, of course, to submit it to his government without delay. He expressed personal sympathy for the American view. For a few moments the two men permitted their minds to wander and to dwell on the roseate possibilities for the reaction of Russian public opinion to the proposed American-Japanese action. Ishii's mind must also be supposed to have been dwelling most intently on the effects which this proposal would have on the interests and ambitions of the various elements that made up his own government; but he was far too tactful a man to show this. When he departed, the Secretary of State was still quite comfortable in his mind about the Japanese reception of the proposal.

At 2:00 p.m. that day (July 8), the British Ambassador called on the President, apparently in another matter. Wilson appears to have told him, on this occasion, nothing whatsoever of the decision that had been taken. But later that afternoon it dawned on Lansing that the Japanese would immediately tell the other Allied governments about the American approach and that great resentment would ensue if, in the meantime, they had heard nothing directly from Washington. He at once exposed these reflections in a note to the President [1] and obtained the latter's approval to his apprising the British, French, and Italian envoys, in strictest confidence, of what had been decided. This was done the following morning (Tuesday, July 9), in three separate interviews at the Department of State. [2] No record of these interviews is available. There is reason to believe that the reaction of Lord Reading, in particular, was one of outraged astonishment, partly over the manner in which the decision had been taken, partly because of Lansing's studied ambiguity about the part the western Allies were to take in the proposed action.

In early afternoon there was a Cabinet meeting. Remaining after the others had left, Lansing told the President of Reading's reaction. Both men, evidently, were irritated by it. (Wartime strain and weariness was, by this time, breeding its characteristic asperities.

[1] *Foreign Relations, The Lansing Papers*, Vol. II, *op.cit.*, pp. 372–373.
[2] Lansing MSS, *op.cit.*, Desk Diary.

Wilson and his Secretary of State had both now worked themselves into a high state of suspicion of British motives and resentment of British pressures in the Siberian problem.) Not long after Lansing had returned to his desk at the State Department the three Allied envoys (the other two plainly marshalled by Reading for this purpose) appeared in a body, demanding to know

> whether the Allied Governments were not to take part in the initial landing of troops at Vladivostok or whether it was our [i.e. the American] purpose to confine the enterprise to Japanese and American troops.

Lansing replied that he had never discussed the matter with the President and could see no object in doing so until Japanese approval had been obtained, at which time the United States government would be glad to consult with the western Allies. Sharp exchanges ensued. Lansing charged that in failing to consult the Allies the Americans were only doing what had been done to themselves on many occasions. Reading found this statement offensive; and he insisted that the Allies ought to participate in the initial landing. To this Lansing replied

> . . . that this seemed to me rather a matter of national pride and sentiment than a practical question; that I could not understand why this subject should be raised and that it showed to me the wisdom of the course which we had taken in not consulting all the Allied Governments before we had acted as apparently there would have been delay in discussing the details . . . [3]

It is impossible to note this passage without drawing attention to the extraordinary workings of the American mind in matters of inter-Allied relations. For six months the Allied governments had pleaded with the United States government to join them in some action relating to Siberia. Now Washington, having made its own decision without consulting them, was determined to act with utmost precipitation. Two days was even too short a time; and the need for haste was cited as justification for not consulting the Allies at all. But beyond that, one cannot fail to note Lansing's contemptuous rejection of the British view as a "sentimental" one. Five days before, in drawing up his own memorandum for the President on the Siberian question, Lansing had justified the entire change of

[3] *Foreign Relations, 1918, Russia,* Vol. II, *op.cit.,* pp. 269-270.

American policy by the proposition that the seizure of Vladivostok by the Czechs "had materially changed the situation by introducing a *sentimental* element into the question of our duty."[4] The July 6 decision had cited "sentimental grounds" as dictating the American action. Now Lansing complained precisely that Reading's attitude was a matter of sentiment. More than once, in this acrimonious conversation, he returned to this charge. "I was not disposed," he said,

to consider the sentimental phase but only the expedient side of the question. . . . I thought expediency should control and that if expedience was opposed to British participation that, to my mind, ended it, . . .

Sentiment, when it came to determining American actions; expedience, when it came to judging the behavior of America's Allies —this is the principle that appears to flow from Lansing's reactions on this occasion.

Lord Reading was, for obvious reasons, unappeased by Lansing's position. With difficulty he was restrained, the following day, from telegraphing to his government a stinging report on the matter which, the President considered, would have made a good deal of trouble.[5] Even without this report, the irritation in London was intense. Without delay, on the 10th, the British government matched the American step by taking unilateral action of its own: ordering the British garrison battalion at Hong Kong to proceed at once to Vladivostok, and following this shortly by appointing a high-powered British Military Mission to Siberia, under the command of General Alfred W. F. Knox, former head of the British Military Mission in European Russia. To this there was soon added the appointment of Sir Charles Eliot as High Commissioner. Thus the effect of Washington's unilateral action was not to keep the British out of Siberia but to propel them at once into that complicated situation—and this *without* any coordination of policy as between the two governments.

❖

While the American step remained for some days an official secret, the repercussions of it were not long in making themselves felt in

---

[4] See above, p. 395 (italics added).
[5] Lansing MSS, *op.cit.,* Desk Diary, July 10.

the Far East. The Czech seizure of Vladivostok had already exerted on the explosive Far Eastern situation an effect comparable to the removal of the pin from a hand grenade. Together, the two actions —that of the Czechs and that of Wilson—put into motion every single element participating in the Far Eastern situation, and of these there were many. If the situation had been complicated before these happenings, this was nothing compared to what now ensued. Derber and his associates, encouraged by the suppression of the Vladivostok Bolsheviki, at once attempted to establish themselves in Vladivostok as the "provisional government of autonomous Siberia." Horvat, equally convinced that the moment had come, left Harbin in the first days of July for Vladivostok, in order to set up an all-Russian government there. The Vladivostok Czechs, meanwhile, having received an initial donation of Japanese arms, launched an offensive northward along the Amur Railroad, encountering the first serious resistance in the neighborhood of Nikolsk (Voroshilov), some sixty miles along the line. Horvat and his entourage, endeavoring to get to Vladivostok, ran up against the advancing Czechs and were held for some time at the town of Grodekovo, just inside the Siberian border. There he was also checked by an appeal from the French, British, and Japanese Ministers in Peking, insisting that he desist from his political purpose, as apt to embarrass the Czechs.

Horvat's departure, together with a Czech request to be permitted to move Czech units across the Chinese Eastern, threw the delicate situation in Manchuria wide open. The Chinese professed to see in Horvat's departure an abandonment by Russia of her rights in the Chinese Eastern Railway zone and in northern Manchuria generally. They vowed that Horvat would not be permitted to return, and mounted such stumbling efforts as they could to take the territory under their own control. The Japanese played with both Horvat and the Chinese like a cat with mice.

The Czech seizure of Vladivostok and the American proposal had thrown Tokyo, naturally enough, into a veritable agony of decision. The latent differences of opinion within the Cabinet and among influential circles with regard to Japan's policy in Manchuria and Siberia were at once brought to a state of crisis. The General Staff, supported by powerful elements within the Cabinet and elsewhere, favored exploitation of the situation as an opportunity for occupation of northern Manchuria, acquisition of the Chinese Eastern

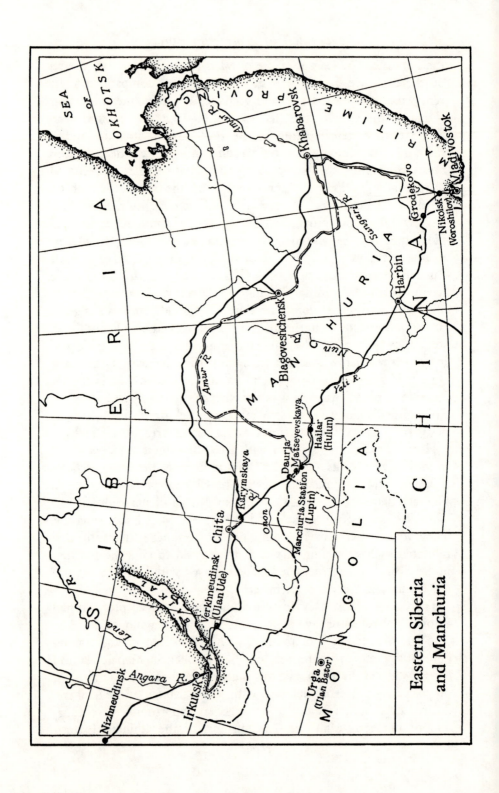

Eastern Siberia
and Manchuria

Railway, and establishment of a dominant Japanese position in eastern Siberia. They were successful, generally, in establishing this as the view of the government as a whole. But how, then, to handle the American request, full of opportunity but also full of embarrassment? To this problem, the General Staff paid little attention. It made the moves; the Foreign Office, to the genuine distress of moderate statesmen such as Goto and Ishii, was left to handle the problem of answering Washington.

While the debate in Tokyo progressed, the Japanese angled in Washington to find out what, in the American view, was to be done about the over-all command of the proposed joint expedition. This, too, had not been thought about in the deliberations of July 6. Queried by Polk, the President decided that the Japanese should have the supreme command. They were so informed by Polk on July 16.[6] There is no evidence that anyone had thought to clear this decision with the War Department.

By this time, hints and rumors of the American proposal had begun to leak, particularly in the Japanese newspapers. It was presumably to counter inaccurate reports of this nature that the President now decided, although the Japanese had not yet replied, to make formal notification to the Allied governments (not to the public) of the American position. The result was the *aide-mémoire* of July 17, handed to the Allied embassies in Washington on that day. Wilson drafted it alone, on his own typewriter. It stands as just about the only evidence of the thoughts with which he viewed the whole problem at that time. He discussed it, apparently, with no one. He had been obliged, he wrote to Charles R. Crane a few days later, "to do some very lonely thinking about the Russian business, . . ."[7] Whatever the degree of obligation, the thinking was certainly lonely. If the President took counsel with anyone else on Russian matters at this juncture, the record does not show it. American officialdom was left no less dependent than the foreign governments on the *aide-mémoire* for its knowledge of Wilson's policy.

On July 24 the Japanese reply was finally made. Lansing was by this time on vacation. Ishii told the Acting Secretary, Frank Polk, that the Japanese government could not limit its force to the sug-

[6] Unterberger, *op.cit.*, p. 76, cites Polk's confidential diary (Polk MSS, *op.cit.*) to this effect.
[7] Baker, Vol. VIII, *op.cit.*, p. 304.

gested 7,000. They would send a division—normally about 12,000 men—and they would reserve the right to send more, if the situation so required. The Ambassador produced the text of a unilateral declaration which the Japanese government proposed to make by way of explanation for its action. It was, from Washington's standpoint, a disturbing document. It named no limit to the force Japan would send. It hinted that more might be sent later—and not just to Vladivostok. It contained a cryptic reference to Japan's "special position"—presumably in Siberia. Worst of all, it expressed Japan's anxiety "to act in harmony with the Allies," by which were meant the British and French.[8]

The Japanese reply came as a distinct shock to the President. It was almost as unresponsive to the American initiative as Wilson's own reaction had been to the proposals of the Allies. At first the President was inclined to withdraw from the entire venture, and he authorized Polk to say so to Ishii.[9] But in the further discussions that ensued, both between Polk and Ishii and between Ambassador Morris and the Japanese Foreign Minister, a break was somehow avoided. The American side contrived to swallow the 12,000 figure; and the question of the despatch of further forces was left enshrouded in a cloud of ambiguity which suited Japanese purposes excellently. In return for this, the Japanese were asked to make modifications in the wording of their proposed declaration.

The Japanese government was understood in Washington to be considering this matter, and Polk and the President were still awaiting a reply on this point when suddenly, in the night from August 1 to 2, the declaration was made public by the Japanese government with no forewarning to Washington at all. Ishii brought a copy of it, as finally issued, to Polk on the morning of August 2. It did indeed contain two modifications that were in accord with the American view; but the fact of its unilateral issuance, without prior notification, was significant.

---

[8] *Foreign Relations, 1918, Russia,* Vol. ii, *op.cit.,* pp. 301–302 and 324–325. The text of this declaration was later modified, before its issuance, in response to American pressure. But it revealed quite clearly what was in the Japanese mind; and Washington had no reason to allow itself to be reassured as to Japanese motives by a mere modification in the wording of a public statement.

[9] Unterberger, *op.cit.,* p. 82, cites the diary of Lansing's secretary Gordon Auchincloss to this effect.

The President stopped in that day, on his way from his early morning golf, to see Polk. Ishii had apparently already been there. The Japanese action had made it clear that a final American decision could no longer be postponed. Either the United States government must withdraw or it must at once take positive action. In either case, it must make public announcement of its position immediately. (Nothing had yet been said to the public about the July 6 decision or the approach to the Japanese.)

The decision at this point does not seem to have been a difficult one or to have caused the President any particular anguish. His mind was evidently already made up. He was prepared to go through with the plan, regardless of the Japanese reaction. He could not now withdraw, particularly after circulation of the *aide-mémoire,* without appearing to abandon the Czechs and without making open confession to the world of a sensational conflict of policy as between the Americans and the Japanese. Whether or not he was fully aware of it, the Japanese had him cornered.

From Polk's office Wilson strolled down the cool, dark corridors of the State, War, and Navy Building to that of the Secretary of War. The upshot of the discussion there was, one must assume, the designation of Major General William S. Graves to command the American Expeditionary Force to Siberia and the issuance of the initial orders looking to the despatch of that force.

General Graves has related in his own memoirs how this order was delivered to him:[10] how, having formerly been Secretary of the General Staff, he had only recently been assigned to command the 8th Division at Camp Fremont, Palo Alto, California; how he had proceeded to this new post earlier in July; how, on the afternoon of August 2, he had received a telegram directing him to proceed at once to Kansas City, go to the Baltimore Hotel, and ask for the Secretary of War; how he had done all this, and how the Secretary of War, who had very little time, had told him of his new designation, had thrust into his hands a copy of the *aide-mémoire* of July 17, and had then said to him:

This contains the policy of the United States in Russia which you are to follow. Watch your step; you will be walking on eggs loaded with dynamite. God bless you and good-bye.

[10] Graves, *op.cit.,* pp. 1-5.

This order was substantially the only political guidance General Graves was ever to receive in the promulgation of his intensely delicate and complicated mission. That it was, even at the time it was presented to him, utterly inadequate to its purpose, that it was still further out of date by the time he arrived in Siberia, and that within two months after his arrival it had lost all conceivable relevance, seems never to have occurred to him. He accepted it with that unquestioning and religious reverence which sterling soldiers normally bear for directives from supreme authority. For one and a half years he would cling to the letter of it with a stubbornness that would drive his Allied colleagues and associates to despair; and he would never cease to regard with baleful suspicion and hostility anyone who professed to have *other* orders or anyone who had the temerity to question the relevance and wisdom of his own.[11]

On the same day that General Graves received these orders, August 3, the President issued to the press a communiqué which represented, in effect, a paraphrase of the key portions of the *aide-mémoire*. On this same day, Japanese and British forces arrived in Vladivostok and began to go ashore. Also on this day, August 3, in addition to giving General Graves his orders, the War Department directed the Commanding General in the Philippines to despatch to Vladivostok, by first available transport, the 27th and 31st Infantry Regiments, stationed there, one field hospital, one ambulance company, and Company "D" 53rd Telegraph Battalion. Graves himself was told to proceed from San Francisco direct to Vladivostok, taking with him 5,000 selected men from the 8th Division at Camp Fremont.

The 27th Infantry, commanded by Colonel Henry D. Styer, arrived in Vladivostok on August 16; the 31st Infantry, a few days later. General Graves, with his men, reached Vladivostok on September 1, travelling in the old transport *Thomas* (now a familiar sight in the Golden Horn). He was amazed to discover, on arrival, that there was no orderly customs and port control. In the course of the ensuing months he was destined to discover things stranger than this.

We shall follow no further the adventures of General Graves in

[11] In a telegram to Polk of July 31, Lansing, then on vacation, warned against Graves's appointment as commander of the Siberian expedition. He had heard, he said, that Graves "has not the tact and diplomacy . . . to deal with so delicate a situation where the Commanding Officer requires other than military ability." (Polk MSS, *op.cit.*) Plainly, no heed was paid to this warning.

the wonderland to which he had now been admitted; but we will do well, in noting his arrival there, to consider some of the elements of the situation which he found before him, and to compare them with the terms of the *aide-mémoire,* which still constituted his basic instruction and his sole policy guidance.

The Japanese, having once embarked on what amounted to a unilateral policy, now turned out to have in Siberia, instead of 7,000 or even 12,000, some 72,000 troops—ten times the number originally envisaged by the President and six times the number which he had later shown himself willing to consider. In addition, the Japanese had despatched an entire division of some 12,000 men to the Chinese Eastern Railway zone, where, by this time, they had acquired complete control, in part through direct action by their own forces and in part by exploitation of the helpless position of the Chinese government.

In eastern Siberia, Bolshevik resistance had by this time been practically destroyed, through the combined efforts of the Japanese and the Czechs, in the entire area from Vladivostok to Irkutsk. The junction between the eastern and central bodies of Czechs, which Graves had been supposed to support with his force, had actually been achieved—as it so happened—on the day prior to his arrival in Vladivostok, when the two Czech forces met in the neighborhood of Chita. This rendered immaterial the central feature of Graves's orders, so far as the Czechs were concerned. Meanwhile, the vague plans for drumming up shipping with which to evacuate the Czechs from Siberia, as formed at the Supreme War Council meeting in early June (see above, p. 311), had been cancelled at British initiative (apparently without remonstrance from the American side) on July 11, in view of the inauguration of the westward action of the Vladivostok Czechs.[12] There was now no plan whatsoever for the removal of the Czechoslovak forces from Siberia; no shipping of any sort had been set aside for this purpose.

Not only had the original thought of evacuating the Czechs to France now been effectively dropped, but the main body of the Czechs, at the western end of the Trans-Siberian, were now engaged in activities of a wholly different nature, which found no recognition

---

[12] Notification of this intention was made to the State Department on July 12. See *Foreign Relations, 1918, Russia,* Vol. II, *op.cit.,* p. 275 (paraphrase of Balfour's telegram of July 11).

whatsoever in Graves's orders. In alliance with White Russian forces, these Czechs had thrown themselves with vigor and with initial enthusiasm into the struggle against the Bolsheviki in the Urals-Volga area, in the attempt to implement the scheme so hopefully cultivated in French and British circles, of a junction, through Yaroslavl and Vologda, with Allied forces operating from Archangel. They had succeeded, during the months of July and August, in taking Kazan and Ekaterinburg. They were now confidently awaiting the Allied help that was never to come. But actually, the tide was already turning against them. Trotsky's vigorous and determined effort to whip up a real Red Army was beginning to bear unexpectedly rapid fruit in the accumulation of a serious Soviet force in the Volga area. A German-Soviet agreement, concluded on August 27th, had freed still more of the Soviet units for operations against the Czechs. By the time of Graves's arrival the Czechs, together with their White Russian allies, had not only reached the limit of their punch in that area but had actually over-extended themselves in relation to the growing strength of their opponents. They were thus not only engaged in a civil war, for which the Wilsonian plan had made no provision at all, but their effort was doomed to be, from this time on, increasingly an unsuccessful one. In these circumstances, the failure of the Allies to send any appreciable aid was bound to produce great bitterness. And this feeling was bound to be directed particularly toward the Americans who were known to have entered Siberia in some force. Had the American government not made, after all, a particular show of its friendship for the Czech cause?

As for the Russian efforts at self-government which General Graves was directed to "steady," these were difficult—to put it mildly —to discover. Approximately twenty-four different governments or political authorities now functioned on the territory that had constituted the pre-war Russian Empire. Some of these attempted to draw a claim to legitimacy from the elections to the Constituent Assembly in the preceding November; but in most instances, the claim of popular sanction was tenuous. Most of these authorities were locked in a desperate civil struggle against the Bolsheviki—a struggle which had now become deadly and embittered in the extreme, and marked on every hand by cruelties and bestialities sickening to recount. In these circumstances there was little room for efforts at self-government. The anti-Bolshevik factions were grievously dis-united among themselves; and those with which Graves had to deal in Siberia had, it must be confessed, very little connection indeed with democracy or self-government. Ironically enough, the only local election that seems to have taken place in Siberia in the summer of 1918 was one held in Vladivostok itself at the end of July, under the benevolent aegis of the Czechs and the Allied marines. To every-one's horror, it yielded an unquestionable Bolshevik majority. This, in turn, was the ironic consequence of two revealing circumstances, for both of which the Allies were responsible: on the one hand, due to local Allied influence in previous months the Bolsheviki had had no opportunity to alienate the populace to the same extent as else-where by their usual extremities and cruelties; on the other hand, the activities in that locality of the Derber and Horvat factions, whom the Allies had obligingly admitted to the scene, had made an ex-tremely unfortunate impression and had caused general disillusion-ment with the anti-Bolshevik cause. In the prevailing circumstances, no one dreamed of permitting the Vladivostok Bolsheviki to reap the fruits of their electoral victory by controlling the city; this would, obviously, have created a wholly impossible situation. Thus the only instance in which General Graves might conceivably have acted to "steady any efforts at self-government" was precisely one in which any such action would have been completely contrary to the other main requirement of his orders: the support of the Czechoslovaks.

MURMANSK AND ARCHANGEL

We have seen (p. 366) that from the latter part of May British plans with respect to the northern ports had been based on a scheme which envisaged (1) the holding of the Murmansk base and the expansion of operations there as a means of pinning down the Ger-man army in Finland, and (2) the establishment of a further base at Archangel, where Czechs and local Russian forces were to be trained and from which point an operation would be launched to effect a juncture with the Czech and other Allied forces in Siberia. This remained, undeviatingly, the basis of British plans throughout the summer of 1918. It found reflection in all British statements, and notably in the Supreme War Council paper of July 2, which spoke of an Allied occupation in Murmansk and Archangel "in order to retain the bridgeheads into Russia from the north from which forces can eventually advance rapidly to the center of Russia." Despite the fact that the United States government never agreed in any way to such a scheme, measures to implement it were put in hand, from the British and French side, as early as mid-May, and were systematically pursued, with such small and inadequate forces as were available, from that time on. It became the basis of a formal request from General Poole to the Czech command, to the effect that the Czechs should move westward with a view to seizing Perm (the present Molotov) and Vyatka (Kirov) and effecting a junction with the Allied forces advancing from Archangel.[13] This scheme thus became the strategic basis of the entire Allied effort in the north.

We have also seen that in mid-July President Wilson—acting reluctantly, against his own better judgment and that of his military advisers, and only with a view to conciliating the European Allies—agreed to yield to the judgment of the Supreme Command (i.e., Foch)

. . . in the matter of establishing a small force at Murmansk, to guard the military stores at Kola, and to make it safe for Russian forces to come together in organized bodies in the north.

He was not prepared to go beyond this. In particular, he was not prepared to have American forces "take part in organized intervention in adequate force from Murmansk and Archangel." He warned that these forces would be withdrawn if

. . . the plans in whose execution it is now intended that they should cooperate should develop into others inconsistent with the policy to which the Government of the United States feels constrained to restrict itself.

This language was odd and ambiguous, woefully inadequate as a description of military purpose. Mention was made, in the positive sense, only of Murmansk; it was left unclear whether the President intended that American forces should participate in any operations whatsoever at Archangel.

The reference to guarding military stores at Kola was, and remains, baffling. Kola was an unimportant village at the head of the

[13] The transmission of this request, as well as the fact of the Czech effort to comply with it, is confirmed by a message from Harris, then at Novo-Nikolayevsk, to the American Legation at Peking of August 16, 1918, to be found in the Harris MSS, *op.cit.* The Czech effort to meet this request was probably the main cause of the deterioration of their military position, in the late summer of 1918, in the Urals and western Siberian area.

Murmansk inlet; but the term was sometimes used to denote the Murmansk region as a whole. There was no accumulation of military stores there; where the President had gotten the idea that there *was* one is a complete mystery. The only appreciable accumulation of such stores had been at Archangel, three or four hundred miles distant. These had, by this time, been hauled off to the interior by the aroused Bolsheviki. In this respect, Wilson's statement can stand as an example of the danger of issuing such statements, as he did in this instance, without staff assistance of any sort.

As for "making it safe for Russian forces to come together in the north," this phrase was founded on the characteristic Wilsonian ambiguity about the reality of Soviet power. It was, at that time, quite safe for *anti-Bolshevik* Russian forces to come together at Murmansk, now held by anti-Bolshevik forces. It was equally safe for *communist* Russian forces to come together at Archangel, where the Bolsheviki were in full control. It was absurd to suggest that there could be any one place in which it would be safe for *both* to attempt to come together. If one spoke of befriending the Russians, then the question—as Lenin had so aptly stated it—was only: what Russians? But for the Allies to make any answer to this question meant precisely to intervene in Russian domestic affairs, which Wilson was determined, for his part, not to do.

The wording of the *aide-mémoire* of July 17 made plain only one thing: the United States did *not* believe in or agree with the British plans for penetration into the Russian interior from Archangel or Murmansk, and was *not* prepared to see American forces used in the implementation of such schemes. Guard duty at Murmansk?— yes; guard duty at Archangel?—possibly, though not specifically so stated; participation in expeditions into the interior?—definitely no. This was the President's formula of mid-July 1918, so far as the American forces were concerned.

Again—as in the case of Siberia—this was, let us note, a unilateral dictum, not a negotiated compromise. At no time did any responsible American official, knowing the President's mind and bearing his authority, attempt to talk out with responsible British officials the differences here involved or to adjust the wording of the statement to meet Allied views. No forewarning was given to the British of the President's decision; they had, accordingly, no opportunity to comment on it, to raise questions about it, to plead for modifications in its wording. They were to have full command (this was never questioned) over the American forces involved; but they had no voice in defining the purposes to which the forces in question were to be put. The President's formula was put to them not in privacy but in a round-robin communication circulated to all the Allied governments, and on a take-it-or-leave-it basis: if you want to use American forces in the north, here is what you may use them for. The British were left with the choice of accepting the forces on these terms, hoping that somehow things would work out for the best, or suspending an operation they had already inaugurated and starting the argument all over again, from the beginning, with the elusive and unapproachable President.

No effort appears to have been made to see that the limitations defined in the American *aide-mémoire* were ever subsequently discussed with the British at the military level, with a view to their being taken into account by the British commanders in their further dispositions. Nothing in the conduct or statements of the British commanders, at the time or subsequently (and at least two of them wrote detailed memoirs of the period), suggests that they had any clear understanding of the American government's position or that they permitted themselves to be appreciably restricted in the use they made of American units by what little they thought they knew of it.[14] Nor does any effort even appear to have been made to effect any modification in the orders of Captain Bierer of the *Olympia* who, as we have seen, was operating entirely under British command and whose marines were already ashore at Murmansk.

[14] General Maynard reveals in his memoirs, *op.cit.,* a lack of understanding for the American position which is little short of fantastic, and which led him into highly unfair judgments of the American performance.

Field Marshal Lord Ironside, who was British Commander at Archangel from the end of September, relates in his memoirs (*Archangel 1918–1919,* Constable, London, 1953, pp. 33–34) how he attempted without success in October 1918 to induce Lt. Col. George E. Stewart, ranking officer of the American contingent, to accept full command over one of the two "fronts" that had been formed, against the Bolsheviki, in the area south of Archangel. This would have been an international command, embracing not only American units but those of other nationalities as well. Stewart based his refusal to accept on the grounds that it would exceed his instructions. This did not alter the fact that his men were already being employed in combat deep in the interior, under British command, and would continue to be so employed in future. Ironside suspected, in view of this reply, that Stewart had secret instructions from the United States government, which he was unwilling to divulge. It is more probable that Stewart was simply bewildered by the conflict between the President's words and the uses to which the American units were now being put.

By failing, in this way, to follow through on the implementation of his own decision, the President contrived to get the worst of all possible worlds: he irritated the British and French with his *obiter dicta* and drew onto himself, ultimately, the blame for the failure of the entire venture (on the grounds that the United States contribution had been too little and too late); he did *not* prevent the United States units from being used for precisely the purposes for which he said they should not be used; nor did he withdraw them, as he said he would, when they were thus used; yet he did prevent them from having any proper understanding of the purposes for which they *were* being used; finally, he rendered the United States vulnerable to the charge, which Soviet propagandists have never ceased to exploit, of interfering by armed force in Soviet domestic affairs.

One cannot refrain from noting, in this sad set of circumstances, the example of one of Wilson's signal weaknesses as a wartime statesman. This was his evident belief that words, on his part, were enough, even in matters of inter-Allied collaboration; that he had merely to give the general political line on a given question and things would then flow automatically, without further attention on his part, from what he had said. He seems to have had no idea of the continuing process of persuasion, persistence, vigilance, and follow-up that would have been necessary, at this stage of the war, to press decisions through the vast, cumbersome ramifications of the Allied machinery for making war and for coordinating the various national efforts.

The British, on the other hand, were ill-advised to accept the services of the American battalions when they had no intention of using them in accordance with the President's conditions. One gains the impression that the Americans were regarded by many of the British, throughout this episode, not as partners with whom a real and intimate understanding was to be sought, but rather as stupid children, to be "gotten around" in one way or another—to be wheedled into doing things they were not expected either to desire or to understand. What was important, in the view of this portion of British officialdom, was not whether the Americans really understood what they were doing; what was important was that they should be coaxed and cajoled into doing these things, whether they understood them or not. Individual Americans, including the President, may have given provocation for such an approach; and in some instances (Archangel was one of them) it may be said to have been successful, in that the main British desideratum—the despatch of the forces—was achieved. But it was nevertheless unwise. Americans were not always as insensitive to this approach as they might appear to be; and this accounted for many of the negative reactions which the British encountered among them. A policy founded on a better understanding of the American character would have insisted on the most detailed and explicit understanding and agreement on the American side with respect to any operation in which Americans were to take part, and would have demanded, as well as accorded, greatest punctiliousness in the observance of it. In ninety-nine cases out of a hundred, this demand would have been met.

❖

Let us now note what happened in the Russian North, in the wake of the President's decisions.

The result of Maynard's actions in the final days of June was, as we have seen, to confine the Bolshevik forces to the area below Kem, some three hundred miles south of Murmansk. This assured to the British both naval (from the White Sea) and military control of the approaches to Murmansk, and thus stabilized the military situation in that area. The action was immediately followed, as recounted above, by a regularization of the relationship between the Allies and the local Russian authority, in the form of the agreement of July 6.

With the Murmansk situation thus taken care of, General Poole's attention now turned to Archangel. Here, the extremely late endurance of heavy ice in the neck of the White Sea (into early July) would have made impossible any earlier action, even had the forces been available. But in early July the ice was finally breaking up, and naval access to the port was now technically possible.

With the break between Murmansk and Moscow, the attitude toward the Allies of the Bolshevik authorities in Archangel, headed by the fiery military commissar, M. S. Kedrov (page 18), became hostile and suspicious in the extreme. By the latter part of June the Archangel Bolsheviki were already objecting strenuously to the continued presence there of the British naval icebreaker and issuing warnings that any attempt by any further Allied naval vessel to enter the port would be regarded as a hostile act and met with

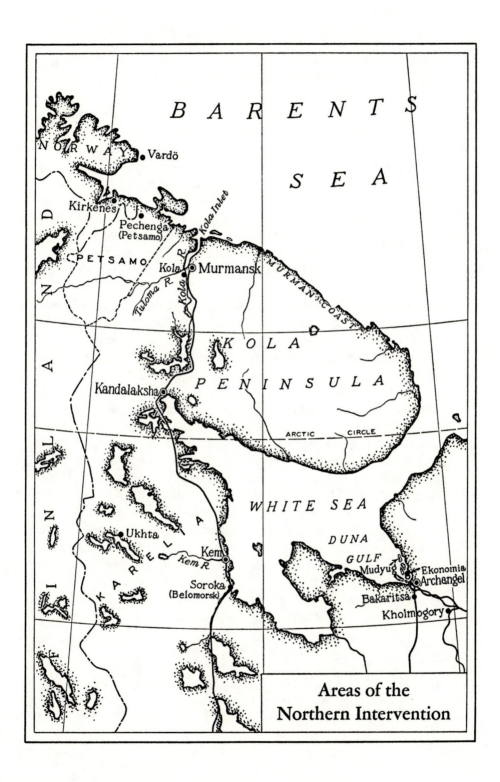

Areas of the
Northern Intervention

armed action. In mid-July the British were compelled to withdraw the icebreaker, the Archangel Soviet having refused to take responsibility any longer for its safety.[15]

Lacking the strength for a full-fledged invasion, the British set about with vigor and urgency, through secret agents, to stimulate an uprising by the anti-communist forces in Archangel, to be coordinated with the arrival of an Allied landing force. Throughout the last two weeks of July, these efforts proceeded with great intensity. The fact that they were taking place remained no great secret from the Soviet authorities, although they seem not to have uncovered the exact channels through which the conspiracy was developed.[16] This was, it will be recalled, the period immediately following delivery to the Allied governments of the President's *aide-mémoire* of July 17.

The first of the tiny Allied contingents other than British, sent pursuant to the Supreme War Council decision of early June, arrived at Murmansk on July 26. It was a French colonial infantry battalion, numbering only a few hundred men. It was enough, however, together with the ripening of the political preparations, to permit the launching of the Allied action. On the afternoon and evening of July 31 a force of some 1,500 men, selected from the various national units at Murmansk, sailed from that port for Archangel, in company with a small naval task force. General Poole and his staff were accommodated in the naval yacht *Salvator*. The force included the airplane carrier *Nairana* (which served as flagship for Admiral Kemp), the light cruiser *Attentive*, two submarine chasers and six armed trawlers, all British; likewise the French heavy cruiser *Amiral Aube* (which had previously attempted without success to get through the ice to Archangel), two British transports, and a number of smaller Russian vessels, drawn from the Murmansk base.

On the morning of August 1, the Allied flotilla approached the fortified island of Mudyug, off the delta of the Duna River, and

[15] See Cole's messages of June 21 and July 15, *Foreign Relations, 1918, Russia*, Vol. II, *op.cit.*, pp. 486–487 and 497.

[16] On July 20, the Soviet authorities even captured a small British reconnaissance detachment, all naval personnel, which had attempted to land on the shore of the White Sea near Archangel. (*Ibid.*, pp. 500–502.) With difficulty they were persuaded by the Allied representatives in Archangel to refrain from executing the captured men. Five of the British sailors were sent to Moscow and imprisoned there for a long period.

succeeded—in what must surely have been one of the earliest of combined air-sea operations against land defenses—in overcoming the resistance of the batteries there, the powder magazine of one of them being set on fire by a bomb from one of the *Nairana's* seaplanes. An effort was made by the Soviet commanders to block further passage of the flotilla by sinking two icebreakers in the channel of the delta; but it was clumsily carried out, and the Allied vessels passed the barrier without serious difficulty.

News of these events created great excitement in the city of Archangel, and at once set in motion the wheels of the anti-communist *Putsch*. The undertaking was entirely successful, and practically bloodless. The Soviet military forces evacuated the vicinity in panicky haste. By morning of the following day, August 2, the city was effectively in the hands of White Russian elements, the leaders of whom had been in close touch with the British for some time past. By noon a new government, under the presidency of the Popular-Socialist leader N. V. Chaikovsky, had been established.

That same evening the Allied vessels arrived off the city. At eight p.m. General Poole went ashore, to be greeted by what appeared to be a demonstration of delirious enthusiasm on the part of the population. The operation, thus far, had cost the expedition no casualties.

The Bolshevik forces that had evacuated the city were not negligible, and they were still in the immediate vicinity. The first task for Poole's tiny force was obviously to make contact with them and to establish something resembling a provisional defensive front around the port area. In this operation the Amercian marines from the *Olympia,* restless from long inactivity at Murmansk, participated enthusiastically. Seizing an engine and some cars at Bakaritsa, a marine lieutenant, supported by a handful of men, set out to pursue the retreating Soviet forces down the railway line. He succeeded in chasing them seventy-five miles before the Russians were able to gain sufficient lead to burn a bridge. That the participants in this happy escapade had any knowledge of the President's recent expression of unwillingness to have American troops participate in organized intervention into the interior from Murmansk and Archangel, or that it would have meant much to them had they known it, seems doubtful in the extreme.[17]

---

[17] For the account of this incident see the curious volume entitled *The History of the American Expedition Fighting the Bolsheviki, Campaigning in North Russia,*

Despatch of American Forces

While Poole was endeavoring to consolidate his military position at Archangel, the wheels of the American and British military machinery moved in a rather hasty and perfunctory recognition of the President's undertaking. The 1st, 2nd, and 3rd Battalions of the 339th Infantry, the 1st Battalion of the 310th Engineers, the 337th Field Hospital and the 337th Ambulance Company, all then in England en route to France, were designated for duty in North Russia and were turned over, in effect, to the British for further disposition. The entire force numbered about 5,500 men.

The 339th Infantry consisted mostly of young recruits, many of them of Polish-American origin, from Michigan and Wisconsin. It was sometimes called "Detroit's Own." It had had some rudimentary basic training at Camp Custer before departure for England; but it was of course wholly without combat experience. Upon being turned over to the British in England for service in North Russia, the men were supplied with British winter clothing and (much to their disgust) with Russian rifles. They were then embarked from Newcastle, on August 25, in three British transports bound for Murmansk.

The Spanish influenza, which had been raging with devastating effect through armies and through civilian populations in that final winter of the World War, broke out on all three ships. The medical detachment was present, but someone had forgotten to put the medical supplies aboard. By the time the vessels reached Arctic waters, both passengers and crews were ravaged by this acute and often fatal illness.

Meanwhile General Poole's tiny force at Archangel had begun to experience serious military difficulty. A wireless message was therefore sent to the three transports, ordering them to skip Murmansk and to proceed directly to Archangel. They arrived there and made fast on the Bakaritsa side on a dark, rainy afternoon—September 4, 1918. The arrival was subsequently described, by one of the participants, as follows:

The troopships "Somali," "Tydeus," and "Nagoya" rubbed the Bakaritza and Smolny quays sullenly and listed heavily to port. The American doughboys grimly marched down the gangplanks and set their feet on

---

1918–1919, compiled by three of the officers of the 339th U.S. Infantry (Captain Joel R. Moore, Lieutenant Harry H. Mead, and Lieutenant Lewis E. Jahns) and published in 1920 by The Polar Bear Publishing Co., Detroit, Michigan.

the soil of Russia, . . . The dark waters of the Dvina River were beaten into fury by the opposing north wind and ocean tide. And the lowering clouds of the Arctic sky added their dismal bit to this introduction to the dreadful conflict which these American sons of liberty were to wage with the Bolsheviki during the year's campaign.[18]

Hospital space was available for only about thirty of the stretcher cases. Laboriously, the remaining sick were carried off, through the rain, to an old barracks, where they were laid, in their clothes, on board bunks. A number of them died that way.

Of the healthy, one battalion, the 2nd, was detailed for duty in the Archangel area. Another was despatched up the Duna River to be placed under the command of a British general charged with the capture of Kotlas, some three hundred miles distant. The third was hustled off up the railroad in boxcars, that same evening, to join the British General Finlayson (now of World War II fame) in his unsuccessful effort to push through to Vologda. Within less than twenty-four hours from the time of their landing, these latter were in contact with something called the enemy, nearly a hundred miles from Archangel, deep in the forest, occupying combat outposts where they stood knee-deep in water. And who was the enemy? A poster, purporting to represent orders from British General Headquarters informed them. The enemy were Bolsheviki and Germans. The Bolsheviki were

. . . soldiers and sailors who, in the majority of cases are criminals. . . . Their natural, vicious brutality enabled them to assume leadership. . . .

And as for the Germans:

. . . The Bolsheviks have no capacity for organization but this is supplied by Germany and her lesser Allies. The Germans usually appear in Russian uniform and are impossible to distinguish.[19]

The nearest Germans, on available evidence, were actually four to five hundred miles away.

Again, as in the case of Siberia, we shall not pursue further, in this volume, the fate of these young Americans who were propelled, in circumstances so bewildering, without in fact having the faintest

[18] *Ibid.*, p. 11.
[19] *Ibid.*, p. 219.

idea of what it was that they were supposed to be doing, into the hardships and horrors of a foreign civil war in the endless swamps and forests of the Russian Arctic. If, on that day in September 1918, anyone in distant Washington knew what was occurring with them and thought to compare it with the President's injunction that they were not to interfere in internal Russian affairs and were not to be used for intervention from Archangel into the interior, the record holds no indication of it. The combined bureaucratic barriers of two great military establishments now lay across the five thousand miles that separated them from those of their fellow countrymen who had recruited them and despatched them from their native shores. They were effectively removed from both the responsibility and the attention of official Washington. They were now, in the most painfully literal sense of the term, the forgotten men.

❖

We see, then, that in each case—in the Russian North as in Siberia—whatever merit may have resided in the President's decisions of July 1918 concerning America's course of action in those areas, was largely forfeited by the manner in which the decision was developed. In the one case, it was the diplomatic implementation that was faulty; in the other, the military. Whatever may be said for the wisdom of the American government in its approach to these problems, there is little to be said for its procedures.

The fact is that in both cases the situation was, from the American standpoint, already virtually out of control when Wilson finally made up his mind. People had only *appeared* to await his decisions. Actually, they had not done so. British, Japanese, Czechs, Russians, sometimes even Americans, while going through the motions of consulting official Washington, had taken their actions before they received the answer. In most cases, they had had no choice but to do so.

Had Wilson been able to survey the scene of 1918 as we are able to survey it today, he would have had to recognize that when great forces have come into motion in world affairs, either in war or in developing crisis, no government, however great its prestige or its military power, can hope to keep them under control and then to direct their motion by months of silence, followed by a single vague and cryptic declaration. It takes a different order of statesmanship

—one marked by the most anxious and careful following of events and by a determination to act upon the situation unintermittently by every conceivable means—to shape to one's own purpose the mighty and incessant process of change that forms the relationships between nations in troubled times.

CHAPTER XIX

JULY AND THE FINAL BREAKUP

THE implementation of the decisions taken by the British and French governments in May and June and by the United States government in the first days of July would have sufficed, in any event, to produce ultimately a complete rupture of the uneasy half-relationship which the Allied governments had maintained, up to that time, with the Soviet government. This process was precipitated, however, by the tragic and dramatic turn taken by political events within Russia during the month of July.

The Czech uprising, leading as it did to the sudden and unexpected success of the anti-communist movement throughout central Siberia, naturally gave great impetus to underground opposition activity in the other parts of Russia. In Moscow and Petrograd, the entire month of June was marked not only by intense fermentation among these groups themselves, involving hot debate, frantic efforts to compose differences, and the cultivation of a wide variety of schemes and plots for the overthrow of Soviet power, but also by intensified approaches to the representatives in Russia of both German and Allied governments, and appeals for their support and collaboration. Whereas it was, for the most part, the groups at the extreme right of the political spectrum that tended to turn to the Germans, it was those of the center and the non-communist left who approached the Allies. Most prominent among these latter were the "Union for the Regeneration of Russia," a multi-party grouping uniting a number of elements running all the way from moderate Kadets and ex-officers to right-wing S-R's, and the "Union for the Defense of Fatherland and Freedom," a militant, relatively unideological organization, headed by that extraordinary mixture of terrorist, novelist, and adventurer: Boris Savinkov. The latter, an S-R by past political affiliation, had been for a time Minister of War in the Provisional Government. He had now struck out independently and had formed this highly conspiratorial organization, composed largely of former officers.

As the awareness of the Siberian events, on the one hand, and the inter-Allied decisions of May and early June in the matter of intervention, on the other, grew upon the Allied representatives in Russia, their interest in all these Russian opposition groupings increased apace. The French were the most eager with advice and offers of support—also the least discreet. Noulens, on the occasion of a visit to Moscow in mid-June, personally cultivated contacts with opposition leaders there and was rash enough, shortly thereafter, to address to a number of the opposition groups—all now outlawed by the Soviet government and consequently operating quite illegally—a semiofficial letter, purporting to give the views of the Allies on the manner in which Russian domestic-political affairs would have to be arranged if there were to be any successful collaboration with the Allies. This scheme, needless to say, left no room anywhere for the Bolsheviki, and envisaged, by implication, their overthrow.[1]

With the Union for the Regeneration of Russia, the French contacts were particularly close. At some time during the month of June, French representatives appear to have given the Union to understand that intervention was soon to take place, and to have divulged to its agents the essence of the Franco-British plan for effecting a union between the intervening force at Archangel and the advancing Czechs, with the view to forming a solid front from the White Sea to the Pacific. The Union, reviewing its own plans in the light of this information, came to the conclusion that central Russia, i.e., the Moscow region, would probably be occupied by the Germans as soon as the Allies moved, and accordingly shifted the center of its militant underground activity away from Moscow, mainly to the south and the east. Savinkov, on the other hand, who appears to have become party to the same information, took a more fateful decision, the results of which we shall observe shortly. It was to throw his entire organization into an effort to seize the territory immediately northwest of Moscow, where the junction between the Czechs and the Archangel forces would have to be effected.

[1] A. Argunov, *Mezhdu dvumya bolshevismami* (Between Two Bolshevisms), Paris, 1919, pp. 3–7, as cited by Bunyan, *op.cit.*, pp. 182–185.
See also Vishnyak, *op.cit.*, p. 140.

It was evidently his thought that by so doing, he would place himself in a key position once the intervention became a fact.

The main opposition groups were obviously penetrated, to some degree, by Soviet agents. Either by this means or through imperfect security on the part of the Allied representatives themselves,[2] the Soviet leaders also became aware, at some time in June, of the Franco-British scheme for linking up the anti-communist movement in Siberia with the intervention in the Russian North. Coming as it did on the heels of the news of the arrival of General Maynard and his force at Murmansk and of the break between Moscow and Murmansk, this news hit the Moscow leaders hard. It spelled, unquestionably, the end of any hopes they may have had that the French and British might in some way be dissuaded from the desire to intervene. From this time on, their hopes—such as they were—were laid on the possibility (quite shrewdly calculated, in the light of Wilson's views) of splitting the Americans from the other Allies on this issue. Their behavior through the crucial days of July must be judged in the light of this awareness on their part of Franco-British intentions.

Meanwhile, preparations were going forward, in the latter part of June, for the Fifth All-Russian Congress of Soviets, scheduled to open in Moscow on July 4. It would be the first Congress of this sort to be held since mid-March, when the Fourth Congress had assembled to ratify the Brest-Litovsk Treaty. The only parties to be represented at this Congress would be the Bolsheviki and the Left S-R's, all other parties now being banned from participation in the Soviet system.

The Left S-R's had split off from the main body of the Social-Revolutionary Party at the time of the Bolshevik seizure of power. For a time, they had participated in the Soviet of People's Commissars, a body which—with many reservations—might be compared to the cabinet under the western parliamentary system. This arrangement had not survived the Brest-Litovsk crisis; but the Left S-R faction, now functioning as an independent party, had continued to participate in many local soviets and to be represented in the central

[2] Noulens recorded in his memoirs, Vol. II, *op.cit.*, p. 121, his belief that the French interpreter he used on the occasion of his visit to Moscow was a Soviet informer at the time.

The Francis MSS, *op.cit.*, make plain the fact of Soviet knowledge, as early as July 8, of the plan to land at Archangel (Chicherin mentioned it to Poole on that date).

Congress of Soviets. Its leaders were a wild-eyed group, neurotics and romanticists, remnants of the extreme terroristic wing of the pre-war revolutionary opposition—more radical, in many respects, than the Bolsheviki themselves. Prominent among them was Maria Spiridonova, a young woman consumed by political passion, the very embodiment of revolutionary fanaticism.[3]

Ever since March the Left S-R's had been in bitter opposition to the Bolsheviki over the issue of the Brest-Litovsk Treaty. They urged denunciation of the treaty and proclamation of a revolutionary war to the death against the Germans. They opposed the Bolsheviki sharply on this issue. With the advent of summer, the conflict between them and the Bolsheviki was compounded by a difference of opinion over problems of food procurement, in the face of the spreading famine in central Russia.

In late June, the feelings of the Left S-R's about the tie with Germany became for some reason intensified, and grew to fever pitch.[4] As the month came to an end there were repeated signs that the leaders of the faction, whose most essential characteristic for years in the past had been the violent refusal to adjust to *any* political situation, Tsarist or revolutionary, were beginning now to manifest, in relation to the Soviet regime, the same tendencies to violence and terrorism by which they had been driven under the Tsars.

The Congress opened on July 4, in the huge hall of the Bolshoi Theater in Moscow. The atmosphere was no less sultry than that of the Potomac on which, that very same day, Wilson and Lansing were making their excursion to Mount Vernon. For two days, the Left S-R's filled the hall with the most violently inflammatory attacks on the Germans and the Bolsheviki, accompanied by open threats that they would take direct action if their views were not met. The Counselor of the German Embassy, Riezler, witnessing the session from a box, became the personal object of threats by S-R orators, and of hostile demonstrations on the floor. Lenin, whose revolutionary soul could not suppress an undercurrent of sympathy for this manifestation of political extremism and hatred of the imperialists,

---

[3] Spiridonova was greatly respected in the revolutionary movement as one reputed to have suffered special cruelties and indignities at the hands of the Tsarist police— even to the point of being violated by a group of her Cossack jailers.

[4] The reasons for this escape this writer; possibly German reprisals against the peasantry in the Ukraine had something to do with it. The S-R's were particularly closely connected with the peasantry.

replied tactfully, on the 5th, to the Left S-R attacks, treating Spiri-donova with marked personal gentleness but yielding nothing in substance and challenging the S-R's, the last of Bolshevism's political associates, to break with the Soviet system if they wished. On a vote, the Congress upheld the Bolsheviki; the S-R resolution, calling for denunciation of the treaty, was rejected.

The following day, July 6, two men, both Left S-R's, called—on a pretext—on the German Ambassador, Count Mirbach, in his Em-bassy. Received by him in his drawing room, they suddenly opened fire with revolvers, shot Mirbach dead, and fled through a window.[5] The act, the purpose of which was to provoke a break with the Ger-mans, served as a signal for an attempt at a general Left S-R uprising in Moscow.

The uprising, as wildly conceived as the assassination, was quickly suppressed by the Bolsheviki. But the shock of the Mirbach murder was great, both on Soviet-German and Soviet-Allied relations. Lenin and Sverdlov (then Chairman of the Central Executive Commit-tee), on learning of the assassination, came at once, at German in-sistence, to the distracted German Embassy and made formal apolo-gies. But the Germans were rightly skeptical of the real degree of Soviet regret, and the occurrence naturally raised the question whether the German Embassy should not thenceforth have its own military guard, drawn from the German army. To the Allied repre-sentatives, already jittery from exposure to a long series of rumors about alleged German intentions to occupy Moscow or Petrograd, the thought of any such introduction of armed German units into the Soviet capital was bound to be deeply disturbing.

In addition to this, the Soviet government, in announcing the as-sassination, blamed it—immediately and unhesitatingly—on the Allies, describing the assassins as "two scoundrels—agents of Rus-sian and Anglo-French imperialism."[6] In this there was not a word of truth. The Left S-R's were capable of anything; but the one thing they happened not to be guilty of at this juncture was the cultivation or acceptance of support from any foreign faction whatsoever. The

[5] A graphic account of this tragic event will be found in Gustav Hilger (and Alfred G. Meyer), *The Incompatible Allies, A Memoir-History of German-Soviet Relations, 1918–1941*, The Macmillan Co., New York, 1953, pp. 3-6. The building in which this occurred has since served as the Italian Embassy. As Hilger has indicated, the memory of this assassination, reinforced by the long-ineradicable bloodstain on the drawing room floor, has lived on in the folklore of Moscow's diplomatic society.

[6] Bunyan, *op.cit.*, p. 213.

baselessness of the charge was at once exposed by the unabashed acceptance by the Left S-R leaders of full political responsibility for the deed. The assassination, they formally announced, had been carried out pursuant to a resolution of their Central Committee.[7] This effectively disposed of the effort of the Bolsheviki to make the French and British scapegoats for the deed. But the fact that the attempt had been made to do so was of course not lost on the French and British representatives in Moscow and Vologda, who were made to feel in this way the menacing quality of the hatred and bitterness now borne them by the leaders of the Soviet regime.

The excitement and confusion produced by the Mirbach murder was compounded by the outbreak on the same day of another uprising, conducted this time by Savinkov and his organization, in several cities to the north and east of Moscow, notably Yaroslavl. The occurrence of the two actions on the same day was purely coincidental; there seems to have been no connection whatsoever between the two enterprises. The Yaroslavl uprising was a much more serious matter, militarily speaking, than the Left S-R action in Moscow. It was two weeks before the Soviet forces succeeded in retaking Yaroslavl. Bloodshed and reprisals were severe on both sides. This was now full-fledged civil war, with no quarter given. The Bolsheviki alone, after recapture of Yaroslavl, executed more than 400 persons there by way of vengeance.

For the Yaroslavl uprising, too, the Allies were blamed by the Bolsheviki. There was more justification, this time, for the suspicion. There is no reason to doubt that the French and British had given support and encouragement to Savinkov, generally. Nor would they have been in any way averse, in principle, to using his organization to assist in the establishment of the juncture between the Czechs and the Archangel operation, had it been possible to do so. But again it happens to be doubtful, in point of fact, that this particular operation on Savinkov's part was directly inspired by the French and British. That it was intended by Savinkov to fall in with the Allied action is unquestionable. "Our aim," Savinkov stated in his memoirs,

was to cut off Moscow from Archangel, where the Allies proposed to land a force. According to that plan, the Allies, having landed at Archangel,

---

[7] In public testimony (July 10), Spiridonova stated proudly, "I organized the assassination of Mirbach from beginning to end." *Ibid.*, p. 219.

could very easily take Vologda and menace Moscow if Yaroslav were in our hands.

... But the Allies did not come.[8]

But in these memoirs, Savinkov said nothing specific about the uprising having been planned by or specifically coordinated with the Allies. Several years later, having fallen into Bolshevik hands, he became the victim and leading figure of what was in effect the first of the great Soviet show trials. Here, confessing in the usual extravagant manner, he charged the French with responsibility for the whole affair. "Noulens," he said on that occasion,

sent me a telegram from Vologda in which he definitely stated that the landing would take place between the 3rd and the 10th of July . . . and insisted that we begin the insurrection on the 5th day of July. . . . Thus the French were closely connected with the affair but deceived us.[9]

Obviously, such testimony—by a man who knows that his only chance for life lies in saying what his captors want him to say—has no intrinsic credibility.[10] And in this instance, the allegation was most implausible. There is good reason to suppose that the French Consul General of that time in Moscow, M. Grenard, was closer to the truth when he wrote, later, that Savinkov embarked on the venture on his own initiative and in violation of a pledge he had given to the Allies not to act independently of the other Russian parties. It is even possible that Savinkov's premature action was deliberately provoked by the Bolsheviki through the spreading of false rumors leading him to believe that Allied intervention was more imminent than was actually the case. This would have been a very astute move on the Soviet side, for the prematureness of Savinkov's action enabled the Bolsheviki to deal with it separately and to suppress it before the Allies landed in Archangel.[11]

[8] B. Savinkov, *Borba s bolshevikami* (The Struggle against the Bolsheviki), Warsaw, 1920, pp. 24–28, as cited in Bunyan, *op.cit.,* p. 181.

[9] *Ibid.,* p. 181, footnote 38.

[10] Savinkov, whose death sentence was promptly commuted to ten years' imprisonment, committed suicide in prison some months later.

[11] The Francis MSS, *op.cit.,* reveal that in the last days of June Noulens wired to General Poole in Murmansk, inquiring of the latter's plans for military operations. In his reply, despatched June 30, Poole stated—according to Francis—that he expected to land at Archangel "soon" with a considerable number of troops. The exact wording of this message is not available; but it may be regarded as out of the question that Poole named any such dates as the 5th to 10th of July as the prospective time of landing. Maynard and his tiny force were busy, at that time, consolidating the British hold on the Murmansk Railway as far south as Soroka. There

George Kennan, 1848-1924

THE CENTURY MAGAZINE, 1888

Ambassador Francis and Counselor of Embassy J. Butler Wright in the Ambassador's Ford. Philip Jordan at the wheel

The Ipatyev house in Ekaterinburg, where the Tsar's family were confined

The Final Breakup

It is easy to see how these happenings, together with the reports of continued Czech successes in Siberia and of the defection of the Murmansk Soviet, all taking place at a time when central Russia was in the grip of a famine of growing intensity, produced a crisis of Soviet power scarcely to be equalled until the day, twenty-three years later, when German forces—this time the forces of Hitler—would again be knocking at the gates of Moscow. July 1918 was Bolshevism's darkest hour in the entire period of war and intervention. The situation of the Soviet regime, politically isolated, hemmed in on all sides by hostile armies, itself devoid as yet of any sizeable armed force, and faced with both famine and armed revolt in the area nominally under its control, was desperate; and it appeared even more desperate than it was.

In defense of the Allied plans for intervention it must always be recalled that at this moment it appeared to the Allied representatives as though the Bolsheviki, by their doctrinaire extremism, their reckless disruption of the old army, and their insistence on antagonizing all the non-proletarian elements of Russian society, had dug their own political grave. "The Soviet Government," Francis wrote to his son Perry on July 30,

---

was no telling when this operation would be completed. The agreement with the Murmansk Soviet—one of the prerequisites to the Archangel landing—had not yet been concluded. The French colonial detachment, which Poole was actually later to use for the move on Archangel, had not even sailed from western Europe. Poole had no force whatsoever available, at the end of June, for an attack on Archangel, and could not conceivably have undertaken to carry out such an attack at any specific time in the first part of July. (See telegram, Francis to SECSTATE, No. 315, July 3, 1918; *ibid.*)

On July 5, furthermore, Francis transmitted, as a favor to the British, a message to General Poole from one of the leading British agents in Russia, MacLaren, which throws an interesting light on the whole subject of the coordination of the Archangel landing with the actions of the opposition groups. In this message, MacLaren told of arriving at an understanding with a representative of the Union for the Regeneration of Russia whereby the tiny local force of that organization at Vologda (some 300 men) would attempt to seize Vologda in coordination with the Archangel landing. MacLaren asked what measures Poole wanted carried out with respect to the Russian transportation system, both defensive and offensive, in conjunction with the landing. It was imperative, he said, that he should have immediate instructions—otherwise, in the absence of definite instructions, the local Russian organization might make a premature move on the strength of false information. Such false information, he said, was already being spread by Trotsky; and he named as an example the rumor that the station "Mandon" on the Archangel line had already been seized by the Allies. This message, despatched on the very eve of the Savinkov uprising, shows that the British political agents were not only aware of the danger that local Russian forces might be provoked into taking premature action, but convinced that rumors designed to have this effect were already being spread from the Soviet side.

[437]

is expiring at last—in fact to use its own words it has been a corpse for four or five weeks but no one has had the courage to bury it.[12]

Even Sadoul, in whose mind the passionate wish for the survival of Soviet power was normally father to the thought, fell into black despair; and while he blamed the situation on the hostility of Allied policy rather than on the extremism and the utopian experiments of the Bolsheviki themselves, letter after letter from his pen in this period testifies to his belief that Soviet power was doomed. It is important to remember that in the French and British missions, it was men convinced that Soviet power was practically a thing of the past and that its fall could not fail to be followed by further German penetration into central Russia, who pursued with such intensity, in the summer of 1918, the schemes for a linking of the Archangel forces with the Czechs. Great as was their dislike for what they had seen of Bolshevism, it was primarily the re-creation of resistance to Germany on which they set their eyes.

❖

In Vologda, life had by this time become relatively relaxed. Summer had at last arrived. Francis and Philip Jordan lived in the clubhouse, together with the Brazilian Chargé and the Siamese Minister. A mess was operated there for the remaining American personnel, all of whom had now found quarters elsewhere in the little town. The Ford, sent on by flatcar from Petrograd, was now available; and while the procurement of gasoline was a real problem, and the roads nothing to boast of, the vehicle gave an added touch of flexibility to the confining, provincial life. Philip, anxious to get the Ambassador out of doors after his severe illness of late April (which had aged him markedly), found a grass-covered field, under the walls of the monastery at the edge of town. This he converted into a makeshift golf links. He would go along in advance and plant stakes, to take the place of holes; Francis and his personal secretary, Mr. Earl M. Johnston, would then follow along, trying to make the balls hit the stakes, and shouting *"Beregi,"* the nearest thing to a translation of "Fore," at such astounded Russians as happened to cross their path.

In the evenings there was bridge or poker in the Embassy. Francis took an eager interest in the progress of his housemates and staff in

[12] *Ibid.*

the various games that he enjoyed. He had attempted, he wrote to his son in early June, to teach them the Log Cabin game,

. . . but have only practiced up to this time the double deal and the draw of six cards. The old poker players think that fours are more difficult to procure than three pair consequently I have compromised and three pairs now beat only a full house. Have induced them to play blazes also but not kilters nor skip straights—especially skip straights around the corner which experienced players find great difficulty in learning . . .[13]

When the interest in cards had exhausted itself, conversation tended to become desultory. Thoughts turned to distant, and widely disparate, homelands. The Brazilian and the Siamese would argue, listlessly, as to which of their countries had the largest snakes; after which, Francis' voice would again be heard through the fog of cigar smoke: "Now when I was Mayor of St. Louis—let's see, that must have been in 1888—Philip, how many times was I Mayor of St. Louis? . . ." Thereupon the Siamese's head would nod, and the Brazilian's thoughts would turn to the boulevards of Paris, and the young American Secretary of Embassy would stare wistfully through the open window to the world outside, where the soft, unsettling half-light of the northern summer night still bathed the poplars, where the wail of a locomotive whistle drifted across the sleeping countryside, and where a faint clatter of hurried footsteps along a cobbled street bespoke, somehow, the mystery of the vast, distracted, passion-ridden Russian land.

The events of July broke with rude abruptness upon this provincial idyl. For some time—ever since the death of Summers, in fact—Chicherin had been courting Francis in the desperate hope of dividing him from his Allied colleagues, and luring from him information as to what was going on in the Allied camp. To mark the Fourth of July, a flowery missive was despatched, ringing all the changes (later to be rung with meager success by the American Communist Party) on the similarity between the revolutionary origins of the two governments. An abortive Russian-American Friendship Society was even established in Moscow, under the chairmanship of Borodin (later to become prominent as representative of Russian communism in China), who had spent some time before the war in the United

---

[13] *Ibid.*, letter, Francis to son Perry, June 4, 1918.

States. Voznesenski was despatched to Vologda to take Francis' political temperature and to say reassuring things to him.

There is a certain pathetic quality about these approaches, as one examines the evidences of them today. It was not that there was not much opportunism and desperation behind them, not that they were faithful reflections of the views of Lenin and Trotsky; but one senses that in Chicherin's mind, no more immune than any other to the power of contradiction, there was a certain weariness with revolutionary defiance and violence, and a sneaking wish that something might really come of it all: that Francis might really conceive a sympathy for the Russian Revolution and infect his compatriots with it, that somehow the fresh vigor and good will of America might be added to the genuine social idealism that so many still discerned in the Bolshevik movement. One gains the impression, from the evidences of Chicherin's personal diplomacy at this time, that he was the one man on the Soviet side who really cared, for long-term as well as short-term reasons, what the Americans thought of the Bolshevik effort to create a new Russia.

However this may be, his attempt to improve matters came too late. Since the beginning of May, Francis' suspicions, based on acceptance of the thesis of Soviet duplicity and excessive German influence, had become fixed. There had now been evoked, in the Governor's behavior, the elaborate reflex of dissimulation ingrained by a thirty years' immersion in the maneuvers of American domestic politics. He had sized up the situation; he knew—or thought he did —what they were trying to do to him. They would see, now, that two could play at this game. He received Voznesenski (whom he described privately as having "the cheek of an army mule") with a sly affability, and teased him without mercy. When Voznesenski, on the occasion of his first visit, fished for information as to whether the Allies had decided to intervene in the near future, Francis told him he did not know, but that on the occasion of his next visit "I would not be as candid with him again and . . . would not tell him whether I knew or not." [14] And then, on the occasion of the last visit (June 30), he tantalized the unfortunate man still further by saying that "if Allied intervention had been decided upon, I did not know it."

This, he later explained, disingenuously, in a letter to Poole,

[14] *Ibid.,* letter to son Perry, June 23.

while true was for the purpose of preventing the hurrying-up preparation that is apparently being made to resist Allied intervention if it should occur. . . .[15]

Along with these outwardly amiable exchanges, there were mounting signs of tension as the relationship between the Soviet government and the Allies deteriorated. In the last days of June, Kedrov, the political commissar at Archangel, descended on Vologda and removed from office the pro-Allied municipal administration, relations with which Francis had assiduously cultivated. This action aroused some indignation among the local populace. To suppress any further pro-Allied tendencies, in light of the growing danger of intervention at Archangel, new Soviet internal security units, animated by a proper degree of hostility toward the Allies, were despatched to Vologda in the first days of July.

On the Fourth of July, Francis gave a reception for the members of the diplomatic corps and a number of the friendly municipal officials and local residents. To his surprise and delight, Philip Jordan succeeded in producing a very creditable punch and adequate quantities of sandwiches, from sources of supply which remained a mystery even to the Ambassador. The Victrola, which had done duty at Francis' diplomatic dinners, was again brought out, and there was dancing in the garden to its squeaky notes. It was the last time the Vologda inhabitants of that generation would have a chance to witness the social amenities of doomed capitalism.

On this occasion, Francis delivered a public address,[16] which he subsequently handed to the press and allowed to be published as "an address to the Russian people." In the main, it was politically unexceptionable, quite along the lines of President Wilson's statements. But it reiterated the refusal of the United States to recognize the Brest-Litovsk peace; and this must have hit painfully into the midst of the conflict between the Bolsheviki and the Left S-R's at the Congress of Soviets, beginning in Moscow that same day. The statement that "We will never stand idly by and see the Germans exploit the Russian people and appropriate to Germany's selfish ends the immense resources of Russia" could only have sounded to the fevered Soviet ear as another threat of the imminent intervention. And the very mode of Francis' action—addressing himself directly to the

[15] *Ibid.*, Francis to Poole, July 1.
[16] Francis, *op.cit.*, pp. 240–242.

Russian people over the head of the regime—was certainly resented in Moscow.

Meanwhile, a minor incident in Moscow, unimportant in itself, had contrived to symbolize in a curiously prophetic way the pattern of coming events. John Lehrs, Vice Consul and interpreter of the Consulate General in Moscow, had gone to the Foreign Office on June 27 to discuss with Karl Radek a renewal of the licenses entitling the American consular officials to bear firearms. Radek had treated him with flagrant discourtesy, even to the point of having his lunch brought in and consuming it silently, paying no attention to Lehrs and leaving him to look on. When the repast was over, Lehrs finally succeeded in bringing up the matter of the licenses, pointing out that the Soviet government had just issued a decree to the effect that anyone found bearing firearms without a license would be shot on the spot. Radek's reply was that

Dzerzhinski refuses to give licenses to you; he says he does not see why he should give such licenses to foreign counter-revolutionists; . . .

At this, Lehrs lost his temper and a scene ensued.[17]

Together, Poole and Chicherin succeeded in patching the matter up. Lehrs was transferred to Vologda to avoid further difficulties. But the incident, occurring only a week before the Mirbach murder, is interesting both in that connection and in another connection, to be described shortly.

The news of the events of July 6—the Mirbach murder and the outbreak of the uprisings in Moscow and Yaroslavl—broke with stunning effect on the diplomatic corps in Vologda. The cause for anxiety in Mirbach's murder was obvious. Yaroslavl was a city halfway between Moscow and Vologda; disorder was striking close to home. All the Allied envoys were now seized with the fear that Moscow might be occupied by the Germans; that the intervention might come too late; that the hand of the assassin, having dealt with the German, would now be turned against themselves. On the night of the 7th, Francis despatched a wire to Washington (it never arrived), urging that the date of the Archangel landing be advanced.

On the next morning, Monday, July 8, the diplomats in Vologda found themselves cut off from all communication with Moscow. The

---

[17] Francis MSS, *op.cit.,* memorandum, Lehrs to Poole, June 29.

Yaroslavl rebellion had broken all the connections. The little colony had been joined, on the 7th, by the British Chargé d'Affaires, F. O. Lindley, who had succeeded in making his escape through Finland to England in March, and had now been returned to Russia to take over major responsibility from the discomfited Lockhart. The principal Allied chiefs of mission—American, French, Italian, and British —now began to meet daily, under Francis' chairmanship as doyen, just as they had done in other troubled times. They were all agreed, by this time, on the vital urgency of the Archangel landing. A joint telegram was drawn up, which Francis despatched on the night of the 8th to Admiral Kemp, pleading that this action be expedited.

The following day, Tuesday, the diplomats received a desperate appeal from the insurgents at Yaroslavl begging for Allied assistance. There was nothing to be done but to despatch another telegram to Murmansk, which they did.

By this time, telegraphic connection between the Embassy at Vologda and the Department of State had been completely severed. The trouble at Murmansk had disrupted the last available channel. Unbeknownst to Francis, his telegrams had for some time not been going through. Of those the Department had been sending to him, only a portion had reached him in the last few days. Now, on July 9, he received the last such message he was to receive while on Bolshevik-held territory. From this time on, he would be quite cut off from any direct means of communication with his government.

The following morning (July 10), Francis was thrust once more— as in the previous February—into a difficult ordeal of decision as to his own movements and those of his Allied colleagues. A message was received in the morning from Chicherin, addressed to Francis as Dean of the Diplomatic Corps, and reading as follows:

Taking into consideration the present situation and possibility of danger for representatives of Entente powers Soviet Government looks upon Moscow as town where security of named representatives can be assured. Considering as its duty safeguarding ambassadors' security Government sees in their coming to Moscow a necessity. We hope that highly esteemed American Ambassador will appreciate this step in friendly spirit in which it is undertaken. In order to execute this measure and to remove any difficulties People's Commissariat for Foreign Affairs delegates to Vologda as its representative, Citizen Radek.[18]

[18] Francis, *op.cit.*, pp. 245-246.

[443]

This document was received by the Vologda diplomats with a mixture of derision and indignation. Noulens later referred to it, in his memoirs, as "this burlesque document which . . . invited us to entrust our security to the place where circumstances had just demonstrated it would be the least assured." [19] Not only were they, in the light of Mirbach's murder, decidedly not impressed with the advantages of Moscow from the standpoint of personal security,[20] but they strongly suspected that one of the motives of the Soviet government in asking them to come to Moscow was to hold them as hostages against any eventualities. In this, they were no doubt partly right, although the Soviet leaders were probably sincere in the belief that, Mirbach's murder notwithstanding, protection of the diplomats would be easier in Moscow than in Vologda, where Soviet authority—particularly at this moment during the Yaroslavl uprising —was tenuous.

At the behest of the corps, Francis drafted a reply, despatched to Chicherin the following day (July 11). Here, Francis asked why the further residence of the corps in Vologda was considered unsafe. "We have no fear," he stated,

of the Russian people, whom we have always befriended and whom we consider our Allies, and we have full confidence in the population of Vologda. Our only anxiety is concerning the forces of the Central Empires with whom we are at war and, in our judgment, they are much more likely to capture Moscow than Vologda. We realize that in a country suffering as Russia is at present there are unreasonable and desperate men, but we are confident that they are not more dangerous at Vologda than elsewhere. At Moscow, on the other hand, we hear that the Germans have already received permission to introduce their troops to safeguard their representatives, and in any case the town is directly threatened by the Germans. If you mean by your message that the government of Soviets has taken without consulting the Allied Missions the decision that the latter should come to Moscow and that you are sending Mr. Radek to carry such a decision into execution, we desire to inform you that we consider that would be offensive to us and we would not comply therewith.[21]

[19] Noulens, Vol. ii, *op.cit.,* p. 144.

[20] Both of Mirbach's murderers were reported to be officials of the dread Cheka; and it was with forged documents of identity from the Cheka that they had succeeded in gaining admission to the German Embassy. (Hilger, *op.cit.,* p. 3.)

[21] Francis, *op.cit.,* p. 246.

Immediately after the despatch of this message, Francis had the entire exchange translated into Russian and handed to the local press. The local Vologda paper had an extra edition on the streets before evening. The move was an astute one on Francis' part, as it appealed to local pride and the strongly anti-Soviet sentiment among the Vologda population; but it was, again, highly offensive to the Soviet authorities.

Radek arrived in Vologda the following day (July 12) at noon. To appreciate the impact of his arrival, it is necessary to call to mind his unique personality, so familiar to many an early foreign resident in the Soviet republic. He was a short man, of startling and yet not unattractive ugliness, with wide protruding ears, a face framed with a monkey-like fringe of beard (which gave him a Puck-like aspect), and large yellow teeth from which there incessantly hung an incongruous Dutch pipe. He seemed to love to embellish this exterior with various outlandish forms of clothing. Equally conversant in German, Polish, or Russian (he was of Polish-Jewish origin), he was a man of great brilliance and wit, coupled with a breath-taking insolence and a biting and profoundly critical approach to all human phenomenon, great and small.

On arrival in Vologda, Radek at once got into touch with the local communist authorities, who may be presumed to have shown him, not without indignation, the newspaper extra of the day before. His first step, in any case, was to clamp down a rigid censorship on the local press and to forbid the publication of any further material of this sort from the embassies. He then made an appointment, by telephone, to see Francis at 4:00 p.m. When he arrived, one hour late, Embassy officials, now including Lehrs, were taken aback to find him wearing a military cartridge belt, from which there was appended an enormous pistol. This was presumably his revenge for the altercation with Lehrs. In any case, following so hard on the heels of Mirbach's murder, this demonstration was scarcely reassuring.

The diplomatic corps was again in session in Francis' office when Radek arrived. Francis went out to the anteroom to greet his Soviet guest. He, too, was startled at Radek's appearance (he swore that the next time they met he would have his own gun on the table). He invited Radek to come in and talk with the corps as a body; but

Radek refused, on the grounds that the Soviet government did not recognize the ambassadorial quality of Noulens. Francis thereupon talked alone with him and with Arthur Ransome, the English correspondent, who had accompanied him as interpreter. Radek reaffirmed that the purpose of his visit was to arrange for the removal of the diplomatic corps to Moscow. When Francis, after a long discussion, made it clear to him that the members of the corps were not prepared to move, Radek replied, "I will station guards around all your embassies. And no one will be permitted to go in or out without a passport."

"We are virtually prisoners, then?" Francis asked.

"No," Radek replied,

you are not virtually prisoners, you can go in and out and the chiefs [of mission] can all go in and out, but when you desire anybody to come in here, you will have to tell the local Soviet the name of the man and they will give him a pass to enter through your guards.[22]

Radek was as good as his word. The guards appeared the following morning. In this way there was inaugurated that curious system of personal supervision, designed to serve simultaneously the purposes of protection, surveillance, and isolation from the local community, without which no American ambassador was permitted to exist in the Soviet Union until after the death of Stalin in 1953.

The next day (July 13) brought a new exchange of communications with Chicherin. The latter was emphatic in denying that the Germans were threatening Moscow, or that they had received permission to introduce their troops there.[23]

For two or three days, agitated exchanges continued between the diplomats, on the one hand, and Radek and Chicherin, on the other. When Francis showed signs of wavering in the face of Chicherin's conciliatory attitude, the French and British stiffened his back (according to Noulens) by showing him the derisive personal observations about himself which Radek had included in his telegrams to

[22] *Ibid.*, pp. 247–248.
[23] The following evening (July 14) the German Chargé did indeed present to Chicherin a demand for the stationing of a company of German soldiers in Moscow for the guarding of the Embassy. The fears of the diplomats were therefore not wholly idle. The Soviet government refused, however, to accede to this demand. Much to the disgust of the German Embassy in Moscow, the matter was not energetically pressed in Berlin. Mirbach's successor, Helfferich, found the situation anything but reassuring, and remained in Moscow—a terrified man—for only a few days. The Germans then withdrew the entire mission from Soviet territory.

Moscow. (The Allied agents had lifted these messages—through processes known best to themselves—from the local telegraph offices.)

At the same time, curiously enough, Chicherin's confidence in the relative good will of the Americans was similarly shaken by the receipt in Moscow of the text of the agreement concluded on July 6 between the Murmansk Soviet and the Allied commanders. The inclusion of the signature of Captain Bierer on this document came as a sharp surprise to the Soviet leaders who had, up to this time, supposed the Murmansk operation to be a purely British show. They had no means of knowing that Bierer had no political instructions of any kind from his own government and considered himself entirely under British command.

❖

In just these days, while Francis sparred with Chicherin over the future of the Vologda diplomats, the continuing process of revolution in which the Bolsheviki had now involved themselves found expression in one more development which, like the suppression of the Constitutent Assembly, did not immediately affect western interests but shocked western opinion and drove perceptibly deeper the psychological wedge that was already coming to separate the peoples of the western world from the new revolutionary power in Russia.

The former Tsar, Nicholas II, had been interned together with his family and household from the late summer of 1917 to the spring of 1918 at Tobolsk, on the Irtysh River in western Siberia. The treatment accorded to the imperial party there, while marked by ups and downs, had not been unendurable.

At the end of April 1918, the family was moved to Ekaterinburg (the present Sverdlovsk), in the Urals. There is reason to suppose that this move was ordered by the Soviet leaders with a view to the eventual execution at least of the Tsar himself, though the exact modalities had not yet been determined.

At Ekaterinburg the family were confined in a gloomy brick edifice, formerly the home of a local businessman by the name of Ipatyev. Here, their treatment deteriorated markedly; they were obliged to endure not only overcrowding and prison food but also personal humiliation and insult at the hands of their guards.

The outbreak of the Czech uprising naturally brought to a head the question of the fate of the imperial family. While Ekaterinburg,

situated on the northern branch of the Trans-Siberian, was not initially involved in the uprising, by early July it was threatened from
three sides by Czech and White forces, pressing both to liberate the
Tsar and to advance toward Archangel, where the Allies were expected to intervene. The early fall of the city was regarded by the
Soviet military authorities as unavoidable.[24] In these circumstances,
the local Communists evidently received from Moscow authority to
take whatever steps they might find necessary to prevent the imperial
family from falling into anti-Bolshevik hands. Although an evacuation of the family to central Russia would still appear to have been
possible in mid-July, the decision was taken by the Urals Regional
Soviet, on July 12, to kill the entire family and household.

During the night of July 16 the members of the imperial party
were awakened and told to come into the cellar. This they did, unaware as yet of the fate that awaited them. The party included, in
addition to the imperial couple and their children, the family doctor
and three servants. The Tsar arrived bearing in his arms his son, the
Tsarevich, aged thirteen, who was too ill to walk.

What followed has been so well told by Mr. William Henry
Chamberlin, in his history of the Russian Revolution,[25] that it remains only to recall his account:

The Tsar stood in the middle of the room, at his side the Tsarevitch
sat in a chair; on his right stood Doctor Botkin. The Tsarina and her
daughters stood behind them near the wall; the three servants stood in
corners of the room. Yurovsky told the Tsar (there is no clear record
of the precise words which he used) that he was to be put to death. The
Tsar did not understand and began to say "What?" whereupon Yurovsky
shot him down with his revolver. This was the signal for the general
massacre. The other executioners, seven Letts and two agents from the

[24] Allen Wardwell tells in his diary on June 15, 1918, how he paid a visit that
day to Radek's office, where he was shown maps illustrating the course of the civil
war. When Radek stepped out of the office for a few moments, Wardwell took
occasion to ask a younger Soviet military officer, who was present, about the situation
of Ekaterinburg. His answer was: "Oh, we are going to lose that." (Wardwell
MSS, *op.cit.*, Diary.)

[25] William Henry Chamberlin, *The Russian Revolution 1917–1921*, The Macmillan
Co., New York, 1935. The above account is taken entirely from Vol. II, Chapter
XXIV, pp. 84–95 of this work, entitled "The End of the Tsarist Family." I have also
had access to the digest, prepared by N. D. Sokolov (the official investigator, subsequently, of the murder), of the report by General M. K. Dietrichs, who commanded
the forces that captured Ekaterinburg, to the Dowager Empress Maria Fedorovna,
about the occurrence. A handwritten copy of this digest, in Russian, will be found
in the Harris MSS, *op.cit.*

Cheka, emptied their revolvers into the bodies of the victims. The Tsar fell first, followed by his son. The room was filled with shrieks and groans; blood poured in streams on the floor. The chambermaid, Demidova, tried to protect herself with a pillow, and delayed her death for a short time. The slaughter was soon ended; Yurovsky fired two additional bullets into the body of the Tsarevitch, who was still groaning and the Letts thrust bayonets into any of the victims who still showed signs of life.

When the telegram reporting the execution reached the Soviet leaders in Moscow, the following day, they were assembled in a meeting devoted to the discussion of quite other matters. The message was handed to Lenin. He read it and passed it on to the others. There was a moment of silence, and a swift sharp glance passed among the members of the group. Then, without a word of comment, they returned—by tacit accord—to the business of the day.

The Soviet leaders had, of course, by this time, burned their bridges. This new responsibility did not materially increase, as they saw it, the burden they already bore. No trace of pity for the victims of this action stirred in their consciousness. Two decades later one of their number, Trotsky, would suffer—as only a devoted parent can —at the realization that his own son had probably been destroyed by Stalin; and the suffering would be rendered more poignant by the reflection that the young man had been completely non-political. That this caused Trotsky to repent his share in the responsibility for the happenings of the night of July 16–17 in Ekaterinburg is doubtful. Such is the revolutionary mentality.

News of the killing of the Tsar was announced by the Soviet government in Moscow on July 25. Nothing was said, in this announcement, about the killing of the family. Rumors of the Tsar's execution had been circulating in the Russian capital for some time—even before the event. Ekaterinburg fell to the Whites on the same day the announcement was made in Moscow. The traces of the murder were at once uncovered, and the true circumstances learned, by the Whites. The news was not long in trickling through to Allied officialdom in Russia.

Allied reactions in the final days of July and the immediately ensuing period must be judged, then, in the light of the fact that to the other causes of western revulsion to the ideas and behavior of the Bolsheviki, there was now being added, in bits and pieces of news and rumor, the knowledge of this sickening, cold-blooded slaughter

of helpless people whose position was as much the product of historical circumstance, and as little the result of their own doing, as were
the social realities on which Marxist thought professed to be based.

✧

To return to events in Vologda: on July 17th a British officer,
Captain McGrath, arrived there from Archangel, empowered by
General Poole to request the Allied diplomats, on the General's behalf, to leave for Archangel, as their continued presence in Vologda
might hamper his military plans. McGrath was evidently authorized
to inform the principal Allied chiefs of mission, including Francis,
of the plans for an Allied landing at Archangel at the end of July or
the beginning of August. In the face of this request, the chiefs of
mission decided to make all preparations for departure, to be ready
to move at a moment's notice, but to remain for the time being in
Vologda and to wait for more definite news about the plans for the
landing.

In this tenuous state matters rested until July 22nd, when the
following extraordinary message, revealing very clearly Soviet pre-
monitions of the forthcoming landing, was received from Chicherin:

> I entreat you most earnestly to leave Vologda. Come here. Danger ap-
> proaching. To-morrow can be too late. When battle rages, distinction of
> houses cannot be made. If all smashed in your domiciles during struggle
> of contending forces responsibility will fall upon your making deaf ear
> to all entreaties. Why bring about catastrophe which you can avert? [26]

For the diplomats, this settled it. They decided to leave for
Archangel at the earliest possible moment. They were afraid, however, that if they told Chicherin their destination was Archangel,
authorization might not be forthcoming to the local railway authorities for their removal. Francis therefore replied, ambiguously:

> Thank you for your telegram. We fully appreciate the uninterrupted
> interest you have taken in our personal safety and have decided to follow
> your advice and are leaving Vologda.

The following morning the diplomats moved back into their
special trains, which had been standing for months on the Vologda
siding. There followed two days of confused exchanges with the

[26] Francis, *op.cit.*, p. 253.

Soviet authorities about the question of locomotives for the diplomatic party. At times it looked as though the diplomats would not be permitted to depart at all. When locomotives were finally produced, shortly after midnight on the morning of Thursday, July 25th, the diplomats watched anxiously to see which end of the train they would be attached to, fearing that the intention might be to haul them off to Moscow, after all. These fears, fortunately, were idle. At two in the morning the trains pulled out, northbound, in the early northern dawn, on the line to Archangel.

The party arrived at the Bakaritsa terminal, across the river from Archangel, the following morning. Here there ensued nearly forty-eight hours of uninterrupted confusion and wrangling with the local Soviet authorities. The latter were now well aware that some sort of action against Archangel was imminent; they were, in consequence, highly nervous about the arrival of the diplomatic trains. There seemed to be endless sources of disagreement: whether the diplomats could remain at Archangel, whether they could communicate with their governments (these questions were both decided in the negative), on what sort of vessels and under what sort of protection they should be removed, what should be done about their baggage and passports. The shadowboxing was made more elaborate and more agonizing by the fact that neither side was inclined to mention what was uppermost in everyone's mind. There were tense moments when it looked as though the diplomats would be held, after all, as hostages.

While all this was going on, the Allied party continued to live on the train (except the British, who casually moved out onto a houseboat provided by their consul). From the train windows the Americans could look out across the wide river to the distant skyline of Archangel, where exactly one week later the Allied force would be landing. Finally, in the wee hours of the night from Saturday to Sunday, the clearance was given and arrangements were made for them to leave at once in two Russian vessels, to be escorted by a Soviet armed trawler. A note of comedy was added at the last moment, when the bewildered members of a British economic good will mission, whom some unsuspecting department of the British government had trustingly despatched to Russia in the midst of the confusion and who had got as far as Moscow before discovering into what a hornets' nest they had wandered, emerged from a passenger train just arrived from the interior, and, charging down the dock, leaped on board with the others, endlessly relieved to be escaping from the fantastic world whose favor they were supposed to have cultivated. At four a.m. the vessels cast off and proceeded down the delta. By midmorning they were clear of the islands. Course was then laid for Kandalaksha (now held, of course, by the British) on the western shore of the White Sea.

The voyage lasted into the following day. For a time that night, Francis stood on the deck, gazing at the northern horizon. Poetry had never been his bent, and he was now far removed from the time of life when romantic strings are struck in the human breast by the prospect of natural beauty; yet even he could not remain oblivious to the splendor of the Arctic night. The sea was as smooth as glass. The sky was cloudless. The sunset, burning in the northern sky, moved gradually to the east as it transformed itself, with undiminished brilliance, into the sunrise.

The turmoil and violence of revolutionary Russia, by which Francis had been surrounded unintermittently for some seventeen months, was now left behind. Of Russia itself he had not seen the last; for he was destined to undergo one more brief tour of service in Allied-held Archangel before being taken away, a sick and aging man, on the *Olympia*. But he now had completed his service under the Red flag. In the face of all the besetting complexity of his problems, in the face of the paucity of guidance and encouragement from Washington, and in the face of real danger to his person, he had done his duty as he saw it, with persistence, fidelity, and courage. He could depart with good conscience.

It would be fifteen years, now, before another American ambassador would set foot on Soviet soil and another period of direct Soviet-American relations—less colorful, outwardly more orderly, but burdened by this time with an even greater weight of conflicting commitment on both sides—would be ushered in.

CHAPTER XX

THE END AT MOSCOW

All too clearly I saw that the role of hostages, which had originally been destined for the Ambassadors, would now be reserved for us.—Bruce Lockhart, concerning the period following departure of the ambassadors from Vologda

IT is difficult to imagine what the western chanceries envisaged as the likely fate of the Allied officials left in Moscow, once the intervention had begun; nor is it possible to ascertain, from the available record, whether particular thought was given to this question at all. While the more senior of the Allied officials in Russia were aware, by the time the ambassadors left Vologda, that something was brewing in the north, neither the English nor the Americans had any proper notification from their governments as to what was planned or any instructions as to how they should conduct themselves vis-à-vis the Soviet authorities in the face of such a situation. Poole, in fact, had been out of touch with his government since the beginning of July—the stoppage of his telegraphic messages having evidently been occasioned, as in the case of Francis, by the break between Murmansk (the telegraph relay point) and Moscow. But even had he been in touch with the State Department, it is doubtful that he would have received any forewarning of the contemplated Allied step. The matter was in British hands; and it is not at all certain that even official Washington knew the troops were to be landed at just that time.

The first days following the departure of the ambassadors from Vologda passed peacefully enough in Moscow, though with considerable nervousness on both sides. All were uneasily aware that something was about to occur which would have an important and unpredictable effect on the status of the Allied representatives there. Chicherin, anxious not to precipitate difficulties, expressed to Poole the hope that relations would not be impaired by the envoys' depar-

[453]

ture; Poole and the other consular officers assured Chicherin that they saw no reason why the political situation should be affected; the *Izvestiya* hopefully published both statements.

But no one was comfortable. The Allied representatives strongly suspected that behind all the politeness they were already, in reality, hostages. On the morning of July 26, the consuls visited Chicherin in a body and proposed the immediate departure via Archangel of all Allied military personnel—still a fairly numerous contingent, mostly French and Italian. Chicherin was serious and "studiously polite." [1] He voiced agreement in principle, but indicated that others would have to be consulted. After three days of inconclusive conferences and exchanges, Chicherin informed Poole, on the 29th, that in view of the situation at Archangel the military contingent would not be permitted to leave through that port, and its departure would have to be indefinitely delayed. [2]

This was serious. It meant that the Allied military personnel, and probably the others as well, were indeed hostages.

That night, Lenin spoke at a joint session of the Moscow Soviet and various labor union bodies in the capital. By arrangement with Chicherin, the Allied consuls were permitted to have a representative present. It was a long and violent speech. The first part of it consisted largely of a bitter attack on the British. Recognizing that a time of most serious danger had arrived for Soviet power, Lenin laid this largely to the intrigues of the British and French with the Russian opposition parties. Charging the British and French with responsibility for the Czech uprising, [3] greatly exaggerating the scale of British operations at Murmansk, and dwelling at length on British intrigues at Baku (where British agents were now busy trying to counteract Turkish-German influence), Lenin went on to allege that British-French imperialism "which for four years has covered the world with blood in the effort to achieve world domination," had now mounted

[1] Lockhart, *op.cit.*, p. 304. The Soviet refusal to permit the Germans to bring in a uniformed German guard for their embassy had led the Germans to put pressure on Moscow for the expulsion of the Allied military missions. The Allied desire to have them removed presumably reflected the realization that their usefulness was ended.

[2] *Foreign Relations, 1918, Russia*, Vol. I, *op.cit.*, p. 648.

[3] As evidence for this, Lenin cited sums allegedly passed to the Czech Corps by British and French representatives in Russia. He seems either to have failed to understand, or to have deliberately concealed, the fact that the Czech force had been accepted as an integral part of the French army. There was, in the light of this fact, nothing in any way unnatural in the fact that the Corps should have received financial support from British and French sources.

an operation to "throttle" the Soviet republic and to plunge Russia into an imperialist war. In this way, the Russian civil war had merged, Lenin said, with war from outside:

The uprising of the *kulaks,* the Czechoslovak mutiny, the Murmansk movement—this is all one war, descending upon Russia. . . . We have again gotten into war, we *are* at war, and this war is not only a civil war— it is now Anglo-French imperialism which opposes us; it is not yet in a position to launch its legions against Russia: geographic conditions stand in the way; but it gives all that it can—all its millions, all its diplomatic connections and forces—to the support of our enemies.[4]

With sinking hearts, the Allied consuls listened to the report their representative brought back from this meeting. What did this mean? Was a state of war considered to exist? Were they on enemy territory?

Thirty years later, Poole observed:

We've now got used to this idea of cold war—or "no war, no peace," as Trotsky said—but thirty years ago we thought in the black-and-white terms of international law—either you were at war or you were at peace.[5]

Poole himself, at that moment in 1918, favored ignoring Lenin's speech. Why, he argued, precipitate an issue?[6] But the others were all for an insistence on clarification. Together, they called on Chicherin (July 30). Was this, they inquired, a declaration of war? Did it imply the rupture of the existing *de facto* relations? Were they to leave?

Chicherin was evasive. What existed was, he explained, a "state of defense" rather than a state of war. It need not "necessarily" imply a rupture of relations.

The consuls were not satisfied. They would expect, they said, an explanation. Otherwise, they would depart.

While they were still in Chicherin's office, the latter received a message telling of the assassination (by a young S-R) of the German commander in the Ukraine, Field Marshal v. Eichhorn. To the amazement of the foreign representatives, Chicherin, the most sedentary of men, reacted to this news by rising from his desk and doing a little dance of glee around the room, waving the message in the air. "You

[4] Lenin, *Socheneniya, op.cit.,* Vol. 28, *July 1918–March 1919,* pp. 1–13. The last quoted passage occurs on pp. 12–13.

[5] Columbia University Oral History Project, Butler Library, New York; transcript of recorded reminiscences of DeWitt C. Poole.

[6] *Loc.cit.*

see," he observed, "what happens when foreigners intervene against the wishes of the people." [7] To the consuls, glumly aware of the probable impending advent of their forces on Russian soil, the impression conveyed by this incident was not a happy one.

The following day, Karakhan admitted to the Japanese Consul, Ueda, that the Allied representatives were all being held as hostages. This was confirmed, two days later, by Radek. Chicherin, on the other hand, wrote to Poole on August 2 that negotiations had been opened with the Germans looking toward the provision of safe-conduct for the departure of the Allied missions via Finland. The fact is that there was already considerable difference of opinion within the Soviet government as to how the Allied officials should be treated—Chicherin favoring their prompt release, the Party and secret police favoring their detention and, at a later date, their incarceration or, in some instances, even execution. Increasingly, now, the Allied officials would be the victims of the vacillations of Soviet policy occasioned by these differences and the lack of coordination between the Foreign Affairs Commissariat and the secret police.

On the 3rd, Poole held a solemn meeting of all the American officials and residents. They numbered about a hundred, all told. He told them he feared intervention was imminent (unbeknownst to him, it was actually already taking place) and urged them all to depart. He would try, he said, to arrange as soon as possible for their evacuation via Finland.

The next morning (August 4), the blow fell. The news of the Archangel landing spread like wildfire through the city, occasioning great excitement. No one knew the scale or exact purpose of the incursion. The assumption was that there would now be some sort of an Allied march on Moscow.

The effect on the Soviet leaders was not long in making itself felt. On the morning of the 5th some 200 British and French nationals were arrested and placed in confinement in a building on the Smolenski Boulevard. Poole, in company with his Swedish and Japanese colleagues, at once called on Chicherin and Karakhan. The Soviet officials stated that the private Allied nationals would be held as hostages, but that the French and British consular officers would not be arrested.

---

[7] Lockhart, *op.cit.*, p. 305. It was Poole who recalled (in his orally recorded reminiscences, *op.cit.*) Chicherin's little jig.

No sooner had Poole and the others returned to their offices when they learned that the consular officers, contrary to Chicherin's assurances, had also already been taken into custody by the police. The latter had not even hesitated to violate the British consular premises; they had carried out the arrests within the building, apparently oblivious to the clouds of smoke belching from the chimneys from the packages of secret files that had been tossed, at the last moment, into the stoves. The arrests appear to have been ordered by the local Party authorities, without the knowledge of the Foreign Office.[8]

Later in the day Poole received a long letter from Chicherin, obviously written before the latter had knowledge of the arrest of the consuls. It was a measure of the importance Chicherin still attached to American opinion that he should have taken time out to write this letter at what must have been a crushingly busy moment.

After detailing the Soviet complaint against the intervention and asking Poole to inform his government "that a wholly unjustifiable attack and obvious act of violence has been launched against us," Chicherin reiterated the assurance that the diplomatic immunity of the official representatives would be respected.[9]

All this, and particularly the revelation of Chicherin's helplessness vis-à-vis the police, was for Poole the breaking point. He saw no possibility of continuing to carry on without jeopardizing the interests he was there to represent. He had, now, no one to turn to. The Ambassador was gone. There was no communication with Washington. The decision was his. The following day he burned his codes, closed his office, turned the premises over to the custody of his Scandinavian colleagues (provisionally, the Swedes; permanently, the Norwegians), and placed himself and his nationals under the latter's protec-

---

[8] See *Foreign Relations, 1918, Russia,* Vol. I, *op.cit.,* p. 652. The consular officers themselves were released the following day, on the intercession of their Swedish colleague. Wardwell, who applied himself from that time on with untiring devotion to the welfare of the Allied nationals, also succeeded in arranging for the immediate release of some of the women. But it was many weeks before all of these Allied citizens would regain their liberty.

[9] Yuri V. Klyuchnikov & Andrei Sabanin, *Mezhdunarodnaya politika noveishego vremeni v dogovorakh, notakh, i deklaratsiyakh* (International Politics of Recent Times with Documents, Notes, and Declarations), Izdaniye Litizdata NKID, Moscow, 1925, Part II, pp. 162–163. (For a full English translation, see Degras, Vol. I, *op.cit.,* pp. 93–95.)

In this letter, Chicherin also asked Poole, perhaps rhetorically, for enlightenment as to British intentions: "What does Great Britain want from us? . . . the destruction of the most popular government the world has ever seen? . . . counterrevolution?"

tion, such as it was (the neutral representatives had plenty of trouble themselves in dealing with the aroused Bolsheviki). He immediately asked for a train and safe-conduct for the Americans, for exit via Finland.

❖

Meanwhile the junior officials who had been left behind at Vologda were also having their troubles. The Bolsheviki, aware that something was about to happen at Archangel, were determined that no Allied influence should remain at Vologda. Kedrov, the all-powerful commissar for the Northern Region, was at once sent to Vologda, after the ambassadors had left, to clean up the situation.

Francis had left his Third Secretary of Embassy, young Norman Armour, to hold the Embassy building in Vologda, to look after the few remaining Americans there, and to serve, if necessary, as a channel of communication to Poole. On August 1, Kedrov sent word to Armour that Vologda was unsafe—he must leave at once for Moscow. A special train, it was said, would be ready the following evening, for all the remaining Allied personnel. The communication was peremptory. There was no doubting that Kedrov meant business. Armour, nevertheless, decided not to board the train except under duress. He spent the day of the 2nd burning the remaining official files, but kept two of the cumbersome old code books then in use. Then he settled down to wait for the Soviet authorities who, he knew, would come to evict him.

Looking around the empty premises, in the evening, as the zero hour drew near, he saw that someone had left an old top hat in a corner. This he placed—as a parting shot—in the empty safe, twirled the combination dials, got a batch of official red tape, and sealed the receptacle up as impressively as possible. (He heard later that the Communists worked for five hours to get the safe open, and finally blew it up.)

During the night the authorities arrived, bringing thirty or forty armed men with machine guns. Armour and the other remaining Allied nationals were marched down and placed on board a train where, under heavy guard, they endured an odyssey of several days before arriving in Moscow. On the way, Armour—now uncertain as to whether they would ever be freed—sat for many hours burning the heavy code books, page by page, in the little samovar chimney at the end of the car, while British and French friends stood guard to warn of any communist approach.[10] On August 8, the Vologda party joined the other Americans in Moscow.

❖

Three weeks passed before the American contingent could leave Moscow. The Finnish frontier was, in the last analysis, the only conceivable route of exit. This meant that safe-conduct had to be obtained, through neutral governments, from the Germans and the Finns. The little group of Allied officials became, in this period, progressively isolated and made to feel the hostility of Soviet officialdom. Repeatedly, their quarters were abruptly requisitioned and they were sent scurrying about for other shelter. Wardwell, basking in the still perceptible warmth of Robins' reputation, was relatively well treated (though he, too, was at least once evicted from his diggings), and he utilized to good advantage the standing and freedom this gave him. Daily, he visited the imprisoned French and British, looked after their needs, took their messages, interceded with the Soviet authorities for their release or their comfort.

The Allied officials were variously affected, according to their political views and their previous knowledge of Allied intentions, by the news that trickled through, in just those days, of the Archangel landing. None were happy. Even those who had favored intervention were shocked at the frivolous manner in which the action was undertaken. On the 10th, Lockhart, calling on Karakhan, found the latter's face wreathed in smiles. It had just been learned in the Kremlin that the total force of the expedition that had landed in Archangel was only a few hundred men. Lockhart was thunderstruck at the implications of this news. He had, at the end, favored intervention, but only in adequate strength. He recognized at once, as did the other hostages in Moscow, that an intervention with inadequate forces would be disastrous to Allied prestige in the Soviet capital. "It was a blunder," he observed in his reminiscences,

comparable with the worst mistakes of the Crimean war. . . . It raised hopes which could not be fulfilled. It intensified the civil war and sent

[10] For the official account of Armour's experiences, see *Foreign Relations, 1918, Russia*, Vol. 1, *op.cit.*, pp. 669–670. Remaining data are from Armour's personal account to me.

thousands of Russians to their death. Indirectly, it was responsible for the Terror. Its direct effect was to provide the Bolsheviks with a cheap victory, to give them new confidence, and to galvanise them into a strong and ruthless organism.[11]

The Americans, largely innocent of any knowledge of Allied plans, were even more bewildered. Wardwell gave vent to his feelings in his diary at the end of August. The text of the President's communiqué of August 3, repeating much of the *aide-mémoire,* had now finally trickled through to Moscow. "We cannot understand," Wardwell wrote,

just what America's attitude is in regard of intervention. . . . We hear Americans have landed in Archangel and are also coming in from the East with the Japanese. The American statement . . . seems hardly frank; they say they are not in favor of intervention, but are coming in solely to protect Allied military supplies at Archangel and to protect the Czecho-Slovaks from the armed German and Austrian war prisoners.

This explanation, Wardwell went on to observe, was "utter rot." The Czechs were fighting the Red Army, not Germany and Austria. The war prisoners were few and unimportant. How, then, was one to understand the American attitude?

. . . Are we going on to support the Czechs, who, at the moment, are the most formidable enemies of the Bolsheviks, or are we to back down and leave the Czechs stranded, or are we trying to straddle the two questions? It looks a good deal like the latter and the questions cannot be straddled, they must be met. . . . If we are fighting these people let's say so and get it over . . .[12]

It was not until the night of August 26–27 that the necessary clearances could be obtained and the special train bearing most of the remaining American residents (some ninety-five persons, mainly personnel of the former Consulate General, the Y.M.C.A., and the National City Bank's Russian branch) despatched from Moscow. Wardwell and Poole both decided not to leave with the others: Wardwell, because one of his Red Cross staff, Mr. J. W. Andrews (later to be president of Liggett and Myers Tobacco Company), had been stricken with rheumatic fever and was hospitalized and unable to travel; Poole, in part because he thought his influence might yet

[11] Lockhart, *op.cit.,* p. 308.
[12] Wardwell MSS, *op.cit.,* Diary entry of August 27.

be useful to his Allied consular colleagues, whose safety and eventual liberation from Russia were by no means assured, and in part—he being young and rash and adventurous—out of sheer curiosity to see what was going to happen and a feeling that it might be useful to his government if he stayed. The courageous action of these two young Americans in remaining at their posts, and the comfort and aid they subsequently contrived to afford to their Allied colleagues, earned for them the lasting gratitude of the latter and their governments.

Armour pleaded to be allowed to remain with them; but he paid the penalty for being the youngest in rank, and was ordered categorically to take charge of the party of evacuees, and accompany them to Finland. Arriving at Petrograd on August 28, he and his charges were detained in the yards there. The city, famine-stricken, terrorized, deserted now by at least a half a million of its former inhabitants, was only the wraith of the great teeming capital that had existed on the banks of the Neva the year before. The cold hand of the Terror was already chilling and laming the place, inflicting upon it that strange species of blight—a lifelessness, a furtive drabness, a sense of the sinister lurking behind a peeling façade, and everywhere a hushed, guarded inscrutability—which seems to be the effect of the communist touch on any great urban area. Dismayed and appalled, the American evacuees, living in their train in the railway yards, wandered through the stricken city, along semi-deserted streets, over pavements already beginning to be grass-grown, among buildings already fading from neglect. Some of the Americans endeavored to seek out old Petrograd acquaintances, only to be met with frightened faces, fingers hastily placed before the lips, doors slammed abruptly in their faces.

If Poole and Wardwell had looked forward to a relative respite from trouble and responsibility once the American party had been sent out, they were doomed to disappointment. The Americans had not been gone four days (they were, in fact, still in Petrograd) when the heavens fell. In Petrograd, at 11:30 a.m. on August 30, the head of the local Cheka, Uritski, was shot dead in front of the secret police headquarters by a young military cadet of Baltic origin. The news, reaching Moscow in the afternoon, caused intense consternation and anger among the Bolsheviki. Lenin spoke that evening at a workers' meeting at the former Mikhelson plant in the southern section of Moscow. The violence of his feelings was reflected in the demagoguery—extreme even for him—of his language. The issue was now drawn, he argued, between the parasitic banditry of the property-owning classes and their British and French allies, "masquerading under the slogans of freedom and equality," and the working proletariat. "There is only one of two ways out for us: either victory or death." [13]

As he left the building on completion of his speech, Lenin was shot twice—once in the neck, once in the chest—by a young woman, a Left S-R, Dora Kaplan. At death's door, seemingly, he was taken away to the hospital.[14]

Bolshevik fury now knew no bounds. The steady hand of Lenin himself was temporarily absent. The others, frightened and infuriated, were left to themselves. Their reaction was to launch a campaign of terror as savage and bloody and undiscriminating as anything the modern world has seen. To the Cheka units all over the country word went out to go to the limit. Chekists showing mercy were themselves to be shot. The results were appalling. In Petrograd alone over 500 persons—none even charged with complicity in either of the assassinations—were executed within two days after Uritski's murder. Similar retribution was taken all over Russia. Everywhere, the air was filled with tales of execution, incarcerations, tortures, and excesses of every kind, only too many of them true. Terror was now, for the first time since the Revolution, ubiquitous and unrestrained—the dominant element in the situation.

This new shock could not fail to affect the position of the Allied hostages in Russia. On the day after the murder and assault (August 31) an armed group of aroused Communists stormed into the

[13] Lenin, Vol. 28, *op.cit.,* pp. 71–73. In this speech, incidentally, Lenin made further reference to the United States which revealed either his ignorance of American reality or his utter disregard for it. "Let us take," he said, looking around for an example of the hypocrisy of the western world in its professed attachment to the principles of equality and brotherhood, "America, the freest and most civilized of all. There they have a democratic republic. And so what? A handful not of millionaires but of billionaires rules over everything, and the entire people remains in slavery and subjection. If the factories, plants, banks, and all the riches of the country belong to the capitalists, and alongside the democratic republic we see a serflike enslavement of millions of toilers and an impenetrable destitution— then, one must ask, where does one find here your famous equality and brotherhood?"

[14] Lenin's escape from death was little short of miraculous. Had the bullet that struck his chest deviated a fraction of an inch from the course it took, death would have been certain. As it was, he recovered relatively rapidly.

Petrograd British Embassy building, still occupied by a remnant of the British staff. The senior of the British officials, Captain Francis N. A. Cromie, former Assistant Naval Attaché, attempted to bar the way, only to be told that if he did not stand aside, he would be "shot like a dog." He then opened fire himself and killed two of the intruders before perishing himself, in the encounter.[15] The remainder of the staff were imprisoned in most wretched circumstances, first at the Cheka headquarters and then in the Fortress of St. Peter and St. Paul.

In Moscow, too, the effect on the situation of the remaining Allied nationals was drastic. Lockhart was arrested on the day of the Cromie murder, held overnight in Lubyanka (headquarters of the Moscow Cheka and subsequently of the entire Soviet secret police system), forced to undergo a harrowing confrontation *à deux* with the doomed Dora Kaplan just prior to her execution, and then released again the following morning.

Shaken and horror-stricken at the flood of events, the little band of Allied officials still at large met that day in the premises of the former American Consulate General, where Poole was living and where Wardwell had now joined him. They glumly debated what they should do if they found themselves in Cromie's position, and came to no agreement.[16] The little group were by this time almost wholly isolated. They were, as a rule, no longer received at the Soviet Foreign Office. It was dangerous for them to see their Russian friends. Cut off, uninformed, surrounded with the most menacing official hostility, they awaited whatever might befall them. In horror at what was transpiring, Poole addressed to the Department a message (to be sent through the Norwegians) setting forth the ghastly plight into which intervention had brought the moderate Russians and those friendly to the Allied cause. Some alleviation might pos-

---

[15] Legend has it that the mob had been aroused over a report that Uritski's murderer had taken refuge in the English Club (an institution which had no connection with England beyond the name). The Soviet version was that Cromie, after shooting the others, shot himself. The English version was that he was shot by the intruders. I have not been able to establish the precise facts. The body, reputedly barbarously mutilated, was recovered from the Cheka, two or three days later, by the Dutch and Danish representatives and given a hero's burial, from the English Church.

[16] Poole later recalled with admiration Wardwell's firmness and courage on this occasion. Though he deplored the events that had produced this tension, Wardwell insisted that the others must now stand morally behind Cromie's action and face the situation with equal dignity and courage. "We must do nothing," he said "which would discredit Cromie." (Columbia University Oral History Project, *op.cit.*)

sibly be produced, he thought, if the neutral governments would protest publicly.

. . . The other and truly efficacious course is a rapid military advance from the north. Our present halfway action is cruel in the extreme. Our landing has set up the Bolshevik death agony.[17]

On September 2, Chicherin, reporting to the Central Executive Committee on the state of Soviet foreign relations, described the deterioration of relations with the Allies, reiterating the usual charges of Anglo-French instigation of the Yaroslavl insurrection and other disorders, and explaining the reasons for internment of the British and French citizens. In this connection he added that the Soviet attitude toward American citizens was "entirely different."

. . . although the United States Government also was compelled by its Allies to agree to participate in intervention, so far only formally, its decision is not regarded by us as irrevocable.[18]

This mild statement reflected Chicherin's own opinion. But it did not reflect the mood of the Cheka and of Soviet officialdom generally, in the face of which the position of the remaining Americans was now precarious and disagreeable in the extreme.

On September 4 Lockhart was again arrested—this time for an imprisonment of many weeks. The air was full, by this time, of the tales and evidences of slaughter and horror on every hand. Poole, now shocked to the point of desperation, took pen in hand that day and addressed a letter to Chicherin, protesting futilely against the terror. "It is impossible for me to believe," he wrote,

that you approve of the mad career into which the Bolshevik government has now plunged. Your cause totters on the verge of complete moral bankruptcy. . . . You must stop at once the barbarous oppression of your own people.[19]

Wardwell followed this up some days later (September 8) with a similar letter, saying that the American Red Cross—"an association whose object it is to relieve human suffering"—could not allow this

---

[17] *Foreign Relations, 1918, Russia,* Vol. I, *op.cit.,* p. 682, from telegram of September 3, 1918.

[18] Degras, Vol. I, *op.cit.,* p. 104. Chicherin was not aware, of course, that General Graves had arrived in Vladivostok the preceding day, or that two American infantry regiments had been there earlier. Nor could he know that American units would be going ashore at Archangel two days later.

[19] *Foreign Relations, 1918, Russia,* Vol. I, *op.cit.,* p. 683.

"unwarranted slaughter" to pass unnoticed. In the name of the "simplest principles of humanity and of justice which must be the basis of any form of government which has at heart the best interests of the people," he added his protest to that of Poole.[20]

Poole's note was not acknowledged. It is not likely that Chicherin understood his motives. Chicherin subsequently told someone, Poole recalled later,

. . . that he didn't understand why I had written him this challenging note. He could only surmise that I had hoped to bring reprisal of some kind, perhaps my arrest, in the hope . . . that this would precipitate serious intervention by the United States.[21]

To Wardwell, Chicherin did reply, some days later (September 11). The reply was a long and impassioned letter, bitterly charging the American Red Cross with indifference to the cruelties perpetrated by the enemies of Bolshevism. "In the passion of the struggle tearing our whole people," Chicherin wrote,

do you not see the sufferings, untold during generations, of all the unknown millions, who were dumb during centuries and whose concentrated despair and rage have at last burst into the open . . . ? . . . Do you not see the beauties of the heroism of the working class, trampled under the feet of everybody who were above them until now, and now rising in fury and passionate devotion and enthusiasm to recreate the whole world and the whole life of mankind? [22]

Poor Chicherin! Among all the individual revolutionary enthusiasms of this early day, there was none purer or more selfless than his, and none destined for more bitter disappointment.

On the 6th, two days after Lockhart was taken for the second time, orders went out for the arrest of the remaining Allied officials, other than the Americans. General Lavergne, French Consul General Grenard, and a number of others were meeting with Poole, in the building of the former American Consulate General (next to the English Church, on the Bryusovski Pereulok), when the agents of the Cheka proceeded to the execution of their task. Not wishing to violate the American building, now under Norwegian protection, the police squad waited on the street, outside the gate. When the

[20] *Ibid.*, pp. 685–686.
[21] Columbia University Oral History Project, *op.cit.*
[22] *Foreign Relations, 1918, Russia*, Vol. 1, *op.cit.*, pp. 714–715.

Allied officials left, the attempt was made to take them into custody. Poole, seeing what was going on, rushed out, dragged his colleagues back through the gate, and forbade the police to enter the premises. The police respected this inhibition but surrounded the premises with a permanent armed guard, cut off the water and electricity, and settled down to a state of siege. Only Poole and his cook were permitted to go in and out.

The siege endured about a fortnight. The police were not aware that the basement of the building was used as a storage place for the remaining supplies of the American Red Cross—a circumstance which greatly simplified the food problem—nor were they aware that a single water faucet in the basement continued for some inexplicable reason to flow. The internees maliciously fortified their guardians in this latter ignorance by ostentatiously dragging out the bathtubs to catch rain water whenever the heavens were obliging enough to provide any.

After a week of fruitless effort to bring about a termination of the siege, Poole made a trip to Petrograd to enlist the help of the Norwegians, whose representatives had remained in that city. When he returned (September 15), things had become very ugly indeed. The weather had now turned cold and raw. The guard, fed up with their chilly, wet vigil, cast bitter glances at the house and muttered that the time had come to go in and finish things off. That they were quite capable of doing this could not be doubted. News of the American participation in the two interventions had, moreover, at last reached Moscow; and the edge of Soviet hostility was now, for the first time, turned full force against the Americans. On the 17th all the remaining Y.M.C.A. personnel, headed by Mr. Paul Anderson, were arrested. It was clear that Poole's hours of freedom were now numbered.

It was in these circumstances that Poole received, by messenger from Chicherin, an instruction addressed to him by the United States government. The Embassy at Paris, knowing no other way of relaying this message to Poole, had thoughtfully had it broadcast by radio, and the Soviet monitors had picked it up. It directed Poole categorically to leave at once—by any possible route.[23] It was, unquestionably, an act of kindness on Chicherin's part to pass it on to him.

[23] The text of the message will be found *ibid.*, p. 671.

Poole was now wholly isolated. Almost all of his Allied friends were under arrest or detention. He could aid them no further. He had no staff, no assistant, no access to the authorities, and no prestige. The Cheka were now quite uncontrollable from the standpoint of the Foreign Affairs Commissariat. Their patience with Poole was plainly running out. Chicherin's action had been a hint.

Poole decided to accept the instruction. He had, indeed, no choice. He succeeded, without difficulty, in obtaining from the Foreign Affairs Commissariat through his neutral colleagues the papers necessary for his exit across the border. But he dared not let the Cheka know of his plans. After first getting the cook to smuggle a small bag of belongings out of the besieged building, he sauntered casually out of the front door, on the morning of September 18, saluted amicably the young communist virago who commanded the guard detachment, and disappeared into the city. Recovering his bag at a prearranged spot, he made his way across town to the railway station, and sat there, concealed among the masses of humanity encamped, as always, on its slimy floors, until the train left in the evening.

Arriving in Petrograd the next day, Poole threw himself on the mercies of the Norwegians. He was housed for the night in the old American Embassy building on the Furshtatskaya, which Francis had left only six months before. The following morning, accompanied by two Norwegians—a vice consul and a courier—he proceeded by train to the Finnish frontier at Byeloostrov. It was the 20th of September. A cold autumnal rain streamed down on the pine-forested suburbs, with their long avenues of deserted, boarded summer cottages. At the frontier, the senior Soviet official turned out, happily, to be one who had been bribed with $1,000 to permit the first trainload of Americans to pass through. We will let Poole tell the rest in his own words:

The Russian officer in command . . . and the Norwegian vice consul were apparently good friends, and they went to his office and talked. I walked impatiently up and down the platform. I could look down across a creek and see a squad of Finnish soldiers on the other side . . . marking the frontier. I grew more and more impatient, so after a while I burst into the room where these two men were, to the evident annoyance of the Russian, and said: "Look here, you say I can go. Well, I want to go." So with annoyance he said all right, and we walked down the hill in the drizzling rain. They stopped at the beginning of the little bridge that spanned the creek and I walked through the middle where a Finnish officer was waiting. . . . Thank Heaven when I identified myself the officer said: "Yes, I am expecting you, and you can enter Finland."

I hadn't had any sleep for a long time because of those Red Guards around the consulate general, and I think when I heard this last good news I kind of passed out for a minute. I was standing there and the next thing I knew this Finnish officer said to me very nicely. . . . "Don't you want to come in out of the rain?"

I looked and saw that my two Norwegian friends were already back where we had come from. So I must have been standing there for quite a while. So I went into the little shelter where the Finnish guard was gathered . . .[24]

It was later learned, from the Norwegian courier who had remained at the Soviet frontier station, that orders for Poole's arrest reached the officer in charge just ten minutes after he passed through.

✧

Wardwell and the remaining members of the Red Cross Mission were now all that remained in Moscow of the official, or semiofficial, American group.[25] By October 5, Andrews was sufficiently restored that he could be moved, albeit on a stretcher. He and Wardwell proceeded that day to Petrograd. There was a long delay there, and it was not until October 17 that they proceeded, with the morning train, as Poole had done a month before, to the frontier at Byeloostrov. Four were in the party that morning: Wardwell himself, Andrews (still on a stretcher), a Red Cross physician, Dr. Davidson, and a British trained nurse, Miss Kean (daughter of a Scottish pastor), who had also remained to take care of Andrews.

Iron gates had now been mounted at each end of the little bridge where Poole had passed—one for the Finns, one for the Bolsheviki. There were no difficulties, this time, with the Soviet border control. The magic aura of Raymond Robins still hovered benevolently over the little party and its relations with the Soviet authorities. The Soviet gate was opened. Wardwell paid 600 rubles to have the baggage taken to the middle of the little bridge. The party followed. The Soviet gate was closed again. Some husky Finns appeared, un-

[24] Columbia University Oral History Project, *op.cit.*
[25] Mr. Paul Anderson and the other remaining Y.M.C.A. men were released and permitted to depart shortly after Wardwell's departure.

The Vologda diplomats on the day of their entrainment for Archangel, July 23, 1918

Seated, l-r: Italian Chargé Torretta, French Ambassador Noulens, Ambassador Francis, Serbian Minister Spaleikovitch, Japanese Chargé Maruono, British Chargé Lindley; standing, l-r: Brazilian Chargé Kelsch, French Counselor Dulcet, and Chinese Chargé Chen-Yen-Chi

Deserted, grass-grown Petrograd, 1918. The storming of the Winter Palace took place here one year earlier

Letter from the British Foreign Secretary to the American Ambassador commending Wardwell, Webster, and Poole

Consul DeWitt C. Poole

locked their gate, lifted Andrews up and disappeared with him and Miss Kean, locking the gate behind them.

For an hour and a half Wardwell and Davidson sat forlornly on the railway ties of the little bridge (from which the tracks had now been removed), confined between the two strife-torn worlds of thought and feeling which no one had been able to hold together.

This was a moment to which, in view of the danger and strain and anxiety of the recent weeks, one had long looked forward; yet now that it was here it was like a death. The sky was leaden; a cold wind blew from the northwest. The wooden shelter on the Finnish side was deserted. Above, on the Soviet side, the figure of a Red Guard, rifle slung on shoulder, greatcoat collar turned up against the wind, was silhouetted against the low scudding clouds. The little stream, hurrying to the Gulf of Finland, swirled past the wooden pilings and carried its eddies swiftly and silently away into the swamps below. Along the Soviet bank a tethered nanny goat, indifferent to all the ruin and all the tragedy, nibbled patiently at the sparse dying foliage.

At last the Finns reappeared, rolling a handcar, and opened the gate. Wardwell and Davidson, with their help, moved the baggage over and placed it on the handcar. The Finnish gate now clanked down again behind them—one more link in that iron curtain that was to constitute through coming decades the greatest and saddest of the world's political realities.

Slowly, pushing the handcar before them, the little group disappeared down the track—into the comforts and problems and preoccupations of another life.

EPILOGUE

LESS than a month after Wardwell passed into Finland, World War I came to an end. With this development, the stated reasons for the presence of American forces in Russia lost what little validity they might previously have had. To the extent there might have been substance behind the fears that, in the absence of intervention, the war stores in Russian harbors would fall into German hands, or the northern ports would be subject to German attack, or Siberia would be seized for the Germans by the war prisoners, such substance was finally nullified by the collapse of the Central Powers and the termination of hostilities. As for the Czechs, they had, as we have seen, long since effected the junction of their forces in Siberia; all that now prevented their departure for their homeland was the absence of Allied shipping and their involvement in the Russian civil war. The American forces had scarcely arrived in Russia when history invalidated at a single stroke almost every reason Washington had conceived for their being there.

The United States government had, then, little to show, at the end of the first year of the Soviet-American relationship, for its efforts to cope with the problems posed for it by the Russian Revolution. Not only had it committed several thousands of its soldiers to a military involvement on Russian soil which had now lost what rationale it might once have had and which could not, in the circumstances, have been more confused, more futile, or more misleading, but it had sacrificed to this dubious undertaking the slender thread of communication with the new government in Russia which had existed in the form of the official and semi-official staffs left after the Revolution on the territory held by the Bolsheviki.

To say that this was unfortunate is not to suggest that grave impediments to a fruitful development of Soviet-American relations would not have been present in any case. The violent ideological preconceptions of the Soviet leaders; their hatred of the capitalist world; their dizzy illusions of the imminence of world revolution;

their lack of any serious intention of cultivating a constructive and permanent relationship with the capitalist West; the childish delight they took in taunting and insulting the western governments; the cynicism, opportunism, and absence of good faith that marked their methods of dealing with the non-communist world; plus all the various anti-social tendencies that they were inheriting, without re-alizing it, from the Russian officialdom of earlier times—the govern-mental xenophobia, the exaggerated concern for prestige, the com-pulsive fear of foreign observation and influence, the persistent tendency to over-suspiciousness, secretiveness, dissimulation, and de-ception in dealing with an outside force—all these traits of the Soviet official personality would have been present in any case, to bedevil even the most faithful and enlightened of American efforts to moderate the differences and to reduce the gap.

Whether, in these circumstances, anything could have been achieved had the American staffs remained in Russia and the Amer-ican troops not arrived there, is a matter of conjecture. The events recounted above would suggest that these prospects were not utterly hopeless—that some possibility of achievement existed, if only be-cause this is a changing world, where people influence others and are influenced by them in unexpected ways, and where things are constantly moving on, creating new opportunities as older ones lose their reality.

It was precisely this possibility—the most important that could be imagined from the standpoint of the long-term future of both the Russian and American peoples and indeed of mankind generally—that was sacrificed to the slender and evanescent baubles of the mili-tary intervention; and never, surely, in the history of American diplomacy has so much been paid for so little. Compared to this price, the incidental disadvantages of the American action—the further poisoning of the Soviet attitude and the confusing of the his-torical record—were minor.

The reasons for this failure of American statesmanship lay, as the reader will have observed, in such things as the deficiencies of the American political system from the standpoint of the conduct of foreign relations; the grievous distortion of vision brought to the democratic society by any self-abandonment—as in World War I—to the hysteria of militancy; the congenital shallowness, philosophical and intellectual, of the approach to world problems that bubbled up from the fermentations of official Washington; and the pervasive dilettantism in the execution of American policy. How pleasing it would be if one were able to record, in concluding this volume, that these deficiencies had been left behind, along with all the individual undertakings and adventures of 1918—to be recaptured, like these, only by the labor of the historian; to take on, like these, that deceptive quaintness which the passage of time bestows on all human situations, however tragic; to be contemplated, now, from a safe distance, as the components of dead situations, only partially relevant to our own.

APPENDICES

ACKNOWLEDGMENTS

SELECTED BIBLIOGRAPHY

INDEX

APPENDICES

Lt. Col. Raymond Robins to the Secretary of State: [1]

Washington, July 1, 1918

Sir: Pursuant to your request I have the honor to present to you herewith a brief printed statement of my recommendations concerning the Russian situation.

It seems to me that in all the confusion of statement and conclusion surrounding the Russian situation the following propositions are reasonably clear:

First, that Germany hesitates to employ in Russia armed forces in sufficient number to subjugate the land but desires—as clearly indicated by a consistent course of conduct in Urkainia, Finland and the Baltic Provinces—to establish so-called governments of law and order which are too weak to support themselves in the great class struggle but which may be maintained and controlled by German force.

Second, that through such governments Germany hopes to control and utilize Russian resources and, if possible, Russian man-power against the Western Allies in this war, and to conclude the war with Russia completely under the economic dominion of Germany.

Third, that forcible Allied intervention opposed by the Soviets would be essentially analogous to what Germany is doing in the Ukraine, in Finland and in the Baltic Provinces.

Fourth, that such intervention unless welcomed by the great mass of the Russian people would be destructive in principle of the entire basis of President Wilson's democratic war policy.

Fifth, that forcible Allied intervention, if uninvited by the Soviet power, will certainly be opposed and will result in civil war.

Sixth, that forcible Allied intervention can not be justified upon grounds of military necessity, and will not prevent but will hasten and make easy the consummation of Germany's war aims in European Russia.

Seventh, that American economic co-operation with Russia will open the way for effective Allied intervention with force and the creation of an actual fighting front opposed to Germany in Russia.

[1] *Foreign Relations, The Lansing Papers,* Vol. ii, *op.cit.,* pp. 365-372.

Appendices

The recommendations enclosed herewith are stated with as much brevity as possible.

Respectfully,

RAYMOND ROBINS

[Enclosure]

Statement of Recommendations Concerning the Russian Situation

American Economic Cooperation With Russia

I.—RUSSIA WILL WELCOME AMERICAN ASSISTANCE IN
ECONOMIC RECONSTRUCTION

America's democratic war aims are such as to make allied intervention by force in Russia inconceivable unless desired by the great mass of the Russian people. Thus far there has been no expression of any such desire, but there is now presented in the invitation coming from the responsible head of the Soviet Government for America's coöperation in economic reconstruction, the opportunity for taking a vitally important preliminary step toward complete economic and military coöperation in the creation of an effective Eastern front. This suggestion should be considered solely as a war measure, uninfluenced by altruistic concern for the Russian people.

The Russian people and their leaders are learning by bitter daily experience the necessity of organizing resistance to German power. When the peace written by Germany at Brest-Litovsk was signed the condition of the old army was such that it was utterly incapable of resisting any organized force. Demobilization was the first indispensable prerequisite for the creation of an effective force with which German power could be opposed. The next step is the reconstruction of the economic situation. Modern armies cannot survive unsupported by economic and industrial organization.

It was upon the plea of the necessity for economic reconstruction that the peace, frankly described as shameful, was accepted. The leaders of the Soviet Government realize that their social-economic revolution must fail, and that Russia will inevitably fall under the complete domination of autocratic Germany unless immediate and effective assistance in the reconstruction of economic life can be obtained. Their faith in the formulas of International Socialism naturally repels the suggestion of friendly coöperation with so-called Imperialistic and Capitalistic Governments, but the compelling realities and necessities of life have led in this case, as in many others, to readjustment and compromise. Hence the present suggestion coming from the responsible head of the Soviet Government which is an earnest request for America's coöperation in the internal reconstruction of economic life.

It is my sincere conviction, if this suggestion is acted upon and such economic reorganization is accomplished as is needed to equip and support a revolutionary army, that such an army can and will be formed and that in such event the assistance of armed forces of the Allies will be gladly accepted by the Soviet Power. This Power can not be expected to countenance Allied intervention until convinced that the intervening force will not be used to destroy it.

II.—GENERAL PURPOSES OF AN ECONOMIC COMMISSION

The aims of an Economic Commission sent to Russia to coöperate in the problem of economic reconstruction will be—

First. To so reconstruct commercial distribution as to assure the consumption of Russian resources in Russia where they are vitally needed, thus preventing such resources from being used for the support of the German people and the German armies.

Second. To control the use and disposition of surplus resources and through such control to prevent such use in the service of Germany.

Third. If possible to re-establish trade with Russia upon a basis which, while facilitating economic reconstruction in Russia, will at the same time furnish to the Allies for use in England and France necessary products shipped from Russia via Archangel, which otherwise would necessarily be brought to England from more distant ports requiring longer voyages and consequently a greater use of tonnage.

Fourth. To convince the Russian people that the interests of Russia and the Allies in overthrowing German autocracy are identical, and that American assistance is given solely with a view to hastening the day when Russia will be able to aid the destruction of the German menace.

Fifth. To encourage and assist in the organization of a voluntary revolutionary army, creating behind such an army the necessary organization for its economic support.

Sixth. To convince the leaders of Revolutionary Russia, whoever they may be, that the Allied Governments have no imperialistic purpose in Russia and will gladly send forces to assist the Russian people in opposing the aggression of German force; and through coöperation with these leaders, to obtain their consent to sending Allied troops which in coöperation with Russian forces may be sufficient to reestablish the Russian front.

Seventh. To obtain an accurate understanding of the fundamental social forces at work in Russia and to keep the American and other allied governments advised of the actual facts controlling the development of the Russian, social, economic and political revolution.

III.—THE ECONOMIC PROBLEM

Russia is not suffering so much from a lack of resources as from the breakdown of the ordinary processes of distribution. The Russian peasant finds himself with a large quantity of grain and a large amount of depreciated paper currency. If he takes his grain to the local center of trade he finds none of the necessities of his life for sale, and can not exchange his grain except for more depreciated paper money. Consequently the grain is not brought to market. In several instances where shipments of manufactured articles needed by the peasants have been sent to villages, theretofore suffering from the lack of grain, abundant supplies of grain have at once been brought from the surrounding country by the peasants to be exchanged for the manufactured articles.

While this is typical of the situation in many provinces, other neighboring provinces are facing famine conditions because of crop failures or other reasons, and have no grain with which to sow their fields or to feed their people. In a district near Samara, the handling of such a situation was attempted by the local peasant's coöperative society. Going to the peasants who lacked the seed wheat with which to sow their fields, this organization proposed to procure the necessary seed-wheat, provided the peasants would advance the price of the grain which the society promised to deliver within a fixed period of time. Many of the peasants, ignorant of all methods of business involving even the simplest form of credit, refused this offer made solely in their own interest. A unit of the American Friends Society, which has been doing excellent work in that district, determined to bridge the gap; and sending a man to Omsk found no difficulty in purchasing the necessary seed-wheat, and after procuring the same transported and sold it to the peasants without loss in a majority of cases.

Meanwhile, the factories in the industrial centers have in many cases continued their operations and have produced manufactured articles that are lacking in the country districts. In illustration: The J. M. Coates Company, which produces 60 percent of all the cotton thread produced in Russia, and which has large factories in Petrograd, continued its operations up to the end of February, 1918, and at that time had on hand the largest stock of manufactured products its books had ever shown. Owing to difficulties of communication, transport, and hauling, the distributing branch of the business had not been functioning. That efficient production is possible under Soviet rule has been demonstrated by the experience of the International Harvester Company which has largely increased its producing efficiency during the past six months under Soviet rule. This experience was made possible through tactful handling of a very difficult situation which resulted in effective coöperation from the Soviet authorities who in order to get results were willing when faced with the practical necessities of the situation, to modify the rigid formulas of their economic theory. No doubt the experience of this company is exceptional, but the tactful handling of daily problems as they arise through a competent American Economic Commission will be the most effective method of accomplishing similar results in like cases.

IV.—GOVERNMENT COOPERATION

Obviously nothing can be accomplished without the coöperation of governmental power. The commission must, therefore, go if it goes at all, willing to deal with the leaders of Revolutionary Russia actually in power, without regard to their principles or formulas of economic, social, or political life, so long as such leaders sincerely desire to recreate forces in Russia which will be used in resisting the force of German arms. Seeking such coöperation, the members of this commission will be asked to advise regarding problems of a most practical and controlling nature. They will be able to exert powerful influence to prevent large commercial transactions with Germany. All of this work will from necessity be done under Government control and protection. Their advice re-enforced by the un-compromising facts of life will lead inevitably to the modification, adjust-ment, and softening of the hard and impossible formulas of radical social-ism; and because of the necessity of finding it, a practical basis for progress will be found. The Russian Revolution has now reached the stage where it is to be controlled, not by theory, but by the unyielding necessities of life. This fact is becoming each day more clear to the radical socialistic group now in control of the Soviet Government.

It is apparent from the informality of the suggestion inviting American coöperation that formal recognition of the Soviet Government is not a necessary prerequisite to coöperation. Acting upon this informal invita-tion, a commission can proceed to Russia and be placed in direct touch with the entire situation without further formality.

American coöperation will give the Allies effective and controlling in-fluence upon the internal situation. Such coöperation will be able to direct the forces supporting the Soviet Power against Germany. If effective, coöperation will ultimately compel the continued utilization against the Russian people of tyrannical German force, thus preventing German coöperation and increasing the bitter resentment against Germany which is steadily gaining ground in Russia. If the economic life of Russia can be sufficiently organized to make possible the support of an effective army, this growing resentment will surely crystallize in the organization of an army which will effectively oppose the German menace in Russia.

V.—ORGANIZATION OF COMMISSION

Through coöperation with the Government the work of such a Com-mission will be concerned with:—

(1) Railway control, management and operation;
(2) Reorganization of credit and finance, governmental and commercial;
(3) Commercial distribution of grain and manufactured articles in exchange for grain;
(4) Food administration and control;
(5) Shipping and foreign trade, with particular reference to Allied war needs;
(6) Industrial management and control in co-operation with labor;
(7) Reorganization of manufacturing and coal mining industries;
(8) Development of agriculture;
(9) Prevention, or utilization, of speculative markets;
(10) Education;
(11) Propaganda.

To accomplish substantial results the most competent organizing and technical ability will be required. Members of the Commission must be men of liberal views and sympathetic understanding, capable of meeting fact conditions with practical ability to achieve results under difficult and complex circumstances.

Under the control of the Commission it will be necessary to create an extensive organization with representatives in all important centers of Russian life. For this purpose the distributing and sales organizations of large business concerns, both American and English, which have heretofore been organized in Russia and which are now in danger of being disorganized should be utilized and reorganized to meet the actual demands of the situation. There are many such organizations in Russia as, for instance, the New York Life Insurance Company, the J. M. Coates Company, and the International Harvester Company.

The organization thus created by the Commission will co-operate in the various local centers with various Russian agencies, including the local Soviets, the Peasants' Co-operative Societies and the local Zemstvos where they are functioning. Thus the commercial and industrial needs necessary for re-creation of commercial life may be effectively ascertained. Through co-operation in railway management the opportunity will be created of transporting manufactured goods from the place of production to the place of consumption. The Commission will be able to control the disposition of manufactured goods by the use of American credit and upon transportation of such goods to the local centers will, with them, be able to control the disposition of large food products.

These products should of course be primarily used for consumption in Russia and will be transported to the centers where food products are lacking. Any surplus will be available for export.

If export trade with the Allies can be re-established upon such a basis as to result in economic use of tonnage in bringing from Archangel products required in England and France it should be possible to exchange for these products to ship to Russia agricultural and other tools and machinery and manufactured products. This trade should be in the absolute control of the Commission, so that the distribution of the goods sent to Russia will be, in so far as possible, under the control of the Commission. With American credit and American goods the Commission will be able to control the disposition of Russian resources, vitally needed by Germany. In this connection it is encouraging to note that there are authentic reports to the effect that Germany has been endeavoring to make large purchases of American bank notes for the purchase of grain from the Ukraine peasants. This fact indicates that Germany has not at her disposal the goods required by the Ukrainian peasants for which they would be willing to exchange their grain. Effective organization combined with the use of American credit and the control of American goods should effectively prevent the commercial exploitation of Russia by Germany during the balance of the war.

The work of this Commission will be so extensive that the burden of responsible supervision should not be placed upon any of the departments of the Government already so greatly overburdened with work. In order to meet this situation and at the same time to obtain proper co-ordination it is suggested that a separate and independent department of the Government be created under the Overman Act; that at the head of this department there should be a man enjoying the absolute confidence of the President, who shall be responsible only to the President; that there be associated with him representatives of the various Government departments having vital interests connected with the prosecution of the war which may be related to the work of the Commission.

The Commission should be responsible only to this independent department and, through it, responsible to the President. This department should be granted an appropriation by Congress adequate to effectively carry on its work. The very large amount of money which will be required is indicated by the character of the work to be done.

Independent facilities of communication in cipher should be established between the Commission and the department to which it is to be responsible.

Time is of the utmost importance. The Commission should be organized as quickly as possible and should proceed to Russia via Archangel so as to reach the center of European Russia without unnecessary delay.

RAYMOND ROBINS

July 1, 1918.

Appendices

The Secretary of State to the Allied Ambassadors:

Aide-Mémoire [1]

The whole heart of the people of the United States is in the winning of this war. The controlling purpose of the Government of the United States is to do everything that is necessary and effective to win it. It wishes to cooperate in every practicable way with the Allied Governments, and to cooperate ungrudgingly; for it has no ends of its own to serve and believes that the war can be won only by common counsel and intimate concert of action. It has sought to study every proposed policy or action in which its cooperation has been asked in this spirit, and states the following conclusions in the confidence that, if it finds itself obliged to decline participation in any undertaking or course of action, it will be understood that it does so only because it deems itself precluded from participating by imperative considerations either of policy or of fact.

In full agreement with the Allied Governments and upon the unanimous advice of the Supreme War Council, the Government of the United States adopted, upon its entrance into the war, a plan for taking part in the fighting on the western front into which all its resources of men and material were to be put, and put as rapidly as possible, and it has carried out that plan with energy and success, pressing its execution more and more rapidly forward and literally putting into it the entire energy and executive force of the nation. This was its response, its very willing and hearty response, to what was the unhesitating judgment alike of its own military advisers and of the advisers of the Allied Governments. It is now considering, at the suggestion of the Supreme War Council, the possibility of making very considerable additions even to this immense program which, if they should prove feasible at all, will tax the industrial processes of the United States and the shipping facilities of the whole group of associated nations to the utmost. It has thus concentrated all its plans and all its resources upon this single absolutely necessary object.

In such circumstances it feels it to be its duty to say that it cannot, so long as the military situation on the western front remains critical, consent to break or slacken the force of its present effort by diverting any part of its military force to other points or objectives. The United States is at a great distance from the field of action on the western front; it is at a much greater distance from any other field of action. The instrumentalities by which it is to handle its armies and its stores have at great

[1] *Foreign Relations, 1918, Russia,* Vol. II, *op.cit.,* pp. 287–290.

cost and with great difficulty been created in France. They do not exist elsewhere. It is practicable for her to do a great deal in France; it is not practicable for her to do anything of importance or on a large scale upon any other field. The American Government, therefore, very respectfully requests its associates to accept its deliberate judgment that it should not dissipate its force by attempting important operations elsewhere.

It regards the Italian front as closely coordinated with the western front, however, and is willing to divert a portion of its military forces from France to Italy if it is the judgment and wish of the Supreme Command that it should do so. It wishes to defer to the decision of the Commander in Chief in this matter, as it would wish to defer in all others, particularly because it considers these two fronts so closely related as to be practically but separate parts of a single line and because it would be necessary that any American troops sent to Italy should be subtracted from the number used in France and be actually transported across French territory from the ports now used by the armies of the United States.

It is the clear and fixed judgment of the Government of the United States, arrived at after repeated and very searching reconsiderations of the whole situation in Russia, that military intervention there would add to the present sad confusion in Russia rather than cure it, injure her rather than help her, and that it would be of no advantage in the prosecution of our main design, to win the war against Germany. It can not, therefore, take part in such intervention or sanction it in principle. Military intervention would, in its judgment, even supposing it to be efficacious in its immediate avowed object of delivering an attack upon Germany from the east, be merely a method of making use of Russia, not a method of serving her. Her people could not profit by it, if they profited by it at all, in time to save them from their present distresses, and their substance would be used to maintain foreign armies, not to reconstitute their own. Military action is admissible in Russia, as the Government of the United States sees the circumstances, only to help the Czecho-Slovaks consolidate their forces and get into successful co-operation with their Slavic kinsmen and to steady any efforts at self-government or self-defense in which the Russians themselves may be willing to accept assistance. Whether from Vladivostok or from Murmansk and Archangel, the only legitimate object for which American or Allied troops can be employed, it submits, is to guard military stores which may subsequently be needed by Russian forces and to render such aid as may be acceptable to the Russians in the organization of their own self-defense. For helping the Czecho-Slovaks there is immediate necessity and sufficient justification. Recent developments have made it evident that that is in the interest of what the Russian people themselves desire, and the Government of the United States is glad to contribute the small force at its disposal for that purpose. It yields, also, to the judgment of the Supreme Command in the matter of establishing a small force at Murmansk, to guard the military stores at Kola, and to make it safe for Russian forces to come together in organized bodies in the north. But it owes it to frank counsel to say that it can go no further than these modest and experimental plans. It is not in a position, and has no expectation of being in a position, to take part in organized intervention in adequate force from either Vladivostok or Murmansk and Archangel. It feels that it ought to add, also, that it will feel at liberty to use the few troops it can spare only for the purposes here stated and shall feel obliged to withdraw those forces, in order to add them to the forces at the western front, if the plans in whose execution it is now intended that they should cooperate should develop into others inconsistent with the policy to which the Government of the United States feels constrained to restrict itself.

At the same time the Government of the United States wishes to say with the utmost cordiality and good will that none of the conclusions here stated is meant to wear the least color of criticism of what the other governments associated against Germany may think it wise to undertake. It wishes in no way to embarrass their choices of policy. All that is intended here is a perfectly frank and definite statement of the policy which the United States feels obliged to adopt for herself and in the use of her own military forces. The Government of the United States does not wish it to be understood that in so restricting its own activities it is seeking, even by implication, to set limits to the action or to define the policies of its associates.

It hopes to carry out the plans for safeguarding the rear of the Czecho-Slovaks operating from Vladivostok in a way that will place it and keep it in close cooperation with a small military force like its own from Japan, and if necessary from the other Allies, and that will assure it of the cordial accord of all the Allied powers; and it proposes to ask all associated in this course of action to unite in assuring the people of Russia in the most public and solemn manner that none of the governments uniting in action either in Sibereia or in northern Russia contemplates any interference of any kind with the political sovereignty of Russia, any intervention in her internal affairs, or any impairment of her territorial integrity either now or hereafter, but that each of the associated powers has the single object of affording such aid as shall be acceptable, and only such aid as shall be acceptable, to the Russian people in their endeavor to regain control of their own affairs, their own territory, and their own destiny.

It is the hope and purpose of the Government of the United States to take advantage of the earliest opportunity to send to Siberia a commission of merchants, agricultural experts, labor advisers, Red Cross representatives, and agents of the Young Men's Christian Association accustomed to organizing the best methods of spreading useful information and rendering educational help of a modest sort, in order in some systematic manner to relieve the immediate economic necessities of the people there in every way for which opportunity may open. The execution of this plan will follow and will not be permitted to embarrass the military assistance rendered in the rear of the westward-moving forces of the Czecho-Slovaks.

Washington, July 17, 1918.

ACKNOWLEDGMENTS

The author wishes to acknowledge his indebtedness to the following publishers:

To Harcourt Brace and Company, New York, for permission to quote from *Russian-American Relations, March 1917–March 1920, Documents and Papers,* compiled and edited by C. K. Cumming and W. W. Pettit, 1920.

To Hodder and Stoughton, London, for permission to quote from *The Murmansk Venture* by Major General C. Maynard, c. 1928.

❖

The author wishes to acknowledge his indebtedness to the following persons, for permission to quote from hitherto unpublished material:

To Francis L. Berkeley, Jr., Curator of Manuscripts of the Alderman Library at the University of Virginia, Charlottesville, and to the School of Law Library at the University of Louisville, for Justice Louis D. Brandeis' letter of May 11, 1924.

To Allen W. Dulles, for Secretary Lansing's memoranda to President Wilson of March 18 and July 4, his letter to George Kennan of May 28, his telegram to Frank Polk of July 31, and the items from the Desk Diary.

To Thomas Francis, for Ambassador Francis' letters to Felix Cole of June 13; to his son Perry of June 4, 23, and July 30; to DeWitt C. Poole of June 13, 15, 19, 20, and July 1, 1918.

To Chihiro Hosoya for his memorandum "Origin of the Siberian Intervention, November 1917–August 1918."

To John A. Lehrs for his memorandum of June 29, 1918.

To Sir Robert Bruce Lockhart, for his communications to the Foreign Office of March 5, April 13, and May 8, 1918.

To Mrs. DeWitt C. Poole, for Mr. Poole's letters to Ambassador Francis of May 24, June 3, 5, 15, 1918; and to David Otto Tyson, March 10, 1948.

To Lady Salter, for Arthur Bullard's letter to DeWitt C. Poole, May 6, 1918; his report to George Creel of May 9, his letter to Edgar Sisson of May 12, 1918, and the paper entitled "Dealing with the Bolsheviki."

To Dr. Charles Seymour, for the Edward House diary items of March 18 and August 17, 1918.

To Herbert Bayard Swope, for his letter to President Wilson of April 1, 1918.

Acknowledgments

To Mrs. Allen Wardwell and Edward R. Wardwell, for Allen Wardwell diary items of February 28; March 5, 6, 12, 16, 28 and 29; May 8, June 15, and August 27, 1918.

To Mrs. Woodrow Wilson, for her note to President Wilson of March 18, 1918; and President Wilson's letter to Herbert Bayard Swope of April 2; his note to Lansing of July 3, 1918, and the note to Tumulty for Crane of May 11, 1918.

To Sir William Wiseman, for his telegram to the Foreign Office of June 15, 1918.

❖

The author wishes to acknowledge his indebtedness to the following persons for giving him the benefit of their valuable memories and impressions of the events with which this volume deals, and in some instances for reading portions of the manuscript:

J. W. Andrews

The Honorable Norman Armour

George W. Bakeman

The Honorable John K. Caldwell

The Honorable Felix Cole

Malcolm Davis

Harold H. Fisher

The Honorable Felix Frankfurter

Professor George C. Guins

Read Lewis

Professor Otakar Odlozilik

The Honorable William Phillips

Professor Leonid I. Strakhovsky

George M. Vesselago

SELECTED BIBLIOGRAPHY

~~~~~~

MANUSCRIPTS

The following collections were used in the preparation of this volume:

In the Library of Congress:
Hermann Hagedorn–W. B. Thompson Papers
George Kennan Papers
Robert Lansing Papers
Breckinridge Long Papers
Roland S. Morris Papers
Elihu Root Papers
Woodrow Wilson Papers

In the Library of Princeton University:
Arthur Bullard Papers

In the Missouri Historical Society, St. Louis:
David R. Francis Papers

In the State Historical Society of Wisconsin, Madison:
Alexander Gumberg Papers
DeWitt C. Poole Papers
Raymond Robins Papers

In the Library of the University of Chicago:
Samuel N. Harper Papers

In the Library of Yale University, New Haven:
Edward M. House Papers
Frank L. Polk Papers
Sir William Wiseman Papers

In the Butler Library, Columbia University, New York:
Oral History Research Office, transcript of recorded reminiscences of
DeWitt C. Poole;
Archive of Russian and Eastern European History and Culture, Allen
Wardwell Papers.

In the Archives of the American National Red Cross, Washington:
Various papers.

[488]

Bibliography

In the Archives of The Johns Hopkins University, Baltimore:
Frank Goodnow Papers

In the Hoover Institute and Library, Stanford University, Stanford:
American Red Cross Mission to Russia, 1917; Papers
W. L. Darling Papers
General M. K. Dieterich Papers
Papers on the American Railway Mission to Russia (John Frank Stevens)
Ernest Lloyd Harris Papers; files of the American Consul General in Vladivostok for the period 1918–1920
Dmitri Leonovich Horvat, *Memoirs* (manuscript)
M. Kolobov Papers

PUBLIC DOCUMENTS

Publications of the United States Government consulted in the preparation of this volume included:

Bolshevik Propaganda, Hearings before a Subcommittee of the Committee on the Judiciary, United States Senate, 65th Congress, Third Session (1919).

Papers Relating to the Foreign Relations of the United States: The Lansing Papers, 1914–1920, Volume II (1940).

Papers Relating to the Foreign Relations of the United States: 1918, Russia (three volumes), (1931, 1932).

The National Archives of the United States Government:
Foreign Affairs Branch
War Records Division; Record Groups 120, Records of the American Expeditionary Forces, and 45, Naval Records
Justice and Executive Branch

BOOKS

Non-periodical sources consulted in the preparation of this volume included:

Ralph Albertson, *Fighting without a War: An Account of Military Intervention in North Russia,* Harcourt Brace & Howe, New York, 1920.

Paul B. Anderson, *People, Church and State in Modern Russia,* The Macmillan Co., New York, 1944.

Alexis N. Antsiferov, *The Coöperative Movement in Russia during the War: Credit and Agricultural Coöperation,* Yale University Press, New Haven, 1929.

A. Argunov, *Mezhdu dvumya bolshevizmami* (Between Two Bolshevisms), Paris, 1919.

Bibliography

Henry Baerlein, *The March of the Seventy Thousand*, Leonard Parsons, London, 1926.

Ray Stannard Baker, *Woodrow Wilson, Life and Letters* (eight volumes), Doubleday, Doran and Co., Inc., Garden City, N.Y., Volume VII, *War Leader, April 6, 1917–February 28, 1918* (1939) and Volume VIII, *Armistice, March 1–November 11, 1918* (1939).

N. Barou, *Russia Co-operation Abroad: Foreign Trade 1912–1928*, P. S. King & Son, Ltd., London, 1930.

Eduard Beneš, *My War Memoirs* (Tr. Paul Selver), George Allen & Unwin Ltd., London, 1928.

A. Berezkin, *S SHA—Aktivny organizator i uchastnik voennoi interventsii protiv Sovetskoi Rossii (1918–1920 gg)* (USA—Active Organizer and Participant in Armed Intervention against Soviet Russia 1918–1920), State Publishing House for Political Literature, Moscow, 1952.

Maria Botchkareva (with Isaac Don Levine), *Yashka: My Life as Peasant, Officer and Exile*, Frederick A. Stokes Co., New York, 1919.

Elsa Brändström, *Among Prisoners of War in Russia and Siberia*, Hutchinson & Co., London, 1929.

Robert Browder, *The Origins of Soviet-American Diplomacy*, Princeton University Press, 1953.

William Adams Brown, Jr., *The Groping Giant: Revolutionary Russia as seen by an American Democrat*, Yale University Press, New Haven, 1920.

James Bunyan, *Intervention, Civil War, and Communism in Russia: April–December 1918, Documents and Materials*, The Johns Hopkins Press, Baltimore, 1936.

James Bunyan and H. H. Fisher, *The Bolshevik Revolution, 1917–1918*, Stanford University Press, Stanford, 1934.

Edward Hallett Carr, *A History of Soviet Russia, The Bolshevik Revolution 1917–1923*, (four volumes), The Macmillan Co., New York, Volume I (1950) and Volume III (1953).

William Henry Chamberlin, *The Russian Revolution* (two volumes), The Macmillan Co., New York, 1935.

Tao-hsing Chang, *International Controversies over the Chinese Eastern Railway*, The Commercial Press, Ltd., Shanghai, 1936.

George Chicherin, *Two Years of Foreign Policy: The Relations of R.S.F.S.R. with Foreign Nations, from November 7, 1917 to November 7, 1919*, Russian Government Bureau, New York, 1920.

A Chronicler (John Cudahy), *Archangel: The American War with Russia*, A. C. McClurg & Co., Chicago, 1924.

Winston S. Churchill, *The Aftermath: The World Crisis, 1918–1928*, Charles Scribner's Sons, New York, 1929.

Bibliography

W. P. and Zelda K. Coates, *Armed Intervention in Russia, 1918–1922,* Victor Gollancz Ltd., London, 1935.

Correspondance diplomatique se rapportant aux relations entre la République Russe et les Puissances de l'Entente, 1918, Publié par le Commissariat du Peuple pour les Affaires Etrangères, 1919.

C. K. Cumming and Walter W. Pettit, *Russian-American Relations, March, 1917–March, 1920: Documents and Papers,* Harcourt, Brace and Howe, New York, 1920.

Edmund Dane, *British Campaigns in the Nearer East 1914–1918: From the Outbreak of War with Turkey to the Armistice,* Hodder and Stoughton, London, 1919, Volume II, *The Tide of Victory.*

Jane Degras, compiler, *Calendar of Soviet Documents on Foreign Policy 1917–1941,* Oxford University Press for Royal Institute of International Affairs, London, 1948.

Jane Degras, Editor, *Soviet Documents on Foreign Policy* (three volumes), Oxford University Press for Royal Institute of International Affairs, 1951, Volume I, *1917–1924.*

A. I. Denikin, *Ocherki russkoi smuty* (Sketches of the Time of Trouble in Russia), J. Povolozky & Cie, Editeurs, Paris, c. 1923, Volume II.

Blanche E. C. (Mrs. Edgar) Dugdale, *Arthur James Balfour, First Earl of Balfour, K.G., O.M., F.R.S.,* Hutchinson & Co., Ltd., London, 1936 (two volumes).

Louis Fischer, *Men and Politics, An Autobiography,* Duell, Sloan and Pearce, New York, 1941.

Louis Fischer, *The Soviets in World Affairs, A History of the Relations Between the Soviet Union and the Rest of the World 1917–1929* (two volumes), Second Edition, Princeton University Press, 1951.

David R. Francis, *Russia from the American Embassy,* Charles Scribner's Sons, New York, 1921.

I. I. Genkin, *Soedinennye Shtaty Ameriki i SSSR—Ikh politicheskie i ekonomicheskie vzaimootnosheniya* (The United States of America and the USSR—Political and Economic Relations between Them), State Social-Economic Publishing Co., Moscow-Leningrad, 1934.

N. N. Golovin, *Rossiiskaya kontr-revolyutsiya v 1917–1918 gg* (Russian Counterrevolution, 1917–1918), Prilozheniye k "Illyustrirovannoi Rossii," 1937, Volumes II, III, and IV.

William S. Graves, *America's Siberian Adventure, 1918–1920,* Jonathan Cape & Harrison Smith, New York, 1931.

J. O. Hannula, *Finland's War of Independence,* Faber & Faber, Ltd., London, 1939.

William Hard, *Raymond Robins' Own Story,* Harper & Brothers, New York, 1920.

[491]

Bibliography

Paul V. Harper, Editor, *The Russia I Believe In: The Memoirs of Samuel N. Harper, 1902–41*, University of Chicago Press, 1945.

Gustav Hilger (and Alfred G. Meyer), *The Incompatible Allies: A Memoir-History of German-Soviet Relations 1918–1941*, The Macmillan Co., New York, 1953.

Max Hoffman (Tr. Eric Sutton), *War Diaries and Other Papers*, Martin Secker, London, 1929.

Erwin Hölzle, *Der Osten im Ersten Weltkrieg*, Leipzig, 1944.

Herbert Hoover, *The Memoirs of Herbert Hoover; Years of Adventure 1874–1920*, The Macmillan Co., New York, 1951.

Lord Ironside, *Archangel, 1918–19*, Constable & Co., Ltd., London, 1953.

Philip C. Jessup, *Elihu Root* (two volumes), Dodd, Mead & Co., New York, 1938, Volume II, *1905–1937*.

Eugene M. Kayden, *The Coöperative Movement in Russia during the War: Consumers' Coöperation*, Yale University Press, New Haven, 1929.

Mikhael Sergeevich Kedrov, *Bez bolshevistskogo rukovodstva (iz istorii interventsii na Murmanye)* (Without Bolshevik Leadership), Izdatelstvo "Krasnaya Gazeta," Leningrad, 1930.

Mikhael Sergeevich Kedrov, *Za sovetski sever* (The Struggle for a Soviet North), Leningrad, 1927.

V. M. Khvostov and I. I. Mints, under editorial direction of V. P. Potemkin, *Istoriya Diplomatii* (The History of Diplomacy), Volume II, *Diplomacy in Recent Times (1872–1919)*, State Publishing House for Political Literature, Moscow, 1945.

Margarete Klante, *Von der Wolga zum Amur: Die tschechische Legion und der russische Bürgerkrieg*, Ost-Europa Verlag, Berlin, 1931.

Yuri V. Klyuchnikov and Andrei Sabanin, Editors, *Mezhdunarodnaya politika noveishego vremeni v dogovorakh, notakh, i deklaratsiyakh* (International Politics of Recent Times with Documents, Notes, and Declarations), Izdaniye Litizdata N.K.I.D., Moscow, 1925.

I. K. Koblyakov, *Ot Bresta do Rapallo* (From Brest to Rapallo), State Publishing House for Political Literature, Moscow, 1954.

V. Kral, *O kontrrevolyutsionnoi i antisovyetskoi politike Masarika i Benesha* (Concerning the Counterrevolutionary and anti-Soviet Politics of Masaryk and Beneš), State Publishing House for Foreign Literature, Moscow, 1955.

Jaroslav Kratochvíl, *Cesta revoluce*, Praha, 1928.

A. Ye. Kunina, *Proval Amerikanskikh planov zavoevaniya mirovogo gospodstva v 1917–1920 gg.* (Failure of the American Plans for World Domination, 1917–1920), State Publishing House for Political Literature, Moscow, 1954.

Bibliography

Robert Lansing, *War Memoirs of Robert Lansing*, Bobbs-Merrill Co., New York, 1935.

V. I. Lenin, *Sochineniya* (Complete Works), Fourth Edition, State Publishing House for Political Literature, Moscow, 1950, Volume 27, *February–July 1918;* Volume 28, *July 1918–March 1919.*

David Lloyd George, *War Memoirs of David Lloyd George,* Ivor Nicholson & Watson, London, 1936, Volumes v and vi.

R. H. Bruce Lockhart, *British Agent,* G. P. Putnam's Sons, London and New York, 1933.

G. Mannerheim, *Erinnerungen,* Atlantis Verlag, Zurich, 1952.

Clarence A. Manning, *The Siberian Fiasco,* Library Publishers, Inc., New York, 1952.

Peyton C. March, *The Nation at War,* Doubleday, Doran & Co., Inc., Garden City, New York, 1932.

T. G. Masaryk, *Die Welt-Revolution: Erinnerungen und Betrachtungen 1914–1918,* Erich Reiss Verlag, Berlin, 1925.

C. Maynard, *The Murmansk Venture,* Hodder & Stoughton, Ltd., London, c. 1928.

Anatole G. Mazour, *Finland Between East and West,* D. Van Nostrand Co., Inc., Princeton, 1956.

Rudolf Medek, *The Czechoslovak Anabasis across Russia and Siberia,* The Czech Society, London, 1929.

A. I. Melchin, *Amerikanskaya interventsiya v 1918–1920 gg* (The American Intervention, 1918–1920), Military-Naval Publishing Co., Moscow, 1951.

Paul N. Milyukov, *Rossiya na Perelomye* (Russia at the Crossroads), Imprimerie d'Art Voltaire, Paris, 1927.

James R. Mock and Cedric Larson, *Words that Won the War: The Story of the Committee on Public Information 1917–1919,* Princeton University Press, 1939.

Joel R. Moore (with Harry H. Mead and Lewis E. Jahns), *The History of the American Expedition Fighting the Bolsheviki: Campaigning in North Russia 1918–1919,* The Polar Bear Publishing Co., Detroit, 1920.

Henry Newbolt, *History of the Great War based on Official Documents by Direction of the Historical Section of the Committee of Imperial Defence,* Longmans, Green & Co., London, 1931, Volume v, *Naval Operations.*

Vladimir Nosek, *Independent Bohemia: An Account of the Czecho-Slovak Struggle for Liberty,* E. P. Dutton & Co., New York, 1918.

Joseph Noulens, *Mon Ambassade en Russie Soviétique, 1917–1919,* Librairie Plon, Paris, 1933 (two volumes).

[493]

Bibliography

Frederick Palmer, *Newton D. Baker: America at War* (two volumes), Dodd, Mead & Co., New York, 1931.

Ján Papánek, *Czechoslovakia,* International Universities Press, New York, 1945.

P. S. Parfenov, *Grazhdanskaya voina v Sibiri* (The Civil War in Siberia), State Publishing House, Moscow, 1924.

P. S. Parfenov, *Uroki proshlogo, grazhdanskaya voina v Sibiri 1918, 1919, 1920 gg.* (Lessons of the Past, Civil War in Siberia 1918–1920), Harbin, undated.

Sophia Rogoski Pelzel, *American Intervention in Siberia 1918–1920,* University of Pennsylvania Press, Philadelphia, 1946.

Charles Pergler, *America in the Struggle for Czechoslovak Independence,* Dorrance & Co., Philadelphia, 1926.

Albrecht Philipp, Editor, *Die Ursachen des deutschen Zusammenbruchs im Jahre 1918,* Deutsche Verlagsgesellschaft für Politik und Geschichte, Berlin, 1925.

Paul S. Reinsch, *An American Diplomat in China,* Doubleday, Page & Co., Garden City, New York, 1922.

Edward Alsworth Ross, *The Russian Soviet Republic,* The Century Co., New York, 1923.

Jacques Sadoul, *Naissance de l'URSS,* Editions Charlot, Paris, 1946 (Volume 1).

Jacques Sadoul, *Notes sur la Révolution Bolchevique,* Editions de la Sirène, Paris, 1920.

Jacques Sadoul, *Quarante Lettres de Jacques Sadoul,* Librairie de l'Humanité, Paris, 1922.

Konstantin W. Sakharow, *Die tschechischen Legionen in Sibirien,* Heinrich Wilhelm Hendriock Verlag, Berlin-Charlottenburg, 1930.

B. Savinkov, *Borba s bolshevikami* (The Struggle Against the Bolsheviki), Warsaw, 1920.

Frederick Lewis Schuman, *American Policy Toward Russia since 1917: A Study of Diplomatic History, International Law, and Public Opinion,* International Publishers, New York, 1928.

Gregori Semenov, *O sebe, vospominaniya, mysli i vyvody* (About Myself, Memories, Thoughts and Conclusions), China, 1938.

Charles Seymour, *Intimate Papers of Colonel House* (four volumes), Houghton Mifflin Co., New York, 1928, Volume III, *Into the World War,* Volume IV, *The Ending of the War.*

Edgar Sisson, *100 Red Days: A Personal Chronicle of the Bolshevik Revolution,* Yale University Press, New Haven, 1931.

B. Solodovnikov, *Sibirskie avantyury i General Gaida* (The Siberian Adventures and General Gajda), Prague, undated.

Bibliography

Pitirim Sorokin, *Leaves from a Russian Diary*, E. P. Dutton & Co., New York, 1924.

Leonid I. Strakhovsky, *Intervention at Archangel: The Story of Allied Intervention and Russian Counter-Revolution in North Russia 1918–1920*, Princeton University Press, 1944.

Leonid I. Strakhovsky, *The Origins of American Intervention in North Russia (1918)*, Princeton University Press, 1937.

Emil Strauss, *Die Entstehung der tschecheslowakischen Republik*, Orbis-Verlag A.G., Prague, 1935.

M. Tikhomirov, *Vneshnaya politika Sovetskogo Soyuza* (Foreign Policy of the Soviet Union), State Publishing Co., Moscow, 1940.

Leo Trotzki, *Mein Leben*, S. Fischer Verlag, Berlin, 1930.

Lev Trotski, *Kak vooruzhalas revolutsiya* (How the Revolution Armed Itself), Supreme Military Editorial Council, Moscow, 1923.

Lev Trotskii, *Sochineniya* (Complete Works), Moscow, 1926, Volume XVII.

Betty Miller Unterberger, *America's Siberian Expedition 1918–1920: A Study of National Policy*, Duke University Press, Durham, 1956.

Elena Varneck and H. H. Fisher, *The Testimony of Kolchak and Other Siberian Materials*, Stanford University Press, Stanford, 1935.

V. Victoroff-Toporoff, *La Première Année de la Révolution Russe (Mars 1917–Mars 1918), Faits-Documents-Appréciations, avec un Tableau hors Texte des Partis Politiques Russes*, Imprimerie G. Iseli, Berne, 1919.

M. V. Vishnyak, *Vserossiiskoye uchreditelnoye sobraniye* (The All-Russian Constituent Assembly), Izdatelstvo "Sovremenniya Zapiski," Paris, 1932.

Rüdiger von der Goltz, *Meine Sendung in Finnland und im Baltikum*, Verlag von K. F. Koehler, Leipzig, 1920.

Richard von Kühlmann, *Erinnerungen*, Verlag Lambert Schneider, Heidelberg, 1948.

Erich von Ludendorff, *Ludendorff's Own Story*, Harper, New York, 1919 (Volume II).

Voroshilov, *Stalin i krasnaya armiya* (Stalin and the Red Army), Voenizdat, 1937.

John Ward, *With the "Die-Hards" in Siberia*, George H. Doran Co., New York, 1920.

Robert D. Warth, *The Allies and the Russian Revolution*, Duke University Press, Durham, 1954.

John W. Wheeler-Bennett, *The Forgotten Peace (Brest-Litovsk, March 1918)*, William Morrow & Co., New York, 1939.

John W. Wheeler-Bennett, *The Treaty of Brest-Litovsk and Germany's Eastern Policy*, Clarendon Press, Oxford, 1940.

Bibliography

D. Fedotoff White, *Survival: Through War and Revolution in Russia*, University of Pennsylvania Press, Philadelphia, 1939.

John Albert White, *The Siberian Intervention*, Princeton University Press, 1950.

Chitoshi Yanaga, *Japan since Perry*, McGraw-Hill Book Co., Inc., New York, 1949.

J. D. Yanson, *Foreign Trade in the U.S.S.R.*, G. P. Putnam's Sons, New York, 1935.

A. Zaitsev, *1918 God* (The Year 1918), Ocherki po istorii Russkoi Grazhdanskoi Voiny, 1934.

Clara Zetkin, *Reminiscences of Lenin*, International Publishers, New York, 1934.

Ye. M. Zhukov, Editor, *Mezhdunarodnye otnosheniya na dalnem vostoke (1870–1945)*, (International Relations in the Far East, 1870–1945), State Publishing House for Political Literature, 1951.

INDEX

[497]

Index

Index

Index

Index

Index

Index

Index